AdI
Annali d'Italianistica
The University of North Carolina at Chapel Hill
Chapel Hill, NC 27599-3170
http://www.ibiblio.org/annali   e-mail: annali@unc.edu

Annali d'italianistica, Inc., was founded at the University of Notre Dame in 1983. In 1989 it moved to the Department of Romance Languages and Literatures at the University of North Carolina at Chapel Hill.
Annali d'italianistica is an independent journal of Italian studies directed and edited by eminent scholars,
whose names and academic affiliations appear on the journal's editorial boards.
Annali d'italianistica, Inc., is non-profit organization.

FOUNDER & EDITOR IN CHIEF
Dino S. Cervigni
The University of North Carolina at Chapel Hill, Professor Emeritus
ASSOCIATE EDITOR
Anne Tordi, PhD, *The University of North Carolina at Chapel Hill*

CO-EDITORS
Norma Bouchard, *San Diego State University*
Alessandro Carrera, *University of Houston*
Carmine Di Biase, *Jacksonville University*
Valerio Ferme, *University of Colorado at Boulder*
Massimo Lollini, *Oregon University*
Dennis Looney, *The University of Pittsburgh*
Federico Luisetti, *The University of North Carolina at Chapel Hill*
Gaetata Marrone, *Princeton University*
Cristina Mazzoni, *The University of Vermont*
Luca Somigli, *The University of Toronto*
John Welle, *The University of Notre Dam*

© 2015 by Annali d'Italianistica, Inc.
ISSN 0741-7527

ISBN-13: 978-0692556580 (Annali d'italianistica, Inc.)
ISBN-10: 0692556583

ADVISORY BOARD

Andrea Battistini, *Università degli Studi di Bologna*
Francesco Bruni, *Università di Venezia*
Giuseppe A. Camerino, *Università del Salento*
Paolo Cherchi, *University of Chicago*
Louise George Clubb, *University of California, Berkeley*
Vincenzo De Caprio, *Università della Tuscia, Viterbo*
Giulio Ferroni, *Università della Sapienza, Roma*
Valeria Finucci, *Duke University*
John Gatt-Rutter, *La Trobe University (Melbourne)*
Walter Geerts, *Universiteit Antwerpen*
Antonio Lucio Giannone, *Università del Salento*
Willi Hirdt, *Universität Bonn*
Christopher Kleinhenz, *Univerisity of Wisconsin, Madison*
Edoardo A. Lèbano, *Indiana University*
Alfredo Luzi, *Università di Macerata*
Albert N. Mancini, *The Ohio State University*
Olimpia Pelosi, *SUNY-Albany*
Ennio Rao, *The University of North Carolina, Chapel Hill*
Paolo Valesio, *Columbia University*
Rebecca West, *The University of Chicago*
Antonio Vitti, *Indiana University, Bloomington*

Annali d'Italianistica
Volumes 1-21 are available for free consultation:
www.archive.org/details/annaliditalianis212003univ

Editorial Policy
Annali d'Italianistica seeks to promote the study of Italian literature in its cultural context, to foster scholarly excellence, and to select topics of interest to a large number of Italianists. Monographic in nature, the journal is receptive to a variety of topics, critical approaches, and theoretical perspectives. Each year's topic is announced ahead of time, and contributions are welcome. The journal is published in the fall of each year. Manuscripts should be submitted electronically as attachments in Word. Authors should follow the MLA style for articles in English; articles in Italian should conform to the *AdI* editorial style. Visit the journal's website (www.ibiblio.org/annali) for further information. For all communications concerning contributions, address the Editor, *Annali d'Italianistica*, The University of North Carolina at Chapel Hill, Chapel Hill, NC 27599-3170, or email: annali@unc.edu.

Notes & Reviews
This section occasionally publishes essays and review articles on topics treated in previous volumes of *Annali d'Italianistica*.

Italian Bookshelf
Italian Bookshelf is edited by Dino S. Cervigni and Anne Tordi. The purpose of *Italian Bookshelf* is to identify, review, and bring to the attention of Italianists recent studies on Italian literature and culture. *Italian Bookshelf* covers the entire history of Italian literature and reviews books exclusively on the basis of their scholarly worth. To this purpose, junior and senior colleagues will be invited to collaborate without any consideration to academic affiliation and with an open attitude toward critical approaches. Contributions to this section are solicited. Scholars who intend to contribute are encouraged to contact the editors. Book reviews, to be submitted electronically, should be sent to the Editor. For inquiries, post <annali@unc.edu>.

The Journal's Website: www.ibiblio.org/annali
The tables of contents of all issues are available online. As of volume 16 (1998), each issue's introductory essay and all book reviews are available online with their full texts. As of the 2008 issue, book reviews are published exclusively online.

In Memory of Mario Marti
(1914-2015)
Scholar Teacher Mentor

The most senior of all the Italianists in the world, and a much admired scholar, teacher, and mentor, Mario Marti died on February 4, 2015, in Lecce. His funeral was celebrated in the Church of San Lazzaro on the following day. His wife, Franca, his daughter, Chiara, and his son Benedetto survive him. He was only a few months shy of his 101st birthday, having been born on May 19, 1914 in a small town near Lecce. He attended the *Liceo Classico Colonna* in Galatina (LC), and graduated from the *Scuola Normale Superiore* of Pisa in 1938 with a dissertation on Leopardi, under the directorship of Luigi Russo. After teaching in a *liceo* in Rome and commuting weekly to the newly formed Università di Lecce for many years, he finally returned to his native Salento, was chair of Department, and *Rettore* of the University from 1968 until 1981.

A specialist primarily of the Middle Ages, the Renaissance, and Leopardi, Mario Marti — a philologist, a critic, and a lover of Italian culture — has written on virtually all centuries of Italy's literary culture and on many aspects of his native Salento. Scholars of the Middle Ages know him and will remember him with much appreciation for his studies on the *dolce stil nuovo*, Dante, and Boccaccio. His editions (e.g., *I poeti del dolce stil nuovo*; Giovanni *Boccaccio, Opere Minori in volgare*) are indispensable research tools. He has been a constant contributor to the *Giornale storico della letteratura italiana* until the very last years of his life. Including all his books, editions, essays, and reviews, his bibliography exceeds 1,000 scholarly pieces. He remained active until the last year of his life.

Mario Marti distinguished himself, in my view, for two characteristics. He deeply loved Italy's literary history and culture, and he always nurtured, encouraged, and supported his many disciples, friends, and colleagues. I met him when I first visited Lecce in the mid-1970s. I was humbled when he presented himself very modestly as a scholar of the time before Dante. After that first encounter, I paid him a visit annually with few exceptions. He received friends and colleagues with much warmth in his comfortable apartment in Lecce, within walking distance from his beloved University. Always encouraging and supportive, Mario Marti showed much interest in his visitors' research. I saw him for the last time in May 2014, when he had just completed his 100th birthday. His health was failing, but his mind was very lucid and his speech very clear. All of us — he, his wife, my wife, and I — engaged in a very pleasant conversation for about an hour.

Together with his many friends and colleagues I will deeply miss him. I will remember him for his scholarship and dedication to the study of Italian literature, for his support of so many of us, for his warmth, for his modesty.

Dino S. Cervigni

AdI 2017.
Violence Resistance Tolerance Sacrifice in Italy's Literary and Cultural History

From ancient philosophers — Heraclitus ("All things come into being through strife") — to Petrarch ("Sed sic sine lite atque offensione nil genuit natura parens") and beyond, people have often believed that nothing occurs without violence, struggle, and even war. The Hebrew Bible presents the *lex talionis* (the eye-for-an-eye code of justice), but also the command not to hate one's brother and to love neighbors (Lev. 19.17-18). The New Testament contains Christ's injunction to love one's enemies. And yet, even in the Gospels one comes across striking statements, "I did not come to bring peace, but a sword" (Matthew 10.34), and also, "The one who has no sword must sell his cloak and buy one" (Luke 22.36). Even inanimate nature — the physical locus within which we humans live — often appears in all its frightening aspects almost as often as in its benevolent and nurturing manifestations. Thus, from the beginning of humankind's history to the present time, violence in all its manifestations and human responses to it — resistance, tolerance, compassion, and sacrifice — have accompanied and guided human beings. And yet, human responses to violence include not only additional violence and resistance to it, but also acceptance, tolerance, compassion, and sacrifice. Here are some of the questions which the phenomenon of violence brings up: What is violence, which are its roots, and how can it be assessed? Should humans embrace it, seek to resist to it, control it and overcome it, or should they also allow to be overcome by it in some form of sacrifice?

I am inviting scholars to engage in the analysis of violence, resistance, tolerance, and sacrifice within the context of Italy's literature and culture. Interested scholars are asked to define their approach theoretically and ethically, analyze the roots and consequences of violence — whether it be physical, verbal, mental, or psychological — and point out its consequences. Theoretical essays, drawing from various disciplines, are also most welcome. Thus AdI 2017 seeks to investigate whether any forms of violence are acceptable, or, rather, whether all forms of violence should be condemnable; and whether the only violence that may be somewhat fruitful, although always condemnable, is the violence which is inflicted, not upon others, but upon ourselves and which we are willing to bear for the benefit of others, as Christians believe that Christ did. Unquestionably, violence changes individuals, communities, and societies, which may seek to resist to it, tolerate it, or become victims of it. Confronted by violence, people have even immolated themselves.

Thus additional issues to be pondered are: Has historical violence created enduring literary and cultural expressions leading to peace or only to more violence? Has the representation of violence in literature and art glorified violence, created a vicious circle, or sought to break the virtually unstoppable spiraling of brutal force? What role have compassion and sacrifice played, and what role should they play in a violent world such as ours? Neither religious nor secular literature can claim on the unequivocal condemnation of violence in human lives. And yet, even outside religious literature, Italy's literary culture offers many examples — fictional and historical — of a non-violent life, from Boccaccio's Griselda to Galileo Galilei and Spiro Tozaj/Michele Tallarico in Gianni Amelio's *Lamerica*. Thus the issue to confront will always be: What is the best way to stop the vicious circle of violence?

Essays are due in the fall of 2016. The volume will appear in the fall of 2017. Please submit your proposal to Dino Cervigni, editor (annali@unc.edu), or either guest editor: Chiara Ferrari (Chiara.Ferrari@csi.cuny.edu) and Olimpia Pelosi (onuvola@aol.com).

ANNALI D'ITALIANISTICA
Volume 33, 2015

THE GREAT WAR & THE MODERNIST IMAGINATION IN ITALY
GUEST EDITORS
LUCA SOMIGLI & SIMONA STORCHI

17 **Luca Somigli and Simona Storchi**
Introduction.
The Great War and the Modernist Imagination in Italy

1. INTELLECTUALS & THE LEGITIMATION OF THE WAR

31 **Marja Härmänmaa**
Gabriele D'Annunzio and War Rhetoric in the *Canti della guerra latina*

53 **Cristina Gragnani**
Lacerba e *Il figlio alla guerra*: agli estremi dell'interventismo intellettuale?

75 **Michael Subialka**
Modernism at War: Pirandello and the Crisis of (German) Cultural Identity

2. WRITERS AND ARTISTS AT WAR

99 **Allison Cooper**
Giuseppe Ungaretti's Disanimate Modernism

115 **Stefano Bragato**
F. T. Marinetti's Construction of World War I Narratives (1915)

131 **Umberto Rossi**
Broken Images of a Defeat:
Gadda, Comisso, Malaparte, and the Rout of Caporetto

151 **Davide Bellini**
Kobilek di Soffici: dalla guerra-gioco alla narrazione di una comunità

169 **Alberto Comparini**
Sbarbaro e la rappresentazione negativa della Grande Guerra:
per una lettura modernista dei "trucioli di guerra" (1917-1919)

187 **Maria Elena Versari**
Avant-garde Iconographies of Combat:
From the *Futurist Synthesis of War* to *Beat the Whites with the Red Wedge*

3. THE INTERNAL FRONT

205 **Selena Daly**
Constructing the Futurist Wartime Hero: Futurism and the Public, 1915-1919

223 **Enrico Cesaretti**
Domestic Fronts: Bringing the Great War Home
in Pirandello's *Novelle per un anno*

241 **Sarah Pesenti Campagnoni**
La guerra (in) tradotta. Informazione, propaganda e immagini dal fronte

4. GENDERING THE WAR

259 **Barbara Meazzi**
Annie Vivanti e la Grande Guerra: stupro, aborto e redenzione in *Vae Victis!*

275 **Lucia Re**
Women at War: Eva Kühn Amendola (Magamal)
– Interventionist, Futurist, Fascist

309 **Katia Pizzi**
From Marinetti's *L'alcòva d'acciaio* to Giani Stuparich's *Ritorneranno*:
Gender, Nationalism, Technology and the Italian Great War

5. The Great War between History and Myth

321 **Simona Storchi**
Ardengo Soffici's *Rete mediterranea*:
The Aesthetics and Politics of Post-war Modernism

341 **Jennifer Griffiths**
Enrico Toti: A New Man for Italy's Mutilated Victory

355 **Silvia Contarini & Pierpaolo Naccarella**
La difficile memoria della Grande Guerra
nella rivista comunista "Rinascita" (1944-1968)

ITALIAN BOOKSHELF
Edited by
Dino S. Cervigni and Anne Tordi

As of the 2008 issue, book reviews are published exclusively online. Please visit the journal's website for the complete text: www.ibiblio.org/annali

GENERAL & MISCELLANEOUS STUDIES

385 Christian Thorsten Callisen, ed. *Reading and Writing History from Bruni to Windschuttle. Essays in Honour of Gary Ianziti*. Burlington (VT): Ashgate, 2014. Pp. 257. (**Marta Celati**, *University of Oxford*)

387 **Franco Cassano.** *Southern Thought and Other Essays on the Mediterranean.* **Ed. and trans. Norma Bouchard and Valerio Ferme.** New York: Fordham University Press, 2012. Pp. 212. (**Anthony Tamburri**, *John D. Calandra Italian American Institute, Queens College, CUNY*)

390 **Marcella Croce.** *The Chivalric Folk Tradition in Sicily. A History of Storytelling, Puppetry, Painted Carts and Other Arts.* Jefferson (NC): McFarland, 2014. Pp. 210. (**Andrea Privitera**, *University of Western Ontario; Università di Padova*)

392 **Domenico De Martino, a cura di.** *Una lingua e il suo vocabolario.* Firenze: Accademia della Crusca, 2014. Pp. 132. (**Daniela D'Eugenio**, *Graduate Center, City University of New York*)

395 **Donatella Fischer, ed.** *The Tradition of the Actor-Author in Italian Theatre.* London: Modern Humanities Research Association and Maney Publishing, 2013. Pp. 220. (**Laurie Shepard**, *Boston College*)

397 **Francesca Italiano and Irene Marchegiani.** *Percorsi: l'Italia attraverso la lingua e la cultura.* 3rd ed. Upper Saddle River (NJ): Pearson, 2014. Pp. 592. (**Daria Bozzato**, *Kenyon College*)

399 *Journal of Italian Translation* 7.2 (Fall 2012) and 8.1 (Spring 2013). (**Luciano Parisi**, *University of Exeter*)

399 *Misure critiche. Rivista semestrale di letteratura e cultura varia.* Nuova serie, anno XII, 1, gennaio-giugno 2013, pp. 229. (**Tommaso Pepe**, *Florida State University*)

402 *Sicily and Scotland. Where Extemes Meet.* **A cura di Graham Tulloch, Karen Agutter & Luciana D'Arcangeli.** Leics : Trubadour Publishing, 2014. Pp. 160. (Enrico Bolzoni, *Université de Poitiers*)

404 *Studi d'Italianistica nell'Africa australe / Italian Studies in Southern Africa* 27.1 (2014). Pp. 114. (**Lidia Ciccone**, *Independent Scholar*)

406 **Silvia Valisa.** *Gender, Narrative, and Dissonance in the Modern Italian Novel.* Toronto: University of Toronto Press, 2014. Pp. 239. (**Andrea Sartori**, *Brown University*)

MIDDLE AGES & RENAISSANCE

408 **Marco Santoro.** *I Giunta a Madrid: vicende e documenti.* Biblioteca di Paratesto 9. Pisa: Fabrizio Serra Editore, 2013. (**Graziano Ruffini,** *Università di Firenze*)

414 **Lucia Battaglia Ricci.** *Scrivere un libro di novelle. Giovanni Boccaccio autore, lettore, editore.* Memoria del tempo 39. Ravenna: Longo Editore, 2013. Pp. 243. (**K. P. Clarke,** *University of York*).

416 **Douglas Biow.** *On the Importance of Being an Individual in Renaissance Italy: Men, Their Professions, and Their Beards.* Philadelphia: University of Pennsylvania Press, 2015. Pp. 311. (**Sharon McHugh,** *New York University*)

418 **Igor Candido.** *Boccaccio umanista. Studi su Boccaccio e Apuleio.* Ravenna: Longo, 2014. Pp. 165. (**Filippo Gianferrari,** *The University of Notre Dame*)

420 **Francesco Ciabattoni and Pier Massimo Forni, eds.** *The* Decameron *Third Day in Perspective.* Toronto: Toronto University Press, 2014. Pp. 268. (**Brandon K. Essary,** *Elon University*)

422 **Grupo Tenzone.** *Le dolci rime d'amor che io solea.* Madrid: Rosario Scrimieri Martìn edizioni 2014. Pp. 201. (**Anna Maria Cantore,** *Università degli Studi di Bari*)

425 **Julia Hairston, ed. and trans.** *The Poems and Letters of Tullia d'Aragona and Others: A Bilingual Edition.* Toronto: Center for Reformation and Renaissance Studies, 2014. Pp. 352. (**RoseAnna Mueller,** *Columbia College Chicago*)

427 **Luca Lombardo.** *Boezio in Dante: La Consolatio philosophiae nello scrittoio del poeta.* Filologia medievali e moderni, Serie occidentale. Volume 4. Venezia: Edizioni Ca' Foscari, 2013. Pp. 704. E-book. (**Julia Bolton Holloway,** *University of Colorado, Boulder*)

429 **Molly M. Martin and Paola Ugolini, eds. and trans.** *Veronica Gambara: Complete Poems, A Bilingual Edition.* The Other Voice in Early Modern Europe. Toronto: Center for Reformation and Renaissance Studies. 2014. Pp.186. (**RoseAnna Mueller,** *Columbia College Chicago*)

431 **Amyrose McCue Gill and Sarah Rolfe Prodan, eds.** *Friendship and Sociability in Premodern Europe: Contexts, Concepts, and Expressions.* Toronto: Center for Reformation and Renaissance Studies, 2014. Pp. 318. (**Delphine Montoliu,** *CNRS, CLLE-Université Toulouse Jean Jaurès Laboratory*)

433 **Caterina Mongiat Farina.** *Questione di lingua. L'ideologia del dibattito sull'italiano nel Cinquecento.* Ravenna: Longo, 2014. Pp. 164. (**Laura Benedetti,** *Georgetown University*)

435 **Daragh O'Connell and Jennifer Petrie.** *Nature and Art in Dante: Literary and Theological Essays.* Dublin: Four Courts Press, 2013. Pp. 248. (**Massimo Lollini,** *University of Oregon*)

437 **Carlo Ossola.** *Autunno del Rinascimento. Idea del tempio dell'arte nell'ultimo Cinquecento.* **Prefazione di Mario Praz.** Biblioteca di Lettere Italiane, Studi e Testi.

LXXII. Firenze. Leo S. Olschki Editore. 2014. Pp. 425. (**Federica Conselvan**, *Università "La Sapienza" di Roma*)

439   Francesco Petrarca. *Rerum memorandarum libri.* **A cura di Marco Petoletti.** Firenze: Le Lettere, 2014. Pp. 524. (**Paolo Rigo**, *Università degli Studi Roma Tre*)

441   **Rocco Rubini, ed.** *The Renaissance from an Italian Perspective: An Anthology of Essays 1860-1968.* Ravenna: Longo Editore, 2014. Pp. 254. (**Tessa Bullington**, *University of North Carolina at Chapel Hill*)

443   **Manuela Scarci, ed.** *Creating Women: Representation, Self-Representation, and Agency in the Renaissance.* Toronto: Centre for Reformation and Renaissance Studies, 2013. Pp. 205. (**Cristina Mazzoni,** *University of Vermont*)

445   *Shakespeare and the Italian Renaissance: Appropriation, Transformation, Opposition.* **Ed. Michele Marrapodi.** Burlington, Vermont: Ashgate, 2015. Pp. xi + 373. (**Carmine Di Biase**, *Jacksonville State University*)

447   **Matteo Soranzo.** *Poetry and Identity in Quattrocento Naples.* Farnham-Burrington: Ashgate, 2014. Pp, 169. (**Emma Grootveld**, *KU Leuven, Research Foundation Flanders*)

449   **Chris Wickham.** *Sleepwalking into a New World: The Emergence of Italian City Communes in the Twelfth Century.* Princeton: Princeton University Press, 2015. Pp. 305. (**Michael Sherberg**, *Washington University in St. Louis*)

451   **Jan M. Ziolkowski, ed.** *Dante and Islam.* New York: Fordham University Press, 2015. Pp. 372. (**Ellie Emslie Stevens,** Independent Scholar)

SEVENTEETH, EIGHTEENTH, AND NINETEENTH CENTURIES

453   **Luigi Capuana.** *The Dragon's Nest and Other Stories and Plays Selected from his Five Collections of Fairy Tales.* **Ed. and trans. Marina Cocuzza and Joseph Farrell. Illustrations by Giovanna Nicotra.** Mineola (NY): Legas, 2014. Pp. 148. (**Ennio Rao**, *University of North Carolina at Chapel Hill*)

454   **Natalie Crohn Schmitt.** *Befriending the* Commedia dell'Arte *of Flaminio Scala*: *The Comic Scenarios.* Toronto: The University of Toronto Press, 2014. Pp. 328. (**Joseph Farrell**, *Professor Emeritus, University of Strathclyde*)

456   **Alice Crosta.** *Alessandro Manzoni nei paesi Anglosassoni.* Bern: Peterlang, 2014. Pp. 248. (**Nicla Riverso**, *University of Washington*)

459   **Eugenio L. Giusti.** *The Renaissance Courtesan in Words, Letters and Images. Social Amphibology and Moral Framing (A Diacronic Perspective).* Milano: LED Edizioni Universitarie di Lettere, Economia e Diritto, 2014. Pp. 96. (**Clara Stella**, *The University of Leeds*)

461   **Crystal Hall.** *Galileo's Reading.* New York: Cambridge University Press, 2013. Pp. 254. (**Daniele Macuglia**, *Morris Fishbein Center for the History of Science & Medicine, University of Chicago*)

463 *La lingua di Galileo.* Atti del Convegno: Firenze, Accademia della Crusca, 13 dicembre 2011. **A cura di Elisabetta Benucci e Raffaella Setti.** Firenze: Accademia della Crusca, 2013. Pp. 140. (**Franco Gallippi**, *Istituto Italiano di Cultura a Toronto*

465 Giovanni Meli. *The Poetry of Giovanni Meli. A Bilingual Anthology (Sicilian/English).* **Ed., Introd., and trans. into English verse by Gaetano Cipolla.** Pueti d'Arba Sucula/Poets of Arba Sicula Vol. 14. Mineola (NY): Legas, 2015. Pp. 356. (**Ennio Rao**, *University of North Carolina at Chapel Hill*)

466 **Giuseppe Parini,** *Il Mattino (1763) – Il Mezzogiorno (1765),* **a cura di Giovanni Biancardi, introduzione di Edoardo Esposito, commento di Stefano Ballerio,** Pisa-Roma, Fabrizio Serra Editore, 2013. Pp. 310. (**Matteo Fadini**, *Università di Trento*)

468 **Giuseppe Parini,** *Odi,* **a cura di Mirella D'Ettorre, introduzione di Giorgio Baroni,** Pisa-Roma, Fabrizio Serra Editore, 2013. Pp. 279. (**Matteo Fadini**, *Università di Trento*)

470 **Eugenia Paulicelli.** *Writing Fashion in Early Modern Italy: From* Sprezzatura *to* Satire. Burlington VT: Ashgate, 2014. Pp. 261. (**Cristina Mazzoni**, *University of Vermont*)

472 **Rachel A. Walsh.** *Ugo Foscolo's Tragic Vision in Italy and England.* Toronto: University of Toronto Press, 2014. Pp. 218. (**Emanuela Pecchioli**, *SUNY, Buffalo*

TWENTIETH AND TWENTY-FIRST CENTURIES: LITERATURE, FILM, THEORY, CULTURE

474 **Giosuè Allegrini and Lara-Vinca Masini.** *Visual Poetry: L'avanguardia delle neoavanguardie: mezzo secolo di poesia visiva, poesia concreta, scrittura visuale.* Milano: Skira, 2014. Pp. 478. (**Massimiliano Delfino**, *Columbia University*)

476 **Pierpaolo Antonello.** *Dimenticare Pasolini. Intellettuali e impegno nell'Italia contemporanea.* Milano-Udine: Mimesis, 2012. Pp. 163. (**Monica Jansen**, *Utrecht University — University of Antwerp*)

478 **Nir Arielli.** *Fascist Italy and the Middle East, 1933-40.* New York: Palgrave Macmillan, 2013. Pp. 257. (**Norma Bouchard**, *San Diego State University*)

480 **Massimo Bontempelli.** *Watching the Moon and Other Plays.* **Ed. and trans. Patricia Gaborik.** New York: Italica Press, 2013. Pp. 127. (**Jonathan R. Hiller**, *Adelphi University*)

482 **Vincenzo Cardarelli.** *L'epistolario Cardarelli-Bacchelli (1910-1925). L'archivio privato di un'amicizia poetica.* A cura di Silvia Morgani. Perugia: Morlacchi, 2014. Pp. 562. (**Paolo Rigo**, *Università degli Studi Roma Tre*)

485 *Cronache dal cielo stretto. Scrivere il Nordest.* **A cura di Cristina Perissinotto e Charles Klopp. Prefazione di Elvio Guagnini.** Udine: Forum, 2013. Pp. 270. (**Thomas Harrison**, *University of California, Los Angeles*)

487 **Vilma De Gasparin.** *Loss and the Other in the Visionary Works of Anna Maria Ortese.* Oxford: Oxford University Press, 2014. Pp. 320. (**Stefano Bellin**, *University College London*)

489 **Lorenzo Del Boca.** *Italy's Lies: Debunking History's Lies So That Italy Might Become a "Normal Country."* **Trans. Ilaria Marra Rosiglioni.** Studi e Testi 2. New York: Bordighera, 2014. Pp. 226. (**Marcello Messina**, *Universidade Federal do Acre*)

491 **Luca Di Blasi, Manuele Gragnolati, and Christoph F. E. Holzhey, eds.** *The Scandal of Self-Contradiction. Pasolini's Multistable Subjectivities, Traditions, Geographies.* Wien-Berlin: Turia + Kant, 2012. Pp. 327. (**Francesca Parmeggiani**, *Fordham University*)

493 **Francesco Durante, ed.** *Italoamericana: The Literature of the Great Migration, 1880-1943.* Ed. (American edition) Robert Viscusi. New York: Fordham University Press, 2014. Pp. 997. (**K. E. von Wittelsbach**, *Cornell University*)

495 **Alain Elkann.** *Racconti.* Milano: Bompiani, 2014. Pp. 443. (**Olimpia Pelosi**, *State University of New York at Albany*)

497 **John Gatt-Rutter.** *The Bilingual Cockatoo: Writing Italian Australian Lives.* Melbourne: Hybrid, 2014. Pp. 237. (**Patrizia Sambuco**, *Monash University*)

499 **Antonio Lucio Giannone,** *Fra Sud ed Europa. Studi sul Novecento letterario italiano.* Martano-Lecce: Edizioni Milella 2013. Pp. 253. (**Anna Maria Cantore**, *Università degli Studi di Bari*)

501 **Danielle Hipkins and Roger Pitt, eds.** *New Visions of the Child in Italian Cinema.* Bern: Peter Lang, 2014. Pp. 342. (**Patrizia Bettella**, *University of Alberta*)

504 **Ernest Ialongo and William M. Adams, eds.** *New Directions in Italian and Italian-American History: Selected Essays from the Conference in Honor of Philip V. Cannistraro.* New York: John Calandra Italian American Institute, 2013. Pp.128. (**Francesca Muccini**, *Belmont University*)

506 **Giulia Iannuzzi.** *Fantascienza italiana. Riviste, autori, dibattiti dagli anni Cinquanta agli anni Settanta.* Milano: Mimesis, 2014. Pp. 359. (**Luciano Parisi**, *University of Exeter*)

508 **Giulia Iannuzzi.** *Sotto il cielo di Trieste. Fortuna critica e bibliografia di Pier Antonio Quarantotti Gambini.* Milano: Biblion, 2013. Pp. 185. (**Luciano Parisi**, *University of Exeter*)

510 **Lucienne Kroha.** *The Drama of the Assimilated Jew: Giorgio Bassani's Romanzo di Ferrara.* Toronto: University of Toronto Press, 2014. Pp. 313. (**Emiliano Perra**, *University of Winchester*)

512 **Daniela La Penna.** "La promessa d'un semplice linguaggio". *Lingua e stile nella poesia di Amelia Rosselli.* Roma: Carocci, 2013. Pp. 207. (**Laura Ferro**, *Università La Sapienza*)

514 **Daniela La Penna, ed.** *Meneghello. Fiction, Scholarship, Passione civile.* Special supplement to *The Italianist* 32. Reading: University of Reading, 2012. Pp. 247. (**Elisa Segnini**, *University of British Columbia*)

516 **Francesco Lioce.** *Dalla* Colonia felice *alla "colonia Eritrea". Cultura e ideologia in Carlo Dossi.* Napoli: Loffredo, 2014. Pp. 138. (**Fabrizio Miliucci**, *Università degli Studi Roma Tre*)

517 **Stefania Lucamante.** *Forging Shoah Memories. Italian Women Writers, Jewish Identity and the Holocaust.* New York: Palgrave Macmillan, 2014. Pp. 291. (**Inge Lanslots**, *KU Leuven, University of Leuven*)

519 **Bernadette Luciano and Susanna Scarparo.** *Reframing Italy. New Trends in Italian Women's Filmmaking.* West Lafayette, Ind.: Purdue UP, 2013. Pp. 245. (**Francesca Parmeggiani**, *Fordham University*)

522 **Manuela Marchesini.** *La galleria interiore dell'Ingegnere.* Torino: Bollati Boringhieri, 2014. Pp. 188. (**Martina Mazzetti**, *Università degli Studi di Firenze*)

524 **Matteo Marchesini.** *Da Pascoli a Busi. Letterati e letteratura in Italia.* Macerata: Quodlibet, 2014. Pp. 535. (**Fabrizio Miliucci**, *Università degli Studi Roma Tre*)

525 **Lucy M. Maulsby.** *Fascism, Architecture and the Claiming of Modern Milan, 1922-1943.* Toronto: University of Toronto Press, 2014. Pp. 247. (**John Foot**, *University of Bristol*)

527 **Andrea Mirabile.** *Multimedia Archaeologies. Gabriele D'Annunzio, Belle Époque Paris, and the Total Artwork.* Amsterdam: Rodopi, 2014. Pp. 215. (**Enrico Minardi**, *Arizona State University*)

530 *Morte a Venezia. Thomas Mann/Luchino Visconti: un confronto.* **A cura di Francesco Bono, Luigi Cimmino, Giorgio Pangaro, Soveria Mannelli.** Catanzaro: Rubbettino, 2014. Pp. 238. (**Alessandro Tinterri**, *Università di Perugia*)

533 *NEMLA Italian Studies. Journal of Italian Studies, Italian Section, Northeast Modern Language Association* 36 (2014). Special issue. *Italy in WWII and the Transition to Democracy: Memory, Fiction, Histories.* **Ed. Franco Baldasso and Simona Wright.** Pp. 235. (**Nicola Lucchi**, *New York University*)

535 **Federico Pacchioni.** *Inspiring Fellini: Literary Collaborations behind the Scenes.* Toronto: University of Toronto Press, 2014. Pp. 237. (**Ryan Calabretta-Sajder**, *University of Arkansas, Fayetteville*)

537 **Elio Pagliarani,** *Tutto il teatro,* **a cura di Gianluca Rizzo,** Venezia, Marsilio, 2013. Pp. 366. (**Mimmo Cangiano**, *Duke University*)

539 **Federica Pedriali, ed.** *Gadda Goes to War. An Original Drama by Fabrizio Gifuni.* Edinburgh: Edinburgh University Press, 2013. Pp. 167. (**Francesca Facchi**, *University of Toronto*)

542 *Per Franco Scataglini. Indagini di poesia*. Atti del Convegno: Urbino, 9 maggio 2012. **A cura di Tiziana Mattioli.** Rimini: Raffaelli Editore, 2013. Pp. 172. (**Gabriele Scalessa**, *University of Warwick*)

543 *Per Nino Pedretti. Vòusi*. Atti del Convegno, Urbino, 30 novembre 2012. **A cura di Gualtiero De Santi, Tiziana Mattioli, Manuela Ricci.** Rimini: Raffaelli Editore, 2013. Pp. 152. (**Gabriele Scalessa**, *University of Warwick*)

545 **Giuseppe Polimeni**, ed. *Lingua letteraria e lingua dell'uso. Un dibattito tra critici, linguisti e scrittori ("La Ruota" 1941-1942)*. Firenze: Accademia della Crusca, 2013. Pp. 128. (**Mary J. Migliozzi**, *Indiana University*)

547 **Laura Rorato.** *Caravaggio in Film and Literature. Popular Culture's Appropriation of a Baroque Genius*. London: Modern Humanities Research Association and Maney Publishing, 2014. Pp. 226. (**Giacomo Tagliani**, *University of Siena*)

550 **Frank Rosengarten.** *Through Partisan Eyes: My Friendships, Literary Education, and Political Encounters in Italy (1956-2013). With Sidelights on My Experiences in the United States, France, and the Soviet Union*. Firenze: Firenze University Press, 2014. Pp. 207. (**Charles Klopp**, *Ohio State University*)

552 **Grace Russo Bullaro and Elena Benelli**, eds. *Shifting and Shaping a National Identity: Transnational Writers and Pluriculturalism in Italy Today*. Kibworth (UK): Troubador, 2014. Pp. 230. (**Meriel Tulante**, *Philadelphia University*)

554 **Monica Seger.** *Landscapes in Between: Environmental Change in Modern Italian Literature and Film*. Toronto: U of Toronto, 2015. Pp. 196. (**Massimiliano Cirulli**, PhD candidate, *University of North Carolina at Chapel Hill*)

556 **Giuseppe Sgarbi.** *Lungo l'argine del tempo. Memorie di un farmacista*. Ginevra: Skira, 2014. Pp. 148. (**Olimpia Pelosi**, *State University of New York at Albany*)

559 **Hugh Shankland.** *Out of Italy. The Story of Italians in North East England. The story of Italians in North East England*. Kibworth Beauchamp: Troubador Publishing Ltd, 2014. Pp. 344. (**Giusy Di Filippo**, *University of New Hampshire*)

560 **Anthony Julian Tamburri**, ed. *Meditations on Identity / Meditazioni su identità*. New York: Bordighera, 2014. Pp. 116. (**Lidia Ciccone**, *Independent Scholar*)

563 **Francesco Trento e Aureliano Amadei.** *Twenty Cigarettes in Nasiriyah*. [No city:] FourCats Press, 2014, Pp.173. (**Federica Colleoni**, *University of South Florida, Tampa*)

565 **Antonio Vitti**, ed. *Lezioni di cinema e di regia*. Firenze: Società Editrice Fiorentina, 2013. Pp. 327. (**Anita Virga**, *University of the Witwatersrand*)

566 **Katrin Wehling-Giorgi.** *Gadda and Beckett: Storytelling, Subjectivity and Fracture*, London, Legenda, 2014. Pp. 164. (**Alberto Comparini**, *Stanford University*)

BRIEF NOTICES BY ANNE TORDI

569   Pier Paolo Argiolas, Andrea Cannas, Giovanni Vito Distefano, and Marina Guglielmi. *Le grandi parodie Disney, ovvero I classici fra la nuvole.* Cagliari: Edizioni NPE, 2013. Pp. 197.

569   **Vincenzo Ferrara.** *Dialettismi italiani nei lessici bilingui.* Acireale-Roma: Bonanno Editore, 2013. Pp. 288.

570   **Paolo Regio,** *Sirenide*, Edizione, Introduzione e Note **a cura di Anna Cerbo**, Università degli Studi di Napoli "L'Orientale", Dipartimento di Studi Letterari, Linguistici e Comparati, Sezione Romanza. Collana Testi XII. Napoli: University Press, Photocity Edizioni, 2014. Pp. 1096.

571   **Franco Ricci.** *The Sopranos. Born Under a Bad Sign.* Toronto: University of Toronto Press, 2014. Pp. 324.

571   *"Umana cosa è aver compassione degli afflitti..." Raccontare, consolare, curare nella narrativa europea da Boccaccio al Seicento. Atti del Convegno di Torino per il settimo centenario di Boccaccio (12-14 dicembre 2013).* A cura di **Erminia Ardissino, Guillermo Carrascòn, Davide Dalmas, Patrizia Pellizzari**. Numero monografico di *Levia Gravia. Quaderno annuale di letteratura italiana,* XV-XVI (2013-2014), Alessandria, Edizioni dell'Orso, 2015. Pp. 706.

573   **Alessandro Vettori.** *Giuseppe Berto: la passione della scrittura.* Venezia: Marsilio Editori, 2013. Pp. 207.

POETRY & FICTION

573   **Angela M. Jeannet.** *Il paese di Nuova Speranza. Un'italiana negli States.* No city: Dumes: 2015. Pp. 205.

573   **Angela M. Jeannet.** *Tre fratelli.* Narrativa Aracne 31. Ariccia (RM): Aracne, 2015. Pp. 178.

573   **MISCELLANEOUS**

Carte di viaggio. Studi di lingua e letteratura italiana 7 (2014). Pp. 144. [Pisa-Roma. Fabrizio Serra Editore. 3015]
Cultura e prospettive 22 (gennaio-marzo 2014). Pp. 192.
Cultura e prospettive 23 (aprile-giugno 2014). Pp. 192.
Cultura e prospettive 24 (luglio-settembre 2014). Pp. 192.
Esperienze letterarie 39.3 (2014). Pp. 138.

Luca Somigli and Simona Storchi

Introduction: The Great War and the Modernist Imagination in Italy[1]

Since the publication of Eric Hobsbawm's *Age of Extremes* in 1994, it has become commonplace to speak of a "short twentieth century" — the "secolo breve," to use the Italian expression that became the title of the 1995 Rizzoli translation of Hobsbawm's book. This expression explicitly recognizes the ruptural and age-defining impact of the First World War. In fact, in this reading of modern European history, which has by now become common, the Great War marks the beginning of a period of often violent transformation that closed (at least in Hobsbawm's account) with the Fall of the Berlin Wall and the first Gulf War. Cultural historians have also remarked on the transformative effect of the war on everyday life, as the subtitle of Modris Eksteins's *Rites of Spring: The Great War and the Birth of the Modern Age* (1989), reminds us. As Eksteins remarks, values such as speed, newness, inwardness or transience precede the war; indeed, these values were also some of the keywords of pre-war European Modernism. And yet, in order for them to take hold beyond the confines of intellectual circles and artistic debates, "an entire scale of values and beliefs had to yield pride of place, and the Great War was [...] the single most significant event in that development" (Eksteins xiv). More recently, Antonio Gibelli has made a similar argument specifically for Italy, describing the war as "an accelerated and violent course in modernity" (10) that transformed the relationship between individuals and state, produced and expanded new technologies and new forms of social organization, blurred the boundaries between natural and artificial, and revolutionized the perception of space and time.[2] Eksteins and Gibelli provide the two poles within which the essays of this volume move: on the one hand, they aim to investigate the transformative impact of the war on all aspects of cultural life; on the other, they remain rooted in the specificities and particularities of Italy.

Following the Franco-Prussian war of 1870-71, the forty-odd years of general peace in Europe — interrupted now and then by the flare-up of conflicts on its Balkan fringes or on its imperial edges, as in the case of the Italo-Turkish War of 1911-12 — may have lured its populations into a false sense of security

---

[1] We would like to thank Dino Cervigni for his comments and suggestions on this introductory essay and for all his help in assembling the volume.
[2] Unless otherwise noted, all translations are ours.

that made the outbreak of the Great War all the more shocking. However, the specter of war had never disappeared from the European scene. Indeed, on the eve of the armed conflict, the discourse of the artistic and literary avant-garde was thoroughly steeped in the rhetoric of war and had been so for quite some time. Before they were mobilized, writers and artists already saw themselves locked in a deadly struggle with enemies that, as Milton Cohen writes, included "the forces of artistic reaction, the hostile press, the conservative academies, the reactionary critics, the smug, self-satisfied bourgeoisie" (160). These battles, as Cohen points out, were not new to the 1910s, for they had evolved through skirmishes throughout the nineteenth century. Yet, by the early 1910s, as the modernist innovation intensified, its language turned increasingly to war and violence (160), as evidenced by the 1909 Futurist manifesto, a text that exuded aggressiveness and famously declared war "the sole cleanser of the world" (Marinetti, *Critical* 14). From the "slap in the face of public taste" invoked by Burliuk, Kruchenykh, Mayakovsky and Khelbnikov in their manifesto of the same title (Caws 230), to the "blasts" launched against numerous adversaries, including England and France, in Wyndham Lewis's Vorticist manifesto, aggressiveness became an integral component of the language of an avant-garde intent on attacking the institutions of bourgeois life. In this context, modernists across Europe greeted the mobilization of 1914 with enthusiasm, either welcoming the war as a "purifying fire" that would "clean out" Europe's decay and bring about palingenesis and regeneration, or finding creative inspiration in life at the front (Cohen 163; Griffin 153). The war constituted an opportunity for avant-garde artists to take the fusion of art and life to its extreme consequences, while the technological innovations it fostered challenged artists to find the appropriate idiom to represent this new reality. At the same time, the toll taken by the war on European modernists in terms of artists killed or severely wounded, both physically and psychologically, was immense. With rare exceptions, the war destroyed the modernists' mood of buoyant optimism about the future and their beliefs about the war's role in bringing about that future. These sentiments were replaced by the representation of trauma and by an apocalyptic imagery, which highlighted the loss of idealism undergone by artists as the war came to be experienced in its full atrocity (Cohen 165). Finally, as Cohen notes, Modernism itself became a war casualty: it did survive, but it lost its international character and became permeated by the classical values of balance, restraint and order (165). Thus, the relationship between war and Modernism was complex and multi-directional. The modernist rhetoric of war permeated the discourse of interventionism and served to justify the war effort both during the conflict and in retrospect, during its aftermath; yet, at same time, the reality of war in the trenches and on the battlefield, and the very real consequences for individual lives, profoundly affected and shaped the various forms of modernist poetics. Indeed, the war brought into relief the untenability of any simple and straightforward distinction between "tradition" and "the modern." In this regard, analyzing discourses of legitimation of the war, Jay Winter points out the convergence of the formal experimentation championed by the avant-garde during the pre-war years and a more conventional approach, steeped in traditional values — such as patriotism, propaganda and the glorification of the war dead — which were disseminated by elite and popular culture before and during the war (Winter 3).

An approach that takes into account the many facets of the cultural responses to the First World War is particularly suitable to an analysis of the Italian situation and will contribute to a rethinking of how Italian Modernism reacted to and was shaped by the First World War. Mario Isnenghi's influential book, *Il mito della grande guerra,* systematically explores the attitudes and reactions of Italian intellectuals before and during the war. What characterizes the Italian situation vis-à-vis that of the rest of Europe is the vocal and active support for intervention on the part of a large number of avant-garde and modernist intellectuals, writers and artists — a support that, to a certain extent, influenced their response to the actual war experience. For the modernist intellectuals who supported Italian intervention, the war represented the realization of a series of myths which had been at the center of the aesthetic-political debate since the beginning of the century and which, to an extent, had defined the relationship between art and politics since then. These coalesced around a cluster of themes: the religion of the fatherland, the critique of the ruling class and of the bourgeoisie, the quest for a new social order, the aspiration to a spiritual, cultural and moral renewal (Adamson 264). The interventionism championed by the Italian cultural elites was linked particularly to an avant-garde culture steeped in the "mito della Grande Italia," as Emilio Gentile calls it. This myth manifested itself in radical nationalism and in the call for a political, moral and cultural revolution that would regenerate the Italians, form a solid national conscience, and prepare Italy to be a protagonist in history and a leader in modern civilization (*La Grande Italia* 92). As Gentile rightly notes, this myth of national regeneration was at once cultural and political, as the rebellion against bourgeois culture extended to liberal democracy and took the form of a totalizing aspiration to a national regeneration inspired and led by art (*L'apocalisse* 191-92). Indeed, the sometimes complementary and sometimes contradictory interpretations of the war before, during and after actual military engagement — the "fourth war of Independence," the "capitalist war," the "mutilated victory," the cradle that nurtured the Fascist spirit, to name only a few — all hinge around the perceived need of forging a national identity and a mission for Italy and its people. In this sense, in Italy the avant-garde legitimized the war and vice-versa. For the war became the event that defined a generation of avant-garde intellectuals and sanctioned the reconciliation between art and the praxis of life which, according to Peter Bürger, was at the core of the avant-garde experience. As some of the essays in this volume demonstrate, the reflection on and the representation of the war catalyzed some of the defining issues thematized by Modernism, such as the relationship between the artists and the institutions of culture and between the artist and tradition; the question of cultural memory; the role of the sacred; the mythical and the metaphysical with respect to positivist discourses of modernity; the status of technology within modern society (Somigli e Moroni 12). Above all, the war put into question the role of the modern intellectual. Ultimately, the ability to verbalize or visualize war determined the status of the artists and their capacity to understand, confront and survive the forces of modernity that they had helped to unleash.

I. *Intellectuals and the Legitimation of the War*
When in 1914 F. T. Marinetti published the Italian translation of his 1913 poem *Le Monoplane du Pape*, he astutely changed the subtitle of the book from the "political novel" of the French version to the more pointed and topical "prophetic novel."[3] If not the war itself, the poem certainly anticipates the rhetorical strategies that served, in the various intellectual circles favoring intervention, to legitimize Italy's entry into the war. Pitting the youthful Italian volunteer "red shirts" against the ultra-Catholic Austrian soldiers along a frontline very much like the one that two years later would divide the two nations, Marinetti imagines a conflict that is cultural and religious before it is political, opposing, on the one side, a liberal, secular, vigorous Italy still steeped in the values of the Risorgimento (hence, the reference to the Garibaldinian uniform), and, on the other, a bigoted, senescent Austria-Hungary, about to collapse under the weight of its traditions and superstitions. Indeed, the notion of a conflict not only between two blocks of nations united by political and military alliances but, rather, between two opposing and perhaps incompatible views of the world, orients much of the discourse surrounding intervention. The essays in this section consider some articulations of that fundamental distinction.

More often than not, the rejection of the obligations of the long-standing treaty linking Italy to the central powers, Germany and the Austro-Hungarian Empire, was legitimized, not on the basis of the material and political benefits resulting from an alliance with the countries of the Triple Entente, but rather on the basis of the cultural and even "racial" incompatibility between Italians and the peoples of the Germanic nations, and of the close genetic links of Italy to France. As Cristina Gragnani explains in her essay, the war propaganda reactivated and endowed with new meaning an opposition that, already in the 19th century, had fractured European culture along broad trans-national lines: the opposition between *civilisation* and *Kultur*, between — at least from the point of view of the interventionist majority that favored an alliance with France — the

---

[3] The date of publication of the translation is, however, controversial. As Cammarota notes in his bibliography of Marinetti's writings, the volume was apparently not distributed before May 1916, although excerpts appeared in various periodicals between September 1914 and October 1915 (57).

Latin cult of measure, harmony and dialogue, and the Germanic cult of order, strength and hierarchy.[4] Indeed, Gragnani's essay shows the resilience and the power of this rhetorical strategy by noting how it cut across cultural, political and generational boundaries, remaining productive both before and after Italy's entry into the war. For instance, this cultural opposition orients the narrative of sacrifice for the nation in Anna Franchi's novel-pamphlet *Il figlio della guerra* (1917), and it grounds the interventionist discourse of the contributors to the avant-garde journal *Lacerba*, in particular of its editor Giovanni Papini, even though his aggressive nationalism and cultural elitism is otherwise quite distant from Franchi's socialist and feminist politics, which have solid Mazzinian and Republican roots.

The same rhetoric underlies also the poetic production of the leading writer in the interventionist campaign, Gabriele D'Annunzio, well after Italy joined the war. Marja Härmänmaa's analysis of D'Annunzio's *Canti della guerra latina*, written between 1914 and 1918, demonstrates how the opposition between the civilizing mission of the Latin peoples — among whom Italians stand out as heirs of Roman culture — and the barbarism and bestial savagery of what she calls the "Teutonic 'Other'" serves to tie together a number of different strands of the interventionist discourse, from the critique of Giolittian non-interventionism to irredentism. A perhaps more complex version of this opposition is to be found in Pirandello's short story, "Berecche e la guerra" (1915), the subject of Michael Subialka's contribution. Here, the protagonist's disillusionment with the German culture that had formed him and his generation (significantly opposed to that of his son, who vehemently supports France and volunteers to fight in its army) does not translate into an adversarial and dogmatic form of patriotism — although Berecche does feel the stirrings of an ambiguous "Latin sentiment" — but rather into a nationalism that is both capacious enough to value the contributions of other cultural traditions to that of the nation, and honest enough to acknowledge that Italy's motives for intervention may be as material and pragmatic as the motives that led Germany and the Austro-Hungarian Empire to precipitate the war.

II. *Writers and Artists at War*

As Winter notes, the art and literature produced during and in response to the First World War were characterized by an apocalyptic stance, which, by focusing on eschatology, utilized the language of the sacred to recast its message (145). Incorporating and elaborating some the darkest and most pessimistic responses to modernity characteristic of Western Europe's culture of the *fin de siècle*, the apocalyptic imaginary outlined by Gentile as constitutive of the cultural responses to the war (*L'apocalisse*) found its ultimate expression in the

---

[4] Such categories were of course considered exactly in the reverse in the German cultural world. See for instance Eksteins 76-82.

crisis of the ability to transmit experience. According to Walter Benjamin, who gave voice to this crisis in his essay "The Storyteller," the First World War had marked the culmination of a process of erosion of the ability to communicate experience, and this erosion, he felt, characterized the modern age. At the end of the war, Benjamin observed, men "returned from the battlefield grown silent — not richer, but poorer in communicable experience" (84). Yet many intellectuals who had had a direct experience of the war refused to be silenced by it. Their narrations foreground a meta-narrative element, as war writing became bound up with a reflection on the modes of communicating experiences that appeared to be incommunicable. As the traumatized self of the soldier/narrator/witness had to find a suitable voice to express the sense of destruction, de-humanization, loss and existential precariousness brought about by the war, the narrative of the conflict became bound up with modernist modes of writing, to such an extent that, in the Italian case, some of the works that defined literary Modernism were associated with war writing. These were characterized by intense subjectivity, fragmentation and linguistic experimentation, all part of an effort to convey the sense of ontological doubt and existential instability and a larger sense of crisis. The front became a physical as well as a metaphorical locus, a "psychologically and spiritually desolate place," as Allison Cooper argues in her essay, "in which one confronted the most pressing crises of modernity." In particular, she focuses on the notion of disanimation in relation to Giuseppe Ungaretti's war poetry. During the Great War, Cooper argues, disanimation conveyed the feeling of alienation arising from an awareness of a lack of unitary subjectivity or experience, caused by the mechanization of the conflict. It also emphasized the dehumanizing effect of the war and the inability of language to communicate that effect, thereby foregrounding the ineffability of the war experience, which reduced human beings to aphasia and posited an erasure of the self. Yet, Cooper argues, Ungaretti's language of loss, founded in death and born of aphasia — physical, emotional and epistemological as well as verbal — is ultimately turned into a reconstitutive tool that guarantees survival. Similarly, in his analysis of Camillo Sbarbaro's *Trucioli*, Alberto Comparini notes how the poet resists the mechanical and de-humanizing character of the war by anchoring his self to nature, thus defeating the cycle of death engendered by the conflict and claiming for nature a metaphysical dimension capable of restoring the relationship between the self and the world fractured by war.

The magnitude and novelty of the war experience, as Umberto Rossi notes in his article on Gadda, Comisso and Malaparte's accounts of the rout of Caporetto, required a rethinking of the literary strategies employed to convey its narration. A radically modern experience on a technologized battlefield, Rossi argues, lent itself to modernist modes of narration. These could be highly subjective journals or memoirs, as in the case of Gadda and Comisso, or a reportage by a collective subject — "il popolo dei soldati" — as in Malaparte's pamphlet *Viva Caporetto!*

Introduction: The Great War and the Modernist Imagination in Italy 23

Those avant-garde artists and writers who had actively supported the Italian intervention as the war broke out in Europe often used the narration of the conflict as an ideological tool to foreground an artistic agenda strictly interrelated with those ideas of palingenesis and national regeneration that had underpinned the interventionist cause. As Davide Bellini demonstrates in his essay, Ardengo Soffici's war memoir, *Kobilek*, sought to construct a war narrative that could convey a cross-class experience aimed at a wide readership. With *Kobilek* Soffici moved away from the avant-garde rhetoric that had characterized *Lacerba* and towards a rethinking of the modes for narrating the conflict, modes that would incorporate the immediacy of the journal entry into a more structured account. Such a mixed narrative economy allowed the space for a reflective narration, which explored not only the war action, but the psychology of the soldiers as well as their regional characteristics, to such an extent as to become, Bellini argues, the self-narration of a whole national community (see also Isnenghi, *Il mito della grande guerra* 193-95).

Reporting his experiences on notebooks, sheets, articles and *tavole parolibere*, Marinetti — Stefano Bragato explains — adopted a novel strategy, entailing a diversification of textual production, intended for capturing different aspects of the war experience and aimed at conveying them to different audiences. Each medium was utilized with a strategically different purpose and contained cultural and stylistic references aimed at a variety of backgrounds. With Marinetti, as with most modernist writers engaged directly with the war, reporting from the front became an ideological as well as a literary operation. The presumed autobiographical character of the war narrative was assumed to confer authority to the description of the events, yet Marinetti's prose appeared to be blurring the boundaries between reality and fiction. The narration itself of the war assumed a central role and, as such, became more important than the facts it recounted. Being turned into a propaganda tool, which required a rethinking of compositional strategies and autobiographical techniques, the writing self underwent an operation of textualization, in line with the avant-garde pledge to reduce the distance between art and life. Thus reality became aestheticized.

The futurists demonstrated that the self-promotional techniques deployed during the war had far-reaching influence, but also that the artistic idiom developed by futurist artists to represent the war had an ideological as well as an iconographic malleability which exposed it to appropriation by the international avant-garde in different political contexts. In her article, Maria Elena Versari traces the influence of Carlo Carrà's *Futurist Synthesis of War* on El Lissitzky's *Beat the Whites with the Red Wedge* (1920). The futurist visual experimentation gained currency in post-revolutionary Russian art as an innovative art form that suited the values of the Russian revolution. In particular, the Russian artists that championed the futurist style, such as Lissitzky and Malevich, acknowledged its potential to speak to the masses, pointing to the force that emerged from the

Russian Revolution. The transposition of the visual language of war in Carrà's work to that of the Russian Revolution in Lissitzky's *Beat the White with the Red Wedge*, a powerful syncretic assemblage of war symbols and revolutionary metaphors, shows the continuity between the language of war and post-war political and ideological propaganda, demonstrating how the war fought in the trenches and on the artistic front resulted in an internationalized idiom whose main quality was the ability to speak to the masses.

III. *The Internal Front*

As we noted above, much of the historical research of the last quarter century has emphasized the transformative effect of the war on every aspect of everyday life. While these transformative effects may have been felt more sharply by the men in the trenches and on the battlefields, they also affected the lives of those who stayed behind — the internal front, as it were, to which the essays in this section are dedicated. Indeed, as Enrico Cesaretti shows in his reading of Pirandello's short stories that directly reference the war, the account of the rupturing impact of the conflict on the daily life of the men and women on the home front — the fathers and mothers, friends and lovers, children and siblings of the men on the theater of war — constituted a privileged means to articulate some of the central themes of modernist literature, from the difficulty of endowing individual experience with order and meaning to the sense of the fragility of the subject in the face of forces beyond their control.

Stephen Kern has famously argued that the over-exposure to physical and sensorial stimuli on the war front translated into daily reality the fragmentation of modern experience already expressed in the arts by the Cubist avant-garde (287-312). While Kern's thesis is undoubtedly true, the role played by the Futurist avant-garde in giving form to the war experience should not be underestimated, especially in the case of Italy. In an essay on the soundscape of the war, Selena Daly has in fact convincingly suggested that the pre-war theorization and practice of an aesthetic use of the sounds and noises of modernity — think of Russolo's famous "noise-tuners" — offered the Futurists "a defense mechanism employed at the front in order to cope with the extremity of the situations unfolding around them." In her contribution to this volume, Daly considers how, at the same time, the war allowed Italian audiences to integrate into *their* experience Futurism itself, which went from being a phenomenon usually met with general scorn and ridicule by mainstream readers and gallery- and theater-goers, to being a respected and widely celebrated cultural movement. If the vehement patriotism of the Futurists — many of whom served (and in some cases died) in the war — reassured the public regarding the seriousness of what it had until then generally considered as little more than artistic buffoons, this credit in turn became an incentive for Marinetti and his fellow avant-gardists to develop new ways of reaching their audiences, culminating with the short-lived experience of the Futurist political party.

Visual media were another important instrument in the process of turning the war events into coherent narratives to influence public opinion. "The Great War was the first event to be multiplied iconographically by the extensive use of photography," writes Gibelli (11), and the same can be said perhaps even more persuasively for the twentieth-century visual medium par excellence: cinematography. Sarah Pesenti Campagnoni's essay documents the growing importance of photography and cinema on several levels, to support the war effort and the process of memorialization in its aftermath. The Italian army, like its European counterparts, quickly understood the potential of visual media to produce a "channel of empathic communication with the audiences on the internal front," and thus developed numerous strategies to use cinema and photography as means to legitimize the war effort and to amplify the crucial themes of sacrifice for the nation and support for the troops at the front. The essay also discusses the difficulties encountered in this effort — what the author calls the "invisibility of modern warfare," characterized by mostly empty battlefields and long periods of inaction in the trenches, so that the crucial event of the encounter with the enemy remained invisible and the recounting of it was entrusted to the testimony of the survivors rather than to images captured on film.

IV. *Gendering the War*
In an essay on British women and World War I, Claire Buck has compared the marginality, until recent years, of women's writing about the conflict, to the marginality to which they were pushed back in the workplace after 1918, when the men returning from the front reclaimed jobs and occupations temporarily taken over by women during the shortage of male labor power caused by conscription. Her provocative statement holds true for Italian culture as well. Frequently invoked as either victims to be avenged by their male protectors or as themselves nurturers of their menfolk fighting at the front, women seldom managed to make their voice and position heard in a significant and, perhaps more importantly, lasting way. In this respect, the debate that flourished in 1916-17 in *L'Italia futurista* on the "donne del posdomani" ("women of the future"), to quote an article by Rosa Rosà, is instructive. Rosà lucidly identified in the war a turning point in the recognition of the equality of women with men: "There is no need to say again that at this point women have replaced men in jobs that up until now we believed only men could perform, and enjoy salaries that until now women had never managed to get through *honest* work. Women are useful now — very useful" (113).[5]

---

[5] "Inutile ripetere, che in questo istante milioni di donne hanno assunto — al posto di uomini, lavori che fin ora si credeva solo uomini potessero eseguire — riscuotendo salari che fin ora il lavoro *onesto* della donna non aveva mai saputo ottenere. Sono utili ora, le donne, utilissime."

And yet, this utopian moment, as Silvia Contarini describes it in *La Femme futuriste* (312), comes to an end with the war and its aftermath. Indeed, Contarini's observation regarding the "disappearance of the question of women from the social and political scene" of post-war Italy can be applied not only to the Futurist movement, which in this sense egregiously failed in its self-avowed role of renewer of Italian social and political life, but to Italian culture as whole. In the words of social historian Anna Bravo, "old roles were resumed, and the women forced back into traditional peasant silence, leaving the men to monopolize the claim to war honours" (qtd. Wood 17).

The intellectual experience of Eva Kühn Amendola, the subject of Lucia Re's essay, offers a good example of the contradictions produced by this moment of fluid and unstable gender relations. Born in Lithuania and educated in Russia, England and Switzerland — and thus a true representative of the cosmopolitanism characterizing pre-war European intellectual life — Kühn settled in Italy after marrying Giovanni Amendola, who would become an influential politician and anti-Fascist. During the war she contributed to numerous Futurist periodicals, writing under the pseudonym of Magamal. Her creative and political writings witness to the great effort made by women intellectuals to use Marinetti's movement to re-think gender norms and roles; but they also point to the failure of that project in the face of the visceral masculinist ethos of their male colleagues, the ambiguities of the Futurist political program, and, perhaps more importantly, the increasing closure of public space to women after the war.

More often, women were invested with a powerful symbolic function, as the (passive) object at stake in the struggle with the enemy: the female body — be it that of a lover or of a mother — is in effect the symbolic site of national identity. This is the case, for instance, in two works otherwise characterized by remarkable thematic and aesthetic differences: F. T. Marinetti's *L'àlcova d'acciaio* (1921), with its celebration of the "guerra-festa," and Giani Stuparich's *Ritorneranno* (1941), an elegiac Triestine *tranche de vie*. As Katia Pizzi argues, the two works find a common ground in an ideological discourse that situates women firmly back in the private space of the maternal, thus re-establishing the gender binary threatened by the war in the ways so clearly perceived by Rosà. The nation itself is turned into a female figure in need of protection on the part of the male soldier.

A more faceted and complex version of this conflation of woman and nation is to be found in Annie Vivanti's novel *Vae Victis!*, based on her 1915 play *L'invasore* and inspired by the reports of war rapes during the German invasion of Belgium. As Barbara Meazzi shows, Vivanti's narrative shifts the focus from the consequences of the rape and ensuing pregnancies on the victims to the social body: the "contamination" of the body of the two women is quite literally the contamination of the national community — something that can be avoided only through a further violation of the female body, either through abortion or suicide. Nonetheless, through their choices (in particular Chérie's decision not to abort the enemy's child), Vivanti's women are given agency. As Allison Scardino Belzen rightly notes, "as stand-ins for Belgium, they were vanquished. As female characters, they found the strength to absorb and respond to the violence committed against them by the Germans" (141). Thus, as the war turned the female body into a parallel battlefield of competing ideologies of nation, race, gender and the self, modernist female writers offer "an embodied, feminist critique of trauma and the identity politics of war and war narratives" (Goodspeed-Chadwick 1). In this context, the female body stands in as a "textual marker" or symbol of female identity, which allows for the creation of a space for female characters and foregrounds female views and experiences that have traditionally been foreclosed (Goodspeed-Chadwick 1-5).

V. *The War Between History and Myth*
The immediate post-war years saw a process of mythologization of the war, particularly on the part of the veterans engaged in the process of elaborating the war experience both on a personal and political level. The testimony of artists, writers and intellectuals also contributed substantially to the memorial culture of the war, which was extensively used in post-war discourses of national identity and reconstruction. In this particular context, the body of the soldier underwent an extensive narrative processing aimed at dealing, on the one hand, with the wounding, mutilation, shock and trauma experienced in the trenches and, on the other, with the symbolic resignification acquired by the soldier's corporeal sacrifice on the altar of the nation. As Ana Carden Coyne has argued, after the war, the soldier's body, particularly the wounded and maimed body, became associated with discourses of national and cultural reconstruction and was incorporated in memorial culture and rituals (see also Wittman). This process is exemplified by the mythologizing of the one-legged cyclist Enrico Toti, whose disabled body, as Jennifer Griffiths argues in her article, became a symbol of national struggle in the Great War. As a war hero whose disability preceded the war and who died in battle, he occupies a peculiar position both in the memorial culture of the First World War and in the sacralization of the soldier's body. Acclaimed as a hero throughout and after the war and during the fascist years, he was the subject of several monuments that made use of neoclassical and Christian artistic idioms, thereby creating a mythical language of heroism and sacrifice that associated his body with metaphors of the nation.

The avant-garde artists returning from the war used their experience to rethink the connection between art and politics and reassess the integration between art and the praxis of life, particularly in its critique of the institutions of bourgeois art. As Walter Adamson notes, the war reconfigured the strategic outlook adopted by avant-garde modernists, who moved away from self-supporting groups and towards alliances with revolutionary political movements or regimes antagonistic to prevailing capitalism or commodity culture (344). In

Italy, the return to order that characterized the international post-war artistic scene was expressed in terms of a return to tradition as the reinterpretation of the classical heritage in strong national terms, allowing for a politicization of aesthetics which was key in the alignment of the avant-garde with Fascism during the inter-war years. In that respect, as Simona Storchi shows in her essay, Ardengo Soffici was a crucial figure in the theorization of the interconnection between aesthetics and politics, which he used to claim a strong role for the artist as the spiritual guide of the new nation emerging from the war. As Storchi demonstrates, Soffici used his magazine *Rete mediterranea*, published in 1920, as a platform to voice his politicized version of aesthetics, using his position both as an artist and as a veteran to gain legitimacy for his aesthetic-political program.

The development of a memorial culture of the Great War during the fascist regime is well documented (Griffin; Gentile, *Il culto del littorio*, *La grande Italia*, *Le origini*). Fascism used the war as an ideological repository, incorporating it in the construction of its own mythology and self-justification. Fascism also used the memorial culture of the war in the ritualization processes which underpinned its sacralization of politics, as Emilio Gentile has defined the vision underlying the complex system of myths, symbol and rituals at the core of the political practice of the fascist regime (*Il culto del littorio*). However, after the Second World War and the fall of the fascist regime, the interpretation of the Great War underwent a revision. The culture of the left in particular, as Silvia Contarini and Pierpaolo Naccarella explain, carried out a critique of the Great War and of the motivations for intervention. In their article on the treatment of the First World War in the communist periodical *Rinascita* between the 1940s and the 1960s, they chart the fluctuations in the assessment of the war within Italian communist historiography, which reflected changes in party leadership and the evolution of the politics of the PCI in the post-war years. Throughout the three decades of *Rinascita* which the two authors analyze, the war was assessed negatively, mainly as a fundamentally imperialist and bourgeois war, which in Italy was imposed on a population that was either passive or actively against it, and which caused profound damage to the country, particularly the South. Yet, throughout the post-World-War-Two years, the First World War was also seen as having had a positive function, as it contributed to an awakening of the masses and to their development of a political awareness. In any case, Contarini and Naccarella note that the interpretations of the Great War carried out in *Rinascita* over three decades tended to serve the political needs of the present. Such processes of revision and reappropriation contributed, together with the memorial culture, to the transformation of the Great War into a *lieu de mémoire*, as noted in Mario Isnenghi's multi-volume work on memory places in Italian culture. According to the social framing of the collective memory of the event, the Great War became bound up with the construction of the post-war nation, engendering a process of memorialization in which the memory of the war was kept alive while at the same time progressively removed from the reality of the war itself and turned into a political myth (Isnenghi, "La grande guerra").

University of Toronto   *University of Leicester*

Works cited

Adamson, Walter L. *Embattled Avant-Gardes. Modernism's Resistance to Commodity Culture in Europe*. Berkeley: U of California P, 2007.
Benjamin, Walter. "The Storyteller." *Illuminations*. Ed. Hannah Arendt. Trans. Harry Zorn. London: Pimlico, 1999. 83-109.
Buck, Claire. "British Women's Writing of the Great War." *The Cambridge Companion to the Literature of the First World War*. Ed. Vincent Sherry. Cambridge: Cambridge UP, 2005. 85-112.
Bürger, Peter. *Theory of the Avant-Garde*. Trans. Michael Shaw. Minneapolis: U of Minnesota P, 1984.
Carden-Coyne, Ana. *Reconstructing the Body. Classicism, Modernism, and the First World War*. Oxford: Oxford UP, 2009.
Caws, Mary Ann, ed. *Manifesto. A Century of Isms*. Lincoln: U of Nebraska P, 2001.
Cohen, Milton A. "Fatal Symbiosis: Modernism and the First World War". *The Literature of the Great War Reconsidered. Beyond Modern Memory*. Ed. Patrick J. Quinn and Steven Trout. Basingstoke: Palgrave Macmillan, 2001.
Contarini, Silvia. *La Femme futuriste. Mythes, modèles et représentations de la femme dans la théorie et la literature futuristes*. Nanterre: Presses Universitaires de Paris 10, 2006.
Daly, Selena. "Futurist War Noises: Confronting and Coping with the First World War." *California Italian Studies* 4.1 (2013). http://escholarship.org/uc/item/8fx1p115
Eksteins, Modris. *Rites of Spring: The Great War and the Birth of the Modern Age*. New York: Doubleday, 1989.
Gentile, Emilio. *L'apocalisse della modernità. La grande guerra per l'uomo nuovo*. Milano: Mondadori, 2008.
_____. *Il culto del littorio*. Roma: Laterza, 1993.
_____. *La Grande Italia. Ascesa e declino del mito della nazione nel ventesimo secolo*. Milano: Mondadori, 1997.
_____. *Le origini dell'ideologia fascista 1918-1925*. Bologna: Il Mulino, 1996.
Gibelli, Antonio. *L'officina della guerra. La Grande Guerra e le trasformazioni del mondo mentale*. 1991. 3rd ed. Torino: Bollati Boringhieri, 2007.
Goodspeed-Chadwick, Julie. *Modernist Women Writers and War. Trauma and the Female Body in Djuna Barnes, H.D., and Gertrude Stein*. Baton Rouge: Luisiana State UP, 2011.
Griffin, Roger. *Modernism and Fascism. The Sense of a New Beginning under Mussolini and Hitler*. Basingstoke: Palgrave Macmillan, 2007.
Hobsbawm, Eric. *Age of Extremes. The Short Twentieth Century, 1914-1991*. London: Micheal Joseph, 1994.
Isnenghi, Mario. "La grande guerra". *I luoghi della memoria. Strutture ed eventi dell'Italia unita*. Ed. Mario Isnenghi. Roma-Bari: Laterza, 1997: 273-309.

———. *Il mito della grande guerra.* Bari: Laterza, 1970.
Kern, Stephen. *The Culture of Time and Space 1880-1918.* 1983. Cambridge: Harvard UP, 2003.
[Lewis, Wyndham]. "Manifesto." *Blast* 1 (1914): 9-43.
Rosà, Rosa. "Le donne del posdomani." 1917. *Una donna con tre anime.* Ed. Claudia Salaris. Milano: Edizioni delle Donne, 1981. 113-14.
Scardino Belzer, Allison. *Women and the Great War: Femininity under Fire in Italy.* New York: Palgrave Macmillan, 2010.
Somigli, Luca, and Mario Moroni. "Modernism in Italy: An Introduction." *Italian Modernism. Italian Culture between Decadentism and Avant-Garde.* Ed. Luca Somigli and Mario Moroni. Toronto: U of Toronto P, 2004. 3-31.
Winter, Jay. *Sites of Memory, Sites of Mourning. The Great War in European Cultural History.* Cambridge: Cambridge UP, 1995.
Wittman, Laura. *The Tomb of the Unknown Soldier, Modern Mourning, and the Reinvention of the Mystical Body.* Toronto: U of Toronto P, 2011.
Wood, Sharon. *Italian Women's Writing 1860-1994.* Atlantic Highlands (NJ): The Athlone P, 1995.

Marja Härmänmaa

Gabriele D'Annunzio and War Rhetoric in the *Canti della guerra latina*

1. *Introduction: D'Annunzio between Poetry and Politics*

In the period following Italian unification, Francesco De Sanctis stressed the civil responsibility of writers. According to De Sanctis, an intellectual must not remain in an ivory tower, but must interact with the surrounding reality, and assume responsibility for culture and society. The message was fully understood by Giosuè Carducci, who during his lifetime was strongly engaged socially and politically. In a similar vein the so-called "generation of 1914," i.e., writers born around the 1880s such as F. T. Marinetti or Giovanni Papini, who had studied the sociologists Vilfredo Pareto and Gaetano Mosca, felt the urge to contribute to the direction of the nation. Yet, before them, the idea of socio-political engagement had probably reached its peak with the words and deeds of Gabriele D'Annunzio.

In addition to recognizing him as a writer, history remembers D'Annunzio as the founder of both modern political style and discourse (Alatri; Bàrberi Squarotti, "D'Annunzio scrittore 'politico'"; De Felice; De Felice and Gibellini; Ledeen; Perfetti, "D'Annunzio, ovvero la politica come poesia"). D'Annunzio initiated his political career as a member of parliament in 1897, and concluded it with the occupation of the city of Fiume (in Croatian, Rijeka) on the Dalmatian coast, where he, as a reaction to the humiliating treaty of Versailles, established a corporatist state under his leadership after the First World War (12 September 1919 to 18 January 1921). However, regardless of his activity, and with the exception of the constitution of the state of Fiume ("Carta del Carnaro"), D'Annunzio never wrote an explicit political programme.[1] A glaring example of his rather apolitical attitude is the way he suddenly changed his political position in the parliament from the Right to the Left. As an explanation he simply declared himself to be "beyond right and left" and instead "going towards life" (Andreoli, *Il vivere* 306-12; Ledeen 6; Woodhouse 163-93). Nevertheless, it is possible to identify a solid thread in D'Annunzio's politics: namely, his

---

[1] Giorgio Bàrberi Squarotti has rightly stated that politics in D'Annunzio's writings is never reasoning or analysis, but always literary "invention." For D'Annunzio, politics is only an occasion to experiment with a different kind of writing (Bàrberi Squarotti, "D'Annunzio scrittore 'politico'" 320-21).

unquestionable love for the fatherland. Like many others in the pre-First World War years, D'Annunzio was a nationalist dreaming of a strong, imperialistic Italy that would have importance on the international level (Gentile 86-94; Perfetti, *Il movimento nazionalista in Italia*). He expressed these aspirations in different pre-war writings. These political articles are collected in *Armata d'Italia* (1888), the first militaristic poems are now in *Odi navali* (1893), and the poems about the Italian-Turkish war in Libya (January 1912) are in *Merope*, also entitled *Canzoni della gesta d'oltremare* (1911-1912).

When the First World War began in August 1914, Italy was nominally allied with the Central Powers. However, after a period of neutrality, it finally entered the war on 23 May 1915 as an ally of France and the United Kingdom. During the neutrality stage, many intellectuals were in favour of the country's participation in the war with France (Isnenghi). Immediately when the war broke out, D'Annunzio also began to promote Italy's alliance with France and the country's intervention against Austria-Hungary.[2] In May 1915 he returned to Italy from France, and during the so-called "maggio radioso" (Radiant May, 2-20 May 1915), he delivered various speeches that are included in the collection entitled *Per la più grande Italia*. Furthermore, both before and during the war, he wrote several poems and rhythmic prose pieces that are now in the collection entitled *Canti della guerra latina*.[3]

2. Canti della guerra latina

Initially entitled *Gli inni sacri della guerra giusta*, the aforementioned collection was retitled *Asterope* when it was included in the larger poetic collection *Laudi del cielo, del mare, della terra e degli eroi* in his *Edizione dell'opera omnia* in 1932. Like the other four volumes of the cycle — *Maia, Electra, Alcyone, Merope* — *Asterope* (or *Sterope*) took the name of one the Pleiades, specifically the one who, according to one version of the legend, married Mars. However, he finally decided to change the title to *Canti della guerra latina*. *Canti* contains 18 works of lyric poetry and rhythmic prose, the first two of which are in French. D'Annunzio wrote them all between 1914 and 1918, and thus they are his last poems (Andreoli, "Canti" 1331-32).[4]

---

[2] In addition to the two first poems of *Canti*, D'Annunzio wrote three articles in favour of Italy's intervention. The articles, published in France, are: "Fluctibus et fatis," published in *Le Journal* of 30 September 1914; "La très amère Adriatique," published 25 April 1915, in *Le Figaro*, and "Le ciment romain," published in *La Petite Gironde* 30 April 1915, (Woodhouse 286). The articles are analysed also by Tosi (129-30).
[3] For this essay I have used the edition of *Biblioteca Italiana Zanichelli* [BIZ], DVD-ROM for Windows.
[4] Until now *Canti della guerra latina* has not aroused much scholarly attention. The most important studies are the essay of. Bàrberi Squarotti, "Le immagini della guerra," in which some pages are dedicated to *Canti*, and Bertazzoli's article "*Merope* e *Asterope*. Testi lirici per la patria in armi." Also Costa and De Michelis dedicate a chapter to *Canti*.

As the titles of the collection well indicate, the first poems were written in order to urge Italy's participation in the First World War, while the later ones glorify the conflict in order to sustain the country's willingness to fight. Therefore, these are celebratory poems with a persuasive intention. Before they were collected in a single volume in 1933, most had been published between November 1915 and November 1918 in the leading Italian newspaper *Il Corriere della Sera*, which, after a short period of neutrality, favoured Italy's intervention in the war.[5] According to Mario Isnenghi, the fact that the Italian press constantly published D'Annunzio's writings made him the country's semi-official war orator, who significantly influenced the opinion of the middle-class reading public that was supposed to lead the country (106).

Inspired by the theory of the so-called new rhetoric, my aim in this article is to analyse D'Annunzio's war rhetoric in *Canti della guerra latina* (Lo Cascio; Meyer; Perelman and Olbrechts-Tyteca; Perelman). I shall concentrate on the way in which D'Annunzio represents himself as orator; the enemy and the war; and the kind of rhetorical strategy he uses in order to persuade the reader about the justice and necessity of the conflict.

3. The Elected People
The First World War marked a turning point in both D'Annunzio's life and his literary production. On the one hand, the gunshots in Sarajevo offered an opportunity for the indebted dandy, who had been forced to move to France in order to escape his creditors in 1910, not only to return to the beloved fatherland, but also to change his life. With the outbreak of the war D'Annunzio bid farewell to the pre-war "vita leggera," when he was famous most of all for his love affairs and luxurious life-style, and prepared to become a national hero, the spiritual guide of the country, *Il Vate* of the Italians.[6]

Right after the declaration of war, Luigi Albertini, D'Annunzio's close friend and editor in chief of *Il Corriere della Sera*, asked him to write an article in support of Italy's neutrality. Instead, on 13 August D'Annunzio published in *Le Figaro* a poem entitled "L'Ode pour la résurrection latine," in 11 parts and 231 verses that grandiosely initiated his interventionist campaign; curiously, the following day the poem was also published in *Il Corriere della Sera* marking a

---

[5] "Ode pour la résurrection latine" and "Sur une image de la France croisée peinte par Romaine Brooks," the poems that open the collection, were first published in the French newspaper *Le Figaro* on 13 August 1914 and on 5 May 1915, respectively (Andreoli and Lorenzini 1332, 1336; Costa 229).
[6] It is worth recalling that once Italy entered the war, D'Annunzio volunteered to serve on the frontlines at the age of 52, where his legendary endeavours made him undoubtedly one of the bravest men in the war. About D'Annunzio's life, see especially Andreoli, *Il vivere inimitabile*; Woodhouse.

change in the newspaper's attitude towards the conflict (Woodhouse 273).[7]

Regardless of his nationalistic convictions, it is nevertheless appropriate to ask to what extent his desire to consolidate a sort of cult of personality incited D'Annunzio to engage in political life. In "L'Ode pour la résurrection latine," which is also the first poem of *Canti*, D'Annunzio explicitly verbalizes the transformation the war provoked in him: "Je ne suis plus en terre d'exil, / je ne suis plus l'étranger à la face blême, / je ne suis plus le banni sans arme ni laurier. / Un prodige soudain me transfigure, / une vertu maternelle / me soulève et me porte" (strophe 1). Likewise, he specifies his role as interpreter of the fervent vocation of the French and Italian peoples: "Je suis une offrande d'amour, / je suis un cri vers l'aurore, / je suis un clairon de rescousse / aux lèvres de la race élue" (strophe 1). Thus, before the formation of the interventionist coalition in Italy in September, D'Annunzio appropriated for himself a leading position in it by volunteering to God: "Me voici. Envoyez-moi, Seigneur" (strophe 2).

On the other hand, as Raffaella Bertazzoli has indicated, *Merope* first and then *Canti* marked a change in D'Annunzio's production. Instead of using literary invention in which he juxtaposes great but often imaginary endeavours to the misery of the "terza Italia," or escapes to future utopias from the antiheroic world of Umberto I, D'Annunzio finally focuses in his war poetry on present reality, on the ultimate heroic moment for the fatherland that the war represents to him (Bertazzoli 253). Nevertheless, Italy's cultural and military history does occupy an important position in *Canti*. In addition to being a mosaic of quotations of his previous texts, *Canti*, as well as his other interventionist writings, combines different ideological and political traditions of the country (Isnenghi 106-07). Unlike in his previous works, however, D'Annunzio here demonstrates no nostalgia. Instead, history and tradition are overtly exploited to stress Italy's special role in the world. In terms of rhetorical analysis, Italy's great past serves as the authority to which D'Annunzio appeals in order to sustain his point of view.[8] As the poems of *Canti* were all published first in *Il Corriere della sera*, the primary readership to whom they were targeted was therefore the cultivated middle class that could both understand and appreciate his erudite rhetoric.

In addition to references to Michelangelo, Garibaldi or the Risorgimento, a special position in D'Annunzio's rhetoric is reserved for Dante. Among the Italian poets of the twentieth century, D'Annunzio, perhaps better than anyone

---

[7] The poem was greatly appreciated by French writers, in particular by Maurice Barrès, Romain Rolland, and Paul Adam (Tosi 24-25; Andreoli, "Canti della guerra latina" 1328).

[8] The choice of an authority in a persuasive text is crucial. To defend a certain opinion, the author needs to know which positions the public would accept, which positions must be defended and how these positions should be defended. In other words, the author must be aware of the public's innate "identity": their interests, values and beliefs (Lo Cascio; Perelman).

else, was familiar with Dante's works. Consequently, his literary production is full of Dante's poetic motifs, direct quotes, terms and locutions, symbols and characters. Dante as a persona is present in D'Annunzio's works in the form of chastener or pilgrim. Often he appears with characteristics that derive from the Christian tradition, such as purifier, mediator, liberator or comforter (Balducci; De Michelis 34-35; Di Poppa Volture 249-56; Härmänmaa "L'immagine dell'inferno"; Scorrano 11-38; Valesio 87-114). Similarly in *Canti*, Dante has a dual role. On the one hand, several references to the poet stress the value of the Italian tradition, as in "Salmi per i nostri morti 1" (1918), in which D'Annunzio remembers Dante's statue in Trento as a symbol of the city's Italian character: "Mia nell'alpe è la città che Dante cuopre" (strophe 46). On the other hand, Dante, and especially his *Inferno,* function as a vehicle in different analogies D'Annunzio creates in order to underscore horror and disgust. In "Per i combattenti" (1918), by using both Dante's terminology, and with a comparison to *Inferno*, he emphasizes how the neutralists have dishonoured the war:

> Ma dall'immondo Barbaro la viva
> guerra sepolta fu come carogna
> truce, posta a marcire nella fogna
> buia, stivata nell'orrenda stiva,
> soffocata nel tossico fumante
> e rituffata nella lorda pozza
> come quell'ira che del fango ingozza
> nello Stige implacabile di Dante.
>
> (strophes 25-26)

Among the historical periods which D'Annunzio in one way or another references in his argumentation strategy, ancient Rome is especially important. The glorification of Roman history, placing the eternal city as a model for the arts and for social life and the idea of the Italians as its successors, culminated when Fascism adopted the cult of Rome, or *romanità*, to serve its ever more aggressive political goals. The popularity of ancient Rome had already experienced a sharp rise in the Risorgimento. Among others, Giuseppe Mazzini justified his nationalistic and imperialistic ideas about the Italian mission in the world by elevating the concepts of the Italians as heirs of all the values Rome represented and the significance of the *urbe* for Western civilization. Successively, in the young nation-state, the patriotic bourgeoisie began to use Rome metaphorically. The Roman Empire was considered to be a part of Italy's national history, and the sole period of cultural domination and prosperity before the Renaissance. The symbol of Rome went hand in hand with patriotic feelings and it was particularly cherished by those who dreamed of a strong, united and imperialistic Italy (Arthurs; Canfora, *Ideologie del classicismo*; Cracco Ruggini and Cracco; La Penna; Treves; Visser).

As John Woodhouse has revealed, as early as 1895 D'Annunzio planned to write a poetic prose piece about the magnificence of the Latin race beyond which "there is only barbarism" (274). He never finished the volume, but the myth of Rome is constantly present in D'Annunzio's writings (Cagnetta; Canfora, "Sull'ideologia del classicismo dannunziano"; Luti). In his interventionist campaign and in *Canti*, the "Latin resurrection" is one of the main arguments with which D'Annunzio justifies the war.[9] In "Fluctibus et fatis" he writes about the extraordinary character of Latin culture that is "nécessaire à la noblesse du monde, comme le rythme intérieur à tout être vivant" (842). Thus, D'Annunzio's war is in fact "une lutte de races" between the Latins and Teutons (840), a holy conflict between the elected people to whom belongs the role to lead civilization, and disgusting animal savagery: "Nous sommes les nobles, nous sommes les élus; / et nous écraserons la horde hideuse" ("L'Ode pour la résurrection latine," verses 211-12).[10]

Rome is usually present in the poems in an abstract form of "spirit" or "idea." In the last poem entitled "Cantico per la vittoria," published a day after the armistice on 12 November 1918, the locution "the poem of Rome" is the metaphor of the Roman heritage in the city of Dubrovnik (in Italian, Ragusa) on the Dalmatian coast that, according to D'Annunzio, belonged to Italy: "o Ragusa; / e tu bevi il carme di Roma" (strophe 17).

In addition to the cultural heritage, and in harmony with the nineteenth-century tradition, Rome also served D'Annunzio as a model of imperialism and aggressive foreign policy. In "L'Ode pour la résurrection latine," Rome is the stimulus that inspires the poet, the first-person narrator, to urge Italy to combat. When the poet understands his mission as promulgator of the Latin renaissance, he hears the horses of the Dioskouri neighing, which is to be understood as a symbol of the country's unrestrained will to fight: "Et j'entends les chevaux des Dioscures hennir" (v. 42). Successively, he hears the steps of the goddess Victory on the pavement of the ruins of the ancient city of Ostia. The poet turns to Victory to get help and strength to deliver his message: "ô Vierge, accompagne mon message, affermis ma voix!" (v. 84). Instead, in "Per la gloria," published in *Il Corriere della Sera* in December 1915, the analogy with the Roman past serves to arouse the wrath of a historical defeat: "Ma tu fa, Dio d'Italia, che al tuo cenno / gittiam nelle bilance lor cortesi / un ferro ancor temibile, che pesi / più della spada barbara di Brenno" (strophe 40).[11]

---

[9] The war offered an opportunity for France to redress the humiliating defeat in the Franco-Prussian War of 1870, and for Italy to gain international prestige and territories in the north.
[10] The same idea of the elected people is already present in the poem "Canto per la nazione eletta" (1899).
[11] Brennus, to whom D'Annunzio refers, was a chieftain of the Senones, who defeated the Romans at the Battle of Allia in 390 BC. In 387 BC he led an army of Cisalpine Gauls in the attack on Rome and captured most of the city. Brennus's sack of Rome was

4. About "the Old People"

What Isenghi calls "the intellectual use of the war" as a remedy to collective and individual pathologies was widespread in pre-First World War Europe. In Italy the idea of war as the solution to socio-political problems was particularly cherished by those who were disappointed with unification and the political life of the country. In interventionist writings, this so-called internal enemy was composed, first, of all the neutralists who opposed Italy's involvement in the conflict and successively of the defeatists, who were ready to accept the humiliating treaty of Versailles (Isenghi 107; Wohl). For D'Annunzio too, the enemy is primarily internal. In the rhetorical context in which *Canti* is to be located, Italy's government and the neutralists are the chief constraint that prevents the realization of the war. When representing the internal enemy, D'Annunzio polemically relies on both moral and physical concepts such as ignominy, fear, cunning, and animalism. Still, most of all, the enemy within is labelled as "the old people." As the war turns into a battle between the generations, D'Annunzio's position is similar to that of the pre-war interventionist coalition in which the most active groups, especially Papini, were those who claimed to represent "the Italian youth" and "the younger generations." They considered the war as an opportunity to destroy the unheroic Giolittian regime, cast away the restrictions of bourgeois existence and open the way towards an ill-defined but radically different future (Wohl 168). [12]

In "La très amère Adriatique" (25 April 1915) D'Annunzio overtly blames the political class for poor rule since unification, thanks to which Italy was still a second-class international power:

L'Italie, en vérité, après cinquante ans de malheurs, d'erreurs et d'efforts, mal gouvernée par des vieillards fourbes ou ineptes qui n'étaient que les restes des temps serviles ou bien les charbons étaient du petit feu de la petite révolution, l'Italie n'a pas encore montré au monde *ce qu'elle est réellement*.

(848; italics in original)

In "L'Ode pour la résurrection latine," D'Annunzio points to the enemy who are people "vêtu d'ignominie e de paix," characterized by "l'astuce et la

---

the only time the city was occupied by a non-Roman army before it fell to the Goths in 410.

[12] The Prime Minister of the Italian government during the neutrality period was Antonio Salandra (1853-1931). He was preceded by Giovanni Giolitti (1842-1928). All in all, the politicians of the period were born in the 1850s and even the 1840s. They were thus 10-20 years older than D'Annunzio, and 30-40 years older than Giovanni Papini (1881-1956), the most efficient propagator of the so-called generational thinking. After the war, the idea of the youth revolution became an essential element of Fascism (Wohl). The emphasis upon youth was also a very important theme in D'Annunzio's later politics (Ledeen 10).

peur," "vaches baveuses, / [qui] ruminaient le mensonge" (strophe 4).[13] Thus, Italy is "corrompue et polluée par les mains des vieillards" (strophe 4). In "Per la gloria" (1918) the "blandi parassiti" and "i delicati porci" (strophe 25) who murmur in "un mercato immondo" (strophe 24) persuade Italy to ignore war and the enemy's threat and wish to conserve the country as the innocent and inoffensive "Italietta" of the old, lazy and cowardly people: "Sèrbati a noi, sèrbati a noi perfetta / pe' lunghi ozii che a noi farà la pace / candida. Non ti giova il dado audace / trarre. Ma dormi su' tuoi lauri e aspetta" (strophe 33). In "Cantico per l'ottava della vittoria" (1918), written after the armistice, the defeatists are present with "il sogghigno dei vigliacchi" (strophe 2). The Poet invokes the personified Truth (Verità) to create the ode against the Italian government: "O domatrice di fuochi, foggiami tu quest'ode / e scagliala verso Roma; ché la mia mano prode / mi trema e condurla non posso" (strophe 3).

5. *The Dalmatian Ladies*

For both D'Annunzio and many other interventionists, one of the main nationalistic, political, ideological, cultural and to some extent economic rationales of the war consisted in assuring Italy a prominent role in international politics and in annexing the so-called *terre irredente*.[14] The territorial advantages, together with national aggrandizement, were also the main reasons for the Prime Minister Antonio Salandra and the foreign minister Sidney Sonnino, supported by King Vittorio Emanuele III, to involve Italy in the conflict against Austria.[15]

Similarly, in D'Annunzio's rhetoric, the chief political argument was to seize territories in Istria and on the Dalmatian coast, "de reconquérir avec la santé de son poumon gauche," as he put it in "Fluctibus et fatis" (840).[16] In "La très amère Adriatique" he supports his claims by reference to the supposed geographical continuity between the Alps and the Adriatic Sea, established by the divine will and human justice:

C'est que la possession de l'Adriatique, puisqu'on peut dire que l'Adriatique est le fils des Alpes et presque la continuation creuse de la plaine du Pô. Elle nous appartient par droit divin et par droit humain: par Dieu qui façonne les figures terrestres de manière que

---

[13] It is worth noting that D'Annunzio published "L'Ode" in August, right after the declaration of the war, and before the interventionist coalition was organized in September.

[14] These were territories in the north, northwest and northeast of Italy that were populated by Italian-speaking people or were connected to Italy by secular historical, linguistic or cultural ties.

[15] Instead, Giovanni Giolitti, the socialists and the Catholics opposed the intervention (Wohl 170).

[16] See also D'Annunzio's speech entitled, "Parole dette agli esuli dalmati ricevendo in dono il libro che afferma, dimostra e propugna l'italianità della Dalmazia, stampato in Genova" (7 May 1915), 31-34.

chaque race y reconnaisse sa destinée, et par l'homme qui multiplie la beauté des rivages en y dressant les monuments de sa noblesse et en y gravant les signes de ses plus hauts espoirs.

(851)

Even though the Dalmatian coast physically belongs to the Balkan region, its history was nevertheless Latin ("Le Ciment romain" 856). For this reason Italy's geographical and spiritual unification would be fulfilled only with the annexation of the areas that once were the Emperor Augustus's 12th region, and of which the Italian monuments are evidence ("La très amère Adriatique," 851). In addition to historical reasons, D'Annunzio details Italy's role as saviour in the region during times of political turbulence. Indeed, only Italy (with her conquest of Dalmatia) was able to offer a geopolitical solution to the territorial claims of the different Yugoslavian nations inside the Austrian-Hungarian Empire: "Elle [L'Italie] seule, en cette heure miraculeuse, a dans son poing la clef de fer qui ouvrira la porte étincelante de l'Avenir aux nations jougoslaves régénérées, réconciliées et fédérées" ("Le ciment romain," 854).

In the highly allusive *Canti*, the geopolitical reasons often fade away, but they are crucial topics in two poems. In "Salmi per i nostri morti 1" (1915), published in November 1915, by the end of the first and rather unfortunate year of the war, D'Annunzio explicitly declares: "Mie tutte le città del mio linguaggio, tutte le rive delle mie vestigia. Mando segni e portenti in mezzo ad esse" (strophe 47). Expelling the enemy from Italian territory becomes the rationale of the war: "E tu dicevi: 'Io trionferò. Io romperò il nemico nella mia terra e io lo calcherò sopra i miei monti. Io spartirò le Giudicarie, misurerò la valle dell'Isonzo, riscolpirò le rosse Dolomiti'" (strophe 45). In the last poem of *Canti*, "Cantico per l'ottava della vittoria," published for the first time in *Il Corriere della Sera* on 12 November 1918, a day after the armistice, some strophes are dedicated to the Dalmatian cities that Italy wished to annex. In the emotional images D'Annunzio personifies the cities as beautiful women who implicitly await Italian male heroes to rescue them, whereas references to Italian architecture, art and analogies with Venice make it clear to the reader that the cities are in fact Italian:

> E le città di Dalmazia si scingono sul mare
> cantando dai bei veroni veneti, bionde e chiare
> nell'ambra di Vettor Carpaccio.
>
> (strophe 10)
>
> E Zara è la prima, [...]
> tutta bella al davanzale della sua Riva Vecchia,
> ridorata come quando Venezia si rispecchia
> nell'oro sciolta dal caligo.
>
> (strophe 11)
>
> O Traù, mia dolce donna, tu che sei tra le donne
> dàlmate la più dorata!

> Sei nelle tue colonne come il fuoco nell'alabastro.
>
> (strophe 14)

At the end of the war, the peace treaty of Versailles signed in June 1919 was a disappointment to Italy, which did not get the territories she had claimed and that were promised to her in the treaty of London – including the aforementioned Dalmatian cities. By foreseeing the difficulties in the peace treaty already in "La preghiera di Sernaglia," published in *Il Corriere della Sera* on 24 October 1918, D'Annunzio presents the atrocious image of the personified and "mutilated Victory." In the famous slogan that became popular after the war, especially among the Italian irredentists and nationalists, the potential national trauma is metaphorically represented by the physical pain of "smashed knees" and "clipped wings":

Vittoria nostra, non sarai mutilata. Nessuno può frangerti i ginocchi né tarparti le penne. Dove corri? dove sali?

(strophe 63)

6. *Livestock and Sexual Orgy*

The First World War also marked a substantial change in the way D'Annunzio represented warfare. Like his contemporary Giovanni Pascoli in "La favola del disarmo" (1906), D'Annunzio, too, in his previous works, had stressed cruelty, slaughter and rape as constitutive elements of war. In the poem "Il sangue de le vergini" (1894) he depicts an imaginary war as a primordial outburst of a death instinct and will to conquest, an exercise of absolute violence without any logical reason or ethical motivation, a mere stage of humans' perennial cruelty ("Il sangue de le vergini"; Bàrberi Squarotti, "Le immagini della guerra" 195-201; Pascoli). The incentive for the hostilities between the two peoples is the sinister hatred bequeathed from father to son: "L'odio per cui feroci / tutti gli esseri pugnano, l'odio grande e immortale / che arde il sangue de gli uomini, mettea ne' loro cigli / un foco. Ed era l'odio il terribile male / che avean da i primi padri ereditato i figli" ("Il sangue de le vergini," vv. 153-157).

After the imaginary conflicts, the real war entered D'Annunzio's literary production with *Merope* (1911-1912). In this collection of epic poems, D'Annunzio reports real events in the Libyan war that are often taken from newspapers. Thanks to many details, including the names of actual Italian soldiers, the poems bear resemblance to a war documentary (Bàrberi Squarotti, "Le immagini della guerra," 203). Similar to "Il sangue de le vergini," the constitutive elements of war in *Merope* are hatred, revenge and violence. In "Canzone dei Dardanelli" (1912) D'Annunzio dedicates several verses to the cruelty of the enemy who has "crucified" the captured Italian soldiers, "cut their bodies with an axe," "turned them in black clot," "impaled the living ones with the skin of the chest pulled down like a red apron," "stitched their eyelids with needle and twine" or "buried them in sand up to the neck" (vv. 160-75). The detailed description transforms the enemy's brutality into the true rationale of warfare and ultimately serves to arouse in the Italians the paramount hatred that is "midolla della vendetta," and the pre-condition of fighting (vv. 175-76).[17]

The bittersweet revenge that "ride ne' denti suoi di giovin lupo" makes killing the enemy easy and exculpatory ("Canzone dei Dardanelli," vv. 152-153). In "Canzone della Diana" (1911), in order to further justify their merciless shooting, D'Annunzio represents the Turks not as humans but as mere dogs, and for this reason a stray shot turns into a cardinal sin:

> Occhio alla mira ferma, o cristiani.
> Solo chi sbaglia il colpo è peccatore.
> Vi sovvenga! Non uomini ma cani.
> Per secoli e per secoli d'orrore,
> vi sovvenga! Dilaniano i feriti,
> sgozzan gli inermi, corrono all'odore
> dei cadaveri, i corpi seppelliti
> dissotterrano, mùtilano i morti,
> scempiano i morti. Straziano i feriti,
> gli inermi, i prigionieri, i nostri morti!
> (vv. 157-166; Bàrberi Squarotti, "Le immagini della guerra" 205)

In "Fluctibus et fatis" D'Annunzio still stresses the need for the same hatred towards a repressive and threatening enemy: "Et celui-là même ne manqua aucune occasion d'enseigner et d'exciter la haine nécessaire contre l'ennemi invaincu qui toujours nous serre du côté gauche, du côté du Coeur, et ne nous permet de respire qu'avec un seul poumon" (838). The enemy is infamous and aggressive, cruel and covetous (840). The "homme teuton" (842) is constantly pushed by evil to expand toward Italy: "Une malefaim perpétuelle les pousse de leurs plaines sablonneuses et de leurs forêts glacées vers nos vignobles, nos vergers, nos cités claires, nos golfes tièdes" (841). For this reason the Italians have the obligation to fight him in a war that is a "supreme combat" for the existence and freedom of the Italian race: "il s'agit de combattre le combat suprême contre une menace imminente de servitude et d'extermination" (840).

In *Canti*, the same brutal enemy is present in "L'Ode alla nazione serba" (1915). D'Annunzio wrote the poem after the complete annihilation of the Serbian army during the autumn of 1915 in a joint offensive by Austria-Hungary, Germany and Bulgaria (Zoric). The defeat offered D'Annunzio an occasion to express once again his persistent loathing of Austria-Hungary, which he represents as a merciless executioner of innocent and defenceless civilians: "Il boia d'Asburgo, l'antico / uccisor d'infermi e d'inermi, / il mutilator di fanciulli / e di femmine" (vv. 22-25).

---

[17] The horrors are based on news articles of which some were published in *Le Matin* and *Le Journal* between 23 and 26 October 23 1911 (Andreoli and Lorenzini 1318).

In *Canti*, as in *Merope*, the enemy is often depicted as an animal. In "Salmi per i nostri morti 1" this cruel animalism is first conveyed implicitly with the image of the enemy with prey in its teeth: "Tu spezzi le mascelle del nemico e gli fai gittar la preda di tra i denti" (strophe 23). Successively, D'Annunzio explicitly transforms the war into a battle between a herd of beasts and pure justice: "Condotte come mandre, spartite come branchi sono le sue schiere. Le tue son come sacrificii di giustizia, son come olocausti di purità, son come offerte da ardere interamente" (strophe 24). The most extensive representation of the external enemy is in "L'Ode pour la résurrection latine," in which he is colourfully depicted with the traditional connotations of barbarism. The Teutonic "Other" is likened to livestock, whose existence is scarred by sexual orgy and alcohol abuse. To make him further and concretely disgusting, D'Annunzio liberates his fantasy and completes the image with a rotting carcass that the stinking two-headed vulture, a parody of the two-headed eagle of Austria, vomits:

> La force barbare nous appelle
> au combat sans merci.
> Comme la horde traînait
> dans ses chariots couverts de peaux fraîches
> les concubines innombrables
> pour les rassasier de carnage
> et les enivrer d'hydromel,
> ainsi elle amène toutes les hontes
> derrière ses hommes comptés en bétail à deux pieds,
> pour qu'ils couchent avec toutes dans leur sang épais
> qui est le rouge frère de la boue,
> tandis que le vautour à deux têtes,
> le maître puant au double cou dénudé,
> pousse son cri lugubre et rejette
> la charogne mal digérée.
>
> (vv. 133-145)[18]

However, compared to both the previous war poems and the interventionist writings, in *Canti* D'Annunzio's war rhetoric changes radically. First of all, the enemy image is completely different from the one in *Merope*. In *Canti*, denigrating Austria-Hungary in such an unambiguous way as in "L'Ode" is an exception. Usually, D'Annunzio uses abstract terms such as "enemy," and most of all "barbarism," when it is not even clear whether he is referring to the internal or external enemy or to an intangible "cosmic force." As a matter of

---

[18] The image of a vomiting two-headed eagle is already present in "Canzone dei Dardanelli" (1912): "La schifiltà dell'Aquila a due teste, / che rivomisce, come l'avvoltoio, / le carni dei cadaveri indigeste!" (vv. 73-75). The term "horde" with reference to the German and Austrian enemy appears already at the end of "Fluctibus et fatis" (843).

fact, in *Canti*, with the exception of "L'Ode" and "L'Ode alla nazione serba," he does not explicitly point out that the true physical enemy against whom the Italians fight is the Austro-Hungarian Empire.[19] On no other occasion does he disparage or accuse the real external enemy, Austria-Hungary, in the manner of modern war propaganda, of which he made ample use in *Merope* and the interventionist articles.

Second, the Italians do not feel hatred in the First World War. On the contrary, even before Italy's involvement in the war, D'Annunzio completely changed his stand, and in the speech in Quarto near Genova, he instead blesses those who abandon hatred: "Beati quelli che, avendo nel petto un odio radicato, se lo strapperanno con le loro proprie mani; e poi offeriranno la loro offerta" ("Orazione per la sagra dei Mille" 20).[20]

Last but not least, unlike in *Merope*, in which D'Annunzio offers a detailed description of the righteous and justified shooting of the enemy, the Italian soldiers do not kill in the First World War as reported and represented by the *Canti*. This substantial change found in D'Annunzio's portrayal of the enemy, or rather the lack of an enemy, is a consequence of the way D'Annunzio represents the nature of the war and its rationale in *Canti*. With few references to existing places, the First World War trenches, in fact, turn into a metaphysical and metatemporal space of pain and sorrow, disaster, death and sacrifice, which the Italian soldier reaches with a pure heart only to sacrifice himself. Regardless of the real territorial claims, in the poems of *Canti*, the First World War becomes a transcendental experience of purification and ultimately the gateway to resurrection and immortality.

7. *The Holy Harvest*

In the *Canti* (as in *Merope* earlier), D'Annunzio abandons the rhetorical *dispositio* of antithesis, realized often with a juxtaposition of Italy's glorious past, whether antiquity, medieval communes, the Renaissance or the Risorgimento, and the deplorable present time after unification (Bertazzoli 249). Instead, right after the first shots are fired, he represents the war as an epiphanic moment, a veritable occasion for the renaissance of the Latin people. At the beginning of "L'Ode pour la résurrection latine," D'Annunzio depicts the recent outbreak of war as an abstract, cosmic experience, both beautiful and horrifying: "Quelle horreur et quelle mort / et quelles beautés nouvelles / sont partout éparses dans la nuit?" (vv. 1-3) Successively, he stresses the idea of war as an

---

[19] However, for instance, in "Per la gloria" (1915) there is an implicit allusion to the Austrian-Hungarian Empire: "Duro nemico: in vento di Croazia / è polvere di guasto, afa d'incendio. / Ogni bellezza ei tiene in vilipendio" (strophe 29). Thus, the external enemy is still present in *Canti* even though in an abstract form.

[20] The "Orazione per la sagra dei Mille" (5.5.1915) is the famous speech D'Annunzio delivered in Quarto for the inauguration of the statue honouring Garibaldi's expedition, and with which he started his interventionist campaign in Italy.

occasion for a Latin rebirth with an analogy to agriculture, the basic activity humans must undertake in order to survive and a symbol of a new beginning. All of Part IX, the last section of "L'Ode," is dedicated to the image of war as harvest to which D'Annunzio invites the women. The fiercely fighting men on the frontline are compared to ears in the wind, whereas the fundamental elements of "bread" and "hunger" are metonymies of the new life that will begin in the battlefields:

Car, pour les Latins, c'est l'heure sainte / de la moisson et du combat. O femmes, / prenez les faucilles et moissonnez! / Apprêtez le pain nouveau / à la faim nouvelle! Vos hommes / frapperont fort, serrés comme les épis, / dans la bataille, rang contre rang, / comme les blés drus sous le vent d'est.

(vv. 215-22)[21]

However, the sublimation of the war culminates with its representation as Christian sacrament. The reasons for exploiting religion in war propaganda are naturally manifold; according to Giorgio Bàrberi Squarotti, by doing so D'Annunzio had particularly in mind a Catholic readership. In an Italy where the political ideology and official war propaganda were mainly secular, and the Pope was strongly against the war, D'Annunzio's religious rhetoric served to convert in favour of war those Catholics who were still strongly connected with the pacifist Church (Bàrberi Squarotti, "Le immagini della guerra" 213).

On the other hand, across the Western world, the use of religious rhetoric in politics, hailing from the French revolution, had consolidated its position during the nineteenth century. Together with the nationalistic ethos, politics was transformed from rational planning and decision making into enthralling and fanatical passion peppered with religious pathos. The nation became the fatherland, and the fatherland became the new divinity of the modern world. The term "martyr," that until then had only had a religious connotation began to be used to indicate political values, human feelings and sacrifices (Chabod 3-83). In the penultimate strophe of "La Marseillaise," Claude Joseph Rouget de Lisle sanctifies the fatherland: "Amour, sacré de la patrie / conduis, soutiens nos bras vengeurs." In Italy, some fifteen years later Ugo Foscolo ends his *Dei sepolcri* in a similar vein: "ove fia santo e lagrimato il sangue / per la patria versato" (vv. 293-94). Successively, in justifying his nationalist ideas, Giuseppe Mazzini made ample use of religious terminology that reflected his religious concept of nation, fatherland and politics in general (Mazzini).

By continuing the "religion of the Fatherland" indicated by Mazzini and the Risorgimento in D'Annunzio's political discourse, the distinction between the

---

[21] Some verses later D'Annunzio calls Victory a fierce harvester: "O Victoire, moissonneuse farouche" (v. 223). Soldiers are seeds for the new world: "Vous êtes la semence d'un nuoveau monde" (v. 229). In "All'America in armi" (1918) there is the same image of war as harvest (strophes 9-10).

sacred and the profane often faded (Ledeen 8-9). In his war poems religious terminology and thematics entered for the first time in "Canzone del sangue" (1911), and successively in the rest of the poems in *Merope*. As a result, the colonial war in Libya against the Turks becomes a necessary, right and holy new crusade in which the Christian Italians are fighting against the Muslim Turks ("Canzone del sangue"; Bàrberi Squarotti, "Le immagini della guerra" 204-07).

The Christian religion is also a powerful rhetorical device in D'Annunzio's prose propaganda in favour of Italy's intervention in the First World War. In March 1915, the invitation to deliver the speech in Quarto, offered the exiled D'Annunzio the possibility to return to Italy with glory and dignity. In addition to initiating D'Annunzio's interventionist campaign in Italy, the speech revealed the main rhetorical strategies with which he would successively sublimate the war: the Christian elements run the gamut from biblical phrases to a blasphemous parody of the Sermon on the Mount, and the speech concludes grandiosely with nine blessings of D'Annunzio's own ("Orazione per la sagra dei Mille" 11-20; Woodhouse 288-89).

In *Canti* D'Annunzio's manipulation of the Christian religion reaches an indisputable peak. The poems are full of religious terminology, symbols, images and direct quotes from the Bible. Some of the poems are entitled "prayers" or "psalms," and some of them also follow the technique of the biblical psalms. When representing the soldiers' suffering, D'Annunzio finds analogies in the Bible. In "La preghiera di Doberdò," a wounded soldier is compared to Bartimaeus, the blind beggar of Jericho (strophe 34). The functional religious language transforms the war into a myth and collective sacrifice and, by using Christian symbols, D'Annunzio convinced his audience that Italy was participating in a holy expedition (Bertazzoli 260; Ledeen 9).[22]

The war is holy, "sacra guerra" ("Per i morti del mare," v. 2), because it is fought for the existence of the Italian race, for the sanctified fatherland and for Latin culture. The abstract enemy in the war becomes a blasphemous monster, who burns churches, breaks altars and profanes holy relics: "Hanno arsi i duomi di Dio dove battezzammo i nostri nati, portammo le nostre bare, prostrammo il nostro cuor tristo. // Hanno abbattuto i nostri altari, fonduto le nostre campane, contaminato le nostre reliquie, maculato le specie di Cristo" ("La preghiera di Sernaglia," strophes 29-30). Not only are many of the poems prayers directed to a merciful and protective God, but also, in order to justify the war, D'Annunzio appeals to God, who therefore becomes the supreme authority in his rhetoric: "Dio di gloria, tu fa questo giudizio / della gloria, tu giudica di noi / per la palma, considera gli eroi, / guarda alla fede e pesa il sacrificio" ("Per la gloria," strophe 4). As the war is the fulfilment of God's will, the "true God" is present

---

[22] The Christian religion is present so extensively that Giorgio Bàrberi Squarotti has rightly stated that in *Canti* the First World War is transformed into a true celebration of Christian religious rites (Bàrberi Squarotti 201, 211).

where soldiers and civilians are suffering the most: "[...] e tutto armato di dolor t'avanzi / ed imprendi, nel giorno che t'è innanzi, / il taciturno tuo combattimento; // quivi è l'Iddio verace, / e sia lodato" ("Per i cittadini," vv. 41-45).

The motif of war as Christ's renewed sacrifice in each wounded soldier is also to be found in other war poets, such as Vittorio Locchi, Clemente Rebora and Giuseppe Ungaretti (Bàrberi Squarotti, "Le immagini della guerra" 213). By comparing the war to the birth of Jesus Christ, D'Annunzio emphasizes the idea of "advent," a new and undoubtedly glorious era in Italy's history that will begin in the trenches.[23] The holiness of the war culminates in "Il Rinato" (1918), in which D'Annunzio describes the rebirth of Christ amidst the horrors in the trenches as a promise of a new and better world in which "the light will hinder the darkness":

> S'ebbe natività nella trincea
> cava il Figliuol dell'uomo; e solo quivi,
> messo in fasce da piaghe, si giacea.
>
> (strophe 5)
>
> [...] E sanguinava in fasce; ed il rossore
> si dilatava come immenso raggio,
> sicché tutti i ghiacciai parvero aurore,
> tutte le nevi parvero il messaggio
> dei dì prossimi, l'ombra fu promessa
> di luce, il buio fu di luce ostaggio.
>
> (strophes 9-10)

8. *Towards Immortality*

Regardless of its holiness, D'Annunzio's war is nevertheless devastating and horrible. In "Per la gloria" (1915), he dedicates several stanzas to the sacrifices of the civilians (strophes 17-20); in "Per i cittadini" (1918) the first person narrator shows the interlocutor the trenches full of suffering:

> ecco t'appare
> più vicina dei sogni
> la trincea tetra, la penosa bolgia,
> tra maceria e steccaia
> il fango imputridito
> le piaghe non fasciate
> i morti non sepolti / gli smorti vólti
> dei vivi senza sonno
> fitti nel limo sino all'anguinaia.
>
> (strophe 2)

---

[23] A section of five poems in *Canti*, all published in January 1915, is indicatively entitled "Preghiera dell'avvento."

Instead of hiding blood, D'Annunzio continually emphasizes the constant presence of death in the war. In "La canzone del Quarnaro" (1918) in order to arouse courage and to challenge death, he glorifies it as merry company: "Siamo trenta d'una sorte, / e trentuno con la morte. / EIA, l'ultima! / Alalà!" (strophe 1).[24] Yet this kind of profanation is an exception, as usually D'Annunzio encompasses death with an aura of sanctity.

According to Raffaella Bertazzoli, D'Annunzio discovered the idea of the "beautiful death" on the battlefield in Nietzsche's *Zarathustra* (Bertazzoli 259). In "Salmi per i nostri morti 1" he indeed compares the brightness of death to a victory: "Una corona brilla sopra esse, come sopra la chioma delle vergini. Il sorriso precede la prodezza, e riappare dopo l'agonia. La morte è chiara come una vittoria" (strophe 25). Dying on a battlefield in the holy war for the sanctified fatherland also means the sanctification of the victims: "E allora udita fu dall'alto una voce senza carne, che diceva: 'Beati i morti.' Fu intesa una voce annunziare: 'Beati quelli che per te morranno'" (strophe 50). Finally, dying in war is the gateway to immortality, as the dead ones are promised resurrection: "Senza sudarii tu, senza lenzuoli, / li seppellisci ed io li dissotterro./ Rifioriranno ai tuoi novelli soli, / alla nuova stagione ch'io disserro" ("Il rinato" vv. 52-55). As the victims pantheistically meld in soil, water and wind, they become part of the holy fatherland:

> Ma presi erano nella terra, tenuti erano dalla terra, profondati in essa, intrisi con essa, carname con zolle, ossame con selci.
> E morivano. E come i corpi loro formavano il tuo corpo, così gli spiriti loro facevano il tuo fiato, o Patria, il tuo fiato possente.
> ("Salmi per i nostri morti 1," strophes 36-37)

Thus, dying on the battlefield is the only right way to die.[25] It was also the way D'Annunzio himself wanted to die in order to be liberated from the prison of the body and to become one with the beloved fatherland:

> Son nel carcere dell'ossa, nei lacci delle vene,
> e non diffuso nei vènti, nelle acque, nelle arene,
> in tutte le tue creature.
> Con una meravigliosa gioia tesi le mani

---

[24] Il Quarnaro, or Kvarner, is a bay in the northern Adriatic Sea, located between the Istrian peninsula and the northern Croatian littoral mainland. Since antiquity the Quarnaro has been considered the extreme limit of Italy's geographical territory. It is also mentioned by Dante: "Sì come Pola presso del Carnaro, / che Italia chiude, e i suoi termini bagna." (*Inferno* 9.114). During the end of the nineteenth and the beginning of the twentieth century, the Quarnaro was one of the symbols used by both Italian and Slavic nationalists.

[25] About D'Annunzio's rather complicated idea of death, and about his constant death drive, see Härmänmaa "The Seduction of Thanatos."

a rapir la morte. E sempre diceva ella: "Domani."
("Cantico per l'ottava della vittoria," strophes 27-28)[26]

9. Conclusion

D'Annunzio has been described as the founder of modern political discourse, which he was able to refine as a member of parliament, an interventionist and as commandant in Fiume. In answer to the challenges of the emerging mass society and the democratic system, he transformed political actions into dramatic ones in which people actively participated. Consequently, his political discourse was most of all geared to arouse enthusiasm; instead of a rational analysis of social problems, it was melodramatic and poetic, based on myths and symbols rather than on facts. By speaking directly to the people, posing questions, and asking for their participation, D'Annunzio made the crowd an active part of his speeches (Bàrberi Squarotti "D'Annunzio scrittore 'politico'"; Ledeen 8-9, 202; Leso 736-41; Perfetti, "D'Annunzio, ovvero la politica come poesia").

Similarly, in *Canti della guerra latina* the aestheticization of war was perfected. In harmony with D'Annunzio's political rhetoric, the *Canti* are emotional, allusive, metaphorical and evocative. To justify the war D'Annunzio used an ample spectrum of rhetorical devices that vary from the myth of Rome to the Christian religion, from barbarian threat to youthful revolution. Thanks to this rhetorical variety, the poems appealed to different social groups in Italy, sealing the political success of the author.

D'Annunzio coveted a civilizing mission that, together with his love of his country, led him to politics. His speeches in favour of Italy's intervention during the "maggio radioso" aroused great enthusiasm in the audience (Woodhouse 288-94). Furthermore, the fact that he was also a valiant war hero undoubtedly consolidated his popularity. By his deeds, D'Annunzio showed that his boldness was something more than mere rhetoric, and in this way he bridged the gulf between intellectuals and the masses.

University of Helsinki

Works Cited

Alatri, Paolo. "Ideologia e politica in D'Annunzio." *D'Annunzio a Yale*. Atti del Convegno, Yale University, 26-29 marzo 1988. Ed. Paolo Valesio. Milano: Garzanti, 1989. 23-34.
Alighieri, Dante. *La divina commedia*. Ed. Fredi Chiappelli. Milano: Mursia, 1960.
Andreoli, Annamaria. "Canti della guerra latina." D'Annunzio, *Versi* 1326-32.
―――. *Il vivere inimitabile. Vita di Gabriele D'Annunzio*. Milano: Mondadori, 2000.
Andreoli, Annamaria, and Niva Lorenzini. "Note." D'Annunzio, *Versi* 1332-58.
Arthurs, Joshua. *Excavating Modernity. The Roman Past in Fascist Italy*. Ithaca: Cornell

---

[26] D'Annunzio repeated the same idea about "la morte mancata" in *Il notturno*. See Härmänmaa, "The Seduction of Thanatos."

UP, 2012.
Balducci, Maria Giulia. "Funzionalità del simbolo dantesco nel sistema metaforico dannunziano." *Rassegna dannunziana* 13 (1988): 28-35.
Bàrberi Squarotti, Giorgio. "D'Annunzio scrittore 'politico'." *Quaderni dannunziani* 1-2 (1987): 319-48.
_____. "Le immagini della guerra." *D'Annunzio e la guerra*. Ed. Francesco Perfetti. Milano: Mondadori, 1996. 195-218.
Bertazzoli, Raffaella. "*Merope* e *Asterope*. Testi lirici per la patria in armi." *D'Annunzio a cinquant'anni dalla morte*. Atti dell'XI convegno internazionale di studi dannunziani. Vol. I. Pescara: Centro nazionale di studi dannunziani in Pescara, 1989. 247-64.
Cagnetta, Mariella. "Idea di Roma, colonialismo e nazionalismo nell'opera di D'Annunzio." *Quaderni del Vittoriale* 23 (September-October 1980): 169-86.
Canfora, Luciano. *Ideologie del classicismo*. Torino: Einaudi, 1980.
_____. "Sull'ideologia del classicismo dannunziano." *Quaderni del Vittoriale* 23 (September-October 1908): 56-72.
Chabod, Federico. *L'idea di nazione*. Roma: Laterza, 1961.
Costa, Simona. *D'Annunzio*. Roma: Salerno Editrice, 2012.
Cracco Ruggini, Lellia, and Giorgio Cracco. "L'eredità di Roma." *Storia d'Italia*. Vol. 5. *I documenti*. Ed. Ruggiero Romani and Corrado Vivanti. Torino: Einaudi, 1973. 3-45.
D'Annunzio, Gabriele. "All'America in armi." *Canti della guerra latina. [BIZ].* DVD-ROM.
_____. *Armata d'Italia. Prose di ricerca II*. Ed. Annamaria Andreoli and Giorgio Zanetti. Milano: Mondadori, 2005. 1923-86.
_____. *Canti della guerra latina. Biblioteca Italiana Zanichelli [BIZ]*. Ed. Pasquale Stoppelli. Bologna: Zanichelli, 2010. DVD-ROM.
_____. "Canto per la nazione eletta." *Elettra. [BIZ].* Ed. Pasquale Stoppelli. Bologna: Zanichelli, 2010. DVD-ROM.
_____. "Cantico per l'ottava della vittoria." *Canti della guerra latina. [BIZ].* DVD-ROM.
_____. "Cantico per la vittoria." *Canti della guerra latina. [BIZ].* DVD-ROM.
_____. "Canzone dei Dardanelli." *Merope. [BIZ].* Ed. Pasquale Stoppelli. Bologna: Zanichelli, 2010. DVD-ROM.
_____. "Canzone del sangue." *Merope. [BIZ]* Ed. Pasquale Stoppelli. Bologna: Zanichelli, 2010. DVD-ROM.
_____. "Canzone della Diana." *Merope. [BIZ].* Ed. Pasquale Stoppelli. Bologna: Zanichelli, 2010. DVD-ROM.
_____. "La canzone del Quarnaro." *Canti della guerra latina. [BIZ].* DVD-ROM.
_____. "Le ciment romain." *Scritti giornalistici II* 853-57.
_____."Fluctibus et fatis." *Scritti giornalistici II* 837-43.
_____. *Merope (Canzoni della gesta d'oltremare). [BIZ].* Ed. Pasquale Stoppelli. Bologna: Zanichelli, 2010. DVD-ROM.
_____. "L'ode alla nazione serba." *Canti della guerra latina. [BIZ].* DVD-ROM.
_____. "L'Ode pour la résurrection latine." *Canti della guerra latina. [BIZ].* DVD-ROM.
_____. *Odi navali. [BIZ].* Ed. Pasquale Stoppelli. Bologna: Zanichelli, 2010. DVD-ROM.
_____. "Orazione per la sagra dei Mille." *Prose di ricerca I* 11-20.
_____. "Parole dette agli esuli dalmati ricevendo in dono il libro che afferma dimostra e

propugna l'italianità della Dalmazia, stampato in Genova" *Prose di ricerca I* 7-10.
_____. "Per i cittadini." *Canti della guerra latina. [BIZ].* DVD-ROM.
_____. "Per i combattenti." *Canti della guerra latina. [BIZ].* DVD-ROM.
_____. "Per i morti del mare." *Canti della guerra latina. [BIZ].* DVD-ROM.
_____. "Per la gloria." *Canti della guerra latina. [BIZ].* DVD-ROM.
_____. *Per la più grande Italia. Prose di ricerca I.* 3-157.
_____. "La preghiera di Doberdò." *Canti della guerra latina. [BIZ].* DVD-ROM.
_____. "La preghiera di Sernaglia." *Canti della guerra latina. [BIZ].* DVD-ROM.
_____. *Prose di ricerca I.* Ed. Annamaria Andreoli and Giorgio Zanetti. Milano: Mondadori, 2005.
_____. "Il Rinato." *Canti della guerra latina. [BIZ].* DVD-ROM.
_____. "Salmi per i nostri morti 1." *Canti della guerra latina. [BIZ].* DVD-ROM.
_____. "Il sangue de le vergini." *Intermezzo di rime. [BIZ].* Ed. Pasquale Stoppelli. Bologna: Zanichelli, 2010. DVD-ROM.
_____. *Scritti giornalistici II.* Ed. Annamaria Andreoli and Giorgio Zanetti. Milano: Mondadori, 2003.
_____. "La très amère Adriatique." *Scritti giornalistici II* 847-52.
_____. *Versi d'amore e di gloria II.* Ed. Annamaria Andreoli and Niva Lorenzini. Milano: Mondadori 2001.
De Felice, Renzo. *D'Annunzio politico: 1918-1938.* Roma: Laterza, 1978.
De Felice, Renzo, and Pietro Gibellini, eds. *D'Annunzio politico.* Atti del Convegno, Il Vittoriale, 9-10 ottobre 1985. Milano: Garzanti, 1987.
De Michelis, Euralio. *Tutto D'Annunzio.* Milano: Feltrinelli, 1960.
Di Poppa Volture, Enzio. *Il Padre e i Figli. Dante nei maggiori poeti italiani dal Petrarca a D'Annunzio.* Napoli: Morano, 1970.
Foscolo, Ugo. *Dei sepolcri. [BIZ].* Ed. Pasquale Stoppelli. Bologna: Zanichelli, 2010. DVD-ROM.
Gentile, Emilio. *La grande Italia. Il mito della nazione nel XX secolo.* Rome: Laterza, 2011.
Härmänmaa, Marja. "L'immagine dell'inferno: la rappresentazione metaforica di Volterra in *Forse che sì forse che no* di Gabriele D'Annunzio." *Atti del XVI Congresso dei Romanisti Scandinavi: Roskilde, 24.-27.8.2005.* Ed. Michel Olsen and Erik Zwiatek. <http://diggy.ruc.dk/bitstream/1800/8454 /1/Artikel73.pdf >
_____. "The Seduction of Thanatos." *Decadence, Degeneration and the End: Studies in the European* fin de siècle. Ed. Marja Härmänmaa and Christopher Nissen. New York: Palgrave, 2014. 276-302.
Isnenghi, Mario. *Il mito della grande guerra.* Bologna: Il Mulino, 1997.
La Penna, Antonio. "La tradizione classica nella cultura italiana." *Storia d'Italia.* Vol. 5. Ed. Ruggiero Romani and Corrado Vivanti. Torino: Einaudi, 1973. 1319-72.
Ledeen, Michael A. *The First Duce: D'Annunzio at Fiume.* Baltimore: Johns Hopkins UP, 1977.
Leso, Erasmo. "Momenti di storia del linguaggio politico." *Storia della lingua italiana.* Vol. 2. Ed. Luca Serianni and Pietro Trifone. Torino: Einaudi, 1994. 703-55.
Lo Cascio, Vincenzo. *Grammatica dell'argomentare. Strategie e strutture.* Scandicci: La Nuova Italia, 1991.
Luti, Giorgio. "D'Annunzio giornalista e l'idea di 'classicismo.'" *Quaderni del Vittoriale* 23 (September-October 1980): 11-25.
Mazzini, Giuseppe. *Doveri dell'uomo* (1860). <http://www.liberliber.it/ biblioteca/m/ mazzini/index.htm>
Meyer, Michel. *Questions de rhétorique: langage, raison et séduction.* Paris: Librairie

Générale Française, 1993.
Pascoli, Giovanni. "La favola del disarmo." *Odi e inni. [BIZ].* Ed. Pasquale Stoppelli. Bologna: Zanichelli, 2010. DVD-ROM.
Perelman, Chaïm. *L'Empire rhétorique. Rhétorique et argumentation.* 1977. Paris: Librairie Philosophique J. Vrin, 2002.
Perelman, Chaïm, and Lucie Olbrechts-Tyteca. *The New Rhetoric. A Treatise on Argumentation.* Notre Dame: U of Notre Dame P, 1971.
Perfetti, Francesco. "D'Annunzio, ovvero la politica come poesia." *D'Annunzio e il suo tempo.* Ed. Francesco Perfetti. Genova: SAGEP, 1992. 369-85.
_____. *Il movimento nazionalista in Italia (1903-1914).* Roma: Bonacci, 1984.
Scorrano, Luigi. *Modi ed esempi di dantismo novecentesco.* Lecce: Adriatica Editrice Salentina,1976.
Tosi, Guy. *La Vie et le rôle de d'Annunzio en France au début de la grande guerre, 1914-1915: exposé chronologique d'après des documents inédits.* Paris : P. U. F., 1961.
Treves, Pietro. *L'idea di Roma e la cultura italiana del secolo XIX.* Milano: Riccardo Ricciardi Editore, 1962.
Valesio, Paolo. *Gabriele D'Annunzio: The Dark Flame.* New Haven: Yale UP, 1992.
Visser, Romke. "Fascist Doctrine and the Cult of *Romanità*." *Journal of Contemporary History* 27 (1992): 5-22.
Wohl, Robert. *The Generation of 1914.* Cambridge, MA: Harvard UP, 1979.
Woodhouse, John. *Gabriele D'Annunzio. Defiant Archangel.* Oxford: Oxford UP, 2001.
Zoric, Mate. "L'"Ode alla nazione serba," i suoi contenuti poetici e politici e la sua fortuna." *D'Annunzio politico.* Atti del Convegno, Il Vittoriale, 9-10 ottobre 1985. Ed. Renzo De Felice and Pietro Gibellini. Milano: Garzanti, 1987. 285-310.

Cristina Gragnani

Lacerba e *Il figlio alla guerra*: agli estremi dell'interventismo intellettuale?

In questo saggio metto a confronto due esperienze dell'interventismo intellettuale che appartengono ad ambiti culturali distanti tra loro: la rivista d'avanguardia letteraria e artistica, espressione di un nazionalismo di destra, *Lacerba* (1913-1915),[1] e il romanzo-pamphlet rivolto soprattutto alle donne della socialista, femminista e mazziniana Anna Franchi, *Il figlio alla guerra* (1917). Non suggerisco che vi siano stati rapporti diretti tra i lacerbiani e Anna Franchi. Lo scopo principale di questa analisi è mostrare come due discorsi interventisti generati in ambiti diversi tra loro in termini di sfera politica di riferimento, di poetica, di momento storico, di generazione, di *readership* e di visione della guerra convergano tuttavia su alcune strategie retoriche e anche su alcuni temi centrali.

Durante i suoi ultimi dieci mesi di *battage* interventista, il foglio fiorentino *Lacerba* fomenta l'impazienza dei suoi lettori nei confronti di un governo che frena la corsa del paese verso la sua occasione di palingenesi e di affermazione in ambito internazionale. Concepito nel 1916 e terminato nel giugno del 1917, il romanzo-pamphlet autobiografico e semi-epistolare *Il figlio alla guerra* di Anna Franchi intende rinforzare le motivazioni dell'intervento nel fronte interno e contrastare il clima di scoraggiamento generale del difficile secondo anno di conflitto.[2] Il suo scopo più esplicito è persuadere le donne a seguire l'esempio delle madri eroiche dei combattenti del Risorgimento, capaci di nascondere ansia e lacrime a beneficio della patria e di comprendere il valore del proprio sacrificio.[3]

---

[1] *Lacerba* nacque dall'iniziativa di Giovanni Papini e Ardengo Soffici quando, nel 1913, si staccarono dalla per loro troppo moderata *Voce* prezzoliniana, allineata con l'idealismo crociano, per creare una rivista in cui l'arte e la letteratura, intese come strumenti per contestare la cultura ufficiale, fossero in primo piano. Come nota Somigli, "the hallmark of *Lacerba* was a form of polemical writing aimed at demolishing, often more through the strength of its rhetoric of pugnacious sarcasm then through real argumentation, bourgeois social institutions, moral conventions and the intellectual establishment" (475). Con lo scoppio della prima guerra mondiale, la rivista cambiò rotta e da periodico prevalentemente artistico e letterario divenne sostanzialmente foglio di propaganda interventista. Per una bibliografia estesa su *Lacerba* rimando al volume di Del Puppo *Lacerba 1913-1915*.

[2] La metà del 1916 segnò un momento di scoraggiamento generale e di pessimismo nel paese in guerra (Monticone 36-37; Procacci 69).

[3] La trama del romanzo è essenziale e assolve la doppia funzione di fornire esempi di virtù patriottica e di fare da cornice a lunghe e accorate digressioni ideologiche. La storia

La retorica dei lacerbiani anticipa la carneficina e la celebra da un punto di vista estetico e filosofico. Al momento della scrittura del *Figlio*, invece, il massacro è in atto e la società ne sta soffrendo le tragiche conseguenze da lunghi mesi. L'entusiasmo di Giovanni Papini per una guerra che ridurrà provvidenzialmente il numero degli abitanti del mondo ("La vita non è sacra" 225; "Amiamo la guerra" 274) suona grottesco mentre è in corso la decimazione di un'intera generazione. Franchi non aderisce alla retorica nichilista di *Lacerba*. Piuttosto incoraggia le madri (e attraverso loro anche i loro figli soldati e il resto del fronte interno a non perdere di vista le ragioni dell'intervento: la guerra è giusta e va combattuta fino in fondo.[4]

Molto è stato scritto su *Lacerba* e i suoi fondatori; ma ancora poco si sa dell'autrice del *Figlio alla guerra*. Nota nell'ambito dei *Gender Studies* per il suo controverso romanzo, *Avanti il divorzio* (1902), scritto in sostegno della campagna socialista per il divorzio, Anna Franchi (Livorno 1867-Milano 1954) è stata un'intellettuale prolifica e versatile.[5] Cresciuta in una famiglia di forte tradizione mazziniana e repubblicana, allo scoppio del conflitto la scrittrice entra subito nel solco dell'interventismo democratico e si mobilita per l'entrata in

---

è narrata in prima persona e incorpora un gruppo di lettere che il figlio della narratrice le spedisce dal fronte. La narratrice racconta la propria attesa del figlio e le proprie ansie, riflette sulla società dell'Italia in guerra e racconta aneddoti raccolti negli ospedali presso cui assiste i soldati. La forte presenza dell'elemento ideologico che sovrasta quello narrativo è dovuta anche al fatto che il libro include i testi di conferenze che Franchi aveva dato presso il Reale Conservatorio di Milano (Malaguti http://www.letteraturadimenticata.it/Franchi.htm) e anche articoli usciti in precedenza in alcuni quotidiani.

[4] Come Franchi documenta nella sua autobiografia, fu l'editore Emilio Treves a commissionarle il romanzo (*La mia vita* 304). *Il figlio alla guerra* sembra voler imprimere nelle donne (e attraverso le donne anche nelle loro comunità e nei loro figli combattenti) la motivazione a tener duro in un momento in cui una pace non sembrava accettabile. In questa fase della guerra, percepita come un punto di non ritorno, molti intellettuali pnsarono di dover sostenere il governo nello sforzo bellico per tenere il morale alto e alimentare la motivazione a combattere e resistere fino alla vittoria. Come scrive Henry Kissinger in *L'arte della diplomazia*, "una volta entrati in guerra, i leader d'Europa furono talmente ossessionati dal fratricidio e sconvolti dalla distruzione di una giovane generazione che la vittoria divenne l'unico obiettivo possibile" (161).

[5] Nella sua lunga vita, Franchi ha pubblicato romanzi e racconti, biografie, drammi e libri per l'infanzia e per l'adolescenza. È stata inoltre giornalista, critica letteraria, traduttrice e storica dell'arte. A cavallo tra i due secoli scorsi ha militato, pur non prendendone mai la tessera, nell'alveo del Partito Socialista Italiano. Il suo attivismo non si è limitato alla campagna pro-divorzio, ma si è esteso anche alla lotta per i diritti dei lavoratori e delle lavoratrici. È noto, ad esempio, il suo impegno in supporto alle trecciaiole di Firenze durante i moti del biennio 1896-1898, e per la propaganda della Camera del Lavoro (Gigli, 2008: 87-90). Per una bibliografia aggiornata su Anna Franchi si vedano Gragnani e Gigli 2014.

Lacerba e *Il figlio alla guerra*: agli estremi dell'interventismo intellettuale? 55

guerra dell'Italia (Gigli 2008: 91).⁶ Sposa la causa della quarta guerra d'indipendenza e aderisce alla propaganda antitedesca degli Alleati. La sua retorica interventista presenta forti legami con il discorso nazional patriottico risorgimentale e si avvale dei principi dell'etno-antropologia positivista per demonizzare il nemico.⁷

L'accostamento di un periodico d'avanguardia che chiude alla vigilia dell'intervento⁸ con un romanzo d'impianto narrativo tradizionale, uscito a guerra inoltrata, può sembrare un azzardo. I percorsi intellettuali dei protagonisti di queste due esperienze dell'interventismo intellettuale non potrebbero essere

---

⁶ Con l'espressione "interventismo democratico" ci si riferisce "[all']opera di quegli intellettuali che vogliono l'Italia in guerra contro gli imperi centrali nel 1914 per diffondere una concezione liberale e democratica dello stato e dei rapporti sociali-umani. [...] L'interventismo democratico afferma che la difesa/espansione della democrazia può dipendere dalla canna del fucile. Il patriottismo repubblicano prevede la democrazia in armi così come la possibilità di esportare principi democratici" (Marconi 274). Gli interventisti democratici, che formavano una élite intellettuale, si riconoscevano nel mazzinianesimo e vedevano la guerra come il completamento del Risorgimento. Uno degli esponenti di maggior spicco di questa corrente dell'interventismo intellettuale era Gaetano Salvemini, direttore dell'*Unità*. Durante il periodo della propaganda interventista Franchi collaborava anche al "Popolo d'Italia", fondato da Mussolini, dove venne in contatto con l'interventismo del sindacalismo rivoluzionario. Nell'autobiografia racconta di aver collaborato con Filippo Corridoni (*La mia vita* 286).

⁷ Franchi aderisce a una rappresentazione razzista del popolo tedesco che condivide, ad esempio, con i membri della Lega Antitedesca di Genova (Montesi 61-80) e con le collaboratrici della rivista nazionalista "L'unità d'Italia", tra cui Beatrice Sacchi, Teresa Labriola e Anna Maria Mozzoni (Guidi 94-95). Stabilire rapporti di gerarchie tra i popoli basandosi sul concetto di razza era tipico della cultura ottocentesca. Alla fine del diciannovesimo secolo in Italia, come nel resto d'Europa, era comune basare il senso d'identità nazionale sull'etnicizzazione e razzializzazione dei gruppi nazionali, secondo una concezione biologica della razza. Sia Alberto Burgio che Pierre André Taguieff fanno risalire l'affermazione di questa tendenza, che Taguieff chiama "racialisme", con il consolidarsi dell'antropologia (Burgio e Casali 11 e Taguieff). Federico Niglia nota come il discorso sulle razze latina e germanica fosse stato centrale nell'ambito dell'antropologia italiana durante il ventennio precedente lo scoppio della guerra e come tale dibattito fosse "presto fuoriuscito dall'ambito scientifico e si era tramutato in una lotta per la giustificazione di presunta superiorità razziale. La battaglia degli italiani era così diventata una battaglia per la tutela del 'primato' italiano, latino e mediterraneo dall'affermazione della superiorità nordica" (Niglia 119). Al tempo dell'entrata in guerra dell'Italia, i concetti di razza e nazione tendono a sovrapporsi e il "razzialismo" permea la propaganda interventista

⁸ *Lacerba* chiude i battenti il 22 maggio 1915, a due giorni dall'intervento, ufficialmente perché la missione di promuovere l'entrata in guerra dell'Italia era finita. Comunque, Somigli osserva anche che il bilancio della rivista a quel punto era problematico e questo avrà contribuito alla decisione di interrompere le pubblicazioni (474).

più diversi: sovvertitori, Papini e Soffici, del pensiero e dell'arte tradizionale e reduci dall'immersione nella Parigi avanguardista d'inizio secolo; paladina, Franchi, del realismo in arte e letteratura; antisocialisti Papini e Soffici; giornalista impegnata in campagne vicine al Partito Socialista e attivista in prima linea, Franchi. Distanti tra loro sono anche i rispettivi bacini di lettura. *Lacerba* s'indirizzava a letterati, aspiranti letterati o giovani intellettuali del ceto medio alto, sensibili al tema del rinnovamento dell'arte e della società, attratti dalla cultura irrazionalista del passaggio tra i due secoli; Franchi, con *Il figlio*, si rivolgeva a un pubblico composto di vari strati della borghesia più o meno istruita e in particolare al pubblico femminile.[9]

Tuttavia, un'analisi in parallelo di queste due espressioni così diverse dell'interventismo intellettuale rivela quanto il discorso sulla guerra, per quanto generato in ambiti culturali distanti tra loro, faccia riferimento a un repertorio retorico e a un immaginario in gran parte comune. In questo articolo mi concentro su quattro aree tematiche che riguardano sia *Lacerba* che *Il figlio*: la retorica antitedesca, il populismo interventista, la dialettica vecchi/giovani e la celebrazione estetico-filosofica della guerra collegata a sua volta al tema della guerra rigeneratrice.

L'interventismo intellettuale italiano, di qualsiasi appartenenza politica, non può essere considerato separatamente dall'antigermanesimo diffuso dalle campagne degli Alleati, basato sul contrasto *civilisation* e *Kultur*[10] radicato anche nell'etno-nazionalismo ottocentesco che identifica razza, cultura e nazione. L'idea della guerra come scontro di civiltà, alla base di tanta propaganda visuale dei paesi alleati, si basava sul concetto francese di *civilisation* intesa come eredità della cultura latina fondata sul senso della misura e sulla ragione, contrapposta alla *Kultur* tedesca rappresentata come l'esatto opposto e cioè come tendenza alla brutalità e alla barbarie. Secondo

---

[9] Era presumibilmente, in gran parte, lo stesso pubblico che leggeva periodici femminili, romanzi didattici e galatei. Ma non è escluso che Franchi e Treves avessero in mente anche i soldati al fronte come possibili lettori dato che il titolo evocava sia le madri che i figli combattenti.

[10] Faccio qui riferimento alla coppia antitetica dei termini *Kultur* (riferito alla germanità) e *civilisation* (riferito alla tradizione latina), uno degli elementi più salienti della propaganda di guerra durante il primo conflitto mondiale. Nell'ambito della storiografia sulla Grande Guerra, i due termini sono spesso impiegati nelle loro rispettive versioni francese (*civilisation*) e tedesca (*Kultur*). Come nota Peter Brugge, nell'Ottocento, si fa strada in Germania l'idea del contrasto tra *Kultur* e *Zivilisation* che viene poi utilizzato come strumento retorico per giustificare la guerra franco-prussiana (113). Sul versante tedesco, per *Kultur* s'intendeva l'autenticità espressiva, la creatività, la forza dello spirito, da contrapporsi alla *Zivilisation*, che indicava gli aspetti esteriori del vivere quali la democrazia, la politica, il diritto di voto e veniva identificato con la Francia. Con la prima guerra mondiale, il binomio "cultura" versus "civiltà" viene usato a scopo di propaganda sia dalla Germania che dagli Alleati.

Lacerba e *Il figlio alla guerra*: agli estremi dell'interventismo intellettuale? 57

questa linea di propaganda, la principale funzione della guerra doveva essere quella di fermare l'avanzata degli imperi centrali per impedire che la *Kultur* fosse imposta con la forza distruggendo la civiltà e negando la libertà dei popoli.[11]

Su tale opposizione si fonda l'antigermanesimo di Franchi nel *Figlio alla guerra*. Nonostante i sentimenti irredentisti espressi dall'autrice nel pamphlet *Città sorelle* (1916) e in due libri per giovani scolari, nel *Figlio* il fuoco si sposta sulla Germania.[12] La campagna anti-austriaca rimane un tema importante del libro, ma passa in secondo piano rispetto alla propaganda anti-tedesca. Franchi sposa l'idea della guerra di civiltà, dello scontro tra bestialità e ragione:

Non più cavalleria, non più patti, non più riguardi; poiché una parte del genere umano ha risvegliato la dormiente bestia umana, pensi l'altra parte, alla quale ancora rimane un barlume di ragione, a non trarre dal ragionamento una perniciosa debolezza.

(*Il figlio* 197-98)[13]

Nel prendere questa posizione Franchi aderisce allo slogan messo in circolazione dai paesi alleati della "guerra che porrà fine a tutte le guerre", allineandosi con gli interventisti democratici e con quei socialisti che vedevano nella guerra una via per contrastare il militarismo e l'espansionismo degli imperi centrali così da garantire una pace duratura e ricostruire il mondo su nuove basi. Consapevole di rivolgersi a un pubblico socialmente misto e composto in gran parte di donne, Franchi traspone il concetto di scontro tra barbarie e civiltà su un

---

[11] Sia la propaganda tedesca che quella degli Alleati intendeva la guerra come missione storica. La propaganda tedesca presentava la guerra come mezzo necessario a difendere lo spirito germanico; la pubblicistica bellica degli Alleati giustificava la guerra come mezzo necessario per proteggere la civiltà dei popoli latini e dei loro alleati dalla *Kultur* tedesca che, a partire dall'invasione del Belgio e della Francia, cominciò a essere intesa come brutalità bestiale e barbarie. Un noto poster di reclutamento diffuso negli Stati Uniti nel 1917 offre una chiara rappresentazione visiva del contrasto *Kultur/civilisation* visto dalla parte del blocco degli Alleati. Raffigura un gorilla con in testa un elmetto tedesco con la scritta "Militarism" e con in mano una clava con su scritto "Kultur"; nell'altro braccio, tiene prigioniera una donna con le vesti strappate, allegoria del Belgio e della Francia come nazioni oppresse o, più in generale, della libertà violata. Dietro alle spalle della bestia, dall'altra parte dell'oceano, si vedono le rovine di architetture gotiche che evocano i paesi invasi. Il poster di Harry R. Hopps è consultabile presso la Library of Congress Prints and Photographs Division (http://www.loc.gov/pictures/item/2010652057/).

[12] Si tratta di *A voi soldati futuri dico la nostra guerra* del 1916 e di *Le guerre dei nonni e le nostre* del 1922.

[13] Esprimono un'ansia simile le parole di Ardengo Soffici in "Intorno alla gran bestia": "Nessuno ignora ormai quale sia il fine di coloro che hanno preparato l'attuale conflitto. Il predominio della razza teutonica, in Europa per ora, nel mondo se possibile, in seguito" (245).

piano nazionale e mitico per renderlo più immediatamente assorbibile alla sua *readership*. Il contrasto tra *civilisation* e *Kultur* si risolve in un confronto tra italiani (di razza latina) e tedeschi (di razza barbara). Uno degli scopi è affermare la legittimità dell'uso della violenza da parte di un popolo civile che per natura e cultura tenderebbe a rifiutarla, nei confronti di un popolo brutale che, se non fermato, rischia di compromettere la pace e la libertà nel mondo intero. Dal momento che i combattenti italiani sono identificati con i soldati romani e i tedeschi con la loro controparte barbara, la guerra in corso è per Franchi guerra giusta come lo erano state quelle dell'antica Roma. La rievocazione del passato rimane vaga e s'impernia su una serie di parole chiave che portano il discorso su un piano mitico anziché storico:

> Là ai confini, sulle vette dei monti carpitici da una secolare razza di prepotenti e di pirati, sulle zolle aride di quel Carso che fu per i romani la porta oltre la quale tentarono di chiudere le belve, uno stillicidio di sangue nostro impregna e neve e sassi di indelebili macchie d'odio; là dove, liberi latini, divennero schiavi, un giorno, oggi liberi latini combattono per strappare l'ultimo anello arrugginito dal sangue di una vecchia catena.
> (*Il figlio* 37)

Secondo questa impostazione binaria, i soldati tedeschi (la categoria include anche gli austriaci) sono descritti in termini di una furia "fatta di strage per amor di strage, di punizioni sanguinarie, di distruzione sistematica, di strazianti carneficine allo scopo d'incutere spavento" (*Il figlio* 32). Gli italiani, al contrario, rimangono generosi anche nel contesto sanguinario della guerra che sono costretti a combattere.

In linea con l'interventismo democratico, per Franchi la guerra è necessaria per contrastare il militarismo e l'imperialismo tedesco che incarnano valori negativi del passato e che già le guerre del Risorgimento e ancora prima la Rivoluzione francese avevano combattuto:

> Ma soprattutto noi combattiamo il passato; questa guerra fa parte di un succedersi di ribellioni, è ancora l''89, è il '70, è il più grande episodio del Risorgimento, è la guerra del popolo che vuol rompere ogni catena di servaggio. Imperialismo, militarismo, e tutte le forme di regresso, tutti i ricordi di un barbaro passato, tutti si combattono adesso.
> (*Il figlio* 116)

Le motivazioni all'interventismo offerte da Giovanni Papini nell'articolo "Le cinque guerre" non si discostano di molto. Dopo aver elencato le cinque ragioni per volere l'intervento italiano — "guerra ideale, guerra irredentista, guerra imperialista, guerra rivoluzionaria, guerra finta" ("Le cinque guerre" 89) — Papini precisa che la guerra promossa da *Lacerba* è quella "ideale" e cioè quella che si deve combattere per contrastare la Germania, la cui minaccia è un pericolo per la pace oltre che per la civiltà:

> La guerra ideale è quella che si dovrebbe fare per ragioni, diciamo così, di civiltà —

Lacerba e *Il figlio alla guerra*: agli estremi dell'interventismo intellettuale? 59

ragioni europee. La Germania è un pericolo per la pace, per la cultura, per la libertà dello spirito, per la concezione della vita per tutto quello che noi — italiani intelligenti — vogliamo ed amiamo. L'egemonia tedesca — cioè il sopravvento del militarismo, mercantilismo, pedantismo, religiosismo ecc. — sarebbe un disastro per i nostri valori. Perciò l'Italia deve cooperare colle altre nazioni più vicine al suo spirito — Francia geniale, Inghilterra liberale, Russia pazza — alla domatura dell'odiosa Germania.

(89)

Nel far coincidere gli italiani e i tedeschi con gli antichi romani e i barbari, Franchi propone una lettura in chiave mitica del contrasto *Kultur/civilisation*. Papini invece si mantiene sul piano dello scontro culturale tra Francia e Germania e incita la comunità intellettuale che fa capo al cenacolo fiorentino a sostenere la Francia per ragioni di affinità e debito culturale. Dopo aver illustrato il contributo della nazione d'oltralpe alla cultura italiana ed europea, Papini afferma:

Tutta la Francia è un esercito contro un paese da poco civilizzato che deve a lei e all'Italia quel poco di buono che ha fatto nel mondo. Noi, in quanto artisti, in quanto pensatori, in quanto poeti, in quanto italiani ci sentiamo colla Francia contro i nostri nemici.

("Ciò che dobbiamo alla Francia" 252)

La diversa strategia comunicativa è dovuta ai due distinti ambiti socio-culturali cui *Lacerba* e Franchi fanno riferimento e anche alle diverse epoche in cui i loro rispettivi discorsi interventisti erano prodotti. Al tempo di *Lacerba* si dibatteva sull'opportunità o meno di allearsi con la Francia, mentre al tempo del *Figlio* la scacchiera degli schieramenti era già disegnata. Ciò che accomuna le due esperienze è il tentativo di decostruire il mito della superiorità culturale tedesca, forte in età giolittiana e ancora vivo nel secondo anno di guerra, di ribaltare cioè la percezione positiva della propensione all'ordine e del progresso tecnologico del popolo tedesco e, più in generale, di contrastare il pangermanesimo (Niglia 115).[14] Nell'ultimo numero della rivista Soffici scriveva:

---

[14] Sia *Lacerba* che *Il figlio* evocano grossolani stereotipi per costruire il nemico come inferiore o pericoloso. Nel *Figlio*, un intero capitolo è dedicato a una famiglia tedesca costretta a lasciare l'Italia al momento della dichiarazione di guerra alla Germania. Dopo essersi rimproverata per aver, anche solo momentaneamente, provato compassione per il dolore di questa famiglia nel dover tornare in patria, la narratrice passa a elencare le caratteristiche negative del popolo tedesco, tutte rappresentate dai membri della famiglia in questione: le donne sono civette e di facili costumi; gli uomini sottomessi alle donne o addirittura ritardati. Anche Papini si era occupato del tema dei tedeschi presenti in Italia, nell'articolo "Fuori i tedeschi!" in cui scriveva che, in caso di entrata in guerra dell'Italia, ci si sarebbe dovuti mobilitare per cacciare tutti i tedeschi presenti sul suolo nazionale perché, come aveva appena dimostrato il caso del Belgio, la presenza del nemico sul territorio sarebbe stata troppo pericolosa. Ogni tedesco in Italia, afferma Papini, sarebbe un potenziale contatto con le classi dirigenti e militari degli imperi centrali per preparare

– Disprezziamo il militarismo e l'imperialismo quali ce li ha rivelati la Germania del Kaiser. [...]
– Disprezziamo la disciplina e *l'esprit de troupeau*.
– Disprezziamo l'organizzazione e stimiamo la Germania inferiore alla stessa Turchia perché appunto di questa organizzazione si fa vanto principalmente e arma.

("Memento" 163)

Franchi attribuisce al militarismo, all'organizzazione e al senso delle gerarchie la natura barbara e spietata della ferocia tedesca:

Io credo che i soldati lanciati in paese di conquista possano divenire anche feroci; ma se talvolta di questi casi avvengono non sono però il resultato di una ferocia organizzata, comandata, voluta da alti facitori della guerra.

(*Il figlio* 91-92)

Su *Lacerba* è Thomas (Angelo Cecconi) a individuare nell'hegelismo la radice comune del marxismo e del militarismo, esprimendo un rifiuto sommario di tutto quanto abbia a che fare con il pensiero tedesco responsabile di aver determinato una cultura brutale ("Tedescheria immanente e... invadente" 123). Solo Nietzsche, già punto di riferimento per le precedenti avventure intellettuali papiniane, si salva perché è identificato come nemico della cultura tedesca.[15] Dal canto suo, Franchi attribuisce a Marx, Bismark e Guglielmo II lo sfruttamento dell'ideale della fratellanza universale per ingannare gli altri popoli e convincerli a sottomettersi senza combattere:

La fratellanza oltre la razza e oltre i confini sarebbe una magnifica idealità, ma i fatti hanno dimostrato che Bismark, Marx, Guglielmo II di questa idealità si sono serviti per preparare con l'indebolimento dei popoli il tradimento e la conquista. Non un imperatore teutonico ha pensato la conquista, ma il popolo tedesco tutto.

(*Il figlio* 34-35)

Un'altra caratteristica comune alla retorica del *Figlio* e di *Lacerba* è l'insistenza sulla mancanza d'individualità del popolo tedesco, che lo induce a seguire acriticamente la propria classe dirigente favorendo l'affermarsi del deleterio

---

l'invasione (54-55). Papini non rifugge nemmeno dall'indugiare sul carattere "antipatico" dei tedeschi, odiati o mal sopportati in tutti i paesi in guerra ("Contro la neutralità" 260).
[15] Dopo la virata interventista di *Lacerba*, si susseguono nella rivista numerose dichiarazioni che mirano ad allontanare Nietzsche dalla cultura tedesca. Ad esempio, in "Due parole ai tedeschi", Soffici lo definisce un filosofo polacco (263). In "Breve risposta a un tedescante", sempre Soffici scrive: "Circa Nietzsche ho letto tutto e lo considero il filosofo antitedesco per eccellenza" (44). In "Ciò che dobbiamo alla Francia", Papini lo definisce "l'unico grande tedesco venuto dopo il '70" e precisa che Nietzsche preferiva comunque la cultura francese a quella tedesca (252).

Lacerba e *Il figlio alla guerra*: agli estremi dell'interventismo intellettuale?

militarismo:[16]

> Ma il popolo tedesco non ha ancora il gusto della personalità, del pensiero individuale; l'impero tedesco non è fatto di popolo, è fatto di poche teste e di molte braccia. Un uomo vuole, pochi lo secondano, gli altri obbediscono.
>
> (Il figlio 119)

Anche Soffici insiste sulla rigidità e la tendenza all'ubbidienza dei tedeschi:

> Le idee del tedesco mancano di elasticità: sono limitate e brutali. Ciò spiega la sua capacità d'azione, specie materiale. Ciò spiega anche la sua ordinazione sociale. [...]. Il tedesco non ha dubbi perché non ha il senso della complessità della vita. Egli va per la sua strada come un treno. E come una locomotiva, non discute il macchinista.
>
> ("Sulla barbarie tedesca" 291)

Per contrasto, uno degli elementi portanti dell'interventismo di *Lacerba* e del *Figlio* è la costruzione dell'identità del popolo italiano come naturalmente contrapposto alla vigliaccheria e alla sonnolenza della classe dirigente.[17] *Lacerba* insiste sull'inerzia del governo che disonora il paese, mentre il volere del popolo andrebbe nella direzione opposta e auspica un ruolo attivo dell'Italia nella guerra, vista come occasione di trasformazione profonda dell'Europa:[18]

---

[16] Per un'interpretazione personale del contrasto tra tedeschi e italiani si veda la poesia di Pietro Jahier *Wir Müssen*, in cui il poeta mette a confronto le diverse motivazioni che spingono italiani e tedeschi a lavorare e a uccidere: per gli uni lo scopo della vita è la vita stessa; per gli altri, il fine ultimo è consumare, produrre e ammazzare per produrre di più: "Noi per VIVERE lavoriamo / VIVERE / non molto consumare per molto produrre / per poi Müssen ammazzare / per molto riprodurre e molto riconsumare / e di nuovo Müssen ammazzare" (165).

[17] Come nota Emilio Gentile, l'idea del contrasto tra libertà individuale e annientamento dell'individuo nel militarismo derivava dal clima generato dalla guerra franco-prussiana. Allora s'identificava con il contrasto Francia/Prussia. In seguito l'idea si è allargata ai popoli latini e ai tedeschi intesi come imperi centrali: "Dopo il 1870 [...] Francia e Germania cominciarono a essere percepite come due civiltà contrapposte e antagoniste. Civiltà francese e civiltà tedesca: l'una figlia della Rivoluzione francese, della concezione della nazione fondata sul libero e volontario consenso dei cittadini, vincolata alla salvaguardia della libertà e dei diritti dell'individuo; l'altra cresciuta con il militarismo autoritario, l'affermazione del primato della nazione e dello Stato potenza, come organismi che si integrano reciprocamente avendo le loro solide fondamenta nella forza permanente e immutabile della razza, entro la quale si svolgeva la vita effimera dei singoli individui come cellule di un grande corpo sociale, che aveva una sua coscienza e una sua volontà superiore, si imponeva agli individui attraverso la disciplina del dovere etico, si incarnava nella figura dell'imperatore e dell'aristocrazia militare" (111).

[18] Nel comunicato "Dichiarazione" si legge: "Il governo italiano il quale sta in questo momento disonorando e rovinando il paese con l'insistere nessuno sa perché, in una neutralità ormai imbecille, non perde nessuna occasione per dichiarare che questo suo

Il nostro governo è stolto, o vile, o traditore. Mentre l'intera nazione in angoscia sempre crescente attende da lui un moto e una parola che risponda alla sua muta ma concorde domanda [...]. Siamo ancora impigliati nei "se" e nei calcoli delle possibili eventualità, mentre gli avvenimenti precipitano togliendo ogni giorno alla nostra nazione una possibilità di riscatto e di gloria, ed esponendola invece al disprezzo del mondo civile, degli stessi suoi figli migliori.

("Appello" 273)

Anche Franchi rappresenta l'intera nazione come favorevole alla guerra e indignata nei confronti del governo, anche se per ragioni diverse rispetto a *Lacerba*. Nel *Figlio*, più che come desideroso di gloria, il popolo italiano è caratterizzato come puro, coraggioso, incline alla giustizia e convinto della necessità della guerra riparatrice di torti e vergogne secolari e recenti, nonché come salvaguardia della libertà di tutte le nazioni sotto lo scacco della minaccia tedesca. Al contrario del popolo tedesco, quello italiano mostra indipendenza di giudizio e di sentimento e fa da contraltare alla classe dirigente che, per viltà e obbedienza alle ragioni della Realpolitik, aveva rischiato di trascinare l'Italia nel disonore contro il volere della gente:

Il popolo ha visto il pericolo che minacciava la civiltà del mondo; ha sentito, il popolo, che la lotta era immane perché bisognava combattere non solo per l'Italia, ma con tutti e per tutti i popoli ansiosi di libertà, per tutte le migliori liberazioni avvenire, per la rinascenza nostra, per la rigenerazione della stessa razza tedesca.

(Il figlio 118-19)

Simili sono anche le strategie retoriche che Franchi e i lacerbiani usano per condannare la classe professorale, colpevole, insieme ad altri gruppi, di aver coltivato il mito della superiorità culturale tedesca e degli avanzamenti tecnologici della Germania, promuovendo la neutralità. Più violento verbalmente appare Soffici:

La vile canizza giolittiana, l'ignobile, losco, vomitativo Giolitti; gli analfabeti dell'"Avanti", i preti, i giornalisti venduti, i generali bulowiani, la melma fetente universitaria, professorale, filosofica; la ciurmaglia, bavosa, laida del senato [...]

("Sulla soglia" 156)

Franchi chiama in causa chi nella società avrebbe avuto i mezzi culturali necessari per comprendere l'entità della minaccia ed è rimasto invece accecato

---

modo di comportarsi davanti agli avvenimenti che trasformeranno la faccia d'Europa, corrisponde perfettamente al desiderio della maggioranza del popolo italiano. Noi non crediamo che questa sia la verità, eccettuati i preti, una parte dei socialisti e pochi trippai amanti del quieto vivere a costo di qualunque umiliazione, nessuno in Italia approva l'inerzia che il governo c'impone, che ci snerva e che ci condurrà alla più abietta depressione morale, se non, alla fine, a una reazione esasperata che a parecchi potrà costare assai caro" (265).

Lacerba e *Il figlio alla guerra*: agli estremi dell'interventismo intellettuale? 63

da una pericolosa fascinazione per l'efficienza industriale della Germania:

> Chi in Italia amò i tedeschi con una specie di ammirazione per le loro qualità d'industriali dimostrò di non aver mai capito la razza. La colpa è un po' di molta gente: scienziati e professori, industriali e uomini politici... Prepararono la rovina del mondo, e della strage un po' tutti siamo responsabili. [...] Adesso è inutile recriminare, bisogna vincere, difendere l'avvenire [...].
>
> (*Il figlio* 35)

Se il popolo evocato da *Lacerba* voleva la guerra per riscattare l'Italia in ambito internazionale e perché non gli fosse negata l'opportunità di rigenerarsi nel "bagno di sangue" che si andava preparando, quello narrato da Franchi auspicava l'intervento per difendere la libertà universale e proteggere l'umanità dalla minaccia tedesca. In entrambi i casi, il popolo chiamato in causa nel discorso interventista è una proiezione ideale (Isnenghi 102; Tosi 88). È infatti poco realistico pensare che le classi più basse fossero inclini alla guerra. Al contrario, come osservano Alberto Monticone e Giovanna Procacci, tra gli altri, le masse erano rimaste sostanzialmente estranee ai motivi dell'intervento e avevano subito la guerra come *corvée* o come disgrazia. Contadini e operai avevano lasciato le loro occupazioni preoccupati che le loro famiglie rimanessero indigenti (Monticone 36; Procacci 53). Quello italiano era senza dubbio un fronte interno diviso.[19]

In entrambi i casi è dunque in atto un simile paradosso: da una parte il popolo reale, contrario all'intervento al tempo di *Lacerba* e provato da una guerra non voluta ai tempi del *Figlio*; dall'altra, la proiezione ideale del popolo che funziona sia come fattore motivante alla guerra per i lettori borghesi della rivista, sia come termine di paragone per mettere in evidenza la viltà e lo squallore della classe dirigente in *Lacerba* come nel *Figlio*. Al tempo della scrittura del *Figlio*, con l'Italia in guerra da due anni per volere del governo Salandra, l'insistenza di Franchi sul fatto che fu il popolo a volere l'intervento nel maggio 1915 ha probabilmente anche la funzione di diminuire nelle lettrici e nei lettori il senso che la partecipazione dell'Italia al conflitto fosse stata a tutti gli effetti un'imposizione dall'alto.

Che questa caratterizzazione del popolo fosse problematica non sfuggiva nemmeno a chi la proponeva. Dopo aver affermato la volontà dell'intera nazione di andare in guerra, il comunicato "Dichiarazione" di *Lacerba* concede che questo sentimento possa riguardare solo una minoranza, ma precisa anche che si tratta di una minoranza rilevante, quella intellettuale. Tenendo i piedi in due staffe, la redazione di *Lacerba* (probabilmente Papini) esalta il valore dell'élite nei confronti delle masse che diventano così portatrici di un significato sempre

---

[19] Come nota Alberto Asor Rosa, in Italia, a differenza di altri paesi quali la Francia, "la condanna popolare della Guerra non trova la sua espressione letteraria perché i *populisti* sono tutti schierati per la Guerra" (Asor Rosa 73).

cangiante, persino all'interno dello stesso articolo:

> Comunque, e anche ammettendo che, secondo le convinzioni di palazzo Braschi e della Consulta, il nostro popolo sia davvero il popolo più stolto, vile e nullo della terra, è bene si sappia a Roma e pertutto che se la maggioranza approva il contegno del nostro governo, c'è tuttavia un certo numero d'italiani i quali non l'approvano assolutamente e non intendono affatto assumerne la responsabilità morale.
>
> ("Dichiarazione" 265)

Anche Franchi, dopo aver celebrato il patriottismo spontaneo e persino atavico del popolo italiano, ammette il ruolo degli intellettuali nell'indurre nelle masse l'entusiasmo della guerra:

> [D]elle intenzioni del governo il popolo poco sapeva, e infine la massa si fa sempre una coscienza attraverso gli entusiasmi che sa sollevare la minoranza intellettuale.
>
> (*Il figlio* 7)

La definizione di "populismo" di Francisco Panizza, che insiste sul processo ambiguo di nominazione (*naming*) del popolo e del suo *altro*, può essere applicata al processo retorico in atto sia in *Lacerba* che nel romanzo di Franchi. Secondo Panizza, il populismo è

> an anti-status quo discourse that simplifies the political space by symbolically dividing society between the people (as the underdogs) and its *other*. Needless to say, the identity of both "the people" and *the other* are political constructs, symbolically constructed through the relation of antagonism, rather than sociological categories. Antagonism is thus a mode of identification in which the relation between its form (the people as signifier) and its content (the people as signified) is given by the very long process of naming — that is, of establishing who the enemies of the people (and therefore the people itself) are.
>
> (Panizza 3)

La rappresentazione del popolo come favorevole all'entrata in guerra dell'Italia è collegata, sia in *Lacerba* che nel *Figlio*, alla narrazione del cosiddetto "maggio radioso",[20] presente sia nella rivista che nel romanzo, anche se con alcune differenze. *Lacerba* parla delle manifestazioni di piazza che precedettero l'entrata in guerra dell'Italia in tempo reale, durante il mese di maggio del 1915, e incita i lettori a sostenere l'intervento e a partecipare al clima di rivolta in atto; Franchi, che in quel tempo aveva partecipato in prima persona ai cortei di maggio e che scrive *Il figlio* a un anno di distanza, ricorda questo periodo in una serie di flashback. Entrambi i testi fanno riferimento al possibile ritorno al

---

[20] L'espressione "maggio radioso" indica il periodo che va dal 13 al 24 maggio 1915 e cioè dalle dimissioni temporanee del primo ministro Antonio Salandra all'intervento italiano. Durante questo breve tempo le piazze italiane furono animate da manifestazioni interventiste e anche da cortei neutralisti.

Lacerba e *Il figlio alla guerra*: agli estremi dell'interventismo intellettuale? 65

governo di Giolitti durante quei giorni caldi perché, proprio a maggio, si era sparsa la voce, poi risultata attendibile, che il re avesse chiesto all'ex primo ministro di tornare a capo dell'esecutivo. Questo avrebbe significato l'attuazione della politica giolittiana sulla guerra, vale a dire il prolungamento delle relazioni diplomatiche con l'Austria e un ulteriore ritardo dell'intervento italiano, se non la rinuncia all'entrata in guerra.[21] *Lacerba* metteva in guardia i suoi lettori sulle conseguenze che tale sviluppo nella politica estera italiana avrebbe comportato per il paese e gridava all'infamia. Come è noto, le cose andarono diversamente. Giolitti rifiutò l'incarico, Salandra rimase al governo e dichiarò la guerra all'Austria. Nel *Figlio*, Franchi rievoca quel periodo insistendo sul fatto che il rischio di trascinare l'Italia nella vergogna era stato scongiurato solo per un soffio.

L'anti-giolittismo era stato uno dei temi principali di *Lacerba* fin dall'inizio delle sue pubblicazioni. I lacerbiani contestavano l'intero operato del primo ministro, a prescindere dalla sua posizione sulla guerra. Uno degli scopi della rivista era scuotere la cultura e la società italiana dal torpore in cui le politiche giolittiane avevano, secondo i collaboratori del giornale, gettato il paese. La polemica interventista s'innestava dunque in *Lacerba* su un discorso già avviato.[22] Il caso di Franchi è diverso. Prima dello scoppio della guerra non aveva manifestato ostilità nei confronti del governo Giolitti e la sua critica all'ex primo ministro si limitava al suo neutralismo.

Nonostante questa sostanziale differenza, colpisce, nelle parti del *Figlio* dedicate al "maggio radioso" e all'antigiolittismo, l'evocazione delle stesse energie giovanili cui fa riferimento *Lacerba*, la stessa dialettica vecchi/giovani che animava la rivista. Le motivazioni al sostegno della guerra di Franchi rimangono ideologiche e legate al suo retroterra risorgimentale e alla sua

---

[21] Il 9 maggio 1915, Giovanni Giolitti, preoccupato che il primo ministro in carica Antonio Salandra e il ministro degli esteri Sydney Sonnino avessero già deciso per l'intervento, si recò a Roma. Circa trecento deputati e cento senatori depositarono il loro biglietto da visita fuori dalla sua abitazione romana come voto simbolico a favore di un suo ritorno al governo. Il giorno dopo, ricevuto dal re, Giolitti ribadì che a suo avviso era necessario proseguire le trattative con l'Austria e rinunciare all'entrata in guerra. Dopo aver appurato che la decisione di entrare in guerra non avrebbe incontrato sufficiente consenso in parlamento, Salandra decise di dimettersi, lasciando a Vittorio Emanuele III la responsabilità di risolvere la crisi. Il re interpellò Giolitti per formare un nuovo governo, ma questi rifiutò. Il parlamento, nonostante avesse espresso volontà contraria all'intervento, sapendo che il re invece era a favore, il 20 maggio votò i pieni poteri al governo Salandra (*La storia d'Italia* 681-82 e 684).

[22] Come suggerisce Luca Chiti, l'interesse dei lacerbiani nel promuovere la guerra non era estraneo a ragioni di politica interna, in quanto rappresentava gli interessi dell'élite che si opponeva a Giolitti (205). Secondo Giovanna Procacci, la guerra fu alla fine dichiarata da Salandra per "ricreare il blocco di destra sconfitto dal riformismo giolittiano" (12).

adesione all'interventismo democratico. Tuttavia, nel ricordare i cortei del maggio 1915 sembra riferirsi (e aderire) a un ribellismo giovanile di stampo lacerbiano:

> Eppure io stessa ho provato quello che provava la gioventù italiana, quando un governo di inetti o di traditori minacciava di trascinare l'Italia in una sleale politica di vergogna; io stessa ho plaudito alla gioventù ribelle alla vergogna. Quella mattina di maggio, quando la notizia di un richiamo del Giolitti fece sollevare la popolazione onesta e veramente italiana in un solo scatto di indignazione [...] quasi senza volere, mentre con Cesare Battisti tra loro, passavano per la via Manzoni, a Milano, gli allievi del Politecnico gridando un grido di morte, ho esclamato "Bravi!"
>
> (*Il figlio* 3-4)

I giovani che gridano "Morte a Giolitti!"[23] sono, come i figli di Franchi,[24] studenti universitari e probabilmente futuri ufficiali volontari. Tra di loro ci sono di sicuro lettori di *Lacerba* e *La Voce* che respirano l'aria di propaganda anche violenta che emana dalle due riviste.[25] Esprimendosi a proposito del ruolo della *Voce* nella propaganda interventista, Prezzolini afferma che la rivista doveva rivolgersi ai giovani colti (per lo più studenti universitari) che costituivano il suo più consistente bacino di lettura ("Facciamo la guerra" 4). A coloro cioè che, come ufficiali volontari dell'esercito, avrebbero potuto mediare tra gli intellettuali, detentori della complessità delle ragioni della guerra, e gli strati più bassi e meno istruiti della popolazione. Rappresentavano, secondo la formulazione di Gaetano Mosca, uno dei maestri di Prezzolini, il "secondo strato", il livello intermedio tra i due gruppi sociali. Mario Isnenghi nota come anche *Lacerba*, nata dalla costola più avanguardista e iconoclasta della "Voce", all'atto pratico si proponeva un ruolo simile a quello descritto da Prezzolini (125).

---

[23] Franchi chiarisce che si trattava di questo grido nella sua autobiografia, *La mia vita*: "Ma nello stesso giorno, mentre con i colleghi che si trovavano in sede, dalla finestra dell'Associazione sventolavo una bandiera, acclamando i giovani che in folla si recavano sotto le finestre della 'Trento e Trieste', in prima fila scorsi i miei due figli, Gino e Ivo. / Era il momento in cui si gridava: '*Morte a Giolitti*'. [...] M'avvicinai e, per un impulso sciocco, come ne hanno le mamme [...] dissi: / – Che fate qui voi due? Andate a casa. / – O bella! E perché? Vai tu, a casa, sora Annina" (289).

[24] Al tempo della scrittura del romanzo, due dei figli di Franchi, Ivo e Gino, erano ufficiali volontari. Gino morirà tragicamente nella battaglia del Monte San Gabriele, nel settembre del 1917.

[25] È interessante che Franchi menzioni il "grido di morte" del corteo quando più volte Papini parla in *Lacerba* della possibilità dell'uso della violenza da parte del popolo. Ad esempio, nella conclusione di "Appello" il riferimento è esplicito e sottolineato dai caratteri maiuscoli: "La parola degli scrittori, dei pensatori e degli artisti può ancora avere la sua efficacia, prima che contro i vecchi, i pusilli e gli invalidi che ci rappresentano davanti al mondo divenga necessaria la VIOLENZA" (273).

I giovani al cui grido si unisce la narratrice sono membri plausibili di questo secondo strato. Non a caso il romanzo di Franchi include una componente epistolare costituita da una serie di lettere a lei indirizzate dal figlio, un giovane ufficiale volontario che si trova in prima linea. Pur rifiutando l'idea della "guerra-festa" comune a tanti poeti-soldati,[26] nemmeno lui sembra immune da un linguaggio quasi marinettiano nelle sue descrizioni delle battaglie. A proposito della morte in trincea, pur senza intenti celebrativi, parla di "fracassamento di cranii", "spezzatura di membra che talvolta volano in aria come le membra di quei burattini che si dislocano per divertire i ragazzi" (*Figlio* 66-67). Più avanti, il giovane soldato esalta la bellezza della poesia della guerra a scapito di quella della natura, aderendo, almeno dal punto di vista estetico, alla pedagogia marinettiana e papiniana:

> Non ti accorgi che divento poeta? Però debbo confessare che tutta la grande poesia della natura perde d'importanza di fronte alla poesia meravigliosa della nostra guerra. Vorrei dire alla lirica superba — anche sonora — di questa azione da giganti.
>
> (Figlio 97-98)

Papini, in "Amiamo la guerra", indugia proprio sulle suggestioni estetiche dei suoni di guerra. In questo caso la bellezza della musica prodotta dal cannone scaturisce dal suo prevalere sulla voce dei neutralisti, su certi vezzi poetici e sulle proteste popolari contro la guerra; nel caso del figlio si riferisce piuttosto alle motivazioni ideali del conflitto:

> Com'è bella, da monte a monte, la voce sonora e decisa dell'artiglieria! Come ricopre bene, coi suoi tonfi lunghi e larghi, i pistolotti degli avvocati, i razzi dei poeti e i boati delle folle incattivite!
>
> (274)

In un'altra lettera, il figlio parla di "orrenda meraviglia" riferendosi alla possibile strage imminente e sembra aver metabolizzato la decostruzione papiniana della sacralità della vita:

> È la poesia del dolore, della morte, della disperazione, ma è una grandiosa poesia. Nessun poeta può cantarla mai in tutta la sua grandezza. Oggi ho un fremito nell'anima. Sento che qualche cosa di meraviglioso si annuncia. Dico meraviglioso, ma non so, può anche essere orrenda meraviglia, fatta di strage. Che importa? Può essere la morte. Che cosa inutile la vita.
>
> (*Figlio* 281-82)

---

[26] Derivata dall'omonimo arazzo del 1925 di Fortunato Depero e collegata al mito marinettiano della "guerra sola igiene del mondo", l'espressione "guerra festa" ha avuto una certa fortuna negli studi sulla letteratura di guerra in riferimento all'esaltazione della guerra come opportunità di purificazione e rigenerazione sociale ed esistenziale (Isnenghi 169; Cortellessa 115; Tosi 110).

La dialettica vecchi/giovani caratteristica di *Lacerba* è un tema presente anche nel *Figlio*, come ad esempio nell'aneddoto che ha per protagonisti un giovanissimo aspirante combattente e un "vecchio" azzimato che ricorda i borghesi opportunisti bersagliati da *Lacerba*:

Un ragazzo di diciassette anni tira un carretto e canta una canzone di guerra. Un uomo azzimato di una certa età lo segue crollando la testa fino a che non ce la fa più e lo redarguisce.
Un dialogo dei più graziosi. Il monello aveva delle arguzie feroci contro il vecchio pacifista e [...] pareva che volesse fare al pubblico un'orazione contro i vecchi ormai votati al sacrificio delle idealità.
— Dica, ma alla guerra ci vo io, sa? Che gliene importa a lei? La pelle è mia; sicuro che se fossi una vecchia carcassa come lei, farei a meno di andare alla guerra, ma io sono giovane.

(*Figlio* 41-42)

La tirata contro i vecchi di Agnoletti su *Lacerba* è senz'altro più cruda e dettagliata, ma esprime sentimenti simili:

I vecchi fanno schifo. Non vogliono vendicare il Belgio, obbligo per noi morale [...]; non vogliono liberare gli italiani schiavi. Non vogliono pigliare le terre nostre. [...] Questi vilissimi vecchi son sordi: non sentono battere le ore della storia. Questi vecchi putridi hanno due ideali e basta: il canile e la mangiatoia.

(Agnoletti 8)

La quarta area tematica riguardante sia *Lacerba* sia *Il figlio* di cui mi occupo è il mito della guerra rigeneratrice, alla base di molto interventismo avanguardista. *Lacerba* aderiva a un modello di esaltazione della guerra per la guerra in linea con lo slogan marinettiano "guerra sola igiene del mondo", come grido d'insofferenza verso il presente, impeto di ribellione contro il giolittismo e spinta al superamento di una crisi esistenziale che accomunava un'intera generazione d'intellettuali (Isnenghi 92).[27] Papini invocava il "caldo bagno di sangue nero" come necessario salasso per l'umanità, così che questa potesse ritrovare energie nuove e rinascere purificata:

Ci voleva alla fine un caldo bagno di sangue nero dopo tanti umidicci tiepidumi di latte materno, di lacrime fraterne. Ci voleva una bella innaffiatura di sangue per l'arsura d'agosto e una rossa svinatura per le vendemmie di settembre e una muraglia di svampate per i freschi di settembre.

("Amiamo la guerra" 274)

---

[27] Più che l'antigermanesimo manifestato soprattutto da Soffici, secondo Isnenghi sono i due articoli di Papini già menzionati, "La vita non è sacra" e "Amiamo la guerra", a fornire una chiave di lettura più veritiera dell'interventismo di *Lacerba*. A questi si può aggiungere, ad esempio, "Picchia e non ascolta", sempre a firma di Papini.

Lacerba e *Il figlio alla guerra*: agli estremi dell'interventismo intellettuale?

L'avanguardia prebellica italiana si era nutrita di una serie di gridi violenti di guerra che si erano succeduti fin dall'inizio del Novecento. Come nota Isenghi,

[t]utta la Belle Époque — l'età giolittiana in Italia — è punteggiata di questi fervidi saluti alla guerra che torna: 1904, 1911, 1912, 1914, 1915. Vi potremmo riconoscere una costante, che è psicologica e ideologico-politica, esistenziale e sociale. Da "Questa grande guerra sembra fatta per noi", nel *Regno* del 1904, alla "Guerra sola igiene del mondo e sola morale educatrice", nel 1909, nella *Battaglia di Tripoli* "vissuta e cantata" da Filippo Tommaso Marinetti (1911-1912), nel 1915; dall'*Ode alla violenza* dei futuristi al "caldo bagno di sangue nero" di Giovanni Papini su "Lacerba", a "Facciamo la guerra" e "Salute al nuovo mondo!" di Giuseppe Prezzolini sulla "Voce" nel 1914.

(Isenghi 7)

La convinzione che la guerra avesse un potere di trasformazione tale da poter dar vita a una nuova Europa, imprimere una scossa innovatrice alla società e scuotere le coscienze individuali al punto da risolvere la crisi esistenziale che affliggeva molti intellettuali di inizio secolo era un tratto comune a tanti collaboratori di *Lacerba* e *La Voce*. Giuseppe Prezzolini, ad esempio, si esprimeva sulla *Voce* riguardo alla guerra accostando immagini di morte e nascita:

Il mistero della generazione di un nuovo mondo europeo si compie. Forze oscure scaturite dalla profondità dell'essere sono al travaglio ed il parto avviene tra rivi mostruosi di sangue e gemiti che fanno fremere.

(Prezzolini 1)

In realtà, non si trattava di un mito emerso improvvisamente con le avanguardie letterarie e artistiche del periodo prebellico. Come ha mostrato Emilio Gentile, il tema della guerra rigeneratrice aveva radici ottocentesche. L'idea della guerra come necessaria interruzione dell'effetto di snervamento prodotto da troppo lunghi periodi di pace risaliva agli anni del conflitto franco-prussiano e aveva radici nello storicismo, nel positivismo, nel darwinismo sociale e nell'idealismo (Gentile 111 e 113). Secondo Gentile l'entusiasmo per la guerra come occasione di rinnovamento era comune a molti soldati. Nonostante il generale malcontento nei confronti dell'entrata in guerra dell'Italia,

non erano stati pochi, o erano stati comunque una numerosa minoranza, specialmente giovani, coloro che all'inizio della Grande Guerra avevano esultato ed erano partiti volontari ed entusiasti convinti che stesse iniziando una nuova era per l'umanità, che gli individui e la nazione sarebbero stati rigenerati dal sangue, e che dalla guerra sarebbe nato un mondo nuovo, più sano e più nobile negli ideali delle nazioni.

(Gentile 12)

L'interventismo di Franchi sembra estraneo alle invocazioni alla guerra dei letterati avanguardisti. Pur rimanendo convinta della necessità dell'intervento e del fatto che la pace sarebbe la scelta peggiore perché condurrebbe ad altre guerre, la voce narrante del romanzo non ne esalta né giustifica la barbarie e non ne celebra la qualità estetica (se non attraverso la voce del figlio). Nel passo che segue si sente piuttosto un senso di stanchezza e sopraffazione:

Passano uno dopo l'altro, uguali e tristi i giorni, senza conforto, senza che nulla faccia presagire la fine di tanta barbarie. [...] Mai tante armi micidiali furono create in una volta, mai si levarono tanti lamenti di invocazione. Ogni mattina con l'alba la speranza viene attraverso i vetri a risvegliarci. La speranza non [...] ha deposto quel suo vezzo malvagio di deridere queste povere creature del mondo, fragili esseri in balìa della cieca deità che dal caos ebbe vita, che al caos ci chiama e che dicono il Destino.

(Figlio 203-04).

Siamo certamente lontani dalla retorica papiniana della guerra come necessario mezzo drastico di depopolazione del mondo e dalla celebrazione estetica della carneficina di "Amiamo la guerra" (274). Tuttavia, a un esame più attento, si vede come nemmeno *Il figlio* sia completamente estraneo all'idea della guerra rinnovatrice di energie per gli individui e anche per l'intera razza. Del resto, come già accennato, l'esaltazione della guerra come rimedio storico e come spinta propulsiva all'evoluzione era parte della cultura europea della seconda metà dell'Ottocento, cultura che aveva fatto da humus a correnti artistico-letterarie e di pensiero diverse tra loro. A partire dal 1870,

[la] schiera dei cantori delle virtù della guerra divenne numerosa e varia, includeva reazionari e rivoluzionari, religiosi e atei, idealisti e positivisti. [...] La guerra era considerata un evento appartenente alla naturale condizione dell'uomo, sempre possibile nella perpetua lotta per l'esistenza, e l'ascensione verso forme superiori di civiltà.

(Gentile 113)

Se pure obliquamente, anche Franchi, in un'occasione, presenta il conflitto in termini di rinascita nazionale e individuale e accetta il principio, ispirato a una visione evoluzionista della storia, del necessario ritorno ciclico delle guerre nella vita delle nazioni. Il potere rigeneratore della guerra ha un impatto anche sul figlio della narratrice. Prima di arruolarsi, era un ragazzo debole e distratto, come i suoi coetanei. Tuttavia la guerra ha infuso nuova energia in un'intera generazione e, nelle parole di Franchi, in tutta una razza:

Non mi pareva tanto diverso dai suoi compagni; così che talvolta pensavo tra me alla possibile insussistenza di tutte le conclusioni scientifiche sulle razze, e quasi sentivo che una reazione potente sarebbe venuta ove uno di quei fatti imperiosi che nella vita dei popoli accadono a più o meno lontane riprese di anni, avesse posto la razza nostra nella condizione di dover mettere in giuoco la propria energia.

(Il figlio alla guerra 9)

Le parole di Papini riguardo al necessario ritorno delle guerre per il progresso dei popoli sono più esplicitamente violente di quelle di Franchi e non

Lacerba e *Il figlio alla guerra*: agli estremi dell'interventismo intellettuale? 71

suggeriscono un'adesione al pensiero della "guerra giusta" che invece fa da sfondo a tutto l'interventismo di Franchi.[28] Inoltre, il passo che segue risale a prima dello scoppio della guerra. Vale tuttavia la pena leggerlo in parallelo a quello tratto dal *Figlio* appena citato per evidenziare quanto, pur da punti di vista distanti tra di loro, sia *Lacerba* che il romanzo di Franchi avessero assorbito spunti e suggestioni da un sostrato comune:

Guerra interna e Guerra esterna — Rivoluzione e Conquista: ecco la nostra storia. Per l'una e per l'altra noi siamo quello che siamo — cioè superiori ai figli delle bertucce.

("La vita non è sacra" 224)

Le motivazioni della propaganda di *Lacerba* e del *Figlio* sono diverse fra loro, sia da un punto di vista ideologico che da un punto di vista cronologico. La rivista invocava la guerra per affermare la supremazia culturale italo-francese rispetto alla Germania e per creare le condizioni per la partecipazione dell'Italia al grande evento globale che avrebbe cambiato il volto dell'Europa.[29] Lo scopo principale del *Figlio* era rendere la guerra un evento accettabile da parte di chi non era mai stato favorevole all'intervento, oppure da parte di chi era diventato fortemente contrario alla luce degli sviluppi tragici del conflitto ormai visibili a tutti. Nonostante queste differenze sostanziali, l'analisi in parallelo dei numeri interventisti di *Lacerba* e del *Figlio alla guerra* mostra come nel discorso sulla guerra, sia che fosse di area avanguardista e nazionalista e diretto a una élite intellettuale come la rivista di Papini e Soffici, o invece legato alla tradizione realista e rivolto a una *readership* più vasta ed eterogenea, con speciale attenzione al pubblico femminile come il romanzo di Franchi,[30] convergessero strategie retoriche e temi comuni.

Temple University

---

[28] Anche se il motivo della "guerra giusta" non rimane completamente fuori dalla retorica papiniana, si veda ad esempio il già citato articolo "Le cinque guerre" in cui parla di "guerra ideale" per contrastare l'avanzare degli imperi centrali.
[29] "Papini tente de gagner les consensus de l'opinion publique pour que le pays saisisse ce moment unique, au nom de trois objectifs vitaux: la renaissance, l'accomplissement territorial et la revanche de l'Italie — aussi bien dans sa dimension spirituelle que dans le concert des puissances européennes. L'enjeu politique et la revendication d'une spécificité culturelle visent à préserver l'italianité" (De Paulis-D'Alembert 57).
[30] L'analisi di un testo come *Il figlio alla guerra* impone naturalmente considerazioni di genere. Il contributo delle scrittrici alla letteratura di guerra (pamphlets, romanzi, poesie, articoli di giornale) è stato largamente ignorato. Per quanto si tenda ad associare femminismo (e femminilità) con il pacifismo, la maggior parte delle donne che hanno scritto sulla guerra erano interventiste. Oltre a Franchi, tra le autrici che hanno prodotto testi di propaganda vanno ricordate almeno Annie Vivanti, Willy Dias, Haydée, Matilde Serao e Carolina Invernizio. Una voce fuori dal coro è stata quella di Ada Negri. Mi occupo del rapporto tra scrittrici italiane e prima guerra mondiale in un progetto di libro in corso di lavorazione.

Opere citate

Agnoletti (Agnoletti Ferdinando), *Colpi di pungolo*, "Lacerba", III, 1 (1915): 6-8.
Burgio Alberto e Luciano Casali (a cura di), *Studi sul razzismo italiano*, Bologna, CLUEB, 1996.
Asor Rosa Alberto, *Scrittori e popolo: il populismo nella letteratura italiana contemporanea*, Torino, Einaudi, 1988.
Brugge Peter, *The Nation Supreme: The Idea of Europe 1914-1915*, in *History of the Idea of Europe*, a. c. di Ole Wæver, Kevin Wilson e Jan van der Dussen, London, Routledge, 1995 (revised edition), 83-150.
Chiti Luca, *Cultura e politica nelle riviste fiorentine del primo Novecento: 1903-1915*, Milano, Loescher, 1972.
Cortellessa Andrea, *Le notti chiare erano tutte un'alba*, Milano, Mondadori, 1998.
De Paulis-D'Alembert Maria Pia, *Giovanni Papini: culture et identité*, Toulouse, Presses Universitaires du Mirail, 2007.
Del Puppo Alessandro, *Lacerba 1913-1915*, Bergamo, Lubrina, 2000.
Franchi Anna, *Avanti il divorzio*, a c. di Elisabetta de Troja, Palermo, Sandron, 2012.
_____. *A voi soldati futuri dico la nostra guerra*, Milano, Vallardi, 1916.
_____. *Il figlio alla guerra*, Milano, Treves, 1917.
_____. *Le guerre dei nonni e le nostre*, Milano, Vallardi, 1922.
Gentile, Emilio, *L'apocalisse della modernità: la Grande Guerra per l'uomo nuovo*, Milano, Mondadori, 2008 (nuova edizione 2014).
Gigli Lucilla, *Latino e calza. Educazione ed esperienze biografiche ne "La mia vita" di Anna Franchi*, "Espacio, Tiempo y Educacion" 1 (1) (2014), 97-113. http://dx.doi.org/ 10.14516/ete.2014.001.001.005
_____. *"Noi vi seguiremo senza vacillare": Anna Franchi, la propaganda, la letteratura*, "Storia e problemi contemporanei" 49 (2008), 87-100.
Gragnani Cristina, *Un io titanico per un'"umile verità": ideologia e disegno letterario in "Avanti il divorzio" di Anna Franchi*, in Ombretta Frau e Cristina Gragnani, *Sottoboschi letterari: sei case studies tra Otto e Novecento: Mara Antelling, Emma Boghen Conigliani, Evelyn, Anna Franchi, Jolanda, Flavia Steno*, Firenze, Firenze University Press, 2011, 85-113.
Guidi Laura, *Un nazionalismo declinato al femminile 1914-1918*, in *Vivere la guerra*, a c. di Laura Guidi, Napoli, CLIO, 2007, 93-118.
Isnenghi Mario, *Il mito della grande guerra: da Marinetti a Malaparte*, Roma, Laterza, 1970.
Jahier Piero, *Wir Müssen*, "Lacerba", III, 22 (1915): 165.
Kissinger Henry, *L'arte della diplomazia*, Milano, Sperling & Kupfer, 2004.
La crisi di fine secolo, l'età giolittiana e laprima guerra mondiale, vol. 19, in *La storia d'Italia*, consulenza e coordinamento di Massimo L. Salvadori, Novara, DeAgostini, 2005.
"Lacerba", Milano, Mazzotta, 1970 (http∫ØØhdlÆhandleÆnetØ2027ØmdpÆ3901503 8642453).
Malaguti Elena, *Anna Franchi*, Malaguti, http://www.letteraturadimenticata.it/ Franchi.htm.
Marconi Pio, *Dalla libertà alla sicurezza*, in *Filosofia giuridica della guerra e della pace*, a c. di Vincenzo Ferrari, Milano, FrancoAngeli, 2008, 269-315.
Montesi Barbara, *"Il frutto vivente del disonore": i figli della violenza, l'Italia, la Grande Guerra*, in *Stupri di guerra: la violenza di massa contro le donne nel Novecento*, a c. Di Marcello Flores, Milano, Franco Angeli 2010. 61-80.

Monticone Alberto, *Problemi e prospettive di una storia della cultura popolare nella prima guerra mondiale*, in *Operai e contadini nella Grande Guerra*, a c. di Mario Isnenghi, Bologna, Cappelli, 1982, 33-39.
Neal, *Tedescheria immanente e... invadente*, "Lacerba", III, 16 (1915), 123-26.
Niglia Federico, *L'antigermanesimo italiano. Da Sedan an Versailles*, Firenze, Le Lettere, 2012.
Panizza Francisco, *Populism and the Mirror of Democracy*, in *Populism and the Mirror of Democracy*, a c. di Francisco Panizza, London, Verso, 2005, 1-31.
Papini Giovanni, *Amiamo la guerra*, "Lacerba", II, 20 (1914), 274-75.
_____. *Le cinque guerre*, "Lacerba", III, 12 (1915), 89-90.
_____. *Ciò che dobbiamo alla Francia*, "Lacerba", II, 17 (1914), 249-52.
_____. *Contro la neutralità*, "Lacerba", II, 18 (1914), 257-61.
_____. *Fuori i tedeschi*, "Lacerba", III, 7 (1915), 54-55.
_____. *Picchia e non ascolta*, "Lacerba", III, 16 (1915), 121-22.
_____. *La vita non è sacra*, "Lacerba", I, 20 (1913), 223-25.
Prezzolini Giuseppe, *Facciamo la guerra*, "La Voce", 26 agosto 1914, 1-6.
Procacci Giovanna, *Dalla rassegnazione alla rivolta: mentalità e comportamenti popolari nella grande guerra*, Roma, Bulzoni, 1999.
Soffici Ardengo, *Intorno alla gran bestia*, "Lacerba", II, 16 (1914), 245-47.
_____. *Sulla barbarie tedesca*, "Lacerba", II, 22 (1914), 291-92.
_____. *Breve risposta a un tedescante*, "Lacerba", III, 6 (1915), 44-45.
_____. *Sulla soglia*, "Lacerba", III, 20 (1915), 155-57.
_____. *Memento*, "Lacerba", III, 22 (1915), 163.
Somigli Luca, *Lacerba (1913-14); Quartiere Latino (1913-14); L'Italia futurista (1916-18); La Vraie Italie (1919-20)*, in *The Oxford Critical and Cultural History of Modernist Magazines: Europe 1880-1940*, part I, a c. di Peter Brooker, Sacha Bru, Andrew Thacker e Christian Weikop, Oxford, Oxford University Press, 2013. 469-90.
Taguieff Pierre-André, *Quand on pensait le monde en termes de races*, "L'Histoire", 12 dicembre 2013.
Tosi Giuseppe, *Gente sciupata e superba. Motivi privati dell'interventismo nella Grande Guerra: Serra, Gadda, Soffici e Jahier*, MLN (Italian Issue), 1 (2004), 84-108.

Michael Subialka

Modernism at War:
Pirandello and the Crisis of (German) Cultural Identity

Critics have elaborated several different conceptual approaches which they use to divide and categorize the multiple strands of modernist writing in the Italian context. Despite their differences, however, these approaches have also tended to result in similar alignments or groupings of modernist figures, distinguishing between the political avant-gardes like the Futurists and the seminal Italian modernists of introspection, Italo Svevo and Luigi Pirandello. While some critics have focused on the strong political and nationalist elements that seem to set the Futurists apart, others have focused on the specific sense of pessimistic crisis and how Svevo and Pirandello respond by elaborating a correspondingly pessimistic worldview. But the conclusion in both cases has been a confirmation of the same basic division of the Italian modernist scene. My contention here is that a reexamination of Pirandello's literary engagement with World War I complicates this general picture, revealing key ways in which Pirandello is in closer continuity with the nationalist elements of modernism than has sometimes been acknowledged.

In Pirandello's war stories, a crisis of cultural identity brings strong elements of nationalism into contact with the pessimistic worldview for which the writer is known. At the same time, this nationalism is situated in a discourse of transnational cultural identity, linking it to Risorgimento philosophical thought, while, in terms of Pirandello's family history, it connects to a personal commitment to a unified Italy free from foreign rule. I argue that by drawing these nationalist elements together with his humoristic outlook, Pirandello integrates his pessimistic worldview with a simultaneous commitment to an ethics of interpersonal compassion and a desire for spiritual renewal at a national level. This attitude sets him apart from his modernist contemporaries.

1. *Italian Modernism between Traditionalism and Nationalism*
In order to understand how Pirandello's war stories help us to gain new insight into the relationship among the conflicting impulses at work in Italian modernism, one must first clarify the conceptual models that articulate those impulses. Two critical approaches have focused on different impulses in the modernist imagination, but both result in similar ways of grouping the most prominent figures of Italian modernism. One approach is offered by Luca Somigli, who

makes use of Emilio Gentile's notion of "modernist nationalism" to articulate the distinction between avant-garde artists like the Futurists and writers like Svevo and Pirandello: the Futurists (and other avant-garde groups, like the writers for *La voce*) are engaged in a project of political renovation with nationalist aims (82-83); in contrast, Svevo and Pirandello focus on the dissolution of the subject and its connection to the world, culminating in a "universe empty of meaning" (86). In this view, the optimistic or positive project of the modernist nationalists contrasts with the metaphysical and psychological pessimism of Svevo and Pirandello.[1]

This grouping thus coincides with the interpretative "line" drawn by Renato Barilli, who maintained that Svevo and Pirandello (in contrast to Carlo Emilio Gadda) mark the high point of Italian modernism because they achieve the best "balance between tradition and innovation [...]" (6; my translation). But, as this characterization suggests, Barilli's focus is less on the role of an optimistic nationalist project than on the question of how modernism relates its radical innovation to the tradition coming before it. This difference puts Barilli's framework in dialogue with the position charted by Robert Dombroski, who has suggested in his comparison of Svevo and Pirandello to Gadda that we must focus on how these writers view the function of their writing in the context of the modern crisis that gives rise to it. He argues that for both Svevo and Pirandello a seemingly nihilistic vision of the modern world is actually overcome through the subject's literary reflection (the autobiographical impulse): "[their] novels illustrate in different ways how art can revive a world deadened by modernization and how the reified subject can regain its lost humanity through the artful reconstruction or management of reality's negative aspects" (2003, 102). In this sense, it is not their pessimism that unifies Svevo and Pirandello but rather their attempt to use innovative new forms of writing to regain something that is lost in the modern world.

I suggest that Barilli and Dombroski offer an approach to Italian modernism that aligns with a key concept developed by Frank Kermode (though neither of them dialogues with the scholar of English modernism directly). I have in mind Kermode's distinction between traditionalist and anti-traditionalist modernists.[2] In his view, both are unified by a deep sense of ongoing crisis that is articulated in apocalyptic terms (103). However, for the traditionalist modernists, including Yeats, Pound, Eliot, and Joyce (104) — and, I would add, following Pericles Lewis (2007, 166), Svevo — this crisis unfolds in continuity with the lost past. In

---

[1] This reading shows how modernists like Svevo and Pirandello relate to what Harrison characterizes as a moment of "nihilistic idealism" across Europe in the years before World War I (8).

[2] Key elements of Poggioli's influential *Theory of the Avant-Garde* align with Kermode's picture of the anti-traditionalist elements of modernism. For Poggioli, the avant-garde is both an historical movement (associated with figures like Marinetti) and a spirit of futurity in aesthetic production, which he links to romanticism.

contrast, for the anti-traditionalists, the perpetual renovation of the world uproots the modern moment from all historical continuities, leading to a perpetual novelty built out of crisis. This impulse toward total novelty sets them apart from the traditionalists, who articulate a deep sense of rupture and loss, going so far as to deconstruct traditional forms of representation to express that modern crisis, but for whom this sense of loss is grounded in a desire for some form of order.

Thus, just as Somigli has shown how the notion of modernist nationalism can help us understand the different ways in which various Italian writers compare with one another, I contend that Kermode's notion of modernist traditionalism can likewise help us to understand a key element uniting various interpretations of Italian modernism — like those articulated by Barilli and Dombroski. In the former case, the strong impulse of a nationalist political project suggests a separation between the active, optimistic movement of a group like the Futurists, on the one hand, and the much more introspective and pessimistic view of writers like Svevo and Pirandello. In the latter view, the distinction is not one of optimism and pessimism but rather focuses on the response to crisis and the ways in which that response attempts to reestablish some form of order or to balance the radical innovation of modernist form with the desire for meaning — a desire typical of more traditional forms.

Both of these conceptual approaches to modernism are integral to my reading of Pirandello's short stories from the period of World War I. He mixes elements of a pessimistic, almost apocalyptic, view with a nationalist outlook; at the same time, his commitment to an ethics of compassion reveals a sense in which this pessimism is not as total as we might think — his universe is not, perhaps, completely empty of meaning. In fact, in "Berecche e la guerra" (1915) ["Berecche and the War"] and "Colloquii coi personaggi" (1915) ["Conversations with Characters"], Pirandello affirms the interventionist aspirations of his young contemporaries, like the Futurists. At the same time, he envisions the war as an inescapable rupture of Italy's links with German culture, creating an identity crisis that is nevertheless productive precisely insofar as it is required in order to construct a more robust Italian cultural identity. Yet his affirmation of interventionism coincides with a humorous poetics that relativizes historical conflicts and ironizes commitments to political and practical aims. What emerges is thus a deeply ambivalent modernist imagination, which spans from these short stories to Pirandello's broader corpus — torn between the traditionalist's aspirations to achieve authentic forms of identity, the nationalist's aspiration for cultural renewal, and a humorous compassion that sees these aspirations as both meaningful (serious) and futile (laughable).[3]

---

[3] In this sense my analysis of Pirandello agrees with the need, expressed by Somigli and Moroni, to develop a broader notion of modernism in the Italian context in order to account for its multifaceted nature (5).

2. Cultural Identity Crisis: German Philosophy and the Extents of Nationalism

"Berecche e la guerra" is an ideal place to start if we want to account for how Pirandello's poetics of humorous compassion combines a moderate form of modernist nationalism with strong elements of modernist traditionalism. The 1934 publication of the story was preceded by an authorial note that explicitly thematizes those elements. It highlights the importance of humor in combining patriotism with the crisis of personal and cultural identity brought by the war:

> Raccolgo in questo XIV volume delle mie *Novelle per un anno* il racconto in otto capitoli *Berecche e la guerra*, scritto nei mesi che precedettero la nostra entrata nella guerra mondiale. Vi è rispecchiato il caso a cui assistetti, con maraviglia in principio e quasi con riso, poi con compassione, d'un uomo di studio educato, come tanti allora, alla tedesca, specialmente nelle discipline storiche e filologiche. La Germania, durante il lungo periodo dell'alleanza, era diventata per questi tali, non solo spiritualmente ma anche sentimentalmente, nell'intimità della loro vita, la patria ideale. Nella imminenza del nostro intervento contro di essa, promosso dalla parte più viva e sana del popolo italiano e poi seguito da tutta intera la Nazione, costoro si trovarono perciò come sperduti; e, costretti alla fine dalla forza stessa degli eventi a riaccogliere in sé la vera patria, patirono un dramma che mi parve, sotto quest'aspetto, degno d'essere rappresentato.
>
> (*Novelle per un anno*, III, 572)

> I'm placing *Berecche and the War*, a story in eight chapters written in the months preceding our entry into the World War, with this XIVth volume of my collected *Stories for a Year*. It reflects the case I witnessed, with astonishment to begin with and almost laughingly, then with compassion, of a studious man educated like so many others at that time in the German fashion, and especially in the disciplines of history and philology. During the long period of our alliance Germany had, for such people, become not just spiritually but also in their thoughts and feelings, as an intimate part of their lives, their ideal native land. As our intervention against her, called for by the most vital and sound part of the Italian people and then accepted by the whole nation, became imminent, they therefore felt, as it were, lost; and, compelled in the end by the very force of events to take back their true native land to themselves, they suffered a crisis which, from this aspect, seemed to me to be worthy of representation.
>
> (Dashwood 25)

While the story itself was elaborated in several phases over a period that seems to have stretched between 1914 and 1917 (Dashwood 3), the fictional setting places the entire narrative in the days of Italy's neutrality after the initial outbreak of war — before the decision in favor of intervention, which finally occurred in the spring of 1915. Pirandello evidently uses this setting as an opportunity to focus on a moment of upheaval and crisis. Throughout the story, a general cultural crisis is enacted through the "case" that the author claims to have witnessed; the psychological disintegration of the protagonist, Berecche, thus stands in for the experience of a whole class of people and becomes indicative of the broader national crisis. These cultural elites, who were formed "in the German fashion," adopting the rigorous methods of German history and philology (like Pirandello himself, who received his doctorate in Romance philology from Bonn), find themselves displaced. The vitality and health of the interventionists have uprooted these studious young men from their "ideal native land," creating a feeling of loss and confusion as they search for a way to "take back their true native land to themselves." The crisis of personal and national identity is clearly directed toward finding new foundations for a meaningful identity.

The plot of the story weaves these themes of national and personal identity crisis together in a humorous way. Divided into eight short chapters, the story traces the transformations in the protagonist's attitude toward his ideal homeland after Italy's declaration of neutrality following the German invasion of Belgium; this news shatters him psychologically, strains his personal relationships, and splits his family into factions as his son and future son-in-law advocate for intervention against Austria-Hungary and Germany. This fracturing leads Berecche to revise some of his opinions, gradually admitting not only the faults of Germany's bellicose actions but also his willingness to fight alongside his son. After his son, Faustino, leaves home to volunteer in France, the story ends with Berecche brashly determining that he will teach himself to ride horseback so that he can fight by Faustino's side. But the old man does not know how to ride, and he falls off in a comical catastrophe that lands him in the hospital, temporarily blind — a condition he thus shares with his youngest daughter, Margheritina, who was born blind. The inner breakdown of Berecche's preconceived notions about Germany, his blustering struggles with his family and friends, and his own fervor and incompetence, all create a sympathetic caricature of a man who belongs to another era and who struggles to adapt to the shift in alliances and the call to national solidarity that accompany the outbreak of the Great War.

By situating his story in terms of the categories of his theory of humor, Pirandello connects this "case" to his broader poetics in ways that resonate with his two most important modernist novels, the earlier *Il fu Mattia Pascal* [*The Late Mattia Pascal*] (1904) and his film novel, written contemporaneously with "Berecche," *Si gira...* [*Shoot!*] (1916, republished with revisions under the new title *Quaderni di Serafino Gubbio operatore* [*The Notebooks of Serafino Gubbio, Cinematograph Operator*] in 1925).[4] By the time Pirandello collected "Berecche" in 1934, this poetics was also manifest in his revolutionary theatrical pieces, like *Sei personaggi in cerca d'autore* [*Six Characters in Search of an Author*] (1921, revised and republished in 1925). In these works, traditional narrative and theatrical forms are fragmented or deconstructed in ways that reflect a broader

---

[4] De Castris has argued that these novels should both be thought of as experimental, with *Si gira...* (*Quaderni di Serafino Gubbio operatore*) being the most advanced stage of Pirandello's formal innovations (124). For Dombroski, Pirandello's modernism reaches its novelistic maturity in *Il fu Mattia Pascal* (2003, 92).

crisis of representation.⁵ This is what Manuela Gieri has analyzed as Pirandello's effort to establish a modern "counter-tradition" (295), which is nevertheless to be situated in historical continuity with earlier breaks with tradition, specifically Baudelaire's response to modernity (297-303). Likewise, in "Berecche," jumps in the setting, a loose movement in and out of characters' subjective perspectives through techniques such as free-indirect discourse, and moments of discontinuous or confusing reflection all participate in that same impulse toward formal innovation. The specific wartime crisis relating to the German cultural elements of Italian national identity is thus connected integrally to Pirandello's modernist poetics.

In "Berecche," there appears to be a conflict between the nationalist rejection of German culture and the affirmation of an Italian cultural identity, on the one hand, and the broader modernist project that deconstructs notions of stable identity, on the other. My argument is that in order to make sense of this conflict, we will have to develop a clearer account of the precise nature of nationalism within the story. As Julie Dashwood has convincingly argued, the identity crisis in "Berecche" involves a rejection of the German cultural tradition that puts special weight on the German "method" of thought. She conceives this method as belonging to positivist philosophy and philology as well as to the Hegelian picture of world history as a progressive development of spirit (*Geist*) (1). This German "method" is perhaps epitomized by a passage where Berecche re-evaluates the lessons taught by his German professors of Romance philology; there, the rigorous method that has come to dominate his life (III.579 [33]) is associated with "alcune affermazioni tedesche, che offendevano in lui non soltanto la logica ma anche, in fondo in fondo, il suo sentimento latino" (III.586) ["some German assertions which not only offended his sense of logic but also, in his heart of hearts, his latin sentiment" (38)].

But the nature of the Italian nationalism in this "Latin sentiment" needs to be qualified in terms of Berecche's subsequent reflections, which also will challenge our assumption that his crisis leads him to reject German philosophy. In fact, Berecche immediately goes on to laud a group of earlier German thinkers, from before the existence of a nation called Germany: "Goethe, Schiller, e prima Lessing, e poi Kant, Hegel... Ah, quand'era piccola, quando ancora non era, la Germania, questi giganti! E ora, gigante, ecco qua, s'è buttata, pancia a terra, con le mani afferrate sotto il petto e un gomito qua, sul Belgio e in Francia, l'altro là su la Russia in Polonia" (III.586-87) ["Goethe, Schiller, and first Lessing and then Kant, Hegel... Oh all these giants, when Germany was small, when she was not

---

⁵ The connection between Pirandello's experimental forms, in narrative and theater, and modernism has been discussed by numerous critics. From the decay of modern Rome (Luperini 17, 25) to the disruption of linear narrative form (Gardair 53-55) to the link between Pirandello's theater and avant-garde procedures of deconstructing theatrical tradition (Verdone 50, Livio), the bibliography on this topic is expansive.

yet Germany! And now she is a giant, and has flung herself belly down on the ground, hands clasped under her chest, with one elbow here, on Belgium and in France and the other there, on Russia and in Poland" (39)]. In opposition to the small-minded brutality of his contemporaries' German nationalism, Berecche sees in classical and romantic German thought a literary and philosophical perspective that transcends national boundaries.

Berecche's outlook here draws on a notion of national pride, his "latin sentiment," that is evidently meant to be consistent with a broader poetic and philosophic spirit — one which, notably, directly includes Hegel. For this reason I suggest that we should consider Pirandello's war story as being situated in a Risorgimento tradition of viewing Italian culture in similarly transnational terms. That tradition was perhaps expounded most forcefully by a key Risorgimento philosopher, Bertrando Spaventa (brother of Silvio, the Neapolitan political revolutionary). Spaventa argued against close-minded nationalism, insisting that the new Italy must be an iteration in a larger, collective process of world history where the spiritual life of nations coincides:

[...] nel mondo moderno, all'opposto dell'antico, la vita di ciascuna nazione si muove come all'aperto insieme con quella delle altre; ciascuna è non solo se stessa, ma anche l'altra; anzi non è veramente se stessa, che in questa relazione e intima unità colle altre. [...] Così la nazionalità non ha più lo stesso significato di prima. Non apparisce più come qualcosa che è dato naturalmente e immediatamente e dirò quasi ciecamente da un inesorabile destino; ma come un prodotto assolutamente spirituale, come il posto che ciascun popolo piglia da sé, per sua propria e conscia energia, nello splendido banchetto della nuova vita.
(9-10)

[...] in the modern world, in contrast to the ancient world, the lives of all nations move together, unconcealed. Each nation is not only itself but also the other. Indeed, it is not really itself except insofar as it is related to and intimately unified with the others. [...] As such, the meaning of nationality is altered. It no longer appears as something that is given naturally and immediately (I will even say blindly) by an inexorable destiny, but rather as an absolutely spiritual product. It is the place that each people occupies on its own — through its own conscious energy — at the splendid banquet of new life.
(49)

For him, as for his contemporary Francesco De Sanctis (whom Pirandello studied closely), Hegelian philosophy became a key element to help ground the revolutionary aspirations of Risorgimento patriotism (Rubini 11, Hoffmeister 65, Piccone 99). They saw a continuity running from the Italian Renaissance and the philosophy of Giambattista Vico through to Hegel and the Risorgimento; this continuity corresponded to the close relation between Italian and European culture and thought in an ideal new world order where all free peoples were related.[6]

---

[6] Pirandello's contemporary, and sometimes antagonist, Benedetto Croce, likewise envisioned a continuity between the Renaissance, Risorgimento, and early-20th-century

Reading "Berecche" in continuity with this Risorgimento tradition reveals a key sense in which the traditionalism of Pirandello's modernist stance coincides with a notion of modernist nationalism. It is worth looking at Emilio Gentile's definition of that concept more carefully here:

> What distinguished this nationalism, what made it modernist, was its intention to reconcile intellectual culture, or *spiritualismo* (spiritualism) — understood here generically as the primacy of culture, ideas, and feelings — with mass industrial society, an intention that aimed at opposing and avoiding the negative effects brought in the wake of modernity, such as materialism, skepticism, hedonistic egoism, egalitarian conformism, etc. — all that modernist nationalism identified with the rationalist and individualistic tradition of the Enlightenment. Toward that end modernist nationalism argued the necessity of accompanying the industrial revolution and modernization with a "revolution of the mind" in order to form the sensibility, the character, the conscience of a new Italian who could comprehend and confront the challenges of modern life, who could firmly adhere to the superiority of the mental forces that would assure unity and collective identity to the nation in the face of the development of material and technological forces.
>
> (60)

Unlike the Futurists (or other avant-garde nationalists), Pirandello does not embrace technological modernity and industrialization as the tools to forge a new Italian nation. As critics have pointed out in relation to his key modernist texts, such as the novel he first published during the Great War, *Si gira...*, Pirandello's stance is directly opposed to the mechanization of human life, which is captured in the recurrent metaphor of the film camera as a great black spider devouring the actors' vitality.[7] It is in this sense that Pirandello fits with what Kermode has identified as traditionalist modernism, referring to how some modernists' revolutionary and new poetic forms are nevertheless complementary to the past (112), which they view as a "source of order" (115).

Yet, even if Pirandello is opposed to technological modernity, his vision of nationalism fits with key aspects of Gentile's definition, particularly with the sense that modern "materialism, skepticism, hedonistic egoism, egalitarian conformism, etc." need to be overcome with spiritualism in Italian intellectual culture.[8] Strikingly, this intellectual culture is rooted in non-Italian sources,

---

Italian culture; he believed that the Risorgimento represents the reawakening of the rational and religious spirit of the Renaissance (16). As Rubini has argued, this stance participates in a broad trend in Italian idealism, from Spaventa through Giovanni Gentile, of attempting to link Italian thought with the currents of European thought (18).

[7] This metaphor has been the subject of expansive critical attention. Here it is enough to mention in passing the most recent study to focus on this novel, which takes its title from that metaphor: Michael Syrimis's *The Great Black Spider on its Knock-Kneed Tripod: Reflections of Cinema in Early Twentieth-Century Italy*.

[8] The connection to spiritualism runs deep throughout Pirandello's corpus. One facet that has been much discussed is his recurring interest in the spiritualist school of Theosophy

following on the Risorgimento tradition of conceiving the modern spirit in a transnational scope. As such, we might say that the way in which Pirandello's text exhibits nationalism is itself colored by a form of traditionalism, one that understands the unity of the nation in less restricted ethnic terms than the definitions of thinkers such as the Futurists.

3. *A Family Affair: Risorgimento Struggle as an Intergenerational Task*

The link to the Risorgimento and the notion of a transnational Italian identity is not simply a matter of philosophy. In "Berecche," as well as in "Colloquii coi personaggi," Pirandello articulates a highly personal vision of patriotic sentiment that is rooted in family ties. This vision explicitly links those patriotic ideals to the tradition of the Risorgimento, grounding Pirandello's nationalism in the idea of an incomplete task left for the "sons" by their forefathers — and, in "Colloquii," left by their foremothers, as well.[9] At the same time, it exhibits further links to the transnational conception of Italy as coming into its own not as an isolated unit but in community with other modern nations.

In a central moment of "Berecche," the protagonist and his family discover a letter left by his son, Faustino, who has gone off to join the French in their fight against the Germans. As the letter makes clear, his aim is not specifically to support the French but rather to take action, to show that Italy's young sons will not sit idly as the world around them is at war (III.613-14). The letter is long and sentimental, over-developing an extended metaphor where Italy is depicted as a maidservant thrust from one master to another, lost and in search of her rightful place. As the tearful response of the whole family (until then bitterly divided against itself) reveals, the letter also appeals to the patriotic sentiments of Pirandello's readers. We are no doubt meant to agree with their family friend, Mr. Fongi, whose statement ends the chapter: "Nobilissimo... nobilissimo..." (III.614) ["So noble... so very noble" (60)].

The letter's call to action and its insistence on the valor and strength of young Italian men certainly resonate with aspects of the Futurists' modernist nationalism. Likewise, Pirandello's own comments in the author's note align with that project, focusing on the health and vitality of the interventionist cause; these

---

(Ragusa 22-30, Illiano 78, Costanzo). However, as Thomas notes, we should not rush to think that Pirandello was himself a Theosophist (77).

[9] It is essential to note the importance of the women patriots in this story, as their role is indicative of the changes in family structure and notions of national civic participation brought by the Risorgimento experience. As d'Amelia has shown, these shifting gender roles include an expanded significance for a woman's role as mother (as opposed to being a wife first and mother second), which gives rise to a whole discourse on motherhood with far-reaching implications for Italian modernity in the 20th century (115-16). The key role of the mother and her feminine perspective in "Colloquii" indicates a clear overlap with this discourse (Subialka 81-84). I am grateful to Ursula Fanning for reminding me of the relevance of d'Amelia's work to this particular topic.

youths pushing for change are "[la] parte più viva e sana del popolo italiano" (III.572) ["the most vital and sound [healthy] part of the Italian people" (25)]. Indeed, the Futurists themselves would seem to be included among those who are praised in this passage. Yet the ideal depicted in Faustino's letter also speaks directly to the incomplete task of the Risorgimento and to the idea that the new generation must fight to finish that revolution, to break Italy free of her subservience to the Austrian Empire. In this sense, the connection to the Futurists' modernist nationalism is only partial; there are other ideas at work in the kind of patriotic identity that Pirandello has in mind.

In fact, Italy's task in the Great War is linked explicitly to Pirandello's family history and a notion of intergenerational struggle, as we see in "Colloquii coi personaggi," a short story in two parts, both published in the *Giornale di Sicilia* in 1915, while the first part was collected together with "Berecche e la guerra" in 1919. This story envisions an intergenerational connection not only to the Risorgimento but to the revolts of 1848 against the Bourbon monarchy.[10] After the announcement of Italian intervention, the narrator/protagonist/author, Pirandello, is worried to the point of being unable to write, presumably because his (actual, autobiographical) son, Stefano, will depart shortly to fight on the front lines (III.1143).[11] In the second half of this story, which Pirandello never republished during his life, the author receives a visit from his recently deceased mother, who comes bearing advice to help him in his time of worry and distress. She couches her lessons in a beautiful sequence of memories of her own parents and their patriotic resistance to the foreign occupation of Sicily (III.1147-51). Her son, she explains, will have to endure and suffer, for it was he who wanted this war, even though he knew it would be his son who would have to fight in it. Here, the family metaphor from "Berecche" — Italy with her sons — is made into an autobiographical call to complete the revolutionary task of his forefathers' struggles against foreign rule.

The patriotic project of this form of nationalism is leagues away from the Futurists' theorization of Italian supremacy or their insistence on bloodletting as a form of national purification.[12] It is much closer to what the historian David

---

[10] That intergenerational story was traced at great length in Pirandello's 1913 novel, *I vecchi e i giovani* [*The Old and the Young*], but it is made even more explicitly autobiographical in "Colloquii."

[11] "Colloquii coi personaggi" is also printed in volume III of *Novelle per un anno* and so is likewise cited parenthetically in the same form as quotations from "Berecche."

[12] Marinetti describes the regenerative power of bellicose bloodletting in many places. One succinct statement comes in a chapter of *Democrazia futurista* (1919) entitled "Il cittadino eroico, l'abolizione delle polizie e le scuole di coraggio" [translated from an earlier appearance of the text, as a speech to the Chamber of Labor in Naples on June 26, 1910, as "The Necessity and Beauty of Violence"]. There, he writes: "Quanto all'elogio della guerra, non costituisce certo, come si è preteso, una contradizione coi nostri ideali, né implica un regresso verso le epoche barbare. A chi ci rivolge accuse simili, noi rispondiamo

Gilmour has recently described as an ongoing militarism that emerged from the unification movement and dominated the agendas of the Piedmont kings (263-64). In this reading, the eagerness for intervention, as well as the fervor for colonial projects in Africa, represents the continuation of a policy and mentality of militarism set in motion by a unification that proceeded militarily and over a short time span rather than as a gradual process of cultural cohesion (266-67). Yet in Pirandello's stories this effort to achieve cultural cohesion is decidedly not an effort to establish a self-sufficient, separate notion of the Italian people. Completing the process of emancipating "Italian" regions from the rule of foreigners (previously the Bourbons, now the Austrians) does not entail the kind of radical notion of Italian superiority that distinguishes other avant-garde writers and their version of modernist nationalism.

4. *Distance vs. Immersion: Pirandello's Compassionate Modernism*
Just as Pirandello's stories reconceive nationalism, shifting from rigidity and delineated self-sufficiency to a version of national identity rooted in a more open notion of the nation's spiritual progress, so too do they shift the notion of personal identity. From the collapse of a solipsistic notion of the self-contained subject emerges an impulse toward connection, an effort to understand, and a compassion for shared suffering. This shift is written into the particular mode of humorous double-vision that Pirandello deploys in his writing, and it is most visible in the contrast between two modes of mitigating the suffering of the war. While the stance of "philosophical" reason pushes characters toward an ideal of distanced detachment, a more compassionate alternative pulls them toward immersing themselves in the lives of others.

The humor in "Berecche e la guerra" goes beyond the obvious ways in which the protagonist is made comical, the ways in which his efforts to construct his own identity continually fail. In Pirandello's famous essay *L'umorismo* [*On Humor*]

---

che alte questioni di salute e di igiene morale dovevano necessariamente esser risolte *appunto per mezzo della guerra*, prima di qualsiasi altra. — La vita della nazione non è forse simile a quella dell'individuo che combatte le infezioni e le pletore mediante la doccia o il salasso? Anche i popoli, affermiamo noi, devono seguire una costante igiene di eroismo, e concedersi gloriose docce di sangue! [...] / Noi crediamo che soltanto l'amore del pericolo e l'eroismo, possano purificare e rigenerare la nostra razza" (445-46, emphasis in original) ["As far as praising war is concerned, it certainly does not represent — as some have claimed — a contradiction in our ideals, nor does it imply any regression to a barbaric age. To anyone who makes that sort of accusation against us, our response is that important questions of health and of moral health ought, of necessity, to be resolved precisely by having recourse to war, in preference to all other solutions. Is not the life of the nation rather like that of the individual, who fights against infection and high blood pressure by means of the shower and the bloodletting? Peoples too, in our view, have to follow a constant, healthy regime of heroism, and indulge themselves with glorious bloodbaths! [...] / We believe that only a love of danger and heroism can purify and regenerate our nation" (61-62)].

(1908) he defines his poetics by describing humor as a special type of mirror in which we see, all at once, two types of reflections of the same root image (126-27 [113]). That is, we simultaneously perceive the way in which something is ridiculous and laughable and also the inner reason for which it is serious and pathetic (in the non-pejorative sense of that term, as moving our pathos). The most famous image that he uses to develop that notion of humor is one of an old woman done up with so much makeup that she looks like an exotic parrot. The immediate reaction is laughter: she is not fooling anyone, and she looks positively ridiculous. But, at the same time, in humorous reflection we perceive a pathetic inner image of this woman, we understand her beneath that surface image and see how she is struggling to keep herself looking young. (Pirandello posits the possibility that she has a younger husband whose love she is desperately trying to keep alive.) This pathetic image is described as pushing the initial, surface reflection not simply further but *deeper* (127 [113]). Humorous reflection operates at both levels simultaneously. Berecche's blustering "reasoning," his brash certainty that reading an old book about riding horses would be enough to make him an advanced rider, and the scenes of family turmoil at home, all result in laughter; but, as Pirandello has pointed out in his author's note, this laughter is followed by a sense of "compassione" (III.572) ["compassion" (25)].

Humorous compassion involves moving from a distanced (surface) vision to a deeper insight into a character's psyche; likewise, Pirandello's depiction of the Great War utilizes both perspectives to highlight the ways in which the individual copes with the mass scale of suffering. While it is true that the story's humor involves an escape into detached and distant vision, what critics have described in general as a Pirandellian "philosophy of distance" (Guarna 13), I contend that the efficacy of this distancing effect is challenged by the narrative. The philosophy of distance alone results in a kind of solipsistic vision of the hunkered-down subject whose only defense against modernity is retreat into a philosophical stance of detachment. Pirandello's writing could thus seem to depict a universe empty of meaning, as Somigli has characterized it, putting it on par with the solipsistic self-analysis of Svevo's Zeno. But that, it turns out, is only half of the story.

The philosophy of distance is an approach to life articulated by numerous Pirandellian characters, particularly in the series of meta-fictional short stories that culminates in "Colloquii coi personaggi." In these stories, male *raisonneur* characters adopt methods of extracting themselves from suffering by relativizing the importance of their experiences in the present. This approach is achieved through a combination of historical and spatial reductions — zooming out to make the present look historically insignificant (a mere blip in an endless flow of time) or spatially miniscule (a mere speck of dust on a speck of dust in the infinite void of space). The inventor of the phrase, "the philosophy of distance," is a character from "La tragedia di un personaggio" ["A Character's Tragedy"] (1911), Dr. Fileno, who has written a book of that name where he describes his method as looking through a reversed telescope and proudly touts the method's achievement of making him numb to the pain of his daughter's death. Similarly, in the first half of "Colloquii coi personaggi," an unnamed male *raisonneur* character advises Pirandello to detach himself from his stress over his son, Stefano, on the front lines and his concern over the patriotic justification of the war. He insists that the historical account of the war will change over time, that what seems just and necessary in one moment can seem unjust or not worth the effort in another, and that these struggles and their ideals are not what matter in life (III.1142). According to this view, the pressing commitments of today recede in the distance of time.

Likewise, in "Berecche" the protagonist repeatedly makes use of a distancing effect to allay his worries and calm his nerves. As his inner confusion and turmoil deepens, this method becomes more necessary, but also less convincing. One of the most interesting of these instances is a moment right after his son, Faustino, has returned from an interventionist demonstration where he was arrested. Berecche reflects on his daughter Margherita's inner faith and devotion, which he sees as something enviable and solid in contrast to his own flailing attempts to grasp onto the light of reason (III.593 [45]). It is in this context that Berecche suddenly retreats from the pain of his life, and the impossibility of resting peacefully in either his little light of reason or a childlike faith. He turns instead to a distanced view of the earth relative to the vast expanses of space: "La vede per gli spazii senza fine, come forse nessuna o appena forse qualcuna di quelle stelle la può vedere, questa piccola Terra che va e va, senza un fine che si sappia, per quegli spazii di cui non si sa la fine" (III.595) ["He sees this little planet Earth in endless space, as perhaps none or maybe just one of those stars can see it, going on and on, for no known purpose, in that space whose end is unknown" (46)]. What follows is a very long reflection on the perspective that an intelligent being out in the stars would have on this little grain of sand and the supposedly important cares of its infinitesimal inhabitants. Following on that, Berecche contextualizes the experience of this moment relative to the historical time of all human events, seeing the present recede to a point. Human suffering, the deeply important moment we live through, will all be reduced to a speck; our lived experience might seem fundamental now, but it will fade in historical time and vanish in the distance of celestial spaces.[13]

---

[13] The same perspective is applied in the prototypically humorous Pirandellian work, his first modernist novel, *Il fu Mattia Pascal*, where the second preface, which he labels "philosophical," paints the same basic picture as a way of describing the decentered condition of humanity after the Copernican revolution (*Tutti i romanzi* I, 323-24). These articulations of human finitude and their pessimistic outlook for culture are clearly tied to the tradition of cultural pessimism that Dienstag has identified with the figure of Leopardi, as well as with the metaphysical outlook in philosophers like Schopenhauer and Nietzsche (55). Guarna's analysis of the link between Pirandello and Leopardi makes much use of the instance of Copernicus as a figure of humorous reflection (59-62).

But the philosophy of distance espoused by these *raisonneur* characters should not be confused with Pirandello's own outlook, for his perspective is, as we have said, double. In fact, in "La tragedia di un personaggio," the narrator explicitly rebukes Dr. Fileno for his failure to consistently apply his reverse telescope to his own life (I.824). In "Colloquii," the narrative goes a step further, implicitly contrasting the unnamed male character's perspective of distance against the very different perspective of a second, much more concrete character, the ghostly apparition of Pirandello's own, recently deceased mother. As we have already seen, his mother situates the suffering and struggle of World War I in the context of an intergenerational engagement in the many battles to forge an independent Italian identity. But unlike the cosmic view that relativizes the present struggle by positioning it as a blip in an overwhelmingly large historical panorama, here the connection to the past grounds the Great War as part of a continuous effort to which the author's community and family have been committed. Far from stripping the present struggle of its force, this perspective gives it even more significance precisely by reaffirming the conjunction of its social and deeply personal dimensions.[14]

That connection to the personal sphere is indicative of the other side of Pirandellian humor, its immersive impulse. In "Colloquii" this impulse emerges in the mother figure's insistence that one must use the senses to immerse oneself in the life of others.[15] Her final words, carried on the wind through Pirandello's garden, offer a clear alternative to the distanced, philosophical approach: "Guarda le cose anche con gli occhi di quelli che non le vedono più! Ne avrai un rammarico, figlio, che te le renderà più sacre e più belle" (III.1153) ["Look at things also with the eyes of those who no longer see them! From this a sorrow will come, son, that will render them more sacred and more beautiful" (104)]. This immersive alternative to the distanced escape of the male character results in an ethos of compassion that, interestingly, is still a form of escape from the overwhelming suffering of the present. But instead of escaping by rendering the present meaningless (by rendering it laughable in its vanity), the immersive view

---

[14] Dashwood even asserts that Berecche is not a philosophical thinker at all, saying his effort to create a stable identity revolves around managing his social spaces and personal relationships (13-14). While I would not go this far, it is at least clear that characterizations like Guarna's, which treat the philosophical stance of distanced vision as the central facet of Pirandello's poetics/aesthetics (13, 19), surely exclude something essential, and more essentially human.

[15] The immersion of oneself into the perspective of another is especially fundamental to the poetics of Pirandello's mature theatrical work (Caponi-Doherty 76; Ferrucci 8). But a similar focus also emerges earlier, in the short stories and in his novels (Subialka 87). Caesar has argued that his interest in the actress's immersive multiplicity also corresponds to a problematic gender dynamic in Pirandello's outlook (245-47), though Bini suggests that this relationship is more complicated and, indeed, points to how the feminine, and specifically Marta Abba, Pirandello's lead actress and "muse," becomes a key locus of resistance to the masculine logic that Pirandello's views problematize (86).

offers a form of redemption for the suffering of the present in an appeal to the shared care that the narrator feels for those he loves. It is their way of seeing the world, colored by their own, personal, histories of struggle, that render the world more beautiful and also more sacred.[16]

This combination of the personal and the sacred in an immersive alternative to philosophical distance is likewise the closing note in "Berecche e la guerra." While Berecche's riding accident reveals his sudden patriotism to be laughable, it also opens him to a new experience of shared suffering. Instead of fighting in the war alongside his son, Faustino, he is plunged into the darkness of temporary blindness; but in this way he comes to a new understanding of his youngest daughter's experience of life. Moreover, his shared experience of her darkness becomes a metaphor that allows Berecche to overcome his philosophical distance, not by discarding the insights of his historical relativism but precisely by uniting those insights with a more immersed, compassionate view:

Forse non sa neppure Margheritina che lì dirimpetto c'è un villino con una Madonnina a uno spigolo e un lampadino rosso acceso. Che è il mondo per lei? ecco, ora egli può intenderlo bene. Bujo. Questo bujo. Tutto può cambiare, fuori, diventare un altro, il mondo; un popolo sparire; ordinarsi altrimenti un intero continente; passare, anche vicina, una guerra, abbattere, distruggere... Che importa? Bujo. Questo bujo. Per Margheritina, sempre questo bujo. E se domani, là in Francia, Faustino sarà ucciso? Oh, allora anche per lui, senza piú quella benda, con gli occhi di nuovo aperti alla vista del mondo, sarà tutto bujo, sempre, così, anche per lui; ma forse peggio, perché condannato a vederla ancora la vita, questa atrocissima vita degli uomini.
Torna a stringersi forte al petto la sua cechina sempre chiusa nel suo silenzio nero; mormora:
– E di questo, figliuola mia, di tutto questo, siano rese grazie alla Germania!

(III.621-22)

Perhaps Margheritina doesn't even know that opposite there's a little house with a little Madonna at one corner and a little red lamp burning. What does the world mean to her? Well, now he can well understand. Darkness. This darkness. Everything outside can change; the world can become something other; a people disappear; a whole continent be redrawn; a war pass close by, to overthrow and destroy... What does it matter? Darkness. This darkness. For Margheritina, always this darkness. And if Faustino is killed, tomorrow, there in France? Oh, then, for him as well, even without that bandage, with his eyes open

---

[16] The idea that an immersion in life can render the world more sacred or charge it with some special value and meaning recurs in key places across Pirandello's corpus. The most obvious example may be the final scene of Pirandello's last novel, *Uno, nessuno e centomila* [*One, No One, and A Hundred Thousand*] (1926), which sees the protagonist give up his claim to stable identity in favor of a vitalistic, mystical embrace of the external world (*Tutti i romanzi* II, 902). Van den Bossche argues that this novel, together with an example such as *Si gira...* as well as other modernist texts such as Svevo's *La coscienza di Zeno*, exhibits the way in which vitalist philosophies inform the modernist impulse, which he relates to the emphasis modernism places on the unreliable narrator (248).

again to see the world, everything will be darkness, always, like this, for him as well; but perhaps worse because he will still be condemned to see life, this atrocious life of men.
He again hugs his little blind daughter, forever enclosed in her dark silence, to his chest; he murmurs:
"And for this, my little girl, for all this let thanks be given to Germany!"

(65-66)

Elements of Berecche's distanced perspective are present here: he sees the war as something foreign, invisible; its outcome can change, whole peoples could be destroyed, but in the darkness it makes no difference. However, in contrast to his earlier perspective, where that distance was a result of projecting himself outward into the stars to look down at the world, here it is achieved through a touching moment of unprecedented closeness with his child. What he understands well is that the same world seen through other eyes can be radically different; the things that seem so important, the things that obsess his reasoning and define his identity, can also be invisible, matters of indifference.

While that does not change the atrocity of war, it does change Berecche's priorities. He knows that what really matters for him is his son, Faustino; the world is not destined to remain dark, unless his son never comes home. Likewise, he can now say out loud to his daughter that Germany, far from the "ideal fatherland," is in fact to blame. What we witness in this scene is thus Berecche shifting from his identification with German culture — but not to a notion of Italian identity instead. What replaces his affective tie to Germany are the human relationships most important to his life. The ability to see through his daughter's eyes completes the disintegration of his former sense of identity by transferring his care from an abstract ideal to the people with whom he shares his life, and in whose suffering he also shares.[17]

5. Conclusion: Vulgarity and Spiritual Renewal

It is in light of this ethics of compassion that we should understand Pirandello's perspective on the war. The philosophical view of war's vanity does not nullify the motives that push nations to war. Though from a distance those motives might look different — reduced in significance, or cast in a more suspicious light by different historical circumstances and perspective — from within the lived experience of an individual or a nation, those motives still matter. In Berecche's case (as in Pirandello's), they matter for deeply personal reasons; they are motives rooted in care for loved ones and dedication to the historical task handed down by one's ancestors.

---

[17] In this sense I am in firm agreement with Mariani's assessment that "Pirandello's whole concept of *umorismo* affirms, in fact, that his art springs from a matrix that is deeply ethical, not merely preoccupied with questions of form" (12). De Castris also analyzes *Si gira...* with an eye to the tension between compassion and "dramatic" objectivity (135).

So what, then, should we make of the ironic final line that Berecche utters about the Germans? It is clear that he has flipped about-face and come to blame them for the war. But what is particularly relevant for us is the reasoning behind that blame. As Berecche expresses it earlier while he watches Faustino sleep in his bed, after he comes home late from a demonstration where he had been detained, all of the carnage and destruction being wrought is purposeless. Here he does not mean it in terms of the distanced, cosmic perspective, but rather in a very material sense: "No: questa non è una grande guerra; sarà un macello grande; una grande guerra non è perché nessuna grande idealità la muove e la sostiene. Questa è guerra di mercato [...]" (III.598) ["No: this is not a great war; it'll be a great slaughter; but it isn't a great war because it isn't based on and sustained by any great ideals. This is a war about economic interests [...]" (48)]. The war is, on top of its inherent destructiveness, vulgar. Unlike the "noble" sentiments of his son, rooted in the Risorgimento ideals of a free Italy, Germany's attack is purely pragmatic, moved by materialism. We may be led to think, once again, of Emilio Gentile's definition of modernist nationalism as a movement seeking to reverse the nihilistic tendencies of modernity's culture of materialism. The spiritual cause of Italian freedom is raised in contradistinction to that impulse.

But unlike the more fervent Italian nationalists, Pirandello does not hesitate to turn that same accusation against Italy, as well. Thus in his final play, *I giganti della montagna* [*The Mountain Giants*] (1937), Pirandello scripts what is often read as a caricature of the Fascist party's cultural failures, their blindness and deafness to the communication of higher truth in artistic form.[18] Likewise, in other works his view is decidedly opposed to the tendencies of modern mechanization, in the film industry but also more broadly, which are seen to strip life of its vitality and reduce action to a commodity, a function of base materialism.[19] Fusing the spiritual impulse of modernist nationalism with the modernist traditionalist's sense of crisis as a loss of and yearning for past forms of order, Pirandello also draws from a deep sense of compassion that colors those modernist impulses in unusual ways.

As such we can say that Pirandello aligns with neither the Futurists nor Svevo. While his work is colored by aspects of modernist nationalism, he never

---

[18] In an appendix that Marta Abba wrote to accompany the unfinished play in Pirandello's *Maschere nude* [*Naked Masks*], she describes his vision for the finale as a demonstration that the gold and power of the Giants is meaningless when confronted with the power of the actors' fantasy, their world of art (II.1371-2). Some critics such as Sciacca have seen the play's denunciation of political power as accidental — one manifestation of Pirandello's overarching unmasking of the vanity of human life (15-16). But as I have argued here, such views overstate the degree to which Pirandello's worldview corresponds to the most negative moments of his humorous double vision.

[19] As Dombroski has articulated it, Pirandello's negative view of modernity is rooted in a typically modernist outlook on the "impoverishment of human existence" wrought by cultural materialism (1992, 23).

embraces the more radical Futurist notions that coincide with their optimism — their vision of war as a cleanser, a bloodbath to purify the nation. But the association of Pirandello's outlook with Svevo does not take into account the important differences in how their pessimism is expressed. This difference is encapsulated in the ending to Svevo's most famous novel, written in the wake of the Great War, *La coscienza di Zeno* [*Zeno's Conscience*] (1923). There, the narrator concludes his self-analysis by withdrawing to the cosmic level in a way that is reminiscent of Pirandello's philosophy of distance. But what he envisions is a future where the world's contagion, humanity, is wiped clean by humanity's own destructive impulses:

Forse traverso una catastrofe inaudita prodotta dagli ordigni ritorneremo alla salute. Quando i gas velenosi non basteranno più, un uomo fatto come tutti gli altri, nel segreto di una stanza di questo mondo, inventerà un esplosivo incomparabile, in confronto al quale gli esplosivi attualmente esistenti saranno considerati quali innocui giocattoli. Ed un altro uomo fatto anche lui come tutti gli altri, ma degli altri un po' più ammalato, ruberà tale esplosivo e s'arrampicherà al centro della terra per porlo nel punto ove il suo effetto potrà essere il massimo. Ci sarà un'esplosione enorme che nessuno udrà e la terra ritornata alla forma di nebulosa errerà nei cieli priva di parassiti e di malattie.

(442)

(Perhaps, through an unheard-of catastrophe produced by devices, we will return to health. When poison gases no longer suffice, an ordinary man, in the secrecy of a room in this world, will invent an incomparable explosive, compared to which the explosives currently in existence will be considered harmless toys. And another man, also ordinary, but a bit sicker than others, will steal this explosive and will climb up at the center of the earth, to set it on the spot where it can have the maximum effect. There will be an enormous explosion that no one will hear, and the earth, once again a nebula, will wander through the heavens, freed of parasites and sickness.)

(436-37)

Svevo's pessimistically comical explosion highlights a vision of human evolution as self-annihilating, speaking to the nihilistic pessimism often attributed to the modernist writer, and the related yearning for a return to order, even if that return here is figured as an apocalyptic end to humanity itself. In contrast, as we have seen, Pirandello's distanced vision of the world encompasses elements of war's destruction and human life's insignificance — a distanced vision, however, that is also brought back to earth, so to speak, by his commitment to an interpersonal ethical stance rooted in compassion. Pirandello's nationalism is different from the Futurists'. His traditionalism is different from Svevo's. In his combination of the two elements, Pirandello charts a modernist course that moves between the extreme points of an artificial optimism and a nihilistic pessimism.[20]

---

[20] The characterization of Futurist optimism as "artificial" comes from Marinetti's own writings and has been analyzed in detail by Poggi, who focuses on how it is manufactured to coincide with Futurist political commitments (267-68) but also argues that this optimism "never fully repressed its negative counterpart" (xi). Marinetti's opposition to pessimism

It would be interesting to examine the implications of Pirandello's view of the war for the way in which we understand the relationship between Pirandello's modernism and the high aestheticism of a decadent like D'Annunzio.[21] There is little doubt that key aspects of Pirandello's stance reflect those of his oft-antagonist. Likewise, it would be fruitful to examine how the unique aspects of Pirandello's modernism place him in relation to German thinkers at the time, such as Max Scheler and Martin Heidegger. For the former, war emerged as a necessary experience in the constitution of a people from a phenomenological perspective; for the latter, as is well known, the ethics of care becomes a dominant aspect of his existentialist system.[22] The intersection of these modes of thought bears striking resemblance to aspects of Pirandello's conception of war and his response to it on an experimental level.

Though pursuing those connections falls outside the scope of my discussion here, it nevertheless seems fitting to conclude with a gesture outward — to link Pirandello's ideas to those developing and circulating in the German cultural sphere. For, as I hope to have made clear, his Italian nationalism is rooted in a longstanding tradition of openness to European thought in general and to German idealism and existentialism in particular. But more than that, it seems telling that in the wake of World War I, when Pirandello more fully embraced his career-defining focus on the stage, it was frequently Germany that provided both inspiration and an understanding reception. If Berecche's cultural identification with German method could not withstand the crisis of war, that is not to say that

---

in all its forms is repeated throughout his writings. In an essay on "L'uomo moltiplicato e il Regno della macchina" ["Extended Man and the Kingdom of the Machine"] (published as part of *Guerra sola igiene del mondo* in 1915), for example, he asserts: "Il nostro franco ottimismo si oppone così, nettamente, al pessimismo di Schopenhauer, di quel filosofo amaro che tante volte ci porse il seducente revolver della filosofia per uccidere in noi la profonda nausea dell'Amore coll'A maiuscolo" (301) ["This frank optimism of ours is thus diametrically opposed to the pessimism of Schopenhauer, that bitter philosopher who so often proffered the tantalizing revolver of philosophy to kill off, in ourselves, the deep-seated sickness of Love with a capital L" (88)].

[21] As Lewis has shown, D'Annunzio's position is deeply tied to a mode of modernism interested in actualizing a project of cultural renewal (2000, 210-11); likewise, Mirabile argues that D'Annunzio's work bridges our concepts of decadentism and modernism (19). The link Gieri describes between Pirandello and Baudelaire similarly could be used to explore how the aestheticism of decadence and the aestheticism of modernism relate.

[22] Scheler and Heidegger were both prominent German philosophers, though the former's fame has not weathered the test of time quite as well as the latter's. Both responded against the tradition of Kantian idealism, though in different modes. The contemporary philosopher Hans Blumenberg links them in his analysis of the concept of care (and Heidegger's use of the myth of Care crossing a river to build humans out of clay), focusing on their visions of war and the struggle against metaphysical despair (145-57). There is rich ground here for comparison with Pirandello.

Germany could not emerge as a preferable locus of cultural refinement again.[23] We could thus think of Pirandello's humor in conjunction with a characterization that the Austrian philosopher, Edmund Husserl, made in a letter to his student, Arnold Metzger, in the wake of the Great War:

> [...] my writings, just as yours, are born out of need, out of an immense psychological need, out of a complete collapse in which the only hope is an entirely new life, a desperate, unyielding resolution to begin from the beginning and to go forth in radical honesty, come what may.
>
> (360)

We might likewise think that Pirandello's willingness to tolerate ambivalence, his eagerness for multiple perspectives, and his compassionate humor reveal both a flexibility and a practical interest in reconstituting the shattered subject in a new light. His unmasking may reveal emptiness, but it also provides the grounds for a kind of honesty that allows him, and us, to carry forward. In this sense, his modernist deconstruction of the subject and its world is not, finally, a negative project.

St Hugh's College, University of Oxford

---

[23] Here, of course, it is important to keep in mind that Pirandello did not live to see WWII. Pirandello's ongoing attachment to Germany, and rich German reception, has been discussed by multiple scholars (see Büdel and De Michele). Pirandello's "exile" to Germany in response to disappointment with Mussolini is considered by daVinci Nichols and O'Keefe Bazzoni (61).

Works Cited

Barilli, Renato. *La linea Svevo-Pirandello.* Milano: Mursia, 1972.
Bini, Daniela. *Pirandello and His Muse: The Plays for Marta Abba.* Gainesville, FL: UP of Florida, 1998.
Blumenberg, Hans. *Care Crosses the River.* Trans. Paul Fleming. Stanford: Stanford UP, 2010.
Büdel, Oskar. "Pirandellos Wirkung in Deutschland." *Der Dramatiker Pirandello.* Ed. F. N. Mennemeier. Cologne: Kiepenheuer & Witsch, 1965. 209-39.
Caesar, Ann Hallamore. *Characters and Actors in Luigi Pirandello.* Oxford: Oxford UP, 1998.
Caponi-Doherty, Gabriella. "'Sono una donna non sono una statua': Character Identity and Actor Resistance in *Diana e la Tuda.*" *Pirandello Studies* 33 (2013): 68-78.
Costanzo, Samantha. "Pirandello, Theosophy and the Tantalus Syndrom." *PSA: The Journal of the Pirandello Society of America* 23 (2010): 43-69.
Croce, Benedetto. *Poeti e scrittori del pieno e del tardo Rinascimento.* 2 vols. Roma: Laterza, 1945-52.
Dashwood, Julie. "Introduction." Pirandello. *Berecche and the War* 1-23.
d'Amelia, Amelia. "Between Two Eras: Challenges Facing Women in the Risorgimento." *The Risorgimento Revisited: Nationalism and Culture in Nineteenth-Century Italy.* Ed. Silvana Patriarca and Lucy Riall. London: Palgrave Macmillan, 2012. 115-33.
daVinci Nichols, Nina, and Jana O'Keefe Bazzoni. *Pirandello and Film.* Lincoln: U of Nebraska P, 1995.
De Castris, Arcangelo Leone. *La storia di Pirandello.* Roma: Laterza, 1971.
De Michele, Fausto. "*Sei personaggi in cerca d'autore* nel polisistema letterario di lingua tedesca. Un esempio di *primary translation?*" *Pirandello e la traduzione culturale.* Ed. Michael Rössner and Alessandra Sorrentino. Roma: Carocci Editore, 2012. 37-45.
Dienstag, Joshua Foa. *Pessimism: Philosophy, Ethic, Spirit.* Princeton: Princeton UP, 2009.
Dombroski, Robert. "The Foundations of Italian Modernism: Pirandello, Svevo, Gadda." *The Cambridge Companion to the Italian Novel.* Ed. Peter Bondanella and Andrea Ciccarelli. Cambridge: Cambridge UP, 2003. 89-103.
_____. "Pirandello's Modernity: Epistemology and the Existential of Theatre." *Pirandello and the Modern Theatre.* Ed. Antonio Alessio, Domenico Pietropaolo, and Giuliana Sanguinetti-Katz. Canadian Society for Italian Studies, 1992. 23-34.
Ferrucci, Carlo. *La musa ritrosa: Pirandello e Marta Abba.* Bologna: CLUEB, 2010.
Gardair, Jean-Michel. *Jean-Michel Gardair legge* Il fu Mattia Pascal *di Luigi Pirandello.* Fossombrone: Metauro Edizioni, 2001.
Gentile, Emilio. "The Conquest of Modernity: From Modernist Nationalism to Fascism." Trans. Lawrence Rainey. *Modernism/Modernity* 1.3 (1994): 55-87.
Gieri, Manuela. "Luigi Pirandello between Modernity and Modernism." *Italian Modernism: Italian Culture between Decadentism and Avant-Garde.* Ed. Luca Somigli and Mario Moroni. Toronto: U of Toronto P, 2004. 294-306.
Gilmour, David. *The Pursuit of Italy: A History of a Land, Its Regions, and Their Peoples.* New York: Farrar, Straus and Giroux, 2011.
Guarna, Mario. *La filosofia del lontano: la natura filosofica dell'umorismo in Pirandello.* Acrireale: Bonanno, 2010.
Harrison, Thomas. *1910: The Emancipation of Dissonance.* Berkeley, CA: U of California P, 1996.

Husserl, Edmund. *Husserl: Shorter Works*. Ed. Peter McCormick and Frederick A. Elliston. Notre Dame: U of Notre Dame P, 1981.
Illiano, Antonio. "Pirandello's Literary Uses of Theosophical Notions." *A Companion to Pirandello Studies*. Ed. John Louis DiGaetani. New York: Greenwood Press, 1991.
Kermode, Frank. *The Sense of an Ending: Studies in the Theory of Fiction with a New Epilogue*. Oxford: Oxford UP, 2000.
Lewis, Pericles. *The Cambridge Introduction to Modernism*. Cambridge: Cambridge UP, 2007.
_____. *Modernism, Nationalism and the Novel*. Cambridge: Cambridge UP, 2000.
Livio, Gigi. *Il teatro in rivolta: Futurismo, grottesco, Pirandello e pirandellismo*. Milano: Mursia, 1976.
Luperini, Romano. *Luigi Pirandello e Il fu Mattia Pascal*. Torino: Loescher, 1990.
Mariani, Umberto. *Living Masks: The Achievement of Pirandello*. Toronto: U of Toronto P, 2008.
Marinetti, Filippo Tommaso. *Critical Writings*. Ed. Günter Berghaus. Trans. Doug Thompson. New York: Farrar, Straus and Giroux, 2006.
_____. *Teoria e invenzione futurista*. Ed. Luciano De Maria. Milano: Mondadori, 1968.
Mirabile, Andrea. *Multimedia Archaeologies: Gabriele D'Annunzio, Belle Époque Paris, and the Total Artwork*. Amsterdam: Rodopi, 2014.
Pirandello, Luigi. *Berecche and the War*. Trans. Julie Dashwood. Market Harborough: Troubador, 2000.
_____. "A Conversation with My Mother." Trans. Miriam Aloisio and Michael Subialka. *PSA: The Journal of the Pirandello Society of America* 26 (2013): 97-107.
_____. *Maschere nude*. 2 vols. Milano: Mondadori, 1958.
_____. *Novelle per un anno*. Ed. Mario Costanzo. 3 vols. Milano: Mondadori, 1985-1990.
_____. *On Humor*. Trans. Antonio Illiano and Daniel P. Testa. Chapel Hill: U of North Carolina P, 1974.
_____. *Tutti i romanzi*. Ed. Giovanni Macchia and Mario Costanzo. 2 vols. Milano: Mondadori, 1973.
_____. "L'umorismo." *Saggi, poesie, scritti varii*. Ed. Manlio Lo Vecchio-Musti. Milano: Mondadori, 1960. 15-160.
Poggi, Christine. *Inventing Futurism: The Art and Politics of Artificial Optimism*. Princeton, NJ: Princeton UP, 2008.
Poggioli, Renato. *The Theory of the Avant-Garde*. Trans. Gerald Fitzgerald. Cambridge, MA: Harvard UP, 1968.
Ragusa, Olga. *Luigi Pirandello: An Approach to his Theatre*. Edinburgh: Edinburgh UP, 1980.
Rubini, Rocco. "(Re-) Experiencing the Renaissance. Introduction." *The Renaissance from an Italian Perspective: An Anthology of Essays. 1860-1968*. Ed. Rocco Rubini. Ravenna: Longo, 2014. 7-20.
Sciacca, Michele F. *Pirandello: "I giganti della montagna."* Stresa: Centro Studi Rosminiani, 1974.
Somigli, Luca. "Italy." *The Cambridge Companion to European Modernism*. Ed. Pericles Lewis. Cambridge: Cambridge UP, 2011. 75-93.
_____, and Mario Moroni. "Modernism in Italy: An Introduction." *Italian Modernism: Italian Culture between Decadentism and Avant-Garde*. Ed. Luca Somigli and Mario Moroni. Toronto: U of Toronto P, 2012. 3-31.
Spaventa, Bertrando. *La filosofia italiana nelle sue relazioni con la filosofia europea*. Ed. Alessandro Savorelli. Roma: Edizioni di Storia e Letteratura, 2003.

———. "Italian Philosophy in Relation to European Philosophy." Trans. Michael Subialka. *The Renaissance from an Italian Perspective: An Anthology of Essays. 1860-1968*. Ed. Rocco Rubini. Ravenna: Longo, 2014. 45-110.
Subialka, Michael. "Pirandello's Mother: Feminine Perception and Double Vision." *PSA: The Journal of the Pirandello Society of America* 26 (2013): 71-95.
Svevo, Italo. *La coscienza di Zeno e 'continuazioni'*. Ed. Mario Lavagetto. Torino: Einaudi, 1987.
———. *Zeno's Conscience*. Trans. William Weaver. New York: Penguin, 2001.
Syrimis, Michael. *The Great Black Spider on its Knock-Kneed Tripod: Reflections of Cinema in Early Twentieth Century Italy*. Toronto: U of Toronto P, 2012.
Thomas, Johannes. "*Il fu Mattia Pascal*. Per un'analisi metacritica." *Pirandello e la traduzione culturale*. Ed. Michael Rössner and Alessandra Sorrentino. Roma: Carocci Editore, 2012. 65-78.
Valdemarca, Gioia. "La macchina mostruosa. Zeno come cyborg." *Italo Svevo and His Legacy for the Third Millennium*. Ed. Giuseppe Stellardi and Emanuela Tandello Cooper. Troubador: 2014. 213-25.
Van den Bossche, Bart. "Unreliability in Italian Modernist Fiction: The Cases of Italo Svevo and Luigi Pirandello." *Narrative Unreliability in the Twentieth-Century First-Person Novel*. Ed. Elke D'hoker and Gunther Martens. Berlin: Walter De Gruyter, 2008. 247-58.
Verdone, Mario. "Pirandello e il futurismo." *Pirandello e le avanguardie*. Ed. Enzo Lauretta. Agrigento: Centro Nazionale Studi Pirandelliani, 1999. 45-54.

Allison Cooper

Giuseppe Ungaretti's Disanimate Modernism

For a generation of twentieth-century thinkers, the "front" came to connote more than the ravaged physical landscape of such World War I battlefields as the Somme, Ypres, Verdun, and Caporetto. For many, the front also came to represent figuratively the psychologically and spiritually desolate place in which one confronted the most pressing crises of modernity: those culture-shaping issues that had their origins in, among other things, the period's accelerated industrialization, the discovery of the unconscious, and the death of God. Over the last quarter century, Anglophone and Francophone cultural historians like Paul Fussell, Modris Eksteins, Jay Winter, Stephane Audoin-Rouzeau, and Annette Becker have argued that the First World War and, especially, conflicts along its Western Front, tested the notions of progress and ontological authenticity that had characterized Western European society at the end of the nineteenth century, finding evidence in the poetry of Wilfred Owen, Siegfried Sassoon, and Robert Graves, and in the literature of Henri Barbusse, Erich Maria Remarque, and Virginia Woolf, among others.[1] Yet few of these scholars, or the writers whose works they cite, have concerned themselves with the devastating conflicts along the Italian front, where the country bordered the Austro-Hungarian Empire. This situation has changed in the past decade with important contributions to the field by Mark Thompson, whose English-language *The White War* describes the World War One experience from an Italian perspective, and Emilio Gentile, whose *L'Apocalisse della modernità* extends the work of such historians as Mario Isnenghi and Giorgio Rochat through a cultural analysis of the conflict. And yet there is still more to be said about the crisis of representation that troubled wartime authors and artists in Italy as they sought to depict subjectivities gravely affected by the conflict and by literary and artistic movements like Futurism that preceded and, arguably, precipitated it.

Walter Benjamin suggested in "The Storyteller" that the Great War led to an impoverishment of communicable experience — a particularly apt insight in relation to the wartime works of Italian soldier poets and painters like Giuseppe Ungaretti and Carlo Carrà. "Was it not noticeable at the end of the war,"

---

[1] See Fussell's *The Great War and Modern Memory*; Eksteins's *Rites of Spring: The Great War and the Birth of the Modern Age*; Winter's *Sites of Memory, Sites of Mourning*; and Stephane Audoin-Rouzeau and Annette Becker's *14-18, retrouver la Guerre*.

Benjamin wondered, "that men returned from the battlefield grown silent — not richer but poorer in communicable experience?" (84). He noted that "A generation that had gone to school in a horse-drawn streetcar now stood under the open sky in a countryside in which nothing remained unchanged but the clouds, and beneath these clouds, in a field of force of destructive torrents and explosions, was the tiny, fragile human body" (84). The manufactured horrors of war, Benjamin intimated, pushed death beyond the reassuring boundaries of nature and into the realm of the unspeakable. The Great War, he implied, denaturalized the relationship between human beings and the material world (a relationship that also forms the basis of language) and effectively rendered them speechless.

The silence Benjamin alluded to figuratively was, in the case of many combatants, literal. Some 20,000 Italian soldiers suffered from psychiatric maladies brought about by the conflict and prevalent among these was aphasia, the inability to produce speech in the aftermath of trauma (Gibelli 451). Reduced to little more than matériel by the war, soldiers diagnosed with aphasia were subsumed by a Taylorist system that processed them as quickly as possible in order to return them to the field, where they were utilized once again as human material in the ongoing conflict (Gibelli 452). This was equally true of soldiers suffering from other types of psychiatric problems. It was at the Ospedale Neurologico Militare in Ferrara that Carrà and Giorgio de Chirico, both soldiers suffering from depression and poor physical health, engaged in their short-lived collaboration on *pittura metafisica* (Baldacci 358-72). The war's reduction of human subjects to material is reflected in works like Carrà's *Solitudine* and de Chirico's *Il grande metafisico*, which depict solitary human figures in their most elemental forms. Participants in society's first real example of total war, Italian soldiers were regarded as little more than equipment, a fact memorably illustrated in Ernest Hemingway's *A Farewell to Arms*, one of the only English-language novels to depict the fighting along the Italian front.[2]

As Ungaretti, de Chirico, Carrà, and other Italian writers and artists confronted firsthand a war that subordinated violently some one and a half million of their contemporaries to machines and emerging technologies, they simultaneously had to come to terms with the aesthetic legacy bequeathed to them by the "first" Futurism, with its destabilizing notions of dynamism, flux, and interpenetration that were intended to break down previously distinct

---

[2] In a terse exchange about the Italians' expected retreat after their ruinous defeat at Caporetto, Henry, the novel's American protagonist who has joined the Italian military effort as a volunteer, asks a superior officer: "Tell me, I have never seen a retreat — if there is a retreat how are all the wounded evacuated?" The officer's reply makes clear the subordination of the soldiers in the field to the matériel of battle: "They are not," he says. "They take only as many as they can and leave the rest." Henry then wonders, "What will I take in the cars?" "Hospital equipment," the officer answers (*A Farewell to Arms* 187).

metaphysical categories of subject and object. As the futurists sought to "obliterate traditional distinctions between the organic and the inorganic, between sentient beings and the physical and mechanical world" (Poggi 20), their feverish embrace of the products of industrialization and apparent abnegation of the self in the name of progress raised broad questions about the reification of the individual.[3] These questions took on new meaning in the face of World War One's *Materialschlacht* — a strategy that converted the individual into an object to be used like any other (canons, ammunition) for the sake of war, and that effectively overturned Kantian notions of man as an end in himself.[4]

An important aesthetic device employed by the aforementioned figures is the representation of otherwise animate objects as devoid of life or spirit, or what we might call, after Ungaretti, "disanimation" — an Anglicization (and nominalization) of the Italian "disanimato" that appears in his wartime poem "Sono una creatura." Meaning "sfiduciato," "esanime" or "privo di vita, di anima" (*Dizionario italiano ragionato* 541), "disanimato" first appears in Italian literature with early translations of Virgil's *Aeneid* into the vernacular, where it was employed to render the Latin "exanimis" (*Aen.* 10.840). In Virgil's epic, the occasional use of "exanimis" in place of the more common (and, one might argue, clinical) "mortuus" sustains an important undercurrent of individual, human pathos throughout the poem's description of the struggle to launch a new Roman empire.[5] Dante also employs "disanimato" in the *Divina Commedia*, where it evokes the liminal state of the pilgrim as he makes his way through purgatory (*Purg.* 15.135). During the Great War, disanimation quietly conveys in a range of texts and artworks the human pathos that arises from a modern state of alienation that had its origins in the era's increasing awareness of a lack of a unitary subject, or of unified experience. Poems such as those collected in Ungaretti's *Il porto sepolto* (1916), for example, generate their own internal necessity and coherence (disturbing or ambiguous as it may be) in the absence of any external order. "Sono una creatura" reclaims the adjective "disanimato" for Ungaretti's own poetics in order to underscore an irreversible awareness of the disparity between consciousness and the objects of consciousness, or between self and world.

---

[3] For more on Futurism's treatment of the relationship between humans and machines see Blum, Poggi, Salaris and Schnapp.

[4] For more on technology's role in undoing Kant's concept of rational human beings as an end in themselves, see Adorno's *Negative Dialectics* (361).

[5] See, for example, Marcello Adriani's translation, in his *Volgarizzamento dell'Eneide di Vergilio*, of "At Lausum socii exanimem super arma ferebant / flentes, ingentem, atque ingenti vulnere victum" (10.841-42) with, "Li compagni ne portavano il disanimato Lauso, sopra l'armi, piagnendo," as cited under the entry for "disanimato" in the early seventeenth-century *Vocabolario degli Accademici della Crusca*.

In this article I explore the way in which several of Ungaretti's wartime works utilize a negative poetics characterized by spectral beings and corpses to reinstate a violent process of subtraction in which life is removed, leaving behind only the shadow of the self, or an inanimate object. This disanimation mirrors the way that meaning is unhinged from language in Ungaretti's poetry, leaving only a meaningless symbol behind. In this way, his poems call attention to the ontological and linguistic crises of the early twentieth century through a dialectics of deficit. Paradoxically, I argue, disanimation also enables Ungaretti's poetry to transcend its elegiac function through an aesthetic mitigation of the violent historical moment that it describes — demonstrating, as Rebecca Comay has observed, how "worded grief can preempt the very loss that occasioned it" (3).

Born and raised in Egypt, though of Italian parentage, Ungaretti was an active participant in the vibrant, cosmopolitan culture of early twentieth-century Paris. Arriving in France in 1912, the twenty-four-year-old poet attended lectures at the Collège de France and, in 1914, graduated from the Sorbonne with a thesis on the French romantic writer Maurice de Guérin. In France, he was befriended by many of the principal authors and artists of the Parisian avant-garde, including such figures as Guillaume Apollinaire (whom he considered one of his closest friends in Paris), Pablo Picasso, Giorgio de Chirico and Blaise Cendrars. Ungaretti also developed friendships with many representatives of the Florentine and Futurist avant-garde movements, who traveled frequently to Paris to promote their own cultural initiatives. It was his acquaintance with members of these movements that led to the first publication of his poems in Italy, in the Florentine journal *Lacerba*.

Inspired by the Futurist avant-garde's call for the creation of modern artistic practices in Italy and the cultural renewal that was to attend these, *Lacerba*'s founders desired to establish a similarly vigorous, yet distinct, avant-garde movement in Florence.[6] The publication quickly became a forum in which the frequently opposing positions of early twentieth-century intellectuals were articulated and elaborated, with contributions reflecting the radically changing cultural and political climate of Italy between 1913 and 1915, the years of its publication. The values of the journal, as established in its inaugural issue, were brevity, forthrightness, vitality, creativity, and wit, along with the privileging of paradox over consistency or logic, the fragment over the whole, and individualism and rebellion over contemporary institutions and ideologies ("Introibo" 1).

Given the similarities of their values and projects, collaborations between the Florentine avant-gardists and the Futurists, based largely in Milan, were frequent. The journal maintained its distinctiveness from the latter, however,

---

[6] Adamson (166-80) provides a useful overview of the role that *Lacerba* and other literary journals played in the culture of avant-garde Italy.

through its policy of welcoming numerous contributions from outsiders, including Apollinaire and Picasso, as well as other Parisian figures like the poet Max Jacob and the cubist sculptor Alexander Archipenko. Also included were regular contributions from such figures as Aldo Palazzeschi, a gifted and iconoclastic poet involved both with Futurism and the Florentine avant-garde. It was Palazzeschi who, along with *Lacerba*'s co-founders Ardengo Soffici and Giovanni Papini, encouraged Ungaretti to publish his early work in the journal (Adamson 172).

Ungaretti's participation in the experimental literary undertakings of the Florentine avant-garde contrasts with his post-World War I exploration of the relationship between classic and contemporary Italian poetry. This investigation would cause him eventually to look to the work of figures like Petrarch and Leopardi for inspiration as he pursued an aesthetic that would restore, after the rupture called for by the Futurists, a "temporal continuity" between classic Italian poetry and the poetry of the postwar period (Saccone 270). The poet's collaboration on the postwar literary journal *La ronda* (1919-1923) naturally invites us to associate him with the so-called *ritorno all'ordine*, given the journal's programmatic call for a return to classicism and rejection of the avant-garde movements that had reigned in the years before the war. But Ungaretti's project did not involve a simple return to tradition; it offered, rather, a discriminating assessment of the predicament of the Italian avant-garde.[7] He wished to restore duration — conceived of as temporal depth — and memory to the poetic word. The Futurists, who emphasized the contemporaneousness of words (expressed in the practice of *parole in libertà*) and the most provisional aspects of reality, were, Ungaretti would observe, "dimentichi che ogni atto profondamente umano (e quindi la poesia) emana dall'illusione di vincere la morte" (*Vita d'un uomo: saggi e interventi* 173). Without this illusion, Ungaretti observed further, we poets "trascureremmo di trasfondere le nostre ispirazioni in qualche sostanza di durata, e saremmo dannati a produrre opere vuote di qualsiasi mistero" (*Vita d'un uomo: saggi e interventi* 173).

Disanimation is one of the principal means by which Ungaretti's wartime poetry countered the contingent, provisory nature of Futurist and avant-garde aesthetics, as well as the contingent nature of life in the trenches. It reinstates death, absence and loss as eternal conditions — the backdrop, so to speak, against which life and art engage, anticipating the image of war made vivid by Benjamin in "The Storyteller." Among his early poems, "Chiaroscuro" (published in *Lacerba* in 1915) represents the writer's first attempt to use the spectral to explore lyrically the uncertain state of the modern, alienated subject. Written in Milan, where Ungaretti moved in the summer of 1914 following the outbreak of war, the poem alludes to the suicide, a year earlier, of his Arab

---

[7] See Saccone and Baroncini for more on Ungaretti's relationship to prewar avant-garde movements and the return to order.

friend Moammed Sceab. A childhood companion of Ungaretti's in Egypt, Sceab moved to Paris with the poet in 1912, where the two lived in the same apartment building. The suicide, which Ungaretti attributed to Sceab's increasing sense of geographical and psychological dislocation, was eventually to become the central theme of a second poem of Ungaretti's of 1916 — discussed later in this essay — entitled "In memoria." Considered together and within the broader context of *Allegria di naufragi*, Ungaretti's 1919 collection of wartime poems, "Chiaroscuro" and "In memoria" function as essential interpretive keys to the poet's treatment of the conflict and its seemingly simultaneous dissolution of civilization, culture, and the self.

In "Chiaroscuro," Sceab returns figuratively from the dead and his apparition becomes an occasion for the poet to consider the tenebrous relationship between life and death. Reference to an unnamed apparition is made as the poem's speaker contemplates a cemetery, the tombs of which fade from vision in the falling darkness of evening and reemerge in the dim light of dawn. The poem's Dantesque, indistinct atmosphere, produced through a pattern of imagery revolving around the play of light and dark (chiaroscuro), establishes the cemetery as a locus of in-betweenness, its partial concealment and revelation achieved through subtle gradations of tone, expressed in a preponderance of adjectives and nouns like "nero," "giorno," "tetro," "oscurità," "torbido," and "chiaro":

> CHIAROSCURO
> Anche le tombe sono scomparse
>
> Spazio nero infinito calato
> da questo balcone
> al cimitero
>
> Mi è venuto a ritrovare
> il mio compagno arabo
> che s'è ucciso l'altra sera
>
> Rifà giorno
>
> Tornano le tombe
> appiattate nel verde tetro
> delle ultime oscurità
> nel verde torbido
> del primo chiaro
>
> (*Vita d'un uomo: tutte le poesie* 15)

The function of the apparition in the poem emerges through a comparative reading of the definitive and original versions of "Chiaroscuro." In the definitive version, adopted by Ungaretti in 1919 (and reproduced above), the poet alludes obliquely to his friend Sceab, declining to elaborate on the cause of the latter's suicide or how it has affected him personally. As a consequence, the reader remains suspended in the ambiguity established so effectively by the poem's dark imagery. In contrast, in the original version of "Chiaroscuro" (the one that appeared in *Lacerba*), the lines "Mi è venuto a ritrovare / il mio compagno arabo / che s'è ucciso l'altra sera" are followed by the verses: "È stato sotterrato a Ivry / con gli splendidi suoi sogni / e ne porto l'ombra." Unlike the indirect reference to Sceab in the final version of the poem, the additional verses in the original underscore the enduring effects of Sceab's death upon the poet. Ungaretti's evocation of the specter thus forms an aperture of sorts, with Sceab's persistent presence emerging as an effect of memory, resistant to the eradicating forces of time, culture and history.

Freud's *Totem and Taboo* (1913) is particularly useful in understanding disanimation because the book links the discovery of the unconscious — an event that many historians have identified as a particularly tumultuous moment in early twentieth-century culture — to the figure of the ghost, itself a form of disanimation. Freud accomplishes this by suggesting that the ghost symbolizes the existence of two states within the individual. "One," he wrote, "in which something is directly given to the senses and to consciousness (that is, present to them)," and another "in which the same thing is latent but capable of reappearing" (93). These two states, Freud argues, correspond to perception and memory, or consciousness and unconsciousness. The disconnect that Freud identifies between conscious and unconscious mental states is reproduced in Ungaretti's poetry through the device of disanimation, which fosters the poetic expression of a particular sense of self-estrangement.

The original version of "Chiaroscuro" was written in an anticipatory moment, after Italy had joined the war but before Ungaretti was mobilized. It establishes the overarching theme of *Il porto sepolto*, his first collection of poems (subsequently absorbed into *Allegria di naufragi*), published near the Italian front a few months after the poet was called to arms in 1915. In "Chiaroscuro" the poet had described somberly how he bore within himself, not unlike the tombs featured in the poem, the shadowy remains of that which had been buried ("sepolto"), namely the memory of his friend Sceab. Ungaretti explores this dynamic more fully in *Il porto sepolto*, where he establishes himself as the custodian of a sense of self, and of a culture and civilization, that were increasingly being effaced by the war. The spectral and disanimate figures in the poems evoke a world emptied of life and meaning, whose sense is restored only through the imagination of the poet. This theme is apparent in the collection's opening poem, "In memoria," another elegy to Sceab that also addresses the poet's concerns about the alienating forces of modern life and the role of poetry in negotiating these.

"In memoria" continues the melancholy contemplation of death initiated in "Chiaroscuro," absorbing and refining those rejected verses of the original version of the latter that alluded to Sceab's final resting place and to his death's effects on the poem's speaker. Sceab's spectral presence assumes historical qualities in the poem — a transformation that enables the poet to allude to the specific cultural and psychological causes of his friend's suicide. As suggested above, Ungaretti perceived these to have their origins in Sceab's estrangement from his own culture as well as that of France, his adoptive country. Regarding the deaths of Sceab and others, Ungaretti would eventually observe that "si sentivano lontani dalla loro civiltà, senza potersene interamente staccare e senza potere interamente appartenere ad un'altra" (*Vita d'un uomo: tutte le poesie* XXVI). "In memoria" conveys this estrangement in a mournful and restrained tone not unlike that of "Chiaroscuro," contrasting Sceab's noble, colorful past with his nearly anonymous finish in a Parisian cemetery:

IN MEMORIA
Locvizza il 30 settembre 1916

Si chiamava
Moammed Sceab

Discendente
di emiri di nomadi
suicida
perché non aveva più
Patria

Amò la Francia
e mutò nome

Fu Marcel
ma non era Francese
e non sapeva più
vivere
nella tenda dei suoi
dove si ascolta la cantilena
del Corano
gustando un caffè

E non sapeva
sciogliere
il canto
del suo abbandono

L'ho accompagnato
insieme alla padrona dell'albergo
dove abitavamo
a Parigi
dal numero 5 della rue des Carmes
appassito vicolo in discesa

> Riposa
> nel camposanto d'Ivry
> sobborgo che pare
> sempre
> in una giornata
> di una
> decomposta fiera
>
> E forse io solo
> so ancora
> che visse

(Vita d'un uomo: tutte le poesie 21)

    The confrontation in "Chiaroscuro" between death and memory becomes in "In memoria" a conflict between cultural or psychological alienation — closely linked to death, yet distinct in its implication of a sort of living death — and poetry. We see this shift in the poet's observation that Sceab "non sapeva / sciogliere / il canto / del suo abbandono," which suggests Ungaretti's belief in the power of poetry (*canto* signifying either "song" or "poem") to ease grief and isolation. The verses imply that, by arbitrating anguish, poetry gives voice to that which would otherwise disappear into the void — those murky depths that in "Chiaroscuro" swallow up the cemetery's tombs. The elegiac function of "In memoria" prevents Sceab from disappearing entirely into the graveyard at Ivry. The poem's final verses, "E forse io solo / so ancora / che visse" (a reworking of the verse "e ne porto l'ombra" from the original version of "Chiaroscuro"), likewise assert Sceab's existence, and therefore thwart the very obscurity (nothingness) that they lament.

    Ungaretti's inclusion of "In memoria" in *Il porto sepolto* — for the most part a volume of wartime poetry — might appear to be an anachronistic choice. The elegy to Sceab refers to experiences in the poet's life made remote by his friend's death, the passage of time, and geographical distance, as well as by the bleak conditions Ungaretti faced on the Carso as he composed it and other poems. Yet not only did Ungaretti include the poem in the collection; he selected it to open it. Moreover, through his careful notation of its place and date of composition (Locvizza, 30 September 1916), he underscores its relationship to other poems in the collection such as "Fratelli" (Mariano il 15 luglio 1916) and "San Martino del Carso" (Valloncello dell'Albero Isolato, il 27 agosto 1916) — both clearly identifiable examples of trench poetry whose principal subjects are the war and its effects on the individual. But the subject of "In memoria" — the dissolution of the self and, by extension, of entire civilizations and cultures that survive only in the poet's imagination — prefigures the apocalyptic theme of death and rebirth through poetic invention that runs throughout *Il porto sepolto*.

In Ungaretti's wartime poetry, the motif of the corpse, like that of the specter in "Chiaroscuro" and "In memoria," serves to mourn even as it paradoxically reaffirms life. The brief poem "Veglia" recounts a terrible night passed alongside a comrade's grotesque corpse, and culminates almost defiantly in an affirmation of life conterminous with poetic expression:

>
> VEGLIA
> Cima Quattro il 23 dicembre 1915
>
> Un'intera nottata
> buttato vicino
> a un compagno
> massacrato
> con la sua bocca
> digrignata
> volta al plenilunio
> con la congestione
> delle sue mani
> penetrata
> nel mio silenzio
> ho scritto
> lettere piene d'amore
>
> Non sono mai stato
> tanto
> attaccato alla vita
>
> (*Vita d'un uomo: tutte le poesie* 25)

Here, as in "In memoria," poetry counters the absolute nothingness of death through an act of communication: here the speaker's letters, "piene d'amore." Despite its finality — or perhaps because of it — the poem's corpse provokes an assertion of life. Stefano Velotti has described this paradox in the following terms:

Il cadavere ha questa speciale virtù: posto per un verso oltre il confine della vita, e per altro verso (nella sua visibilità) ancora a cavallo tra la vita e la morte (le due dimensioni più difficili da pensare) ci fa scorgere un "oltre" incomprensibile, che funziona da cartina al tornasole per segnalare l'elemento vitale (invisibile) in cui siamo immersi.
(Unpublished paper)

"Veglia," "Chiaroscuro," and "In memoria" all incorporate spectrality to lament the alienating forces of modern life (and especially war) that reduce humanity to nonbeing, but align poetic expression with an assertion of being.

Ungaretti's ghosts and cadavers open up the poetic text to meanings that language may only express with great difficulty, pushing, to borrow the words of Colin Davis, "at the boundaries of language and thought" (379). The fullest expression of this dynamic occurs in *Il porto sepolto*'s "Sono una creatura," which utilizes disanimation to describe the war's dehumanizing effects and the near inability of language to communicate such effects. Composed in the midst of the battle between Italian and Austro-Hungarian forces for Monte San Michele, a stronghold of the Austrian defense that was seized eventually by the Italians (the day after the composition of "Sono una creatura," in fact), the poem likens the frustrated cry of its speaker to a taciturn stone, suggesting a process of petrification in which the human voice is figuratively "turned to stone." Using the words "totalmente disanimata," the poem describes a condition of lifelessness and immobility, in which both language and being seem emptied of meaning.[8]

The first section of the poem opens with a simile that compares the poet's pain to the craggy peak of Monte San Michele:

> Come questa pietra
> del S. Michele
> così fredda
> così dura
> così prosciugata
> così refrattaria
> così totalmente
> disanimata

(*Vita d'un uomo: tutte le poesie* 41)

The next section repeats the figurative term of the simile and completes it by supplying the literal term:

> Come questa pietra

---

[8] The word "pietra" suggests a wide variety of literary allusions, both historical and contemporary. Italo Calvino's essay "Leggerezza" addressees the notion of "petrification" in literature. Calvino writes, "In certi momenti mi sembrava che il mondo stesse diventando tutto di pietra: una lenta pietrificazione [...] Era come se nessuno potesse sfuggire allo sguardo inesorabile della Medusa" (8). In contrast to the petrification enacted by Medusa's gaze, Calvino cites Eugenio Montale's artful juxtaposition of the weighty and the light in his poem "Piccolo testamento": "[...] è una professione di fede nella persistenza di ciò che sembra più destinato a perire" (11). He might well have applied this observation to Ungaretti's poem, in light of its life-affirming title ("Sono una creatura") and its final lines ("la morte / si sconta / vivendo"). Ungaretti's use of the motif also evokes the Dante of the *rime pietrose*: "Così nel mio parlar voglio esser aspro / com'è ne li atti questa bella petra, / la quale ognora impetra / maggior durezza e più natura cruda [...] " (170-71). Dante also uses a simile of the stone in *Rime* C 12 ("la mente mia [...] è più dura che petra") and in the *Convivio* 2.1.3 ("Coloro che non hanno vita ragionevole alcuna sono quasi come pietre"). Finally, Ungaretti's use of the simile echoes the role of the stone in the songs of the troubadors, who used it to convey the difficulty of expressing emotions. In their poetry "la pietra" always relates to death and unhappiness, and is therefore an early example of negative poetics.

> è il mio pianto
> che non si vede

Presenting its figurative term first, "pietra," the poem then expands on it, increasing poetic suspense as the reader anticipates the literal term, "pianto."[9] Where logic and syntax would suggest that the literal term of the comparison should appear first, Ungaretti's inversion of terms in the poem, together with the delayed introduction of the second term, suggests that a natural relationship between the "real" (the referent) and the "imaginary" (the linguistic sign) has been upset. The poem laments the loss of this relationship, even while simultaneously proposing a new one to take its place.

A strong pattern of tactile imagery — expressed in the adjectives "fredda," "dura," and "prosciugata" — conveys the stony peak's austerity. Through the rhythmically increasing syllabification of these words, and the repetition of the correlative "così," the first section of the poem builds to a crescendo that culminates with the word "disanimata," thereby dramatically making explicit either the peak's or the stone's inanimate qualities that were only implied by the preceding adjectives. The speaker presents the lament, linked to the word "disanimata" by the simile, as removed from the human being in which it logically ought to have its origin. Weeping — the primary meaning of "pianto" — is unique because it mediates between pure emotion and language, but it is here frustrated, going unnoticed: "il mio pianto / che non si vede." This image further communicates the speaker's alienation by suggesting that traumatic experience has led not only to an inability to communicate, but also to an erasure of the self. The full horror of the speaker's situation is communicated in these lines. The cry and, by extension, pain, that goes unnoticed forcefully communicates the poet's aphasia, which seems to result from the ineffability of experience.[10]

In "Sono una creatura," Ungaretti further underscores the diminishing power of language through the word "così." As the marker of a correlative, we might expect "così" to compare terms dialectically in order to create new and revitalized meaning. Here, the correlative suggests its opposite by marking a language that is cold, hard, and apparently drained of meaning. At the same time, it proposes a new language that has its foundation in death and is therefore appropriately ascetic. As an intensifier, "così" also works to deepen the

---

[9] See Harrison for an additional interpretation of Ungaretti's inversion of syntax and how it characterizes his poetic voice (67).

[10] This symbolic value of the stone is borne out not just within the context of its comparison to the speaker's cry, or in the literary traditions to which it alludes, but also in its popular usage, where it is associated with a widely used *modo di dire* — *metterci una pietra sopra* — that means to discontinue discourse on a given subject. The idiom has its origins in the gravestone ("pietra") that permanently seals a tomb, and is therefore also closely related to the idea of death.

comparison between the rocky peak and the poet's pain. This intensification is extraneous, however, since the terms of the simile are clear and meaningful in and of themselves. The repetitive "così" then becomes an excessive description of the inanimate stone, suggesting a compulsive drive towards death, or towards a language that can express death, which culminates with the total dispiritedness of lines seven and eight. The lines' seemingly compulsive march towards death asks the reader to contemplate not just physical death, but also the death of meaning. And yet, the poem does successfully communicate with its audience, if only through a negative discourse that thematizes, structurally and semantically, the extreme alienation of the individual.

If the principal theme of the first two sections of "Sono una creatura" links the failure of language to death, then its third and final section counters that message by emphasizing the poet's manipulation, or escape, from death through poetic invention:

> La morte
> si sconta
> vivendo

Here, Ungaretti questions the inevitability of death, or at least its finality, by choosing to end the poem instead with "vivendo." In doing so, he raises questions about death's "authority" over life and simultaneously casts doubt upon the symbolic order of language. This is reinforced by the poem's title, "Sono una creatura," which plays counterpoint to the despondent tone of the poem and reinforces its final emphasis upon the restrained victory of life.

The tension between death and life shapes Ungaretti's wartime poetry, and finds its purest expression in disanimation. Steeped as it appears to be in the Great War's violence, disanimation would seem to represent a purely negative principle. This is not the case, however, for its very presence constitutes a confrontation with the circumstances of loss: the events of the war in particular and, more generally, the experience of modernity. Poems like "Chiaroscuro," "In memoria," "Veglia," and "Sono una creatura" represent more than just the deadening sensation felt by the poet in the face of loss, however. They also give rise to a confrontation between the emptiness resulting from loss and the plenitude produced from a dialectical discourse that eludes synthesis. The poem's narrator mourns that which has been lost — Sceab, a fallen comrade, and his own sense of self — yet those losses are precisely what make the poems possible. Mourning takes place as the emotional energy previously directed toward the aforementioned figures is displaced onto the poem itself. Yet that displacement is barely removed from the poem's narrator, who uses poetic language to reconstitute himself. Thus, by way of poetic expression, the love previously reserved for a lost object is ultimately displaced onto the self, a fundamentally positive gesture that guarantees the latter's survival.

A richly ambiguous device, disanimation is uniquely suited to the complex mental and aesthetic exigencies of a generation of Italian authors and artists. Their firsthand experiences during the Great War led them to devise new literary and visual languages capable of expressing a sensibility radically different from those associated with the prewar avant-garde movements. It is with this in mind, perhaps, that scholars of early twentieth-century Italian culture ought to evaluate the works of the postwar *ritorno all'ordine*, often associated with a revalorization of traditional aesthetic values and, in particular, with the return of the individual as art and literature's primary subject. The return of the individual, yes, but to echo Benjamin, one that now stands alone in a world radically changed by the war.

Bowdoin College

Works Cited

Adamson, Walter L. *Avant-Garde Florence: From Modernism to Fascism*. Cambridge: Harvard UP, 1993.
Adorno, Theordor. *Negative Dialectics*. New York: Seabury Press, 1979.
Alighieri, Dante. *Dante's Lyric Poetry*. Trans. K. Foster and P. Boyde. London: Oxford UP at the Clarendon Press, 1967.
―――. *The Divine Comedy of Dante Alighieri. 2: Purgatorio*. Trans. John D. Sinclair. New York: Oxford UP, 1961.
Audoin-Rouzeau, Stephane, and Annette Becker. *14-18, retrouver la Guerre*. Paris: Éditions Gallimard, 2000.
Baldacci, Paolo. *De Chirico: 1888-1919, La metafisica*. Milano: Leonardo Arte, 1997.
Baroncini, Daniela. *Ungaretti e il sentimento del classico*. Bologna: Il Mulino, 1999.
Benjamin, Walter. "The Storyteller." Trans. Harry Zohn. *Illuminations: Essays and Reflections*. Ed. Hannah Arendt. New York: Schocken Books, 1968. 83-109
Blum, Cinzia. "Rhetorical Strategies and Gender in Marinetti's Futurist Manifesto." *Italica* 76.2 (1990): 196-221.
Bürger, Peter. *The Decline of Modernism*. Trans. Nicholas Walker. University Park: Pennsylvania State UP, 1992.
Calvino, Italo. *Lezioni americane: sei proposte per il prossimo millennio*. Milano: Arnoldo Mondadori Editore, 1993.
Carrà, Carlo. *Solitudine*. 1917. Private Collection, Zurich.
Comay, Rebecca. "The Perverse History: Fetishism and Dialectic in Walter Benjamin." *Research in Phenomenology* 29 (1999): 51-62.
Davis, Colin. "Hauntology, Spectres and Phantoms." *French Studies* 59.3 (2005): 373-79.
De Chrico, Giorgio. *Il grande metafisico*. 1917. The Museum of Modern Art, New York.
"Disanimato." *Dizionario italiano ragionato*. Firenze: G. D'Anna, 1987.
"Disanimato." *Vocabolario degli Accademici della Crusca*. Ed. Mirella Sesa, Umberto Parrini. Accademia della Crusca. Scuola Normale Superiore. 31 October 2014. < http://vocabolario.sns.it/html/_s_index2.html>.
Eksteins, Modris. *Rites of Spring: The Great War and the Birth of the Modern Age*. New York: Houghton Mifflin Company, 1989.

Fagiolo dell'Arco, Maurizio, ed. *Realismo magico: pittura e scultura in Italia, 1919-1925*. Milano: Mazzotta, 1988.
Freud, Sigmund. *Reflections on War and Death*. New York: Moffat, Yard and Company, 1918.
_____. *Totem and Taboo*. Trans. James Strachey. New York: W. W. Norton & Co., 1950.
Fussell, Paul. *The Great War and Modern Memory*. New York: Oxford UP, 1975.
Gentile, Emilio. *L'apocalisse della modernità: la Grande Guerra per l'uomo nuovo*. Milano: Arnoldo Mondadori, 2008.
Gibelli, Antonio. "Guerra e follia. Potere psichiatrico e patologia del rifiuto nella Grande Guerra." *Movimento operaio e socialista* 3.4 (1980): 441-64.
Harrison, Thomas. "D'Annunzio's Poetics: The Orphic Conceit." *Annali d'italianistica* 5 (1987): 60-73.
Hemingway, Ernest. *A Farewell to Arms*. New York: Charles Scribner and Sons, 1929.
"Introibo." *Lacerba* 1 Jan (1913): 1.
Isnenghi, Mario, and Giorgio Rochat. *La grande guerra: 1914-1918*. Bologna: Il Mulino, 2008.
Leed, Eric. "La legge della violenza e il linguaggio della guerra." *La Grande Guerra: esperienza, memoria, immagini*. Ed. Diego Leoni and Camillo Zadra. Il Mulino, 1986. 19-46.
Lyttelton, Adrian. "Society and Culture in the Italy of Giolitti."*Italian Art in the 20th Century: Painting and Sculpture, 1900-1988*. Ed. Emily Braun. Munich: Prestel-Verlag, 1989. 23-31.
Poggi, Christine. "Dreams of Metallized Flesh: Futurism and the Masculine Body." *Modernism/Modernity* 4.3 (1997): 19-43.
Saccone, Antonio. "Ungaretti, Reader of Futurism." *Italian Modernism: Italian Culture Between Decadentism and Avant-Garde*. Ed. Luca Somigli and Mario Moroni. Toronto: U of Toronto P, 2005. 267-93.
Salaris, Claudia. *Dizionario del futurismo: idee provocazioni e parole d'ordine di una grande avanguardia*. Roma: Editori Riuniti, 1996.
Schnapp, Jeffrey. "Propeller Talk." *Modernism/Modernity* 1.3 (1994): 153-78.
Thompson, Mark. *The White War: Life and Death on the Italian Front, 1915-1919*. New York: Basic Books, 2008.
Ungaretti, Giuseppe. *Vita d'un uomo: saggi e interventi*. Ed. Mario Diacono and Luciano Rebay. Milano: Mondadori, 1997.
_____. *Vita d'un uomo: tutte le poesie*. Ed. Leone Piccioni. Milano: Mondadori, 1969.
Velotti, Stefano. "Dare asilo all'ignoranza." Unpublished article, 2000.
Virgil. *The Aeneid*. Trans. Allen Mandelbaum. Berkeley: U of California P, 1981.
Winter, Jay. *Sites of Memory, Sites of Mourning*. Cambridge: Cambridge UP, 1995.

Stefano Bragato

F. T. Marinetti's Construction of World War I Narratives (1915)

When in May 1915 Italy entered the war, Marinetti had just joined the Italian army as a soldier. With other Futurist artists,[1] he had enrolled in the Battaglione Lombardo Volontari Ciclisti Automobilisti (VCA), a newly formed auxiliary corps which fought alongside the Alpini in the mountain region of Lake Garda from October to December 1915. The days in the VCA marked a significant step in Marinetti's development as an intellectual, since for the first time he came face to face with war as a soldier. Previously, he had experienced war only as a news correspondent for the French newspaper *L'Intransigeant*, first during the Italo-Turkish conflict in Libya in 1911, which he described in *La battaglia di Tripoli* (1912),[2] and then during the siege of Adrianople in 1912-1913, which would inspire his first words-in-freedom poem *Zang Tumb Tumb* (1914). Marinetti narrates the VCA experience in a number of texts belonging to different literary genres: two notebooks, a set of loose sheets, two newspaper articles and three *tavole parolibere*. In this article, a comparative analysis of these texts shows the extent of the impact that the Great War had on Marinetti's literary activity.

Among other things, the First World War introduced into Marinetti's war writing a significant autobiographical element. As a life-writing literary space, his personal notebooks thus started playing a key role within his methods of literary composition. This is evident from the study of his World War I notebooks written in 1915, which worked as a particular kind of source text for developing the other VCA narratives. As I will argue in the article, Marinetti's 1915 notebooks were conceived in the first place as drafts for these other VCA texts, rather than as plain, "neutral" autobiographical daily chronicles. Despite being a private literary space without external addressees, the notebooks are affected by some degree of autobiographical unreliability, which they share with the other VCA writings. This unreliability shows that in spite of their appearance as factual diaries recounting a war experience where Marinetti would do no more than jot down plain daily notes, Marinetti's notebooks constituted in fact a proper experimental

---

[1] They were: Umberto Boccioni, Anselmo Bucci, Luigi Russolo, Mario Sironi, Antonio Sant'Elia, Ugo Piatti, Carlo Erba and Achille Funi.
[2] Marinetti's Libyan chronicles, written in French, were published daily in *L'Intransigeant* from 25 to 31 December 1911, and then collected in the volumes *La bataille de Tripoli* (1912) and *La battaglia di Tripoli* (1912, Italian translation by Decio Cinti).

laboratory, where he knowingly put together narratives which diverged from the actual experience, and which he subsequently manipulated for composing or assembling together with further works.

The First World War therefore prompted a new method of composing autobiographical war literature, in which his notebooks functioned as a place where memories are "actively constructed" rather than just "passively gathered." Marinetti's war notebooks of 1915 were sophisticated and elaborate aesthetic creations, already imbued with a degree of Futurist imaginary and ideology. Their textuality was then reworked by Marinetti in order to compose the newspaper articles and the *tavole parolibere*, which together with the 1915 notebooks will constitute the objects of my inquiry. The reworking was done following two different rhetorical strategies, which were finely tuned to fit the expectations of the two sets of readers for whom these writings were intended, namely, a general audience and a cultural elite. This compositional method will also be employed by Marinetti in subsequent works about World War I and beyond.

Marinetti and War

It is difficult to overstress the centrality of war and in particular of World War I in Marinetti's thought and in Futurist aesthetics. The ninth "commandment" of the foundational manifesto of Futurism specifically points to the celebration of war as one of the primary aims of any Futurist artist (*Teoria e invenzione* 11). In *La battaglia di Tripoli* and especially in *Zang Tumb Tumb*, to glorify war meant to portray its external manifestations (sounds, colors, shapes, actions) and to leave aside human feelings and thoughts as well as any interpretations of it. This aim entailed a primarily aesthetic approach to war, deriving in part from the principles of the technical manifestoes (especially the "distruzione dell'io" and the pursuit of the "sensibilità lirica della materia," stated in the *Manifesto tecnico della letteratura futurista*; *Distruzione della sintassi. Immaginazione senza fili. Parole in libertà*; and *Lo splendore geometrico e meccanico e la sensibilità numerica*). Marinetti conceived and described war as an extraordinary spectacle and display, the best one ever created by man, which the Futurist artist was to observe and could only accurately represent through the techniques of Futurist writing.

When it comes to glorifying the First World War, however, the situation is different. Even before its outbreak, Marinetti felt this war as *his* war, since in addition to aesthetic significance it brought with it political and ideological implications. Marinetti was an anti-Austrian and an irredentist: before the conflict he had promoted Italy's intervention by proselytizing in the streets and in theaters and by engaging in a massive propaganda campaign using his publishing house, Edizioni futuriste di "Poesia." Even after its end, World War I continued to be a central preoccupation in Marinetti's literary and political activity, as he fought for an appropriate social recognition for its veterans. The very outbreak of the Great War, therefore, constituted the realization of a part of the Futurist program: fighting, describing, and glorifying the war became an imperative for Marinetti and his fellow Futurists. As he saw it, the Great War was the "ultimate avant-garde artwork" (Re 84).

Another new element that distinguished the Great War from both the Libyan and the Balkan conflicts was Marinetti's personal involvement. In 1915 he was no longer a news reporter describing a bombardment, but a soldier himself, fighting for his life in the cold trenches of the Garda mountains. War was no longer an external phenomenon to be carefully observed and described; now it was a personal event affecting his own daily existence. The Great War, in other words, introduced into Marinetti's war writing a new autobiographical element, which modified the way war was experienced and narrated; unlike in his previous works, its glorification was now carried out from within, since the writer and the fighter were the same person. The texts narrating the VCA experience therefore marked a new, important stage in Marinetti's war writing, since for the first time he recounted his own war actions.

Marinetti's Experience in the VCA
Formed in the spring of 1914, the Battaglione Lombardo Volontari Ciclisti Automobilisti left Milan for Peschiera del Garda on 21 July 1915, and at the end of September reached the border town of Malcesine, on the eastern side of Lake Garda. On 13 October the volunteers arrived at the base camp of Redecòl, on Mount Altissimo, where they joined the Alpine battalion "Verona."[3] They were involved in several military operations, the most important of which was the capture of Dosso Casina, a big Austrian entrenchment of key strategic importance taken on the night between 24 and 25 October. The resonance of the battle was such that it was reported in a feature illustration published on the front page of *La Domenica del Corriere* on 14 November 1915. The battalion was then disbanded on 6 December, and as a result Marinetti and his fellow Futurists returned to Milan.

Even though it officially started its operations in July, the VCA had its first armed encounter with the Austrians beginning only in mid-October. In his writings, Marinetti provides a detailed account only of the two weeks from 13 to 27 October, giving no information about the subsequent days. The narration mostly recounts single episodes of that experience, from the first patrolling duties on 13 October to the dangerous water duty of 27 October, including the capture of Dosso Casina on 24-25 October and other military tasks. Marinetti's narration is spread out over a number of texts, each containing one or more of these episodes. Although their forms and literary genres vary, they all share a descriptive approach; Marinetti mostly writes war chronicles recounting battles, patrols, shootings, individual or collective actions, seldom mentioning feelings,

---

[3] It is rather ironic that Marinetti joined the war on a bicycle, i.e., that very vehicle he scorned as a symbol of slowness and *passatismo* in the foundational manifesto of Futurism (*Teoria e invenzione* 9).

emotions, thoughts, and reflections concerning the events.[4]

1. Notebooks. The first place in which Marinetti recounts his actions at the frontline are two notebooks, subsequently published in 1987 (*Taccuini* 4-42).[5] It is possible that during this period Marinetti wrote a few other notebooks, which, however, remain unaccounted for (Bragato). The two extant notebooks contain both texts and drawings, and record three episodes which took place in those weeks: the sight of the first wounded man of the battalion on 22 October (notebook 1782), the account of the night between the 26th and the 27th, spent in an outpost near the Austrian trenches (notebook 1781), and that of a water duty carried out on the following day (notebook 1781). These notes were probably written at the front, as the hasty, rushed and sometimes rather confused handwriting seems to suggest. Their style is mostly nominal and telegraphic, punctuation is poor, as if Marinetti wanted to quickly record as much information as possible — indeed, Raimondi compared him to a film director storing film footage every day (XLI). As mentioned above, these notebooks gather only the data of phenomena and events (Raimondi XLVI; Benedetti 230-31). It is possible to recognize this descriptive approach also in the particular focus these texts take on the soundscape of the war, which is profusely conveyed by means of words and onomatopoeias. It has been argued that this focus on soundscape served as a coping mechanism for Marinetti to negotiate the difficulties of life in the trenches (Daly, "Futurist War Noises" 8-11).

2. Loose sheets. A detailed chronicle of the days 22-27 October, divided by dates, can be found in 36 loose sheets which have been published in 1997 in an article entitled "36 pagine dimenticate e inedite del diario di guerra di F. T.

---

[4] References to the VCA experience are also in the manifestoes *Orgoglio italiano* (*Teoria e invenzione* 502-3) and *Il Futurismo e la Guerra* (*Teoria e invenzione* 560-61), but since they consist of very short accounts without any links with the above writings they have been left out from my analysis.

[5] The notebooks are kept at the Beinecke Rare Book and Manuscript Library, Yale University, archive "Filippo Tommaso Marinetti papers GEN MSS 130," box 45, folders 1781-1782. Although the covers and some pages are missing, they are in a fairly good condition. Written in pencil (except for the sheets 1r, 2v-4r, 10v, 12v of the notebook in the folder 1782, which also present writings in black pen), they both measure mm 150x100 and have lined pages; over a few pages Marinetti drew a vertical line with a blue pencil, a distinctive trait to which I will come back shortly. The notebook 1781 has 21 pages, the notebooks 1782 has 13 pages and contains also a postcard with an illustration of the Garda region. They are published in the current edition of Marinetti's notebooks, which includes materials written in 1915, 1917-1921, 1926, all kept at the Beinecke Library. Partly because of some editorial constraints and because it was made from microfilms, the edition is affected by various issues related to philological accuracy (Bragato), among which is the exclusion of consistent portions of text. A selection of these portions was published in 1992 ("Unpublished Diaries" 25-40).

Marinetti."[6] My examination of the manuscripts led me to hypothesize that they consist of a subsequent rewriting of the 1915 notebooks, a fair copy carefully written at a desk (Bragato), and I therefore will treat them as a fragment of a subsequent version (possibly a more comprehensive fair copy) of Marinetti's notebooks.[7]

3. Newspaper articles. The experience in the VCA is also recounted by Marinetti in two newspaper articles published in *La Gazzetta dello Sport* on 31 January and 7 February 1916, both entitled "Quinte e scene della campagna del Battaglione Lombardo Volontari Ciclisti sul lago di Garda e sull'Altissimo. Annotazioni episodiche di F. T. Marinetti." They are structured as two parts of a single narration and presented as a "behind the scenes" report of those days, as also stated in the summary on the first page of the 31 January issue ("F. T. Marinetti narra le vicende della campagna dei Volontari Ciclisti milanesi al fronte trentino"). The first article covers the period from the departure from Milan in July to the first war action on 13 October, whereas the second narrates the events of the two weeks from 13 to 27 October, and therefore displays some notable links with the notebooks and "36 pagine."

4. *Tavole parolibere*. Unlike the newspaper articles, the three *tavole* referring to the days in the VCA do not report Marinetti's entire experience but focus only on single events. The first *tavola*, "Con Boccioni a Dosso Casina," describes the difficult night of 26-27 October, spent by Marinetti at the head of a lookout party very near the Austrian trenches; its focus is on the many night noises constantly unsettling him and his comrades. It was published on 25 August 1916 in *L'Italia futurista*, in an issue entirely dedicated to the recent death of Boccioni (17 August).[8]

The difficulties encountered by Marinetti and Boccioni (the physical and

---

[6] The sheets measure mm 310x210 and are kept at the Marinetti archive at the Beinecke Library, box 40, folder 1696. As "36 pagine" consists only of a transcription (with a few errors) of the autograph text without any paratextual information, the critical reception of these sheets has been rather confused, to the extent that they have been considered as an alternative version of the 1915 notebooks (Bellini 18), as portions of them which had been left out of the 1987 edition (Benedetti 229; Cammarota 108), or as little sheets ("foglietti") written in the trenches (Salaris 167-68). In addition, because of the unusual font of the journal which makes the digit "6" very similar to a "0," the article has sometimes been quoted as "30 pagine dimenticate e inedite" (Benedetti 229; Salaris 326).

[7] As I have been able to observe in my archival survey, in all his notebooks Marinetti used to draw a vertical line on sections of text that he would employ for composing other subsequent works. In the two 1915 notebooks this line can be found in those very passages that also appear in "36 pagine," with which the notebooks share a very similar wording.

[8] Most probably, this *tavola* was originally entitled "Una notte in sentinella sull'Altissimo," as it seems to come from the first pages of the first (1 June 1916) and second (15 June 1916) issues of *L'Italia futurista*, where this title appears in the section "Nei prossimi numeri." Marinetti probably decided to publish it in this issue with a different title, in honor of his friend.

emotional impact of the bitter climatic conditions, the danger of slipping on the icy ground, etc.) during a water duty on 27 October are the subject of the second *tavola*, "Corvée d'acqua sotto i forti austriaci," published in *L'Italia futurista* on 8 July 1917. For many years it was featured in Marinetti's public performances, as is evident from the records in his notebooks.

The last *tavola* is a drawing entitled "Battaglia a 9 piani," published on 8 January 1916 in the journal *Vela latina*.[9] By merging together events that happened on different days (19, 23 and 24 October), in this cross section Marinetti represents a mountain battle simultaneously fought on nine different levels. Various features of this *tavola* have attracted critical attention[10]; however, an interesting feature that has so far gone unnoticed is its potential Dantesque reference. The funnel shape of the *tavola* seems to recall one of the most fascinating visual representations of Dante's *Inferno*, namely, Botticelli's *Chart of Hell* (c.1485-c.1500).[11] In Botticelli's illustration two oblique lines converge at the bottom of the picture to form a funnel, which is horizontally divided into nine sections representing the nine circles of Hell. With a remarkable adherence to Dante's text, in each circle the damned are portrayed undergoing their specific punishment and different episodes of the poem are represented. Although he was never explicitly mentioned after the pre-Futurist works (published in *Scritti francesi*), Dante constituted a central presence throughout all Marinetti's literary activity, providing narrative structures and themes (as well as hidden references), from the foundational manifestoes *Fondazione e Manifesto del Futurismo* and *Uccidiamo il chiaro di luna!* (Baldissone, *Filippo Tommaso Marinetti* 47-48), to the private poems *Poesie a Beny*, where his wife Benedetta is associated with Beatrice (Baldissone, "Beatrice e Marinetti. Da Dante a Venezianella" 121-38; Baldissone, *Benedetta Beatrice* 149-76), up until his very last novel *Venezianella e Studentaccio* (Valesio, Introduction XLVII, LXXVIII-LXXIX, LXXXIII, XCI), published posthumously. Given both this Dantesque legacy and Marinetti's attention to numerology, the similar structures of "Battaglia a 9 piani" and

---

[9] A typographically set version in French (entitled *Bataille à 9 étages du Mont Altissimo*) subsequently came out in 1919 in the volume *Les Mots en liberté futurists* (95). It was then republished with minimal variations in 1925 in the collection *Nuovi poeti futuristi* (Caruso and Martini 1: 49). In this article I will focus on the Italian version.

[10] Focusing on its particular indexical attributes, John White has seen in this *tavola* "a work of specific anti-Austrian propaganda, not an impartially presented battleground" (150). Johanna Drucker defined it as a typographically ordered description of the chaos of the battle (131), a position that has recently been challenged by Selena Daly, who has focused instead on Marinetti's attempt to "futurize" the mountain landscape in order to reconcile it with the chiefly urban nature of Futurism ("The Futurist Mountains" 327-31).

[11] The chart is one of ninety illustrations made by Botticelli for a codex of the *Commedia* commissioned by Lorenzo di Pierfrancesco de' Medici. It "furnishes a panoptic display of the descent made by Dante and Virgil through the 'abysmal valley of pain'" (Parker 84). I thank Paola Nasti for the idea I am developing in this section, which was suggested to me during a seminar held at the University of Reading.

Botticelli's *Chart of Hell* may not be coincidental. The resemblance between the two can be seen, in my opinion, as a rhetorical device aimed at raising the literariness of the *tavola*, by creating a further intertextual level that can be grasped and appreciated only by educated readers. As I will discuss in the following pages, this is part of Marinetti's strategy of adjusting the narratives of his VCA experience differently according to the two different kinds of readership they address.

Textual Links among the VCA Writings
1. The textual analysis of the VCA writings shows that the notebooks and "36 pagine" worked as source texts for the composition of the newspaper articles and the *tavole parolibere*. This is evident, for example, in the third level of "Battaglia a 9 piani":

i nostri 149 invisibili uah uah uah uah partenza di treni suicidi su ponti aerei fragili fatalità di rumori rotaie convergenti in un unica stazione ogni 27 secondi PLUM PLUUM PLUUM

In this passage, Marinetti is describing cannon shells (caliber 149) shot by the Italian artillery on the left-hand side. They are shot across Lake Garda and reach the Austrian trenches on the right-hand side, as if an invisible rail bridge connected the two mountains. The Austrian trench becomes then like a station to which these shell-trains arrive every 27 seconds. When they explode, they produce a noise similar to that of big trains ("PLUM PLUM"). The comparison between shells and trains is expressed by an urban metaphor, a feature that is widely identifiable in "Battaglia a 9 piani" (Daly, "The Futurist Mountains" 327-31).[12] The source of this idea can be identified in a notebook drawing illustrating shells shot from a "batteria italiana" on the left-hand side of the page which land on a mountain on the right-hand side, producing the same noise of the *tavola*, "PLUM PLUM" (*Taccuini* 16). On the top left corner of the notebook page, moreover, Marinetti mentions a "lampo di specchio al sole," which can be related to the "raggio solare tubocalorifero" written on the top left corner of "Battaglia a 9 piani"; finally, in both the notebook and the *tavola* Lake Garda appears at the bottom of the page.

All of this is shared by a passage in "36 pagine":

Giorno 23 e Notte 23-24

---

[12] This metaphor is, however, not exclusive to Marinetti. It can also be found in a notebook entry that Boccioni wrote in those days (22 October: "Sulla nostra testa passano i 149 sibilando come direttissimi," *Taccuini futuristi* 201) and in a letter he addressed to Vico Baer (22 October: "Passano a cinquecento metri sulle nostre teste i proiettili da 149 che danno l'impressione di treni direttissimi" *Gli scritti editi e inediti* 382); and it is also mentioned by Luigi Russolo in his studies on war noises ("[i] grossi calibri [producono] un rumore simile a quello di un treno che passi non molto lontano" 45).

Alba. 149 nostri, treni suicidi su arcate rotte di grandi ponti di ferro aerei che scavalcano il lago. – Dall'Altissimo [Italian trench] al Colle del Bal [Austrian trench]. […] 1° raggio di sole che rade le altissime vette s'aggrappa, trema, poi scatta giù lunghissimo e m'infilza sull'orlo del precipizio.

(80-81)

This passage is also the source text of the following section in the first article of the *Gazzetta dello Sport*:

Dall'Altissimo, al disopra delle nostre teste, partono ora come treni pesanti che striscino sui binari di grandi ponti incurvati, le grosse granate dei nostri 149. Convergono tutte al di là del lago, con orario preciso, come ad un'unica stazione, a quel trincerone austriaco di Colle del Bal.

(14)

It is evident that both this passage and the one in "Battaglia a 9 piani" come from the text in "36 pagine," which is reworked in different ways in order to produce two different outputs as a *tavola parolibera* and a newspaper article.

A few features of these rewritings show the different procedures followed by Marinetti for their composition. In the making of the *tavola*, the source material of "36 pagine" is poured into a rather complex rhetorical structure, whereas the newspaper article is much plainer. In "Quinte e scene" the comparison between shells and trains and between the Austrian trench and a train station is expressed with two similes ("come treni pesanti"; "come ad un'unica stazione"), whereas in the *tavola* Marinetti uses metaphors ("treni suicidi"; "convergenti in un'unica stazione"), which abolish the conjunction "come" and leave on the page just the second term of the comparison. Moreover, the expression "treni suicidi" of the *tavola* (which conveys the idea of trains designed to crash and explode) becomes in the article "treni pesanti," with a consistent loss of metaphorical power. Furthermore, the metonym "nostri 149," which in "Quinte e scene" indicates the guns ("le grosse granate dei nostri 149"), in "Battaglia a 9 piani" signifies the shells ("149 nostri"), making thus a further logical leap. Similarly, "arcate rotte di grandi ponti di ferro" (in "36 pagine") is a more rhetorically condensed expression than "binari di grandi ponti incurvati" (in the article): the curved quality of the bridges shifts from a noun ("arcate") to a more explanatory noun plus adjective ("ponti incurvati"). Finally, the temporal cluster "ogni 27 secondi" of the *tavola* becomes in the article "con orario preciso," which is in fact less precise. Besides the different literary genres to which "Battaglia a 9 piani" and "Quinte e scene" belong, their dissimilar rhetorical structures have to do, in my opinion, with the different reading publics these works are addressed to; Marinetti speaks on the one hand to a Futurist cultural elite and on the other to a more general public (Daly, "The Futurist Mountains" 324). These works come from the same source text ("36 pagine"), which is strategically reworked in different ways according to their different addresses.

2. "Con Boccioni a Dosso Casina" also shares some textual references with a drawing in a notebook page. The drawing is entitled "Capoposto di notte" and describes that very same night between 26 and 27 October, when Marinetti was at the head of a lookout party (*Taccuini* 20-21). Both texts refer to that night's coldness and darkness with similar wordings, and especially focus on the many noises unsettling the volunteers. According to Daly, this *tavola* reveals an "unusually contemplative side to Marinetti" ("The Futurist Mountains" 331), which can be especially observed in multiple references to silence ("silenzio quasi totale," repeated four times, in bold typescript; "buio totale + silenzio totale"). It is, however, interesting that those references are not to be found in the corresponding notebook drawing, and therefore they were probably introduced only during the composition of the *tavola*. Rather than intentional manifestations of a contemplative side, I believe that they can therefore be seen as rhetorical devices introduced by Marinetti in order to emphasize the noises of that night, relying on a specific contrastive procedure which is widely used in descriptions of silence and noise (Manzotti 17-19).

This night comes two days after the capture of Dosso Casina, the most important war action of the VCA corps. This is how Marinetti reports it in the second article of the *Gazzetta dello Sport*:

Alle sette riprendiamo la marcia sulla mulattiera, e incontriamo finalmente gli alpini, coi quali ci lanciamo all'assalto delle trincee e dei reticolati di Dosso Casina, mentre i 149 dell'Altissimo intensificavano il loro tiro ben diretto. Notte meravigliosa, quella della nostra vittoria. I nostri muscoli esigevano il sonno e il riposo, ma la gioia di valutare l'enorme bottino di munizioni e di vettovaglie conquistate, ci diede la forza di costruire nuove trincee durante tutta la notte.

(15)

Marinetti is at the forefront, bravely fighting alongside the Alpini, the toughest and most famous regiment of the Italian army. However, if we compare this passage to the corresponding one in "36 pagine," a few issues seem to arise.

Si apre il fuoco alle 11.
Fuoco a volontà, tra l'intrico indiavolato dei reticolati austriaci già sfondati dai 149 dell'Altissimo. Gli Austriaci sono fuggiti già in parte. Ciò che rimane cede e ruzzola giù verso Malga Zures. Bottino di munizioni, zappe, picconi. Subito in trincea. Poi tutti a scavare caverne, ripari.

(84)

It is rather surprising that both texts lack a detailed description of the battle of Dosso Casina, which is only generically mentioned. If the glorification of war is a cornerstone of Futurist art, one would perhaps expect Marinetti to narrate extensively the most important action of his 1915 war experience, rather than just quickly touch on it. In order to clarify this point, we can turn to Boccioni's and Bucci's accounts of those days. The Futurists, who were in the "terza compagnia," were supposed to work together that night with the "seconda compagnia," but they had lost track of them. This is the account of the two painters:

(Boccioni) La seconda compagnia è trovata bisogna raggiungerla. S'è unita agli alpini. S'è espugnata Dosso Casina [...]. Verso le 8 girato Dosso Remit troviamo gli alpini di sentinella sdraiati con già nelle mani materiale abbandonato dagli Austriaci. Entusiasmo. Incontriamo sempre Alpini.
Arriviamo a Dosso Casina. Attraversiamo reticolati sfondati, trincee superate. Gioia. Saliamo sul monte.

(*Taccuini futuristi* 212-13)

(Bucci) I nostri della prima e seconda compagnia son già da due ore al trincerone [i.e., Dosso Casina] con settanta volontari alpini. Il capitano è al trincerone. Il trincerone è preso. "Gli austriaci?" Fuggiti lasciando tutto il bottino. [...]
"Spicciatevi. Bisogna arrivare in tempo per il contrattacco!"
Si vola. È la salita sopra un colle tondo, coronato di sassi come un calvario.

(Bellini 119)

As Boccioni and Bucci's excerpts demonstrate, the Futurists did not take part in the battle of Dosso Casina, since by the time they reached the combat zone the fighting was already over; the "trincerone" had already been conquered by the first and the second companies together with the Alpini. Hence, it seems safe to argue that the reason Marinetti does not describe the battle is simply that he was not there: he was too late.

The reliability of Marinetti's World War I reports comes therefore into question. By stating in "Quinte e scene" that he fought in the battle of Dosso Casina, Marinetti constructs a fictional narrative of those events, creating an alternative memory. This is an important point, because it seems to suggest that in spite of the alleged "behind the scenes" nature of this newspaper article, its aim is not to recount faithfully autobiographical World War I events; rather, it is to give prestige to the Futurist movement by portraying Marinetti and his fellows as war heroes. In other words, I believe that rather than a war chronicle, "Quinte e scene" is chiefly a propaganda operation in which praising the bravery of the volunteers is much more important than giving a truthful account of the war. Most significantly, this enterprise is carried out in a national newspaper with a wide circulation; in those years the *Gazzetta dello Sport* was published weekly with a print run of about one hundred thousand copies per issue (Farinelli et al. 441-42). Marinetti could not report to such a broad audience that he had missed the most important battle of the day because he was late; instead, he needed the public narrative of those events to portray him as fighting in the frontline. Because of the propagandistic nature of this text, moreover, it was essential for it to be easily read by anyone. This is why Marinetti employs an accessible style, very different from the highly rhetorical one of the *tavole parolibere*; the readers of the *Gazzetta dello Sport* had to be able immediately to understand and enjoy Marinetti's "autobiographical" story.

Furthermore, by depicting himself and his companions as successful war heroes Marinetti introduced into the representation of the battle a degree of Futurist imagery (linked to the ideas of boldness and toughness) intimately bound with Futurist ideology. He conveyed the concept that the Italians won the battle because they fought with a Futurist disposition. This kind of narrative publicly reinforced the idea of Futurism as a positive and powerful sensibility, the most appropriate for the new civilization of the twentieth century. Hence, in the making of "Quinte e scene" the audience shapes both style and content, as propaganda influences the rhetorical structure of the article and prompts the introduction of fictional elements.

The text in "36 pagine," which unlike the newspaper article is set in the context of a personal literary space (the subsequent version of a notebook), however, raises further issues regarding Marinetti's reliability. In "36 pagine," Marinetti once again does not bring himself to record that he missed the battle of Dosso Casina; rather, he refers to it with a sentence ("si apre il fuoco alle 11. Fuoco a volontà") which can still suggest his presence in the battle, but through the use of an impersonal verbal form it can ambiguously and simultaneously refer to both his participation and distance from it.

A close reading of these passages extends the question of their reliability as autobiography from Marinetti's public accounts to his private notebooks. This is very significant, since it could have a bearing on the critical status of the notebooks themselves within his oeuvre. Why does Marinetti need to construct an alternative war narrative even in the notebooks?

3. "Corvée d'acqua sotto i forti austriaci" offers a similar instance of inventive rewriting. This *tavola* describes Marinetti and Boccioni carrying a big and heavy bag of water from one campsite to another. Once again, its source can be identified in a notebook drawing, which portrays the scene mentioned above. The water duty also appears toward the end of the second article of the *Gazzetta dello Sport*:

Io, Boccioni e Sironi facevamo la corvée dell'acqua, preoccupatissimi di non romperci ingloriosamente una gamba scivolando sul ghiaccio.

(15)

Here the whole episode is squeezed into a single, very generic sentence, which, unlike the drawing in the notebook and the *tavola,* also features Mario Sironi, thus creating an alternative version of the event. Another account of this day is in Boccioni's notebook:

Viene ordine di andare in corvée d'acqua. Malcontento generale. Cap. monticelli di pessimo umore. Sottotenente Marelli intontito. Andiamo in una vallatella dove sono le cucine. Il terreno è sconvolto dai 149 dell'Altissimo. Frammenti di granate dappertutto. Evito la corvée, sono esausto.

(*Taccuini futuristi* 218)

The autobiographical reliability of Marinetti's narration must again be put into question: Boccioni states that he avoided the *corvée*. Nonetheless, Boccioni appears not only in Marinetti's newspaper article and in the *tavola parolibera*, which are aimed at an external readership, but also in the drawing in the notebook, i.e., a private literary space that is not destined to be shared with an audience. The passages analyzed so far are just a few examples of the inconsistency that can occasionally be found among Marinetti's World War I autobiographical writings.

The Meaning of the VCA Experience
This examination has revealed at least two features of Marinetti's procedures when composing World War I narratives, namely, that he reworked his 1915 notebooks in different ways in order to draft further writings, and that his accounts of his VCA experience hold some degree of fictionality.

1. The textual source of Marinetti's public writings about the VCA experience can thus be traced to the notebooks and to "36 pagine." Different narratives, and therefore different memories of World War I events, were constructed, tailored, and circulated to various reading constituencies. Hence, in Marinetti's writings the VCA experience — his very first direct encounter with war — does not have a clearly identifiable meaning in itself; rather, it takes on a different meaning in each text. In the three *tavole parolibere*, for example, complex rhetorical devices and Futurist writing techniques are extensively used since these texts are addressed to a cultivated reading public mostly made up of supporters of Futurism, who are cognizant of the procedures and purposes of Futurist art and are thus able to appreciate the complex representational strategies embedded therein. In these accounts, Marinetti's entire VCA experience acquires meaning (and an aesthetic one at that) insofar as it allows him to craft pieces of high Futurist poetry that glorify the Great War. This is also evident from a letter Marinetti sent to his Futurist friend Francesco Balilla Pratella on 31 October 1915. In this period, the Futurists used to communicate through a postcard, whose format had been especially designed by Francesco Cangiullo, which consisted of one page divided into sections with seven headings. Under the section "guerra" Marinetti writes:

GUERRA 8 giorni sotto il fuoco
vita meravigliosa torturata
dal freddo acutissimo (1000 metri)
= 3 poemi paroliberi splendidi

(*Lettere ruggenti a F. Balilla Pratella* 57)

Unlike the *tavole parolibere* referred to in the postcard, the narrative constructed in "Quinte e scene" is meant to be read by a largely popular audience, which is expected to be neither familiar with nor versed in obscure Futurist writing performances but is thought to be eager to consume an entertaining war story. For this reason, Marinetti's style becomes plain and accessible. By presenting a narrative of Futurist heroism and bravery, Marinetti publicly conveyed the idea that Futurist ideology was positively invested in nationalist discourse, dynamically engaged with modern warfare, and that it "matched" the sensibility of the new century. In the *Gazzetta dello Sport*, the whole VCA experience takes on meaning only insofar as it allows Marinetti to engage in Futurist propaganda.

2. Marinetti's VCA experience takes on a distinctive meaning even in his war notebooks of 1915. The emergence of the autobiographical component in Marinetti's modes of representation of the war, as I hope to have shown, is one of the most important innovations brought about by the outbreak of the First World War into his writing practice. At the same time, however, the reliability of the text remains problematic. It has been suggested that one way to understand an unreliable story can be to hypothesize an extra-textual pact between the author and the reader (Lejeune 12-22). Moreover, it has been pointed out that the purpose of an autobiography is not to report truthfully the historical details of a life, but rather to portray and to communicate to a reader a consistent self (what D'Intino calls "il blocco monolitico di una personalità" 246; also Smith and Watson 122-29 and Weintraub X-XIII). The creative act of writing, therefore, becomes a central element in the making of both the text and the individual self it depicts. While this idea could certainly apply to Marinetti's public writings about his VCA experience (even though they are not proper autobiographies), it is less plausible where his private notebooks (and "36 pagine") are concerned, since they do not necessarily imply an external reader. Nonetheless, these notebooks are also affected by Marinetti's autobiographical unreliability, as I hope to have shown. Introducing fictional elements into private texts that are the source of a series of public writings is an important point that must be accounted for. This approach can suggest a new way of reading Marinetti's notebooks, and can shed light on the relationship between Marinetti's war experience and its textual transposition.

As I stated at the beginning of this essay, my thesis is that Marinetti's 1915 notebooks were composed at the very outset as literary drafts to be used for composing future "autobiographical" works. Therefore, he writes about the battle of Dosso Casina not because he actually took part in it, but because he is jotting down a tentative narrative for a future work. He draws himself and Boccioni carrying a bag of water not because this actually happened, but because it is good material for an "autobiographical" *tavola parolibera*. The lack of reflections, thoughts and expressions of feeling found in the notebooks can also be seen as a consequence of this technique; as a source of future literary works narrating the war, the notebooks must focus only on the representation of its external phenomena, keeping any reference to human emotions off the page. In "36 pagine," Marinetti occasionally does mention hunger, cold, lack of sleep and lack of supplies (80-82). Far from being complaints, however, these episodes of physical hardship are inserted into the narration with the specific aim of stressing the exceptional endurance and resilience of the Futurist volunteers, as will also be the case in "Quinte e scene," "Con Boccioni a Dosso Casina" and "Corvée d'acqua sotto i forti austriaci." Hence, Marinetti's 1915 World War I notebooks can be regarded as the first building blocks of a specific method of literary composition, their function being not to record events but rather purposefully to design memories which can be creatively readapted in later autobiographical writings, according to the perceived needs of the readership. Thus, they already show the same Futurist imagery which is to be found in the public writings, and which is intimately bound to the Futurist ideology these writings aim to convey. Besides the newspaper articles and the *tavole parolibere*, the First World War takes on a specific meaning even in the notebooks: it is the source of literary drafts which can then be creatively reused.

This new reading of Marinetti's notebooks can contribute to a better assessment of the impact of the Great War on his writing activity. Before 1915, Marinetti's war writing mostly consisted of external descriptions of the war's extraordinary phenomena, and the glorification of war was an end in itself. Once Italy entered the First World War, instead, the sheer representation of war also became a tool to reach further exogenous and endogenous goals of crafting examples of Futurist heroism, with the aim of circulating Futurist propaganda to a wide, popular audience, or of creating drafts with an autobiographical dimension to be subsequently rearranged and manipulated in further war-inspired writings. The autobiographical shift introduced by the Great War, therefore, bestowed on Marinetti's notebooks a primary position within his literary activity. In order to narrate his 1915 war experience, he had to develop a new, specific compositional method that relied on them as a place for the creation of autobiographical (sometimes fictional) drafts. Marinetti would rely on this method also in the making of other future accounts of his WWI experiences, including the self-help manual *Come si seducono le donne* (1917), the "romanzo esplosivo" *8 anime in una bomba* (1919) and the "romanzo vissuto" *L'alcòva d'acciaio* (1921), which narrates the last months of the conflict up to the final Italian victory.

University of Reading

Works Cited

Baldissone, Giusi. "Beatrice e Marinetti. Da Dante a Venezianella." *Il personaggio nelle arti della narrazione*. Ed. Franco Marenco. Roma: Edizioni di Storia e Letteratura, 2007. 121-38.

———. *Benedetta Beatrice: nomi femminili e destini letterari*. Milano: Franco Angeli, 2008.

———. *Filippo Tommaso Marinetti*. Milano: Mursia, 1986.

Bellini, Dario. *Con Boccioni a Dosso Casina: i testi e le immagini dei futuristi in battaglia*. Rovereto: Nicolodi, 2006.

Beltrame, Achille. "I volontari ciclisti alla conquista di Dosso Casina e Dosso Remit." *La Domenica del Corriere* 14 novembre 1915.

Benedetti, Andrea. "The War Diaries of Filippo Tommaso Marinetti and Ernst Jünger."

International Yearbook of Futurism Studies 2.1 (2012): 226-52.
Boccioni, Umberto. *Gli scritti editi e inediti*. Ed. Zeno Birolli. Milano: Feltrinelli, 1971.
_____. *Taccuini futuristi*. Ed. Plinio Perilli. Roma: Mancosu, 2004.
Bragato, Stefano. "La situazione filologica dei taccuini di F. T. Marinetti." *Philological Concerns: Textual Criticism throughout the Centuries.* Proceedings of the International Conference organized by the Graduate Students' Association of Italian Studies (GSAIS): University of Toronto, Department of Italian Studies (Toronto, May 2-4, 2013). Ed. Pamela Arancibia et al. Firenze: Cesati, 2015 (forthcoming).
Bucci, Anselmo. *Pane e luna: autobiografia*. Urbino: Istituto statale d'arte, 1977.
Cammarota, Domenico. *Filippo Tommaso Marinetti: bibliografia*. Milano: Skira, 2002.
Caruso, Luciano, and Stelio Maria Martini, eds. *Tavole Parolibere Futuriste (1912-1944): Antologia*. 2 vols. Napoli: Liguori, 1975.
Daly, Selena. "The Futurist Mountains: F. T. Marinetti's Experiences of Mountain Combat in the First World War." *Modern Italy* 18.4 (2013): 323-38.
_____. "Futurist War Noises: Confronting and Coping with the First World War." *California Italian Studies* 4.1 (2013). http://escholarship.org/uc/item/8fx1p115.
D'Intino, Franco. *L'autobiografia moderna: storia, forme, problemi*. Roma: Bulzoni, 1998.
Drucker, Johanna. *The Visible Word: Experimental Typography and Modern Art, 1909-1923*. Chicago: U of Chicago P, 1994.
Farinelli, Giuseppe, Ermanno Paccagnini, Giovanni Santambrogio, and Angela Ida Villa. *Storia del giornalismo italiano: dalle origini a oggi*. Torino: UTET, 2004.
Lejeune, Philippe. *On Autobiography*. Ed. Paul John Eakin. Trans. Katherine Leary. Minneapolis: U of Minnesota P, 1989.
Manzotti, Emilio. "La descrizione: un profilo linguistico e concettuale." *Nuova secondaria* 27.4 (2009): 19-40.
Marinetti, F. T. *L'alcòva d'acciaio: romanzo vissuto*. Milano: Vitagliano, 1921.
_____. "Battaglia a 9 piani." *Vela Latina* 4.1 (1916): 1.
_____. *La battaglia di Tripoli (26 ottobre 1911). Vissuta e cantata da F. T. Marinetti*. Milano: Edizioni futuriste di "Poesia," 1912.
_____. *Come si seducono le donne*. Firenze: Ed. da Centomila copie, 1917.
_____. "Con Boccioni a Dosso Casina." *L'Italia futurista* 1.6 (1916): 3.
_____. "Corvée d'acqua sotto i forti austriaci." *L'Italia futurista* 2.21 (1917): 3.
_____. *Lettere ruggenti a F. Balilla Pratella*. Ed. Giovanni Lugaresi. Milano: Quaderni dell'osservatore, 1969.
_____. *Les Mots en liberté futuristes*. Milano: Edizioni futuriste di "Poesia," 1919.
_____. *8 anime in una bomba*. Milano: Edizioni futuriste di "Poesia," 1919.
_____. *Poesie a Beny*. Torino: Einaudi, 1971.
_____. "Quinte e scene della campagna del Battaglione Lombardo Volontari Ciclisti sul Lago di Garda e sull'Altissimo. Annotazioni episodiche di F. T. Marinetti (I)." *La Gazzetta dello Sport* 31 January 1916: 3. Rpt. Enrico Crispolti, *Bolaffiarte* 79 (1978): 14-15.
_____. "Quinte e scene della campagna del Battaglione Lombardo Volontari Ciclisti sul Lago di Garda e sull'Altissimo. Annotazioni episodiche di F. T. Marinetti (II)". *La Gazzetta dello Sport* 7 February 1916: 2. Rpt. Enrico Crispolti in *Bolaffiarte* 79 (1978): 14-15.
_____. *Scritti francesi*. Ed. Pasquale Aniel Jannini. Milano: Mondadori, 1983.
_____. "Selections from the Unpublished Diaries of F. T. Marinetti: Introduction and Notes by Lawrence Rainey and Laura Wittman." *Modernism/modernity* 1.3 (1994): 1-44.

_____. *Taccuini 1915-1921*. Ed. Alberto Bertoni. Bologna: il Mulino, 1987.
_____. *Teoria e invenzione futurista*. Ed. Luciano De Maria. 7th ed. Milano: Mondadori, 2010.
_____. "36 pagine dimenticate e inedite del diario di guerra di F. T. Marinetti." Ed. Jean-Pierre Andreoli de Villers. *Simultaneità* 1.1 (1997): 78-87.
_____. *Venezianella e studentaccio*. Ed. Paolo Valesio and Patrizio Ceccagnoli. Milano: Mondadori, 2013.
Parker, Deborah. "Illuminating Botticelli's Chart of Hell." *Modern Language Notes* 128.1 (2013): 84-102.
Raimondi, Ezio. "Il testimone come attore." Marinetti. *Taccuini 1915-1921* XXXVII-LVII.
Re, Lucia. "Futurism, Seduction, and the Strange Sublimity of War." *Italian Studies* 59 (2004): 83-111.
Russolo, Luigi. *L'Arte dei rumori*. Milano: Edizioni futuriste di "Poesia," 1916.
Salaris, Claudia. *Marinetti: arte e vita futurista*. Roma: Editori Riuniti, 1997.
Smith, Sidonie, and Julia Watson. *Reading Autobiography: A Guide for Interpreting Life Narratives*. 2nd ed. Minneapolis: U of Minnesota P, 2010.
Valesio, Paolo. "Introduction." Marinetti. *Venezianella e studentaccio* VII-CII.
Weintraub, Karl Joachim. *The Value of the Individual: Self and Circumstance in Autobiography*. Chicago: U of Chicago P, 1978.
White, John J. "Iconic and Indexical Elements in Italian Futurist Poetry: F. T. Marinetti's 'Words-in-Freedom.'" *Signergy*. Ed. Jac Conradie. Amsterdam: John Benjamins Pub. Company, 2010. 129-56.

Umberto Rossi

Broken Images of a Defeat:
Gadda, Comisso, Malaparte, and the Rout of Caporetto

1. *WWI and the Modernist Debate*

The roster of major inventive talents who were not involved with the war is long and impressive. It includes Yeats, Woolf, Pound, Eliot, Lawrence, and Joyce — that is, the masters of the modern movement. It was left to lesser talents — always more traditional and technically prudent — to recall in literary form a war they had actually experienced.
(Fussell 314-15)

About thirty years ago, the concluding chapter of Paul Fussell's *The Great War and Modern Memory*, one of the seminal texts about war literature, separated the memoirists previously discussed by the American critic (Blunden, Graves, Sassoon, and Jones) from the major figures of the Anglo-American modernism. Since then, Fussell's claim has been repeatedly challenged: traces of the Great War have been spotted in the second chapter of Joyce's *Ulysses* by more than one critic (Rossi, "Joyce and the Rebus of War"); different critical assessments of David Jones's uncompromisingly modernist treatment of the Great War in his 1937 poem-novel *In Parenthesis* (slated by Fussell) have been proposed (Rossi, "Il funebre a parte della Guerra"); above all, an interpretation of three of the major modernist writers (T.S. Eliot, Ezra Pound, and Virginia Woolf) as replying with their literary innovations to the war and the catastrophe it represented for liberalism has been authoritatively put forward by Vincent Sherry in his 2003 monograph *The Great War and the Language of Modernism*.[1]

While this realignment of Great War literature with modernism was taking place, another critical transition was coming about, that is, the adoption of the very category of modernism by Italian Studies scholars in Italy and abroad, as represented by such critical works as Somigli and Moroni's *Italian Modernism* (2004), Somigli's chapters in Eysteinsson and Liska's *Modernism* (2007) and *The Cambridge Companion to European Modernism* (2011), and Tortora and Luperini's *Sul modernismo italiano* (2012). This transition is more than the importation of a critical term coming from a different literary tradition (Donnarumma 14): by putting the first half of the twentieth century under the aegis of Modernism, critics are asked to "riflettere sui limiti e sugli sviluppi cronologici, sul gioco inevitabile delle inclusioni e delle esclusioni, sulle

---

[1] Isnenghi discusses how Italian writers and intellectuals dealt with the crisis of liberalism brought about by the war, and devised an array of literary strategies to tackle this issue; it is the main argument of *Il mito della grande guerra*, particularly evident in the discussion of Malaparte and Mariani (354-66).

distinzioni interne, sul suo stesso significato" (15), that is, to rethink that period of the Italian literature and its wider European and global context.

We might see these two processes as two sides of a triangle, one being the renewed relation between modernism and WWI literature in an Anglophone context, the other the relation between Italian literature and modernism. Geometry suggests us that the third side necessarily connects the Great War and Italian literature, though this connection might seem nothing new, at least since Mario Isnenghi's 1967 pioneer monograph *I vinti di Caporetto*, followed by his 1970 magnum opus *Il mito della grande guerra*, which paved the way for a discontinuous series of critical contributions only partially mapped in my monograph *Il secolo di fuoco*.[2] Yet one has to consider the whole virtual triangle to realize that the rethinking of Great War literature vis-à-vis modernism and Italian literature vis-à-vis modernism asks for a reconsideration of Italian Great War literature in the context of Italian modernism. Hopefully this critical direction should not only amount to a renewed understanding of canonical Italian literary texts dealing with the *grande Guerra* — even though such a task is inescapable — but also trigger a redefinition of the corpus and an analysis of poems, memoirs and novels (plus other texts that are more difficult to classify) that have not been sufficiently discussed in the context of war literature. Moreover, this third realignment of Italian Great War literature with the ongoing debate on modernism and the international discussion on war literature may give our classics of war or combat fiction and *memorialistica* a greater visibility in the global space.[3] In fact one has to regret that in the prestigious *Cambridge Companion to the Literature of the First World War* there is no mention of Italian narratives and poetry, though it has striven to adopt a transnational perspective by including chapters on French and German Great War literature.

This essay will deal with four texts that have tried to depict the experiences of their authors during one of the most complex and important events of the Great War on the Italian front, that is, the battle or rout of Caporetto: a historical event, moreover, surrounded by a myth, or black legend (Isnenghi and Rochat 398-406). This focus will compel us to put aside some of the canonical narratives (such as Emilio Lussu's 1938 memoir *Un anno sull'altipiano*), and some that have not been discussed so often (such as the relatively neglected 1930 novel *Vent'anni* by Corrado Alvaro), though their relationship with the main themes of modernism is quite strong. As one focuses on the notorious military disaster of Caporetto, other works come to the foreground, such as Curzio Malaparte's *Viva Caporetto!* (1921), Giovanni Comisso's *Giorni di guerra* (1930) and the first part of Carlo Emilio Gadda's *Castello di Udine* (1934), in addition to his *Giornale di guerra e di prigionia* (1955-1991).[4] Maybe

---

[2] A more updated bibliography can be found in Carta.

[3] As for the distinction between war novel and combat novel, see Jones.

[4] This volume collects Gadda's *Giornale guerra e di prigionia*, published by Sansoni in

only Malaparte's anomalous pamphlet might qualify as modernist if we adopted a strict definition of the term; yet the effort to turn the name of a circumscribed literary current into a general category that can accommodate a whole period of Western literature has led to more open-ended formulations (Somigli and Moroni 12; Levenson 3), allowing us to deal with an apparently traditional memoir like Comisso's or unrevised and posthumously published narratives like Gadda's, which were not meant to be modernist works in the same way his *Pasticciaccio* is (Somigli 91). Moreover, reconnecting Italian modernist texts of the Great War with the specific critical issues of war literature (Rossi, *Secolo* 16-45) may open new interpretive inroads in these works.

I attribute a strategic importance to Caporetto (and its literary depictions) for reasons I have only begun to discuss in an essay on Hemingway's treatment of the rout, which occurred on 24-26 October 1917, and the ensuing chaotic retreat (Rossi, "Notizie").[5] There I argued that if at the beginning of the Great War many saw the army as an organic community (for reasons that may well be different in each belligerent country), nonetheless the rout shattered that community on the Italian side, thus also disintegrating the collective expectations that amounted to a shared story or history. The community reverted to a gray, anonymous mass, where each individual struggled for safety and survival (not only by retreating, but also by surrendering to the enemy, in that being a POW was seen by many Italian soldiers as much less dangerous than fighting); there was no more a community with a common purpose and a shared history (at least this is how many perceived the rout [Isnenghi and Rochat 391-8]). Such a fragmentation of the armed community is paralleled by a fragmentation of perception, as the dimensions of the battle, the innovative tactics used by the Germans and the Austrian-Hungarians, the features of the mountain territory, the use of gas, and the destruction of communication lines prevented most Italian combatants, regardless of their rank and position, from having an overall picture of what was going on. The same happened to the Italian high command in the first hours — possibly days — of the battle (Isnenghi and Rochat 384-6). This situation is mirrored by the fragmentariness of Hemingway's depiction of the battle in *A Farewell to Arms*, and such a destructuration of the diegesis is a good example of one of the overall features of modernist literature, as Levenson comments on "the recurring act of fragmenting unities (unities of character or plot or pictorial space or lyric form)" (3). A fragmented perception of an event which is too great and complex for the cognitive abilities of an individual asks for a fragmented narrative.

Not all the narrative approaches to the Battle admit that an overall picture is very difficult to achieve (as it required a long historiographical research, for

---

1955 (then, in an edition that also included the "Giornale di campagna," by Einaudi in 1965), and the *Taccuino di Caporetto*, posthumously published by Garzanti in 1991.
5 For a discussion which also takes into account Italian writers, see Rossi, *Secolo* 159-72.

which see Schindler Ch. 12; Isnenghi and Rochat 373-406). If one reads George Macaulay Trevelyan's 1919 memoir *Scenes from Italy's War,* one is presented with a linear and quite traditional depiction of the rout of Caporetto, which — because of Trevelyan's sympathetic attitude towards Italy and its people — strives to explain the state of mind of those Italian soldiers who retreated or surrendered almost without fighting in October 1917; he paints his fresco of the rout with the sweeping brushstrokes of nineteenth-century historiography, but — interestingly — he also focuses on "Giuseppe" (169-75), an imaginary soldier that English readers should take for "a type of the *povero fante*" (169) so that they may know what psychological mechanism brought the infantry regiments in the Isonzo valley to abandon their positions in a matter of hours. The attitude of Trevelyan, who — one should add — was not a trench fighter but commanded an ambulance unit in the rear, is quite different from what we find in the pages of Gadda's notebooks.

2. *Gadda: From the Diary to Epiphanic Prose*

Among these, the one that tackles the battle of Caporetto is a part of his *Giornale di guerra e di prigionia*, the memoir "La battaglia dell'Isonzo," whose original purpose was not at all literary: "I particolari dell'Isonzo e della mia cattura, raccolti pro-memoria, in caso di accuse (Narrazione per uso personale, scrupolosamente veridica)" (265). Gadda was well aware that, after the war, he might have to justify his behavior and the surrender of the machine gun unit he commanded. In a footnote he declares: "Non ci si meravigli di questo frammischiamento di fatterelli e tragedie: la realtà fu tale e io la ricordo fotografando" (292) — a photograph of reality sounds like what one might expect from a nineteenth-century *verista*, not a modernist. Yet, when it comes to the crucial phases of the battle, and to those that brought about the abandonment of the trenches and the hasty retreat, which turned into a chaotic rout and disintegrated the whole Second Army, Gadda finds himself in a condition of uncertainty, ignorance and powerlessness:

[...] la nebbia *impediva* la vista dello Slatenik, non che delle antiche posizioni avversarie [...]
Avrei avuto ragione di credere che le linee fossero ancora occupate dai nostri [...]
Finalmente, *parendoci* di aver scorto qualcosa muoversi nella valle [...]
diedi ordine alle mitragliatrici di sparar meno [...] per rivelare la loro presenza e mostrare al nemico che la linea era guarnita, *illudendolo* sull'entità della nostra forza
Credevo [...] che gli austriaci non avessero avanzato molto: il mio animo alternava il *dubbio* con la speranza.
[la baracca] della vetta Krasij sia quella di Kosek *presumo* sia stata in gran parte distrutta dai grossi calibri [...].
seppi (*voce falsa*) che un battaglione alpino era stato mandato sul Krasij [...]. Ciò mi rassicurò: una tal voce era *falsa*.
sentii una grande esplosione; la *attribuii* allo scoppio di qualche deposito di munizioni [...] mentre *di ben altro* si trattava.

Io *non potevo presagire* [...] Ero *dubbioso* e speranzoso.

(287-92; italics mine)

This split between experience and understanding is also a typical feature of modernism, and has been connected with the traumatic character of modernist experiences (Baer 316); one more reason to go beyond Gadda's statements about a photographic realism and to acknowledge the intimately modernist nature of his depiction of the theater of war.

Moreover, it must be underscored that, although the purpose of this memoir was not strictly literary, Gadda's writing is remarkably effective and foreshadows his mature works (Dombroski, "Meaning" 376).[6] One may for instance read this passage, in which the young lieutenant describes the chaotic retreat in the Isonzo valley:

[the soldiers of Gadda's squad] erano stanchissimi, e l'esempio degli altri li scoraggiava. Poiché assistevano alla ritirata disordinata di truppa senza ufficiali, e di ufficiali senza truppa, della brigata Genova, d'artiglieria, di compagnie mitragliatrici. Tratto tratto gruppi di muli stavano caricandosi affrettatamente; qualche mulo isolato vagolava. Ovunque gruppi di soldati, ecc. — incontrammo e ciò finì di spezzarmi il cuore, una batteria di obici da 210 che evidentemente era in via di traino, i pezzi erano abbandonati sulla strada, ricca preda al nemico: non ricordo se avessero gli otturatori o no — Una quantità di granate da 210 erano state appena scaricate sui bordi della strada. Via via incontrammo altro materiale: roba delle ricche cucine e mense ufficiali, ceste di viveri, ecc. —

(294)

In such passages what stands out, however, is the fragmentariness of Gadda's rendering of the battle, which chimes in with the fragmented image of Dublin in *Ulysses*, or London in *The Waste Land*; the depiction of the broken army, reduced to a disorganized throng, recalls the masses that are protagonist of modernist fiction, especially the metropolitan crowds. In the passage quoted above, the disintegration of the army is also metonymically manifested by the abandoned weapons (the howitzers) and equipment.

The collapse of the army, moreover, completely shatters Gadda's heroic, romantic expectations. When he styled himself "Duca di Sant'Aquila" (33) at the beginning of his "Giornale di campagna," the young officer was surely ironic;[7] yet we must not forget that he joined the war as a staunch *interventista*,

---

6 Contini went so far as to declare that Gadda "aveva cominciato da professionista, non da dilettante" with his *Giornale di guerra e di prigionia* (Contini viii).

7 Carta reads the nicknames Gadda used in his *Giornale* as a "strategia testuale per provare a recidere un legame con quanto di sé e del mondo circostante [...] rifiuta" (102); but this game seems to be inspired more by playfulness and self-mocking than by the "sdoppiamento dell'io in un altro sé rimosso" hypothesized by Carta. A different opinion is expressed by Dombroski, who sees Gadda's alter egos as "una figura allegorica che insieme rivela e contiene (protegge) l'autore" (Dombroski, *Barocco* 14).

and yearned for heroic deeds, even self-sacrifice (39). At the end of his "Giornale di prigionia," though, we find the author disheartened and depressed after more than a year wasted in a German POW camp after his capture at Caporetto:

La mia vita è inutile, è quella d'un automa sopravvissuto a sé stesso, che fa per inerzia alcune cose materiali, senza amore né fede.
Lavorerò mediocremente e farò alcune altre bestialità. Sarò ancora cattivo per debolezza, ancora egoista per stanchezza, e bruto per abulia, e finirò la mia torbida vita nell'antica e odiosa palude dell'indolenza che ha avvelenato il mio crescere mutando le possibilità dell'azione in vani, sterili sogni.

(435)

The young patriot who ardently wished to fight and stand out finds out that he is an anti-hero, an *inetto*, a kindred spirit of Svevo's Zeno.[8] But there are passages scattered throughout these diaries that bespeak Gadda's uncertainty about the role he is playing in the Alpini corps, especially his rants about the disorder of his shelter (138), of the Army's bureaucracy (142), of the whole Italian military machine (143), accompanied by his frequent remarks, at times almost hysterical, about the lack of courage and motivation of the soldiers (134-35, 143). The war is not as heroic and successful as it promised to be in the propaganda of the *interventisti*, and this is manifest well before the tremendously humiliating moment in which Gadda's squad, whose retreat has been unexpectedly cut off by the Germans, must sabotage its machine guns and surrender (302-05); indeed Gadda, as Dombroski comments, "feels himself betrayed in his search for identity" ("The Meaning" 377). His tragically disappointing war experience surely calls in doubt the relationship between the artist and tradition (Somigli and Moroni 12), because the ideals of patriotic heroism were a fundamental component of the nineteenth-century artistic and cultural tradition that he (and many other young combatants, not only in Italy) had inherited in their formative years.[9] Gadda's failure as an infantry officer is made even more bitter by the death of his brother Enrico, a former Alpini officer who was awarded a bronze medal in 1916 and a silver medal because, after becoming a fighter pilot, he crashed with his airplane in April 1919. Enrico, whom Carlo Emilio saw as the best and dearest part of himself (*Giornale* 418), was the real hero, and his death during the war steals forever that role from his brother "Gaddus."

---

[8] "Mi manca l'energia, la severità, la sicurezza di me stesso, proprie dell'uomo che non pensa troppo, che non si macera con mille considerazioni, che non pondera i suoi atti col bilancino, ma che agisce, agisce, agisce a furia di spontaneità e di estrinsecazione volitiva naturalmente eseguita" (199).

[9] Of course here I am simplifying a much more complex transition from the cultural and literary climate of the Risorgimento (including the heroic status of the writer seen as a *vate*), to the crisis of romantic, nationalist and heroic values in post-1870 Italy, a context outlined by Somigli in his discussion of *decadentismo* ("In the Shadow" 912-15).

Being or believing to be an anti-hero is the quintessential condition of the modernist character. The fragmentariness of perception is also a relevant issue for modernists, but the fragmentariness of form, as has been highlighted by Levenson, is also part of the picture when we deal with Gadda's treatment of the war. Let us not forget that before his *Giornale* was published in 1955, the Italian public could read the five prose fragments published in *Il castello di Udine* in 1934. The derivation of these pieces from the *Giornale* has been already analyzed by Rodondi; they re-elaborate the earlier, but then unpublished materials, with a denser and more complex prose, but also in a more fragmentary fashion (even though Gadda wrote in an endnote that the pieces "ebbero vincoli di rigorosa unità infino dalla gestazione" "Appendice" 830). All in all the five prose pieces read like genuine epiphanies, moments of dazzling awareness and illumination, searing manifestations of unforgettable and unsettling memories, such as, for example, the exhausting march on the Adamello glaciers (*Castello* 44-46) in which Gadda collapsed "come un vecchio mulo sfinito" (44). These are also traumatic moments, hence to be read in the light of a fundamental aspect of the modern(ist) experience (Baer).

These pieces are as epiphanic as the stories in Joyce's *Dubliners*, whom Gadda acknowledged having read in a letter to Contini (Lucchini 8); if they are connected by ties of rigorous unity, as Gadda wrote in his note, they are as subtle and covert as those interconnecting the stories of Joyce's more famous collection. Here, however, we do not have the vitreous clarity of vision of *Dubliners*. Rather, we are presented with a spasmodic torsion of the narrative structure, in which different places and situations metamorphose into one another, in an original mix of narration and a sort of feverish argumentation. These pieces present us, in a condensed, more refined (but equally emotional) manner, with the same issues that haunt the *Giornale*:[10] the author's feeling of not being up to the situation, the reassertion of the reasons of his *interventismo*, his alienation from the Italian society as represented by the army, the humiliating conditions in the POW lager, above all the sense of loss and bereavement. It is not coincidental that the last piece of the *Castello*, "Imagine di Calvi," ends with the description of the death of lieutenant Attilio Calvi on the Adamello, a sort of avatar of Gadda's brother Enrico (whose death closes the *Giornale*), another hero with whom the author cannot stand comparison.

Another typically modernist theme that plays an important role in Gadda's writings about the war is, of course, the relationship of the artist and the institutions in general, not only the cultural ones, as suggested by Somigli and Moroni (12). Here it is not only a matter of how a writer interacts with critics, publishers, the academia, the cultural establishment (surely an important issue,

---

[10] In this regard Lucchini comments: "Se il rapporto di filiazione [between *Giornale* and *Castello*] è indubbio, non può sfuggire la maggior asciuttezza del dettato seriore, che [...] condensa gli appunti giovanili di guerra [...]" (11).

inasmuch as modernism thematized it in several epochal *Künstlerroman*); it is also a matter of how the modernist artist relates to society in general, his/her alienation, his/her refusal to integrate or conform, his/her discontent. This side of Gadda's work has already been discussed by Isnenghi in his *Mito della grande guerra* (for which see also De Angelis 60-61); one has, however, to highlight, in Gadda's *Giornale* and *Castello,* the importance of the opposition between the front soldiers and the majority of Italians who stayed at home during the war. This issue connects these narratives to the wider, transnational context of Great War literature, as the opposition between the combatants' and the civilians' worlds (the front line vs. the rear/the cities) is found in many WWI narratives (Rossi, *Secolo* 29-31); a remarkable episode belonging to this uninterrupted discursive thread is the meeting with the two prostitutes who do not seem to be particularly sorry for the disaster that has overwhelmed the Italian Army:

Due cocottes piene di sifilide e di sguaiato servilismo pregarono De Candido [uno degli ufficiali prigionieri] di raccomandarle a ufficiali tedeschi. Cola e lui chiesero quale fosse la loro sorte e si fermarono a chiacchierare [...]. Ricordo le sfacciate parole della più piccola delle due svergognate: "Per noi italiani o tedeschi fanno lo stesso", dette con allegria.

(*Giornale* 307-08)

One might easily read this passage as witnessing Gadda's misogyny, but it is also a moment in which Gadda metonymically represents the civilian world — which did not really believe in the war and was only interested in making money out of it — through the two corrupt and repugnant cocottes; moreover, here we have another example of that "refusal of the norms of beauty" which characterizes modernism in general (Levenson 3), and which entails the description of scandalous situations often related to sexuality. However, another reading is possible. If one thinks of the use of more or less covert symbols in modernist fiction and poetry (often signs of a private nature, such as those in Joyce's "Schema Linati"), because "the use of mythic paradigms" (Levenson 3) is only one of those signifying architectures that — in addition to their sometimes bewildering innovative modes of representation — give modernist texts an inner consistency notwithstanding their "rejection of realism" (Somigli and Moroni 12); hence the prostitutes can be easily read as an embodiment of Italy (traditionally represented as a woman), betrayed and forsaken by her soldiers, her territory prostituted to the oncoming Austrians.

Of course, the objection might be raised that we should not see so much construction and literary texture in words hastily written on an exercise book, in a memoir that Gadda had written for practical reasons; the prostitutes are there because Gadda did meet them on 25 October 1917 in Caporetto. But we know that memory is selective, and that by focusing on the two prostitutes — who were not really relevant for the "rational" purpose of the memoir — Gadda was plausibly driven by a complex psychological dynamics (explored in detail by Carta).[11] Hence this small episode should be read as a multi-layered textual construct with a wide potential for signification.

Moreover, it should be clear that modernist literature of the Great War is not simply a literary practice (or a set of literary practices) that tackles the experience of the combatants in the trenches and/or the civilians who were not in the trenches, but were in any case involved in the conflict; modernism should always be understood as an artistic reaction to modernity, to the vast and deep changes affecting the Western society and then the rest of the world since the end of the nineteenth century, brought about by electricity, cars, airplanes, telephone, cinema, and so forth. The rout of Caporetto is one of the chapters of this enormous novel; it was a battle in which the innovative use of some technologies (e.g., poison gases, automatic weapons, telecommunications) enabled the German and the Austrian-Hungarian armies to completely unhinge the Italian lines and capture hundreds of thousands of prisoners. Gadda's perception of the rout, his emotional (often overemotional) reactions, his bewilderment, confusion and despair are the side effects of a most modern feat of logistics, tactics, strategy and technology. Gadda's experience in those days of October was something that asked for a different treatment from a literary point of view. A first answer is the *Giornale*, then there are the highly modernist, epiphanic pieces of the *Castello*. In other words, a radically modern experience on a technologized battlefield leads to a modernist narrative.

3. *Comisso: Technological and Emotional Distancing*
This view is quite clear when one considers the pages where *Giorni di guerra*, Giovanni Comisso's more classical and less expressionistic memoir, deals with the hours in which the collapse of the Second Army took place (*Giorni* 124-45). We do not find Gadda's overcharged emotivity and magmatic language, yet Comisso's elegant and untroubled prose presents us with a fragmentary view of the battlefield:

La battaglia era incominciata alle due, come era stato avvertito dal Comando supremo. Il generale vecchio e sordo non riesciva a sentire l'osservatorio di Maritza che ne dava la notizia e dovetti ritrasmettergliela. [...] Dal Corpo d'Armata, Kirghis, era lo pseudonimo del capo di stato maggiore [...], volle sapere subito la nostra situazione. Il bombardamento cessò dopo poche ore e tutti i comandi avanzati con un senso di sollievo si affrettarono ad avvertirci. [...]

---

11 Carta's analysis of the contradiction between Gadda's almost fanatic devotion to his mission (as a soldier and an officer) and the weakness of his body, which often falls short of Gadda's own heroic expectations, seems to me more sensitive to the contradictory texture of the *Giornale* than Mileschi's reading, which maintains that the inner conflict between Gadda's patriotic (and authoritarian) beliefs and his doubts about them (and their consequences) only arises in his later works.

Dal Rombon telefonarono che lassù nevicava e vi era stato soltanto un grande lancio di razzi bianchi. Anche questa notizia riescì tranquillamente, ma dopo mezz'ora di sosta il bombardamento riprese. [...] quando biancheggiò sui monti le artiglierie iniziarono un tiro che aveva un fragore diverso. Subito ci venne segnalato che tiravano granate a gas asfissiante. Il comando si mise in allarme. Telefonò a destra e a sinistra per averne la conferma. Nessuno poteva garantirlo. [...] "È ritornato dalla linea l'ufficiale che abbiamo mandato e riferisce che i soldati sono tutti al loro posto, col fucile tra le mani e la maschera al volto" [...] comunicò nuovamente Mirtillo [another codename].

(*Giorni* 125-27)

Like Comisso himself, readers do not directly access the front-lines; the writer belonged to a communications unit of the Regio Esercito, which laid telephone cables to connect the trenches and other positions to the commands and managed networks and switchboards. With the benefit of hindsight, we may say that the role played by Comisso exposed him to what was cutting-edge information and communication technology in 1917. Thus the ongoing battle is perceived through an electric medium, the telephone, which on the one hand achieves an immaterial simultaneity (news from distant points of the front-line arrive immediately to the command, where the writer operates the switchboard with his comrades [125]), while it turns the battlefield in an immaterial, acousmatic space of disembodied voices (Chion) that only offer fragments of the whole event. These fragments may be beguiling, as the reassuring news of the soldiers still holding their line after the bombing with gas shells hides a tragic truth: "Quei soldati erano fermi, impietriti dalla morte che la piccola e miserabile maschera non aveva servito a impedire" (127).

Of course the concluding remark was written with the benefit of hindsight and belongs to the moment of telling, not to the moment told; in October 1917 Comisso was not aware that poison gas had exterminated the soldiers in the front-line and that the Italian front was quickly crumbling. When news of the collapse arrives, it comes as a surprise and is not believed: "[...] un'altra stazione telefonò che al *baracchino del dottore*, ai piedi del Rombon, [the enemy infantrymen] già avevano oltrepassata la linea marciando verso Plezzo. Il comando non si convinse" (127). The flux of information carried by the cables is much faster than the ability of the commanding officers to interpret them or devise a reaction. Comisso registers the barrage of news (most of it bad) until the name of a familiar place transforms the so far immaterial battle into a known space: "La batteria di Naradelie telefonò [...]. 'Abbiamo tolto gli otturatori e ci ritiriamo.' [...] Abbandonai il telefono con un brivido che mi prese alla testa. A Naradelie si andava alla sera per fare una passeggiata" (129). Removing the breech bolt of cannons is the last resort of gunners who must hastily abandon their heavy guns, and this means that the situation is desperate. Moreover, Naradelie is within walking distance, hence Comisso — who so far has been a spectator of the battle, or better its listener — suddenly realizes that the enemy is now so close that he can be finally placed in a space the writer has measured with his own body, as he has walked there. No wonder that this realization is shocking.

What follows is a communication breakdown: "La linea era interrotta. [...] il filo si era spezzato. Le comunicazioni ottiche erano impedite dalla nebbia. [...] Il telefono della teleferica non rispondeva. [...] ogni idea di comunicazione fu abbandonata" (130). When a German or Austrian soldier calls from Maritza (134), it is clear that the battle is lost. "Nessuna linea rispondeva più" (135); the shutdown of the telephone network sanctions the disintegration of the community in arms, and we follow Comisso's escape from the Isonzo valley. Interestingly, one of the soldiers — seeing "la cima del Rombon con le gallerie illuminate" — remarks: "Quelli sono ancora lassù e non sanno che noi ci siamo ritirati. Li prenderanno tutti prigionieri" (137). The soldiers still manning the top of Mount Rombon are in the same situation of Gadda on the nearby Mount Krasij: the lie of the land and the communication breakdown have turned the army into a constellation of splinters, unaware of what is really going on around them.

The following pages tell the odyssey of Comisso through Friuli and Veneto with the retreating armies, until he reaches his home city, Treviso (175); it is the longest episode of the memoir (50 pages out of 230), and its depiction of the chaos after the collapse of the front-line is strikingly similar to what can be found in a well-known masterpiece of English-language modernism, Hemingway's *A Farewell to Arms* (chapters 27-32). The atmosphere of the two narratives is, however, quite different, even though many details match. While in Hemingway there is a nightmarish feeling of helplessness and powerlessness, with the slow and thick throng of soldiers and refugees blocking the roads that Frederick Henry's ambulance unit should move along to reach safety, Comisso lives his odyssey as an adventure. What we are presented with is, to quote Isnenghi, a "guerra-festa, [...] avventurosa e, a momenti, godibile," che "può davvero porsi come un *oggi* privo di *ieri*, come un'entrata di slancio, fresca, ricettiva, nella propria vita che comincia" (193).

Thus Comisso's memoir manages to subvert the relationship between the artist and tradition, and it also questions cultural memory (Somigli and Moroni 12). Compared to a writer like Gadda, who still believes in the values and ideals of Risorgimento, Comisso seems to have a sort of post-political, even postmodern attitude to the "great discourses" of nationalism and politics. Isnenghi calls it "un'affascinante testimonianza dell'uomo come animale apolitico" (Isnenghi 191). Such an aloofness allows the author of *Giorni di guerra* to cast a cold glance on the chaos of Caporetto, registering all sorts of comedic episodes — like the looting of chickens and rabbits (158-59) or the requisitioning and maladroit butchering of an ox (170) — with a strong picaresque flavor. Everything is told without any moral qualms, even when the behavior of Comisso and his soldiers is definitely questionable, in a way that reminds of certain pages of another Great War veteran, Ernst Jünger (1895-1998) — a polymath who has recently been admitted to the modernist canon/corpus (Welge 551-56) — especially his ironic 1936 colonial memoir *Afrikanische Spiele*. Here the word *Spiele* (games, but also manner of playing an instrument and reciting) is a tell-tale one, as Isnenghi used it to summarize the sense of Comisso's war memoir, which "si risolve in una serie di *giochi*" (233).

4. *Malaparte: An Aborted Revolution and Revolutionary Prose*

Another modernist approach to Caporetto is to be found in Curzio Malaparte's *Viva Caporetto!*, aka, *La rivolta dei santi maledetti*. The very form or genre of this work is innovative, compared to the previously discussed texts. Gadda's *Giornale* is a diary and Comisso's *Giorni di guerra* is a memoir, both forms being typical of Great War literature in the whole European and American context; even Gadda's pieces in *Il castello di Udine* are not so different from the lyrical, autobiographic prose *frammenti* favored by the young Italian literati of the *Voce* and the *Ronda* (Debenedetti 13-53);[12] but Malaparte's *Viva Caporetto!* is much harder to classify.

This compact book puts forth a thesis like a political pamphlet, arguing that the mutiny of many regiments of the Italian army at Caporetto — which refused to counterattack and stop the advancing German and Austrian-Hungarian forces, and either surrendered or abandoned their positions to go home — was not simply an act of cowardice or fear, but should be interpreted as a military strike, as a stillborn revolution. Yet Malaparte's argument is organized as a narrative. In the first page of the text the author states:

È il libro [...] di un uomo qualunque, che è andato in trincea, fante tra fanti [...]. È il libro di un uomo normale, di un uomo "in carne ed ossa" che tutto ha accettato come un sacrificio, come un dovere istintivo [...].

(49)

Viva Caporetto! is in fact a narrative text, even though it is not a conventional novel; its author seems to have operated a radical transformation of the novelistic form (if this text can be read as a novel), in which the protagonist of the story is not a character or a group of characters, but the whole Italian people at arms: "i soldati di fanteria, i malvestiti, i laceri, i sudici, i buffi e miserabili soldati di fanteria" (85), i "figli di puttane" (122). The main character of this narrative is, to put it in Pirandello's terms, *uno, nessuno e centomila*; actually a few millions. In *Viva Caporetto!* the focus leaves behind a collective subject, as in this passage:

Ficcato nelle buche e nel fango, roso dai pidocchi, gettato all'assalto contro altre buche

---

[12] It must be underscored, however, that the *Castello* was published in a period in which *frammentismo* was making way for those writers who strove to "reinventare in Italia il genere romanzo" (Debenedetti 13).

fangose ed altri uomini pidocchiosi, il popolo dei soldati, dei buoni e degli ignari, si trovò di fronte ad una cosa imprevista, terribile e inafferrabile, a una macchina fatta di formule, di filo di ferro e di canne rigate, di chimica e di balistica, si trovò a cozzare su un muro d'acciaio, di calcoli e di scienza, invisibile e onnipresente, contro cui nulla poteva la sua povera massa urlante, bestemmiante e piangente, fatta solo di carne, d'ossa e di qualità umane.
La morte meccanica uccideva e straziava, sconvolgeva la terra e i boschi, oscurava il cielo, dilaniava le montagne: e gli uomini, piccoli e grigi, cadevano si rialzavano urlando e si gettavano contro la macchina, contro il muro di calcoli e di formule, contro la morte meccanica che uccideva e straziava — tac tac tac.

(78)

Suddenly the focus shifts to an individual one, as in this brief vignette in which an anonymous infantryman (representative of each individual in the whole group, or social class) meets two well intentioned ladies of the Red Cross,

le quali, ogni volta che il fante accettava ringraziando la tazza di brodo o di caffè e la cartolina coi connotati del Re e di Cadorna, esclamavano, contente e commosse: — "Povero soldatino! Quanto sono bravi i nostri soldatini" — senza sapere che "il soldatino bravino e carino", tornando ai carri bestiame della sua tradotta, diceva agli altri innocentemente, con quel sorriso d'ignorante che è una sintesi di tutte le ingenuità: "Ho trovato due troie, in quella baracca, che m'hanno dato un brodo ed una cartolina". —

(125)

The soldier disappears soon after having been conjured up, once he has played his little part in the plot, showing the mutual misunderstanding between members of the lower and higher classes; the story focuses once again on the people, on the collectivity of soldiers, on the *santi maledetti*.

The question of the genre of Malaparte's work has already been discussed by Barilli, who — before suggesting a bold (and not wholly persuasive) comparison of Malaparte's war writings with Dante's *Divine Comedy* (24-31) — achieves much more solidity when he traces them back to journalism (22-24).[13] Thus, interpreting *Viva Caporetto!* as a reportage might not be too reckless a critical move, and one might go so far as to read this book as a forerunner of the American New Journalism of the 1960s and 1970s. Surely this mix of reportage, pamphlet and memoir is firm in its resolve to startle and disturb the public, which is one of the hallmarks of modernist fiction (Levenson 3). Malaparte's style, moreover, rugged and demotic as it is (undoubtedly a journalistic style), is as radical a stylistic experiment as Gadda's own modernist baroque in a time in which the preciousness of the *prosa d'arte* was the fashion (Debenedetti 48).

The originality of Malaparte's prose is the coupling of a journalistic

---

[13] I also find extremely insightful and intriguing Barilli's suggestion that Malaparte might be better understood by connecting him to other European figures of polymaths such as Malraux, Sait-Exupéry, Silone, Sartre, and Camus (31-13). To these names one should probably add Orwell and Alvaro.

language with allegorical images, as, for instance, when he wants to depict general Cadorna's iron-handed, almost fanatic idea of discipline and authority by imagining him clad in an armour:

[...] chiuso nella sua lucente armatura di principî e di tradizioni, alto nella sua aristocratica fierezza degna di un secolo più cattolico e più legittimista, continuava a premere, col pugno pesante, sul dorso dei soldati curvi nel fango [...].
(125)

Or when he wants readers to visualize the revolt of the accursed saints, the infantrymen who went on strike at Caporetto:

I ciompi, i pezzenti, i ribelli, il carname delle undici battaglie, i rifiuti di tutti i settori e di tutti i reticolati, abbandonarono le trincee e si gettarono contro il paese alzando su gli elmi bruni e sui torrenti di popolo grigioverde i trofei e le insegne della santa e cristianissima fanteria: giubbe lacere e sforacchiate, farsetti a maglia unti e pidocchiosi, elmetti contorti dalle scheggie, scarpe sfondate.
(127)

Further, the representation of the rout as an act of rebellion always has a lively narrative tone, sometimes even theatrical, like when Malaparte lets the "figli di puttane" speak, as if addressing the Italian political and military ruling class, which has sent them to die for twenty-nine months:

Noi non vogliamo più combattere [...]. Perché sempre noi? Perché voi che urlate, che imprecate, che insultate, non raccogliete i nostri fucili? Tocca o voi, ora. Difendetela, questa patria che dite di amare.
Provatelo, questo vostro amore: provatelo facendovi insultare, massacrare, fucilare, umiliare dagli uomini e dalle leggi, come lo abbiamo provato noi in tanti mesi di Carso e di Dolomiti. [...] Noi, figli di puttane, non vogliamo più combattere per voi!
(131)

The collective protagonist of this hybrid pamphlet-novel can also talk back — of course as a "we." This is relevant for at least two reasons. First of all, having his collective character, the "santi maledetti" or "figli di puttane," endowed with a voice, Malaparte enhances the narrative features of his text, giving it a diegetic energy that encourages readers to follow the plot of *Viva Caporetto!* as well as its argumentation. Remarkably, such a plot is quite similar to those of other more or less famous combat novels of the Great War (one might quote as examples Alvaro's *Vent'anni* or Sassoon's *The Complete Memoirs of George Sherston*): leaving home and civilian life, being trained, reaching the war theater, seeing more and more signs of death and destruction, entering the wasteland of the trenches; then the first attack, being shocked or wounded or killed, then the realization of what carnage the war actually is, the growing awareness of being no more than *chair à canon* — all of this is a sort of fixed course mirroring the real life experience of the authors and millions of

WWI combatants. But the perspective is different, and those who talk back in the quoted excerpt are not middle-class officers like Lussu, Gadda, or Alvaro (and their British counterparts, Robert Graves, Edmund Blunden, or Siegfried Sassoon), but the ordinary infantrymen, that is, the Italian peasants (workers were too precious for the Italian industries to be sent to the front), wearing the uniform of the Regio Esercito — those peasants who were usually voiceless, as they could not write and spoke a rather shaky Italian.

The presence of these Italian peasants constitutes another relevant modernist feature of the text. Moroni and Somigli suggested that one of the issues thematized by modernism is the emergence of a counterdiscourse of marginalized groups questioning the coherence and unity of modern culture (12). In fact, Isnenghi's *Il mito della grande guerra* (all its fourth chapter, "La truppa," discusses this matter in detail) has made it clear that most Italian soldiers-writers presented the *umile fante* as an illiterate peasant, unable really to understand the reasons of the war, untouched by the patriotic values of the ruling and middle classes (the values of modern liberalism), resigned to obey and fight, at the same time victim and instrument of what Isnenghi labelled "un imperialismo insicuro" (346). Malaparte questions the coherence and unity of what was in 1921 a modern (and victorious) Italy; in fact, for Isnenghi, Malaparte, "[c]apovolgendo il punto di vista sulla guerra, filtrando gli avvenimenti attraverso un'ottica rovesciata, contesta insieme il ruolo sociale del proletariato delle trincee (dalla rassegnazione alla rivolta) e il ruolo degli ufficiali subalterni" (360).

Of course Malaparte's move is not free from contradictions; Isnenghi warns us that, though the writer had joined the war as an infantryman, and came from a working-class family, he was, like Gadda, a staunch *interventista*, and volunteered to fight in France at 16 when Italy had not joined the war yet; he became a lieutenant in 1917; he was trusted and respected by the establishment of the Italian Army (he was a protégé of general Peppino Garibaldi, the grandson of Giuseppe, and Malaparte's commanding officer). Yet the perspective which structures his hybrid book, the point of view of a lower middle-class intellectual who believes that the Italian soldiers' refusal to fight at Caporetto was the harbinger of an oncoming revolution (similar to the one which took place in Russia in that fateful October 1917), and that the *piccolo-borghesi* like him should ally themselves with the proletarians, with the "santi maledetti," not the tottering Italian ruling classes, must necessarily also allow (or appropriate) the point of view of the marginalized peasants who made up most of the Regio Esercito.

No wonder then that Malaparte contrasts the soldiers on their military strike — leaving the trenches and their assigned positions after the collapse of the front-line, throwing away their rifles (they are also called "i *senza-fucile*" 137) and heading home — with the members of the upper and middle classes who thrived behind the front line. The whole tenth chapter describes the terrified and hysterical reactions of those — staff officers, war profiteers, Red Cross dames, shirkers of all sorts, and so forth — who "non riusciva[no] a capire perché i fanti non volessero più combattere e difenderli" (129).[14] To put it in Malaparte's terms:

Il fenomeno di Caporetto è un fenomeno strettamente sociale.
È una rivoluzione.
È la rivolta di una classe, di una mentalità, di uno stato d'animo, contro un'altra classe, un'altra mentalità, un altro stato d'animo.
È una forma di lotta di classe.

(119)

Tellingly, Malaparte's comment on the mayhem during the general retreat is: "[i]l *riso rosso* travolgeva ogni cosa" (137). The "red laughter" hints at the fact that during the retreat many soldiers got drunk on wine found in the houses they ransacked along the way, but it also hints at the Russian revolution which was raging in the same days. The color red creates a metaphoric connection between the Bolshevik revolution and the rebellion of the Italian soldiers, which Malaparte strives to depict as a "rivoluzione iniziatasi il 24 Ottobre del 1917 e *non ancora giunta al suo termine logico*" (139). Besides, an overt parallel between the two events is traced: "I due avvenimenti iniziali — facce diverse di uno stesso fenomeno — la rivoluzione russa e la rivolta di Caporetto, hanno dato origine a due movimenti paralleli, tesi ad un unico termine, ma l'uno e l'altro da un diverso spirito animati" (146). No wonder that Malaparte resorted to revolutionary literary techniques to paint the fresco of such a revolutionary event, so that his debut work should be seen as a manifestation of that wider literary revolution known as modernism.[15]

Malaparte himself was well aware of this climate of impending transformation, of the palingenetic expectations which animated the European society in those years:

Tutti i valori sociali e morali della vita si confusero: tutte le relazioni fra uomo e uomo, tra l'uomo e lo stato, fra l'uomo e la macchina, fra l'uomo e la terra, fra l'uomo e l'infinito, furono riprese in esame. L'uomo, ridivenuto umano, si accinse alla trasformazione della vita.

(144-45)

Such a paragraph spells out an original definition of what we mean by

---

[14] Here Malaparte reformulates in a radical fashion the opposition between the world of the soldiers and that of the civilians which is so common in war literature (Rossi, *Secolo* 29-31).

[15] That Malaparte ultimately supported Fascism does not necessarily make his inclusion in the modernist canon untenable, as the idea of a Fascist modernism has been proposed as dialectically complementary to its anti-authoritarian counterpart (Welge).

modernism: a very interesting rephrasing and interpretation of Ezra Pound's motto "Make it new!"

5. Concluding Remarks

Summarizing our discussion, we may say that these three authors — Gadda, Comisso, Malaparte — lived the same event (or better, different faces of the same event) in very different ways: Caporetto was a disaster and a disgrace to Gadda; an adventure to Comisso; a miscarried revolution to Malaparte. Yet they all had either to tackle the event with unconventional narrative techniques (Gadda through his modernist pieces and his diary, Malaparte through his pamphlet-novel-reportage), or tell with an elegantly classical style a story whose plot is — when it comes to the days of the rout of Caporetto in Comisso's memoir — totally destructured, an episodic odyssey in a disaster area. Saying that these three authors deliberately embraced a modernist approach to narration would be a distortion; probably it is safer to say that they were compelled to invent their own modernist solutions, which show, as we have seen, so many and remarkable points of contact with the experiences of the major figures of modernism active before, during and after the Great War.

We started by outlining a triangular relationship connecting Italian studies, modernism and war literature. After having explored three quite different narratives of the battle of Caporetto and how they may qualify as modernist works — keeping in mind Somigli's insightful contention that we should "speak not so much of modernism as of *modernisms*" ("In the Shadow" 926) in the Italian context — a conclusion may be drawn: a more accurate mapping and a deeper understanding of the relationship among the corpus of Italian Great war narratives, the wider European cultural and artistic context (modernism) and the Italian historical and cultural context enables us to open promising perspectives on such works as the *Giornale di guerra e di prigionia, Il Castello di Udine, Giorni di guerra* and *Viva Caporetto!* The discussion on war literature and modernism, however, may contribute to Italian studies not only by allowing new interpretations of Gadda, Comisso, and Malaparte (possibly well beyond their war narratives); the interaction between modernism, war literature and Italian studies may also help critics to reassess certain marginal texts, such as Alvaro's *Vent'anni* or Palazzeschi's *Due imperi... mancati*, or bring about new readings of more canonical texts (Lussu's *Un anno sull'altipiano* comes unavoidably to mind) or minor texts of canonical authors (such as Marinetti's *L'alcova d'acciaio*).

All in all, we might discover that the road to a better understanding of the Novecento (maybe the real golden century of Italian literature) runs through the dismal trenches and the ravaged no man's land of First World War battlefields. It is time that these territories were thoroughly charted, completing the pioneering exploration carried out by Isnenghi. Like the *recuperanti* — those people, usually living in the areas of northeast Italy where the battles of WWI took place, who earned their living by retrieving metal and explosives from the ammunition and discarded equipment scattered on the battlefields —[16] critics should start scavenging the wastelands created by technologized warfare, looking for the relics of modernity.

Independent scholar

---

[16] A description of this thankless and dangerous job, which was, however, attractive to the poor Italian mountain communities of the 1920s and 1930s, and the life of *recuperanti* in the Asiago plateau, can be found in Mario Rigoni Stern's 1995 novel *Le stagioni di Giacomo*.

Works Cited

Alvaro, Corrado. *Vent'anni*. 1930. Firenze, Giunti, 1995.
Baer, Ulrich. "Modernism and Trauma." Eysteninsson and Liska 307-18.
Barilli, Renato. "*Viva Caporetto!* come opera archetipa." Ed. Carmine Di Biase. *Curzio Malaparte: la rivolta del santo maledetto*. Napoli: CUEN, 1999. 19-39.
Carta, Elisabetta. *Cicatrici della memoria. Identità e corpo nella letteratura della Grande Guerra: C.E. Gadda e B. Cendrars*. Pisa: Edizioni ETS, 2010.
Chion, Michel. *Audio-Vision: Sound On Screen* (1985). Tr. Claudia Gorbman. New York: Columbia UP, 1994.
Comisso, Giovanni. *Giorni di Guerra*. 1930. Milano: Longanesi, 2009.
Contini, Gianfranco. "Nota introduttiva." Gadda. *L'Adalgisa. Disegni milanesi* i-ix.
De Angelis, Giovanna. "Il *Giornale di guerra e di prigionia* di Gadda: il diario di un 'miserabile'. *Bollettino di italianistica* 2 (2006): 219-37.
Debenedetti, Giacomo. *Il romanzo del Novecento*. 1971. Milano: Garzanti, 1987.
Dombroski, Robert S. *Gadda e il barocco*. Torino: Bollati Boringhieri, 2002.
_____. "The Meaning of Gadda's War Diary". *Italica* 47:4 (1970): 373-86.
Donnarumma, Raffaele. "Tracciato del modernismo italiano." Luperini and Tortora 13-38.
Eliot, Thomas Stearns. "The Waste Land". 1922. *The Waste Land and Other Poems*. London: Faber & Faber, 1990.
Eysteinsson, Astradur, and Vivian Liska, eds. *Modernism*. Amsterdam: Benjamin, 2007.
Fussell, Paul. *The Great War and Modern Memory*. 1975. Rpt. Oxford: Oxford UP, 1977.
Gadda, Carlo Emilio. *L'Adalgisa. Disegni milanesi*. Torino: Einaudi 1963.
_____. "Appendice al *Castello di Udine*." Gadda. *Romanzi e racconti* 828-37.
_____. *Il castello di Udine*.1934. Milano: Garzanti, 1989.
_____. *Giornale di guerra e di prigionia*. 1991. Milano: Garzanti, 2009.
_____. *Romanzi e racconti I*. Ed. Raffaella Rodondi, Guido Lucchin, and Emilio Manzotti. Milano: Garzanti, 1988.
Hemingway, Ernest. *A Farewell to Arms*. 1929. London: Grafton, 1977.
Isnenghi, Mario. *I vinti di Caporetto nella letteratura di guerra*. Venezia: Marsilio, 1967.
_____. *Il mito della grande guerra da Marinetti a Malaparte*. 1970. Bologna: Mulino, 2007.
Isnenghi, Mario and Giorgio Rochat. *La Grande Guerra: 1914-1918*. 2000. Milan: Sansoni, 2004.
Jones, Peter G. *War and the Novelist: Appraising the American War Novel*. Columbia: U of Missouri P, 1976.
Joyce, James. *Ulysses*. 1922. Harmondsworth: Penguin, 1984.
Jünger, Ernst. *Afrikanische Spiele*. 1936. Tr. Harbeck, Ingrid. *Giochi africani*. Milan: SugarCo, 1978.
Levenson, Michael. "Introduction." *The Cambridge Companion to Modernism. Second Edition*. Cambridge: Cambridge UP, 2011. 1-8.
Lucchini, Guido. "Presentazione." Gadda. *Il castello di Udine* 7-14.
Luperini, Romano, and Massimo Tortora, eds. *Sul modernismo italiano*. Napoli: Liguori, 2012.
Lussu, Emilio. *Un anno sull'altipiano*. 1945. Milan: Mondadori, 1978.
Malaparte, Curzio. *Viva Caporetto! La rivolta dei santi maledetti*. 1921. Firenze: Vallecchi, 1995.
Mileschi, Cristophe. "'La guerra è cozzo di energie spirituali': estetica ed estetizzazione della guerra in Carlo Emilio Gadda". *Bollettino '900* 1 (I semestre, 2003):

<http://www.boll900.it/2003-i/Mileschi.html>. 28 September 2014. Online.
Rigoni Stern, Mario. *Le stagioni di Giacomo*. Turin: Einaudi, 1995.
Rodondi, Raffaella. Notes to *Il castello di Udine*. Gadda. *Il castello di Udine* 803-27.
Rossi, Umberto. "Il funebre a parte della guerra. Esperienza, mito e strategie narrative in *In Parenthesis* di David Jones." *Il confronto letterario* 2 (2007): 409-32.
_____. "Joyce and the Rebus of War." *Fin de Siecle and Italy - Joyce Studies in Italy/5*. Roma: Bulzoni, 1998. 165-180.
_____. "Notizie dall'area del disastro: una lettura multidisciplinare della disfatta di Caporetto nelle pagine di Hemingway." *Un fascino osceno. Guerra e violenza nella letteratura e nel cinema*. Ed. Stefano Rosso. Verona: Ombre corte, 2006. 55-79.
_____. *Il secolo di fuoco: introduzione alla letteratura di guerra del Novecento*. Roma: Bulzoni, 2008.
Schindler, John R. *Isonzo. The Forgotten Sacrifice of the Great War*. 2001. Tr. Alessandra Di Poi. *Isonzo: il massacro dimenticato della Grande Guerra:* Gorizia: LEG, 2002.
Sherry, Vincent. *The Great War and the Language of Modernism*. Oxford: Oxford UP, 2003.
_____, ed. *The Cambridge Companion to the Literature of the First World War*. Cambridge: Cambridge UP, 2005.
Somigli, Luca. "Italy." *The Cambridge Companion to European Modernism*. Ed. Pericles Lewis. Cambridge: Cambridge UP, 2011. 75-93.
_____. "In the Shadow of Byzantium: Modernism in Italian Literature." Eysteinsson and Liska 911-29.
Somigli, Luca, and Mario Moroni, eds. *Italian Modernism: Italian Culture Between Decadentism and Avant-Garde*. Toronto: Toronto UP, 2004.
Trevelyan, George Macaulay. *Scenes from Italy's War*. Boston: Houghton Mifflin, 1919.
Welge, Jobst. "Fascist Modernism." Eysteinsson and Liska 547-59.

Davide Bellini

Kobilek di Soffici:
dalla guerra-gioco alla narrazione di una comunità

Preambolo: soldato-giocatore o soldato-operaio?
Un bilancio della letteratura sulla Grande Guerra sarebbe incompleto senza un protagonista come Soffici. La sua traiettoria culturale, dalle avanguardie al fascismo, è esemplare di molte contraddizioni del primo Novecento. In Soffici le aperture europee convivono con le chiusure nazionalistiche; il talento artistico ed espressivo non esclude la duttilità politica, talora una vera e propria tendenza a diventare organico al potere.[1] Proprio questa miscela di elementi rende assai significativa la sua testimonianza sul conflitto, che rimane affidata a tre libri: *Kobilek*, *La ritirata del Friuli* ed *Errore di coincidenza*.

Questo intervento è dedicato all'analisi di *Kobilek*.[2] Qui Soffici, tenente del 128° reggimento fanteria nella II armata del generale Capello, racconta le vicende del suo battaglione durante l'agosto del 1917, dalla partenza da Cosbana alla sofferta avanzata sull'altipiano della Bainsizza, attraverso Plava, gli sbancamenti di Palievo, il "pianoro" di Rutarsce. La battaglia terminò con un'affermazione degli italiani, ma le sorti del conflitto si sarebbero presto capovolte con il disastro di Caporetto (Faldella, Silvestri, Weber).

Oggi è disponibile una precisa ricostruzione della vicenda editoriale di *Kobilek* (Bartoletti Poggi). Il nucleo generativo del libro risale al "taccuino" del fronte: appunti presi di getto prima della grave ferita all'occhio che avrebbe costretto Soffici nell'ospedale da campo di Cormons. Si aggiunsero poi le pagine scritte per il *reportage* a puntate uscito sulla "Nazione" di Firenze nell'autunno successivo, e le dimensioni del testo quasi raddoppiarono. Nel 1918 uscì *Kobilek*, per la "Libreria della Voce", con alcuni passi censurati. Nel 1919 venne pubblicata l'edizione Vallecchi. Nel 1928, sempre presso Vallecchi, uscì infine la terza edizione, in cui i brani soppressi dalla censura furono

---

[1] Mangione ha parlato giustamente di "singolare capacità di adesione anche contraddittoria a tendenze ed eventi del reale" (115).
[2] Cito dall'edizione di *Kobilek* del 1966 della casa editrice Vallecchi. Gli altri due libri – *La ritirata del Friuli* fu pubblicato in volume da Vallecchi nel 1919; *Errore di coincidenza* uscì su "Rete mediterranea" tra il marzo e il dicembre 1920 – registrano i fatti successivi alla disfatta di Caporetto, descrivendo le travagliate, e a volte caotiche, manovre di ripiego delle truppe italiane. Per un quadro d'insieme sui diari di guerra di Soffici, cfr. Biondi e Bartoletti Poggi.

ripristinati.

Secondo Vanden Berghe, a questo processo di ampliamento e revisione corrisponderebbe un progressivo infittirsi di reminiscenze letterarie: Apollinaire e gli stilemi futuristi, certo, ma anche Dante, Leopardi, Stendhal, oltre a una "più marcata toscanizzazione" e a un recupero del "gusto ben radicato della descrizione truce ed espressivistica" (154). Rilievi pertinenti, ma non è questa la direzione che cercherò di seguire. D'altronde sulle filigrane letterarie di *Kobilek* è già disponibile una cospicua bibliografia. Anche quando si è cercato di emanciparlo dalla traiettoria futurista e lacerbiana, in effetti, sono stati evidenziati altri influssi d'avanguardia; Adamson, ad esempio, ha sottolineato il modello di Rimbaud.[3]

Ciò che propongo è di analizzare *Kobilek* non tanto in chiave di rimandi intertestuali, quanto come esempio di narrazione ideologica. Con questo libro Soffici raccontava la guerra in maniera avvincente e semplificata, sollecitando nel lettore un'adesione emotiva e acritica al conflitto. Le risorse dello scrittore sperimentale — dai chimismi lirici all'icasticità visiva e sonora — erano senz'altro presenti, ma risultavano inserite in una più solida struttura fatta di realismo prosaico e analisi psicologica *standard*, capace di catturare l'attenzione del pubblico con una narrazione ad alta leggibilità. L'estetizzazione del conflitto funzionava, e in maniera limitata, solo come elemento di distinzione (Bourdieu): assicurando al libro un'etichetta di modernità, compensava il predominio di una scrittura più convenzionale.

Tutto ciò implicava un'idea di guerra in sintonia con l'orizzonte d'attesa di un pubblico nazionale e trasversale, non più modulata sui roboanti proclami di "Lacerba" e sulla cultura di ristrette *élites* intellettuali. Per il grande pubblico, il conflitto non poteva ridursi a gioco vitalistico ed esplosione di colori, *guerre-jolie* incentrata sull'ego del soldato-poeta; era necessario puntare sull'evidenza genuina di sentimenti-base come la paura e l'angoscia, l'istinto di sopravvivenza (in cui immedesimarsi) o la solidarietà (da cui trarre l'effetto edificante). A questo nuovo universo tematico andava ora incontro la penna di Soffici. Il progetto di produzione-ricezione letteraria si adeguava insomma al trauma di un'esperienza bellica che non corrispondeva alle retoriche che l'avevano invocata. Lo ha sottolineato Isnenghi:

---

[3] "*Kobilek* contains none of the irony and brazenness that so permeated Soffici's futurist contributions to "Lacerba." The tone of the war diary is softer, more reflective, and much more reverent [...]. It was as if he sought to become immanent to reality in the manner of Baudelaire and Rimbaud. *Kobilek* is a celebration of war as a poetic fusion of art and life, a plunge into the primal that seeks to escape all traces of bourgeois identity. For Soffici, the war was the moral equivalent of Rimbaud's move to Africa, and *Kobilek* is better described as a Rimbaudian text than a futurist one. Like Rimbaud, Soffici was determined not only literally to merge himself with the natural world of sensations, but also to make his way through it joyously, however hellish it might prove" (Adamson 58).

Kobilek di Soffici: dalla guerra-gioco alla narrazione di una comunità 153

La guerra che gli intellettuali avevano voluta e corteggiata come mobilitazione e pienezza vitalistica delle energie e degli istinti, attivizzazione di tutto l'essere in senso fisico e psichico, dinamismo e spreco supremo, si manifesta e viene descritta tra le masse come fatica statica e uguale, resistenza opaca, inerte rassegnazione.

(337)

Proprio questo dualismo intellettuali-massa, a mio avviso, Soffici cercò di risolvere con *Kobilek*. Lo stesso Isnenghi si sofferma poco dopo proprio su Soffici, che secondo lui

accenna, al principio, a chiamare i fanti partecipi del suo straordinario gioco di muscoli e di nervi, ma poi ripiega più comprensivamente sul riconoscimento di questa doppia verità della guerra: che per gli uni è energica prova intensamente e soggettivamente partecipata, per gli altri è duro sacrifizio rassegnatamente e collettivamente subìto; come per gli uni è coscienza delle cause e dei fini, per gli altri è ubbidienza al proprio destino.

(337)

Eppure mi sembra che in *Kobilek*, più che una "doppia verità", ossia una frattura fra due idee di guerra, si cerchi di raccontare un'esperienza comune, il dramma di uno sforzo condiviso. Pur sottolineando le distinzioni gerarchiche, Soffici vuole rappresentare una guerra di tutti, in cui gli ufficiali condividono con i soldati il fango della stessa trincea e la miseria dello stesso rancio.

Effettivamente siamo abituati a pensare l'esperienza bellica di Soffici sotto il segno del gioco, della gioia, dell'irrazionalismo vitalistico.[4] Si tratta di un aspetto importante del libro, ma non esclusivo. D'altronde alcuni presupposti ideologici sono mutati rispetto agli anni di "Lacerba". Ora non è più pensabile la virulenta polemica anti-borghese della fase precedente. Si tratta di un Soffici diverso, deciso a rivolgersi a un pubblico più ampio e a sollecitare meccanismi di ricezione trasversali. Di lì a pochi mesi, non a caso, si sarebbe scoperto propagandista, con il giornaletto di trincea "La Ghirba" destinato a conoscere ampia diffusione tra i soldati italiani dopo Caporetto.[5] Ovviamente *Kobilek*, per complessità espressiva e strutturale, è qualcosa di molto diverso dagli opuscoli

---

[4] La lettura di Eraldo Bellini, assai valida e documentata, è fra le più significative di questo orientamento. Nella scrittura bellica di Soffici, Bellini sottolinea l'importanza dell'area semantica attinente alla gioia, all'allegria e alla felicità, nel segno di un sostanziale "svuotamento drammatico della guerra". Si tratterebbe appunto di una visione "ludica" dell'evento, che comporta una "rimozione degli orrori della guerra" e "convoglia la narrazione dei momenti più aspri della battaglia verso esiti futuristi". Tuttavia — e la notazione è significativa per il nostro discorso — anche al critico sembra che "Soffici non riesca mai a liberarsi da un senso di responsabilità nei confronti dei suoi fanti" (175-77).

[5] Il generale Capello avrebbe poi sottolineato, rispondendo alle critiche rivoltegli in merito alla trascuratezza della propaganda fra i soldati, lo sforzo economico profuso per stampare il giornaletto di Soffici: dal marzo al novembre del 1918 ne sarebbero stati pubblicati "29 numeri di circa 40.000 copie ciascuno, che al prezzo di oltre 25 centesimi per ogni copia fa salire la spesa complessiva al di là delle 300.000 lire" (27).

di propaganda che circolarono numerosi nel 1917-1918. Ma è pure evidente che con questo libro Soffici cambia direzione rispetto agli atteggiamenti elitari e provocatori che aveva tenuto in precedenza.[6] Adesso gli intellettuali d'avanguardia gli appaiono infatti "membri di *élites* discutibili" che finalmente, grazie all'esperienza interclassista del fronte, possono comprendere le ragioni di diversi attori sociali, benché genericamente definiti: dalla "massa" alla "borghesia" (*Kobilek* 21).

Non si tratta soltanto di un nuovo *milieu* sociologico. Cambia la modalità con cui si sceglie di narrare (e quindi giustificare) il conflitto. Da scrittore di guerra, Soffici tentò di risolvere la stridente contraddizione tra il soldato "giocatore" e il soldato "operaio" — il primo arruolatosi come volontario, l'altro costretto a subire la coscrizione obbligatoria — che è stata approfondita da Eric J. Leed come una struttura antropologica di fondo della Grande Guerra:

> La differenza fondamentale fra lo "spirito ludico" del volontario e gli altri soldati, che invece consideravano la guerra alla stregua di lavoro forzato, stava nelle attitudini contrapposte riguardo la vita al fronte. Per il volontario la vita era qualcosa che acquistava valore tramite il sacrificio; per il lavoratore era qualcosa da preservare ad ogni costo [...]. La realtà fisica e sociale della guerra vanificava l'ideologia di cui il volontario era portatore.
>
> (121-22)

Analizzando le memorie di alcuni combattenti tedeschi, Leed sottolinea come certi volontari

> riconobbero di essere entrati in guerra con "leggerezza", come dilettanti che non potevano essere presi seriamente dai soldati comuni, i cui stivali erano incrostati di realismo. Le loro aspettative si erano formate nel sogno di un tempo passato, un tempo in cui sembrava ancora possibile costruire un'antitesi etica al mondo borghese. Essi avevano creduto che la guerra fosse negazione dell'interesse materiale, e si ritrovarono immersi nientemeno che nella *Materialkrieg*.
>
> (123)

Kobilek è un libro interessante proprio perché rappresenta il punto di svolta per un autore che, abituato a invocare la guerra da giocatore, si scontra con una prospettiva diversa, quella grigia e alienante della guerra tecnologica. Eppure, di fronte a questa realtà, la sua reazione non è di evasione lirica o di scacco esistenziale. Al contrario, Soffici sfrutta l'occasione per lanciare un messaggio ideologicamente proattivo, al limite della propaganda. Sotto la superficie della confezione diaristica, *Kobilek* veicola una narrazione forte del conflitto, capace di enfatizzare la natura interclassista dell'esercito, l'umanità degli ufficiali, lo

---

[6] "Disprezzar la folla è poco [...]. Bisogna inebriarsi dello schifo ch'essa può causare [...]. Gioia veramente futurista di sentirsi un dio davanti a questa merda concittadina — mondiale — che non è neanche possibile odiare" (*Giornale di bordo* I, 186).

Kobilek di Soffici: dalla guerra-gioco alla narrazione di una comunità   155

sforzo comune verso la vittoria. E si trattava di un proposito tanto più urgente quanto più la guerra appariva alienante e tecnologizzata. Di fronte all'orrore disumano della trincea, occorreva umanizzare i suoi protagonisti.

Gli strumenti espressivi utilizzati per raggiungere quest'obiettivo sono molteplici: un'analisi psicologica semplificata e conciliante, sempre pronta a esaltare l'elemento umano in ogni attore del conflitto; un sistema di personaggi che rappresenta tutte le classi sociali, tutte le regioni della penisola e tutti i gradi della gerarchia militare; una struttura testuale che al frammento lirico-descrittivo alterna con efficace puntualità — nonostante l'autodefinizione "giornale di battaglia" — la durata del racconto e l'ideologia del commento.

La guerra poteva arrivare così a un pubblico non più elitario ma medio, che, attratto dal marchio di uno scrittore colto e tuttavia capace di sollecitare il piacere della lettura, assorbiva un'immagine orientata del conflitto, in cui l'esercito diventava metafora della nazione e lo sforzo bellico appariva animato da un *ethos* pre-politico, intriso di buoni sentimenti e capace di primeggiare sul non-senso della guerra di trincea.

"Interesse umano" e scansione narrativa
Non per niente, autorevoli lettori dell'epoca paragonarono *Kobilek* alla memorialistica risorgimentale, sottolineando indirettamente come il fattore umano riuscisse ad avere la meglio sulle atrocità della guerra tecnologica. Se Ungaretti si limitava ad esprimere uno scarno quanto esplicito apprezzamento,[7] Primo Conti scriveva in questi termini a Giuseppe Raimondi: "Ho letto nelle mie lunghe ore di noia il *Kobilek* di Soffici, e l'ho trovato bello, pieno di un calore vasto che si assoda in blocchi di commossa umanità. È un Soffici imprevisto e, a parer mio, importantissimo" (42). Baldini citava esplicitamente *Le noterelle d'uno dei Mille* di Abba (65). Ancora più significativa la lettura di Emilio Cecchi, che nel 1921, al momento di annunciare allo stesso Baldini l'affiliazione di Soffici alla "Ronda", si inoltrava in un paragone sorprendente:

Ho riavuto in mano *Le mie prigioni*, in questi giorni, hai notato che somiglianze di tono ci sono tra certe parti di *Kobilek, La Ritirata* etc. per innocenza, didattismo morale, interesse umano, Soffici somiglia a Pellico in un modo straordinario. È una cosa che fa ridere, sul primo momento; o sembra soltanto un *bon mot*: invece è verissima, e potrebbe servire come spunto di una interpretazione simpaticissima e rivelatrice. Soffici-Pellico. Intendi che Pellico m'è piaciutissimo.

(218; lettera inviata da Roma il 5 ottobre del 1921)

"Innocenza, didattismo morale, interesse umano": dov'era finito lo scrittore manesco e arrogante dei libri precedenti, da *Lemmonio Boreo* a *Giornale di bordo*? Ma l'intuizione di Cecchi introduce un altro problema importante, cui si

---

[7] "Con il *Kobilek* di Soffici, con questo mio *Porto*, con Baldini, non c'è altro dal fronte, di degno" (Ungaretti, *Lettere a Papini*, 31 dicembre 1917, 169).

è già avuto modo di accennare: il genere letterario di *Kobilek*, che non è di tipo puramente diaristico. In *Kobilek*, accanto alla registrazione in presa diretta, c'è la scansione narrativa lunga, che proietta sul passato una consapevolezza più strutturata dei fatti. In certi punti del testo, infatti, è l'autore stesso a dichiarare una discrasia fra tempo degli eventi e tempo della scrittura, mettendo in evidenza delle pause che lo costringono a imporre una scansione più lunga e a filtrare il vissuto attraverso la memoria. Ad esempio il 26 agosto scrive (la sezione precedente recava la data del 18 agosto):

Riprendo questi appunti che le vicende della battaglia m'impedirono di continuare giorno per giorno.
Sono ricoverato in questo ospedale per una ferita all'occhio sinistro cagionatami dallo scoppio di una granata durante l'ultima ora del combattimento, finito vittoriosamente il 23 al mattino con l'occupazione della quota 652 del monte Kobilek.

(45)

Dopo uno spazio bianco, la narrazione riparte dai fatti del 19 mattina. Una scelta simile consente innanzitutto di anticipare l'esito vittorioso della battaglia — soluzione che non sarebbe consentita a una struttura puramente diaristica. In certi punti l'illusione della forma-diario è mantenuta: vengono esibiti tempi verbali più vicini ai fatti, come il presente e il passato prossimo, e si dà rilievo alla prossimità spaziale attraverso i deittici.[8] Nel complesso prevale tuttavia una vera e propria strategia narrativa in cui sono riconoscibili artifici strutturali volti a confezionare una storia avvincente: la durata romanzesca,[9] la drammatizzazione,[10] la *suspense*.[11]

Si tratta non solo di scelte stilistiche ma anche di una diversa ricerca di effetti sul lettore. È il progetto di ricezione a cambiare di segno. Un giornale di

---

[8] "E stamani all'aurora, siamo come ho detto partiti" (9). "Scrivo appiè del muro [...]. Accanto a me [...]. Fra una mezz'ora [...]" (13). "È arrivata la posta. Se le amiche, gli amici potessero immaginare il piacere che fa ricevere un saluto, una notizia qui!" (67).
[9] Alcuni elementi dilatano il tempo narrativo, nel segno tematico dell'attesa o della sfida: è il caso degli estenuanti tentativi di neutralizzare una mitragliatrice austriaca che ostacola la marcia sull'altopiano di Rutarsce. In questo caso l'autore è abile a rendere la frustrazione serpeggiante nella truppa dando voce ad altri personaggi: "Ufficiali e soldati, eravamo arrivati al massimo dell'irritazione. Vecchi fanti, conoscitori a fondo della guerra, si facevan cattivi all'idea che forse un solo uomo era in quella caverna sopra di noi a sbarrarci la via e a tenerci in quel modo grufoloni nella polvere, cotti dal sole, avviliti dalla sete" (70).
[10] Si veda, ad esempio, il concitato episodio in cui Soffici perde contatto con il proprio reparto e rimane intrappolato in un cratere sotto il fuoco dell'artiglieria nemica (89-92).
[11] A un certo punto Soffici si accorge che i suoi uomini non hanno proseguito la marcia in direzione dell'obiettivo stabilito, e cerca di rendere la tensione vissuta in attesa che un sergente rechi notizie dagli altri reparti: "Ci volle un po' di tempo prima che tornasse, ed io lo passai nell'angoscia, pensando che da un momento all'altro il nemico poteva irrompere su noi, tagliati fuori a quel modo, e distruggerci e accerchiarci" (54).

battaglia dovrebbe enfatizzare la soggettività, il carattere irripetibile e sconnesso delle singole percezioni, l'estro dell'artista sperimentale che cattura gli eventi nel loro repentino accadere. Con il suo spazio-tempo costrittivo la guerra di trincea poteva condurre facilmente verso questa opzione: che tuttavia Soffici non adottò, come un acuto recensore (Baldini) ebbe modo di sottolineare.[12] Il diario richiede al lettore più collaborazione nel colmare gli "spazi vuoti" per la costruzione del senso; il processo della lettura è più critico e personale. Invece la scansione narrativa lunga consente di far ritornare personaggi e temi, di costruire un gruppo, di individuare obiettivi e scale di valori; fornisce al lettore una prospettiva già solida con cui giudicare gli eventi. Sull'umoralità dell'impressione o dello squarcio paesaggistico interviene il potere coesivo della memoria, della costruzione identitaria, del commento etico. Il testo trasforma il suo statuto comunicativo. Da diario, da documento di un individuo isolato, diventa narrazione di una comunità.

Sorvegliare e perdonare: la retorica della comunità
La voce narrante, non a caso, non è quella di un *outsider*, bensì di un ufficiale. Soffici è consapevole dello spirito di sacrificio dei soldati e della loro qualità umana. La scrittura mette in rilievo proprio questi elementi e sottolinea la responsabilità di chi occupa i vertici dell'istituzione militare. Si noti la frase ipotetica che chiude questo brano:

Più tardi, in un giro che abbiamo fatto insieme fra i nostri uomini, già sistemati con miracoli d'industria al riparo di qualche asse, dei teli da tenda fissati con nulla lungo un muro, a ridosso di un ciglio, tesi dal peso obliquo del fucile ritto nella melma, abbiamo ammirato tutta la loro inventiva, la pazienza, la calma, e anche la loro bontà e rassegnazione di gente abituata a tutto, mai scorata, se trattata umanamente e con giustizia.

(11)

Umanità e giustizia: sono questi i valori necessari a un ufficiale per tenere alto il morale dei soldati e guidarli verso l'obiettivo. Valori generici, intrisi di filantropico universalismo, adatti a far presa su un grande pubblico. Alla truppa si richiede una virtù passiva come la "rassegnazione", ma si è pure disposti a riconoscerle un *ethos* del lavoro, quasi nel segno di un antico sapere artigianale italico. Più avanti, a completare lo stereotipo identitario, il motivo bucolico si salda con una massiccia dose di buonismo. Soldati italiani hanno portato oleandri presso le sepolture dei caduti: "Gentilezza di cuore del nostro popolo"

---

[12] "È certo che la trincea ha un orizzonte così breve che se uno non riconnette in sé stesso gli avvenimenti nella serie del tempo con un po' di buon umore e di vero estro, l'armonia di qualunque racconto gli è spezzata, nelle pagine gli si fossilizzano i fatti e le impressioni. [...] Ogni ora divora le precedenti, non si ha mai la mente a ragionare ordinatamente lo spazio che ci può essere tra il principio e la fine di qualunque avvenimento, e le giornate vissute ricadono stancamente una sull'altra" (Baldini 65).

(11-12). A dominare è un punto di vista bonario e comprensivo che punta a rendere familiari al lettore gli umori del soldato, talvolta condensandoli in espressioni dal sapore proverbiale:

Volentieri anzi avrebbero chiacchierato e riso, se non fosse stato proibito, come spensieratamente buttavano lungo i sentieri tutto ciò che li impacciava nell'andare — il telo da tenda arrotolato insieme alla mantellina, le pinze tagliafili; persino la gavetta — e ciò malgrado tutte le nostre minacce. Ché il soldato è fatto così: tanto, sa che al momento buono ritroverà tutto, o saprà farne a meno.

(45)

Però Soffici non si limita a descrivere la truppa nel suo anonimato. Sceglie di conferire ai soldati la dignità di personaggi, assegnando a ciascuno un nome, una posizione nell'esercito, un *background* geografico e un profilo caratteriale. C'è il piemontese smanioso e audace, "tutto cordialità e ingenuità, pronto a qualunque incarico, un poco esaltato dall'avventura guerresca, e di cui è difficile dire se agisca con un tal quale eroismo o con una candida incoscienza. [...] Questa passività che c'è imposta non sa capirla" (21). C'è il siciliano goloso e sornione, che si lascia ipnotizzare dagli auspici di un'imminente pace ascoltando le chiacchiere degli ufficiali, "rimasto tutto il tempo rintanato nella sua buca sotterra, a sentire quella parola di pace ripetuta tante volte, e l'enumerazione di tante delizie, mette fuori piano piano il capo come fa la testuggine a pericolo scomparso, e resta lì attento e immoto" (30-31). C'è il bergamasco salace e carnale, che fra oscenità e bestemmie manifesta il suo desiderio di tornare a casa dalla moglie, puntualizzando però, con paesana astuzia: "Eh no! Questi signori ci mandano a casa perché si empia la moglie, ma io non mi fido e non ci casco. Finché dura la guerra, niente figlioli. A pace fatta, oh! allora sì. Boia d'un mondo ladro! Torno a casa, vuoto la botte del vino, sbornie da olio santo, tiro il collo a tutti i polli del pollaio — e ingravido la sposa" (41). C'è il fiorentino calmo e intelligente, "pizzicagnolo" di mestiere (54), capace di conquistarsi la promozione sul campo, ma animato soprattutto da un puro istinto di sopravvivenza (66). C'è, infine, il calabrese alla sua prima vedetta notturna, attanagliato da una paura quasi infantile, che Soffici si premura di confortare con paternalistica condiscendenza:

Domandai allora al povero figliolo perché tremasse e battesse i denti a quel modo. Cominciò col dirmi ch'era pel freddo; ma subito poi confessò che aveva paura. Lo rimproverai un poco schernendolo per tanta pusillanimità che bisognava vincere in tutti i modi al più presto.
Ma quella franchezza, quel terrore ridicolo, quella gioventù, mi empirono il cuore di tenerezza. La guerra mi mostrò ancora il suo volto tragico, e non potendo, come avrei voluto, abbracciare e rimettere a dormire nella sua buca di terra quel fanciullo, rimasi accanto a lui a rincorarlo e consolarlo, a spiegargli il nessun pericolo di quel suo primo servizio, per tutta l'ora del suo turno.
Nell'andarmene, dissi al capoposto di fare in modo che nelle sere successive

Pietracadella fosse comandato di vedetta più presto affinché si abituasse a poco a poco a non temere la tetraggine delle ore estreme della notte.

(18)

La superiorità psicologica dell'ufficiale sul soldato è netta. L'anima del soldato è un mondo semplice, da scoprire e manovrare con delicatezza. Ma anche l'ufficiale prova sentimenti; ha un "cuore" ed è quasi spinto ad atteggiamenti affettuosi, rispetto ai quali risultano tuttavia più efficaci piccoli accorgimenti organizzativi. Anche le risorse stilistiche del brano sono ben calibrate per arrivare a un pubblico standard: si notino il diminutivo "figliolo" e la locuzione attenuativa "[lo rimproverai] un poco", le strutture binarie "freddo"/"paura", "abbracciare"/"dormire", "rincorarlo"/"consolarlo", e l'allitterazione finale dei suoni *t-e*, "non temere la tetraggine delle ore estreme della notte", che con il suo ritmo da filastrocca sembra quasi ammonire il lettore: è facile, al fronte, ritornare preda di arcaiche paure.

Tutte queste figure sono identificabili dal cognome — Borgo, Randone, Badiale, Fondelli, Pietracadella — e a molte vengono riservati spazi di discorso diretto. Il fante non è lasciato nell'ombra dell'anonimato, coerentemente con un progetto ideologico che vuole riconoscere (e in qualche modo tipizzare) l'importanza del contributo di ciascuno alla causa comune. Siamo quindi agli antipodi della scelta di Ungaretti, che dalla "congestione" del cadavere senza nome, in *Veglia*, traeva un'energia etica volta a trascendere la contingenza del conflitto. Viceversa i combattenti di *Kobilek* vengono nominati proprio in quanto parti di un gruppo belligerante, ingranaggi di una comunità specificamente militare. Rendendosi conto del rischio del paternalismo, Soffici si sforza ogni tanto di correggerlo o prevenirlo, sottolineando una sovrapposizione di punti di vista tra ufficiale e soldato. "Guardavo intorno le facce dei miei soldati, fra i quali ero accovacciato, e in tutte leggevo i miei stessi sentimenti" (55). Il valore supremo è quello della comunità, sia pure nel rispetto delle differenze gerarchiche. "Mangiamo il pane da truppa e beviamo il nostro vino allo stesso fiasco" (23). "È difficile dire come questa collaborazione cordiale fra capi e subalterni sia utile e feconda" (42). "Cominciò lo sforzo enorme di noi tutti, maggiori, capitani e subalterni, per regolare più intelligentemente la loro marcia" (86), si dice più avanti a proposito di un momento dell'avanzata.

La retorica comunitaria che Soffici affida alle pagine di *Kobilek*, inscenando lo sforzo degli ufficiali di porsi in sintonia con il vissuto dei soldati, riflette in qualche modo le direttive che, già prima di Caporetto (e a maggior ragione dopo), i vertici dell'esercito italiano avrebbero impartito in materia di gestione comportamentale delle truppe. Così si legge in una circolare riservata di Cadorna ai Comandanti d'Armata, nel luglio 1917, sulla repressione sommaria dei fenomeni di indisciplina:

Chi punisce con la morte, si domandi sempre, in coscienza, se tutto è stato fatto da parte

sua per migliorare moralmente e materialmente le condizioni dei suoi soldati, se oltre il reprimere egli ha saputo prevenire, se egli è stato a continuo contatto con l'animo delle truppe per comprenderne le aspirazioni, i bisogni, le depressioni, il bene ed il male; se, in una parola, egli sente di dominare veramente le forze vive che gli sono state affidate, con quella scienza del cuore umano, senza la quale nessuno è stato mai un condottiero. Non sempre i Comandanti hanno sentito l'obbligo morale, che è anche una necessità pratica, di conquistare un ascendente personale sulle truppe e di saperlo adoperare. Eppure quotidiani esempi dimostrano quanto può l'autorità, quando è sentita come missione.
Dove le truppe parevano depresse, stanche e inquinate da spirito di indisciplina o da teorie sovversive è bastato un uomo di fede e di volontà per infondere in esse un'anima nuova, per mutarne, anche in pochi giorni, il carattere collettivo, e per ridonare ad esse l'efficienza bellica, infiacchita. È una constatazione che deve essere di grave ammonimento per tutti.
La guerra è lunga, metodica, logorante in quanto tende a meccanizzare anche il combattente. È necessario reagire contro il pericolo della depressione di tutti i valori essenzialmente umani del soldato, senza i quali non si combatte e non si vince.[13]

A ciascun ufficiale si richiede "scienza del cuore umano", e Soffici dimostra di possederla proprio fra le pagine di *Kobilek*. Anche di fronte agli episodi di indisciplina, nei momenti più concitati dell'avanzata, il diario documenta l'esemplare umanità del tenente: ruvido nel serrare i ranghi di fronte al pericolo, ma anche pronto a comprendere e assolvere le debolezze umane dei sottoposti. Ecco un brano di *Kobilek* che mostra una singolare coincidenza, lessicale e semantica, con la circolare di Cadorna che si è appena letta. Dopo un incisivo contrattacco austriaco, alcuni soldati indietreggiano scompostamente, ma Soffici e gli altri ufficiali riescono a trattenerli. Il testo alterna resoconto in presa diretta (anche attraverso secchi frammenti di dialogo) e commento ideologico, all'insegna di quel composito statuto formale di cui più sopra si è già parlato:

Insieme al mio capitano, ai miei colleghi sopraggiunti in quel punto, al capitano Guardi ed ai nostri graduati, attraversai il cammino a quei miserabili, urlando.
– Fermi! fermi! Cosa c'è?
– Vengono avanti con la loro cantata...
Col bastone in aria, con minacce e bestemmie, li fermammo di botto quasi tutti. Facemmo far loro dietro-front e li rimandammo al loro posto.
– Su, canaglie. Dovreste esser fucilati!
Ritornarono in sé e risalirono il bosco di corsa com'erano scesi. I due o tre che non s'eran fermati, retrocedettero ad un tratto anche loro, ed umiliati, vergognosi seguirono i compagni su per l'erta.
Questo brutto episodio mi disgustò parecchio; ma in guerra bisogna anche fare i conti con i nervi degli uomini; e del resto quella prontezza nel ritornare al fuoco, quella vergogna d'aver ceduto a un cieco istinto, mi fecero capire che non si trattava di cattivi soldati.

(61)

Anche in questo caso lo stile e il vocabolario appaiono semplificati. Ma è la

---

[13] Cito da Della Volpe (29).

Kobilek di Soffici: dalla guerra-gioco alla narrazione di una comunità

stessa scansione narrativa del semplice "episodio", articolata in un prima e un dopo, a sottolineare la problematicità della guerra, le mille insidie del cuore del soldato e la necessità di "fare i conti con i nervi degli uomini". Il fante è sempre esposto al rischio di cedere alla paura, ma può essere richiamato alla sua radice etica positiva se l'ufficiale fa il suo dovere. Così, quasi nel segno di un pentimento rituale, si può compiere la redenzione di "miserabili" e "canaglie" pronti alla fuga in soldati "umiliati" e "vergognosi", nuovamente ligi al dovere.

L'ufficiale è un mediatore fra il mondo strutturato delle esigenze militari e quello fluido e informale dei bisogni, delle ansie, del "cuore umano" di chi combatte.[14] Pur dalla sua posizione gerarchicamente distinta, egli deve saper comunicare con la truppa, comprenderne le paure e i disagi, manipolare le varie retoriche che gli consentono di entrare in sintonia coi sottoposti: da quella fisico-comica (il bastone, la bestemmia, la battuta volgare) a quella affettiva (la "tenerezza" con cui conforta la recluta di vedetta).

È di importanza decisiva, ai fini del meccanismo narrativo del libro, che proprio il personaggio che dice "io", cioè il tenente Soffici, sia un ufficiale di questo tipo. Eppure *Kobilek* non manca di rappresentare un altro tipo di ufficiale: quello che chiamerei l'ufficiale-eroe, lontano dalla trivialità dei soldati e quasi illuminato da un'aura di santità. Si tratta del maggiore Casati, a cui è rivolta anche la dedica del libro. Nel suo atteggiamento emerge una più forte distinzione di status rispetto alla truppa; egli ha un'aria "di vero Capo" (si noti la maiuscola), un aspetto "nobile e guerriero" (10). Questo tipo di ufficiale non può avere alcun dialogo informale con il soldato. Piuttosto, in lui si manifesta quell'educazione umanistica che gli consente di tenere discorsi convincenti alla truppa, attingendo a una "pienezza d'eloquenza italiana" che fa trasparire l'autorità delle istituzioni.[15] È il prototipo dell'ufficiale eroico, un vero e proprio sacerdote dell'azione militare che mescola carisma aristocratico e saper fare plebeo:

> A quell'aria marziale e nobilesca si aggiungeva ora quel suo fare risoluto da popolano e insieme un carattere come di santità che inquietava. [...] Mantenne questa sicurezza mistica durante tutto il combattimento, provocando in noi tutti che lo seguivamo un senso di riverenza, ma anche di sconcerto, e magari di ripugnanza, quasi che quell'altezza morale scoraggiasse gli ultimi resti del nostro egoismo, della nostra miseria troppo umana.
>
> (105)

Visto il proposito ideologico ed editoriale di un testo come *Kobilek*, sarebbe

---

[14] Certi passaggi sottolineano quasi un'istintiva empatia, una capacità di cogliere immediatamente gli umori del battaglione: "In tutti s'indovinava l'impazienza di andarsene, di allontanarsi al più presto dalla posizione" (15).
[15] "Parla meravigliosamente, con quella chiarezza e forza di lingua propria ai buoni toscani nutriti di ottimi studi e che sanno dar concretezza ed evidenza alle idee più complesse; esprimere le sensazioni più raffinate" (25).

stato impossibile affidare al maggiore Casati la voce narrante. La grande guerra italiana andava combattuta anche da carismatici eroi (retaggio dannunziano?), ma poteva essere narrata soltanto da chi sapeva parlare con la truppa — non solo alla truppa.[16] Si noti infatti il "noi tutti" che, in antitesi all'ufficiale-asceta, accomuna il tenente Soffici agli altri soldati; in questo modo la voce narrante ribadisce di appartenere alla più vasta comunità dell'esercito, e continua a sollecitare la benevola comprensione del lettore.

Lo stile amaro della guerra e le sicurezze del lettore
La "miseria troppo umana" (eco nietzscheana) di chi soffre e combatte minacciato dalle mitragliatrici, cui Soffici senz'altro si accomuna, stimola in effetti un peculiare meccanismo di ricezione. Il lettore è chiamato a immedesimarsi con le debolezze del soldato e, in buona misura, ad assolverle. D'altronde lo stesso Soffici si auto-raffigura in momenti di difficoltà e di paura, quasi sottolineando la propria inerme condizione umana di fronte al pericolo.[17]

Ciò non significa che il tasto sublime-eroico sia del tutto espunto dalle possibilità espressive del libro. Soffici sapeva di non poterne abusare, soprattutto in quella variante demagogico-nazionalistica così inflazionata nel discorso pubblico del tempo.[18] Ma in alcuni selezionati punti il sublime riemerge, affiancandosi così alla patina sperimentale e futurista come secondo elemento di prestigio formale del libro. In questo caso si tratta di una possibilità retorica che nasce dal contenuto stesso della narrazione, e che può strizzare l'occhio a lettori forniti di una tradizionale attrezzatura umanistica. Infatti *Kobilek* parla (anche) di un'avanzata vittoriosa, che si consuma per di più nello scenario quasi mitologico di una leggendaria montagna. Così, nel finale, quando ormai si è consolidata la vittoria, le truppe italiane che sostano assetate sul giogo roccioso

---

[16] L'aura di superiorità che promana dal maggiore Casati non è questione di grado militare. Infatti lo stesso generale Capello viene rappresentato come uomo bonario e cordiale, disponibile a pranzare con i sottoposti e perfino a scherzare sul proprio aspetto fisico (7-9).
[17] Ecco alcune righe tratte dall'episodio del cratere: "Già m'intenerivo immaginando il mio cadavere [...]. Una terribile voglia di piangere mi saliva alla gola" (91-92).
[18] Nonostante si trovino in *Kobilek* molti accenni all'italianità e al patriottismo, i *topoi* più abusati della retorica ufficiale sono accuratamente evitati. Soffici faceva parte della II armata, dove era diffusa l'irritazione verso comizi e cerimonie. Durante l'estate del 1917, scrive Silvestri, parate ed esortazioni si erano intensificate in tutto l'esercito: "Ai conferenzieri specializzati si aggiungevano gli ufficiali superiori ed i generali più audaci che, dando sfogo a segrete ambizioni letterarie, volevano rivaleggiare in abilità oratoria e dialettica con i professionisti della penna e della parola, per accendere nella folla grigia dei soldati la fede e l'entusiasmo. [...] Nella II Armata un certo freno alla logorrea stereotipata era posto proprio dal generale Capello, che il tono retorico e roboante di quelle declamazioni convinceva poco. [...] E si sforzava, a voce e con circolari, di far capire ai comandi dipendenti che per parlare alla truppa bisognava scegliere concetti semplici, persuasivi ed umani" (207).

Kobilek di Soffici: dalla guerra-gioco alla narrazione di una comunità   163

danno vita a una scena di "solennità eschilea", e l'autore si spinge fino al tecnicismo nel proporre il paragone con la tragedia greca.[19]

Più spesso prevale invece un realismo prosaico, coerente con gli stenti e le amarezze del fronte, e per questo poco propenso ad incongrue impennate di tono. Così il diluvio che sferza il battaglione, nella parte più drammatica dell'avanzata, non è declinato in chiave simbolica come lavacro purificatore, ma nella sua miserabile realtà di "fango" avvilente (80). Il prosaico e il banale sono assai diffusi, e lambiscono anche le più sconvolgenti immagini di morte. Si notino gli ultimi due elementi della seguente enumerazione, dedicata a descrivere una distesa di cadaveri: "Di sotto il terriccio ripiovuto su di essi nelle esplosioni immense, uscivano mani gonfie, nere di bruciaticcio, ginocchia infrante, scarpe fangose, spalle verdi o violette, miste ad elmetti squarciati, a mitragliatrici, fucili, baionette in frantumi, tegami e coperte" (83).

Però il lettore, se da un lato dev'essere colpito dall'immagine cruenta, dall'altro va rassicurato attraverso un'adeguata cornice narrativa che smorzi il potenziale di *shock* del racconto bellico. L'obiettivo non è quello di colpevolizzare chi legge o minarne le certezze (specialmente politiche), ma piuttosto di renderlo partecipe dell'atmosfera di sofferenza e tensione che si respira al fronte. Si noti, nel brano seguente, il contrasto tra la crudezza espressiva con cui viene descritta la ferita del soldato moribondo e il veloce, ma risolutivo accenno all'*happy ending* della sua disavventura:

Quando potei rialzar la testa vidi infatti, un poco più basso di me, il corpo d'un uomo che sussultava come in agonia. Attraverso un buco tondo nell'elmetto, forato da una pallottola come fosse stato di cartone, vedevo il sangue rosso palpitare sgorgando dal cervello, mentre altro sangue colava giù da un occhio del disgraziato.
Urlai al portaferiti di condur subito quel moribondo al posto di medicazione in fondo alla valle. I portaferiti accorsero infatti e lo trascinarono via.
(Ho poi saputo che quel soldato non era morto, non solo, ma che "stava benino!").

(71)

Invece gli aspetti politici o economici che hanno scatenato il conflitto restano fuori dall'universo tematico del libro. Nessuna istituzione extra-militare è nominata; non si fa alcun cenno alla monarchia né al parlamento, mentre solo un rapido passaggio viene dedicato alla visita di Bissolati e Amendola, per inserire una polemica digressione sulla "frollaggine" socialista e sui futuri diritti dei

---

[19] "Coro formidabile, scenario, solennità eschilea che sbigottiva l'animo, come se un qualche momento eroico d'antica storia fosse tornato improvvisamente a ripetersi, o si rappresentasse lassù l'ultimo atto di una tragedia grandiosa. Questa immagine teatrale era resa ancora più viva dal gruppo centrale di cui facevo parte. Il terreno, dalle rocce a noi, era pianeggiante, così da formare una specie di palco, e su quello che si sarebbe potuto dire il proscenio, un gruppo di massi che pareva messo là a bella posta per i principali attori del dramma" (131).

combattenti.[20] La guerra viene offerta al lettore come esperienza scontata, necessaria, semplice; un dato da vivere e da accettare su un piano etico (ancor prima che estetico) e non politico.

Tra sperimentalismo e leggibilità
Un esame anche rapido degli altri aspetti linguistici e stilistici del libro conferma come l'obiettivo di Soffici fosse il compromesso tra soluzioni avanguardistiche e una *koiné* espressiva più facilmente accessibile a un pubblico ampio. Soffici è sempre attento a cercare soluzioni equilibrate che stimolino il lettore senza richiedere una decodifica complessa. Le immagini stranianti ci sono, ma sempre sostanziate di una semplicità denotativa e quasi didascalica: elementi presenti, ad esempio, nel brano in cui viene descritta l'indifferenza degli uccelli che cinguettano tra i proiettili e saltellano sul filo spinato (25). O, ancora, nei referenti delle similitudini con cui si cerca di rendere il suono della mitragliatrice, tutti attinti al versante di esperienze familiari e pacifiche, persino erotiche:

Mi colpì la diversità di suono delle pallottole che, a seconda della distanza onde provengono, dell'accelerazione del tiro, può sembrare un fischio, un miagolìo, un ronzìo, e talvolta rassomiglia a quello di un bacio, lungo, fine, e che ha persino qualcosa di dolce e voluttoso. Mi accorsi nello stesso tempo che quando invece battevano nel tronco, nei rami di qualche albero, o nei sassi in cresta al muricciolo, il rumore che facevano era simile a quello di un piccolo petardo, o di quei confetti che da ragazzi si fanno scoppiare per chiasso fra i piedi della gente.

(50-51)

In questo brano troviamo fra l'altro una vera costante del libro, i deverbali in *-ìo*: utili certo a una ricerca fonosimbolica che catturi il dinamismo sonoro dei mille pericoli del fronte, e chiaramente riconoscibili nella loro filiazione pascoliana prima ancora che futurista.[21]

Le metafore possono attingere anche a un immaginario animale, quasi favolistico: "La mitragliatrice seguitava a cantare come un cattivo uccello" (52); oppure domestico e rustico: "le zolle scottavano sotto di me come i mattoni di

---

[20] Qui non è possibile, per ragioni di spazio, affrontare il problema del rapporto di Soffici con il fascismo; ma forse ha ragione Ceva quando mette in guardia dalla facilità con cui, leggendo libri come *Kobilek*, "forse troppo e ingiustamente suggestionati dal suo 'dopo' politico — ci crediamo autorizzati [...] a registrare i prodromi della 'trincerocrazia' fascista, nel suo miscuglio di arroganza e di inganno, insomma l'Italia del ventennio" (108).
[21] Fra le numerose attestazioni: "ticchettìo" (15, 50), "tramestìo" (15), "saltellìo" (20), "rosicchìo" (20), "crepitìo" (22, 59), "brulichìo" (27), "martellìo" (28), "ronzìo" (28, 50, 62), "miagolìo" (50), "sfavillìo" (59), "scatenaccìo" (60), "pigolìo" (62), "spicinìo" (63), "crivellìo" (87), "trapestìo" (88), "sibilìo" (89), "sfrascheggìo" (93), "bisbiglìo" (100), "frastaglìo" (101).

un forno arroventato" (89). Altrove alla mitragliatrice è riferito un selezionato vocabolario di temi verbali, ingegnoso e straniante nel segno di quell'interferenza con il quotidiano che abbiamo già visto: *strepitare* (52), *gracidare* (81), *sputare* (83), *urlare* (88).

Non mancano formule comuni e quasi banali ("pallido come un cadavere" 73), in direzione nettamente contraria ai cromatismi d'avanguardia pur presenti nel libro (si ricordino le già citate "spalle verdi o violette" dei cadaveri). Ciò è funzionale a una precisa poetica di ricezione: rappresentare la guerra come esperienza semplice e ravvicinata, ormai quotidiana necessità del gruppo più che diletto estetico dell'ufficiale-artista.

Certo non si può negare la ricercatezza formale di alcuni punti. Però non si tratta soltanto di stilemi d'avanguardia, come spesso viene sottolineato; al contrario, certi artifici retorici vogliono andare in direzione di una maggiore godibilità del testo, per attirare un lettore incline non tanto alle trovate sperimentali ma magari all'eleganza lirica del dettato. Assegnerei a questa fattispecie diversi casi di allitterazione e omoteleuto.[22] Non manca, del resto, la ricerca di espedienti di prosa ritmica: spesso accade di incontrare unità sintattiche che coincidono con precisi moduli metrici.[23] Sono invece assai rare le frasi nominali, a conferma del prevalere di una sintassi più convenzionale e scorrevole.

Numerosi, infine, i tecnicismi militari.[24] La dimensione della guerra tecnologica andava necessariamente nominata, in ossequio ai propositi documentari del libro; ma solo per mostrare come, sul non-senso di una violenza meccanica e senza volto, prevalesse l'umanità di un esercito in cui il pubblico dei lettori poteva immedesimarsi, uscendo gratificato dal racconto della battaglia.

Conclusione
La guerra raccontata da Soffici in *Kobilek* rispecchia bene il carattere mosso e quasi metamorfico del suo percorso di scrittore. Ma è anche un buon esempio di "concretizzazione" ideologica dell'esperienza militare, attraverso un codice letterario che – contaminandosi con la cronaca e la propaganda – si fa quasi paraletterario. Un autore che aveva esordito sotto il segno di un individualismo

---

[22] "Notte stellata limpida fra le piante tranquille" (58); "questa attesa ardente" (69); "una luce come di storia e di gloria" (77); "vinti da tanta miseria" (84); "nel caldo e chiaro crepuscolo" (96). È evidente, invece, che molte sinestesie (ad esempio "bianchezza del cielo infiammato", 93) andranno più opportunamente ricondotte al retaggio avanguardista.
[23] Si notino i due endecasillabi contenuti nel seguente periodo: "*E al ricordo della lunga delizia* si torce sulla coperta *che abbraccia e morde con comica furia*" (40); ognuno dei quali, fra l'altro, è concluso dal modulo aggettivo + sostantivo.
[24] Fra gli altri: "giberne" (20), "perforatrici" (20), "mine" (28), "granate" (25), "bombarde" (33), "shrapnel" (59), "marmittoni" (48), "otturatori" (60), "torpedini" (61).

provocatorio e aggressivo si trovava a dover narrare un'esperienza drammatica, collettiva, nazionale. Cementando una mitologia della comunità, decideva così di rivolgersi ad un pubblico ampio, sostanzialmente medio, per favorire una lettura basata non tanto sul trauma e sullo straniamento, quanto sull'identificazione e la comprensione. In questo senso, i modelli formali che più lo favorivano non erano quelli puramente soggettivi del diario, ma una scansione narrativa che guardava anche a strutture più solide, capaci di articolare sviluppi temporali e quadri di personaggi. Anche la lingua collaborava in tal senso, producendo una peculiare coesistenza tra punte sperimentali e leggibilità. Allora, i prossimi studi su Soffici – e su tutta l'area degli scrittori "militanti" degli anni Dieci, lacerbiani o vociani che si confrontarono con l'esperienza del conflitto – potranno forse guardare con interesse a questo nesso, probabilmente nevralgico, tra metamorfosi ideologiche e progetto di ricezione, che *Kobilek* rappresenta in maniera così peculiare.

Università di Palermo

Opere citate

Adamson, Walter L. "Soffici and the Religion of Art." *Fascist Visions. Art and Ideology in France and Italy* 46-72.

Baldini, Antonio. "Soffici sul Kobilek." *I libri del giorno* (maggio 1918): 64-66.

Baldini, Antonio, e Emilio Cecchi. *Carteggio. 1911-1959*. A cura di M. C. Angelini, M. Bruscia et alii. Roma: Edizioni di Storia e Letteratura, 2003.

Bartoletti Poggi, Maria. "Nota a *Kobilek*." Soffici. *I diari della grande guerra: "Kobilek" e "La ritirata del Friuli", con i taccuini inediti*. Firenze, Vallecchi: 1986. 43-58.

Bellini, Eraldo. "Soffici, Ungaretti e la guerra." Bellini 175-77.

———. *Studi su Ardengo Soffici*. Milano: Vita & Pensiero, 1987.

Biondi, Marino. "Soffici, la guerra e la memoria fedele." Soffici. *I diari della grande guerra: "Kobilek" e "La ritirata del Friuli", con i taccuini inediti*. Firenze, Vallecchi: 1986. 7-42.

Bourdieu, Pierre. *La distinzione. Critica sociale del gusto*. Bologna: Il mulino, 2001.

Capello, Luigi. *Per la verità*. Milano: Treves, 1920.

Ceva, Lucio. *Teatri di guerra. Comandi, soldati e scrittori nei conflitti europei*. Milano: Franco Angeli, 2005.

Conti, Primo, e Giuseppe Raimondi. *Carteggio. 1918-1980*. A cura di P. Mania. Roma: Edizioni di Storia e Letteratura. Fiesole: Fondazione Primo Conti, 2001.

Della Volpe, Nicola. *Esercito e propaganda nella Grande guerra*. Roma: Ufficio Storico SME, 1989.

Fascist visions. Art and Ideology in France and Italy. A cura di M. Affron and M. Antliff. Princeton: Princeton UP, 1997.

Faldella, Emilio. *Le battaglie dell'Isonzo. 1915-1917*. Milano: Longanesi, 1965.

Isnenghi, Mario. *Il mito della grande guerra*. 1989. Bologna: Il mulino, 2014.

Leed, Eric J. *Terra di nessuno. Esperienza bellica e identità personale nella Prima Guerra Mondiale*. Bologna: Il mulino, 1985.

Kobilek di Soffici: dalla guerra-gioco alla narrazione di una comunità 167

Mangione, Daniela. "Violamammola e allegro giustiziere. Aggressività e vitalismo in Ardengo Soffici." *Sincronie* 6.12 (luglio-dicembre 2002): 111-20.

Mutterle, Anco Marzio. "Ardengo Soffici scrittore di guerra." *Umanesimo e tecnica*: 115-36.

Silvestri, Mario. *Isonzo 1917*. Torino: Einaudi, 1965.

Soffici Ardengo. *I diari della grande guerra: "Kobilek" e "La ritirata del Friuli"*. *Con i taccuini inediti*. A cura di M. Bartoletti Poggi e M. Biondi. Firenze: Vallecchi, 1986.

———. *Giornale di bordo*. Opere, vol. IV. Firenze: Vallecchi, 1961.

———. *Kobilek. Giornale di battaglia*. Firenze: Libreria della Voce, 1918.

———. *Kobilek. Giornale di battaglia*. 1919; 1928; 1937; 1960. Firenze: Vallecchi, 1966.

Umanesimo e tecnica. Studi raccolti in occasione del centenario dell'Istituto tecnico statale per geometri G. B. Belzoni di Padova. A cura di Margherita Piva et alii. Padova: Liviana, 1969.

Ungaretti, Giuseppe. *Il porto sepolto*. A cura di Carlo Ossola. Padova: Marsilio, 1990.

Ungaretti, Giuseppe. *Lettere a Soffici: 1917-1930*. A cura di P. Montefoschi e L. Piccioni. Firenze: Sansoni, 1981.

Vanden Berghe, Dirk. *Ardengo Soffici dal romanzo al "puro lirismo"*. Vol. 1. *Modelli narrativi e poetici*. Vol. 2. *Testi inediti (1908-1910)*. Firenze: Olschki, 1997

———. "La memoria letteraria nell'elaborazione di 'Kobilek'". *Ardengo Soffici dal romanzo al "puro lirismo"*. Vol. 1, *Modelli narrativi e poetici* 150-161.

Weber, Fritz. *Dal Monte Nero a Caporetto. Le dodici battaglie dell'Isonzo (1915-1917)*. Milano: Mursia, 1967.

Alberto Comparini

Sbarbaro e la rappresentazione *negativa* della Grande Guerra: per una lettura modernista dei "trucioli di guerra" (1917-1919)[1]

> Sbarbaro, estroso fanciullo, piega versicolori
> carte e ne trae navicelle che affida alla fanghiglia
> mobile d'un rigagno; vedile andarsene fuori.
> Sii preveggente per lui, tu galantuomo che passi:
> col tuo bastone raggiungi la delicata flottiglia,
> che non si perda; guidala a un porticello di sassi.
> (Eugenio Montale, *Epigramma*)

In questo saggio offrirò una lettura modernista dei "trucioli di guerra" di Camillo Sbarbaro, apparsi sulla "Riviera Ligure" tra il luglio 1917 e il giugno 1919. La scelta di questa scheggia dell'opera dell'autore ligure risponde all'esigenza di descrivere l'orizzonte epistemologico (in termini di realismo e di poetica, di storia letteraria e di reazione estetica) che caratterizzò il primo Novecento, in una finestra temporale che va dal 1910, *annus horribilis* e prefigurazione filosofico-spirituale nell'arte della catastrofe collettiva della Grande Guerra, al 1919, anno del Trattato di Versailles e teatro della cena delle ceneri del primo conflitto mondiale. Inoltre, la mancata adesione da parte di Sbarbaro a quel processo di interiorizzazione etico-civile della guerra non solo a livello politico, ma anche (e soprattutto) a livello letterario, rende la sua produzione artistica di assoluto interesse per quanto concerne la rappresentazione negativa della guerra.

Nella prima parte del mio lavoro esaminerò e discuterò alcune diatribe storico-letterarie che fino ad oggi hanno precluso una lettura modernista dei *Trucioli* (1920), i cui frammenti lirici sono stati ricondotti a correnti artistiche espressioniste e/o impressioniste. In questa sezione proporrò tre linee guida (una geografica, la "Riviera Ligure", una storica, la Grande Guerra, e una teorica, il frammentismo) per affrontare la questione del modernismo in Sbarbaro. Nella seconda parte, dopo una breve introduzione filologica, commenterò alcuni tra i trucioli di guerra più importanti della raccolta; così facendo, mostrerò come la cifra modernista di Sbarbaro non trovi forma solamente attraverso la

---

[1] Il testo qui proposto è costituito dalla rielaborazione di un intervento ("Sbarbaro and the 'trucioli di guerra'") che ho pronunciato al convegno "The Myth of the Great War" organizzato da Fabio Finotti presso il "Center for Italian Studies" dell'Università della Pennsylvania il 24 e 25 aprile 2014. Dedico questo lavoro a Laura, per la sua ostinata pazienza e il suo amore.

Annali d'italianistica 33 (2015). *The Great War & the Modernist Imagination in Italy*

rappresentazione della realtà *per fragmenta*, ma anche attraverso l'utilizzo del monologo interiore — il *medium* che permette all'io sbarbariano di fondere dimensione lirica e dimensione narrativa all'interno del testo letterario.

Sebbene questo saggio abbia un taglio strettamente monografico (Sbarbaro, il modernismo e i trucioli di guerra), ho cercato di fornire alcuni spunti storico-teorici e geografico-culturali per allargare lo spettro di indagine alla polveriera letteraria della "Riviera Ligure" (1895-1919),[2] la cui sperimentazione letteraria contribuì, indirettamente, allo sviluppo del modernismo italiano. La figura di Sbarbaro, quindi, deve essere considerata e letta anche come un punto di partenza, come una sorta di monade benjaminiana da cui ripartire per tracciare un nuovo profilo critico-interpretativo di questa straordinaria stagione primonovecentesca della letteratura italiana.

1. *Problemi di critica letteraria: Sbarbaro, le avanguardie e il modernismo*
Come ricorda Antonello Perli ne *La parola necessaria* (2008), la (s)fortuna critica di Camillo Sbarbaro ha attraversato due fasi: la prima, filologica, che ha trovato una parziale risoluzione con la pubblicazione nel 1985 dell'opera in versi e in prosa dello scrittore ligure, e la bibliografia degli scritti, pubblicata l'anno successivo; la seconda, dicotomica, o, per dirla con Adorno, la dialettica negativa tra "lo Sbarbaro 'poeta' rispetto allo Sbarbaro 'prosatore' e della conseguente sovrapposizione di *Pianissimo* a scapito dei *Trucioli* che ha contraddistinto la più effusa e pregiudicata produzione saggistica e antologica sullo scrittore" (Perli 2008: 7). Se, infatti, la precarietà filologico-testuale dell'opera sbarbariana ha generato (e in un certo qual modo salvaguardato) un interesse sul fronte ermeneutico per i *Trucioli* — un interesse inaugurato dai fondanti, e ancora oggi fondamentali, saggi di Franco Contorbia (1974) e Domenico Astengo (1983) e culminante nel volume di Simone Giusti (1997) e nel prezioso intervento di Pasquale Guaragnella (2011) —, il primato critico e poetico di *Pianissimo* sui *Trucioli* ha condannato le prose di Sbarbaro a una esistenza limbica, a tratti purgatoriale.

Non è certo mia intenzione intervenire sulla *vexata quaestio* del rapporto tra poesia e prosa, o, in termini crociani, tra poesia e non poesia, di Sbarbaro, sulla quale sono stati ampiamente versati fiumi di inchiostro. Tuttavia, è innegabile che l'insistenza della critica su questo scontro teorico-letterario abbia creato una situazione di stasi interpretativa che ha ricondotto la poetica del frammento di Sbarbaro a un principio organizzativo di impronta espressionista e/o impressionista.

Mentre Gianfranco Contini, dopo aver definito Sbarbaro "l'esempio italiano più rigoroso della prosa d'arte frammentistica" (Contini 1968: 726), lo aveva escluso dalla cerchia espressionista vociana (Contini 1988: 89-95) — e così pure

---
[2] Per la storia di questa rivista, si vedano Boero 1980, 1984 e 2003, e Boero-Merlanti-Aveto 2003.

Clelia Martignoni (1995) —, Romano Luperini (1981: 229-230) e Federico Castigliano (2014) considerano lo Sbarbaro prosatore uno scrittore espressionista *stricto sensu*. Giusti (1997: 152-154) e Perli (2008: 59), invece, rileggono la poetica sbarbariana in termini espressivo-impressionistici, riconducendola a quella del "maestro" — come lo definì Luciano Anceschi (1990: 112-113) — di Sbarbaro: Ardengo Soffici.[3]

Luperini ha recentemente corretto la propria posizione, definendo Sbarbaro (poeta) un "autore che, nonostante la matrice vociana, è difficile collocare nell'avanguardia espressionista" (Luperini 2012: 12).[4] Inoltre, egli l'ha inserito nel canone della poesia modernista che, secondo Luperini, Sbarbaro avrebbe inaugurato "insieme ai crepuscolari" e "al primo Montale", "quello compreso fra *Quaderno genovese*, *Accordi* e gli altri testi poetici del quinquennio 1918-1923 che fanno parte di *Ossi di seppia*" (2011: 93). Il nome di Sbarbaro (in questo caso nella duplice veste di poeta e prosatore) compare anche nel "tracciato del modernismo italiano" di Raffaele Donnarumma accanto ai nomi di altri scrittori — Luigi Pirandello, Federico Tozzi, Italo Svevo, Enrico Pea, Alberto Savinio, Giovanni Boine, Guido Gozzano, Marino Moretti, Clemente Rebora, Giuseppe Ungaretti — protagonisti di quella stagione che Donnarumma definisce "modernismo storico" (2012: 21-23).[5]

Per quanto ancora nebuloso e non del tutto chiaro nelle sue molteplici linee direttrici, il richiamo al modernismo quale categoria estetica per rileggere l'opera di Sbarbaro, e, nel nostro caso, i *Trucioli*, mi sembra particolarmente proficuo. Anche se la critica italiana (diversamente da quella anglo-americana) ha distinto, a livello storico e a livello formale, il modernismo dalle avanguardie,[6] il canone modernista italiano è ancora distante da una sua completa affermazione, soprattutto per quanto concerne gli autori minori — minori rispetto ai grandi scrittori modernisti, quali Italo Svevo, Luigi Pirandello, Federico Tozzi e Carlo Emilio Gadda, per i quali la ricerca scientifica ha raggiunto risultati eccellenti.[7] E un autore "minore" come Sbarbaro, e così altri poeti della sua generazione (non solo per motivi anagrafici ma per ragioni

---

[3] Su Soffici e l'impressionismo letterario, si veda Cangiano 2011.
[4] Ivan Pupo notava già nel 1999 una certa convergenza tra le soluzioni "formali e tematiche dell'espressionismo vociano" individuate da Luperini e quelle moderniste di "Luigi Pirandello e Federico Tozzi" (1999: 137, nota 29).
[5] Nell'altra curatela dedicata al modernismo italiano (Moroni-Somigli 2004), il nome di Sbarbaro non è citato né discusso. Picchione inserisce Sbarbaro in un gruppo di scrittori modernisti ("Pirandello, Svevo, D'Annunzio, Campana, Gozzano, Ungaretti, Sbarbaro, Montale, sono inseribili nella cornice generale del modernismo"), senza però giustificare tale ricostruzione storico-letteraria attraverso un'analisi testuale o attraverso una discussione teorica del soggetto sbarbariano rispetto alle filosofie dell'essere degli altri poeti menzionati (Picchione 2012: 25).
[6] Castellana 2010: 27-30, Donnarumma 2012: 15-21.
[7] Minghelli 2002, Donnarumma 2006, Castellana 2009, Baldi 2010.

poetiche e di geografia letteraria) che hanno collaborato attivamente alle pagine della "Riviera Ligure", compaiono all'interno di una (potenziale) rassegna della letteratura modernista italiana solamente in veste citazionale.

La strada verso una lettura modernista di Sbarbaro sembra essere suggerita da diversi fattori. In primo luogo, la dimensione geografico-culturale all'interno della quale il poeta ligure si è affermato, cioè la "Riviera Ligure", teatro di un interessantissimo dibattito, privo però di una linea editoriale ben definita. Ciò è suggerito altresì dal proteiforme materiale letterario pubblicato dai fratelli Mario e Angiolo Silvio Novaro, che ha permesso a Sbarbaro di poter *attraversare* e *sperimentare* la poetica del frammento secondo i proprî bisogni estetici (già iniziata, con esiti diversi da quelli della "Riviera Ligure", sulla "Voce" derobertisiana), senza dover necessariamente rispondere a un manifesto politico-letterario.[8]

Il passaggio alla "Riviera Ligure", o meglio, l'allontanamento dalla "Voce", da parte di Sbarbaro può essere letto sotto diverse lenti diacritiche: l'estetica non strettamente vociana dell'autore; il rifiuto della mitologia bellica; l'amicizia con Angelo Barile; l'apertura dialettica da parte di Mario Novaro a sperimentalismi letterarî di vario genere; la figura di Giovanni Boine — figura molta cara a Sbarbaro e a cui i *Trucioli* devono molto dal punto di vista filosofico e soprattutto linguistico (Zoboli 2006).

Tuttavia, mi sembra opportuno notare che è proprio grazie a questi fecondi ambienti intellettuali — come sarà poi "Solaria", vero e proprio "organo militante del modernismo italiano" (Donnarumma 2012: 23) —, dove "la concezione del lavoro" e il "rapporto tra intenzione e risultato artistico" non presupponevano "la dimensione del gruppo o del movimento organizzato", né comportavano "l'elaborazione di poetiche condivise (e spesso transartistiche), la stesura o la sottoscrizione di manifesti" (Castellana 2010: 28), che l'estetica modernista trovò una prima cellula embrionale a livello geografico-culturale e poté sviluppare, lentamente, una propria identità (per quanto molteplice e multiforme) storico-letteraria.

Il processo poetico che porterà Sbarbaro a definire la prosa come la sua personale "terraferma" (Sbarbaro 1985: 473) è figlio di un attraversamento letterario ed esistenziale frammentario, scrive Castigliani, "contrassegnato da una spiccata propensione per la palinodia e lo sperimentalismo" (2014: 112) che ha comportato l'amaro riconoscimento da parte dello scrittore del fallimento dell'istanza lirica di *Pianissimo* e il *necessario* passaggio al fertile terreno della prosa:

[...] la prosa è venuta cioè configurandosi come "forma" dell'apertura (della scoperta del "mondo" fenomenico, dell'oggetto, della "realtà") necessaria a quell'espressione del mondo intimo del poeta, dell'"io lirico", divenuta e sentita come ormai impossibile o

---

[8] Per una storia della "Voce", si vedano Mazzotti 1995 e Carpi 2009.

impraticabile nei confini di una poetica della negatività del soggettivismo introspettivo.
(Perli 2008: 228)

Abbandonandosi nelle braccia della prosa, come si legge in una lettera indirizzata ad Angelo Barile del 1912 (Sbarbaro 1985: 554), Sbarbaro sperava di poter diventare "un altro", lasciando dietro a sé "la sua vecchia pelle", liberandosi così di "[s]e stesso" (Sbarbaro 1985: 45) e colmando quella "mancata integrazione ontologica tra l'' io' e la realtà'" (Pavarini 1997: 54) che aveva caratterizzato il disincanto estetico di *Pianissimo*. I *Trucioli*, allora, si presentano quale superamento artistico ed esistenziale della dimensione puramente estetizzante e soggettiva della poesia lirica, e vanno intesi quindi come una svolta dialettica ed epistemologica della poetica di Sbarbaro, nella misura in cui egli ha cercato nella commistione tra poesia e narrativa, tra soggettivismo e oggettivismo, una nuova *forma mentis* per rispondere al nuovo orizzonte filosofico venutosi a creare all'inizio del Novecento e sviluppatosi attorno ai poli rifrangenti del 1910 e della Grande Guerra.

Mentre la singolare esperienza di *Pianissimo* era dovuta a una vera e propria "deficienza dell'essere" (Harrison 2014: 109-77), la cui sintomatologia (e teleologia poetica) può essere ricondotta e associata alla crisi del 1910, quando l'improvvisa esplosione di morte (fisica e metafisica) era divenuta icona dell'impossibilità della vita di configurarsi "come valore centrale per l'uomo etico" (Lukács 1967: 121), il passaggio alla prosa (e, nello specifico, al frammentismo) segue un paradigma diverso, legato inevitabilmente alla sconfitta dell'uomo nei confronti della Storia durante la prima guerra mondiale. Se *Pianissimo* figura quale momento dello Spirito Assoluto quando l'arte espressionista diventa — scrive Harrison — "la prefigurazione spirituale di una fatalità indicibilmente tragica, riscontrabile nei toni degli audaci e degli angosciati, dei devianti e dei disperati, nell'arte di una gioventù precocemente invecchiata nell'attesa di una guerra che aveva a lungo sperimentato nello spirito" (2014: 14), e che popolano i versi di Sbarbaro (in *Pianissimo* il poeta-sonnambulo incontra prostitute, ubriachi, disperati che vagano per le strade durante la notte), i *Trucioli* sono la realizzazione, la figurazione dell'arte nello spirito che si fa e diventa storia, e rappresentano un nucleo testuale fondamentale per affrontare la demitizzazione del mito della Grande Guerra in chiave modernista attraverso l'autocoscienza dell'io sbarbariano. Del resto, come ricorda Castellana, "[i]l modernismo [rispetto alle avanguardie] scommette sulla funzione comunicativa della letteratura, e scommette anche sulla convenzione rappresentativa che, per tutto l'Ottocento, era stata l'espressione più compiuta di quella funzione: per lo scrittore modernista il mondo esterno esiste e può essere raccontato, ma solo attraverso lo specchio della coscienza. Una mediazione tra soggettivo e oggettivo è ancora possibile" (2010: 29).

La modalità autobiografica frammentista ricercata da Sbarbaro nei *Trucioli* si presenta come un percorso di carattere epistemologico, come una esplorazione della realtà attraverso una coscienza soggettiva etico-critica diversa, lontana da quelle forme meramente empiriche (seppur affidate a una ipotiposi dell'io lirico, il "sonnambulo", e non a una struttura trascendentale della persona che dice io)[9] ricercate nella raccolta édita nel 1914 per le edizioni della "Voce", e ora votata a una dimensione trascendentale. Se "nel 1910 il primo decennio nell'ultimo secolo del morente millennio viene a concludersi" nel contesto "di uno sconvolgimento talmente filosofico e metafisico" (Harrison 2014: 15) da distruggere le certezze dell'io e la percezione oggettiva della città (luogo deputato, deformato e destrutturato della deambulazione del sonnambulo sbarbariano in *Pianissimo*), il triennio 1917-1919 raccoglie, per Sbarbaro e per gli autori della "Riviera Ligure", una sfida *mimetica* nei confronti del reale e dell'istanza etica della letteratura, come scrive Castellana:

Dopo il 1914-1915, raccontare il mondo significa fare i conti più o meno direttamente con l'evento che più in profondità ha lacerato la coscienza europea nel primo quarto del secolo. Dopo questa data la narrativa subisce una svolta, e se è vero che la guerra non muta la struttura produttiva monopolistica e imperialista dell'economia e della società italiana del 1918, è altrettanto difficile dubitare che essa abbia contribuito a radicalizzare il pessimismo di chi ne aveva compreso l'assurda insensatezza. E va da sé che anche questo è un elemento che divide il modernismo dalle avanguardie, che avevano appunto creduto di vedere nella guerra una forma di "igiene del mondo" e di palingenesi sociale.

(2010: 30)

Il rapporto tra *mimesis* ed etica, in termini di rappresentazione del reale e testimonianza storico-estetica dell'esperienza bellica, costituisce non solo il secondo punto di tangenza tra Sbarbaro e il modernismo, bensì anche il terzo, poiché il *medium*, la struttura formale che soggiace al processo di costruzione letteraria da parte dell'io poetico, il frammento, è intrinsecamente legato alla fenomenologia modernista della realtà dei *Trucioli*.

Procediamo con ordine. Che il realismo, nella cultura occidentale, costituisca da sempre un punto di scontro della critica è stato ampiamente dimostrato da Federico Bertoni in *Realismo e letteratura* (2007), dove lo studioso, passando in rassegna la storia di questa categoria storica, estetica e letteraria, riassume tale diatriba attraverso un sintagma particolarmente appropriato: "parola sfortunata" (17-23). Riferendosi alla *vexata quaestio* del rapporto eziologico tra mondi reali e mondi di finzione, tra mondi di persone e mondi di *personae*, Bertoni, relativamente al romanzo, afferma che

non ha alcun senso, in effetti, dire che un romanzo rappresenta (copia, imita, descrive...)

---

[9] Relativamente al caso di Sbarbaro, si veda Coletti 1997. Per un'analisi storico-letteraria e teorico-descrittiva delle problematiche relative al rapporto tra io trascendentale e poesia moderna, mi si permetta di rimandare a Comparini 2012. Per uno studio generale sulla poesia moderna, rimando a Mazzoni 2005 e Scaffai 2005.

il mondo reale, per il semplice fatto che il mondo rappresentato non preesiste all'atto stesso della rappresentazione, all'atto testuale che lo istituisce: è un mondo unico, irripetibile, inondato da una specifica "tonalità di luce", portato all'esistenza da quell'atto doppiamente creativo che è il rapporto tra l'autore e il lettore. In altri termini, "il testo di finzione non riproduce il reale, ma costruisce dei mondi testuali che non gli preesistono e che non presuppongono una relazione diretta con il mondo d'esperienza del lettore o dell'autore."

(Bertoni 2007: 106)

La lettura di Bertoni può essere effettivamente estesa anche a quei generi letterari misti, dove dimensione narrativa e tensione poetica diventano espressione materiale ed estensione estetica delle due cifre fondanti la prosa poetica del primo Novecento:[10] da un lato, abbiamo la funzione lirica, che agisce a livello testuale quale matrice strutturale e strutturante dell'opera lungo l'asse del soggettivismo; dall'altro, l'ἐμπειρία, la cui azione e presenza lungo l'asse dell'oggettivismo permette all'io narrante di trasgredire le leggi della narrazione proprie dei generi prosaici e contaminare l'esperienza assolutizzante e sublimata dell'io lirico con la natura empirica della realtà.

Questo strenuo tentativo di percezione della realtà *per fragmenta*, che vede impegnati, a livello sincronico e lungo il medesimo spazio letterario, Giovanni Boine (*Frantumi*, 1918)[11] e Camillo Sbarbaro (*Trucioli*, 1920) — i quali si inseriscono a loro volta in quella linea frammentista iniziata dai *Frammenti lirici* di Clemente Rebora (1913) e dai *Canti orfici* di Dino Campana (1914)[12] — non risponde solamente a un principio di ordine estetico. Come sottolinea Francesca Corvi, "nonostante il carattere transitorio e di breve durata della stagione del frammento", la figura di Sbarbaro assurge a "a ruolo di guida e di rinnovamento" della stagione letteraria del primo Novecento, trovando nella "Riviera Ligure" il proprio *locus amoenus*, dove alla sperimentazione stilistica decostruttiva delle avanguardie viene contrapposto un principio costruttivo. In questo senso, Sbarbaro, che "sarà pressoché l'unico a sostenere a lungo la poetica del frammentismo, addirittura fino al 1962, anno della terza ed ultima

---

[10] A riguardo, si vedano Meijer 1984, Macrí 1998, Valli 2001 [1980], Corvi 2005.

[11] Castellana riconosce già nel primo Boine de *Il peccato* una dimensione modernista della sua poetica: "*Il peccato* di Boine (1913-1914) [...] mostra invece la crisi incipiente, ponendosi esattamente sulla linea di confine tra la negazione avanguardistica del genere e il ritrovato interesse (tipicamente modernista) per la forma-romanzo" (Castellana 2010: 25).

[12] "Alcuni dei titoli più dei brani più significativi sulla rivista risultano già indicativi di un nuovo *modus* espressivo che prende campo con continuità proprio sulle sue pagine e anticipa le future poetiche del *frammentismo* e della *prosa d'arte*; oltre ai *Trucioli* di Sbarbaro e ai *Frantumi* di Boine usciti tra il 1915 e il 1919, saranno da segnalare anche il precedente *Frammento* di Bontempelli del 1907, così come i *Frammenti* di Cecchi del 1915 e del 1916; a questi si aggiungono i numerosi frammenti di Ceccardo Roccatagliata Ceccardi apparsi fra il 1898 e il 1917; inoltre lo stesso direttore Mario Novaro intitolerà *Frammento* un suo testo del 1910" (Corvi 2005: 43).

edizione di *Fuochi fatui*, ma anche vigilia dello sperimentalismo, sancito l'anno seguente dalla costituzione del *Gruppo 63*" (Corvi 2005: 46), si pone così quale testimone e paradigma di questa stagione primonovecentesca, dove espressionismo e frammentismo, lirica e narrativa, sfuggono alla morsa destrutturante delle avanguardie, unendosi in un unico movimento dis-armonico, le cui linee di discontinuità sono dovute unicamente dalla multiforme ricerca di una forma letteraria capace di rispondere, e quindi di opporsi, alla frattura sociale, politica, religiosa, artistica e filosofica che colpì la classe intellettuale nel primo ventennio del Novecento.

L'incompiutezza del frammento, allora, non deve essere letta, come ritiene invece Castellana, in termini esclusivamente avanguardistici, nella misura in cui "[i]l ritorno al romanzo indica piuttosto l'esigenza di tornare a concepire la letteratura come mediazione", mentre "l'avanguardia, con la sua poetica del frammento, dell'incompiutezza costitutiva dell'opera, del valore del mero gesto artistico, rifiutava la mediazione in quanto tale." L'operazione letteraria in atto sulla "Riviera Ligure" agisce in una direzione diversa da quella vociana: il frammento rappresenta una forma di mediazione tra narrazione romanzesca e lirica simbolista, che riconosce nelle "contraddizioni forma-contenuto, soggettivo-oggettivo, arbitrario-necessario, razionale-irrazionale, psicologismo-naturalismo" (Castellana 2010: 28) un principio dialettico positivo, catalizzatore di nuove potenzialità conoscitive da parte dell'io e di riflessioni di carattere etico ed estetico nei confronti della realtà.

A partire da questa triplice dimensione modernista (geografica, storica e teorica), nella prossima sezione cercherò di dimostrare come i trucioli di guerra di Sbarbaro raccolgano a livello testuale la necessità esistenziale da parte delle generazione entrante nel secolo breve di affrontare in termini dialettici e di mediazione letteraria la frantumazione del realismo ottocentesco e dell'identità tra io trascendentale e io empirico attraverso una mimesi della realtà *per fragmenta*. La rappresentazione negativa della Grande Guerra, in quanto elemento distorcente (per quanto volutamente *assente* nei *Trucioli*) non solo della realtà — e quindi del rapporto di causa-effetto tra referenti e significati —, ma dei *realia* (da intendere in questo caso in senso propriamente scolastico) e della coscienza rifratta del soggetto sbarbariano — e quindi dei postulati e fondamenti metafisici proprî dell'io conoscente —, diventa il prisma interpretativo da cui partire per una rilettura modernista del frammentismo italiano e della poetica di Sbarbaro.

2. *"La guerra vuol dire": il modernismo di Camilo Sbarbaro*

I "'trucioli di guerra,'" scrive Perli, nell'edizione vallecchiana 1920, sono "diciassette testi (diciotto se si aggiunge il brano [La guerra vuol dire] [...]), "ben undici dei quali apparvero la prima volta nel numero del giugno '19 della *Riviera Ligure*" (Perli 2004: 133): *Marcia* (283-84), *Ho scoperto qui sopra* (285), *Bene issata. Stretta* (286), *La selva buia di scavi* (287), *La lotta che scuote* (288), *L'abetaia è piena di prodigi* (289-90), *Perché nella linea oscura* (291), *Ave, 2 novembre 1917* (292-94), *Sull'erbaglia sommersa* (295-96), *Uscivo dalla trincea* (297-98), *Ci sono ancora gli animali* (299-300), *Avviene che vicino a una bestia* (301-02), *Ormai se qualcuno invidio* (303-04), *Natale a Terres* (305-06), *Franzenfeste* (307-08), *Lüsen* (309-11), *Primavera a Lüsen* (312-13).[13]

Questa sezione bellica occupa senza soluzione di continuità la parte finale dei *Trucioli*, assegnando così all'esperienza della guerra un ruolo centrale per quanto riguarda l'interpretazione del volume e della poetica di Sbarbaro, per il fatto che la frammentazione dell'io si chiude all'insegna del riverbero della Grande Guerra. Non è certo questa la sede adatta per passare in esame l'intera serie di frammenti; quindi, data la specificità del mio oggetto di indagine (la poetica modernista di Sbarbaro), mi concentrerò su alcuni testi particolarmente significativi per sottolineare come la percezione della realtà *per fragmenta* e dei *realia* sia intrinsecamente legata all'azione deformante della catastrofe (individuale e collettiva) della Grande Guerra, e come la fenomenologia dell'io abbia reagito ad essa attraverso un'analisi soggettivo-oggettiva del rapporto tra *mimesis* ed etica, delegando alla natura il proprio ruolo di soggetto conoscente.

Sebbene Sbarbaro abbia deciso di non includere il truciolo *La guerra vuol dire* nell'edizione 1920,[14] ritengo utile partire da esso per mostrare come i riflessi dell'esperienza bellica, anche quando essa viene recuperata in termini dichiaratamente negativi e di *absentia*, abbiano provocato una rottura (a livello estetico ed etico) dei legami tra reale e *realia*. Inoltre, i trucioli di guerra composti dopo questo primo esperimento stilistico sono un suo prolungamento:[15] una ulteriore testimonianza letteraria della "condanna sottile ma totale della guerra e della condizione militare in genere" (Sbarbaro 1985: 542)[16] che l'*incipit* de *La guerra vuol dire* incarna:

---

[13] I numeri tra parentesi corrispondono alle pagine dell'edizione critica dei *Trucioli* (1920), curata da Giampiero Costa per Scheiwiller nel 1990. Per una dettagliata analisi filologica e macrotestuale dei trucioli di guerra, rimando a Perli 2004: 133-135.
[14] "[...] composto nel settembre-ottobre 1917, pubblicato sulla RL [*Riviera Ligure*] del giugno 1919 [...] e non accolto da Sbarbaro in T1920 [*Trucioli* 1920], [fu ristampato] in *Fuochi fatui* terza edizione ed escluso dall'*Opera in versi*." Il truciolo, prosegue Perli, "fu riprodotto da Giampiero Costa prima tra i *Trucioli dispersi* secondo il testo di *Fuochi fatui*, quindi nell'Appendice della sua edizione critica di T1920, col numero [89] e nel testo critico" (Perli 2004: 135).
[15] Perli giustamente rileva che il mancato inserimento di *La guerra vuol dire* nei *Trucioli* risponde a criterî unicamente stilistici e formali: "[...] escluso in quanto abbozzo non sviluppato di una poetica del paesaggio elaborata invece ne trucioli inclusi nel libro, e mera eco del truciolo [*Firenze vuol dire*] e di esso sorta di doppione inespressivo e perciò giustamente sacrificato" (Perli 2004: 137).
[16] La citazione è tratta da un appunto scritto a penna da Sbarbaro sotto la dedica *A Angelo Barile* per l'edizione Vallecchi 1966 delle *Cartoline in franchigia*.

La guerra vuol dire: la pergola solare sospesa sulla terra amorosa di Francia; la fontana ghiacciata che ci venne incontro a Buttrio; le vetrine di Bologna versicolori nella nebbia; a Vigodarzere, tra le sparse ramaglie incristallate dalla galaverna, il sole che cresceva rosso; i secchi di rame colmi che mettevano in mostra il fianco di Mariuta; la notte di Udine; l'estate densa di Fara; Cesuna Bombardata, presepio ridente della neve; le dame di Crocerossa rondini violette; Dueville assordata dai nidi; la luna di Caminetto gelata e al sole di febbraio i buoi pezzati che aravano; a Orsaria i fioretti azzurri in cui riconobbi gli occhi della sorella; il salice piangente, fanciulla in capelli, incontrato in marcia sulla via di Percotto; Soleschiano paesello — monastero; il ciuffetto di fiori bianchicci che trema sul mio capo in trincea.

(Sbarbaro 1990: 362-63)

In questo truciolo l'epifania semantica della guerra viene deprivata di ogni risvolto significativo; essa rimane un puro fono, un rumore, un momento acustico che non può generare identità o distinzione, coppie minime e valori distintivi che permettano all'io di definire se stesso e la realtà circostante. Dopo i due punti, segue una colata nominale che sembra richiamarsi a una fenomenologia impressionista della realtà da parte dell'io; tuttavia, Sbarbaro costruisce abilmente un monologo interiore, grazie al quale l'io narrante riesce a esprimere non solo gli elementi proprî della coscienza sensibile, bensì anche quelli dell'inconscio, che nel testo sbarbariano si manifesta in tutta la sua fragilità, franto dall'esperienza bellica e incapace di articolare una geografia spaziale ed emotiva attraverso i meccanismi della ragione.

Da un punto di vista formale e ideologico, la manifestazione linguistica della guerra è un significante senza significato, privo di referenti semantici e ontologici che possano raccogliere l'istanza e il desiderio conoscitivi dell'io. Mentre l'*incipit* sembra suggerire la produzione di un enunciato dotato di un valore gnoseologico in grado di offrire al lettore e all'io uno spazio letterario dove poter sviluppare un discorso critico sulla realtà e sui *realia*, le parole di Sbarbaro smontano le catene razionali del linguaggio attraverso la fusione di motivi narrativo-oggettivi e lirico-soggettivi nel frammento, il cui potenziale valore semantico, però, è limitato dalla eco della guerra e dai suoi riflessi decostruenti all'interno della coscienza irrazionale dell'io. La demitizzazione della guerra, allora, si presenta in questo truciolo sia come agente passivo, come tropo linguistico che agisce unicamente sul piano della narrazione significante, ma non su quello della narrazione significativa; sia come deterrente dell'istanza etica del discorso letterario, dal momento che la voce dell'io, sebbene escluda a priori ogni processo di interiorizzazione etico-civile dell'evento storico, rimane racchiusa nell'automatismo della condizione alienante e disumana dell'esperienza militare.

Quest'ultimo motivo, ravvisabile nel tremolio dei "fiori bianchicci" sul capo dell'io-soldato in trincea — sineddoche della stasi in quanto luogo deputato all'estenuante immobilità dei soldati, il cui destino mortuario è racchiuso nel fremito del fiore —, ritorna con perentorietà nel primo truciolo della sequenza bellica, *Marcia*:

Mi destai un giorno uomo matricolato. Sulla paglia il vicino innaffiava la cara otite.

Quando mi misero un fucile in mano, dentro mi raggrinzii vergine violentata dal mascalzone.

Pure non è questa vita meno logica dell'altra.
Bussa qualcuno alle porte d'Italia con un maglio lampeggiante.
Ma il viandante-sanguisuga mesce un triste vino dove si scorda.

E chi conduce sono serafini stellati, soavi alcuni come cocotti.
Cinguettano sulle vie polverose le automobili del comando.
Margherite in un prato scoppiano nella notte improvvisi.
Con occhi di condannati a morte guardiamo i tetri paesaggi passare.
Si marcia.
Si fanno sulle porte a ridere le donne sanguinarie.

(Sbarbaro 1990: 283)

Datato ottobre-novembre 1917, e quindi di poco posteriore a *La guerra vuol dire* (settembre-ottobre 1917), *Marcia*, il truciolo che apre la sequenza dei frammenti bellici, raccoglie l'istanza meccanicizzante simbolicamente racchiusa nell'inerzia del soldato in trincea. In questa nuova stazione dell'io, il ritmo del monologo interiore non è più dettato dal riaffiorare, a livello conscio e inconscio, dei ricordi che Sbarbaro associò al proprio ristagnamento esistenziale nel fango e nel sangue, nella morte e nella vita, della trincea. Così facendo, l'io-soldato si confessa nella sua più totale impotenza nei confronti del reale, essendo vittima del movimento meccanico della non-vita: la guerra. Ridotto allo statuto di non-essere, per il quale, come dirà poi Montale, "lo stesso / sapore han miele e assenzio" (Montale 1984: 33), l'io sbarbariano concepisce la guerra e la realtà come un dato oggettivo, inamovibile, il cui moto è scandito unicamente dalla ripetitività della vita militare. In altre parole, la realtà acquisita *per fragmenta* richiede una temporalità diversa, che, per quanto statica e meccanica, presenta un'andatura circolare — cioè, quella della marcia.

Nato dal solco ideologico scavato dal precedente testo, *Marcia* accentua il valore dis-umano della guerra attraverso procedimenti stilistici strettamente monologici. Occupando un unico verso nella terzina finale, il sintagma "Si marcia" svolge una funzione icastica: il significante-guerra, in quanto espressione negativa dell'esistenza, cioè dell'incapacità dell'uomo di poter comunicare secondo piani intersoggettivi e di promuovere così la comunicazione fattuale dei messaggi individuali e sovraindividuali, si manifesta come mera costruzione impersonale, isolata dal resto frammento e carica di un significato negativo, legato alla monotonia del marciare e alla ciclicità della morte.

La frattura dell'io, provocata dall'epifania negativa della guerra, si manifesta altresì nello spazio naturale. La militarizzazione del modulo poetico-esistenziale ha deformato il paesaggio a tal punto che questi è divenuto alieno all'uomo, perdendo così quel valore di "singolarità del reale" che avrebbe permesso al poeta di ricucire i rapporti tra io e mondo, tra io lirico e io trascendentale, e tra referenti e significati. L'io-soldato che aveva abbandonato lo spazio urbano (e con esso la propria dimensione di io-sonnambulo) per sfuggire al principio meccanicizzante della città ("A queste vie simmetriche e deserte / a queste case mute sono simile. / Partecipo alla loro indifferenza, / alla loro immobilità", Sbarbaro 1985: 25) si trova così a dover fronteggiare nuovamente, come scrive Luperini, "la coscienza di una separazione dal passato prodotta dalla perdita di senso del mondo" (2006: 9).

Tuttavia, la cifra modernista che lega l'io al reale, cioè la distorsione della realtà operata dalla coscienza lirico-narrativa del soggetto conoscente nei confronti del mondo circostante, fa sì che la natura possa assumere le forme di un riflesso divergente dell'essere, una scheggia dell'io avulsa dall'inferno della guerra. Mentre in *Pianissimo* i moduli sincronicamente lirici dello spazio, del tempo e dell'io avevano creato un non-spazio dove il soggetto poetico si limitava ad assistere impotente al fallimento della modernità e al suo lento ma progressivo disfacimento (lo spazio urbano assume i connotati di una novella Dite per il linguaggio aspro e dantescamente comico e per le figure che popolano l'universo esplorato dall'io), nei *Trucioli* il soldato-Sbarbaro proietta il proprio desiderio di sé, per quanto deformato e franto, nell'altro, nella natura circostante, cercando nel meraviglioso, nell'inaspettato e nel prodigioso un elemento di rottura del tempo meccanico della guerra:

La selva buia di scavi e d'insidie, sbarrata di vigne spinose, ha, la notte, voci inumane. Starnuti, sghignazzamenti di volatili; che vedo, nel dormiveglia, occhialuti, gozzuti, con occhi di vecchi cattivi. Mi salva dall'incubo lo scricciolo — forse il pezzetto di turchino che di giorno saetta tra i rami e balzella sulla neve — immagine di me nella selva — che sferruzza nelle pause le sue limettine d'argento.

(Sbarbaro 1990: 287)

L'abetaia è piena di prodigi.
Gli altissimi ceri che mi si serrano intorno, sprizzano al sorgere del sole iridi sfavillanti: sono le lagrime di resina di fresco sgorgate, limpide come acqua. I tronchi buttano fumo e par fiato di viventi.

(Sbarbaro 1990: 289)

Infine la nebbiolina annega l'altopiano. Isolotti vi naufragano i cascinali. La luna è un imbuto celestino; e la tinta, contagiosa, crea al paesaggio un'atmosfera irreale.
Sughero, galleggio in questo incerto.
(La guerra dov'è?)

(Sbarbaro 1990: 292-93)

In questa serie di trucioli, la natura prende lentamente le forme dell'io. Nel primo frammento, il soldato è salvato (ma non svegliato dall'incubo del conflitto bellico — così come il sonnambulo non si sveglia dall'incubo della città-inferno in *Pianissimo*) dalla disumanità della guerra, ipostatizzata in questo frammento da una natura oniricamente negativa, la cui alterità positiva, lo scricciolo che "saetta i rami e balzella sulla neve", permette all'io un parziale riscatto etico. Diversamente da *Pianissimo*, però, dove la palingenesi dell'io era possibile attraverso un processo di autoanalisi, un attraversamento etico della propria coscienza (come non ha mancato di sottolineare Testa 2009), nei *Trucioli* l'io cede il proprio primato ontologico alla natura, nella speranza che questa riesca a superare le barriere della storia e della guerra e restituisca al (s)oggetto conoscente la propria identità.

Nel secondo truciolo assistiamo a questo fondamentale passaggio. Sebbene tra *Pianissimo* e *Trucioli* sia ravvisabile una linea di continuità del male storico avvertito dall'io, che si manifesta nell'inferno della città e nell'inferno della guerra, tra il 1914 e il 1920 si registra altresì il passaggio dalla metafisica dell'io alla metafisica della natura, dall'io come soggetto esploratore all'io come soggetto rifratto dalla natura, il cui valore secolarmente salvifico permette all'io di rompere il tempo meccanico e gli automatismi della guerra e fondare un nuovo pensiero metafisico, che tenga conto della labilità semantica dei rapporti tra referenti e significati. Il richiamo al prodigio non lascia dubbi a riguardo: etimologicamente, il prodigio è l'emissione di una voce divina, come ricorda Benveniste nel *Vocabolario delle istituzioni indoeuropee* (Benveniste 1976: vol. 2, 477-84). E un acuto studioso dei lingue classiche quale era Sbarbaro non poteva certo ignorare tale valore epistemologico, che egli attribuisce, volutamente, in una prospettiva laica e terrena, ai prodigi dell'abetaia.

Questo procedimento ascensivo — ma in senso strettamente terreno e orizzontale —, dove l'io registra la presenza della natura racchiusa in uno spazio pervaso da un'"atmosfera irreale" e in termini puramente antropomorfi, culmina nell'interrogativo categorico che chiude il terzo truciolo: dov'è la guerra? Difficilmente si può rispondere a questa domanda senza tener conto dell'esistenza del truciolo da cui siamo partiti, *La guerra vuol dire*.

L'epifania negativa della guerra, demitizzata da una natura umanizzata dai riflessi della coscienza dell'io, fa emergere in Sbarbaro la necessità di trovare una nuova poetica per indagare l'emergenza conoscitiva propria dell'essere dopo che questi ha assistito alla disfatta dell'uomo contro l'uomo durante la Grande Guerra. Sebbene il soldato-Sbarbaro sia uscito dal sonnambulismo della città, egli si trova ad affrontare nuovamente il proprio male di vivere nella dimensione infernale del conflitto tra uomo e uomo; e nel confronto con la natura, riletta secondo una lenta diacritica modernista a partire dai nuovi rapporti instauratasi tra l'io e la realtà a causa della deformazione dei *realia* e dell'inconscio tra il 1914 e il 1919, Sbarbaro riesce a costruire un sistema filosofico nel quale la rivoluzione copernicana dell'essere (il passaggio, già menzionato, dalla metafisica dell'io alla metafisica della natura, dal soggetto lirico di *Pianissimo* al [s]oggetto rifratto dei *Trucioli*) si oppone alla condizione universale del male storico, che ha ridotto l'uomo a un semplice automa, un soldato che *marcia* secondo il ritmo della guerra.

L'operazione anti-trascendente di Sbarbaro mira, da un lato, a recuperare l'autonomia conoscitiva dell'io, demitizzando l'essenza meccanica e assurda della guerra, e, dall'altro, a riconoscere nella natura una nuova forma di conoscenza metafisica, laica e immanente:

Uscivo dalla trincea. Tornavo alla luce, ai paesi innocenti bombardati, alle abetaie arrossate qua e là dalla mitraglia. Era una mattina tiepida e coperta e camminavo, accompagnato ma solo, traverso opere di guerra, gli occhi miopi perduti dietro le macchie della vegetazione; quando udii un suono di campane, fievole.
Ed ecco, per non so quale dimenticanza, di qua e di là con dolce scampanio cominciarono a chiamarsi i paesi invisibili.

Scampanio domenicale quale l'altipiano udiva ieri, quale udirà domani.
Era la vita impassibile che cancellava la guerra come l'erba la fossa recente.

Prolungavo ad arte l'illusione. Sorridevano nel viso nascosto malinconicamente gli occhi miopi, perduti dietro le macchie della vegetazione.

(Sbarbaro 1990: 297)

L'uscita dalla trincea non appartiene più al campo semantico delle azioni iterative e meccaniche. La natura ora è in grado di cancellare la guerra, giacché è riuscita a sopravvivere all'azione degli automi, a quelle mitraglie che hanno arrossato le abetaie, senza però riuscire a distruggerle del tutto. Lo spazio naturale è contaminato unicamente dalla presenza delle opere di guerra dell'uomo, mentre il ritmo delle stagioni dei paesi invisibili si sostituisce lentamente a quello della marcia ("Era la vita impassibile che cancellava la guerra") grazie alla rifrazione della coscienza dell'io, il cui occhio partecipa alla metamorfosi dello spazio e del tempo prolungando "ad arte l'illusione":

Ormai, se qualcuno invidio, è l'albero.
Freschezza e innocenza dell'albero. Cresce a suo modo. Schietto, sereno. Il sole l'acqua lo toccano in ogni foglia. Perennemente ventilato.
Tremolio, brillare del fogliame come un linguaggio sommesso e persuasivo!
Più che d'uomini ho in cuore fisionomie d'alberi.
Ci sono alberi scapigliati e alberi raccolti come mani che pregano.
Alberi che sono delicate trine sciorinate; altri come ceri pasquali. Alberi patriarcali vasti come case, rotti dalla fatica di spremer fuori la dolcezza dei frutti.
C'è l'albero della città, grido del verde, unica cosa ingenua nel deserto atroce.
Ma più di tutti, due alberi ricordo, che crescevano da un letto di torrente, allato, come svelti fratelli.

Essere un albero, un comune albero...

(Sbarbaro 1990: 303)

Come Sbarbaro decide di abbandonarsi nelle braccia della prosa, così l'io dei trucioli si abbandona al "desiderio di essere" (Bottiroli 2013: 288-353) parte di questo nuovo processo conoscitivo. Riprendendo il tema del tremolio dello spazio naturale, inizialmente declinato secondo il ritmo della stasi in trincea, e quindi della morte, Sbarbaro ne muta la funzione, assegnando un significato etico al linguaggio della natura. La preghiera laica che la coscienza dell'io intravvede rifratta nella forma degli alberi ripristina, da un lato, l'idea di "social catena", di amore e fratellanza tra uomo e uomo, che la guerra ha minato, e, dall'altro, favorisce la palingenesi dell'io ("essere un albero, un comune albero..."), ora che questi è "pronto a perder[si]" e ad "abbandona[re]" il proprio passato per "conquista[re]" la "bellezza" della "natura" (Sbarbaro 1990: 295).

In questo ultimo testo assistiamo così al compimento della teoria modernista di Sbarbaro. Il monologo interiore dell'io diviene parte integrante dell'azione rigenerante (a livello epistemologico ed etico) della natura, la cui azione, muovendosi lungo l'asse della mimesi, è volta a ricucire quei legami tra reale e *realia* che la coscienza del soggetto conoscente, in seguito alla frammentazione della realtà causata dell'epifania negativa Grande Guerra, non era più in grado di percepire. La poetica modernista *per fragmenta*, quindi, si inserisce in questo processo letterario quale *medium* mimetico per sopperire alla distanza creatasi tra l'io e il mondo fenomenologico, secondo un principio propositivo (e non distruttivo); e la natura, mutando il proprio statuto ontologico da oggetto a soggetto, partecipa attivamente alla metamorfosi dell'io sbarbariano, favorendone la palingenesi e cancellando le ombre della guerra dalla memoria individuale di Sbarbaro.

3. Conclusione

In conclusione, attraverso un'analisi storica, teorica e testuale ho cercato di mostrare come la poetica di Sbarbaro nei trucioli di guerra segua un paradigma fondamentalmente modernista e come la Grande Guerra sia *responsabile* del mutamento dei rapporti tra io e realtà. A partire dalla frattura etico-sociale avvertita dallo scritture tra il 1914 e il 1919, Sbarbaro ha modificato il proprio sistema filosofico, cercando di trovare nuove soluzioni estetiche e stilistiche per descrivere la realtà. In questo senso, la rappresentazione negativa della prima guerra mondiale è intrinsecamente legata alla poetica del frammento: come la realtà appare intelligibile e caotica, così l'arte, per salvaguardare gli statuti mimetici del testo letterario, adegua la forma al contenuto, nella misura in cui la realtà viene ritratta dall'io poetico *per fragmenta*.

Dallo studio di alcuni dei trucioli più significativi è emerso che attraverso l'utilizzo del monologo interiore Sbarbaro ha cercato di fondere la dimensione lirica e la dimensione narrativa all'interno del testo letterario, in modo tale da esprimere sia i livelli conoscitivi della sfera sensibile sia della sfera inconscia. La realtà frammentaria così prodotta, quindi, si manifesta quale forma rifratta del soggetto, il quale, non potendo agire direttamente su di essa, affida alla natura il compito di registrare i dati dell'io conoscente, fondando così una nuova metafisica dell'essere, dove significati e referenti sono legati tra loro attraverso la dialettica positiva tra io e mondo secondo il ritmo della natura.

Stanford University

Opere citate

Anceschi Luciano, *Le poetiche del Novecento in Italia*, Venezia, Marsilio, 1990.
Angeleri Cara e Giampiero Costa (a c. di), *Bibliografia degli scritti di Camillo Sbarbaro*, presentazione di D. Isella, Milano, All'insegna del pesce d'oro, 1986.
Astengo Domenico, *Sbarbaro e la prima guerra mondiale*, in *Omaggio a Camillo Sbarbaro*, "Resine" ns 5 (settembre 1983), 13-19.
Benveniste Émile, *Il vocabolario delle istituzioni indoeuropee*, edizione italiana a c. di M. Liborio, prefazione di E. Giammarco, Torino, Einaudi, 1976 [1969], 2 vols.
Bertoni Federico, *Realismo e letteratura: Una storia possibile*, Torino, Einaudi, 2007.
Boero Pino (a c. di), *Lettere a "La Riviera Ligure:" 1900-1905*, Roma, Edizioni di Storia e Letteratura, 1980, vol. 1.
_____, *Lettere a "La Riviera Ligure": 1906-1909*, Roma, Edizioni di Storia e Letteratura, 2003, vol. 2.
Boero Pino, Aveto Andrea, Merlanti Federica, *Lettere a "La Riviera Ligure": 1910-1912*, Roma, Edizioni di Storia e Letteratura, 2003, vol. 3.
Boero Pino (a c. di), *"La Riviera Ligure" tra industria e letteratura*, Firenze, Vallecchi, 1984.
Bottiroli Giovanni, *"Noi non apparteniamo a noi stessi": identità e desiderio*, in *La ragione flessibile: modi d'essere e stili di pensiero*, Torino, Bollati Boringhieri, 2013.
Cangiano Mimmo, *La tentazione dell'"impressione": riguardo ai giudizi di Boine su Soffici*, "Poetiche" ns 13 (2-3, dicembre 2011), 269-304.
Carpi Umberto, *"La Voce": letteratura e primato degli intellettuali*, Bari, Dedalo, 2009 [1975].
Castellana Riccardo, *Parole, cose, persone: il realismo modernista di Tozzi*, Pisa, Fabrizio Serra Editore, 2009.
_____, *Realismo modernista: un'idea del romanzo italiano (1915-1925)*, "Italianistica" 39 (1, gennaio-marzo 2010), 23-45.
Castigliano Federico, *Sbarbaro e la forma-frammento*, "Italian Studies" 69 (1, March 2014), 111-26.
Coletti Vittorio, *Prove di un io minore: lettura di Sbarbaro: "Pianissimo" (1914)*, Roma, Bulzoni, 1997.
Comparini Alberto, *Appunti per una storia della poesia moderna italiana*, "Poetiche" ns 14 (36, dicembre 2012), 453-76.
Contini Gianfranco, *Letteratura dell'Italia unita: 1861-1968*, Firenze, Sansoni, 1968.
Contorbia Franco, *Sbarbaro e la Grande Guerra*, in "Resine", Atti del Convegno Nazionale di Studi su Camillo Sbarbaro (Spotorno, 6-7 ottobre 1973), a. c. di A. Guerrini, 1974, pp. 134-57.
Corvi Francesca, *Il frammentismo sulle pagine della "Riviera Ligure": fuochi fatui della*

Sbarbaro e la rappresentazione *negativa* della Grande Guerra 185

prosa novecentesca, "Rivista di Letteratura Italiana" 23 (1-2, gennaio-agosto 2005), 43-46.

Giusti Simone, *Sulla formazione dei "Trucioli" di Camillo Sbarbaro*, Firenze, Le Lettere, 1997.

Guaragnella Pasquale, *A proposito dell'esperienza bellica di Camillo Sbarbaro e di alcuni libri sulla Grande Guerra*, in *La dorata parmelia: licheni, poesia e cultura in Camillo Sbarbaro (1888-1967)*, a c. di G. Magurno, Roma, Carocci, 2011, 37-59.

De Meijer Peter, *La prosa narrativa moderna*, in *Letteratura italiana*, vol. 3, *Le forme del testo, La prosa*, a c. di A. A. Rosa, Torino, Einaudi, 1984, vol. 2, 759-847.

Donnarumma Raffaele, *Tracciato del modernismo italiano*, in *Sul modernismo italiano* 13-38.

_____, *Gadda modernista*, Pisa, ETS, 2006.

Harrison Thomas, *1910: L'emancipazione della dissonanza*, traduzione di Marco Cobedò, Thomas Harrison e Federico Lopiparo, Roma, Editori Internazionali Riuniti, 2014 [1996].

Luperini Romano, *L'autocoscienza del moderno*, Napoli, Liguori, 2006.

_____, *Modernismo e poesia italiana del primo Novecento*, "Allegoria" ns 63 (1, gennaio-giugno 2011), 92-100.

_____, *Il modernismo italiano esiste*, in *Sul modernismo italiano* 3-12.

_____, *Il Novecento: apparati ideologici, ceto intellettuale, sistemi formali nella letteratura italiana contemporanea*, Torino, Loescher, 1981.

Luperini Romano e Tortora Massimiliano (a c. di), *Sul modernismo italiano*, Napoli, Liguori, 2012.

Lukács György, *Il dramma moderno dal Naturalismo a Hofmannsthal*, prefazione di L. Squarzina, Milano, Sugarco, 1967.

Macrí Oreste, *Poetica del frammentismo e genere del frammento*, in *La vita della parola: Studi su Ungaretti e poeti coevi*, a c. di A. Dolfi, Roma, Bulzoni, 1998, 125-32.

Martignoni Clelia, *Espressionismo tedesco e vociano a confronto*, "Autografo" 30 (9, aprile 1995), 21-34.

Mazzoni Guido, *Sulla poesia moderna*, Bologna, il Mulino, 2005.

Mazzotti Artel, *"La Voce" e i "vociani:" il "frammentismo lirico"*, Milano, Marzorati, 1995.

Minghelli Giuliana, *In the Shadow of the Mammoth: Italo Svevo and the Emergence of Modernism*, Toronto, University of Toronto Press, 2002.

Montale Eugenio, *Tutte le poesie*, a c. di G. Zampa, Milano, Mondadori, 1984.

Moroni Mario e Somigli Luca (a c. di), *Italian Modernism: Italian Culture Between Decadentism and Avant-Garde*, Toronto, University of Toronto Press, 2004.

Sbarbaro Camillo, *L'opera in versi e in prosa*, a c. di G. Lagorio e V. Scheiwiller, Milano, Scheiwiller-Garzanti, 1985.

_____, *Trucioli (1920)*, a c. di G. Costa, Milano, Scheiwiller, 1990.

Pavarini Stefano, *Sbarbaro prosatore: percorsi ermeneutici dal frammento alla prosa d'arte*, Bologna, il Mulino, 1997.

Perli Antonello, *Sui "trucioli di guerra" di Camillo Sbarbaro*, in "Collection de l'écrit" 8 (novembre 2004), 129-45.

_____, *La parola necessaria: saggio sulla poetica di Sbarbaro*, Ravenna, Giorgio Pozzi Editore, 2008.

Picchione John, *Dal modernismo al postmodernismo: riflessioni teoriche e pratiche della scrittura*, Macerata, Edizioni Università di Macerata, 2012.

Pupo Ivan, *"Attraversando Contini": appunti sull'eredità di un maestro della critica novecentesca*, in *La critica dopo la crisi*, Atti del Convegno (Arcavacata, 11-13 novembre 1999), a c. di M. Ganeri e N. Merola, Soveria Mannelli, Rubbettino, 2002, 129-41.

Scaffai Niccolò, *Il poeta e il suo libro: retorica e storia del libro di poesia nel Novecento*, Firenze, Le Monnier, 2005.

Testa Enrico, *Il lirismo etico di Sbarbaro*, in *Camillo Sbarbaro in versi e in prosa*, Convegno Nazionale di Studi (Spotorno, 14-15 dicembre 2007), a c. di D. Ferreri, Genova, San Marco dei Giustiniani, 2009, 243-50.

Valli Donato, *Dal frammento alla prosa d'arte, con alcuni sondaggi sulla prosa dei poeti*, Lecce, Pensa Multimedia, 2001. [*Vita e morte del frammento in Italia*, Lecce, Milella, 1980.]

Zoboli Paolo, *Linea ligure: Sbarbaro, Montale, Caproni*, Novara, Interlinea, 2006.

Maria Elena Versari

Avant-garde Iconographies of Combat:
From the *Futurist Synthesis of War* to *Beat the Whites with the Red Wedge*

In the opening pages of his 1916 book entitled *Enseignements psychologiques de la Guerre Européenne*, Gustave le Bon wrote: "Today's war is a fight between psychological forces," adding that "irreconcilable ideals are engaged in battle. Individual liberty rises against collective servitude, personal initiative against statist tyranny, ancient habits of international loyalty and respect for treaties against the supremacy of cannons" (2).

To a reader familiar with twentieth-century art, these words cannot fail to bring to mind the schematic summary of World War I outlined by the Italian Futurists in their graphic manifesto of 1914, *Futurist Synthesis of War* (*Sintesi Futurista della Guerra*) (ill. 1). The image, in turn, by way of formal resemblance, anticipates El Lissitzky's famous propaganda poster created during the Russian Civil War (1917-1920), *Beat the Whites with the Red Wedge* (*Клином красным бей белых*, 1920) (ill. 3).[1]

While scholars of Futurism have long recognized that there must have been some type of link between the two images (see for instance Salaris 178), modernist art historians have, in general, persistently ignored the issue.[2] In any case, we are still left to speculate about how this connection was, in fact, established, and why El Lissitzky, at that time, directly appropriated one of the Italians' most powerful icons.

Futurism against Backwardness
The *Futurist Synthesis of War*, signed by Filippo Tommaso Marinetti, Umberto Boccioni, Carlo Carrà, Luigi Russolo and Ugo Piatti, is the first manifesto of the group to appear as a *tavola parolibera* (free-word table), such as those that Marinetti had collected in his volume of the same year, *Zang Tumb Tuuum*. It was issued as a leaflet in more than 20,000 copies and distributed in November 1914 (Salaris 178), but Marinetti, Boccioni, Russolo and Piatti conceived it some time before, around the middle of September, while in jail. On September

---

[1] Scholars are not unanimous about when the poster was designed, dating it alternatively to 1919 or 1920. See in particular Nisbet 348, Kozlov and, on the subject of Lissitzky's propaganda boards, Clark 199.
[2] One significant exception is offered by Dimitrii Kozlov's recent monograph, which I will discuss in the course of the present essay.

16th, they had staged a demonstration in Milan to support Italy's entry into the War on the side of the Allies, and had burned an Austrian flag (Boccioni 128). Although Italy was still technically allied with Germany and Austria because of a treaty signed several years before, it was, at that time, still cautiously weighing its options. The Futurists were arrested and charged with attempting to disrupt the nation's friendly relations with a foreign state, a considerable offense according to the Italian penal code. They were released five days later, when a judge reduced their imputation to "offense to the flag of a foreign state," but they were required to abstain from any public demonstrations. As Boccioni wrote to his family: "Tutto finirà in nulla, me lo ha detto lo stesso giudice istruttore ma volevano premere su noi per il futurismo e per il terrore che si ripetessero le dimostrazioni. Non ci moveremo più invece, perché abbiamo dovuto firmare impegnandoci per ottenere la libertà provvisoria [Everything will end in nothing, the examining magistrate told me this, but they wanted to press on us because of futurism and for their terror that the demonstrations might reoccur. We won't move further, since we had to sign and bind ourselves in order to be provisionally released]." (Boccioni 128).

The publication of the *Futurist Synthesis* thus became a stopgap for the Futurists' direct involvement in political activity. The manifesto's layout (Ill. 1) is structured as a triangle, whose point, oriented toward the right, pierces a circle. Within the triangle, we can read the names of the Allied nations (some not yet directly involved in the conflict at the time of publication), each identified by a series of psychological qualities. The Central powers are instead comprised within the frame of the circle. At the exact center of the composition, the word "Futurismo" (Futurism), in big letters, fills the angle's point. At the extreme right-hand side of the angle, in smaller fonts, we can read: "contro" (against) and in front of it, already contained in the space of the circle, the word "Passatismo" (Backwardness). "Futurismo contro Passatismo 8 popoli-poeti contro i loro critici pedanti" (Futurism against Backwardness. 8 poet-peoples against their pedantic critics) is the slogan with which the Italian Futurists summarized the values at stake in World War I, merging political and aesthetic discourse.[3] Psychological attributes such as France's "velocità, eleganza, spontaneità" (velocity, elegance, spontaneity); Japan's "agilità, progresso, risolutezza" (agility, progress, resoluteness); Montenegro's "indipendenza, ambizione, temerità" (independence, ambition, and temerity) are thus visually opposed to Germany's "filosofumo, pesantezza, rozzezza, brutalità" (philosophic abstruseness, heaviness, coarseness, brutality); Austria's "bigottismo, papalismo, inquisizione" (bigotry, Papalism, inquisition) and Turkey's complete lack of qualities (indicated with a zero).

---

[3] The first version of the Synthesis, published as a leaflet, reads "8 poeti" while the version subsequently published in Carrà's *Guerrapittura* reads "8 popoli-poeti". The leaflet also lacks any reference to Turkey.

The Futurists' somewhat brazen national characterizations reflect the widespread idea that the war originated in a clash of civilizations. Indeed, war acted as a catalyst for the merging of anthropological classifications and nationalist discourse that had defined the end of the nineteenth century (Giacanelli 394-97). Giovanni Papini, for instance, wrote that same year in the journal *Lacerba*: "C'è un tipo di civiltà contro un altro. O meglio alcuni tipi di civiltà contro un tipo solo che ha dominato per quaranta anni l'Europa; il tedesco" (There's a type of civilization against another. Or, better, some types of civilization against one single type which has dominated Europe for forty years; the German one) (Del Puppo 76). Le Bon himself, in his book, aimed to demonstrate how the current war could not be understood by using traditional logic because it was completely ruled by irrationality and by the Germans' almost religious furor. He wrote: "[...] hallucinated by their dream, the Germanic peoples believe to be, as the Arabs in the past at the time of Mohammed, a superior race, destined to regenerate the world, after conquering it" (3-4).

The visual solution of a pointed triangle piercing the circle of its enemies symbolized therefore Futurist dynamism against the immobile, enclosed and self-referential nature of traditional values or, as we can read on the leaflet itself, the characteristics of the "genio creatore" (creative genius) – elasticity, synthesis, intuition, invention, multiplication of forces, invisible order – against those proper to "cultura tedesca" (German culture) – rigidity, analysis, methodic plagiarism, sum of idiocies, numismatic order. Marinetti and the Futurists probably had the idea of enclosing Germany and its allies within the shape of a circle because of the symbolic values of stillness and constriction associated with this geometric form. This metaphor had already been widely used in the political arena. The Italian nationalist leader Enrico Corradini, for example, had forcefully employed it in a famous speech, *Proletarian Nations and Nationalism* (*Le nazioni proletarie e il nazionalismo*), that he had given in several Italian cities in 1911. "Il cerchio delle nazioni conquistatrici, cerchio economico e cerchio morale," he had said, "è stretto intorno a noi che ci nutrimmo di rinunzie per utopismo filosofico, per cecità popolare e per viltà borghese. Possiamo romperlo, questo cerchio?" (The circle of the conquering nations, a circle that is economic and moral, is closed around us who lived on abstinence because of our philosophical utopianism, our people's blindness, our bourgeois cowardice. Can we break this circle?) (Corradini 40). As for the dynamic force of the triangle or arrow, the Futurists had already used this simple geometric motif in their paintings. We can find it for instance in Russolo's 1911 *Revolt* (*La Rivolta*, oil on canvas, Gemeentemuseum, The Hague) and in several works by Balla dated 1913 (Del Puppo 72). The immediate and more significant precedent for the image of the triangle piercing the circle, however, resides elsewhere.

Well before the beginning of the war, Marinetti had already associated this image with Futurism's programmatic ideology of revolt against the past and its supporters. He had used it as a sort of seal, in French, to accompany his signature in several letters. Giovanni Lista has published the photographs of two of these documents, a message sent to Felix Marc Del Marle and, even more interesting for our discussion, a letter to the French writer Pierre Bure, written on the stationery of the Consulate of His Majesty the King of Italy in Moscow (Lista unpaged).[4] This latter item shows that Marinetti was using this emblem right at the time of his famous voyage to Russia, which took place between the 7th and the 27th of February, 1914 (January 25th- February 14th according to the old Russian calendar). Cesare De Michelis reports that Marinetti used this ideogram-signature in a dedication to Genrikh Tasteven (Henri Tastevin), who, that same year, translated several Italian Futurist manifestos in Russian.[5] De Michelis suggests that El Lissitzky might have seen one of these iconic dedications (the one to Tasteven reads: "Avec mes amis Futuristes Russes contre tous les > Passéismes") and this, in turn, might have directly influenced his idea for the poster (De Michelis 25). I, however, tend to think that the path from the *Futurist Synthesis of War* to *Beat the Whites with the Red Wedge* might have been somewhat less straightforward. And from Moscow and St. Petersburg in 1914, it brings us back, but just for a while, to the Western European battlefield.

Joffre's Angle of Penetration on the Marne
Of the five Futurists who signed the *Futurist Synthesis of War*, Carlo Carrà was the only one that did not spend any time in jail in September 1914. At the time, he was in Varzi, a small town on the outskirts of Pavia. On the 14th of that month, just a few days before the Futurists' demonstration in Milan, he sent a postcard to Marinetti, commenting on the most recent reports coming from the French front. He wrote: "La odierna vittoria Francese mi ha fatto grandissimo piacere. L'Italia, però, rimane eternamente immobile — abbasso l'immobilità!" (Today's French victory has made me very happy. Italy, however, remains eternally immobile — down with immobility!) (Carrà, Postcard to Filippo Tommaso Marinetti). Carrà's reference was to the battle of the Marne (September 5th-12th, 1914), the event that at the time was engrossing the European public with astonishment and excitement. The Franco-British troops, under the command of General Joffre, had finally succeeded in stopping the German army in its swift and, until then, seemingly inexorable progress into French territory.

---

[4] In the message to Del Marle, probably a book dedication, Marinetti inscribed his signature ("FuturMarinetti") within the triangle; in Pierre Bure's letter, he used the icon on top of the letter, as an alternative letterhead, the triangle of "Futurisme" piercing the ribbon of "Passéisme."
[5] In *Futurizm, Na puti k novomu simvolizmu*, Moscow 1914. That same year, Vadim Shershenevich published another anthology of Italian Futurist manifestos, *Manifesty italyanskogo futurizma*, Moscow 1914. For a list of Italian Futurist texts published in Russian, see De Michelis 289.

Joffre's victory was immediately interpreted as the result of a radical change of tactics, which gave birth to "one of the most intellectual [battles] known to military history" (Hanotaux III). Instead of continuing to oppose the Germans all along the border, the Allies retreated and then, when part of the enemy started to move eastward, concentrated their forces and attacked united, in order to break the front and push their way through enemy lines. Joffre continued to pursue this successful strategy throughout the winter of 1914-1915. In his memoirs, he explained: "[...] the main concern was how to break [the front], in order to subsequently exploit the split to the maximum. And there, too, what was important was to identify the breaking points, not for one aim or another, such as in order to re-occupy a certain region, but in a manner that, if the front would break in those particular areas, the enemy would have to face the most serious consequences" (Joffre 60). According to this new tactic, in other words, "once the line is pierced in a point, all the rest will probably fall simultaneously" (Le Bon 223). For Le Bon, the Battle of the Marne was "the most important event in the annals of our country. It shows, once again, the action of human willpower over the supposed fatalities of history" (Le Bon 334). Joffre's strategy soon became the symbol of individual determination against blind force. Again, as Le Bon put it: "In the fight among nations, willpower plays a preponderant role. A battle is mainly a fight of wills. The Battle of the Marne offers a memorable example of this" (Le Bon 27).

As Carrà's postcard shows, the Italian Futurists were among the first to recognize the importance of this battle not just from a military, but also from a strategic and psychological point of view. While they still had to abstain from carrying out other pro-war demonstrations, they did not miss the opportunity to create iconic celebrations of Joffre's tactics. Marinetti later explicitly linked the battle with the Futurists's own interventionist actions, saying: "While the Battle of the Marne was raging and Italy remained completely neutral, we Futurists organized the first two demonstrations against Austria and in favor of intervention" (White 217).

During the winter of 1914-1915, he created a *tavola parolibera* originally titled -*Mountains + Valleys + Roads x Joffre*, but also known with the alternative title *After the Marne, Joffre Visited the Front in an Automobile* (*Après la Marne, Joffre visita le front en auto*). It was published on the first page of a leaflet dated February 11th, 1915, and subsequently included in Marinetti's 1919 book *Les Mots en liberté futuristes*. John White has called this table an "anti-neutralist demonstration" in its own right and, along with Christine Poggi, has identified the way in which Marinetti merged letters, numbers and mathematical symbols with the codes of contemporary cartography (Poggi 230-33; White 216-18). Roughly around the same time, Carrà conceived a visual composition mixing words, collage and graphics, that he attributed to a dream. It is titled *The Night of January 20th, 1915 I Dreamt This Picture (Joffre's Angle of Penetration on the Marne Against two German Cubes)* (ill. 2) and he inserted it in his 1915 visual book, *Guerrapittura* (Poggi 240-41). Carrà drew a triangle (or cone) on the right (indubitably representing "Joffre's angle"), and two vertical parallelepipeds on the left (the two "German cubes"). These geometric figures are separated by a vertical stream (the river Marne), on the side of which Carrà glued a star-shaped clipping, taken from a contemporary newspaper, to signal the site of the battle. On the upper left-hand corner a German cross indicates the enemy's territory. The composition is completed by a series of stenciled words: "silurare" (torpedoing); "63 gradi" (63 degrees); "piano prospettico" (perspectival plane); "Bazaine," a reference to the general responsible for the French defeat at the hands of the Germans at Metz (1870) during the Franco-Prussian War; and a celebratory exclamation "WW" ("viva viva" in Italian). At the bottom, Carrà inserted some elements that recall the visual layout of *Futurist Synthesis of War*, such as a circle full of crickets' chirps with the inscription: "Musica opaca di 2 coppie di grrrrriiiiillliiiii poeti > contro" (Opaque music of two couples of crickets-poets > against). Linda Landis has suggested that the geometric forms in this work refer to three types of reconnaissance aircrafts used during the battle. In particular, the two "German cubes," as Carrà called them, indicate a German Albatros B II, with its two-bay wing structure, and the triangle or cone on the right depicts a French Morane monoplane with its "sharply tapered fuselage" (Landis 64-65). This interpretation, however, is not convincing, since it completely dismisses the meaning of the title that Carrà gave to his work. Moreover, if the triangular shape was to represent the fuselage of a Morane plane, Carrà would have depicted the Morane, with its "tapered fuselage," flying away westward from the two "German cubes" and not moving against or "penetrating" them, as he had sought.[6] In reality, Carrà's *Joffre's Angle* constitutes an accurate visualization of the military maneuvers that took place on the ground at the Battle of the Marne. Following contemporaneous reports of the battle, Carrà offered an abstract rendition of Joffre's troops at the moment in which they were piercing or, to use Carrà's words, "torpedoing" in between the solid blocks of the German divisions, creating a wedge that broke their resistance.

Thus, Carrà's *Joffre's Angle* offers us a key to understanding the abstract visual schema employed in the *Futurist Synthesis of War*. According to what the Futurists wrote on the work itself, they conceived it in jail, on September 20th, roughly a week after the end of the Battle of the Marne, while Italian and foreign newspapers where busy praising Joffre's dynamic tactics, which had changed the fate of the war.

It is quite probable, therefore, that the *Futurist Synthesis of War* coincided with a moment in which the signature-ideogram (Futurism against

---

[6] For a discussion of these two models of airplanes used during the conflict, see Wohl 207-09 and 220. Carrà depicted a warplane, in a much more detailed manner, in another illustration of *Guerrapittura*: *War Sky* (*Cielo di guerra*) (Carrà, *Guerrapittura* 21).

Backwardness) already used by Marinetti, acquired an additional meaning in light of Joffre's celebrated military tactics. The emblem of the Futurists' fight against past values was already conceived as the stylized metaphor of an assault. In the light of Joffre's strategy, that assault gained, in the fall of 1914, an additional resonance, visually overlapping and intertwining cultural ideology and authentic, military tactics in a single, powerful icon.

"The whole thing is mine, words and design"
In 1915, Carrà inserted the *Synthesis*, printed on a double-sized, foldable sheet, as the last diagram of his *Guerrapittura*. We do not know if, or when, the book made its way to Russia, but it is quite possible that Marinetti sent at least the leaflet of the *Synthesis* to some of the artists that, in the spring of 1914, had taken part in the Esposizione Libera Futurista Internazionale. On that occasion, four artists were reunited under the banner of "Russian artists": Alexander Archipenko, Alexandra Exter, Nikolai Kulbin and Olga Rozanova. In 1916, the latter published her own book devoted to the war, which, on the cover, featured a collage of geometric shapes: triangles, squares and circles (Mason 70-77). Natalia Gontcharova, who, according to the gallerist Giuseppe Sprovieri, had also exhibited in Rome at that time (Parton 142), published an illustrated volume devoted to the same subject in 1914.[7] A few years later, in 1918, she wrote to the Futurist poet Francesco Meriano explicitly asking him to send her Carrà's book (Gontcharova, Letter to Francesco Meriano). Indeed, Carrà's *Guerrapittura* became a renowned and successful example of how avant-garde artists engaged with the theme of the war, up to the point that it was even re-published by the Istituto Editoriale Italiano at the end of the war in 1919.

If we examine the information that El Lissitzky has left us regarding his poster *Beat the Whites with the Red Wedge*, however, we find no mention of Carrà's book, or of the Futurists' *Synthesis*. Documentation on the work, in fact, is mainly offered by the artist's own recollections, and even the poster itself is known today mostly through a series of later copies (ill. 3). In a letter in German to Jan Tschichold, dated July 1925, El Lissitzky wrote: "My old works are scattered to the wind. It was all done for the daily needs of the revolution, and I did not collect it [sic]. I am sending you as printed matter by registered mail: 1 POSTER from the period of the war with Poland. It was issued by the Staff on the Western Front. I found at home a completely battered and decayed copy, which I would like to keep for myself, so I am sending you a tracing done in the original colors. The type means: WITH THE WEDGE WITH THE RED STRIKE THE WHITE [sic], but you can see that it cannot be translated. It grows from 4 to 9 words and nothing remains of the sound: KLINOM KRASNYM BYEI BELIKH. The whole thing is mine, words and design"

---

[7] The exhibition catalogue, however, does not mention any work by Gontcharova (*Esposizione Libera Futurista Internazionale* 29-34).

(Lissitzky, Letter to Jan Tschichold 243).

El Lissitzky's characterization of *Beat the Whites with the Red Wedge* as an interaction of words and images reveals the importance that typographical experiments had in his own artistic production in the mid-1920s. In the same period, he wrote an essay retracing the history of modern typography. He highlighted the contribution of Sonia Delaunay and the English magazine *Blast*, but did not even mention the work of the Italian Futurists. Among the Russian artists responsible for typographical innovations, however, he listed Gontcharova, Rozanova and his own mentor in Vitebsk, Kazimir Malevitch. It was only with the advent of the Russian Revolution, according to Lissitzky, that typographic design underwent a radical change: "It is the great masses, the semi-literate masses, who have become the audience [...]. The traditional book was torn into separate pages, enlarged a hundred-fold, colored for greater intensity, and brought into the street as a poster" (Lissitzky, "Our Book" 358).

Lissitzky's idea that Russian propaganda posters, such as *Beat the Whites*, were a direct transposition of the experiments carried out in the avant-garde book reflects the way in which he himself became involved in producing agitprop in Vitebsk in 1919. He arrived there that year, called by the director of the local art school, Marc Chagall, and, in turn, he extended an invitation to Malevitch, who also joined the school soon after (Rakitin 62). Aleksandra Semenova Shatskikh has pointed out that a series of political drawings started to be published in Vitebsk right after the arrival of Lissitzky. One celebrated Leon Trotsky, who, at the time, was the head of the Red Army. In July 1919, the citizens of Vitebsk could see for the first time a series of locally created Russian Telegraph Agency (ROSTA) posters, the famous "window posters" or "wall newspapers," which already graced Moscow's walls and shop windows. Indeed, Semenova has found documentary evidence linking Lissitzky to the design of Vitebsk's ROSTA posters (Semenova Shatskikh 62). Until that time, Lissitzky's style leaned mostly toward folkloric Russian-Jewish models but was also influenced by the experiments in abstraction carried out by Alexandra Exter in Kiev (Semenova Shatskikh 61). With the arrival of Malevitch in Vitebsk, however, he was soon deeply involved in applying Suprematist principles to propaganda.

If Lissitzky, in his 1925 recollections, was reluctant to give any credit to the innovations of the Italian Futurists, Malevitch's attitude toward them was always much more straightforward. He had met Marinetti during the latter's visit to Russia in 1914 (Bowlt 116) and appropriated not only his exclamatory rhetoric and aphoristic manner, but also several of the Futurists' formal and ideological concerns, such as the centrality of intuition, machine aesthetics, anti-academicism, anti-humanism and an interest in the representation of war and aviation. For him, Marinetti was, along with Picasso, one of the "two pillars, the two 'prisms' of the new art of the twentieth century" (Marcadé, "Malevich, Painting, and Writing" 37-38). His theoretical writings of the time show an in-depth understanding not only of the literary production of Italian Futurism, but also of the movement's achievements in painting and, in particular, of Boccioni's theories.[8] To Malevich's mind, Futurism was a general tendency, encompassing Russian and Italian achievements. Following his arrival in Vitebsk, in November 1919, he gave a lecture on the "Latest trends in Art (Impressionism, Cubism and Futurism)," a topic that he had already addressed in his publications (Rakitin 62). Cubism and Futurism were, in point of fact, the main focus of the first two issues of a journal that Malevich had planned together with Exter, Rozanova and others between 1916 and 1917 (Gurianova).

After the Russian Revolution, many Russian Futurists responded enthusiastically to the requests of the new Regime. In all likelihood, the need for new propagandist material also led to a renewed interest in the Italian Futurists' visual experiments. It was at that time that the Soviet authorities showed an unabashed attraction for Marinetti and his movement. Toward the end of 1919, the leader of Futurism met with an envoy from Moscow to discuss the purchase of Italian Futurist paintings for the State collections while, in the summer of 1920, Anatoly Lunacharsky publicly stated that "in Italy there's one revolutionary intellectual, and it's Filippo Tommaso Marinetti" (Versari 579-81). According to other sources, it was actually Lenin himself who pronounced those words (De Michelis 39). Lissitzky probably saw a copy of the *Futurist Synthesis of War* through Malevitch, at the time in which they were both busy working for the Vitebsk propaganda authorities. He might have also seen it earlier in Exter's studio in Kiev, while she herself was developing agitprop designs. Incidentally, before the summer of 1919, and thus while Lissitzky was in Kiev, Exter had re-established contacts with her longtime lover, and one of Carrà's best friends, Ardengo Soffici (Soffici 371).

In an essay titled "Futurism" and published in the Moscow anarchist newspaper *Anarchiia* in 1918, Kazimir Malevich summarized the attitude of many artists regarding Futurism's status within the Revolution's system of values. He wrote: "Cubism and Futurism are the revolutionary banners of art. They are of value to museums, like the relics of the Social Revolution. Relics to which monuments should be erected in public squares. I propose creating in squares monuments to Cubism and Futurism as the weapons that defeated the old art of repetition and brought us to spontaneous creation" (Gurianova 53).

Surprisingly, right at the time of the article published in *Anarchiia*, a public monument had just been erected in Moscow. It restaged, in three-dimensional form, the visual structure of the *Futurist Synthesis of War*.

Monuments to the Red Wedge
The work (ill. 4) had been designed by the young architect Nikolai Kolli and

---

[8] In his book *Ot Sezanna do suprematizma: Kriticheskii ocherk* (*From Cézanne to Suprematism: A critical sketch*, 1920), for instance, Malevich addresses the Italians' idea of the centrality of the spectator within the artwork and the concept of force-lines.

was part of a series of monuments erected, in Lenin's words, "to commemorate the great days of the Russian Socialist Revolution" (Guerman 8). In a document dated April 18th, 1918, the Soviet leader had called for the removal of "monuments erected in honor of tsars and their servants" and the creation of a set of alternative monuments to replace them. The work of the Commission charged with the task started off with some delay, prompting repeated reprimands from Lenin, but a list of personalities to be celebrated with new monuments was finally published in August of that same year (Lenin 209- 10; 234-35; 236-37). Between the end of 1918 and the beginning of 1919 several busts and statues were erected in Moscow and St. Petersburg (Petrograd) in a variety of styles. Some, such as the memorial to Sophia Petrovskaya by Italo Griselli, revealed a distinctive (Italian) Futurist influence (Pacini 1978; Brucciani 2010).[9] Retrospectively, Lunacharsky reported that the monuments designed by "Futurist artists" were "less successful." At the inauguration of Griselli's work, for instance, many people "took a step back, in fear" (Lunacharsky 271). In any case, a certain number of projects created for Lenin's Plan for Monumental Propaganda were distinctively modern in nature. Kolli's was one of them.

Simply titled *The Red Wedge*, Kolli's monument was built, like many others at the time, with ephemeral materials. It consisted of a red triangle vertically inserted as a wedge into a white rectangular block. A very visible crack snakes downward from the tip of the triangle, suggesting that the force of the red wedge has succeeded in breaking the solidity of the white structure. The abstract metaphor was intended to signify the victory of the Red Army over the White, counter-Revolutionary forces. According to Christina Lodder, "by harnessing military and political terminology, which imbued the forms and colors with ideological associations, the monument manage[d] to convey an ideological narrative, which would have been comprehensible to all levels of society, the literate as well as the illiterate. The effectiveness of this approach was later recognized by El Lissitzky, who adopted an almost identical language for his poster, *Beat the Whites with the Red Wedge* of 1920" (Lodder, *Constructive Strand* 193-94).[10]

---

[9] The Tuscan-born Griselli had moved to Russia before the War to carry out some commissioned portraits. He remained in the country during the conflict and for a few years following the Revolution. From 1918 to 1921, he was employed as a professor of sculpture at the School of Art in St. Petersburg. His portrait of Sophia Petrovskaya, heavily influenced by the work of Boccioni, was apparently removed in 1919, following scathing critiques for its daring style (Brucciani 2010). Griselli, who took part in the 1914 Esposizione Libera Futurista Internazionale in Rome, where he exhibited a portrait of Marinetti (*Esposizione Libera Futurista Internazionale* 17), might have also fostered contacts between Italian and Russian artists after the Revolution.

[10] Lodder's chapter, entitled "Monuments to the Masses" (186-218), appears in her book *Constructive Strand in Russian Art. 1914-1937*.

Kolli's *Red Wedge*, and its embrace of an overtly abstract language, however, originated in a much more specific set of circumstances. In some preliminary sketches, the monument's white block bears a visible inscription: "Банды Краснова," meaning "Krasnov's Bands."[11] In a photograph of the monument erected in Moscow, however, only the first word ("bands") is clearly discernible (ill. 4). According to Dimitri Kozlov, the final version displayed a more general inscription referring to the White Army (Kozlov 57). Until now, the originally planned version of the inscription has failed to attract the attention of scholars. It is nevertheless quite significant if we want to understand the way in which Kolli conceived its monument and how it might have affected El Lissitzky some time later. At the time of the monument's inauguration, in the first years of the Civil War, the public in Moscow's Revolutionary Square would have surely recognized the full implications of a reference to Krasnov's forces.

General Peter Krasnov was one of the leaders of the White Army during the Russian Civil War. In May-June 1918, he beat the Red Army repeatedly, marching toward Moscow in the second half of the year. It was at that point, however, that he was defeated, when the city of Tsaritsyn became the main theater of the Civil War. Krasnov put the city under siege, but was overpowered by the resistance of the Red Army's local unit and by the sudden arrival of additional forces from the Caucasus that attacked his troops from the rear. From a visual point of view, the Reds' attack at Tsaritsyn recalls the strategy employed by Joffre at the Battle of the Marne. Already in February 1919, Krasnov was no longer a problem for the Red Army: he retired from the front and went into exile in Germany. In the wake of the Red Army's many previous defeats, the dissolution of Krasnov's units greatly boosted Soviet morale. According to Peter Kenetz: "Whether the eastern and southern fronts could be united depended on the battle for Tsaritsyn. It would have been extremely advantageous for the Whites to establish a common front, and the Bolsheviks did everything within their power to prevent it" (Kenetz 166).

In the end, Kolli's monument did not include any specific references to Krasnov's name, becoming a more general celebration of the unity finally achieved by the Red Army and the disintegration of the Whites' cohesive force. Trotsky had already used the metaphor of the "wedge" in one of his political texts (Kozlov 56) without, however, referring to the Red Army or to a specific military tactic. The idea of the wedge, inserted with force within a solid object

---

[11] One of Kolli's sketches (*Design for an architectural construction*, 1918, black lead and crayons on paper, 30.5 x 22.8 cm) is at the Tretyakov Gallery, Moscow. Because of the similarity between the Russian words Красный ("red") and Краснов (the family name Krasnov), Lodder (*Constructive Strand* 193) reads the inscription as "gangs of the red," a reference to the Red Army, and interprets it therefore as a dedication of the monument to the Red Army.

in order to break its integrity, was nonetheless widespread at the time. Before the end of World War I, for instance, a reporter from the *Manchester Guardian* explained that, for the Allies, "the Russian Revolution is a potent weapon. It is capable of being thrust like a wedge into German unity" (Farbman 46). In 1919, the memory of Krasnov and his army had already been eclipsed by other, more pressing, military events. Still, the idea of a piercing force, capable of breaking the monolithic unity of the enemy, survived. What Kolli succeeded in creating, with his monument, was a new, powerful link between the metaphor of the "wedge" and the identity of the Red Army.

In his famous poster, El Lissitzky appropriated not only Kolli's icon (at the time visible to anyone in Moscow), but also his linguistic metaphor, which identified the "Red Army" as the "Red Wedge." But the reference to a specifically Soviet visual tradition stops here: the layout of *Beat the Whites with the Red Wedge* reproduces with astonishing accuracy the *Futurist Synthesis of War*. Instead of a three-dimensional wedge, we see a triangle which does not pierce a solid rectangular block but, again, as in the Futurists' original, a circle. The triangle is slightly tilted upward, the background is divided into contrasting black and white surfaces, but the underlying structure of the two images is the same. When, in 1926, he retraced his career as a graphic designer, El Lissitzky wrote that "every invention in art is a single event in time, [it] has no evolution" (Lissitzky, "Our Book" 356). Still, his iconic poster overtly positioned itself at the end of a line of development, which was simultaneously formal, historical and ideological. For the general public, the poster's message was understandable because of the continued presence of the Soviet metaphor of the "Red Wedge," but for an artist engaged in translating ideology into form it revealed the appropriation of a distinctively modernist tradition, whose origins lay with the Italian Futurists and their visual experimentations with war.

Carnegie Mellon University

Works Cited

Adamowicz, Elza, and Simona Storchi, eds. *Back to the Futurists. The Avant-garde and Its Legacy*. Manchester: Manchester UP, 2013.

Boccioni, Umberto. Letter to his family, Milan, 22 [September 1914]. *Lettere futuriste*. Ed. Federica Rovati. Rovereto: Egon/Mart, 2009.

Bowlt, John E., ed. *Russian Art of the Avant-Garde. Theory and Criticism 1902-1934*. New York: The Viking Press, 1976.

Brucciani, Patrizio. *Griselli nelle avanguardie (1911-1923)*. Firenze: Nerbini, 2010.

Carrà, Carlo. *Guerrapittura*. Milano: Edizioni Futuriste di *Poesia*, 1915.

———. Postcard to Filippo Tommaso Marinetti, Varzi, 14 September 1914. Getty Research Institute, Filippo Tommaso Marinetti Correspondence and Papers, 1886-1974, Box 2, folder 1.

Clark, Timothy J. "El Lissitzky in Vitebsk." Perloff and Reed 199-210.
Corradini, Enrico. *Il nazionalismo italiano*. Milano: Fratelli Treves, 1914.
Del Puppo, Alessandro. *Modernità e nazione. Temi di ideologia visiva nell'arte italiana del primo Novecento*. Macerata: Quodlibet, 2012.
De Michelis, Cesare G. *L'avanguardia trasversale. Il futurismo tra Italia e Russia*. Venezia: Marsilio 2009.
Drutt, Matthew, ed. *Kazimir Malevich. Suprematism*. New York: The Solomon Guggenheim Foundation, 2003.
Esposizione libera futurista internazionale. Pittori e scultori italiani russi inglesi belgi nordamericani. Exh. cat. Galleria Futurista, Direttore G. Sprovieri, Roma, via del Tritone, 125. April-May 1914.
Farbman, Michael. *The Russian Revolution and the War*. London: National Council for Civil Liberties / The Herald, 1917.
Giacanelli, Ferruccio. "Tracce e percorsi del razzismo nella psichiatria italiana della prima metà del Novecento." *Nel nome della razza. Il razzismo nella storia d'Italia, 1870-1945*. Ed. Alberto Burgio. Bologna: Il Mulino, 1999. 389-406.
Gontcharova, Natalia. Letter to Francesco Meriano, Nièvre, 28 November 1918. Fondo Meriano, Fondazione Primo Conti, Fiesole.
Guerman, Michail. *Art of the October Revolution*. New York: Harry N. Abrams Inc., 1979.
Gurianova, Nina. "The *Supremus* 'Laboratory-House': Reconstructing the Journal." Drutt 45-59.
Hanontaux, Gabriel. *La Bataille de la Marne. Tome I. (23 Août-7 Septembre 1914)*. Paris: Librairie Plon, 1922.
Joffre, Joseph. *1914-1915. La Préparation de la guerre et la conduite des opérations par le Maréchal Joffre*. Paris: E. Chiron, 1920.
Kenez, Peter. *Civil War in South Russia, 1918: The First Year of the Volunteer Army*. Berkeley: U of California P, 1978.
Kozlov, Dmitriĭ. *'Klinom krasnym beĭ belykh' geometricheskaia simvolika v iskusstve avangarda*. St. Petersburg: ESP Press, 2014.
Landis, Linda. "Futurists at War." *The Futurist Imagination. Word + Image in Italian Futurist Painting, Drawing, Collage and Free-Word Poetry*. Ed. Anne Coffin Hanson. New Haven: Yale University Art Gallery, 1983. 60-75.
Le Bon, Gustave. *Enseignements psychologiques de la guerre européenne*. Paris: Flammarion, 1916.
Lenin, Vladimir Ilich. *Écrits sur l'art et la littérature*. Moscow: Éditions du Progrès, 1978.
Lissitzky, El. Letter to Jan Tschichold, Moscow, 22 July 1925. Trans. David Britt. Perloff and Reed 243-44.
_____. "Our Book." *El Lissitzky. Life, Letters, Text*. Ed. Sophie Lissitzky-Küppers. London: Thames, 1968. 356-59.
Lodder, Christina. *Constructive Strand in Russian Art. 1914-1937*. London: The Pindar Press, 2005.
Lunacharsky, Anatoly. "Lénine et l'art." Lenin 269-73.
Marcadé, Jean-Claude. "Marinetti et Malevitch." *Présence de Marinetti. Actes du Colloque International tenu à l'UNESCO*. Ed. Jean-Claude Marcadé. Lausanne: L'Age d'Homme, 1982. 250-65
_____. "Malevich, Painting, and Writing: On the Development of a Suprematist Philosophy." Drutt 32-43.
Mason, Michael Rainer, ed. *Guerres. Natalija Gontcharova, Ol'ga Rozanova, Aleksej*

Kruchenykh. *Trois suites insignes sur un thème.* Geneva/Paris: Cabinet des estampes du Musée d'art et d'histoire /Adam Biro, 2003.

Nisbet, Peter. *El Lissitzky in the Proun Years: A Study of His Work and Thought, 1919. 1927.* Diss. Yale U, 1995. Ann Arbor: UMI, 1995.

Pacini, Piero. "Pietrogrado 1918: una scultura cubofuturista di Italo Griselli." *Critica d'arte* 43 (1978): 153-64.

Parton, Anthony. *Mikhail Larionov and the Russian Avant-garde.* London: Thames, 1993.

Perloff, Nancy, and Brian Reed, eds. *Situating El Lissitzky. Vitebsk, Berlin, Moscow.* Los Angeles: Getty Research Institute, 2003.

Poggi, Christine. *In Defiance of Painting: Cubism, Futurism, and the Invention of Collage.* New Haven: Yale UP, 1992.

Salaris, Claudia. *Marinetti editore.* Bologna: Il Mulino, 1990.

Semenovna Shatskikh, Aleksandra. *Vitebsk. The Life of Art.* New Haven: Yale UP, 2007.

Soffici, Ardengo. Letter to Serge Férat, Poggio a Caiano, 21 May 1919. Ardengo Soffici, Serge Férat, Hélène d'Œttingen, *Correspondance 1903-1964.* Ed. Barbara Meazzi. Lausanne: L'Age d'Homme, 2013. 370-72.

Rakitin, Vasilii. "The Optimism of a Nonobjectivist." Drutt 60-77.

Versari, Maria Elena. "Internazionalismo futurista. Sui rapporti internazionali del Futurismo dopo il 1919." *Il Futurismo nelle Avanguardie. Atti del Convegno Internazionale di Milano.* Ed. Walter Pedullà. Roma: Edizioni Ponte Sisto, 2010. 577-606.

White, John J. "The Cult of the 'Expressive' in Italian Futurist Poetry: New Challenges to Reading." *Back to the Futurists. The Avant-garde and its Legacy.* Adamowicz and Storchi 208-25.

Whol, Robert. *A Passion for Wings. Aviation and the Western Imagination 1908-1918.* New Haven: Yale UP, 1994.

Avant-garde Iconographies of Combat 201

1. Marinetti, Boccioni, Carrà, Russolo, Piatti, *Futurist Synthesis of War*, central page of the manifesto leaflet, 1914, private collection (F.T.M. Marinetti and C. Carrà© 2015 Artists Rights Society (ARS), New York / SIAE, Rome)

2. Carlo Carrà, *The Night of January 20th, 1915 I Dreamt This Picture (Joffre's Angle of Penetration on the Marne Against two German Cubes)*, from *Guerrapittura*, p. 29, 1914, private collection (C. Carrà© 2015 Artists Rights Society (ARS), New York / SIAE, Rome).

Avant-garde Iconographies of Combat 203

3. El Lissitzky, *Beat the Whites with the Red Wedge*, 1919-1920, reprint 1966 offset on paper, Collection Van Abbemuseum, Eindhoven, The Netherlands (Photo: Peter Cox, Eindhoven, The Netherlands) (El Lissitzky © 2015 Artists Rights Society (ARS), New York).

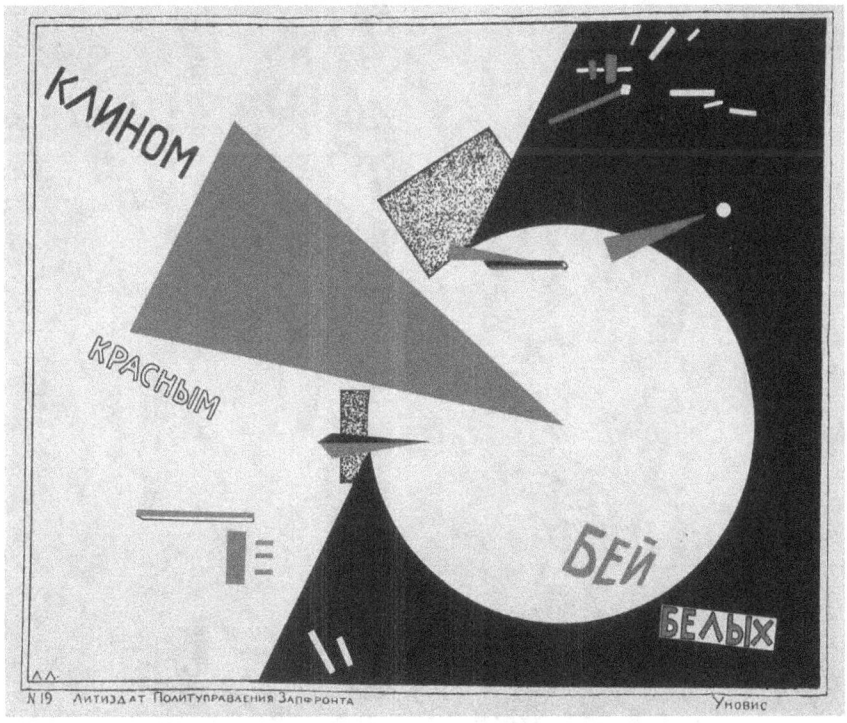

4. Photograph of Nikolai Kolli's monument, *The Red Wedge*, in Moscow (circa 1920).

Selena Daly

Constructing the Futurist Wartime Hero: Futurism and the Public, 1915-1919

1. *Introduction*
The First World War has long been recognized as a challenging period for European avant-garde movements and none of them survived the war completely intact. In many countries, there was a widespread hostility towards any form of art during the war years, but particular disdain was often reserved for the protagonists of avant-garde groups. In the context of Great Britain, James Fox has discussed how art almost completely disappeared from the press, deemed a luxury activity inappropriate for a society at war (49-51). The Vorticists suffered because they were initially reluctant to enlist, leading them to be branded as war shirkers (Black 169-71). Their reputation as "amusing creatures and puzzle painters" could sustain them no longer and journalists wondered "what on earth was up with us that we should ever have been entertained by them" (Collins Baker in Fox 53). Cubism also fell foul of wartime public opinion in France: it was criticized for its internationalist character and was frequently spelt with a Germanic "K" in the popular press, in order to brand it as being in alliance with the enemy (Silver 8-12).

The case of Futurism in Italy was different. Public responses to Futurism actually improved significantly during the years of the Great War, offering a perhaps surprising counterpoint to the dominant narratives in France and Britain outlined above. By analyzing newspaper reports from 1915-1919, this article demonstrates how public and press reactions to Futurism improved significantly as the war progressed, and in addition, how the Futurists sought to render their theatrical and artistic production more accessible to a wider audience during the war years. Although Walter Adamson has noted in passing that "the avant-garde nature of the relationship between futurism and its public did weaken somewhat" in the later war years (862), Futurist scholarship generally identifies such a shift in the Futurist attitude towards the public as a characteristic of "secondo futurismo" from the 1920s onwards. As Claudia Salaris wrote in the catalogue of the 2014 Guggenheim exhibition on the movement, in the early 1920s "the Futurists grew adept at meeting the demands of an increasingly complex and populous society, succeeding in presenting the group as an avant-garde for the masses and specializing in forms of aesthetic communication intended for a wide audience" (43). In fact, attempting to satisfy the public's tastes in art had been part of Marinetti's vision for Futurism since November 1914 and this approach only intensified from 1916 onwards as the war dragged on. A fuller understanding of this shift can only be reached through an examination of the surrounding context of improved press and public reactions towards Futurism following Italy's entry into the war.

The altered press responses to Futurism were initially prompted by the enthusiastic enlistment of many key Futurist figures in the army in May 1915, and particularly by the decision of Marinetti, Umberto Boccioni, Luigi Russolo, Antonio Sant'Elia and Mario Sironi to volunteer for the Lombard Battalion of Volunteer Cyclists and Motorists in May 1915, with whom they saw combat in autumn in the mountains of Trentino at Lake Garda. As a result of the Futurists' voluntary military service, they earned praise and admiration from the press and quickly assumed the status of war heroes. Marinetti, in particular, sought to capitalize on this new-found respect for the protagonists of his movement, and thus began to pursue a more accessible style of art suitable for mass tastes and for the demands of a wartime society. The 1916 and 1917 performances of the "teatro futurista sintetico" genre showcased this new approach in the theater. Initially, it had been Futurist actions which prompted a change in attitude among the press and public, but subsequently it was the public's desire for less extravagant entertainment that pushed the Futurists to modify some of the most provocative elements of their artistic program. The Futurists' heroic status was further cemented in August 1916 with the death of Boccioni while serving with the Italian Army. The final phase of the Futurists' establishment as symbols of Italian military courage and heroism came in 1919 with the staging of the "Grande Esposizione Nazionale Futurista" in Milan and Genoa between March and July 1919. This exhibition marked the re-launch of artistic Futurism after the war, and constituted the culmination of the positive responses to Futurism that had developed during the war, which would have important implications for the movement's trajectory in the 1920s. This article will consider the press responses to these key events during the war (the Futurists' military service; the synthetic theater performances; the death of Boccioni; and the 1919 exhibition) as they succinctly elucidate the transforming relationship between Futurism and the Italian press and public during the years of the Great War.

2. *The Futurists as Volunteer Soldiers, 1915*
When it comes to their perception in the media, Futurism's jingoism served them very well during in the early months of Italy's intervention, as the demands of the nation were immediately placed above the demands of art. As soon as Italy entered the war in May 1915, all Futurist activity stopped. The Futurist leadership marked this moment by publishing the manifesto "Per la guerra, sola igiene del mondo," which declared that "il movimento futurista letterario, pittorico, e musicale è attualmente sospeso, causa l'assenza del poeta Marinetti, recatosi sul teatro della guerra." The manifesto continued:
Finché duri la guerra, lasciamo da parte i versi, i pennelli, gli scalpelli e le orchestre! Son

cominciate le rosse vacanze del genio! Nulla possiamo ammirare, oggi, se non le formidabili sinfonie degli *shrapnels* e le folli sculture che la nostra ispirata artiglieria foggia nelle masse nemiche.

(Marinetti, "Per la guerra")

There was no possibility that the Futurists could be accused of not doing their civic duty. The Lombard Battalion of Volunteer Cyclists and Motorists departed from Milan in early summer 1915 and spent August and September awaiting front-line duty near Lake Garda. In October, they were transformed into an Alpine unit and were involved in the capture of the Austrian position at Dosso Casina. Because of the lack of suitability of bicycles for the mountainous terrain, the Volunteer Cyclists were disbanded in December 1915.[1]

Following the disbandment, Marinetti wrote to Futurist musician, Francesco Balilla Pratella on 31 December 1915, "La stampa è singolarmente migliorata per noi Futuristi" (Marinetti and Pratella 59). The positivity noted by Marinetti is evident in media reports from as early as July 1915. An article commenting on the participation of intellectuals in the war highlighted how these men, the Futurists included, had left to one side "ogni veste di superiorità, per rientrare nelle file di quell'enorme livellatore di uomini che è un esercito in guerra" (Fiorini 655). The Futurists — "bravi giovanotti" — were also praised for having put their interventionist words into action, by volunteering as soldiers (Fiorini 662), which was a common theme in many articles of the time. Valeria Vampa in *Gran mondo* praised the Futurists,

i quali dopo avere tentato con lo sforzo e ben altro con lo scherno di creare una nuova corrente d'idee e di ideali nel campo sconfinato delle arti, dopo aver tentato che non siano stroncate ed offuscate le sfolgoranti ali del genio con i vieti sofismi di decrepite scuole o scuolette, convergono tutta la forza del loro braccio, tutta l'attività del loro intelletto, sui campi cruenti dove tuttavia si decidono i migliori destini dell'umanità.[2]

Similarly, an article of *La libreria economica* claimed the Futurists' war service would be their finest hour:

Chi conosce il loro fervore e la loro audacia non dubita ch'essi compiranno appieno il loro dovere di uomini e d'artisti (poiché per loro le due funzioni s'integrano e s'identificano) e che questo sarà, se non l'ultimo [...] il loro canto più bello e più alto.

(Grammona)

Marinetti was singled out for praise in most reports on the Volunteer Cyclists. *La stampa* journalist Carlo Scarfoglio wrote that Marinetti's volunteering "manifesta una grande forza di volontà, perché [...] non brilla più

---

[1] On the combat experiences of the Lombard Battalion of Volunteer Cyclists, see Daly.
[2] Full bibliographical details for some periodical articles held in the archives consulted for this research project are not available. When relevant, I have added the archive in which these documents are held as part of their entry in the list of works cited.

del fiore velluto della prima giovinezza" (he was 37 at the time). In *Lo sport illustrato della guerra*, Marinetti's sporting prowess and his willingness to live up to his warmongering rhetoric by volunteering were highlighted as worthy of admiration (Codara). The reports that Renzo Codara wrote about the Volunteer Cyclists for *La gazzetta dello sport* were unstinting in their praise for the Futurists of the Battalion. Russolo was lauded as a "soldato docile, obbediente, esemplare" while Marinetti was praised for his "giocondità spensierata" and "geniale esuberanza" (qtd. Bellini 31 and 74). He was also described as a "modello di disciplina agli altri, [che] compie scrupolosamente il suo dovere ed è certamente tra i migliori soldati" (Argenti).

Upon his return to Milan in December 1915, Marinetti sought to capitalize on this unprecedented goodwill towards Futurism from the press. He immediately began a media assault with the aim of raising public awareness of his military service with the Volunteer Cyclists. The Futurists' military service had yielded great dividends and Marinetti realized the importance in continuing to highlight his status as a soldier and veteran of the war in order to maintain the public's favorable opinion of Futurism. He began to publish accounts of his time on the front lines and gave interviews to newspapers.[3] He wrote two articles for *La gazzetta dello sport*, which appeared in January and February 1916, and also produced a manifesto, "Orgoglio futurista," which appeared in the Futurist-aligned magazine *Vela latina* on 15 January 1916.

3. *Synthetic Theater Performances of 1916 and 1917*

Marinetti's revised approach was most evident, however, in the "teatro futurista sintetico" tours of spring 1916, which gave performances in Vercelli, Genoa, La Spezia, Imperia, Pavia, Venice, Livorno, Lucca, Viareggio, Siena, Pistoia, Florence and Naples. At each of these events, a selection of *sintesi* was performed and Marinetti concluded the performance with a speech on his "impressioni sulla guerra." Marinetti had come to the realization that the success of the tour would depend on his own identity as a soldier and on his ability to tap into the patriotic spirit of the audience. Emanuela Scarpellini has noted that plays with war themes were very popular in Milan from 1915, although many were appreciated for their nationalistic sentiments rather than the actual quality of the content (159). In a letter to Pratella of March 1916, Marinetti wrote that unfortunately the short plays by Pratella and Paolo Buzzi had been "*momentaneamente* sacrificati" because "fu necessario non dare che delle sintesi antitedesche e patriottiche e rappresentare almeno un lavoro di [Francesco]

---

[3] Interviews with Marinetti appeared in the following newspapers: *Il giornale del mattino* (Bologna), *Giornale d'Italia* (Rome), *Gazzetta di Messina e delle Calabrie*, and in C. I. Ravida for *Corriere di Mantova*. Photographs of the Futurists in action were also common, *e.g., Domenica del corriere, Gli avvenimenti*, and *Lo sport illustrato e la guerra*.

Cangiullo e di Boccioni che non erano stati mai rappresentati" (61), demonstrating his willingness to compromise Futurism's artistic independence in order to respond to the tastes of the public. Overall, this tour received a positive response from audiences and critics alike. Reviews of the synthetic theater tours in 1916 often refer to the audience's behavior, not least because it was frequently in stark contrast to that which had characterized the Futurist *serate* of the pre-war and interventionist years. Commenting on the premiere of the first tour of "synthetic theater" held in Florence in March 1916, the critic Baccio Bacci observed:

Noto che la folla è migliorata: non si sono ripetute quelle ignobili becerate passatiste che deplorammo sinceramente, allorché fu data al Teatro Verdi una grande serata futurista. Allora trionfò il becerismo e udimmo soltanto il rumore di oggetti che volavano. Ieri sera no. Abbiamo ascoltato, applaudito e anche fischiato. Ma decentemente.

(101)

Although the performance was by no means met with universal approval (Novelli 102), the nature of the dissent was markedly different from that which both the Futurists and critics had come to expect. A significant factor in this newfound positivity was the fact that Marinetti was now a soldier, and that many of the patriotic *sintesi* being performed had been written by Futurist soldiers, such as Boccioni, a reality Marinetti alluded to in his *sintesi* entitled *L'arresto*. It would have been unthinkable for the audience to pelt the performers with objects, as had occurred during the first synthetic tour in 1915. As a member of the army, Marinetti could not be ridiculed as he had been when he had been merely the leader of a provocative and marginal artistic movement. Indeed, Marinetti's status as a soldier was commented upon in reviews; one critic wrote:

Marinetti, Settimelli, Corra, Boccioni, Chiti, sono uomini di talento e di coraggio. [...] Marinetti è reduce dal fronte e vi tornerà a pagare il suo tributo di fede e di sangue. È gente che vive: con rumore, con stranezza, con segni esagerati di esistenza. Ma vive.

(Bacci 101)

The positive reception of Futurist synthetic theater continued in 1917, when there were two performances of the genre held in Florence in aid of military families. The program began with *Il dramma del futurista*, which comprised four *sintesi* by Settimelli and Corra that bore remarkably little resemblance to the enigmatic offerings of the first synthetic theater tour in 1915. As a reviewer commented, "[...] si tratta di un nuovo tentativo di teatro futurista, più accessibile alle menti ed ai gusti degli spettatori che si ostinano a rimaner passatisti" ("Gli spettacoli" 115). The four *sintesi* largely conformed to the norms of traditional dramas and appeared like short one-act plays with a clear narrative structure and traditional staging, all focusing on the figure of Italo, a young Futurist poet and volunteer in the war.[4] The anonymous reviewer for *La nazione* noted that the *sintesi* were "assai applaudite" and that they had "un relativo sapore futurista." Another critic noted that they were "accettati dal pubblico con una certa simpatia" and observed that there were "poche risate ironiche e niente commestibili [...]. Il futurismo progredisce forse perché il pubblico si è un po' più avvicinato a lui" ([no title], *Il nuovo giornale* 116). However, the Futurists were also reducing the distance between themselves and their audiences by appealing to the taste of the masses. These 1917 performances were far more focused on pure entertainment value than had been the case in previous iterations of the genre of synthetic theater, and featured Futurism's first foray into the field of cinema, the most popular of all popular entertainment. While still featuring a war-themed program, the Futurists also addressed the public's need for escapism. This was remarked upon by the reviewer for *Il nuovo giornale*, who wrote:

In uno spettacolo futurista tutto è interessante, anche il pubblico. Questo aveva oggi l'aria di pensare: "Su da bravi futuristi! Non siamo in vena di rissa, né di pugilati! La guerra ahimè altrove e le patate costano un po' care! Siate voi artisti o guastamestieri, non siamo qui per combattere una battaglia letteraria, ma per ridere, sia alle vostre spalle, sia alle nostre!" I futuristi, dal canto loro, per rispondere al desiderio del pubblico, gli hanno ammannito tutta roba di primissima qualità... futurista.

(116)

4. *"Artificial Optimism" and the Death of Boccioni, August 1916*

In August 1916, the Futurist movement suffered a great tragedy when Boccioni died after falling off a horse during a training exercise as part of his military service. The loss of the movement's foremost artistic talent was widely reported on in the Italian media and his dogged commitment to his military ideals garnered him enormous support and compassion, which was unknown to him during his lifetime. As had occurred with the decision to enlist in the Battalion of Volunteer Cyclists, Boccioni's death "sotto le armi" drew praise for the "coerenza [...] in lui tra parola e azione" ("Necrologio"). Readers of reports on Boccioni's death were reminded that once Italy entered the war in 1915, the Futurists "non hanno più sentito che una necessità, superiore e imperiosa: dare tutto alla Patria, al suo avvenire, alla sua grandezza" (Mastrigli). The critic for *Corriere della sera* wrote, "la sua vita, tra queste due milizie, quella della patria e quella dell'arte, aveva raggiunto la sua più perfetta unità" (Simoni in Crispolti 121). Boccioni's death did not bring about a sudden fondness for his art or for Futurism, but it did mark a break from the mockery and dismissal that had

---

[4] The four sintesi were: *I corvi* (published in *L'Italia Futurista*, 18 March 1917), *Uccidiamo il chiaro di luna* (published in *L'Italia Futurista*, 11 March 1917), *Dichiarazione di guerra* (published in *L'Italia Futurista*, 3 April 1917) and *Attacco di aeroplani austriaci*, by Settimelli only (published in *L'Italia futurista*, 10 February 1917).

characterized earlier responses to his work. As one critic remembered, "I quadri e i gessi di Boccioni [...] in Italia vengono benevolmente giudicati come opere indecifrabili d'un simpatico pazzo" (Interlandi). In fact, praise for Boccioni came in spite of his status as a Futurist rather than because of it, and there was a reluctance to engage in aesthetic judgments of his work in the wake of his death. A journalist for *La sera* claimed,

> Certo non oggi si può valutare convenientemente l'opera di questo pittore, che fu artista completo nello spirito bizzarro, nei multipli atteggiamenti, nell'impulsività creatrice, nella vita esteriore. Domani forse, dopo questo sconvolgimento di valori e di idee, gli artisti ameranno e studieranno l'opera di Boccioni.
>
> ("La tragica morte")

Although Boccioni's death prompted an outpouring of praise from sections of the Italian media, Marinetti's own attitude to commemorating Futurism's war dead was rather different. He was fiercely opposed to the "schifosa tendenza che spinge tutti a mettersi comodamente a tavola sul corpo di un artista morto" (Marinetti and Pratella 62; letter of 20 December 1916). Instead, he argued that Futurism had to prove its continued vitality. He instructed Pratella that "*I vivi, i vivi soltanto sono sacri. Il Futurismo*, malgrado l'immensa spaventosa scomparsa del povero Boccioni e di tanti altri, è più vivo che mai" (62). Marinetti objected to special commemorative volumes and obituaries for Futurism's fallen, as he wrote in a letter to Carli in the summer of 1917 (46). In fact, he simply marked Boccioni's death on the front page of the periodical *L'Italia futurista* with an abstract drawing by Giacomo Balla entitled *Il pugno italiano di Boccioni* and Marinetti's own words:

> È morto UMBERTO BOCCIONI caro grande forte migliore divino genio futurista ieri denigrato oggi glorificato superarlo superarlo superarlo durezza eroismo velocità avanti giovani futuristi tutto tutto doloresanguevita per la grande Italia sgombra ingigantita agilissima elettrica esplosiva non lagrime acciaio acciaio!
>
> (1)[5]

This insistence on positivity was nothing new for Marinetti. In the 1911 manifesto "Noi rinneghiamo i nostri maestri simbolisti ultimi amanti della luna," he had declared the need to replace "determinismo scettico e pessimista" with "il culto dell'intuizione creativa, la libertà dell'ispirazione e l'ottimismo artificiale" (306). This "artificial optimism" sustained Futurism through the war years and it was also to define Marinetti's attitude to an art that would be suitable for a post-war society. In an article for *L'Italia futurista* of June 1917, Marinetti was critical of *passéist* critics who were preparing for official commemorations and

---

[5] The issue featured Marinetti's tavola parolibera "Con Boccioni a Dosso Casina" and Boccioni's "Uomo + vallata + montagna" on p. 3, an extract from Boccioni's 'Pittura scultura futurista' on p. 2 and a dedication to him in an article by Carli on p. 2.

historical investigations of the war. He objected to the idea of war heroes, "i numerosissimi autentici eroi della nostra guerra" being subjected to "un bombardamento di discorsi e di statue balorde." Instead, he believed that

L'arte del dopoguerra sarà fatta di libertà, di audacia, di entusiasmo giovanile, di velocità, di varietà di colore e di imprevenuto. [...] Come è necessario ora fare con energia la guerra, senza rievocare nostalgicamente la pace passata e senza piagnucolare, con forza, tenacia e ottimismo fino alla vittoria completa, così si dovrà poi, nei relativi riposi pacifici dell'umanità, lavorare e vivere intensamente aerandosi i cervelli con sempre nuove e inattese forme d'arte ultraallegre, ultrasorprendenti e ultraspensierate, senza rievocare gli orrori della guerra.

("Imbecilli" 1)

5. Re-lauching Futurism: The Great Exhibition of 1919

This is the approach that dominated the "Grande Esposizione Nazionale Futurista" of 1919, which constituted the re-launch of artistic Futurism after the war. In the exhibition catalogue, Marinetti wrote that "il movimento futurista artistico, che subì durante la guerra un rallentamento forzato, riprende oggi il suo dinamismo eccitatore e rinnovatore" (144). The exhibition opened in the Galleria Centrale d'Arte in Milan on 22 March and remained there until 9 May before transferring to Genoa where it opened on 24 May for two months.[6] The planned iterations of the exhibition in Florence and Venice never took place. In July, Marinetti told Gino Soggetti, "L'esposizione a Venezia non ha potuto aver luogo causa lo sfascimento del padiglione costruito al Lido dall'impresario Moretti." Around the same time, Marinetti told Gerardo Dottori (a painter and one of the earliest adherents of Futurism) that the exhibition "verrà aperta a Firenze dopo le elezioni," which took place in November 1919 (qtd. Cialfi and Pesola 35). There is no evidence, however, that this exhibition ever took place. In an article in *Roma futurista* on 4 January 1920, there is a reference to the exhibitions in Milan and Genoa but no mention of a planned event for Florence (Balla et al. 1).

By all accounts the exhibition was well attended. A critic for *Il secolo* remarked on the "enorme successo di curiosità destata dal semplice annuncio della mostra e manifestazioni coll'affluenza di una vera folla" ("Esibizione futurista") and an advertisement in the Futurist magazine *Dinamo* claimed that the exhibition in Milan welcomed 2,000 visitors every day, of which 1,990 were "simpatizzanti intelligenti" while 10 were "critici, professori, pittori passatisti, velenosamente esasperanti" ("Alla mostra"). Press reactions to the exhibition were also on the whole very positive, based on three major factors: the Futurists' status as war veterans; their improved attitude towards the public; and the optimistic outlook of the exhibition. Marinetti told Cangiullo that he considered the exhibition to be "un trionfo grandioso" and continued: "Folla enorme,

---

[6] The exhibition closed at the end of July. See "La chiusura" and Marinetti *Taccuini* 427.

entusiasmo. [...] Tutta la stampa ha marciato. Molti giornali favorevoli."

Before considering the reaction the exhibition garnered in the press, one should examine the vision of Futurism that Marinetti wished the exhibition to embody. As Giovanni Lista has commented, the exhibition marked a "svolta fondamentale del futurismo" (179). This is true both of the Futurists who were included in the show and the works that they exhibited. Works by thirty-five Futurists were exhibited and a further nineteen were represented in the catalogue. Giacomo Balla and Russolo were the only "original" Futurist painters to be included. Others such as Francesco Cangiullo, Fortunato Depero and Sironi had joined the movement after 1912 but were active prior to the outbreak of the war in 1914. The majority of the exhibitors, however, had become affiliated with Futurism only since 1915, and in this respect the exhibition fully adhered to the vision Marinetti had had for Futurism since 1914.

Even before the war, Marinetti's willingness to open up the ranks to new members had angered some of the movement's original protagonists, particularly Carlo Carrà and Gino Severini (Coen 282-88). The expansion of the movement brought about a reduction in artistic quality according to those critical of Marinetti's approach. Severini disapproved of Marinetti's *modus operandi* during the war, writing to Pratella in August 1916 that for Marinetti "l'elemento arte, nel suo valore totale, tende a divenire sempre più piccolo mentre in me è il contrario. Questa è la chiave della nostra divergenza" (qtd. Pratella 71; letter of 23 August 1916). By June 1916, even Boccioni, Marinetti's closest ally, had reservations about Marinetti's strategy, writing to Pratella that "è terribile il peso di dover elaborare in sé un secolo di pittura. Tanto più quando si vedono i nuovi arrivati al futurismo afferrare le idee inforcarle e correre a rotta di collo stroppiandole" (qtd. Drudi Gambillo and Fiori 372; letter of 16 June 1916). Marinetti did not take such concerns seriously, either during the war or after it. His objective in the "Grande Esposizione Nazionale Futurista" was to present his movement as a dynamic and lively force in Italy's cultural life. As Fabio Benzi has pointed out, "più artisti esso coinvolge, tanto più il verbo futurista risulterà vittorioso e condiviso, assorbito da ogni strato della società" (237). The version of Futurism presented in the exhibition was one both intimately connected to the war that had just ended but also one that wished to signal an independence from wartime Futurism. War themes were very prominent in the works on display and one of the "free-word" artists represented was a General in the Italian Army whom Marinetti had known during his military service. In the catalogue, Marinetti declared that Italian Futurism was "l'anima della nuova generazione che ha combattuto contro l'impero austroungarico e l'ha vittoriosamente annientato" (qtd. Crispolti 144); in an article for *Il popolo d'Italia*, he highlighted the fact that almost all of the painters had done "eroicamente il loro dovere sui campi di battaglia" ("L'esposizione nazionale"). However, absent from the roll call of the exhibition was any Futurist who had lost his life in the conflict, including Boccioni and

Sant'Elia. The message was clear: Futurism, and its members, had survived the war intact.

It would appear that Marinetti's strategy was successful. A number of articles on the exhibition presented Futurism as a movement that had been revitalized rather than decimated by the war. According to the critic D. B. for *Perseveranza*, the exhibition constituted "un voler contarsi, a guerra finita, fra i pittori avanguardisti." Although the war had killed some of them, he commented, "ne ha generati molti di nuovo." An article in *La sera* began with the triumphant statement that "La guerra è finita: i futuristi ritornano" ("La mostra di pittura futurista"). Reports responded positively to the Futurists' status as ex-combatants. An article from *Il caffaro* of 25 May 1919 summed up the prevailing response to the Futurist exhibitions. Marinetti told the journalist, P. de G., that some Futurist painters had not been able to participate in the exhibition because they were still on active duty with the Army, leading the reporter to acknowledge that "i futuristi hanno manifestato in ogni campo la loro attività battagliera" and thus he asked, "Come negare tutta la simpatia a questi combattenti di ieri?" Marinetti made sure that the Futurists' military involvement was prominently featured at the exhibitions. At the inauguration of the Milanese show, Mario Carli, a captain with the elite *Arditi* troops, gave a speech about the *Arditi*, which was applauded "alla fine con calore" ("Alla mostra futurista"). His status as a volunteer and the injuries he sustained were both highlighted in the short article. Although his judgment of the exhibition's content was negative, the journalist from the *Rivista di Milano* could not criticize the Futurists' combat record; he acknowledged that Futurism "non ha fatto che la guerra in questi ultimi anni e l'ha fatta da voloroso" ("L'esposizione futurista").

Not only did the exhibition mark a clear break with the protagonists of pre-war Futurism; it also broke with earlier conceptions of Futurist art. Paintings gave way to *tavole parolibere*, which were heavily represented in the exhibition, following a trend that Marinetti had begun during the war years. The exhibition was divided into four sections: "quadri, disegni, complessi plastici, teatro plastico"; "tavole parolibere"; "alfabeto a sorpresa"; and "architettura"; and four trends in Futurist art were identified by Marinetti: "pittura pura"; "dinamismo plastico"; "decorativismo dinamico futurista"; and "stato d'animo colorato, senza preoccupazioni plastiche" (qtd. Crispolti 144). The fact that Boccioni's beloved "plastic dynamism" constituted only one of the four trends (and listed only second, at that) is further evidence of Marinetti's desire to shift the focus from Futurism's pre-war painterly incarnations. Benzi has suggested that Marinetti's mention of a "ricerca di puri valori plastici" under the first heading "doveva suonare come una sorta di proposta di accordi" with Mario Broglio's recently launched magazine *Valori plastici*, which was "l'organo più avanzato in Europa del 'ritorno all'ordine'" (235).

Newspaper reports frequently remarked on a newfound accessibility in the

Futurist artworks, on the curiosity and interest of the members of the public and in turn of the Futurists' improved attitude towards its audience. The hostility towards the Futurists, which had been in evidence in the pre-war years, was almost entirely absent in reactions to the 1919 exhibition, a fact commented on by a number of reports. One journalist reminded readers that before the war people followed Marinetti's movement "con un sorrisetto sulle labbra" ("La mostra di pittura"), while another recalled the situation of just a few years previously when Futurists received nothing but "balorde curiosità o stupido dileggio" from the public (*Le arti*). Now, by contrast people flocked to the exhibition "in una predisposizione dello spirito di benevola, ansiosa e caparbia determinazione di comprendere, disposizione ben diversa da quella di un tempo non lontano!" ("La prima Mostra"). The public was by all accounts eager to engage with the movement. The student newspaper *La fiamma verde* confidently asserted that "il visitatore resta piacevolmente meravigliato di trovarvi, in luogo delle estavagazioni che aveva temuto, delle opere quasi tutte facilmente comprensibili" (Rebizzi), while the *Rivista di Milano* critic agreed but was less enthusiastic of the outcome, writing, "I mezzi di espressione forse nell'intenzione di farsi semplici, sono diventati poveri" ("L'esposizione futurista"). The critics were not incorrect in identifying an attempt by the Futurists to be less opaque in their artwork. This attempt in fact had been an approach advised by Marinetti in 1914 to at least one painter, Gino Severini. Marinetti had long desired that Futurism should not be "limitato a un piccolo cerchio d'intenditori" (qtd. Boccioni 131; letter of 20 November 1914). In order to achieve this, he counseled Severini to paint war-inspired paintings that would be "una espressione talmente forte e sintetica da colpire l'immaginazione e l'occhio di tutti o quasi tutti i lettori intelligenti." Anticipating Severini's possible objections, he clarified that he did not view such an approach as a "prostituzione del dinamismo plastico," although he acknowledged that the proposed new direction for Futurism would probably result in "quadri o [...] schizzi meno astratti, un po' troppo realistici e in certo modo una specie di post-impressionismo avanzato [...] e forse anche un nuovo dinamismo plastico guerresco."

On the other hand, the critic from the Genoese newspaper *Il caffaro* claimed that the visitor would be unable to understand anything of the works on view but that this inability did not matter. Finally appearing to grasp the concept of avant-garde art, he informed his readers that "per intendere un quadro non si vuole che rappresenti qualche cosa: [...] di pittura che tali cose rappresentano ce n'è tanti che non si può dar torto a questi bravi artisti futuristi che hanno finalmente il coraggio di presentarsi in diverso modo" (P. de G.). Marinetti was also praised for his availability to visitors and for his willingness to explain the artworks on display, which was a markedly different approach to that which had characterized the riotous Futurist *serate* of 1910 and 1911. Marinetti was "di una cortesia inalterabile" (P. de G.) at the inauguration of the Genoa leg of the exhibition, moving from one room to the next, rendering the atmosphere "più movimentata" (Ang.).

In fact, references to the positive and dynamic atmosphere of the exhibition were common in reports. The critics responded well to the works on display, judging them to be an appropriate response to the three years of war Italy had just endured. An ability to understand the artwork was, in a way, less important that the viewer's emotional response to it. The critic Ang. from *Il lavoro* was particularly impressed, writing that upon entry into the gallery "siete subito attorniati da una vera ridda di colori. Vi trovate in un vortice nel quale rappresentate centro" and noting that the exhibition delivered "una sensazione di piacere. Sarà forse un piacere che non dà riposo, un godimento un po' eccitante, ma alla fine sempre una sensazione." The works displayed "una gioia di colori e di forme, una gaiezza decorativa, che avvolgono in una atmosfera di ottimismo il visitatore" ("L'esposizione futurista"). There was a sense among the critics that the Futurist movement, as represented by the exhibition, had tapped into the public mood in spring 1919, as Italy emerged from a state of war. According to one, Futurism "ci porta in un mondo nuovo" and another declared that "il futurismo è l'arte sola e vera che saprà imporsi domani" (Guglielmino).

6. *The Diverging Fortunes of Political and Artistic Futurism in 1919*

The almost entirely positive reaction to the 1919 exhibition must have come as something of a surprise to Marinetti. A year previously, in February 1918, in the Manifesto of the Futurist Political Party, Marinetti had taken the extreme decision to divide the movement into two distinct strands: one political and one artistic. He explained this decision, stating:

Il movimento artistico futurista, avanguardia della sensibilità artistica italiana, è necessariamente sempre in anticipo sulla lenta sensibilità del popolo. Rimane perciò una avanguardia spesso incompresa e spesso osteggiata dalla maggioranza che non può intendere le sue scoperte stupefacenti, la brutalità delle sue espressioni polemiche e gli slanci temerari delle sue intenzioni. Il partito politico futurista invece intuisce i bisogni presenti e interpreta esattamente la coscienza di tutta la razza nel suo igienico slancio rivoluzionario. Potranno aderire al partito politico futurista tutti gli italiani, uomini e donne d'ogni classe e d'ogni età, anche se negate a qualsiasi concetto artistico e letterario.

("Manifesto del partito")

However, in the immediate post-war period Marinetti discovered that he had misjudged the public mood. While the 1919 exhibition constituted a coup for artistic Futurism, the political wing did not experience a similar level of success. The first branch of the Futurist Political Party had been formed in Florence on 30 November 1918 and other branches sprang up in cities such as Milan, Naples, and Rome. The number of adherents to these branches was, however, very small. In February 1919, a Roman police report noted that the membership was limited because of scarce publicity and "perché le idee stravaganti propagate dal futurismo politico non si fanno strada, specialmente nella gran massa del pubblico" (qtd. Gentile 84). While their war service and sacrifice had earned them new respectability for, and acceptance of, their cultural pursuits, both theatrical and artistic, among the public and press, the Futurists were unable to translate this changed attitude into broad support for their political ideas.

The diverging fortunes of the political and artistic branches of the movement in spring 1919 meant that already by the summer of that year Marinetti's desire to keep both aspects of the movement alive and running simultaneously was waning. After the exhibition closed in Genoa, he wrote to Dottori that "con la più energica decisione ed elasticità futurista, noi riprendiamo il movimento artistico, senza lasciarci sopraffare dall'attuale caoticissimo momento politico" (qtd. Cialfi and Pesola 35). In October 1919, Giuseppe Bottai complained that Marinetti was uncommitted to the work of the political party, writing that in Rome "molto c'è da lavorare. Marinetti però se ne infischia" (qtd. Gentile 100). However, despite this ambivalence regarding Futurism's political destiny, Marinetti was one of the three Futurists who stood for election on the Fascist list in the November 1919 elections. Mussolini's party performed disastrously, achieving only 1.72% of the vote in Milan (Berghaus 146). The election results mark a decisive turning point for Futurist political engagement. Within two months, Futurism had withdrawn from the political arena, and the Futurist Political Party was no more. In January 1920, at Marinetti's insistence, the journal *Roma futurista*, which had been the mouthpiece of the political party, ceased to engage in political affairs and dedicated itself entirely to the promotion of literary and artistic Futurism. This turn away from political Futurism defined the course of "secondo futurismo" in the 1920s and 1930s. The Futurists' active participation in Italy's war effort on the front lines had an enormous impact on the direction of the movement in the post-war period. Marinetti and his followers moved towards the cultural mainstream, culminating in Marinetti's appointment to the Accademia d'Italia in 1929. In fact, the end to Futurism's marginalization within Italy's cultural marketplace began during the war years as they exploited their new-found identities as volunteers, combatants and veterans. The retreat into art at the beginning of 1920 was a viable possibility for Marinetti not just because of the changes in Italy's politics but also because of the positive reception the movement had garnered and cultivated among the public and the press during the years of the "Grande Guerra."

University of California, Santa Barbara

Works Cited

Adamson, Walter L. "How Avant-Gardes End – and Begin: Italian Futurism in Historical Perspective." *New Literary History* 41 (2010): 855-74.
"Alla mostra futurista." *La sera* [Milano]. 23 March 1919. Libroni, Box 41, Papers of F. T. Marinetti and Benedetta Cappa Marinetti, Getty Research Institute, Los Angeles.
"Alla mostra futurista di Milano." *Dinamo* [Roma]. March 1919, 1.
Ang. "La mostra futurista." *Il lavoro* [Genova]. 25 May 1919. Libroni, Box 41, Papers of F.T. Marinetti and Benedetta Cappa Marinetti, Getty Research Institute, Los Angeles.
Argenti, Filippo. "Coi volontari lombardi sulle rive del Garda." *Idea nazionale* [Roma]. 25 November 1915. Libroni, Box 39, Papers of F.T. Marinetti and Benedetta Cappa Marinetti, Getty Research Institute, Los Angeles.
Bacci, Baccio. [No title] *Il nuovo giornale* [Firenze]. 9-10 March 1916. Rpt. in *Cronache del teatro futurista*. Ed. Giovanni Antonucci. Roma: ABETE, 1975. 101-02.
Balla, Giacomo, Giuseppe Bottai, Gino Galli, and Enrico Rocca. "Programma a sorpresa pel 1920." *Roma futurista* [Roma]. 4 January 1920: 1.
Bellini, Dario. *Con Boccioni a Dosso Casina: i testi e le immagini dei futuristi in battaglia*. Rovereto: Nicolodi, 2006.
Benzi, Fabio. *Il futurismo*. Milano: Motta, 2008.
Berghaus, Günter. *Futurism and Politics: Between Anarchist Rebellion and Fascist Reaction 1909-1944*. New York: Berghahn, 1996.
Black, Jonathan. "'A Hysterical Hullo-bulloo about Motor Cars': The Vorticist Critique of Futurism, 1914-1919." *Back to the Futurists: The Avant-Garde and Its Legacy*. Ed. Elza Adamowicz and Simona Storchi. Manchester: Manchester UP, 2013. 159-75.
Boccioni, Umberto. *Umberto Boccioni: lettere futuriste*. Ed. Federica Rovati. Rovereto: Museo d'arte moderna e contemporanea di Trento e Rovereto, 2009.
"Il caposcuola del futurismo. F. T. Marinetti, volontario." *Domenica del corriere* [Milano]. 11 July 1915. Libroni, Box 39, Papers of F.T. Marinetti and Benedetta Cappa Marinetti, Getty Research Institute, Los Angeles.
Carli, Mario, and Filippo Tommaso Marinetti. *Lettere futuriste tra arte e politica*. Ed. Claudia Salaris. Roma: Officina, 1989.
"La chiusura dell'esposizione futurista." *Corriere mercantile* [Genova]. 25 July 1919. Libroni, Box 39, Papers of F.T. Marinetti and Benedetta Cappa Marinetti, Getty Research Institute, Los Angeles.
Cialfi, Domenico, and Antonella Pesola. *Umbria Futurista 1912-1944*. Arrone: Thyrus, 2009.
Codara, Renzo. "I volontari ciclisti ed automobilisti." *Lo sport illustrato e la guerra* (supplement to *La gazzetta dello sport*). 30 July 1915: 321-23.
Coen, Ester. *Illuminazioni: avanguardie a confronto: Italia, Germania, Russia*. Milano: Electa, 2009.
Crispolti, Enrico. *Nuovi archivi del futurismo: cataloghi di esposizioni*. Roma: De Luca, 2010.
Daly, Selena. "'The Futurist Mountains': Filippo Tommaso Marinetti's Experiences of Mountain Combat in the First World War." *Modern Italy* 18.4 (2013): 323-38.
D. B. "Leonardo Dudreville e la pittura futurista." *Perseveranza* [Milano]. 26 March 1919. Libroni, Box 41, Papers of F. T. Marinetti and Benedetta Cappa Marinetti, Getty Research Institute, Los Angeles.
Drudi Gambillo, Maria, and Teresa Fiori. *Archivi del futurismo*. Roma: De Luca, 1962.

"Esposizione futurista." *Il secolo* [Milano]. 24 March 1919. Libroni, Box 41, Papers of F.T. Marinetti and Benedetta Cappa Marinetti, Getty Research Institute, Los Angeles.

"L'esposizione futurista di Milano." *Rivista di Milano* [Milano]. 5 May 1919. Libroni, Box 41, Papers of F. T. Marinetti and Benedetta Cappa Marinetti, Getty Research Institute, Los Angeles.

Fiorini, Mario. "Il genio in tutte le armi." *Il secolo XX ars et labor*. July 1915: 655-62. Fondo Volontari, Museo della Guerra di Rovereto.

Fox, James. "'Fiddling while Rome is Burning': Hostility to Art During the First World War, 1914-1918". *Visual Culture in Britain* 11:1 (2010): 49-65.

"I futuristi alla guerra." *Gli avvenimenti* [Milano]. 12 December 1915. Libroni, Box 39, Papers of F. T. Marinetti and Benedetta Cappa Marinetti, Getty Research Institute, Los Angeles.

"I futuristi volontari al fronte." *Lo sport illustrato e la guerra* [Milano]. 15 February 1916: 118.

Gentile, Emilio. *"La nostra sfida alle stelle." Futuristi in politica*. Roma: Laterza, 2009.

Il giornale del mattino [Bologna]. [No title] 23 December 1915. Libroni, Box 39, Papers of F. T. Marinetti and Benedetta Cappa Marinetti, Getty Research Institute, Los Angeles.

Il nuovo giornale [Firenze]. [No title] 29 January 1917. *Cronache del teatro futurista*. Ed. Giovanni Antonucci. Roma: ABETE, 1975. 116.

Grammona, Dario. "I futuristi e la guerra." *La libreria economica*. 1 September 1915. Libroni, Box 39, Papers of F. T. Marinetti and Benedetta Cappa Marinetti, Getty Research Institute, Los Angeles.

Guglielmino, Carlo Otto. "L'esposizione futurista." *Il piccolo* [Genova]. 3 June 1919. Libroni, Box 41, Papers of F. T. Marinetti and Benedetta Cappa Marinetti, Getty Research Institute, Los Angeles.

Interlandi. "Boccioni." *Giornale dell'isola* [Catania]. 21 August 1916. Box 5, Umberto Boccioni Papers, Getty Research Institute, Los Angeles.

Lista, Giovanni. "Gli anni dieci: il dinamismo plastico." *Futurismo 1909-2009*. Ed. Giovanni Lista and Ada Masoero. Exhibition catalogue Milano, 6 February – 7 June 2009. Milan: Skira, 2009. 83-180.

Marinetti, Filippo Tommaso. "È morto Umberto Boccioni." *L'Italia futurista* [Firenze] 25 August 1916: 1.

_____ "L'esposizione nazionale futurista che si apre oggi al Cova. Pittori futuristi combattenti e teatro plastico." *Il popolo d'Italia* [Milano]. 21 March 1919. Libroni, Box 41, Papers of F. T. Marinetti and Benedetta Cappa Marinetti, Getty Research Institute, Los Angeles.

_____ "Imbecilli!" *L'Italia futurista* [Firenze] 24 June 1917: 1.

_____. [Untitled article by Marinetti.] *Grande esposizione nazionale futurista*. Exhibition catalogue, Milano, Genova, Firenze, March-May 1919, p. 4. Rpt. in *Nuovi archivi del futurismo: Cataloghi di esposizioni*. Ed. Enrico Crispolti. Roma: De Luca, 2010. 144.

_____. Letter from Marinetti to Soggetti, n.d. but July 1919, Box 1, Folder 1, Gino Soggetti Papers, Getty Research Institute, Los Angeles.

_____. Letter from Marinetti to Francesco Cangiullo, 6 April 1919, Corrispondenza, Fondo Cangiullo, Fondazione Primo Conti, Fiesole.

_____. "Manifesto del partito politico futurista". *L'Italia futurista* [Firenze]. 11 February 1918: 1-2.

_____. "Noi rinneghiamo i nostri maestri simbolisti ultimi amanti della luna." *Teoria e invenzione futurista*. Ed. Luciano De Maria. Milano: Mondadori, 2005, 6th ed. 302-06.

———. "Per la guerra, sola igiene del mondo." May - June 1915. Collezione '900 Sergio Reggi, Archivio della parola, dell'immagine e della comunicazione editoriale (APICE), Milano.

———. *Taccuini 1915-1921*. Ed. Alberto Bertoni. Bologna: Il Mulino, 1987.

Marinetti, Filippo Tommaso, and Francesco Balilla Pratella. *Lettere ruggenti a F. Ballila Pratella*. Ed. Giovanni Lugaresi. Milano: Quaderni dell'Osservatore, 1969.

"Marinetti reduce dal fronte parla della guerra e del futurismo." *Giornale d'Italia* [Roma]. 16 December 1915. Libroni, Box 39, Papers of F. T. Marinetti and Benedetta Cappa Marinetti, Getty Research Institute, Los Angeles.

Mastrigli, Federico. "Per un giovane eroe 'futurista.'" *Quotidiano* [Bari]. 24 August 1916, Box 5, Umberto Boccioni Papers, Getty Research Institute, Los Angeles.

"La mostra di pittura futurista inaugurata oggi a Milano. Futurismo + dopoguerra." *La sera* [Milano]. 22 March 1919. Libroni, Box 41, Papers of F. T. Marinetti and Benedetta Cappa Marinetti, Getty Research Institute, Los Angeles.

"Necrologio." *Emporium*. September 1916. Box 5, Umberto Boccioni Papers, Getty Research Institute. Los Angeles.

Novelli, Enrico (Y). "La 'sintesi teatrale' al Niccolini." *La nazione* [Firenze]. 10 March 1916. *Cronache del teatro futurista*. Ed. Giovanni Antonucci. Roma: ABETE, 1975. 102-05.

P. de G. "L'inaugurazione della mostra futurista." *Il caffaro* [Genova]. 25 May 1919. Libroni, Box 41, Papers of F. T. Marinetti and Benedetta Cappa Marinetti, Getty Research Institute, Los Angeles.

Pratella, Francesco Balilla. *Caro Pratella*. Ed. Gianfranco Maffina. Ravenna: Edizioni del Girasole, 1980.

"La prima Mostra Nazionale Futurista." *Le arti* [Milano], no date but March-April 1919. Libroni, Box 41, Papers of F. T. Marinetti and Benedetta Cappa Marinetti, Getty Research Institute, Los Angeles.

Ravida, C. I. "Marinetti reduce dal fronte." *Corriere di Mantova* [Mantova]. 12 March 1916. Libroni, Box 39, Papers of F.T. Marinetti and Benedetta Cappa Marinetti, Getty Research Institute, Los Angeles.

Rebizzi, Edgardo. "L'Esposizione futurista a Milano." *La fiamma verde: giornale quotidiano illustrato degli studenti italiani* [Milano]. 20 May 1919. Libroni, Box 40, Papers of F.T. Marinetti and Benedetta Cappa Marinetti, Getty Research Institute, Los Angeles.

Salaris, Claudia. "The Invention of the Programmatic Avant-Garde." *Italian Futurism 1909-1944: Reconstructing the Universe*. Ed. Vivien Greene. Exhibition catalogue 21 February – 1 September 2014. New York. New York: Guggenheim Museum, 2014. 22-49.

Scarfoglio, Carlo. "Il Benaco." *La stampa* [Torino]. 28 August 1915: 3.

Scarpellini, Emanuela. "Teatro e guerra." *Milano in guerra 1914-1918: opinione pubblica e immagini delle nazioni nel primo conflitto mondiale*. Ed. Alceo Riosa. Milano: Unicopli, 1997. 153-79.

Silver, Kenneth E. *Esprit de Corps: The Art of the Parisian Avant-Garde and the First World War, 1914-1925*. Princeton: Princeton UP, 1989.

Simoni, Renato. "La scomparsa di un artista di grande ingegno." *Corriere della sera*. Rpt. in *Grande esposizione Boccioni*. Exhibition catalogue, Milano, 28 December 1916 – 14 January 1917: 40-41. Also rpt. in *Nuovi archivi del futurismo: cataloghi di esposizioni*. Ed. Enrico Crispolti. Roma: De Luca, 2010. 117-25.

"Gli spettacoli futuristi al Niccolini," *La nazione* [Firenze]. 29 January 1917. *Cronache del teatro futurista*. Ed. Giovanni Antonucci. Roma: ABETE, 1975. 115.

"La tragica morte del pittore Boccioni." *La sera* [Milano]. 19 August 1916. Box 5, Umberto Boccioni Papers, Getty Research Institute, Los Angeles.

"L'unica soluzione del problema economico in Italia secondo F. T. Marinetti." *Gazzetta di Messina e delle Calabrie* [Messina]. 28 February 1916. Libroni, Box 39, Papers of F. T. Marinetti and Benedetta Cappa Marinetti, Getty Research Institute, Los Angeles.

Vampa, Valeria. "I Futuristi in Azione." *Gran mondo* [Roma]. 25 October 1915. Libroni, Box 38, Papers of F. T. Marinetti and Benedetta Cappa Marinetti, Getty Research Institute, Los Angeles.

Enrico Cesaretti

Domestic Fronts:
Bringing the Great War Home in Pirandello's *Novelle per un anno*

In "Guerra e modernità," the introductive chapter to his *L'officina della guerra. La Grande Guerra e le trasformazioni del mondo mentale*, Antonio Gibelli makes the argument that the Great War not only caused profound scars and traumatic transformations in the external world, in the geographical and physical spaces where the battles were fought but, even more crucially and long-lastingly, it also impacted the inner world of human consciousness and mental structures. As he writes: "Potremmo dire che è nella sfera della soggettività, della mentalità e della memoria, che il cambiamento penetra lasciando i suoi segni irreversibili" (Gibelli 13).

In the years surrounding the war, which, as it happens, both in Italy and elsewhere also coincide with the context of literary modernism, the "irreversible signs" of such changes are expectedly traceable, at different levels of visibility and intensity, in the works of a number of Italian writers and intellectuals.[1] The latter, regardless of their positions as interventionists (the vast majority), fatalists or neutralists, responded to, and tried to come to terms with this cataclysmic event in various ways and through disparate genres in their artistic production. Thus, just to mention a representative few, artists such as Marinetti, with his experimental text *Zang Tumb Tumb* (1914); Ungaretti, with his collection of poems *Allegria di naufragi* (1916); Soffici, with his diary *Kobilek: giornale di battaglia* (1918); Jahier, with his autobiographical memoir *Con me e con gli alpini* (1920); and Palazzeschi, with the solitary pacifism of his meditations in *Due imperi...mancati* (1920), are a few figures commonly associated with the kind of literature directly derived from, dealing with, and/or generated by the

---

[1] The links between the Great War and literary modernism have been widely explored in recent years. There should be no need to recall Paul Fussell's argument that the First World War takes place "within a context of cultural 'modernism,' and indeed is one of its causes" (23). Allyson Booth also observes that "the Great War was experienced by soldiers as strangely modernist and that modernism itself is strangely haunted by the Great War" (6). Finally, Trudi Tate's work has also shown (and, at the same time, problematized) the vicinity and permeability of the categories of "modernism" and "war writing."

First World War.[2]

Most likely because of the absence in his *oeuvre* of a major, well-known text in which the First World War is either a main theme or provides the background to the narrated events, Luigi Pirandello's name almost never comes to mind when one thinks of how the conflict affected the literary and artistic imaginary in these years.[3] Not surprisingly, scholars have underlined his "historical extraneousness" (Gieri 301), his overall focus on individual subjectivities, and his general disengagement from strict ideological and socio-political issues. And yet, it is common knowledge that his works, be they destined for the page or the stage, investigate precisely the effects of modernity's advent on the interiority of individuals. That is, his plays, novels and short stories often capture the sense of alienation and existential disorientation felt during the initial, chaotic, war-torn decades of the twentieth century, a destabilizing time in which traditional values and certitudes came under attack.

The gnoseological dimension of modernity — the thin, unstable borders dividing rationality from madness, the changes in perception of personal identity and, in short, as Dombroski writes, "the ontological status of the Self" in the modern era (*Properties* 88) — are all familiar issues and themes in Pirandello's poetics. It is, perhaps, something more than a curious coincidence and a sign of the Sicilian writer's foreshadowing skills, that a frequently quoted passage in which he describes his nightmarish perception of modern consciousness appears more than ten years ahead of the explosion of the First World War. In "Arte e coscienza d'oggi" (1893), he writes:

> A me la coscienza moderna dà l'immagine d'un sogno angoscioso attraversato da rapide larve or tristi or minacciose, d'una battaglia notturna, d'una mischia disperata, in cui si agitino per un momento e subito scompaiano, per riapparire delle altre, mille bandiere, in cui le parti avversarie si sian confuse e mischiate, e ognuno lotti per sé, per la sua difesa, contro all'amico e contro il nemico.
>
> (880; qtd. in Dombroski, "Pirandellian" 137)

As Dombroski observes, this conflictual, military scenario depicts nothing else but "the advent of modernity: perpetual disintegration and renewal, struggle and contradiction, ambiguity and anguish" ("Pirandellian" 127). In other words, the quotation above suggests that the notion of war as metaphor, as embodiment of the modern, and as emblematic signifier of the times was quite present in his mind. It simultaneously mirrored and helped him define the "tragedy" of the confused and directionless modern human existence. Allyson Booth notes that

---

[2] Of course, this list could be further expanded with names such as Alvaro, Gadda, Lussu, and many others.

[3] One exception (besides the texts I will soon be considering) is the play *Come tu mi vuoi* (1929) which, however, takes place "dieci anni dopo la grande guerra europea" (Pirandello, *Come* 86).

"even at moments when the spaces of war seem most remote, the perceptual habits appropriate to war emerge plainly [...]," and "the dislocations of war often figure centrally in modernist form, even when war itself seems peripheral to modernist content" (4). Booth's words could well apply to Pirandello's case.[4] When the imaginary battle in "Arte e coscienza d'oggi" materialized into a real event, and the war actually exploded, Pirandello certainly could not avoid being affected by it, nor could he refrain from artistically responding to the dramatic events around him.

It is also useful to recall that, from a biographical perspective, Pirandello played a pre-eminent intellectual role in the Italian cultural scene during the war years, and he displayed a patriotic, though divided and tormented, interventionist position. In particular, the conflict impacted him very closely and personally when two of his sons left for the front: first, Stefano volunteered to combat in 1915, was wounded and then taken prisoner by the Austrian army; and then Faustino, who followed him in the war. As a matter of fact, his sons' departure to the front, and Stefano's subsequent, long imprisonment seem to have been a significant source of inspiration for Pirandello on those sporadic occasions in which the war actually plays a relevant textual role in his work and which, predictably, especially attracts the scholar's attention.

A passage in the first of his "Colloquii coi personaggi," a short, two-parts story first published in the "Giornale di Sicilia" on August 17th-18th, 1915, and set in the days preceding Italy's entrance in the conflict, makes one of the most explicit autobiographical references to the event of his son's enrollment in the army. Through the voice of one of the protagonists, a nameless Author, one may begin to form an initial idea of how the war impacted Pirandello's private, domestic sphere, and, by extension, his own mixed feelings of impotence, guilt and exclusion from participating in the unfolding of history:

Mio figlio doveva partire in quei giorni per la frontiera. Della partenza imminente volevo e non riuscivo a sentirmi orgoglioso. Egli avrebbe potuto, come tanti altri della sua età e della sua condizione, sottrarsi almeno per il momento ai suoi obblighi: s'era invece presentato subito, volontario, all'appello [...]. Prima i nostri padri, e non noi! Ora, i nostri figli, e non noi! Dovevo restare a casa, io, e veder partire mio figlio.
(Pirandello, *Novelle* 2686)

In the rest of this essay, I thus wish to address precisely these infrequent, but also potentially revealing, war-inspired stories in the *Novelle per un anno* (from now on *Novelle*), and consider them as something other than just the insignificant, tensionless "burle e bozzetti" Isenghi barely mentions in his book

---

[4] Incidentally, when Booth lists some of the "familiar aspects of modernism," which include "the dissolution of borders around the self, the mistrust of factuality, the fascination with multiple points of view" (4), she could ideally be referring also to fundamental aspects in Pirandello's poetics.

(39).[5] Rather, by viewing them in the light of some of Pirandello's recurring aesthetic principles and "epistemological gestures" (Dombroski, *Properties* 69), my hope is to better justify their legitimate, though marginal, presence in the war-literature of the period and, while discussing their semantic and psychological richness, implicitly highlight some of their eminently modernist qualities.

A Closer Look at the Texts
Besides the above mentioned "Colloquii," there are only four other short stories in the whole corpus of the *Novelle per un anno* whose plot significantly centers around the war.[6] These are, in chronological order, "Frammento di cronaca di Marco Leccio e della sua guerra sulla carta nel tempo della grande guerra europea" (from now on, "Frammento di cronaca"), published in the collection *Berecche e la Guerra* in 1919, but most likely already written in 1916;[7] "Quando si comprende," first published in 1918, in *Un cavallo sulla luna*; "Ieri e oggi," which came out in 1919, and, finally "Berecche e la guerra" (1934), which re-elaborates some parts of the "Frammento di cronaca," and which, however, I shall discuss only tangentially and in conjunction with the latter *novella* (that is, "Frammento di cronaca"), since it has already received in-depth scholarly attention.[8]

By way of introduction, one may anticipate that the departure of a son to the front is a recurring, almost obsessive thematic *leitmotif* in these short stories. For the most part, they develop by following and depicting the multiple, often contrasting effects this event has on an immediate circle of relatives, including parents, siblings, and lovers. Their reactions and behaviors become then

---

[5] Pirandello's presence in Mario Isnenghi's fundamental book, *Il mito della grande Guerra*, is mostly limited to footnotes. In the only instance his name appears in the main text, Isnenghi respectfully liquidates him with: "Lontanissima poi è la capacità di riconoscimento critico dell'esistente dei grandi, da Svevo a Pirandello. Così la tensione si spegne troppo spesso in burle e bozzetti di dimensione novellistica e paesana" (39). In other words, according to Isnenghi, important writers such as Svevo and Pirandello are far from being able to critically assess the real situation and impact of the conflict ("l'esistente"). As a consequence, when they deal with the war in their works, the narrative tension (and, implicitly, the "seriousness" of the topic) is "extinguished" (because they choose to represent the war only in what Isnenghi considers minor literary genres such as "burle" and "bozzetti." Also, no essay is dedicated to Pirandello in Patrizia Piredda's recent collection, *The Great War in Italy. Representation and Interpretation* (2013).
[6] For a list of these war-related stories, see also Gisella Padovani's article.
[7] See "Note ai testi e varianti" in Pirandello, *Novelle per un anno* 3.2, p. 1408.
[8] See especially the fine reading provided by Julie Dashwood in her introduction to the English version, as she notes: "In this novella Pirandello uses the semantics of suffering and madness to convey the state of mind of the protagonist and the world he inhabits" (20).

powerful occasions for the writer to bring up, and, in turn, invite reflection upon some of the salient anxieties, paradoxes and contradictions of the modern human condition confronted with the rupturing times of war.

Some of the questions raised in the first of the "Colloquii coi personaggi" include the possibility and the role of aesthetic creation; the dynamics of artistic representation of reality; the fragmented, split nature of the subject "in un momento come questo [...] giorni di torbida agonia che precedettero la dichiarazione della nostra Guerra all'Austria" (2682-683). In other words, the story is set in a period when the same idea of pursuing intellectual, imaginative, (literary, artistic) work may be considered a shameful, almost frivolous pursuit, in stark contrast with the dramatic seriousness of the events happening in the real world.

As its title indicates, this *novella* is structured on a narrative pattern well-tested by Pirandello. It revolves around the imaginary dialogue between a literary Author who, given the imminent war, has decided to indefinitely suspend his creative activity, and a Character who, because of its own fictional nature, exists "fuori delle transitorie contingenze del tempo." The latter, unaware of, and indifferent to the "orrendo e miserando scompiglio" impacting Europe in those days, reminds the writer that his duty as an artist is to overcome historical contingencies, which, despite their tragic nature, are sooner or later destined to end and, rather, strive to create something eternal, beyond time: "Che contano i fatti? Per enormi che siano, sempre fatti sono. Passano. Passano. [...]. La vita resta" (2685).

It is not difficult to realize that this is one of Pirandello's meta-literary stories, where theoretical questions of poetics and aesthetics are addressed in narrative form.[9] The Character gives voice to Pirandello's recurring distrust of history, which he considered as another rigid form ideally shaped and ordered by the whims of historians. The latter are unable to reflect on and interpret the chaos of real life, which, on the contrary, "si muove con tutti i suoi elementi ancora scomposti e sparpagliati" (Pirandello, "La tragedia" 685). Indeed, the fictional figure of Dr. Fileno, in "La tragedia di un personaggio" (1911), and his ingenious, topsy-turvy "philosophy of the distant" (or of the "inverted telescope") aimed at easing the pain suffered by human beings because of "ogni pubblica o privata calamità" (684), clearly resurfaces in the following passage in "Colloquii," when the Character tells the Author : "Ciò che realmente importa è qualche cosa d'infinitamente più piccolo e d'infinitamente più grande: un pianto, un riso, a cui lei, o se non lei, qualche altro, avrà saputo dar vita fuori del tempo, cioè superando la realtà transitoria di questa sua passione d'oggi" (2686). However, the problem or, at least, a significant complication faced by the Author in "Colloquii" is that his concern and anguish for the fate of his son

---

[9] See also the short stories "Personaggi" (1906), "La tragedia di un personaggio (1911) and, most famously, the play *Sei personaggi in cerca d'autore*.

fighting at the front and for the consequences of the war, continues to affect him after the Character and his suggestions leave the scene. Dr. Fileno, instead, by applying the "inverted telescope" perspective, was able to detach himself from the circumstances and console himself of the recent loss of his daughter. To put it differently, the enormity and tragic nature of this particular historical event is such that it prevents the escapist, exorcizing solution delineated by the Character. The war thus seems to undermine existential defenses, defy poetic strategies and, last but not least, have long-reaching physiological, traumatic effects on the Author. As he states: "Come una tenebra d'angoscia m'aveva rioccupato il cervello [...]. Fuori di questa passione, fuori di quest'angoscia, non potevo per il momento veder più nulla" (2686-687).

These words would not only be appropriate to ideally describe the sort of fear-ridden sensation and impaired, dark vision experienced by a soldier fighting in some mountain trench (thus subtly reminding the reader of a way-of-seeing similar to the one likely experienced by the Author's son at the front). They also suggest that, after all, there is not much difference between the Author and a Character who is, like him, half-blind ("mezzo cieco"), and in need of help ("s'ajutava con gli occhiali" 2682) to truly "see" and decipher reality, be it either a simple note stuck on a door or the "atrocissima vita" (2687) by-produced by the conflict.[10] The distance between Author and Character and, in turn, between Author and son, the latter "sciaguratamente" (2687) conjoined despite their separation, diminishes as the story progresses and, ultimately, the figure of the Author cannot but allude once more to the self-reflexive, multifaceted, and fragmented nature of the typical Pirandellian subject.

"Con chi potevo io veramente comunicare [...] in un momento come quello?" (2687), asks the Author at the conclusion of the first dialogue, evoking at once the particular limitations of his own language to represent reality and convey one's innermost feelings and more general, widespread modernist questions on the problematic relationship between words and things. Let us read his answer, "ombre nell'ombra," in conjunction with the second piece of the "Colloquii," in which the shadow of the Author's recently deceased mother takes the place of the Character while, through a reversal of perspective common in Pirandello's fiction, the figure of the son coincides with the Author. Thus Pirandello's answer suggests that only shadows and specters will be his interlocutors in a world becoming more familiar with feelings of mourning and loss; a world, that is, where death is increasingly undermining the subjectivity of those still living, alienating them even further from reality, and where even the illusion of any existential or epistemological certainty is coming to an end: "È caduto a me, alla mia realtà, un sostegno un conforto [...]. Tu sei e sarai per sempre la Mamma mia; ma io? io, figlio, fui e non sono più, non sarò più..."

---

[10] "Colloquii" begins by reproducing the "Avviso" which the Author stuck on his office door.

(2693-94). Although the memories evoked by the mother as she reminisces about her family's past would seem to shift the attention away from the present, to the heroic period of the "Risorgimento" and the First War of Independence, the Great War makes a forceful reappearance as she communicates to him probably her most important message:

> Ma ecco, per questo appunto sono venuta, figlio mio, per dirti questo, che tu l'hai voluta questa guerra contro tanti che non la volevano e lo sapevi che se poco ti sarebbe costato sacrificare in essa la tua vita, tanto, troppo invece ti sarebbe costato il solo rischio di quella del tuo figliolo. E l'hai voluta. Tu paghi, dunque, di sofferenze più che se fossi andato.
>
> (2693)

In this instance too, the largest and darkest shadow of all, the ongoing conflict, continues to loom. Quite paradoxically, if you wish, the delicate evocation of a loving family figure and of childhood travel memories culminates in a quite abrupt shift to the present in the implicit maternal reminder — which feels more like a scolding — that any attempt to distance oneself, or remove "questa guerra" from one's mind and field of vision, can only be ephemeral and illusory.

Times of War
Temporal and epistemological issues, particularly the manner in which the war and its inhuman toll on soldiers and civilians alter one's inner perception of time — in turn accelerating, slowing, or freezing it in an instant — may be traced in "Quando si comprende" (1918) and "Ieri e oggi" (1919). Although these two short stories were published more or less one year apart, belong to different collections in the *Novelle* (respectively, *Donna Mimma* and *Dal naso al cielo*), and each constitutes a separate and complete narrative on its own, they are nevertheless intimately connected by the content of their plots. Surprisingly, they both revolve around the motif of the "son at the front." As a matter of fact, in a way similar to the "Colloquii," these two stories could arguably even be considered as sections of an ongoing, single narration, yet perceived and told each time from different points of view held by the recurring, common characters. Following this interpretation, one could also view the events narrated in the later short story ("Ieri e oggi") as chronologically anticipating those in the earlier one, thus potentially rehearsing, at an additional and (macro-)structural level, familiar and modernist strategies of Pirandellian perspectival and temporal reversals.

The short, declarative opening line of "Ieri e oggi," "La guerra era scoppiata da pochi giorni" (1362), immediately provides the story with an atmosphere of both finality and anticipation. Readers are literally thrown into the *fait accompli* of the conflict, and simultaneously invited to find out the forthcoming implications of such a recent explosion in the following pages. One of these consequences is that Marino Lerna, together with twelve other young volunteers of a "corso accelerato di allievi ufficiali" (1363), learns that he needs to immediately leave the safety of his training camp in Macerata in order to go to combat on the Podgora front. This unexpected piece of news generates contrasting reactions of "stordimento" and "delusa ebbrezza" in him and his comrades. Everyone, nonetheless, also struggles to maintain a mask of nonchalant confidence: "[…] tornarono a riprendersi con uno studio di mostrare l'uno all'altro che quella loro disinvoltura non era punto affettata" (1363). For example, a fellow soldier named Sarri, "ricco e solo al mondo," certain that death in combat will find him soon, actually devotes himself entirely to enjoying the present and thus just uses his time to satisfy "il gusto più facile, quello bestiale dell'altro sesso" (1364). In his mind, he is already foreseeing and anticipating post-war scenarios, and is disgusted by the ostentatious demonstrations of heroism and patriotism he imagines on the horizon. Consistent with the rebellious identity and behavior he wishes to project (i.e., the mask he is currently wearing), Sarri does not plan to inform anyone of his imminent departure — anyone, that is, but his mistress, Ninì, who followed him from Rome.

Marino Lerna, on the other hand, not only decides to telegraph his parents, but also urges them to visit him to say goodbye in person: "[…] se prendevano il treno delle dieci di sera, avrebbero fatto in tempo a salutarlo prima della partenza" (1365). As the line above, with its abundance of temporal references, may already suggest, the real protagonist during the subsequent farewell episode between parents and son, "uno strazio inutile" (1366), is time itself. On the one hand, we perceive its increased fugacity in these circumstances, and, on the other, how the dramatic force of the events affects its subjective perception, disrupting its linear flow, compressing and mixing the dimensions of past, present and future. From a stylistic perspective, a series of active verbs communicating fast, frenetic movement, and of idiomatic expressions related to speed, emphasize the rushed quality of both the brief familial encounter and the soldiers' departure. Thus, Marino, after dropping his parents at their hotel, "dovette scappar subito in caserma" (1366); later, he returns there "in fretta e furia" (1366), only to run out again to get his combat boots. His comrades arrive "in gran fretta all'albergo" (1367), and then, as the narrative pace intensifies even further and everything seems to be sucked into the void, everyone leaves: "via tutti a precipizio, in carrozza, di gran trotto. […] Più che un distacco, fu uno strappo, una furia, un precipizio" (1367). In contrast, Marino's mother's perception of the events seems associated with a "slower" temporal dimension, and already oriented toward the past. Her concern for her son's fate and possessive, though understandable, desire to hold on to his image — something stable within the impending chaos — anchors her to a "ieri" which, nonetheless, coincides also with her feeling of impotence and "precariousness of existence," as Dombroski remarks (*Properties* 91):

[...] il senso che le facevano tutte le parole, tutti gli atti del suo figliuolo: un senso strano e crudele, di ricordo. — Ogni parola, capisci? Mi fa l'effetto che non me la dica ora, ma che me la diceva ...Così! Mi resta impressa, come se lui già non ci fosse più... Che posso farci? ... Dio... Dio...

(1367)

Her instinctive inclination to "freeze" her feelings and her son's image in an individual memory is a desperate attempt to give an illusory, permanent form to his (and her) identity. But, as every reader of Pirandello knows, there are serious dangers in this process: "Ma guai a fermarti in una sola realtà; in essa si finisce per soffocare, per atrofizzarsi, per morire" (Pirandello, qtd. in Dombroski, *Properties* 70).

At the conclusion of "Ieri e oggi," this motherly, backward-looking approach towards time and reality is thus juxtaposed with that of Ninì, the young prostitute who is also mournful because of the recent departure of Sarri and his fellow soldiers. Contrary to the respectable "signora Lerna," in fact, she gives herself not only literally, to the officers, but also to the eddy of time, namely, she allows her "Self [...] [to] desolve into the All" (Dombroski, *Properties* 91), accepting the "oggi," and, with it, the continuous flux of life. Individuality, in fact, — Dombroski continues — "is, by Pirandellian definition, indistinctiveness" (91):

Non era stata soltanto del Sarri ultimamente, a Roma, la Ninì; era stata anche di altri compagni di lui in quel plotone allievi ufficiali.[...] A mezzogiorno era stata a tavola con loro, con dieci di loro.[...] Glien'avevano fatte di tutti i colori [...]. Avevano volute finanche scoprirle il seno [...] e lei li aveva lasciati fare e toccare, baciare, premere, stringere, strappare, perché se lo portassero, sì, vivo lassù, quell'ultimo ricordo della sua carne d'amore. [...] Ma le era arrivato da parte del Sarri quel terribile schiaffo sulla guancia destra.[11]

By continuing to generously offer her body and, after the train leaves for the front, to cry for everyone's fate ("Lei per uno solo... io per tutti... posso per tutti...anche per suo figlio [...]. 1370), thus rejecting the role Sarri had implicitly chosen for her, Ninì escapes being stuck in a singular, fixed moment and identity, and seems to achieve the paradoxical condition of selfless, "indistinctiveness" mentioned above. It is only natural, therefore, that, in the end, neither tears nor communication can be shared between her and "signora Lerna," two women who react to and cope with the pain and desperation caused by the war's demands in such antipodal ways. Seen by the "signora" "in

---

[11] Interestingly, this same idea of flesh as a mnemonic token of love will reappear, literally materializing itself and with much darker tones, in another short-story related to the First World War: F. T. Marinetti's "La carne congelata" (1922), later republished with slight revisions as "Come si nutriva l'Ardito" in *Novelle con le labbra tinte* (1930).

compagnia d'un giovanotto" just a day after the soldiers' departure, Ninì's response sanctions both the conclusion of the story and the existential chasm that divides them: "— Povera mamma buona e stupida — le disse con quello sguardo. — E non capisci che la vita è così? Ieri ho pianto per uno. Bisogna che oggi rida per quest'altro" (1370).

As its title suggests, at least a partial answer to Ninì's question about the issue of "understanding" life can be found in "Quando si comprende." This story focuses on something that "Ieri e oggi" merely hinted at — the conversation that takes place on the train from Rome to Macerata between afflicted parents about to bid farewell to their son and five other travelers. What emerges in the initial part of the dialogue is each character's tendency to claim the pre-eminence of her/his own personal war-related tragedy — for in fact the conflict is affecting everyone's families — and, in particular, the mother's desperate unwillingness to accept that someone else is able to experience, and actually live with, the same anguish she feels. However, when a "viaggiatore grasso e sanguigno" reverses the perspective and brings up the point of view of his own son, ultimately revealing that he passed away at the front, something changes:

Bisogna non piangere, ridere... o come piango io, sissignori, contento, perché mio figlio m'ha mandato a dire che la sua vita — la *sua* capite? Quella che noi dobbiamo vedere in loro, e non la *nostra* — la sua vita lui se l'era spesa come meglio non avrebbe potuto, e che è morto contento [...]. le labbra livide sui denti mancanti gli tremavano; gli occhi, quasi liquefatti, gli sgocciolavano; e terminò con due scatti di riso che potevano anche esser singhiozzi.

(1473)

These words represent a powerful epiphany for the mother ("trasecolò" 1474). She suddenly understands both the isolated singularity and the egocentric self-centeredness of her anguish: "[...] comprese che non già gli altri non sentivano ciò che ella sentiva; ma lei, al contrario, non riusciva a sentire qualcosa che tutti gli altri sentivano e per cui potevano rassegnarsi, non solo alla partenza, ma ecco, anche alla morte del proprio figliuolo" (1473). When, however, she tries to confirm and solidify this recently acquired knowledge, the simple question she poses to her fellow traveler — "Ma dunque... dunque il suo figliolo è morto?" (1474) — has an even more devastating (and enlightening) effect on the "viaggiatore.". This question confronts him with a factual reality different from the (fictional) one he held to be true and, thus, reveals the fundamental vacuity of his earlier, heroic argument. His own, individual tragedy, then, ultimately manifests itself as he sadly sees beyond the repressive, meaningless artificiality of his own rhetoric and realizes that, indeed, "il suo figliuolo era veramente morto per lui" (1474). At the same time, the traveler's realization of the emptiness existing behind language, of the ultimate incapacity of words to represent experience, is intimately connected to his own experience of the war, to the impact it has on him and, in short, to its modernist capacity to generate, as

Booth writes, a "terrifying tension around the categories of fact and fiction" (12).

Real and Imagined War
The last short story I wish to discuss, Pirandello's "Frammento di cronaca," is among the longest texts in the *Novelle* despite its definition and nature of "fragment."[12] For, in fact, it would seem to represent a particularly fitting example and exploration of such a tension between fact and fiction.

At the beginning of this *novella*, which is divided in eleven parts, we learn that its protagonist, Marco Leccio, is an old, patriotic "veterano garibaldino, reduce di Bezzecca" ("Frammento" 2703). Marco lost both his father and a dear friend during the earlier unification war. Although he cannot be anything but proud of the fact that three of his older sons (he has a total of seven) are already fighting at the front, he cannot bear that his youngest, Giacomino, will soon leave for combat. In the course of the story, the father tries to enlist with his son Giacomino and, once he fails — expectedly, given his age, physical condition, and discordance with modern times —[13] he ends up following the war and "fighting" from his home office, filled with military maps, books, weapons, and relics of the Risorgimento Wars.

Named after the battle fought by Garibaldi in the Third War of Independence, Bezzecca, Marco's daughter, is married to a watchmaker, an "oriundo svizzero tedesco" ("Frammento" 2701), "il signor Livo Truppel," thus creating a peculiar, oxymoronic (and comical) situation at a time when Italians and Austro-Hungarians are fighting on opposite sides. In parallel with the ongoing war, Marco Leccio's own family and home are also sites of conflict and anxiety.[14] After Roman demonstrators attack the German shop in the city center owned by Truppel and his brother Guglielmo, Marco tries to convince the two brothers to change their name to the Italian "Truppa." But Marco's naïve, passionate attempt is seen by Guglielmo Truppel as an action fraught with "ingiurie e minacce" ("Frammento" 2704), and, paradoxically, is followed by the government officials' imposition of a monetary fine upon the Truppel brothers.

Narrated with Pirandello's trademark humor and grotesque tones, this episode serves to immediately define the fiery nature and the lively, patriotic,

---

[12] By the way, the "Frammento" is approximately the same length of "Berecche e la guerra," of which, as noted, it anticipates various themes and motifs.

[13] "Non si sente più sicuro di sé, sente che gli manca un appoggio, l'appoggio solito della propria realtà nel suo figliuolo. [...] esposto alla ridicola realtà, che ha assunto per gli altri, il suo papà che è vecchio e non sa che oggi non si pensa più così, non si va più a spasso vestiti così, con quel cappello di quella foggia, per esempio, e più così non si parla e più così non si ride, e via di seguito" ("Frammento" 2711).

[14] It is not surprising, also given Pirandello's own biographical experience, that the family is often a site of deep tensions and anxieties.

and combative spirit of the old protagonist ("c'è da gridare contro quanti in quest'ora suprema non sentono il loro dovere di italiani" "Frammento" 2704), and the in-between status of the peaceful, meek Livo Truppel. The latter, suddenly perceived as an enemy, realizes that he can no longer go to the Bezzecca anniversary party at Marco Leccio's house, and feels that his own house, too, is becoming a battlefield.[15] He thus decides that he "non avrebbe rimesso piede mai più nella casa del suocero e che se il suocero veniva qualche sera da lui a visitare la figliuola egli [...] oltre il saluto non gli avrebbe rivolto la parola e, dopo il saluto, avrebbe sputato in terra.[...] Truppel promise, giurò per placare il fratello" ("Frammento" 2705).

The conflicting nationalities of the protagonists in this episode suggest that the events taking place in these "bellicose" domestic spaces also constitute a parodical and critical commentary on the sort dynamics associated with the war itself. The repeated act of "sputare in terra" ("Frammento" 2705) performed by Guglielmo Truppel, for example, may make one think at the war generals' obsession with delimiting borders and marking and controlling access to conquered territories. Marco Leccio's stubborn impulsiveness and Guglielmo's refusal to enter Marco's house, in turn, may evoke the irrationality and rigidity of war threats, as well as the lack of tolerance, narrow-mindedness, and self-serving, expedient promises that characterize any conflict. Ambivalence and allusiveness, after all, should not be surprising elements within a narrative context in which the real, undeclared reason behind Marco Leccio's wish to enlist is his love and anguish for Giacomino's fate. In Marco, "fervore patriottico" ("Frammento" 2707), sense of military duty, and belief that "questa è veramente una santa guerra" ("Frammento" 2729), coexist and are juxtaposed with his realization that such a war, with its despiteful modern strategy, has also an economic cause and is among the byproducts of rising capitalist powers. As he tells Livo Truppel while particularly upset about the lack of news from the front: "Bel paese, va' là il tuo! [...]Affarone, la guerra! Anche per gli Stati Uniti di America, sí! Affaroni, affaroni... Sfido io! con questa guerra che non si vede! [...] Migliaia di lire per ogni cannonata, che spesso fa ridere i soldati... Un bel congegno, per tutti i fornitori, questa strategia moderna...." ("Frammento" 2734).

Indeed, Marco Leccio cannot really "see" a war that, because of its modern technological advancements and combat techniques, is so different from the ideal, glorious one he has in mind. Machinery and modern science ("meccanici e [...] farmacisti" 'Frammento" 2722) have taken the place of soldiers' bravery, and have resulted in the increase of casualties and the pointless extension of the

---

[15] This situation of "in-betweennes" will be developed much more in "Berecche e la guerra," whose homonymous protagonist is a "tedescone spatriato" ("Berecche" 2193). The sixth section of "Berecche," entitled "Il signor Livo Truppel," reproduces a substantial part of the first two sections in "Frammento di cronaca."

fighting ("questa macchina stupida e mostruosa della [...] strategia moderna, che mangia vite, strazia carni, e non conclude nulla" "Frammento" 2721). Marco's predilection for old-fashioned weapons ("la bajonetta, l'arma vera, che ha bisogno di coraggio e non di scienza" "Frammento" 2721), for individual acts of valor and past honor codes, and his understanding of the Great War as overlapping with, and direct "prosecuzione e compimento di quella del 1866" ("Frammento" 2709), can only serve to limit and confuse his vision or, at least, to make it far from a clear, univocal one.[16]

Within this context, Marco Leccio's own "guerra sulla carta" conducted from a number of illuminated, flagged maps and relief models displayed in his home office, with the usual assistance of his poor veteran friend, Tiralli, is also a way for him to actually bring this war into view, to paradoxically "see" it and understand it better by (literally and metaphorically) playing around with the notions of light and darkness, alternatively switching one bulb on, and turning another off.[17] From his peculiar temporal perspective, one that oscillates between past memories and present facts, affecting his perception of space and reality,[18] he is thus able to momentarily feed the illusion that he can follow the war's developments, participate in combat, and, as he tells Tiralli, even dictate its future, historical outcome ("Togli via subito codesta bandierina! Kowno resiste e resisterà ancora per un pezzo, te lo dico io" "Frammento" 2720):

Su ciascuna di queste carte pende dal soffitto [...] una lampada elettrica. Cinque lampade elettriche, di sera tutte accese, che fanno un bel vedere. Marco Leccio [...] passa fulmineamente da un teatro di guerra all'altro e vuole che le sue indicazioni, le sue tracce, le sue mosse si vedano e si seguano chiaramente. Di queste lampadine, quattro sono bianche, una azzurra. L'azzurra pende sul teatro di guerra del Trentino, che non è propriamente una carta delle solite, ma una plastica in rilievo di cartapesta colorata [...]. Spegne Marco Leccio le altre quattro lampadine e lascia accesa qua quest'ultima azzurra [...] che conservi e accresca l'illusione della realtà a quel rilievo colorato. [...] Poi serra gli occhi e si sforza di distrarre l'animo dall'immagine del suo figliuolo in pericolo, richiamando gli antichi ricordi della campagna garibaldina lassù.

(2717-18)

In its anticipation of a very similar episode in "Berecche e la guerra," in which

---

[16] Marco Leccio's long list of "materiale bellico [...] obici [...] mortaj da 305 e 420, fucili a tiro rapido, mitragliatrici, dirigibili [...] gas asfissianti, bombe incendiarie [...] tanks, trincee scavate a macchina, blindate [...]." ("Frammento" 2721-22) evidently communicates his deep anxiety about the "development of new weapons technology" (Tate 6).

[17] Since Marco Leccio is trying to re-live his wishes and fantasy of war in the present via the maps, a notion similar to the one of "acting out" mentioned by Mariani in her article could perhaps accompany his "seeing" (166).

[18] "E non è già che quel lago di Garda e quelle valli e quei monti siano così piccoli perché finti [...] no: così piccoli sono perché egli li guarda da lontano lontano. [...] nel ricordo" ("Frammento" 2717).

its homonymous protagonist continues to play his childhood game, "Theater of War,", even as an adult, the extended map scene in the "Frammento di cronaca" equally conveys the idea of the constructed nature of history which, as Dashwood observes, "like a map [...] is dependent on the perceptions, motives, choices and omissions of its makers and interpreters, and the validity of those perceptions is fragile and fleeting" (18). After all, maps could be considered a particular kind of adult "war toy," one which enables both Berecche and Marco Leccio to "breake and remake" (Higonnet 116) the facts of history according to their whims, while also having the effect of "domesticat[ing] war [...] remind[ing] us that war is not something that happens far away on a neatly contained 'battlefront' but part of the everyday" (Higonnet 119).

The narrator's observation that the various operations of "strategia moderna" Marco Leccio performs with the help of his maps ("studio indefesso [...] dei punti, delle linee, delle posizioni") are not so different from those of a "duce supremo d'una guerra" ("Frammento" 2723), make me think of yet another approach to these crucial scene[s], especially if one reads them against the backdrop of some of Allyson Booth's fitting remarks on the interrelations between maps, WWI and modernism. Maps, she notes,

provide apt images of the dangerous gap between representation and experience, and they were frequently exploited by combatants as a means for critiquing inadequate or irresponsible representations of war. Many soldiers recognized that the generals' views of war, so often limited to a study of maps, encouraged a dangerous illusion of having access to the material world of battle when, actually, what they had access to was only a series of representations.

(Booth 94)

Furthermore, she continues, while maps are informed by a univocal, one-directional synecdochic logic, one that "relies on the assumption that one knows what smaller space is a part of what larger one," modernist writers' more complex handling of "the relationship between representation and experience [...] thwarts the orderly habits of mind" (Booth 99) such a logic invites, since they show its limitations and inadequacy to appreciate multiple, contradictory perspectives. It goes without saying that Pirandello's "Frammento di cronaca" would seem a particularly good place to test the implications and meditate further on Booth's assertions.

First of all, the fact that what Marco Leccio does in his home study is "non molto dissimile" from what a "duce supremo" (2723) does in his base camp or, in other words, that the (partial) vision and "fantasy" representation of combat produced by an anxious, restless, and emotionally upset old veteran closely recalls those of a general, not only confirms the narrator's ironic and parodical attitude, or the porous, unstable borders between illusion and reality. From a more concrete perspective, the narrator's remark is also another hint at Pirandello's critical attitude and fundamental aversion to the conflict.

That is, Pirandello seems to indirectly question the skills and the often "irresponsible" (Booth 94) conduct of contemporary, WWI military strategists and modern political leaders, especially if, along with Marco Leccio, one also compares the latter's alluded "deafness" in terms of strategy and weaponry to the openly admired, heroic Risorgimento figures whose portraits hang in his office: "ritratti: quello di Mazzini e di Garibaldi [...] di Nino Bixio e di Stefano Canzio e di Menotti, di Felice Orsini e di Guglielmo Oberdan [...].— Va' a dirlo a Joffre, va' a dirlo a French, va' a dirlo a Cadorna!" ("Frammento" 2716/2723).

Secondly, Marco Leccio's idiosyncratic, dreamy, memory-induced and, ultimately, emotional, artistic relationship to his maps — one that considers their accurate interpretation as less relevant than the gratification provided by the coincidental realism of some maneuver; that lets his mind analeptically wander from a material site on paper to a mnemonic one in his consciousness and, finally, that almost neurotically alternates between moments of enjoyment for his table game and frustrated rejection — would seem to indeed ironically question what Booth calls "the narrow logic of a synecdoche" (99).[19] Marco Leccio strategizes in his home office:

Certo, se una mossa prevista da lui in questo o in quel teatro della Guerra [...] s'effettua proprio come lui l'ha prevista, se ne compiace. [...] non badando più nemmeno se la mossa indovinata sia in favore dei tedeschi e a danno degli alleati, perché veramente l'arte, di qualunque genere sia, è il regno del sentimento disinteressato [...]. Ma non è questo! Non vorrebbe far questo Marco Leccio! Gl'importa assai che i duci supremi oggi combattano le guerre come lui, su la carta!

(2723-24)

That same logic seems to be undermined even further towards the conclusion of the novella, when "una mosca maledetta che viene ostinatamente a posarsi su la carta plastica del Trentino" ("Frammento" 2729), a metaphorical image of reason, repeatedly breaks Marco's illusions, conveying both their ephemerality and the difficulty of containing the complex dynamics of war within the representational limits of a map.

Through the vicissitudes of a protagonist who seems to depend on the fragile illusion provided by his maps, and is confronted with their ultimate uselessness, Pirandello, in line with his poetics of humor, implicitly calls attention to the multifarious spaces of war, to war's impact on internal, emotional, subjective landscapes, as well as on external, geographical ones and, in short, to a quintessentially modernist "awareness of and [...] appreciation for

---

[19] In this light, it may be relevant to observe that the absurd death of Marchetto (Marco Leccio's nephew) "mentre raccoglieva i feriti" (2726), is not only juxtaposed to the past, glorious one of Lavezzari (an old "garibaldino" fighter), but also immediately follows the protagonist's realization of the ultimate irrelevance of his game: "[...] stiamo qua a giocare come due ragazzini scimuniti con le carte e le bandierine! Puah!" ("Frammento" 2725).

multiple points of view" (Booth 99).[20] In this sense, similar to Berecche's loss of control and plunge into insanity, Marco Leccio's final, destructive gesture is a sign of "the collapse of his illusions and ideals" (Dashwood 18): "sdegnato, diede un calcio a tutte quelle carte nel suo studio, e non volle più saperne" ("Frammento" 2737).

The blank space on the page separating Marco Leccio's gesture (described by the narrator in a separate paragraph) from his first-person, suddenly truncated reply to Tiralli ("i tradimenti che sono stati finora la...") may well represent typographically such a "collapse." As it points to a communicative failure directly caused by the war, this textual void seems to paradoxically emblematize both an absence and a presence. On the one hand, it cannot but confirm the war's relative marginality in Pirandello's oeuvre. On the other, however, especially if the war is imagined as a sort of trench and "linear wound" on the page, it also cannot but evoke the peculiar front that the Great War opened in Pirandello's private life and domestic sphere, and that, as I have hopefully demonstrated, these modernist short stories have repeatedly attempted to represent.

University of Virginia

Works Cited

Booth, Allyson. *Postcards from the Trenches. Negotiating the Space between Modernism and the First World War*. New York, Oxford: Oxford UP, 1996.
Dashwood, Julie. "Introduction." to Pirandello. *Berecche and the War*. Tr. and Intro. J. Dashwood. Leicester: Troubadour Publishing Ltd., 2000. 1-23. Web.
Dombroski, Robert. "Pirandellian Nakedness." *Luigi Pirandello. Contemporary Perspectives* 125-38.
———. *Properties of Writing. Ideological Discourse in Modern Italian Fiction*. Baltimore: The John Hopkins UP, 1994.
Fussell, Paul. "Introduction: On Modern War." *The Norton Book of Modern War*. Ed. Paul Fussell. New York: W.W. Norton, 1991.
Gibelli, Antonio. *L'officina della guerra. La Grande Guerra e le trasformazioni del mondo mentale*. Torino: Bollati Boringhieri, 1991.
Gieri, Manuela. "Of Thresholds and Boundaries: Luigi Pirandello between Modernity and Modernism." *Italian Modernism* 294-306.
Higonnet, Margaret. "War Toys: Breaking and Remaking in Great War Narratives." *The Lion and the Unicorn* 31.2 (2007): 116-31.
Isnenghi, Mario. *Il mito della grande guerra*. Bologna: il Mulino, 1989.
Italian Modernism. Italian Culture between Decadentism and Avant-Garde. Ed. L.

---

[20] Booth observes that such an awareness is a trait of modernist writers. Joyce, for example, inverts the "common mapping logic" of Dublin in *Finnegans Wake* (99), and Stevens, in his "Thirteen Ways of Looking at a Mockingbird," may implicitly mock the "clear, singular, bird's eye perspective" (100) which Great War's generals adopted when looking at the maps on their desks.

Somigli and M. Moroni. Toronto: U of Toronto P, 2004.
Luigi Pirandello. Contemporary Perspectives. Ed. Gian Paolo Biasin and Manuela Gieri. Toronto: U of Toronto P, 1999.
Mariani, Annachiara. "Solitude and the Fragmentation of Self: The Disillusioned Representation of Man in the Plays of Luigi Antonelli and Luigi Pirandello." *About Face: Depicting the Self in the Written and Visual Arts.* Newcastle upon Tyne: Cambridge Scholars, 2009. 165-74.
Padovani, Gisella. "I temi della maternità, della guerra, della morte in alcuni testi narrativi e teatrali di Luigi Pirandello." in *La Figure de la mère dans la litérature contemporaine.* E-talis 1 (2013). Web.
Pirandello, Luigi. *Come tu mi vuoi.* Milano: Mondadori, 1971.
_____. *Novelle per un anno.* Vols. 1-3. Firenze: Giunti, 1994.
Piredda, Patrizia, ed. *The Great War in Italy. Representation and Interpretation.* Leicester: Troubadour Publishing, 2013.
Tate Trudi. *Modernism, History and the First World War.* Manchester: Manchester UP, 1998.
World War 1 Bridges: http://www.worldwarone.it/2014/01/luigi-pirandello-and-his-berecche-and.html

Sarah Pesenti Campagnoni

La guerra (in) tradotta.[1]
Informazione, propaganda e immagini dal fronte

È noto quanto la Prima Guerra Mondiale abbia segnato l'imporsi di una fondamentale rottura con la tradizione precedente, seguita da un processo di modernizzazione che ha toccato gli ambiti più diversi: dalla politica alla cultura, dalle scienze alle tecnologie industriali, senza dimenticare le arti tutte, impegnate in un rinnovamento estetico e linguistico necessario all'interpretazione della nuova realtà dell'uomo e delle società. Tra i settori più profondamente segnati da questo processo si deve annoverare anche quello mediatico che vede in prima linea fotografia e cinema quali interpreti privilegiati delle trasformazioni in corso.

Nei primi anni del Novecento, lo straordinario potenziale mimetico dei mezzi foto-cinematografici aveva alimentato lo sviluppo di due generi di grande fortuna, il fotoreportage giornalistico,[2] e, poco dopo, l'attualità cinematografica d'informazione (1908-1910), entrambi imperniati sull'idea di una nuova etica della notizia quale testimonianza fedele dei fatti del reale.

L'illusione di realtà suggerita dai mezzi foto-cinematografici al proprio pubblico e sapientemente sfruttata sia in ambito giornalistico che nell'industria del cinema si pone dunque alla base del ruolo fondamentale da essi giocato nel rapido sviluppo dei sistemi di comunicazione (e propaganda) dell'esercito.

Negli anni del primo conflitto mondiale, infatti, lo Stato Maggiore del Regio Esercito e della Regia Marina italiani si impongono tra i principali produttori di immagini della guerra in corso, segnando un momento di profonda trasformazione negli equilibri industriali, estetici e linguistici vigenti.

In queste pagine si cercherà di evidenziare, brevemente, alcuni momenti fondamentali dello sviluppo in senso moderno della produzione fotografica e

---

[1] Con "tradotta" si intende qui sia il convoglio ferroviario militare destinato al trasporto delle truppe, sia l'operazione di trasferimento di senso dalla caotica realtà del fronte alla sua ordinata rappresentazione a mezzo dell'immagine foto-cinematografica. L'ambivalenza di questo termine serve a sottolineare il continuo movimento di uomini e informazioni attraverso il Paese: nonostante la Grande Guerra sia stata fondamentalmente un conflitto statico, migliaia di soldati attraversarono a più riprese larghe parti d'Italia per raggiungere il fronte, passando dalla prima linea alle retrovie e viceversa, esattamente come accadde per le pellicole e gli scatti realizzati in guerra e quindi diffusi dentro e fuori dai nostri confini.

[2] La nascita del fotoreportage giornalistico si lega a due importanti innovazioni tecniche: lo sviluppo della fotografia istantanea e l'introduzione del retino nel mondo dell'editoria, tra i primi anni Ottanta e la fine dell'Ottocento.

cinematografica militare italiana a carattere propagandistico-informativo nel corso del primo conflitto mondiale, osservando, nel dialogo tra questi due media, l'alternarsi di distanze e punti di contatto.

1. Un esercito dietro l'obiettivo: primi approcci militari al medium foto-cinematografico

L'Italia rappresenta un caso di singolare interesse per sondare quei sintomi di rottura della produzione foto-cinematografica d'attualità con la tradizione precedente che troveranno la loro più forte espressione in occasione del primo conflitto mondiale.

Nel 1915, il Bel Paese è infatti reduce da soli tre anni dalla Guerra Italo-Turca (1911-1912), un evento che, oltre ad essere stato oggetto di un forte risalto da parte dell'industria giornalistica e cinematografica, con un'impennata delle produzioni di attualità a tema bellico, segna anche un punto di svolta nella storia della fotografia militare. In questa occasione, infatti, lo Stato Maggiore dell'Esercito italiano dà il via ad una prima campagna fotografica in zona di guerra, portata avanti dal lavoro dei soldati e degli ufficiali del Servizio Fotografico militare, facente parte del Battaglione Specialisti del Genio.[3]

L'attività del Servizio Fotografico sul fronte libico, terrestre e aereo, si incentra, in particolare, sulla riproduzione delle azioni militari più rilevanti e sul reperimento di informazioni strategiche, senza avanzare pretese di esaustività in termini di documentazione storica del conflitto, come avverrà invece nel corso della Grande Guerra.

Prima dei tragici eventi del 1914-1918, inoltre, non si registra un interesse diretto ed esplicito, da parte dell'Esercito italiano, per un impiego del mezzo cinematografico assimilabile a quello descritto in fotografia. Pur esistendo, infatti, un'interessantissima produzione scientifica, militare e civile, rivolta al cinema quale completamento della fotografia nel tempo per lo studio del movimento, l'insegnamento di pratiche chirurgiche, l'indagine di fenomeni fisici o, più semplicemente, a scopo pedagogico, per quanto concerne la produzione di guerra mancherà per lungo tempo un'attenzione specifica dell'Esercito nei confronti delle potenzialità di questo medium. Nelle rare occasioni in cui si

---

[3] Il Battaglione Specialisti del Genio nasce nel 1910 in sostituzione della precedente Brigata Specialisti del Genio che aveva dato i natali alla prima Sezione Fotografica militare italiana il 1° aprile 1896 (Pesenti Campagnoni, *WWI La guerra sepolta*). L'iscrizione della fotografia nel contesto delle tecniche e delle scienze militari non è irrilevante ai fini della comprensione del ruolo attribuitole dall'Esercito italiano. La produzione fotografica militare, indipendente dalle condizioni di pace o di guerra vigenti, si rivolge infatti al miglioramento e completamento delle tecnologie per la conoscenza del territorio (dalle frontiere montane alle coste), lo studio balistico, la cartografia ecc. La fotografia non viene vista dallo Stato Maggiore quale strumento mediatico, veicolo di dialogo tra le strutture militari e la popolazione civile, ma esclusivamente come applicazione tecnica (Galloni).

rivolge al cinema prima della Grande Guerra, l'Esercito dimostra anzi un atteggiamento del tutto indifferente alle sue specificità rispetto al mezzo fotografico, scegliendo di utilizzare l'uno o l'altro esclusivamente in funzione di necessità di ordine pratico.

A conferma di questa prassi, la Regia Marina e il Regio Esercito italiani si impegneranno nella costituzione di specifiche sezioni cinematografiche solo nella primavera del 1916 (con l'Ufficio Speciale della Marina) e nel gennaio del 1917 (con la Sezione Cinematografica del Regio Esercito) e, anche allora, continuerà a mancare un servizio permanente, indipendente dalle necessità della propaganda di guerra, sul modello di quello fotografico.[4] Nonostante l'innovativa presenza di un Servizio Fotografico militare sul fronte del conflitto libico, dunque, la produzione più esplicitamente mediatica e propagandistica sui temi della guerra resta appannaggio, in questa occasione, dell'industria dello spettacolo e dell'informazione.[5]

Questa scissione tra la produzione militare e quella civile, tuttavia, stimola la ricerca di nuove strategie ed estetiche della narrazione del conflitto che si riveleranno fondamentali per la produzione foto-cinematografica militare di poco successiva. Per quanto concerne il cinema, in particolare, gli anni del conflitto libico vedono profilarsi, nelle scelte delle principali case cinematografiche impegnate sul luogo degli scontri, un modello produttivo che, pur professando una piena adesione al reale, deve fare i conti da un lato con i propri limiti tecnici, dall'altro con esigenze estetiche e narrative dettate, oltre che dal mercato, anche da forti inferenze politiche e militari.

La produzione foto-cinematografica realizzata dall'Esercito italiano nel corso del primo conflitto mondiale si inserisce dunque nel solco di importanti esperienze pregresse sia di ambito militare che civile, definendo il proprio potenziale innovativo nella capacità di far dialogare una tradizione visiva non ancora superata con un panorama di forme espressive e mediali in forte espansione. Superata la distanza tra una produzione strettamente documentaria e una prevalentemente attrazionale e spettacolare, infatti, l'attività delle sezioni

---

[4] Come si vedrà di seguito, la vita della Sezione Cinematografica militare è strettamente legata alle necessità del conflitto in corso ed essa sarà pertanto destinata allo scioglimento al momento della smobilitazione dell'Ufficio Stampa del Comando Supremo dal quale era dipendente.

[5] Si ricordano, a tal proposito, i numerosi interventi censori operati dalle autorità politiche, in particolare, in ambito fotografico, e tesi principalmente a mitigare le accuse rivolte ai militari italiani di perpetrare brutalità nei confronti della popolazione araba. L'azione di censura e controllo operata sulla produzione giornalistica e cinematografica civile impone inoltre il divieto di accesso al fronte delle operazioni imposto a fotografi e operatori da parte militare. In ambito cinematografico questo divieto verrà spesso compensato dalla disponibilità di ufficiali e soldati a recitare i propri ruoli per la macchina da presa nelle retrovie, o in contesti ugualmente controllati (Berruti e Mazzei, *Il giornale mi lascia freddo*; Berruti e Pesenti Campagnoni S. *Luca Comerio in Libia*).

foto-cinematografiche militari durante la Grande Guerra si costruisce intorno ad un preciso ed organico intento propagandistico, teso a coniugare l'illusione di realtà suggerita dall'immagine analogica alla sua "ambiguità gnoseologica", che le consente di servire con efficacia progetti narrativi anche molto diversi.

2. Nuovi attori per un evento nuovo

Nel breve volgere del periodo che intercorre tra lo scoppio della Guerra Italo-Turca e la fine della Grande Guerra, l'Esercito italiano si trova dunque impegnato in un processo di progressivo "assorbimento" della produzione foto-cinematografica, non solo per quanto pertiene le sue potenzialità tecnico-scientifiche, già in gran parte sperimentate, ma anche e soprattutto in ambito propagandistico.

Ancor prima del suo intervento a fianco delle potenze dell'Intesa, nel maggio 1915, l'Italia è oggetto di una pesante campagna di propaganda, giornalistica e cinematografica, ad opera, in particolare, dei futuri alleati anglo-francesi. Accanto alle notizie riportate da periodici e quotidiani, le riviste fotografiche e cinematografiche si interessano con evidente curiosità alle novità determinate dalle nuove esigenze della guerra: campagne di documentazione fotografica ad opera di soldati dilettanti,[6] proiezioni itineranti al fronte,[7] riprese effettuate da palloni, aerostati e velivoli d'ogni sorta.

I cinema del Bel Paese ospitano inoltre esotiche attualità sugli eccezionali e colossali avvenimenti della guerra europea in corso accanto a una produzione tutta nostrana di film a soggetto che, facendo proprio un certo clima nazionalistico e nostalgico, rievoca le gloriose campagne risorgimentali[8]

---

[6] Sulle pagine del *Progresso Fotografico* come di altre riviste italiane (*La fotografia Artistica*), francesi (*Photo-Revue*) o inglesi (l'*Amateur Photographer*) si può seguire un percorso di documentazione informale del conflitto, grazie alla collaborazione dei molti fotografi dilettanti attivi al fronte, che, nonostante i divieti delle autorità militari, hanno rappresentato una realtà importante sia in Italia che all'estero. Al di fuori del panorama italiano, resta celebre il concorso fotografico bandito dalla rivista francese *Le Mirroir* che, sin dall'inizio del conflitto, invita tutti i fotografi impegnati sul fronte, ufficiali e non, a spedire i propri scatti promettendo lauti compensi in cambio di materiali in grado di riprodurre un'impressione vera del conflitto (Viaggio, Tomasini e Beurier).

[7] "Già da tempo la cinematografia ha fatto la sua vittoriosa apparizione nelle trincee, dove pare si è definitivamente stabilita, con grande soddisfazione dei soldati che, fra un'azione ed un'altra, si divertono un mondo. Gli inglesi furono i primi che riproducessero nei loro campi le films e le prime macchine di proiezione. Non fu difficile trovare operatori fra i soldati stessi; il successo è stato tanto lusinghiero da indurre il Comando ad applicare il piacevole passatempo su più vasta scala" (Cavallaro 47).

[8] Torna così sul mercato *Nozze d'Oro*, di Luigi Maggi (Ambrosio, 1911), inizialmente censurato per non urtare la suscettibilità austriaca, quindi riesumato in nome di un rinnovato orgoglio nazionale. Proliferano poi titoli irredentisti come *A Trieste – Vincere o morire*, *Trieste o L'Impero della Forca* ecc., accanto a favole patriottiche che sfruttano la figura del bambino quale veicolo per rinsaldare i valori della patria-famiglia e dell'unità nazionale: *Befana di Guerra*, *Il sogno patriottico di Cinessino*, *La guerra e il sogno di*

strizzando l'occhio agli eventi d'attualità.

Con l'ingresso in guerra dell'Italia, il ruolo fondamentale giocato dai media foto-cinematografici si rende ulteriormente evidente nel tentativo di bilanciare l'invadenza della propaganda straniera con una produzione adeguata e in grado di veicolare sapientemente le informazioni e le emozioni del pubblico dentro e fuori dai nostri confini.

Nelle prime fasi del conflitto, tuttavia, l'Esercito italiano non predispone un sistema di produzione di materiali informativi e propagandistici interno: l'idea stessa di propaganda, infatti, disturba tanto i soggetti più diretti della stessa quanto i vertici militari al punto che, ancora dopo Caporetto, si preferirà fare riferimento ad un generico Servizio P. piuttosto che esplicitare un sostantivo naturalmente legato a sgradite pratiche coercitive.[9]

Sarebbe, tuttavia, ingenuo ignorare la forte e costante azione di controllo e veicolamento dell'informazione operata dagli organismi militari sulle strutture mediatiche civili ancor prima dell'inizio della Grande Guerra e nel corso della stessa. In questa direzione si muovono tutta una serie di iniziative che vanno dal rilascio di lasciapassare ad alcuni selezionati operatori dell'industria del cinema per la produzione di film di attualità,[10] alle concessioni in esclusiva di materiali fotografici a editori selezionati per la tempestiva pubblicazione di cataloghi fotografici degli eventi in corso.[11]

Momi ecc. Non sfugge a quest'impeto patriottico neppure il Maciste mitologico di Cabiria, cui saranno affibbiati i panni dell'eroico alpino (Alonge; Faccioli e Scandola).
[9] "Si è chiamato Servizio P. e non servizio Propaganda prima di tutto perché occorre evitare, quanto più ci si avvicina ai riparti di truppa, di parlare di propaganda e propagandisti, parole che acuiscono la naturale diffidenza del soldato, ed in secondo luogo perchè colla parola "Servizio P." si è indicato il complesso servizio della vigilanza, propaganda ed assistenza, che converge ad un unico fine ma che non è costituito dalla sola propaganda" Comando della I[a] Armata, Sezione P, *Funzionamento dell'organizzazione P.*, Circolare n°358, 24 maggio 1918, p. 6.
[10] Resta celebre il caso del fotografo-operatore Luca Comerio, la cui intimità con la famiglia reale e l'ambiente militare gli consente di ritrarre suggestive immagini delle prime operazioni sul fronte italiano. Oltre a *La grande giornata storica italiana "20 maggio 1915"*, realizzato in occasione della seduta parlamentare che si conclude con la dichiarazione di guerra all'Austria, Comerio ritrae anche importanti battaglie come *La Battaglia tra Brenta e Adige*, *La Battaglia di Gorizia*, girato durante le fasi immediatamente precedenti e successive alla conquista della città, oltre alle operazioni militari di *Guerra d'Italia a 3000 metri sull'Adamello*, proseguendo poi il suo lavoro accanto agli operatori della Sezione Cinematografica militare. Speciali concessioni ottennero anche la ditta Ambrosio, per la realizzazione del film *Alla Fronte*, e la coppia Roatto-Rossetti con i film sulle operazioni della Marina: *La Marina da Guerra opera per la vittoria e per la gloria d'Italia* e *Fra i nostri combattenti per una più grande Italia* (Pesenti Campagnoni *WWI La guerra sepolta*).
[11] Oltre alla nota operazione dell'editore milanese Treves con l'opera *La Guerra*, si ricorda anche la serie di fascicoli *Panorami della Guerra* pubblicati dalla ditta Bestetti e

Ben presto, però, questo sistema di delega a terzi della produzione e diffusione di materiali foto-cinematografici a scopo informativo e propagandistico si rivelerà fallimentare, soprattutto in ambito cinematografico, mettendo in forte imbarazzo i vertici militari per i troppo frequenti episodi di speculazione oltre che per le numerose truffe operate ai danni di esercenti italiani e stranieri.[12]

Nel corso del 1916, dunque, lo Stato Maggiore dell'Esercito italiano, nella figura dell'ufficiale incaricato della gestione dei flussi di informazione, il Colonnello Eugenio Barbarich, capo dell'Ufficio Stampa, poi Ufficio Stampa e Propaganda (1917), comincia a riflettere sulla necessità di creare una struttura militare capace di gestire internamente la produzione di materiali foto-cinematografici da diffondersi capillarmente dentro e fuori dal Paese.

Per quanto pertiene la fotografia, la struttura cui questa speciale produzione viene demandata, detta Sezione Fotografica, si presenta quale ramo eccentrico del più antico Servizio Fotografico e viene collocata alle dirette dipendenze del già citato Ufficio Stampa. La distinzione tra la produzione del Servizio Fotografico e quella della Sezione addetta all'Ufficio Stampa viene inoltre formalmente sancita, come si dirà tra poco, dalla diversa destinazione conservativa cui questi materiali sono indirizzati: gli archivi militari, da un lato, e il Museo Centrale del Risorgimento di Roma, dall'altro.

I nuovi soggetti d'interesse individuati dalla fotografia di propaganda investono, in particolare, l'ampio filone dedicato alla catalogazione e denuncia dei danni al patrimonio artistico, architettonico e industriale italiano, l'illustrazione sistematica delle forniture di vettovaglie, armi, materiali da costruzione e d'altro genere, la dimensione tecnologica e industriale del conflitto, lo sviluppo e il funzionamento degli ospedali da campo e delle retrovie, delle navi e dei treni per il trasporto dei soldati e dei feriti, i campi di concentramento ecc. Si ha poi un fiorire di immagini dal sapore meno impersonale, come i molti ritratti e i gruppi di ufficiali e soldati al campo, di

---

Tumminelli. La pubblicazione che ricopre maggiore interesse per le sue caratteristiche estetiche, tuttavia, è sicuramente quella promossa dall'Ufficio Speciale della Marina, *La marina Italiana nella Guerra europea*, pubblicata dagli editori milanesi Alfieri e Lacroix, tra il 1916 e il 1918. Come si vedrà nelle prossime pagine, la pubblicazione di questi cataloghi fotografici rappresenta un interessante compromesso tra un intervento diretto dell'Esercito nella produzione dei materiali fotografici e la delega del lavoro editoriale nonché della commercializzazione degli stessi a editori di fama.

[12] Resta celebre il caso del Colonnello Enrico Maria Barone accusato di aver abusato di una concessione per le riprese al fronte ottenuta allo scopo di illustrare il proprio ciclo di seminari in favore della Croce Rossa. Barone avrebbe infatti venduto a terzi i materiali in questione a scopo di lucro. Il caso Barone susciterà lo sdegno dell'opinione pubblica, rendendo evidente il fenomeno della speculazione sulle immagini di guerra, e, cosa ancor più grave, rompendo il fragile equilibrio tra le case cinematografiche e il Comando Supremo in merito alla gestione delle concessioni per l'accesso al fronte (Genovese 14-20).

infermiere e medici al lavoro, di momenti della quotidianità del fronte e delle retrovie, tutti tesi a ricercare una ricchezza emotiva e una densità simbolica funzionale a farsi veicolo dello spirito di unità nazionale tra il fronte e il resto del Paese.

    A tutti questi temi sono dedicati ampi repertori fotografici che sfruttano, di volta in volta, tecniche differenti, tra le quali si ricorda in particolare l'utilizzo della fotografia stereoscopica, efficace per la sua resa iperrealistica, e quello della diapositiva, ampiamente sfruttata per illustrare gli interventi in favore del conflitto tenuti da intellettuali, politici, personaggi dello spettacolo e reduci.

    La ricerca di un canale di comunicazione empatica con il pubblico del fronte interno rappresenta infatti una delle principali svolte della fotografia come del cinema militare della Grande Guerra, la cui dimensione propagandistica si incentra, principalmente, sull'amplificazione di alcuni temi chiave della campagna di sostegno alla guerra, quali il valore del sacrificio, la bontà d'animo del soldato italiano, il lavoro, il legame simbolico tra Patria e famiglia. Questi scatti devono poter raggiungere il pubblico in modo capillare, sfruttando al massimo le consuetudini culturali delle fasce sociali più diverse: oltre che a coronare articoli e cronache di guerra sulle riviste e i quotidiani d'informazione o a completare l'immagine confezionata nelle pubblicazioni di propaganda della guerra del Regio Esercito e della Regia Marina, dunque, la fotografia viene largamente utilizzata anche nella produzione di cartoline, album, collezioni stereoscopiche tese alla conservazione celebrativa di una memoria familiare che si confonde, di necessità, con quella pubblica.[13]

    È inoltre interessante citare un ulteriore, e certamente moderno, utilizzo del mezzo fotografico al fronte: nonostante i numerosi divieti, infatti, nel corso della Grande Guerra si assiste ad un proliferare di scatti amatoriali, realizzati da soldati, in genere ufficiali, dotati di apparecchi di proprietà di vario formato,

---

[13] Un caso interessantissimo è rappresentato dallo stereoscopio Marzocchi, dal nome dell'ex ufficiale della Sezione Fotografica che lo mise a punto e lo commercializzò. Nel corso del conflitto, Marzocchi operò su molti fronti e, verosimilmente, con apparecchiature diverse, producendo materiali ufficiali e amatoriali. Con la fine delle ostilità decise di proseguire la sua attività di fotografo aprendo uno studio a Milano, la società "La Stereoscopica", insieme a due soci ed ex compagni d'armi: il Conte Revedin e V. Lazzaroni. "La Stereoscopica" si proponeva di commercializzare gli scatti eseguiti da Marzocchi e da altri fotografi al fronte per perpetrare il ricordo della guerra nella memoria del pubblico. I visori Marzocchi e le oltre 700 lastre stereoscopiche della serie "La guerra Italo-Austriaca 1915-1918" ebbero purtroppo scarso successo di pubblico e rappresentano oggi un oggetto piuttosto raro, anche se alcuni esemplari del catalogo Marzocchi si conservano presso l'Archivio Centrale di Stato di Roma, il Museo Galvani di Bologna, il Museo della Guerra Bianca di Brescia, la Fondazione Cineteca Italiana di Milano e il Museo della Battaglia di Vittorio Veneto, che vanta forse la collezione più completa.

come ricordo personale dell'esperienza di guerra.[14] Queste memorie private sono state oggetto di una pesante censura ed è pertanto assai difficile valutarne l'allineamento con la rappresentazione ufficiale del conflitto. Nonostante le pesanti ingerenze censorie, tuttavia, gran parte della produzione fotografica amatoriale sembra rivelare il desiderio di conservare una dimensione più onorevole e umana della guerra, negandone gli aspetti più terribili e assecondando così una non meno rigida censura privata.

3. Lo spettacolo cinematografico al servizio dell'esercito

Accanto alla fotografia, negli anni della Grande Guerra, anche la cinematografia s'impone per la prima volta all'attenzione del Comando Supremo, in virtù della sua eccezionale capacità di parlare al proprio pubblico nei termini di un intenso coinvolgimento sensoriale ed emotivo, fermo restando la fede nella sua già citata vocazione riproduttiva del reale. Come già evidenziato nelle pagine precedenti, negli anni del conflitto libico si era andato consolidando un nuovo genere cinematografico, declinato nella forma del giornale seriale o, in alternativa, del documentario a soggetto, e caratterizzato dalla dichiarata intenzione di essere una trasposizione fedele di avvenimenti d'attualità.

Con lo scoppio del nuovo conflitto europeo, dunque, la formula dell'informazione cinematografica ritorna immediatamente in auge, favorita anche dalle esperienze consumatesi nelle altre nazioni belligeranti. Sin dalla fine del primo anno di guerra, il 1914, si registra infatti un processo di uniformazione dei sistemi di acquisizione dei media foto-cinematografici da parte degli eserciti belligeranti: Inghilterra, Francia, Germania e Impero Austro-Ungarico si dotano prontamente di strutture produttive che, pur essendo organizzate secondo logiche di dipendenza differenti, fanno di fatto riferimento all'esercito per la produzione di documentari e, soprattutto, giornali cinematografici a cadenza periodica, il cui scopo è quello di fornire un racconto diretto, controllato e verosimile, degli avvenimenti in corso.

Per quanto concerne l'Italia, superata una prima fase di esperimenti tesi a sfruttare al massimo strutture industriali già operanti sul territorio, si arriva alla costituzione di una Sezione Cinematografica militare, anch'essa alle dipendenze dell'Ufficio Stampa, solo tra le fine del 1916 e il gennaio del 1917, momento in cui la suddetta Sezione diventa effettivamente operativa. La Marina italiana anticipa di qualche mese questo risultato, affidando la produzione cinematografica ad un Ufficio Speciale (con funzioni in gran parte simili a quelle dell'Ufficio Stampa del Comando Supremo), attivo già a partire dalla primavera del 1916.

---

[14] L'imponente diffusione della fotografia amatoriale è perfettamente incarnata dal modello Vest Pocket della Kodak, istantanea e portatile, largamente pubblicizzata sulle pagine delle riviste di fotografia e non solo come l'accessorio irrinunciabile del soldato al fronte (Basano e Pesenti Campagnoni).

L'affiancarsi di una Sezione Cinematografica alla già esistente Sezione Fotografica rappresenta certamente un momento di svolta fondamentale nella definizione di un rapporto più diretto tra l'Esercito italiano e il pubblico di massa. Questa novità non può tuttavia nascondere il forte debito della giovane produzione d'attualità cinematografica militare con l'industria del cinema italiano e straniero contemporaneo. Pur essendo dotata di operatori militari,[15] infatti, la Sezione Cinematografica, suddivisa in 4, poi 5 squadre destinate ciascuna a coprire un settore diverso del fronte, deve appoggiarsi, per quanto riguarda le fasi della lavorazione e del montaggio del film, nonché per la disponibilità di macchinari e attrezzature, a strutture industriali capaci di soddisfarne il fabbisogno. Esercito e Marina italiani troveranno in particolare nella casa romana Cines, dichiarata "Stabilimento Militare Ausiliario", un punto d'appoggio fondamentale alla loro produzione.

Anche per quanto concerne l'aspetto distributivo, l'Esercito si trova a dover inserire i propri programmi d'informazione all'interno dei normali palinsesti dello spettacolo cinematografico, venendo così a confrontarsi direttamente con i gusti di un pubblico molto esigente e progressivamente sempre più annoiato, al punto da rendere necessario l'obbligo di proiezione prima dei normali spettacoli. Ad acuire il disamore del pubblico verso la produzione di guerra e la sua diffidenza nei confronti della fedeltà al reale dei materiali e delle notizie riportate, contribuiscono poi i già citati episodi di falsi e le frequenti speculazioni che avevano caratterizzato il primo anno di combattimenti.

La comparsa del Regio Esercito tra i principali produttori diretti di immagini da e del fronte rappresenta certo un passo avanti in direzione della conquista di una nuova fiducia del pubblico nei confronti dell'attualità cinematografica di guerra. La maggiore affidabilità della fonte dispensatrice delle informazioni, viene tuttavia controbilanciata, nei timori del pubblico, dal suo potere censorio. La frequentissima discrepanza riscontrabile tra le aspettative del pubblico nei confronti della rappresentazione di guerra e le caratteristiche dei materiali messi effettivamente in circolazione viene dunque spesso attribuita alla volontà militare di "tagliare" certi contenuti, quali, in particolare, quelli relativi alle dinamiche degli scontri veri e propri.

Nonostante l'innegabile azione censoria operata dalle strutture militari su

---

[15] Non si può tuttavia dimenticare che una parte considerevole degli operatori impiegati dalla Sezione Cinematografica italiana, così come accade per altre nazioni, proviene dalle principali case di produzione attive sul territorio, basti pensare al Tenente Cesare Borgini della Gaumont, ad Achille Panni della Luca Comerio, a Silvio Ornano che aveva lavorato per la Kinema Color di Londra e per la Cimino film di Torino, Carlo Quadroni dell'Etna Film, o a personaggi quali Carmine Gallone e Nino Oxilia, che insieme agli operatori Gencarelli e Montuori hanno prestato servizio presso l'Ufficio Speciale della Marina. Pur restando al di fuori delle strutture militari anche il noto pioniere del cinema Luca Comerio presta la sua abilità di cineasta alle necessità della produzione bellica.

informazioni e immagini provenienti dal fronte, fisse o in movimento, bisogna tuttavia specificare quanto questa censura sia stata spesso prevalentemente "positiva", nel senso di propositiva. La maggior parte degli operatori aveva infatti l'obbligo di inserire all'interno dei metri del proprio girato una percentuale, per altro minima, di sequenze relative alla vita più strettamente ufficiale del fronte: personalità militari, visite e cerimonie o altri elementi rilevanti a scopo propagandistico.[16]

La censura più severa era diretta soprattutto in due direzioni: la tutela del morale dei soldati e dei cittadini, per la quale si evitava di mostrare troppo apertamente i morti in pose macabre, i cadaveri dei nostri soldati o le reali condizioni delle trincee di prima linea, prediligendo al contrario sottolineare il numero dei caduti e dei prigionieri nemici o la dimensione cameratesca della vita al fronte. In secondo luogo, era applicata una forte censura a tutti gli aspetti legati alla disciplina militare, cui non si fa cenno né nella documentazione fotografica, né tantomeno in quella cinematografica.

La mancanza effettiva di immagini e sequenze relative allo svolgimento degli scontri e alle dinamiche dei combattimenti (intesi quali momenti di incontro armato tra parti opposte belligeranti) è imputabile, invece, principalmente alle peculiari caratteristiche della modernità di questa guerra. La dimensione fortemente tecnologica e le proporzioni colossali di questo primo conflitto mondiale, segnano infatti una frattura insanabile con l'esperienza bellica precedente. Nonostante la modernità militare avesse già fatto capolino, annunciandosi nel corso di alcuni conflitti minori del '900, è in questi anni che la trasformazione raggiunge la sua piena maturazione, segnando un profondo iato non solo a livello storico, ma anche e soprattutto culturale. La maggior parte dei combattenti della Grande Guerra era partita portando con sé un'idea di battaglia forgiata nella tradizione ottocentesca e riassumibile, sommariamente, nell'equazione valore più sacrificio uguale onore. Lo scontro con la realtà, rappresentata dal configurarsi di un conflitto regolato, in primo luogo, dall'efficienza e modernità industriale dei paesi belligeranti, dal numero dei combattenti schierati, dalla capacità di rinnovare le proprie risorse umane e

---

[16] Nel 1916, ad esempio, gli operatori ammessi dovevano recarsi al fronte dotati di un'apposita tessera di riconoscimento e di due salvacondotti distinti, uno per le retrovie e uno per le zone delle operazioni, entrambi di durata limitata secondo le disposizioni date dall'Ufficio Stampa del Comando Supremo. La ditta doveva inoltre tempestivamente indicare il luogo delle riprese e i soggetti che sarebbero stati cinematografati, tenendo conto che "per ogni mille metri di nastro, duecento metri, al massimo, devono essere impressionati con soggetti indicati dal Comando Supremo". Nonostante i restanti 800 metri fossero naturalmente sottoposti al vaglio della censura, le richieste dello Stato Maggiore non sembrano costituire un vincolo troppo gravoso: fatto salvo l'obbligo di riprendere occasioni e personalità notevoli in visita al fronte, infatti, la scelta degli altri soggetti rimane a discrezione dell'operatore (R. Esercito Italiano, Comando Supremo, Ufficio Stampa. *NORME per i corrispondenti di guerra* 19).

tecnologiche, annullando quasi del tutto il valore del singolo e il senso del suo sacrificio, rappresenta dunque uno degli aspetti più terrificanti dell'esperienza di guerra. Aspetto per altro difficilmente compreso da quanti non esperirono in prima persona il fronte e raccontato quasi con pudore dai reduci, vittime di una sorta di censura interiore.

Tornando al rapporto tra guerra moderna e mezzo cinematografico, questo si trova in gran parte estromesso dall'effettiva possibilità di cogliere in pieno le proporzioni, le dinamiche, nonché il senso della vita di trincea, caratterizzata da spazi angusti e bui, dalla convivenza con la morte (rappresentata sia fisicamente, dai cadaveri abbandonati dentro e fuori dai trinceramenti in attesa di sepoltura, sia in prospettiva, dal pericolo cui gli uomini erano costantemente sottoposti), da attese lunghissime e da una noia in tutti i sensi letale.

L'invisibilità della guerra moderna non corrisponde quindi, nella maggior parte dei casi, a nessun astratto divieto di ripresa, quanto piuttosto ad una concretissima vacuità dal campo di battaglia, al mancato contatto visivo con il nemico, all'impossibilità di restituire una dimensione sonora che, nel buio delle trincee, ha rappresentato uno degli elementi più concreti e significativi dell'esperienza bellica. Nonostante la sua modernità tecnologica, l'impegno etico nel farsi testimone degli eventi in corso e le evidenti necessità della propaganda militare, il cinema non può che dimostrarsi impotente di fronte a questa nuova guerra delle macchine e degli uomini.

Fatta questa premessa, possiamo ora spiegare fino a che punto la guerra riportata nei cine-giornali e nei documentari dell'Esercito fosse in gran parte percepita dal pubblico dell'epoca in quanto falsa o, più precisamente, inverosimile, pur risultando oggi un passaggio fondamentale in direzione dello sviluppo del nuovo genere documentario.

All'impossibilità tecnica del mezzo cinematografico di riprodurre gran parte degli aspetti più sensibili del conflitto in corso (attese, invisibilità del nemico, suoni, difficoltà di percezione dei confini spaziali nonché degli sviluppi evenemenziali), si deve infatti sommare un orizzonte culturale di riferimento che per la maggior parte degli spettatori oscilla tra l'esaltazione della modernità tecnologica e la nostalgia per un'idea di guerra quale succedersi ordinato e causalmente concatenato di battaglie sul modello ottocentesco.

Per quanto concerne l'aspetto della modernità tecnologica, fondamentale anche ai fini di una propaganda tesa a valorizzare gli sforzi del Paese nella direzione di una modernizzazione industriale al passo con le altre nazioni europee, nel corso degli anni questa assume un'importanza sempre maggiore nella rappresentazione fattane dal cinema militare. L'affastellarsi di sequenze e inquadrature che mostrano, in un accumularsi iperbolico, le sempre più incredibili e letali dotazioni dell'artiglieria italiana, rappresentano un aspetto fondamentale all'interno della maggior parte delle produzioni d'attualità. La tensione spettacolare di queste immagini, il cui obiettivo è eminentemente mostrativo, tuttavia, le vincola ad una dimensione estetica che si rifà agli anni precedenti. Al contrario, le sequenze che si cimentano nel difficile compito di raccontare la quotidianità del conflitto e, ancor più, quelle relative alla guerra-guerreggiata, si trovano a dover gestire da un lato la nuova deontologia di fedeltà al reale dell'attualità cinematografica (fedeltà invocata dal pubblico già ai tempi del conflitto libico), dall'altro un'aspettativa spettatoriale che si rifà a un'idea del combattere ormai superata e incongruente rispetto alla realtà del fronte.

La contraddittorietà di questa situazione, tuttavia, viene risolta in molti casi dalla ricerca di soluzioni ibride, che guardano a uno sfruttamento delle potenzialità del linguaggio cinematografico (montaggio e raccordi in primo luogo) in direzione narrativa, pur restando il più possibile fedeli al repertorio di immagini e situazioni ritratti al fronte o, più spesso, nelle retrovie con o senza la collaborazione dei soldati-attori. Si assiste dunque ad una drammatizzazione del reale, non a caso retaggio della tradizione giornalistica, tesa a riprodurne una dimensione in qualche modo già digerita e narrativizzata, funzionale alle esigenze di una propaganda che punta ad una prematura storicizzazione dei fatti in corso.

L'insoddisfazione del pubblico nei confronti di questa soluzione si iscrive dunque, in primo luogo, in una mancata rispondenza con le sue aspettative: pur facendosi racconto, infatti, la guerra cinematografica continua ad omettere dallo schermo quella rappresentazione della battaglia e del nemico che, semplicemente, nella Grande Guerra non si dà. Si possono invece facilmente seguire tutte le fasi di preparazione degli attacchi, dall'arrivo al fronte, alla disposizione delle trincee, dal bombardamento, alla preparazione delle armi. Quel che accade dopo, lungi dall'essere censurato, appartiene all'esperienza di quei pochi che sono sopravvissuti per raccontarlo. Il cinema riprende il racconto dal rientro al campo, quando vengono raccolti i feriti per portarli ai posti di soccorso e, soprattutto, nel momento della sfilata dei prigionieri e del bottino di guerra. Questa svolta dell'attualità dal vero in direzione di una drammatizzazione del reale a mezzo degli strumenti di linguaggio del cinema (e non della messa in scena) segna dunque l'affacciarsi di un nuovo genere: quello documentario.

4. Diversi progetti per la conservazione delle immagini della Storia
La costituzione delle Sezioni Fotografica e Cinematografica in seno all'Ufficio Stampa e Propaganda del Comando Supremo delinea, dunque, il tentativo dell'Esercito italiano di introdursi in modo competitivo e consapevole, anche se spesso con risultati non ottimali, in un universo mediatico assai articolato, complicato da dinamiche di natura economica e commerciale oltre che iscritto in un orizzonte culturale in rapida evoluzione a partire dal quale si definisce un inedito rapporto di fiducia con il pubblico.

Le innumerevoli difficoltà e i frequenti fallimenti che hanno ostacolato il progetto di autonoma produzione di materiali foto-cinematogafici tesi alla propaganda militare dentro e fuori dal Paese, sono la testimonianza di un processo di apertura a nuove forme di comunicazione che vive di fasi alterne e che risente fortemente, soprattutto in ambito cinematografico, di un'eccessiva burocrazia.[17]

Nonostante i numerosi riscontri negativi, tuttavia, la grande circolazione di immagini fisse e in movimento messa in moto dalla produzione e distribuzione militare incide fortemente sul processo di fissazione della memoria visiva della guerra. La circolazione di questi materiali non si arresta, infatti, con il cessare delle ostilità, ma al contrario prosegue cambiando continuamente aspetto e scopo. Smesse le vesti di una propaganda tesa ad esaltare l'attualità della guerra e la sua tensione verso sorti magnifiche e progressive, le immagini del conflitto appena conclusosi si depositano nella memoria comune o vengono riesumate e ricollocate per farsi sostenitrici di nuove battaglie.[18] Uno dei principali sbocchi della produzione fotografica di guerra alla fine del conflitto, ad esempio, è rappresentato dall'ambito commerciale: le immagini del fronte, gli orrori e la devastazione lasciati sul campo della Prima Guerra Mondiale vengono confezionati in serie di cartoline, stereoscopie o lastre da proiezione e vendute accanto a panorami e *diableries* per la fruizione domestica e la conservazione privata. La composizione seriale di questi fondi ricolloca il singolo scatto nel contesto di una più ampia ricostruzione e narrazione della guerra, come già accadeva con le pubblicazioni fotografiche.[19]

Diverso il caso del cinema, dove la mancanza di un mercato d'uso privato (equivalente all'odierno *home movie*) riduce fortemente le possibilità di circolazione dei film di guerra dopo la sua fine al di fuori del raggio d'azione delle principali forze interessate a proseguire l'opera di propaganda nella nuova

---

[17] Nonostante i molti sforzi per migliorarne il funzionamento, la produzione cinematografica militare italiana non riuscirà mai, nel corso della Grande Guerra, a guadagnare il favore del proprio pubblico, non solo a causa della già citata incompatibilità fra le aspettative spettatoriali e le pur innovative soluzioni narrative messe in atto, ma anche per la sua innegabile povertà estetica, specie se confrontata con le più avanzate produzioni anglo-francesi, oltre che per l'evidente difficoltà di tenere il ritmo delle più agili pubblicazioni di articoli e fotografie che rendono immancabilmente obsoleta l'informazione cinematografica.

[18] Il fascismo, in particolar modo, trasformerà la memoria della Grande Guerra in momento fondativo dell'epica nazionale.

[19] Come già accaduto molti anni prima, nel 1866, con la commercializzazione degli scatti realizzati sul fronte della Guerra Civile Americana da Alexander Gardner nel suo *Photographic Sketch Book* (Lee e Young) o con quelli della Guerra di Crimea messi in vendita dall'editore del fotografo inglese Roger Fenton dopo la fine del conflitto (1856), tuttavia, l'interesse del pubblico nei confronti di questi cimeli della recente storia nazionale, al di fuori delle associazioni combattentistiche e di reduci, si dimostra tiepido e si esaurisce molto rapidamente.

veste della celebrazione commemorativa e di una narrazione storico-impressionista incentrata sull'esaltazione della componente più fortemente emotiva e spettacolare del mezzo cinematografico.

La maggior parte dei materiali cinematografici realizzati sul fronte italiano del conflitto (siano essi giornali della guerra, documentari, film di propaganda o scarti di lavorazione) è stata infatti oggetto, a partire dai primi anni del dopoguerra fino ai giorni nostri, di pratiche di riuso prive di ogni genere di regolamentazione, le cui gravissime conseguenze hanno portato, dopo quasi un secolo, alla perdita di gran parte dei film girati dai nostri soldati.

Messo da parte il tema degli utilizzi post-bellici che di questi materiali sono stati fatti, nel corso degli anni, dagli attori più diversi, è interessante soffermarsi brevemente sull'aspetto più squisitamente conservativo. Sin dai primi mesi di guerra, infatti, in Italia come all'estero si registra una straordinaria attenzione nei confronti della novità rappresentata dalla possibilità di documentare visivamente e in modo capillare un evento di così straordinaria portata storica quale fu la Prima Guerra Mondiale. Dagli ambienti sociali e culturali più illuminati emergono velocemente diverse iniziative per la conservazione di materiali, in particolar modo fotografici, con lo scopo di creare una raccolta organica ed esaustiva di immagini della guerra, capace di trasmettere ai posteri la storia e il significato dei terribili eventi in corso.[20] Questa spinta per la democratica costituzione di un archivio visivo della Storia, che richiama, per altro, ben più antiche profezie e aspirazioni,[21] incontrerà tuttavia l'ostilità dell'ambiente politico e militare, anch'esso impegnato in un proprio progetto ufficiale che, alla prova dei fatti, si rivelerà tuttavia ingarbugliato da una serie di questioni di natura burocratica e amministrativa.

Nel 1918 si era assistito ad un'importante trasformazione dell'assetto istituzionale dell'Ufficio Stampa che, oltre a passare sotto il comando del Colonnello Grossi[22] e ad arricchirsi di un nuovo ufficio destinato alla

---

[20] Nel 1916, un gruppo di intellettuali guidati dal milanese Antonio Curti e da Rodolfo Namias, illustre rappresentante della migliore tradizione fotografica italiana e proprietario della rivista *Il progresso fotografico,* presenta un progetto per la costituzione di un Comitato Nazionale volto a contrastare i ritardi, la miopia, gli impedimenti burocratici e le "suscettività gerarchiche" nella gestione ufficiale della raccolta e conservazione di materiali documentari sulla guerra. Questo innovativo progetto verrà tuttavia affossato in favore della Società per la Storia del Risorgimento, sostenuta dall'Onorevole Boselli, cui verranno infine affidati i fondi della Sezione Foto-Cinematografica (Namias. *La documentazione fotografica della nostra guerra potrà riuscire un'opera organica?*; Namias. *Per la documentazione fotografica della nostra guerra* 5).

[21] Si pensi ai famosi Archivi del Film prefigurati dal pioniere Boleslaw Matuszewski o al colossale progetto di Albert Khan, gli *Archives de la Planète*, che, oltre a materiali foto-cinematografici, avrebbero dovuto raccogliere altre numerosissime forme di documentazione del mondo.

[22] Eugenio Barbarich viene infatti promosso a Generale in capo della Brigata Friuli e, successivamente, Capo di Stato Maggiore del Corpo di Spedizione in Bulgaria e

propaganda, vede configurarsi un diverso assetto anche per le Sezioni Fotografica e Cinematografica. Queste vengono infatti a fondersi in un'unica Sezione Foto-Cinematografica, divisa, da un punto di vista amministrativo, tra le esigenze del Comando Supremo, da cui di fatto dipende per la produzione di propaganda, e la disponibilità economica del Sottosegretariato per la Propaganda all'Estero e la Stampa dell'Onorevole Gallenga, che ne finanzia l'attività. Nonostante i compiti di questa nuova Sezione restino sostanzialmente immutati, questa trasformazione acuisce la distanza tra una produzione di propaganda a cavallo tra esigenze militari e politiche, e una di stampo documentaristico e scientifico che rimane, al contrario, di esclusiva pertinenza militare.

Con lo smantellamento degli uffici del Sottosegretariato di Gallenga nel dicembre del 1918, dunque, il finanziamento alla Sezione Foto-Cinematografica e al suo Laboratorio Fotografico viene sospeso e si richiede all'Esercito di raccogliere e spedire a Roma tutti i materiali realizzati con l'aiuto economico del Sottosegretariato stesso. La richiesta di Roma, cui sottostà un accordo precedente, siglato tra il Generale Diaz e l'ex Presidente del Consiglio Boselli, prevede il trasferimento di questi materiali presso le sale del Museo Centrale del Risorgimento, allo scopo di favorire il consolidamento di quella memoria ufficiale della guerra, proposta, per l'appunto, dagli organi della propaganda militare. Questa operazione sembra dunque sostenere un progetto conservativo che, lungi dal volersi il più possibile esaustivo e completo, si propone invece di effettuare una selezione ridotta di materiali rispetto a quelli potenzialmente accessibili.

Una certa mancanza di rigore storico in questa operazione di musealizzazione dei materiali della Sezione Foto-Cinematografica viene prontamente sottolineata, con toni assai poco concilianti, dal Capitano Cesare Antilli, responsabile della Direzione del Servizio Fotografico[23] e, in conseguenza, di tutti i materiali realizzati nel corso del conflitto dal suddetto Servizio, ivi compresa la Sezione Fotografica e il suo Laboratorio. Egli contesta, in particolare, la scelta arbitraria di separare l'archivio della Sezione Foto-Cinematografica, i cui negativi (circa 10.000) sono per altro giudicati molto scadenti, dall'archivio generale dei materiali del Servizio Fotografico, comprendente invece oltre 120.000 negativi di grande qualità. Secondo le rimostranze di Antilli, infatti, la produzione del Laboratorio Fotografico (precedente all'istituzione della Sezione Foto-Cinematografica), di cui Boselli rivendica la proprietà, non ha mai ricevuto finanziamenti dal Sottosegretariato

---

Macedonia.
[23] Il 15 gennaio 1919, la Direzione del Servizio Fotografico militare passa sotto il Comando dell'Areonautica militare insieme a tutti i materiali prodotti, nel corso del conflitto, dal suddetto Servizio, compresi quelli accumulati dalla Sezione Fotografica e dal suo Laboratorio (ex Revedin), tutti affidati al Magazzino Avanzato Materiale Fotografico per la conservazione.

Gallenga che, pertanto, non dovrebbe avanzare pretese in merito.

La questione dei diritti di proprietà sui materiali realizzati dai vari organi in funzione all'interno dell'Ufficio Stampa del Comando Supremo rimane ad oggi poco chiara. Quel che appare certo, invece, è come la mancanza di un progetto di conservazione concordato in armonia tra le forze militari e quelle politiche abbia portato alla quasi completa distruzione dei fondi cinematografici di produzione militare (di propaganda) a fronte, invece, del conservarsi di un imponente archivio fotografico, ancora in gran parte di proprietà dello Stato Maggiore dell'Esercito.

Questi numerosi scatti sono conservati oggi presso le differenti fototeche e gli archivi dell'Ufficio Storico dello Stato Maggiore dell'Esercito, della Marina, del Genio e di altre Armi, presso musei e archivi minori, compresi quelli di istituzioni che hanno ricevuto donazioni da privati in possesso, per le ragioni più varie, di materiali fotografici, militari e non, relativi al conflitto.[24] Il destino dei negativi e positivi cinematografici, al contrario, è stato più inclemente oltre che più incerto.[25]

Conclusioni

Si è infine giunti a conclusione di questo breve excursus dedicato ai momenti fondamentali dello sviluppo della produzione foto-cinematografica militare la cui modernità si iscrive nella svolta squisitamente mediatica dell'utilizzo di questi mezzi quali veicolo privilegiato di informazione ufficiale, da un lato, ed esperimento di drammatizzazione dell'attualità storica a scopo spettacolare e narrativo, dall'altro.

È proprio sulla scia di questa pratica di drammatizzazione dei fatti del reale, dovuta principalmente alle necessità della propaganda, che muoverà i primi passi quel genere documentario i cui natali si fanno generalmente risalire solo alla fine degli anni Venti, grazie alle riflessioni dello studioso John Grierson.[26]

---

[24] Tra questi si cita il fondo Luis Bogino del Museo Nazionale del Cinema di Torino, che annovera numerosi scatti realizzati da Bogino nel corso del suo lavoro per la Sezione Fotografica del Comando Supremo dal giugno 1915 al marzo 1919. Oltre a documentare ampiamente il fronte terrestre italiano, Bogino si distingue per aver lasciato una dettagliata memoria visiva anche della sezione presso la quale operava, ritratta all'opera in più occasioni, con dettagli relativi anche ai laboratori di sviluppo dei materiali fotografici (Basano. "La memoria visiva della Grande Guerra. La collezione fotografica del Museo Nazionale del Cinema." *AL FRONTE* 23-27).

[25] In Italia purtroppo non esiste un fondo cinematografico militare organico e non è al momento noto il destino dei film destinati alle sale del Museo del Risorgimento. I titoli che ci sono pervenuti si trovano custoditi da archivi e cineteche pubbliche e private e si presentano per lo più in forma frammentaria o lacunosa. Le scelte che di volta in volta sono state fatte, in tempi diversi e da numerosi artefici, hanno infatti prodotto una spietata selezione delle immagini passibili di essere salvate e di quelle da consegnarsi all'oblio, a partire dalla valutazione della loro "utilità storica".

[26] In particolare si fa riferimento alla celebre recensione del film di Robert Flaherty

In questa prospettiva, è interessante sottolineare come, dopo un'iniziale indifferenza da parte militare nei confronti del medium cinematografico, considerato nulla più che un perfezionamento, nel tempo, delle risorse tecnico-scientifiche di quello fotografico, si assista nel corso della Grande Guerra ad un atteggiamento sostanzialmente nuovo, che guarda al cinema proprio per la sua differenza mediatica rispetto alla fotografia. Questo sguardo nuovo è inoltre favorito dall'imporsi, negli anni immediatamente precedenti il conflitto, di forme di giornalismo cinematografico in cui la dimensione informativa si mescola con quella spettacolare, capace di parlare a grandi masse di spettatori.

La specificità d'uso individuata per il cinema militare, tuttavia, ne circoscrive l'utilizzo nel tempo e nello spazio alle necessità del conflitto in corso, senza mai prevedere la costituzione di una struttura produttiva permanente, come per il Servizio Fotografico, né altro scopo rispetto a quello della produzione di propaganda. Gli usi tecnico-scientifici della cinematografia militare di guerra (affini a quelli fotografici come la ricognizione aerea del territorio, i film educativi ad uso militare, quelli scientifici ecc.), pur ampiamente attestati e documentati, restano privi di una struttura produttiva di riferimento e sono per lo più opera di operatori del Servizio Fotografico. Di questi materiali, purtroppo, si conserva (o è stato ritrovato) assai poco, e indagare sulla loro storia particolare e sul loro destino conservativo sarà un'interessante sfida per il futuro.

Per la fotografia militare è possibile individuare usi distinti, rappresentanti ciascuno la risposta ad un diverso approccio e utilizzo di questo medium: documento isolato, unità significante all'interno di un flusso di altre immagini (dalle mostre alle cartoline ecc.) o infine elemento illustrativo facente parte di forme mediali più complesse (come la rivista illustrata). La dimensione comunicativa della fotografia e la sua capacità di parlare ad un grande pubblico sembra dunque venire considerata dall'Esercito italiano in modo del tutto discrezionale, quale possibilità secondaria e ridefinibile di volta in volta a seconda delle necessità.

Il cinema, dal canto suo, è visto con maggiore sospetto proprio in virtù delle sue potenzialità comunicative e di coinvolgimento emotivo, ovvero delle sue stesse qualità di medium. Il motore che sembra muovere la produzione cinematografica militare si iscrive nel processo di creazione di una narrazione della guerra in qualche modo già epicizzata, una documentazione sottratta alla lettura storica cui è destinato il documento e votata fin dall'inizio alla costituzione di una memoria celebrativa. In questa prospettiva, si chiarisce dunque il senso del passaggio della produzione cinematografica di propaganda dagli archivi militari a quelli di un istituto preposto specificatamente alla conservazione di questa memoria preconfezionata. Nella stessa direzione

---

Moana, pubblicata da John Grierson sul *New York Sun* l'8 febbraio 1926.

sembrano iscriversi perfettamente anche gli usi successivi che di questi materiali verranno fatti, piegati dalle trasformazioni politiche a servire nuovi racconti mitici del recente passato italiano.

Università degli Studi di Milano

Opere citate

Alonge Giaime. *Cinema e guerra. Il film, la Grande Guerra e l'immaginario bellico del Novecento*. Torino: UTET, 2001.

_____. "L'occhio e il cervello dell'esercito", *Cinema muto italiano: tecnica e tecnologia*. Vol. 1 a cura di Canosa Michele, Carluccio Giulia e Villa Federica. Roma: Carocci, 2006.

Basano Roberta e Pesenti Campagnoni Sarah, a cura di. *AL FRONTE. Cineoperatori e fotografi raccontano la Grande Guerra*. Catalogo di una mostra al Museo Nazionale del Cinema, Torino, 29 gennaio - 31 maggio, 2015. Cinisello Balsamo (Milano): Silvana Editoriale, 2015.

Berruti Sila e Mazzei Luca. "Il giornale mi lascia freddo. I film "dal vero" dalla Libia (1911-1912) e il pubblico italiano." *Immagine. Note di Storia del Cinema*. Ancona: La Cattedrale, 3, 2011. 53-103.

Berruti Sila e Mazzei Luca. "Silent War. 'Newsreels' and 'Cinema postcards' from Country at War." *La costrucció de l'actualitat en el cinema dels orígen*. Girona: A. Quintana e J. Pons, 2012. 261-76.

_____ e Pesenti Campagnoni Sarah. "Luca Comerio in Libia: documenti non ufficiali di una pagina di storia." *Immagine. Note di storia del cinema*. AIRSC, Ancona: La Cattedrale, 4, 2011. 69-94.

Cavallaro Alfonso. A. (Veritas). "Rappresentazioni cinematografiche nelle trincee." *La Vita Cinematografica*. Torino, 4.14 (15 aprile 1915): 47.

Faccioli Alessandro e Scandola Alberto, a cura di. *A fuoco l'obiettivo! Il cinema e la fotografia raccontano la Grande Guerra*. Bologna: Persiani, 2014.

Galloni Marco. "La tecnica fotografica nella Prima Guerra Mondiale." *AL FRONTE. Cineoperatori e fotografi raccontano la Grande Guerra*. 2015: 37-39.

Genovese Nino. "La strana guerra del Colonnello Barone." *Immagine. Note di Storia del Cinema*. AIRSC, Roma: Edizioni dell'Ateneo, 2.10 (aprile-giugno 1985): 14-20.

Lee Anthony W. e Young Elizabeth. *On Alexander Gardner's Photographic Sketch Book of the Civil War*. Berkeley: University of California Press, 2007.

Namias Rodolfo. "La documentazione fotografica della nostra guerra potrà riuscire un'opera organica?" *Il Progresso Fotografico*. Milano: 10 (ottobre 1915): 318.

_____. "Per la documentazione fotografica della nostra guerra". *Il Progresso Fotografico*. Milano: 2 (febbraio 1916): 62.

Pesenti Campagnoni Sarah. *WWI La guerra sepolta. I film girati al fronte tra documentazione, attualità e spettacolo*. Torino: Università degli Studi, Facoltà di Lettere e Filosofia, Fondo di studi "Parini-Chirio", 2013.

Regio Esercito Italiano, Comando Supremo, Ufficio Stampa. *NORME per i corrispondenti di guerra. Prescrizioni per il servizio fotografico e cinematografico*. Roma: Laboratorio Tipografico del Comando Supremo, giugno 1916 / ottobre 1916.

Viaggio Stefano, Tomasini Luigi e Beurier Joelle. *Soldati fotografi. Fotografie della Grande Guerra sulle pagine di "Le Mirroir"*. Rovereto: Museo Storico Italiano della Guerra, 2005.

und
Barbara Meazzi

Annie Vivanti e la grande guerra: stupro, aborto e redenzione in *Vae Victis!*

Lo stupro è stato praticato nel corso della storia come "arma di guerra", fin dai tempi più antichi. L'espressione "arma di guerra", ricorda Anne Dupierreux, sarebbe però recente, perché utilizzata solo a partire dagli anni Novanta del secolo scorso, all'epoca cioè delle guerre in Rwanda e in Bosnia. Per la prima volta, osserva la studiosa, in quella terribile occasione lo stupro sistematico è stato considerato come parte della strategia militare, il che ha consentito di abbattere il muro di silenzio che fino ad allora aveva avvolto le vittime, e di punire i responsabili per aver commesso un crimine contro l'umanità.

In verità, già all'epoca della Prima Guerra mondiale lo stupro "di massa" compiuto dall'esercito tedesco all'epoca dell'invasione del Belgio aveva suscitato vivissime reazioni, anche grazie alla mobilitazione dei comitati suffragisti britannici e americani, e l'opinione pubblica internazionale si ritrovò allora a fare i conti con gli orrori di cui erano state vittime le donne in quanto "non combattenti". Il recupero dell'evento da parte della propaganda di guerra, tuttavia, fu tale per cui più che alle donne ci si interessò soprattutto ai carnefici, dipinti come dei mostri che nulla, né la pietà, né il timor di Dio, avrebbe potuto arrestare.

Malgrado la tragedia delle donne belghe e francesi abbia avuto in Italia un'eco molto ridotta (Schiavon 170), la scrittrice Annie Vivanti, senz'altro a causa del suo cosmopolitismo, dedicò alla vicenda nel 1915 una *pièce* teatrale intitolata *L'invasore,* trasformata nel 1917 nel romanzo *Vae Victis!*, che riscosse un ottimo successo di pubblico e conobbe una decina di riedizioni, fino al 1940. È legittimo interrogarsi sulle ragioni della fortuna di un romanzo che racconta di due donne belghe che, dopo esser state stuprate da soldati tedeschi, decidono l'una di abortire e l'altra di portare a termine la gravidanza. Ci proponiamo pertanto di analizzare *L'invasore* e soprattutto *Vae Victis!*, considerato da Giovanni Venturi come il romanzo sulla "coscienza dei diritti di una scelta e di una scelta femminile" (308), anche se in verità questo ci sembra essere un testo che tratta di questioni legate alla drammatica ineluttabilità della maternità: malgrado la tematica sembri apparentemente moderna, pur prendendo spunto dagli stupri effettivamente subiti dalle donne belghe, e pur presentando qualche variante qualitativamente significativa rispetto alla narrativa popolare coeva, *L'invasore* e *Vae Victis!* propongono — è questa la nostra ipotesi — dei messaggi fondamentalmente conservatori e apertamente eugenici.

La Belgique à feu et à sang — dettaglio della copertina
(*collezione personale*)

1. *La Grande Guerra e il corpo delle donne: storia, stupri e stereotipi*
La copertina a colori della pubblicazione *La Belgique à feu et à sang*, un opuscolo pubblicato nel 1917 da Maxime Vuillaume presso l'editore parigino Rouff, sintetizza perfettamente il messaggio propagandistico diffuso durante la Prima Guerra mondiale contro il nemico tedesco e condensa alcuni stereotipi circolanti all'epoca riguardo ai Tedeschi: in primo piano vediamo un soldato

tedesco sorridente che tiene nella mano destra una spada ancora gocciolante di sangue; ai suoi piedi giacciono un bimbo ferito mortalmente al cuore e una donna colpita alla testa, che tiene tra le braccia il corpo inanimato del figlioletto. Al centro del disegno si intravvedono dei personaggi in fuga, tra cui è riconoscibile una donna che corre tenendo in braccio un bimbo, preceduta da una ragazzina e inseguita da un soldato armato. Sullo sfondo appare una cattedrale e alcune case da cui si innalzano delle fiamme dal color rosso sangue: il fuoco e il sangue evocati appunto dal titolo dell'opuscolo. Raffigurati come dei campioni di violenza e di crudeltà, i soldati tedeschi sono il simbolo della malvagità assoluta perché non solo uccidono i bambini e le loro madri, ma distruggono addirittura le chiese, le case e le opere d'arte.

Pochi mesi dopo l'invasione del Belgio, si cominciano a stilare dei rapporti sugli orrori commessi dai soldati tedeschi, spesso sotto l'effetto dell'alcool (Brownmiller 55); alle donne stuprate viene riservata una posizione non sempre di primo piano e comunque il loro statuto di vittime non è completamente comprovato. Nel *Bryce Report*, pubblicato fin dal 12 maggio 1915, addirittura si insinua che alcune donne non tentarono di sottrarsi agli stupri, e anzi stuzzicarono i soldati con dei comportamenti "provocanti"; più che sulle violenze subite, si insiste sul degrado umano delle truppe tedesche responsabili dei crimini più biechi.

Intorno al 1917, per designare le violenze sessuali subite dalle donne in Belgio all'inizio della guerra, si comincia a parlare di "stupro del Belgio" (Bianchi 94): la sorte riservata alle donne diventa una sineddoche che rimanda alla violenza cui fu sottoposto il Paese e che nega di fatto alle donne del Belgio la possibilità di essere riconosciute legittimamente come vittime. Come sottolineato tra gli altri da Françoise Thébaud, senz'altro a partire dai fondamentali saggi di George L. Mosse, occorre tenere a mente il fatto che il discorso sulla guerra è profondamente sessuato: ecco allora che lo stupro delle donne belghe diventa lo "stupro del Belgio" perché se l'uomo è soldato, la donna è la terra che il soldato difende, e perciò il suo ruolo è quello di assicurare l'inviolabilità del corpo femminile. Così, nel discorso propagandista, l'immagine dell'avversario prende sembianze bestiali: ci riferiamo in particolare ai manifesti diffusi nel corso della campagna di propaganda "*Remember the Women of Belgium*", poi trasformata in "*Remember Belgium*", e al poster raffigurante un enorme gorilla che stringe a sé il corpo di una donna senza vita mentre nella mano destra tiene una clava su cui è scritta la parola tedesca "*Kultur*".[1]

---

[1] Si vedano i disegni dell'olandese Louis Raemaekers per la Wellington House, l'ufficio britannico di propaganda: http://net.lib.byu.edu/~rdh7/wwi/propaganda/ index.html (consultato il 20 novembre 2014); per il secondo riferimento si veda https://armyheritage.org/education-and-programs/educational-resources/education-materials-index/42-information/education-a-programs/170-remember-belgium (consultato il 20 novembre 2014).

Lo "stupro del Belgio" contribuì a lanciare il dibattito sulla legittimità dell'aborto "terapeutico", diverso da quello definito come "criminale" perché praticato per limitare le gravidanze. Persino in Italia, dove si ignorò di fatto il dramma delle donne belghe, si cominciò tuttavia a disquisire di interruzione della gravidanza ammissibile in caso di stupro.

Dobbiamo ricordare, a tale proposito, il nome di Luigi Maria Bossi, che fu il primo docente italiano di ginecologia: amico di Cesare Lombroso, acceso nazionalista, il Bossi era un sostenitore della pratica dell'aborto in caso di violenza sessuale non certo per tutelare i diritti delle donne o per limitare le nascite, ma per difendere i diritti della nazione (Cassata 71-75). In un articolo intitolato "In difesa delle donne belghe e francesi" pubblicato nel 1915 sulla rivista *La ginecologia moderna* da lui diretta, Bossi si dichiarava favorevole all'aborto giacché, in caso di stupro, le donne avrebbero dato alla luce a

figli miseri fisicamente e colle stimmate ineluttabili della degenerazione e cioè o dei deficienti nello sviluppo destinati a vivere a carico della pubblica beneficienza o dei futuri pazzi e delinquenti.

(Ventrone173)

Bossi riprenderà l'argomentazione eugenetica in un saggio del 1917 intitolato *In difesa della donna e della razza. Polemiche - Discorsi - Referendum contro l'egoistico rovinoso Neo-Malthusianismo, contro l'infamia dell'Antiuomo tedesco*, e la svilupperà scagliandosi contro "l'ignominioso barbarismo teutonico" (Bossi 61). Il saggio, pubblicato presso la casa editrice milanese Riccardo Quintieri (che già aveva editato i romanzi italiani di Annie Vivanti, tra cui *L'invasore* e *Vae Victis!*), raccoglie diversi suoi testi tra cui una sua lettera riprodotta nel 1916 dal *Popolo d'Italia* a proposito di un'inchiesta diffusa "fra donne, medici, sociologi, giuristi e letterati" sulla questione della legittimità dell'aborto in caso di stupro. L'autore trascrive anche alcune risposte, tra cui quella di un certo F. M. Zandrino,[2] che sostiene che lo Stato "deve avocare a sé il dovere di soppressione di chi per l'avvenire sarebbe una fonte inesausta e [...] irresponsabile del male e della vergogna sociale" (Bossi 100). Segue un commento di Anna Franchi, socialista, giornalista e femminista, la quale afferma che ogni donna risponderà in modo diverso al quesito, a seconda della propria sensibilità, ma che tutte le donne chiederanno di fucilare "quei bruti". Quando poi verrà "la pace vittoriosa", gli uomini buoni "troveranno conforto per le sventurate vittime e [...] troveranno modo di proteggere la razza latina dall'inquinamento che potrebbero portare questi bastardi della delinquenza [...]"

---

[2] Di Francesco Maria Zandrino parlano Ungaretti e Prezzolini nel 1914, a proposito di un suo intervento indirizzato a *La Voce* e lì pubblicato nel numero del 16 dicembre 1914 (Carteggio 16). Giornalista, forse maestro elementare, Zandrino aveva fatto parte della "Lega antitedesca", di cui era stato fondatore Luigi Maria Bossi nel 1916 (Ventrone IX; Montesi 73-74).

(Bossi 102). Dal canto suo, Anni Vivanti risponde in qualità di autrice de *L'invasore*:

Londra, 29 settembre
Illustre Professore,
E poiché anche a me giunge la sua domanda se la donna violentata dal nemico abbia il diritto all'aborto, io Le rispondo che come si ha il diritto di spegnere un incendio in casa propria, come si ha il diritto di estirpare un cancro dal proprio corpo, una donna ha il diritto di liberarsi dal malefico germe di vita impostole dalla violenza nemica.
(Bossi 109)

2. Annie Vivanti in difesa delle donne belghe
È arrivata da ieri l'altro Annie Vivanti, la grande Annie, [...]. È la creatura più divertente, del resto, che io abbia mai incontrato. Più divertente ancor dei suoi libri, ed è dir gran cosa. Monelleria, incongruenza, un misto di furbizia e di candore, l'*humour* anglosassone venato di emotività ebraica, un istinto di vita potentissimo, addirittura paradossale. Con me essa è a volta umile e protettiva, piena di compunto rispetto e insieme di tenera pietà per tutto quanto v'ha in me d'irriducibile, d'assoluto, diciam pure di tragico, come artista e come donna.
Così diverse, forse per questo non siamo rivali e ci vogliamo bene.

(Aleramo 89-90)

Così Sibilla Aleramo descriveva nel 1927 Annie Vivanti: scrittrice, poetessa e musicista trilingue e cosmopolita, essa fu attiva tra l'Italia, la Gran Bretagna e gli Stati Uniti fin dall'inizio del XX secolo.

Nata in Inghilterra nel 1866, morta a Torino nel 1942, la Vivanti è ricordata oggi quasi solo per l'"amicizia sentimentale" che la legò a Carducci tra il 1890 — data della prima lettera che il poeta le inviò e che fu pubblicata nell'introduzione della sua prima raccolta di poesie intitolata *Lirica* — e il 1907, ovvero fino alla di lui morte. Sarebbe opportuno invece ricordare Annie Vivanti soprattutto per la sua vivace carriera di poetessa e scrittrice bilingue, cantante e musicista:[3] tra i suoi scritti in prosa, in italiano e in inglese, dobbiamo qui citare almeno il suo romanzo più famoso, *I divoratori* (1911), racconto a sfondo autobiografico di una donna che rinuncia alla propria carriera letteraria per seguire e assecondare la figlia, assoluto genio artistico.

Nel 1915, sicuramente colpita dalle sorti delle donne belghe e su richiesta del dottor Bossi, che voleva che si difendesse l'idea dell'aborto "voluto e desiderato dalla violentata" (Bossi 120), Annie Vivanti pubblica la *pièce* teatrale *L'invasore*, rappresentata per la prima volta al Teatro Olimpia di Milano. Il romanzo *Vae Victis!* del 1917 si rifà al dramma teatrale, pur modificandone

---

[3] Rimando alla tesi di laurea magistrale di una mia studentessa dell'Université de Savoie, Giulia Romanelli, intitolata "Riscoprire Annie Vivanti attraverso i *gender studies*. Il caso di *The Hunt for Happiness*", presentata nel marzo del 2013. Inedita, purtroppo, la tesi, ricca di spunti e di materiali originali, merita di essere proseguita in ambito dottorale.

alcuni elementi nella parte finale.

In entrambi i testi, suddivisi in tre parti, si narra la tragica vicenda di tre personaggi femminili, Luisa, sua figlia Mirella e Chérie, la cognata di Luisa, vittime innocenti della brutalità degli invasori tedeschi in preda all'ebrezza, come già si evinceva dal *Bryce Report* che la Vivanti aveva sicuramente consultato essendo anglofona: "Immondi soldati ubriachi — si legge nel romanzo — avevano soddisfatto su di lei [Chérie] le loro lubriche brame — ed eccola lì, spezzata, contaminata, perduta!" (*Vae Victis!* 194).

I Tedeschi, nel romanzo più che nella *pièce* teatrale, sono ritratti come diabolici, perfidi e traditori, lubrici e "libertini", ovvero viziosi; l'esercito tedesco viene stigmatizzato in quanto "orda cenerognola" o "Jene Grigie" (*Vae Victis!* 33) che niente e nessuno può arrestare, pronto a brutalizzare la popolazione civile per rispettare gli "ordini superiori" e per imprimere il "sigillo della Germania" sul paese, ovvero nei ventri delle donne belghe:

"I vostri ordini..." balbettò l'inebriato Feldmann, pronunciando a stento le parole e poggiando la sua mano sulla spalla stessa di Fischer per tenersi ritto, "i vostri ordini... contraddizione diretta con altri ordini... ordini superiori.... che abbiamo ricevuti. Vero?... eh, Von Wedel?" E tentennò la testa, strizzando l'occhio a Fischer. "Sigillo della Germania... da imprimersi sul paese nemico... Sigillo della Germania... [...]"

(*Vae Victis!* 59)

Evidente qui la rielaborazione dell'immagine degli stupri di massa compiuti in vista di una "germanizzazione" dell'Europa: Luisa e Chérie sono infatti considerate come le vittime di un grande complotto (prima ancora che di uno stupro) compiuto sotto gli occhi dell'undicenne Mirella che, traumatizzata, perde l'uso della parola.

Accolte in quanto profughe in Inghilterra, Luisa e Chérie si accorgono — la prima con orrore e la seconda con stupore —, di essere incinte: mentre Luisa reclama l'aborto non solo per liberarsi da una macchia ma anche nella speranza di poter celare l'accaduto al marito, Chérie nel romanzo accetta la maternità, anche se tale decisione la isola socialmente e provoca l'allontanamento definitivo di Florian, suo promesso sposo (nella *pièce*, come vedremo più avanti, Chérie cercherà invece di suicidarsi).

In un finale pesantemente lirico, oltre che prevedibilmente consolatorio, Mirella ritrova l'uso della parola di fronte a Chérie e al bambino, ch'ella crede essere l'apparizione della Madonna e del Bambino Gesù:

Mirella era guarita! Guarita in grazia di Chérie e del bimbo suo, figlio dell'onta, della violenza e del dolore.
... Scossa da un brivido immenso Luisa cadde a ginocchi presso la sua bambina, e ripeté con lei le consacrate parole...
Tremante ed estasiata Chérie stringeva più forte al seno la sua creatura piegando il capo sotto l'ala di quella divina benedizione.

(*Vae Victis!* 208)

Vivanti e la grande guerra: stupro, aborto e redenzione in *Vae Victis!*

Nonostante una qualità stilistica mediocre tipica della narrativa popolare — imperversano il punto esclamativo e le sospensioni, le costruzioni paratattiche e l'iperbole, il fervore e il trasecolamento, i sospiri e gli svenimenti —, il testo della Vivanti contiene alcune peculiarità che lo rendono, malgrado tutto, originale e audace.

La costruzione del romanzo, ad esempio, è particolare, così come lo è la rivelazione della tragedia: assistiamo, nella prima parte, all'arrivo dei soldati tedeschi nella casa dove vivono le tre donne sole e indifese, ma nulla viene detto del dramma incombente; nella seconda parte, ritroviamo Chérie, Luisa e Mirella profughe in Inghilterra: la bambina ha perso l'uso della parola mentre Chérie non riesce a ricordare quello che le accadde la terribile sera dell'arrivo dei Tedeschi. Benché le due parti del testo — e finanche la terza, che racconta del ritorno a casa — corrispondano a due assi temporali in apparenza separati come è consuetudine nella letteratura popolare,[4] il racconto della tragedia, momento topico del romanzo, arriva nella seconda parte sotto forma di analessi, andando così a collegare le due parti. Non che questa scelta narrativa conferisca al romanzo una qualche trasgressività: di fatto, però, la Vivanti introduce una variante che lo singolarizza.

L'analessi comporta poi un'altra variazione sul genere rosa, di solito reticente alle introspezioni psichiche o psicanalitiche, e che consiste nel fatto che nessuna delle tre protagoniste riesce a "dire" la tragedia. Si potrebbe pensare, e in parte è così, a un effetto *suspense*: eppure in quel "non detto" ci sembra di poter ravvisare un timido accenno di esplorazione della psiche delle tre vittime che per un tempo, da semplici caratteri quali sono, sembrano diventare personaggi a tutti gli effetti. Così, Mirella, testimone della tragedia, è muta e si muove come un automa (tanto che la madre pensa che sia impazzita); dal suo canto Chérie annota sul suo diario con precisione i fatti che ricorda, ma poi non riesce a sfondare il muro delle tenebre:

Odo Mirella che strilla e strilla... mi dibatto disperatamente contro le tenebre che m'avvolgono.... Poi, più nulla....
Più nulla.

La nube che grava sul mio cervello, fluttua, si dirada... si risolleva.
È trascorso un istante?... Un'ora? Un'eternità?... L'ignoro! Sento che qualcuno mi solleva... mi trasporta....
Mi sento la testa violentemente rovesciata all'indietro, sento i capelli tesi sulla mia fronte come se qualcuno me li strappasse...
Ed ora il mondo è pieno di orrori indefiniti, di tortura, di strazio lacerante...
E ripiombo nel nulla.
[...].

---

[4] Si pensi al *Figlio dell'anarchico* (1901) della Invernizio per il versante italiano, o a *Monsieur Lecoq* (1869) di Emile Gaboriau sul versante francese, o ancora a *The Valley of Fear* (1915) di Conan Doyle per il versante inglese.

Ancora una volta, l'incoscienza, come una caverna nera, m'inghiotte.

Mi ridesta la voce di Luisa. Pare che mi chiami, mi chiami da lontano...
Poi quella voce si fa più forte... più vicina — ecco! grida il mio nome. Ed apro gli occhi.
Sì, Luisa è china sopra di me. Mi solleva, mi ravvolge in uno scialle, mi trae con sé...
Dove andiamo? Non so. Luisa mi porta fuori di casa, e via per un viottolo sassoso che conduce ai boschi. Non è giorno e non è notte. Forse è l'alba.
Una sete terribile mi consuma, un malore indescrivibile mi dilania, e sempre Luisa mi trascina avanti, e avanti ancora. Non posso andar oltre.

(104-05)

L'intendimento di Chérie si arresta davanti agli "orrori indefiniti", alla "tortura", allo "strazio lacerante", evocative immagini ellittiche e allusive che consentono il coinvolgimento empatico di chi legge. "Non posso andar oltre" è la metafora — certamente semplificata — dell'incapacità a trovare le parole per descrivere una tragedia.

Nemmeno Luisa riuscirà a "dire": nel corso di un'esplorazione nel passato del ricordo compiuta non già dal personaggio, ma da un narratore esterno, al lettore non è dato sapere che cosa le sia realmente accaduto. Il narratore descrive solo il suo arrivo sulla scena del crimine e il ritrovamento dei corpi della figlia e della cognata:

Allora Luisa si sforzò di ricordare, di ricordare quegli eventi di cui pure avrebbe pagato colla vita l'oblio. Cogli occhi chiusi, le membra scosse da brividi, ella impose a se stessa di rivivere le ore più fosche della sua vita....
L'alba del cinque agosto.
... La casa vuota, silenziosa. Gli invasori sono partiti.
Luisa, uno spettro livido nel grigio pallore dell'aurora, esce barcollando dalla sua camera... [...] Poi scende vacillando le scale.
Ed ecco, accasciata ai piedi della ringhiera di ferro — Mirella! Mirella ancora colle braccia legate, colla piccola bocca aperta, ansando breve, a tratti, come un uccellino che sta per morire...
Luisa la solleva, slega e scioglie la sciarpa che la stringe, le spruzza dell'acqua sul viso... e Mirella apre gli occhi.
Ma quelli non sono gli occhi di Mirella! Vi è delirio e frenesia in quelle pallide iridi che si volgono lente intorno alla stanza, che vagano indecise e che d'un tratto si fermano su un punto, folli, intente.
Che cosa mai guardano con quell'espressione di indicibile terrore?
La madre segue quello sguardo e vede una porta — la porta drappeggiata da una tenda rossa che dà in una camera da letto. È questa una camera poco usata dove talvolta un ospite o un paziente di Claudio ha dormito. Ed è su questa porta che lo sguardo allucinato di Mirella si fissa. È aperta la porta; la tenda rossa pende strappata....
Luisa guarda — poi guarda ancora; e non si muove. La luce elettrica là dentro è ancora accesa, una seggiola è rovesciata sul limitare, e là, là sul letto giace qualcuno.... È Chérie!
Chérie nel suo vestito di velo bianco — Luisa vede che è tutto lacero e macchiato di sangue — Chérie, colle braccia alzate e le mani legate alla sbarra del capo-letto. Il largo nastro rosa le è stato strappato dai capelli per legarle così le mani sopra al capo. Ha la faccia graffiata e sanguinante. È immobile. Sembra morta.

... Ah! come trovò Luisa la forza di sollevarla, di richiamarla alla vita, piangendo su lei e su Mirella, correndo disperata, folle, dall'una all'altra delle due creature? Le aveva vestite, inviluppate di scialli. Era riuscita, ora trascinandole, ora portandole, a scendere con loro le scale, a trarle fuori — fuori da quella casa profanata!
Che cosa fare? Doveva chiamare aiuto? Doveva andare gridando la loro vergogna e la loro disperazione per le vie del villaggio?
No, no, no! Che nessuno le veda, che nessuno sappia mai ciò che è accaduto a loro.

(*Vae Victis!* 116-17)

Certo, la descrizione del ritrovamento del corpo di Chérie è pesantemente stereotipata, non fosse altro che nell'uso dei colori: il bianco del vestito della fanciulla vergine e il fiocco rosa che la lega alla sbarra del letto contrasta con il rosso della tenda e quello del sangue. Però, contrariamente a quanto viene talvolta insinuato nei romanzi popolari coevi,[5] le vittime dello stupro qui non sono affatto consenzienti e non vi è altresì nessun compiacimento nell'evocare le atrocità subite dalle giovani donne.

Il "non detto", che è anche il "non saputo" ("No, no, no! Che nessuno le veda, che nessuno sappia mai ciò che è accaduto a loro"), non esime le vittime dall'essere condannate da chi parla al loro posto: Chérie, vittima a tutto tondo, perde la verginità, rimane incinta ed è costretta a rinunciare al matrimonio e alla sua posizione nella società; nella *pièce* teatrale Luisa addirittura rimprovera Chérie: "Tu vuoi essere madre senza essere sposa!" (*Invasore* 142) — inequivocabile e significativo rimando alla vicenda raccontata da Kleist in *Die Marquise von O.*. E così, la scena dell'agnizione, che dovrebbe permettere a Chérie e a Florian di metter fine ai loro reciproci drammi (anche Florian, in quanto soldato, è stato vittima dei Tedeschi), si conclude invece con l'allontanamento del giovane, inorridito non già da quanto ha subito Chérie, ma dal suo stato di impurità:

Eccola lì, la creatura rovinata e infranta! Eccola lì, prona davanti a lui; simbolo della sua patria — della sua patria rovinata e devastata.
Perdute, perdute entrambe!... Spezzate, contaminate, impure.
Ah, invano egli verserebbe per loro tutto il suo sangue e tutte le sue lagrime. Nulla, nulla più varrebbe a salvarle, nulla più varrebbe a rialzarle nella loro primiera gloria e purità! Perduta l'anima della donna, straziata l'anima della patria!...

(*Vae Victis!* 192-193)

Mentre Chérie gli parla del neonato, Florian le rinfaccia i propri tormenti di soldato e quelli dei suoi compatrioti, le rimprovera di non essere morta o di non aver scelto il suicidio. Per Florian il dramma vissuto da Chérie, essendosi fatto carne, è un oltraggio per la nazione, e qui ritroviamo alcuni segni della sessualizzazione del discorso sulla guerra evocati in introduzione:

---

[5] Il tema, tra l'altro, è abbastanza ricorrente nella produzione narrativa di Settimelli o di Marinetti.

"Ed è questo" — gridò sdegnato — "questo che tu trovi a dirmi, quando ritorno a te scampato dagli artigli della morte? Questo, questo tutto il tuo pensiero mentre la nostra patria sanguina, straziata dagli immondi bruti che vi hanno violate entrambe? Ah, maledizione su loro — maledizione eterna su loro e sulla creatura —"
"No!" con uno strillo ell'era balzata in piedi e gli copriva la bocca colle mani. "Noi no! Non maledirlo!... Non maledirlo anche tu quel bambino — che nessuno mai ha benedetto!"
"In nome del Belgio," tuonò forsennato Florian, "in nome delle donne del Belgio violentate e straziate, in nome dei loro figli torturati, dei loro uomini trucidati — io maledico la creatura a cui tu hai dato la vita. In nome dei nostri cuori lacerati, in nome delle nostre città incendiate, dei nostri focolari distrutti, dei nostri altari abbattuti e profanati — lo maledico, lo maledico! Nei nomi sacrosanti di Louvain, di Lierre, di Mortsel, di Waehlen, di Herselt —"
I nomi sacri al martirio e alle fiamme gli sgorgavano dalle labbra accrescendo la furia del suo cuore. La donna gemeva, coprendosi gli orecchi per non udire, per non udire quei nomi tragici e famigliari — il rosario di fuoco e di strazio del Belgio.
Stringendosi il capo fra le mani, ella piangeva: "Che Iddio non ti ascolti! Che Iddio non ti ascolti!"
Ma egli alzava la voce fremente nell'atroce litania: "E Malines, e Fleron, e Notre Dame, e Rosbeck, e Muysen —"
D'improvviso ristette. Un suono — un suono gli aveva colpito l'orecchio. Che cos'era?
Era un breve grido — il breve, fievole grido d'un neonato. (*Vae Victis!* 195)

Di fronte a quel vagito che diventa "pianto dell'umanità" (*Vae Victis!* 196), Florian si rende improvvisamente conto della "desolazione" circostante, ma non per questo accetta di perdonare a Chérie il frutto dell'atroce oltraggio da lei subìto, giacché la contaminazione ha avuto luogo: per colpa di Chérie e del suo essere donna, l'essenza della nazione concepita come comunità parentale (Banti 60-61) è stata colpita nella sua pura essenza. Dato che il suo onore è stato infangato,[6] non le resta che il suicidio o l'emarginazione dalla comunità. E infatti, partito Florian, nella *pièce* Chérie immagina di uccidere il bambino "predestinato al dolore e alla delinquenza" (*Invasore* 179) e di suicidarsi. Qui si ravvisano chiaramente le teorie del dottor Bossi, che scriveva del resto a proposito della *pièce*:

Essa [...] svolse i due casi del diritto e dell'aborto di due infelici belghe, facendo trionfare solo il primo. E pose così in campo anche il caso in cui nella donna vince il sentimento materno sulla ripugnanza, sull'avversione di dare la vita al frutto di un feroce brutale delitto commesso dal nemico invasore.

(Bossi 121)

Il suicidio non ci sarà perché Mirella, vedendola e scambiandola per

---

[6] Banti analizza la sovrapposizione dell'elemento religioso con quello etico nella letteratura risorgimentale, per cui la difesa dell'onore della nazione, che passa attraverso la difesa delle donne della comunità, santifica le guerre che diventano vere e proprie crociate (60), ed è proprio questo il senso del monologo di Florian.

un'apparizione divina, ritrova la parola e di fatto le impedisce di uscire, insieme a Luisa accorsa nel frattempo. Nel romanzo, invece, malgrado il disprezzo di Florian che l'abbandona al suo destino, Chérie torna a sedersi a fianco della culla, pronta a proteggere il neonato e a nasconderlo agli occhi del mondo: "Ed umilmente riprese il suo posto — il posto della donna — accanto alla culla" (*Vae Victis!* 197), il che le permette di trasformarsi da martire impura a "luminosa forma nell'atteggiamento umile e sacro della immortale Maternità" (*Vae Victis!* 208) che restituisce miracolosamente a Mirella la parola.

A proposito del finale, Luigi Maria Bossi afferma di aver consultato il pubblico presente a ogni rappresentazione de *L'invasore*:

Il pubblico ovunque unanime e profondamente commosso plaudì alla tesi sostenuta dal medico che, in contrasto colle affermazioni bibliche del ministro protestante, sosteneva la tesi del diritto all'aborto, nel mentre si mostrò titubante non solo ma sconcertato e quasi irritato di fronte alla volontà espressa di una violentata di voler crescere fino a termine il frutto del delitto del nemico. Non solo, ma il pubblico si mostrò soddisfatto nell'ultimo atto quando apparve descritta l'infelicità di questa giovane donna che volle tenere con sé e crescersi tale frutto, e si vede quindi evitata, sprezzata e vilipesa da tutti, tanto da decidersi al suicidio.

E la Vivanti compì nobilmente un atto di vera abnegazione sacrificando all'ultimo non poco dell'effetto scenico finale del suo dramma, quando appunto, in omaggio, anzi, in olocausto al sentimento di maternità, invece di chiuderlo con il suicidio di colei che seguendo più l'istinto materno che quello patrio, tenne seco il figlio del nemico invasore, lo chiude coll'episodio della riacquistata favella della bambina rimasta muta dal giorno del delitto e che in un impeto di felicità fa esclamare alla madre di essa: "*Sia benedetta la maternità*".

Episodio altamente emozionante e degno della squisita genialità della scrittrice, ma che, strano a dirsi ma molto significativo, indispone molta parte del pubblico che vorrebbe vedere una finale più tragica per la donna che si ostinò a generare il figlio del nemico.

(Bossi 121-22)

Nella conclusione della nota, Bossi insiste, non senza manifestare la propria perplessità, sulla reazione del pubblico che vorrebbe veder morta Chérie. Andando oltre l'apprezzamento nei confronti del genio letterario della Vivanti, egli torna sulla differenza tra la donna che, violentata, vuole abortire e quella che invece desidera portare a termine la gravidanza: quest'ultima, perché animata da un fortissimo sentimento materno, è in grado di eliminare il dramma psichico "dall'onta subita o per lo meno lo attutisce" (Bossi 122); invece la donna che desidera abortire, a prescindere dalla sua situazione e della sua educazione, "versa in condizioni psichiche eccezionali veramente patologiche" (Bossi 122) che potrebbero mettere in pericolo la sua salute, ragione per cui Bossi preconizza la possibilità di praticare l'aborto.

Ecco allora che, se Chérie è considerata colpevole per tutta la seconda parte, e fino quasi alla fine della terza, per non esser morta e per aver scelto di far nascere il "figlio di un tedesco", Luisa, sapendosi colpevole, preferisce condannare se stessa al suicidio o all'aborto, non sentendosi in grado di amare "il figlio di un nemico" che non può mostrare al marito soldato. Sembra che a lei importi solo l'idea di eliminare la conseguenza dello stupro affinché il marito non sappia:

"Pensate... pensate.... che ho un marito...! che m'ama... che combatte per noi nelle trincee! Che un giorno" — la voce le si spezzò in un singulto — "se il cielo è pietoso — tornerà!" Vi fu un attimo in cui nessuno parlò. "E non basta dovergli dire che la sua bambina è impazzita e muta? Volete ch'io gli vada incontro recando in braccio il figlio di un nemico?"
Un profondo silenzio tenne la stanza.
Allora Luisa, stralunata, nel rapido mormorio della demenza, continuò: "Ma io lo sento... lo sento che divento pazza sotto quest'incubo! Pazza, pazza di terrore e d'odio. [...] Dottore! dottore!" — con un grido gli cadde ai piedi — "è un cancro — un cancro vivente ch'è in me! Toglietemelo! Liberatemene!... o mi darò la morte."

(*Vae Victis!* 126-28)

Malgrado l'opposizione del pastore, il dottore decide di intervenire per liberare Luisa, riferendosi chiaramente alle teorie del Bossi:

"A priori", soggiunse il dottore studiando il viso disfatto e il corpo macilento di Luisa, "a priori credo poter asserire che le condizioni mentali e fisiche di questa donna giustificano il mio intervento."

(*Vae Victis!* 127)

Così, mentre Luisa giace a terra svenuta, il dottore insiste presso il sacerdote sul fatto che l'aborto non è un delitto innanzitutto perché il feto non può essere riconosciuto come un essere umano a tutti gli effetti. E poi solo un medico può decidere se praticare o meno un aborto, perché solo lui sa se la donna è in pericolo di vita:

"Tu — tu uccideresti un essere umano?"
"Non è quasi ancora un essere umano", fece il dottore crollando impaziente le spalle. "Per me, questa donna è afflitta da un morbo, da una infermità. Porta in sé un male che va estirpato, un male che corrompe ed avvelena le più profonde sorgenti della vita. Se questa donna in queste stesse condizioni fosse tisica, tu lo sai che si ammetterebbe senz'altro l'intervento. Orbene, essa è malata; essa è psicopatica. Il continuare in queste condizioni mette a repentaglio la sua vita e la sua ragione. Il dottore ha il diritto, anzi, ha il sacrosanto dovere di salvarla — se può."
"A spese della vita umana ch'essa porta in sé?" chiese il Vicario, colla voce soffocata.
"Sì, sì. A spese di questo germe di vita malefico e intossicato."

(*Vae Victis!* 130)

Aggiunge peraltro ancora il medico che la società non può farsi carico di creature nate malate perché concepite con la violenza. Meglio allora evitarne la nascita:

"Se gli eventi seguissero il loro corso, tu lo sai al pari di me ciò che ne risulterebbe. Ammetterai che la creatura concepita nella violenza e nell'alcoolismo sarà probabilmente un anormale, un degenerato, un epilettico." Il dottore additò il divano dove giaceva Luisa livida e svenuta. "E la madre? Guardala! La madre andrà al cimitero o al manicomio."

(*Vae Victis!* 130)

Il dialogo avviene all'insaputa di Luisa, del cui svenimento nessuno sembra curarsi: del resto l'interruzione della gravidanza non è affar suo, bensì del ginecologo esperto in eugenetica:

Per creare degli uomini forti, sani ed equilibrati, utili a se stessi e alle collettività nazionali di cui fanno parte e quindi all'Umanità, sono necessari nei loro generatori non solo degli esseri altrettanto sani ed equilibrati, ma è ancor necessario che l'atto di creazione si compia nelle condizioni di equilibrio psichico, morale e fisico [...]. Dalla violenza sessuale della soldataglia tedesca non sono nati, non possono nascere che esseri atavicamente delinquenti, ed è per questo che il premeditato crimine germanico è tanto più odioso ed irreparabile.

(Bossi XIV-XV)

C'è da chiedersi se Annie Vivanti si accorse delle conseguenze delle idee ch'ella si apprestava a diffondere con i suoi due scritti, ma non è certo, così come non è certo che i suoi contemporanei se ne avvidero. E forse nemmeno il finale mistico-consolatorio dell'attesa del perdono da parte delle vittime — il perdono per essere state stuprate? — dovette stupire le lettrici dell'epoca:

Esse vivono ancora nel lontano villaggetto del Belgio aspettando, invocando l'alba della liberazione.
E con essa il ritorno della speranza, della gioia, del perdono...
Intorno a loro tuona ancora la guerra; turbina la procella.
Ma forse il termine del loro affanno non è lontano.

(*Vae Victis!* 208)

Non ci pare che il romanzo tratti della "coscienza dei diritti" evocata da Giovanni Venturi, perché la sorte che tocca alle due donne violate è subìta, non scelta (o è scelta da altri). Ci sembra piuttosto che, almeno nella *pièce* teatrale, la Vivanti abbia voluto sottoporre al pubblico un caso umano, come richiestole dal dottor Bossi. Nessuna delle due donne, né Chérie, né Luisa, ha preso da sola e consapevolmente la decisione "fatale": entrambe si sentono morire, eppure sono costrette a vivere o a sopravvivere; il loro destino non è tra le loro mani e non spetta a loro scegliere. Non è certo Luisa che sceglie di abortire, ma è il medico che decide per lei l'aborto considerandolo opportuno per la società; nella *pièce* Chérie vorrebbe suicidarsi ma viene salvata dall'arrivo di Mirella, mentre nel romanzo la maternità è descritta come un richiamo a cui non le è possibile sottrarsi: non già quindi una scelta consapevole, ma una "condanna a vita". La voce del "figlio non nato" le promette infatti la vita eterna, implicita ricompensa al martirio conseguente alla scelta della maternità:

La voce di Luisa divenne quasi un grido.
"Chérie, ma non ricordi che il padre di questa creatura è l'abbietto soldato ubbriaco che ti prese e ti legò?... Non pensi che tu — belga — sarai la madre di un figlio tedesco?"....
Ma Chérie non ascoltava nulla, non pensava nulla, non ricordava nulla.
Non udiva che una voce — la voce del figlio non nato — che attendeva da lei il dono della vita.
E quella voce le diceva che nelle superne lande mattutine dove attendono le creature umane che vivranno, non vi sono né belgi né tedeschi, né vinti né vincitori.

(Vae Victis! 153)

Date le numerose riedizioni, deduciamo che il romanzo e la *pièce* dovettero avere un grande successo, senz'altro a causa della problematica: malgrado l'ostracismo di cui sarà oggetto Annie Vivanti durante il fascismo perché di origine ebrea, la *pièce* scavalcherà la seconda guerra mondiale e sarà adattata al cinema nel 1954, con il titolo *Guai ai vinti!*, per la regia di Raffaello Matarazzo,[7] che ambienta la vicenda a Caporetto: mentre anche nel film Luisa abortisce, assecondata da un medico, Clara (il nome italianizzato di Chérie) decide di portare a termine la gravidanza. Il promesso sposo di Clara non riesce tuttavia ad accettare la nascita del bambino, pur sapendo la fidanzata innocente; lei decide allora di lasciare il paese con il figlio, schernita dai suoi compaesani. Durante la fuga, Clara cade da una scala e si ferisce mortalmente: il fidanzato accorre al suo capezzale, la sposa poco prima che lei muoia e le promette di prendersi cura del bambino. Curioso il finale del film: la donna stuprata dal nemico austriaco (così simile ai soldati tedeschi con cui alcune donne italiane avevano avuto delle relazioni per forza, per necessità o per diletto, e che saranno per questo rapate a zero) deve abortire o morire, ma non le è dato di suicidarsi. Il figlio del peccato, però, considerato ora innocente, fa da contraltare al bambino mai nato di Luisa.

Il romanzo, ristampato abbastanza regolarmente fino al 1940, verrà ripubblicato un'ultima volta, sempre da Mondadori, nel 1956, verosimilmente a causa del film: Annie Vivanti era però morta nel 1942 e pertanto il testo non contiene le varianti introdotte nella versione cinematografica. Impossibile sapere se il romanzo non sia più stato ristampato da allora a causa del tema dell'aborto, o a causa delle teorie eugenetiche, o ancora a causa dell'attitudine troppo apertamente mistico-religioso di Chérie che forse non corrisponde più al gusto delle lettrici all'epoca del secondo dopoguerra. Resta il fatto che la *pièce*, il romanzo e finanche il film si interrogano su come gestire la maternità forzata e pur considerando sempre le donne colpevoli e non vittime. Il cammino verso l'emancipazione femminile è però iniziato anche così, con un romanzo che si interroga sull'ineluttabilità della maternità, e soprattutto che immagina che le donne possano dimenticare, in nome della pace e con l'aiuto divino, le violenze

---

[7] Non è stato possibile visionare il film per l'occasione, perché introvabile. Rimandiamo comunque alla scheda, http://www.cinematografo.it/pls/cinematografo/ consultazione. redirect?sch=10081 (link consultato il 28 novembre 2014).

sessuali di cui sono state vittime.

Université Nice Sophia Antipolis

Opere citate e consultate

Aleramo Sibilla, *Amo dunque sono* (1927), Milano, Mondadori, 1982.
Arslan Veronese Antonia, *Dame, droga e galline*, Padova, CLEUP, 1997.
Banti Alberto Maria, *Il risorgimento italiano*, 2004, Roma, Laterza, 2008.
Bianchi Bruna, *Militarismo versus femminismo*, "DEP — Deportate, esuli, profughe, Rivista telematica di studi sulla memoria femminile", 10 (2009), 94-109.
Bossi Luigi Maria, *In difesa della donna e della razza. Polemiche — Discorsi — Referendum contro l'egoistico rovinoso Neo-Malthusianismo, contro l'infamia dell'Antiuomo tedesco*, Milano, Quintieri, 1917.
Brownmiller Susan, *Le Viol*, Paris, Stock, 1976.
Cassata Francesco, *Molti, sani e forti. L'eugenetica in Italia*, Torino, Bollati Boringhieri, 2006.
Dupierreux Anne, *Quand le viol devient arme de guerre. Étude historico-stratégique du viol et des autres formes de violences sexuelles comme arme de guerre*, 15 pp., http://www.youscribe.com/catalogue/presentations/actualite-et-debat-de-societe/politique/quand-le-viol-devient-arme-de_guerre-368943 (consultato il 2 novembre 2014).
Eco Umberto, *Il superuomo di massa*, 1976, Milano, Bompiani, 1978.
Gibelli Antonio, *La grande guerra degli Italiani. 1915-1918*, Milano, Sansoni, 1998.
Marinetti Filippo Tommaso, *Gli amori futuristi*, Milano, Ghelfi, 1922.
McClintock Anne, *Imperial Leather: Race, Gender and Sexuality in the Colonial Contest*, New York, Routledge, 1995.
Montesi Barbara, "*Il frutto vivente del disonore. I figli della violenza, l'Italia, la Grande Guerra*", in *Stupri di guerra. La violenza di massa contro le donne nel Novecento*, a. c. di M. Flores, Milano, Angeli, 2010, 61-80.
Mosse George L., *Nationalism and Sexuality: Respectability and Abnormal Sexuality in Modern Europe*, New York, Howard Fertig, 1985.
Nozzoli Anna, *Tabù e coscienza. La condizione femminile nella letteratura italiana del Novecento*, Firenze, La nuova Italia, 1978.
The Bryce Report - Report of the Committee on Alleged German Outrages appointed by His Britannic Majesty's Government and Presided Over by the Right Hon. Viscount Bryce, London, 1915, www.firstworldwar.com/source/brycereport.htm (consultato il 26 ottobre 2014).
Schiavon Emma, *Stupri di guerra e donne violentate. Tensioni fra reale e immaginario in Italia 1914-2010*, in *World Wide Women: globalizzazione, generi, linguaggi*, vol. 2, a c. di Franca Balsamo, CIRSDe, novembre 2011, 167-76.
Settimelli Emilio, *I capricci della duchessa Pallore*, Rocca S. Casciano, Tip. L. Cappelli, 1918.
Thébaud Françoise, *Penser la guerre à partir des femmes et du genre : l'exemple de la Grande Guerre*, "Astérion", 2 (2004), 11 pp. http://asterion.revues.org/103 (consultato il 02 novembre 2014).

Ungaretti Giuseppe, *Lettere a Giuseppe Prezzolini. 1911-1969*, a c. di M. A. Terzoli, Roma-Bellinzona, Edizioni di Storia e Letteratura, Dipartimento dell'Istruzione e Cultura del Cantone Ticino, I Carteggi di Giuseppe Prezzolini, 2000.

Ventrone Angelo, *La seduzione totalitaria: guerra, modernità, violenza politica (1914-1918)*, Roma, Donzelli, 2003.

Venturi Giovanni, *Serpenti e dismisura: la narrativa di Annie Vivanti da Circe a Naja Tripudians*, "Les Femmes écrivains en Italie (1870-1920): ordre et libertés", a c. di E. Genevois, in *Chroniques italiennes* (1994), 293-309.

Vivanti Annie, *L'invasore*, Milano, Quintieri, 1915.

Vivanti Annie, *Vae Victis!*, Milano, Quintieri, 1917.

Lucia Re

Women at War: Eva Kühn Amendola (Magamal) – Interventionist, Futurist, Fascist

1. Embattled Women, War and Imagination

Before the First World War, women who openly associated with Italian Futurism tended either to be outsiders of some sort, like Valentine de Saint-Point and Mina Loy, or women who, due to their personal life stories and cosmopolitan upbringing, were not conditioned by the normative bourgeois codes of feminine behavior prevalent in Italy and much of Europe at the time. The Lithuanian-born Eva Kühn Amendola (1880-1961), on whom my discussion will be focused, was a deeply non-conformist woman and a multilingual, cosmopolitan intellectual who became an Italian citizen through her marriage with Giovanni Amendola. The couple met in Rome in 1903, when Kühn was still a student. She was a creative writer, essayist and literary translator. There are many gaps and missing links in the story of Kühn's life and futurist activities. What we have left are basically, as is often the case with female artists, writers and intellectuals until after World War Two, fragments and traces — a kind of "ruined map."[1] Yet the texts and documents available allow us to see that her experience, including the difficult, deeply conflicted relationship with her husband, is an example of how Futurism before, during and immediately after the Great War, set some intellectual women's imagination on fire, becoming for them a form of radical existential, aesthetic and then socio-political practice.[2]

Kühn became directly involved with Futurism around 1912, when she lived next door to the great futurist artist Giacomo Balla in Rome's Via Paisiello, and met, among other protagonists of the futurist movement, Umberto Boccioni and the leader of Futurism himself, Filippo Tommaso Marinetti. Her futurist pen name, Magamal, was inspired by a male character in F. T. Marinetti's 1909-1910 novel, *Mafarka le futuriste* (published first in French and almost immediately thereafter in Italian translation as *Mafarka il futurista*).[3] Magamal in the novel is

---

[1] I take the notion of a "ruined map" from Bruno's *Streetwalking on a Ruined Map*.
[2] For a brief biographical profile, see Paolino, "Eva Kühn Amendola: ovvero l'insostenibile tragicità del vivere." On Eva Kühn Amendola and Futurism during the Great War, see also the article (designed for a wider, non-scholarly audience) by Serri. The entries by Garretto, Garzonio and Sulpasso and the article by Di Leo are also useful and informative. Di Leo includes a bibliography of all of Kühn's known published works and translations.
[3] The novel was originally published in French by Sansot. The frontispiece has the date 1909 on it, but on the cover the date is 1910.

Mafarka's beautiful, androgynous younger brother, whose accidental death deeply saddens the protagonist, who adored him, and makes him more determined than ever to go on his allegorical quest to create a semi-mechanical and "post-human" son, who will be invincible. Kühn became a personal friend of Marinetti and eventually she joined the circle of female writers who contributed to the futurist wartime journal *L'Italia Futurista* (1916-1918), where she published the free-word poem "Velocità" in 1916. In the years of the First World War, Kühn became, like most futurists, an ardent interventionist, and a political activist who in the war's extended, turbulent aftermath supported the Futurist Party and the early Fascist movement. Her "Appello futurista al popolo d'Italia" appeared in the journal *Roma futurista* in August 1919. During the war, Kühn was also active on the home front in the assistance to casualties and disabled veterans, and thus became a member of what has been called Italy's "other army." [4]

Although excluded for the most part from the main business of fighting, women in Italy, as elsewhere in Europe, had a primary role in the war effort. Indeed, as historians have increasingly come to recognize, the war effort could not have been sustained without them, and they were very much involved in the conflict. Unlike other belligerent nations, in Italy there was no state-sponsored welfare and even no rationing cards before 1917, so it was civilian initiative — for the most part organized and conducted by women — that provided aid and kept society functioning. Women became full partners in the war, as their time, commitment, work and support proved crucial to Italy's mobilization. As *madrine di guerra*, their letter writing and manufacture of comfort items as well as necessary objects for the men on the front lines proved critical to maintain and boost morale, especially after the devastating defeat at Caporetto. Women learned new skills, worked outside the home in factories and other sites in the public sphere more than ever before, replacing men in several capacities, and taking on unprecedented responsibilities for the duration of the war. The very definition of femininity, female roles and individual identity began to change and expand. Women emerged as capable and even indispensable citizens and fighters in "the other army," and the demand for suffrage thus appeared increasingly justified, while the traditional cultural and political paradigms sanctioning female inferiority were revealed to be outdated and no longer viable.

The mobilization of women in which she partook made Kühn all the more convinced that political militancy was necessary for women like her, along with cultural emancipation. After the war, towards the end of 1918, Kühn was active

---

[4] The notion of women as members of what was effectively Italy's "other army" is discussed in detail by Belzer. In addition to Belzer, see especially Molinari, *Una patria per le donne*. Until the mid-1990s, feminist scholarship on women and the Great War in Italy was more focused on the pacifist and anti-war sentiments prevalent among peasant and working-class women, thus presenting a partial and somewhat skewed image of the role of Italian women in the conflict. For a discussion of this scholarship, see Molinari, *Patria*.

in the local branch (*Fascio*) of the Futurist Party in Rome. In the 1919 general elections, Kühn campaigned for Marinetti's and Mussolini's party as a member of the coalition *Fasci di Combattimento*. At the time, the party had a left-wing and republican, anti-monarchy agenda; it fully supported female suffrage and equal wages for men and women, as well as land reform and workers' rights to strike and unionize. No other party leadership at the time actively encouraged women to participate. Soon, however, as Marinetti and Mussolini temporarily parted ways in 1919 (after losing the elections), and Fascism veered towards the right, Kühn moved away from Fascism towards more anarchic, left-wing positions. Her political militancy coincided with a pattern of "sexual misconduct" and stubborn rejection of bourgeois conformity. For all these things, as we shall see, she paid dearly. Kühn lived and struggled in that particularly chaotic and violent postwar phase of conflict — the *biennio rosso* — when *arditismo*, Futurism, Fascism, socialism, anarchism and feminism alternately converged and mingled or fought each other, in an atmosphere of high hopes for impending revolution and radical social change, followed by bitter disillusionment. She is an example of the risks involved in daring to be a female Futurist and imagining a radically different way of being a woman in modern Italy, and her life demonstrates how World War One interventionist fervor both radicalized and endangered Futurist women. She may be seen, in fact, as the most radical embodiment of the embattled and contradictory position of intellectual women, female activists, and avant-gardists during and immediately after the Great War, when the conflict itself generated new opportunities and roles for women across social classes even as it sowed the seeds of the Fascist regime's backlash against women and feminism that followed after 1922. In this article, I trace Eva Kühn Amendola's path from her formative years and her experience as an emigrée to her relationship with her husband and her involvement with Futurism, interventionism and wartime activities on the homefront. I discuss her literary contributions to *L'Italia futurista* during the war, and her subsequent involvement in the Futurist-Fascist campaign, which was followed by a period of extended confinement and eventually surveillance by the Fascist regime. My discussion looks at Eva Kühn Amendola as a unique individual and in the wider context of women's changing positions during the First World War, especially in the context of other female intellectuals and Futurist women and of the Futurist destabilization of traditional gender roles.

2. The Heroic Optimism of a Cosmopolitan Intellectual: A Ruined Map
Eva Oscarovna Kühn was born in 1880 in Vilnius of an educated family, and spoke both Russian and German at home (only the rural class at the time still spoke Lithuanian after the radical Russification campaign undertaken by the Tsar in the early 19th century). Her mother, whose native language was German, had studied in a Moscow college for young women from the upper classes, and cared deeply about the education of her four daughters, whom she treated as equals of her three sons. The father, who attended university in Dorpat (Tartu, Estonia),

taught in a technical school but was passionate about literature, the arts, music and philosophy. Although he died when Eva was only thirteen, she inherited his interest for Schopenhauer, whom she later translated, and for symbolist and modernist poetry. The family was related to the novelist and radical thinker Leo Tolstoy, whose theories advocating non-violent socialism, non-orthodox and anti-institutional Christianity (he was even excommunicated by the Russian Orthodox Church), land reform, simple agricultural labor, and ascetic vegetarianism (based on ethical grounds) influenced Eva, who became a vegetarian herself. Moreover, Tolstoy's categorical rejection of the state and property fitted into a general anarchist pattern that also influenced her.

She was confirmed in the Lithuanian Waldensian church when she was seventeen, but although she respected the Waldensian traditional values of austerity, she was only nominally religious, according to Spini (309-10).[5] A native speaker of Russian and German, she later learned English, Italian, and French. After the Tsar closed the university at Vilnius in order to put an end to student nationalist demonstrations there, Eva was allowed by her family to go abroad. She was able to study in London when she was only seventeen by giving Russian and German lessons, and on her return to Vilnius she worked for three years as an English and German language teacher in girls' schools. Eager to expand her horizons and flee from the traditional roles still assigned to women in Russian and Lithuanian society, she moved to Zurich, where she studied anthropology, comparative literature, and art history at the university, and started writing critical essays on philosophy, including an essay on Schopenhauer's optimism, which was later published. She argued that Schopenhauer's pessimism is paradoxical in that it coexists with a heroic optimism based on the acceptance of suffering in the phenomenal world as only the first step in a quest for liberation from sorrow and pain, in which compassion and the arts play a key role.[6]

Kühn herself may be seen as an embodiment of this suffering and heroic optimism. Given the prejudices at the time against intellectual women, writing these philosophical essays was indeed an arduous and daring task for a woman, although Zurich, at the time, had one of the few universities in Europe that welcomed women and was open to foreign female students, especially those coming from the provinces of the Russian Empire and from religious minorities. Kühn's beloved Schopenhauer himself was a misogynist who believed in the natural passivity and mental inferiority of women, whom he also thought to be

---

[5] Also, Waldensians were a minority in Lithuania and in Vilnius, which had a largely Catholic population. Vilnius also had a sizeable Jewish community (about 45% of the city's population) that was almost entirely wiped out during the Holocaust and the Second World War.

[6] I refer to Kühn's essay, "L'ottimismo di Schopenhauer," in *Coenobium*, which was also republished with a slightly different title as an appendix to Schopenhauer, *Introduzione alla filosofia e scritti vari*.

child-like and incapable of either authentic esthetic judgment or moral responsibility, and thus not human in a full sense. This prejudice was widely shared in Italy by, among others, Benedetto Croce as well as the entire *La Voce* circle. Indeed, the bias against women was so rampant and ingrained in the second half of the 19th century and through the first half of the 20th century that for women to seek to become intellectuals meant to engage in a real struggle, a figurative war of sorts that deployed the pen in lieu of the sword, and often involved being at war even against oneself.

Self-conflict and self-loathing, and a difficult relationship with one's own gender, characterize the plight of intellectual women such as Kühn at the beginning of the 20th century, and were at the root of some of these women's profound psychic discomfort and suffering, often diagnosed as hysteria, neurasthenia or other kinds of mental illness. Some, like Sibilla Aleramo and the Futurists Valentine de Saint-Point and Enif Robert, among others, attempted to resolve the conflict by fashioning versions of the myth of the individual superiority and androgyny, or hermaphroditism, of exceptional women, construed as being endowed with "masculine" traits and capacities.[7] But even this imaginary solution was deeply unsatisfactory in that it obstructed both the possibility of self-acceptance as a woman and of a non-elitist type of feminism. The war, however, brought a degree of optimism and a sense that women as a group were finally being recognized as fully human, political subjects as well as equal citizens.

Initially at least, her family background and the education she received allowed Kühn to thrive. Kühn's essay on Henry David Thoreau and his "religion of nature" won her a monetary award that allowed her to fulfill her dream of going to Italy. In Rome, where she rented a room with another young woman, she planned to learn Italian and complete a degree in comparative literature. She became a frequenter of Caffè Greco, the most important literary café in Rome and a haunt of intellectuals (Schopenhauer himself had been a habitué in his day), and she also began attending the gatherings of the Roman Theosophical Society. It was at one of the society's meetings in 1903 that she met and became involved with Giovanni Amendola, who was at the time secretary of the society's library, a hub of many cultural initiatives. The two married in 1907. Kühn is indeed usually remembered only as the wife of Giovanni Amendola, a political leader and journalist and one of the most celebrated heroes of the early Italian anti-Fascist movement, and as the mother of Giorgio Amendola, one of the principal communist leaders of post-World War Two Italy. Yet she was anything but a banal or exemplary wife and mother. Her published interventions as a Futurist are few, though a number of her unpublished Futurist poems and essays are held in the Marinetti archives at the Getty center and elsewhere, along with letters. There is, furthermore, evidence that she wrote a novel entitled *Eva la futurista* that was

---

[7] I discuss this phenomenon, especially with reference to Sibilla Aleramo and Matilde Serao, in Re, "Passion and Sexual Difference."

never published, and whose manuscript has been lost. Conspicuous traces remain, however, mostly in between the lines of her husband and son's stories, of her early adherence to Futurism and then Fascism. Even her own memoir, *Vita con Giovanni Amendola*, is made up mostly of letters to and from her husband. Unfinished and composed when she was already in her seventies, the volume was completed and edited by their son Giorgio, and it is largely not her story, but her husband's. Thus far Eva Kühn Amendola has indeed been a shadowy figure, often a mere footnote in accounts of Futurism and in intellectual women's history. Reading between the lines and in the margins of existing texts, and tracing a path among the fragments of the ruined map we have left, may help chart the course of Kühn's trajectory from a feminist perspective, opening up new viewpoints on the significance of her experience as well as that of other women.

3. *"A bear who keeps you in chains"*: Scenes from a Marriage
Giovanni Amendola, around whom so much of Eva Kühn's life rotates, was born in Naples in 1882. He came from a petty bourgeois, large and rather poor family from the province of Salerno. His father, who had been a *garibaldino*, was a *carabiniere*, a member of the state military police. Giovanni Amendola was a contemporary of Marinetti and, like Marinetti, he was a patriot and abhorred Giolitti — at least initially — as well as socialism. Unlike Marinetti, however, Amendola disliked any kind of extremism and he eventually became a representative of the more conservative wing of the Liberal party, which in his mind embodied the best traits of the old, elitist and conservative liberal state. He supported the Libyan war of 1911-12, chiefly as a means of building the moral character of the Italians, though in 1922 he was minister of the colonies in Luigi Facta's cabinet. From 1912, he worked in Rome as a correspondent for the newspaper *Il resto del Carlino*. After earning his *laurea* in philosophy, he became briefly a professor in Pisa, and wrote for *Il Leonardo* and then *La Voce*, becoming, shortly before the war, a journalist for *Il Corriere della sera*. In March 1915, he was drafted and served as lieutenant in a field artillery regiment. Stationed in Padova, he was involved in combat on the Isonzo River, even earning a bronze medal. The experience of combat helped reverse some of his earlier positions, and he became anti-nationalist, though he retained his patriotic idealism. In 1916, he became bureau chief for the *Corriere della sera* in Rome, renounced his academic aspirations and turned to politics. Elected to parliament in 1919 in the district of Salerno for the conservative *Democrazia Liberale* party, he served as the undersecretary of finance for the Nitti government. As minister of colonies under Facta, he initiated the "reconquest" of Lybia, which had been largely lost during the Arab uprising of 1914-15. Soon after the March on Rome in 1922, he founded the anti-Fascist newspaper *Il Mondo*. He officially denounced the Fascists on several occasions, and became one of the principal opponents of Mussolini in the early 1920s, although he hoped eventually to defuse Fascist violence and anti-democratic practices by integrating the Fascists into the government.

Initially, Giovanni Amendola and Eva Kühn shared their passion for Schopenhauer and Theosophy, though Kühn seems to have had reservations about Theosophy from early on, and she especially disliked its spiritual leader, Annie Besant, who claimed to be a clairvoyant (*Vita* 46). Kühn was instrumental in Giovanni's disillusionment with the more questionable, esoteric and corrupt aspects of Theosophy that led to his abandoning the society in 1905, though even in his more advanced philosophical studies he retained the theosophical propensity for moral self-discipline, and the desire to experience the spiritual aspects of the universe and of philosophical abstraction on an intensely personal level. When Kühn was asked to present her essay on Schopenhauer as a lecture for the Theosophical Society in Rome, Giovanni helped her translate into Italian a passage from the *Parerga and Paralipomena*, but she soon became a skilled translator herself and indeed supported herself by doing translations and giving private lessons. She also provided translations into English of articles from the Italian press to a correspondent for a British newspaper. Kühn's and Amendola's romance did not meet with their respective families' approval. As Giorgio Amendola writes in his 1976 memoir, *Una scelta di vita*, she appeared to her husband's petty-bourgeois southern family as "devastatrice, l'intrusa, la straniera" (7). Not only was Eva (nicknamed "la russa") a foreign woman two years older than Giovanni, but she seemed excessively free and autonomous even to her fiancé, who became increasingly punitive and controlling, "a bear who keeps you in chains," as Eva ironically stated in one of her letters (*Vita* 42).

Eva and Giovanni were forced to separate, and Eva was summarily diagnosed as mentally ill, a victim (like the fictional Madame Bovary in Flaubert's novel and indeed many Victorian and early 20th-century non-fictional women) of mysterious so-called "cerebral fevers," or, more likely (by the standards of contemporary medicine), perhaps meningitis, a stroke, or a viral infection that damaged her nervous system. For a whole year Eva was in the hands of doctors and psychiatrists before she was taken back to Vilnius by her mother, and forbidden to communicate with Giovanni. This emotionally wrenching experience contributed to her fragility, periods of depression, headaches, mental exhaustion and, apparently, nervous breakdowns, to which she seems to have been periodically subject. This led to her being diagnosed as suffering from an unspecified mental illness, followed by a series of extended confinements in psychiatric institutions. In *Vita con Giovanni Amendola*, however, Kühn seems to dispute having suffered from mental illness, attributing her condition instead to other, physiological and genetic causes: "Avevo ereditato da mia madre la tendenza a fortissime emicranie con congestioni cerebrali. Anche in seguito, verso i quarant'anni ebbi di nuovo una grave malattia cerebrale, dovuta a cattiva circolazione; essa mi costrinse per lungo tempo in una casa di salute" (75). In the early 20th century, commitment to mental institutions was still not an uncommon way, in Italy and elsewhere in Europe, to discipline and control non-conformist and sexually free women, reputed to be morally or socially inadequate, deviant or otherwise not "normal." Women's hospitalization for mental illness, — often labeled vaguely only as "melancholy" and used coercively as a form of social and political control — increased considerably during the Great War and in the postwar period, almost as much as men's.[8] After the Second World War, however, Kühn was never again hospitalized. In fact, she won a position as Professor of English at the University of Rome and worked uninterruptedly until her death in 1961 as a prolific literary translator.[9]

During her captivity in Vilnius, Kühn started outlining "La pazzia e la riforma del manicomio," an indictment of the coercion, violence, debilitating drugs and repressive methods used against the mentally ill, which she completed later, between 1913 and 1916. Like many of Kühn's other works, it remained unpublished. In this essay, she effectively argued in favor of a kind of modern psychotherapy as well as the use of play, dance, music and theater for therapeutic purposes.[10] When she emerged from the institution in 1905, Kühn was able immediately to find work as a German-language teacher in Vilnius, and was allowed to resume correspondence with Giovanni, who wrote his letters to her in French. Giovanni eventually joined Eva in Vilnius, but, before being allowed to become officially engaged, they had to accept religious instruction by a Waldensian pastor in Vilnius. The couple spent time traveling and studying philosophy and psychology in Germany, supporting themselves with private lessons. Finally, after Giovanni won the competition for a position as secretary in the Ministry of Fine Arts, they were allowed to marry,in the Waldensian Church in Rome, though Giovanni's father granted his permission only in return for a substantial monthly contribution to be paid to him by his son, even after the couple moved from the parents' flat to their own place in Rome's Via del Babuino.

Giorgio, the first son and future communist leader, was born in November

---

[8] Among the scholarly studies on this subject, see Molinari, "Autobiografie" and Paolella. Although confinement in mental institutions was reserved mostly for lower- and working-class women, Molinari shows that educated women, too, were likely to be committed, usually by their families, who deemed them morally and socially inadequate.

[9] In addition to many works by Dostoevsky, Kühn translated works by Maxim Gorky and by the symbolist Lithuanian poet Jurgis Baltrušaitis. She also translated into Italian the important modernist and communist novel *Christ in Concrete* (1939) by the Italian-American Pietro Di Donato, published in 1941 as *Cristo fra i muratori*, though the translator's name appeared in print only in post-World War Two editions (1961; 1973). Recently it has been suggested that Kühn may have worked on the translation jointly with the anti-Fascist Bruno Maffi, whose name could not appear, or even that Maffi might have been the real translator. Kühn translated also several works by Schopenhauer, including a volume containing his reflections on linguistic differences and the inevitable unreliability of translation, *Sul mestiere dello scrittore e sullo stile*. There is, however, no study to date of Kühn as a translator and of the significance of her work of cultural mediation. For a bibliography of Kühn's translations, see Di Leo.

[10] A handwritten version, sixty pages in length signed Magamal, is among the Marinetti papers at the Getty Institute. This essay is discussed by Salaris in "Incontri."

1907, while Ada — who would later became a medical doctor — was born in 1910 after the couple moved to Florence, where Giovanni directed the Biblioteca Filosofica and completed his *laurea* in philosophy. It was at this time that the first conflicts arose, though the couple eventually had two more children: Antonio, born in 1916, and Pietro in 1918. Eva, who in 1907 had published in *Italia moderna* an essay on the theory of language pedagogy, "Il nuovo metodo intuitivo dell'insegnamento delle lingue moderne," had won an English teaching position in a scuola normale femminile and a translation job for the Istituto Internazionale di Agricoltura, through which she earned twice as much as her husband (*Vita* 82). She was thus a precursor of the new, controversial type of "masculinized" working woman that was shortly to emerge during the Great War.

In Florence, around 1910, Giorgio and Eva Kühn were members of the *La voce* circle, and friends of the Papinis and the Prezzolinis. Eva was, in Papini's words, "donna di appassionato spirito, coltissima, che aveva scritto, o stava scrivendo, uno studio assai originale sull'Ottimismo di Schopenhauer" (921). This was indeed unusual for Papini, who among the men of the group was probably the one who held the most profoundly misogynist views of women (whom he considered worthy of being only either sexual objects or obedient wives and mothers), and particular contempt for female intellectuals.[11] The success of the treatise *Sex and Character* by the Austrian Otto Weininger, which was well known and admired in the *La Voce* circle even before its publication in Italian translation in 1912, contributed to reinforce and popularize a vision of woman as essentially inferior in every way, and even as not fully human.[12] Yet Papini hired Kühn to translate Schopenhauer, while Prezzolini gave her a contract to translate a collection of Dostoevsky's stories for the *La Voce* editions (it was published in 1913). She did this work to contribute financially while also taking care of the household and the children, as the family budget did not allow for any domestic help. (Only later, in Rome, were they able to hire a part-time maid paid by the hour.) Giovanni, who was working on his thesis on Kant and other projects — including a monthly about religion as the basis of philosophy called *L'Anima*, co-edited with Papini in 1911-12 — used the only heated room in the house as his studio, yet complained about Eva's inadequacy as a housewife (Amendola, *Scelta* 8). In 1912, Eva was able to publish an essay on Henry George, an egalitarian economist and advocate of land reform and uniformly higher taxation of the rich to be used for social needs, who was a favorite of Tolstoy's. She received high praise for it and encouragement by Gaetano Salvemini, and later even by Marinetti. In 1919, Marinetti used an updated version of her essay, which appeared in *Roma futurista*, to draft the political and economic program for *Democrazia Futurista*. However, he referred to the author as "Il futurista

---

[11] On Papini's misogyny and that of the intellectuals around *La voce*, see Nozzoli.
[12] On the success and influence of Weininger's work in Italy, see Cavaglion.

Magamal"; in other words, as a male rather than a female Futurist.[13]

Working inside and outside the home, Kühn suffered more than ever from the weight of her double burden, a condition that she shared with many working-class women. She felt thwarted in her intellectual and creative ambitions as well as torn between the life of the mind and the financial and domestic duties of home and family. Although they shared many philosophical interests, Kühn and her husband soon began to think quite differently. While Giovanni, who was known among the *vociani* for his "profound moral seriousness" and as "the only man among us" (qtd. in Adamson 129), developed a commitment to an ethics of spiritual and religious discipline and moralism, his wife would soon turn to Futurism. In 1911, Amendola had written that "the rationality of the good is just this harmony and this cohesion of the human person, held in place by the will and thus raised above the chaos of the animal life to the order and clarity of the self" (quoted in Adamson 129). At just about the same time, on the other hand, Marinetti and the Futurists were arguing almost precisely the opposite, espousing a new notion of the self as multiple, dynamic and contradictory, calling for a heightened sense of the real based on the materiality of the body and of perception in all its chaotic complexity, and the dissolution of the traditional metaphysical categories of order and rationality, as well as the bourgeois family and bourgeois morality.

4. *Becoming a Futurist in Pre-War Rome:*
A Path to Gender Insubordination and Literary Creation
By the time the Amendolas moved back to Rome in August 1912, in the midst of patriotic exultation over Italy's "victory" in the war against the Ottoman Empire in Libya and the Dodecanese — a war that was in some ways in the eyes of many Italians a prelude to the Great War — the city was about to become the most important center for Futurism in Italy. Not only did they live (from 1912 until 1917, after which they moved to Via Porta Pinciana) on the same street as Balla, but the Cappa family also lived nearby, including the family's siblings Arturo and Alberto Cappa and their sister Benedetta. The mother, Amelia Cipollina, was, like Kühn, raised as a Waldensian. The father, Innocenzo Cappa, was to suffer from severe shell shock during the war and die shortly thereafter. (Benedetta would write about this tragic experience in her first Futurist novel, *Le forze umane*). Around 1919 Arturo, who spoke Russian and worked as an envoy of the Italian government in the Soviet Union, where he was sent to study and report about "The Bolsheviks", would become a supporter of the left-wing Futurists in Turin, and an associate of Antonio Gramsci and his *Ordine nuovo*, as well as co-founder in 1921 of the Communist party in Liguria and co-editor of the journal *Bandiera rossa*. Alberto, on the other hand, would become co-founder of the Futurist

---

[13] "La riforma fondiaria di Henry George" takes up the entire chapter 20 of Marinetti's *Democrazia Futurista: Dinamismo Politico*, also in *Teoria e invenzione* futurista, 426-31.

political *Fascio* in Rome, in which Kühn would also be involved, and co-editor of the journal *Roma futurista*, to which Kühn contributed. Their sister Benedetta, a student of Balla's, would become a major Futurist artist as well as writer; around 1919 she became Marinetti's lover and, from 1923, his wife. The painter Rougena Zátková, who was like Kühn an émigrée,[14] was also a student of Balla's studio *Il Convento* during the war years, along with her friend Benedetta. The Futurist poet Luciano Folgore and the painter Enrico Prampolini were also active in Rome at the time, along with the Bragaglia brothers (Anton Giulio Bragaglia's *Fotodinamismo Futurista* was published in Rome in 1913). The Futurist Caffè Gropo in via del Tritone was not far from Via Paisiello, along with the Galleria Sprovieri. The Sprovieri was an important venue for Futurist art, concerts, performances and other activities, often one or two every week, especially from 1913 to 1914. The notorious "Funerali del critico passatista Benedetto Croce" took place there in April 1914. The Teatro Costanzi hosted in the foyer Futurist performances and art exhibitions, including Boccioni's in 1913. Eva attended such Futurist gatherings and events, and in 1913, after a reading by Marinetti, Altomare, Cangiullo, Folgore and other Futurists, Marinetti was invited to dinner at the Amendolas'.[15]

By the end of 1914 Futurist activities in Rome became mainly interventionist demonstrations, agitations that Giovanni Amendola decried from the pages of *Il Corriere della sera* as "disordini provocati dai futuristi." The famous Futurist "vestito antineutrale bianco rosso e verde," created by Balla, was worn by Cangiullo and other Futurists, apparently causing a riot. In February and then April 1915 in Rome, Marinetti was detained during another interventionist demonstration at the University of Rome. In the April demonstration, along with Marinetti, Balla, Settimelli, and Bruno Corra, Mussolini was also arrested.

In *Una scelta di vita*, Giorgio Amendola gives us a candid but somewhat resentful portrait of his mother and of the unconventional life of the Amendola family in Rome before the First World War, when Eva became a Futurist and an interventionist:

Che la mia famiglia fosse diversa dalle altre non c'era da dubitarne. Anzitutto perchè c'era mia madre, che era una straniera — russa, dicevano — nata a Vilno in Lituania, allora provincia dell'impero russo. Mia madre aveva i suoi lavori, i suoi amici, la sua corrispondenza personale. Usciva tutti i giorni e trascurava le faccende domestiche, affidate alle donne di servizio, per lo più a ore, che si succedevano rapidamente. Avevo già la sensazione che la mia famiglia fosse diversa non solo da quella dei miei ordinari parenti,

---

[14] A native of Prague and married to a Russian diplomat, Zátková, like Kühn, had settled in Italy at the beginning of the century. From 1919 until her death from tubercolosis in 1923, she was involved in a romantic relationship with Arturo Cappa. Like Kühn, Zátková, using the pseudonym Madame X, became a contributor to both *Roma futurista* and *Cronache di attualità*.

[15] The episode is reported by Salaris in *Luciano Folgore e le avanguardie* 95.

nelle quali le donne se ne stavano a casa, ma anche da quelle delle famiglie degli amici, tutte meno disordinate della nostra.

(8)

A sense of chaos and disorder, and the hateful feeling of being "different" are associated by Giorgio in his memories of when he was a boy with his mother's unconventionality, and her failure to fulfill her duties as mother and housewife. Eva Kühn continued to work assiduously as a translator (both literary and commercial) to alleviate the family's financial difficulties. At the same time, much to her husband's dislike, she opened the family house to her international circle of bohemian friends, writers and artists with "loud manners and clothing." There is, however, in the son's recollection, also a positive sense of the exhilarating freedom and unusual opportunities that his mother's non-conformist life afforded him. She took him often with her when he was a boy to visit their neighbor Balla and his family (Luce Balla, who also became an artist, was the same age as Giorgio) in his studio, which Giorgio remembers as a fabulous, multicolored and lively environment constantly full of visitors. The colors of Balla's paintings (between 1912 and 1914, Balla was doing some of his most innovative abstract work) remained in the child's memory as particularly vivid and pleasurable to look at. Eva also took her son — much to the dismay of her husband's family — to coffee houses, to the theater, to Futurist art shows and even to some of the *serate futuriste*, including a particularly rowdy one at the Salone Margherita, which Amendola remembers resembling a New Year's Eve party, except that tomatoes were thrown instead of confetti. Giorgio also remembered vividly the days of pro-war turmoil and the *maggio radioso*, the joyous interventionist demonstrations to which his mother took him, when together they witnessed, among other activities, the famous oration by Gabriele D'Annunzio from a Via Veneto hotel balcony that shortly preceded Italy's declaration of war against Austria-Hungary.

As a Futurist and a nationalist, Eva would later also became a supporter of D'Annunzio's conquest of Fiume in 1919 (Amendola, *Scelta* 39-40). Although Marinetti had started out with a vehemently anti-D'Annunzio platform, he and D'Annunzio eventually bonded over the so-called "vittoria mutilata" question, and the conquest of Fiume. Kühn had an exchange of letters with D'Annunzio about Fiume, contributing to strengthen the alliance between Futurism and the *poeta-eroe* during the initial, heady days of the Reggenza del Carnaro.[16] Giovanni Amendola was instead decidedly anti-D'Annunzio and deeply despised both the amoral "Vate" and his fans. Giovanni was accused by the ultra-nationalists of being a *rinunciatario* because he allegedly capitulated to the "vittoria mutilata,"

---

[16] A number of letters by Kühn to D'Annunzio dating from 1919 to 1921 are held in the archive of Il Vittoriale degli Italiani. On the alliance between Marinetti and D'Annunzio and the osmosis between Dannunzianism and Futurism during the Fiume invasion see Salaris, *Alla festa della rivoluzione*.

becoming a supporter of Nitti (for whose lists he ran in the 1919 elections).

Interventionist passion and support for early Fascism were not limited to Futurist women, but were widespread among intellectual women with different backgrounds: for example, socialist feminists such as Teresa Labriola (the first Italian female lawyer admitted to the bar, and the daughter of the Marxist thinker Antonio Labriola) and Maria Rygier. Labriola was an ardent interventionist and the founder of the first Patriotic League for Women. She believed that women needed to be active participants in the war effort, and that the war would finally bring women onto the national stage, involving them in the construction of "the new Italy."[17] Rygier, an emigrée born in Krakow, was a socialist journalist and revolutionary, and then an anarchist agitator. She converted from an anti-war stand to interventionism in 1914, and worked with Mussolini in the interventionist campaign undertaken by Mussolini's radical left-wing newspaper *Il Popolo d'Italia*. She believed that the war could be converted into socialist revolution. As a union supporter and a syndicalist, in 1914 she was eventually arrested and jailed for a time. On January 24, 1915 she took part and even spoke publicly at the great interventionist demonstration of the *Fasci d'Azione Rivoluzionaria* promoted by Mussolini and De Ambris. Both these women, like Kühn, are examples of embattled personalities who, during the Great War, fought in their own way and developed radically different models of female behavior and action.

As cultural historians have shown, women through the Great War emerged rather suddenly onto the public scene. They displayed — along with the more traditional female traits of endurance, courage, self-sacrifice and maternal care evident in their aid and public assistance work — the skills and concentration required of labor in factories and other demanding physical occupations, as well as certain "masculine" strengths and qualities of conviction, belligerency and pugnaciousness that tended to undermine, or even invert, traditional gender differences.[18] Men, on the other hand, made vulnerable and often hysterical by the devastating violence of war,[19] and often (at least in the public imagination), displaced by women in their capacity as bread winners or heads of the family, felt emasculated.[20] The many disabled and mutilated veterans, made deaf, mute or

---

[17] These and other women are discussed in De Giorgio The phenomenon of female nationalism and *interventismo* and the debate with women pacifists are discussed by Guidi, who stresses the racialist dimension of women's nationalism as a new phenomenon connected to World War One; however, the origins of racialized nationalism among women may be traced back at least to the Libyan war of 1911. Schiavon offers an overview of the connection between feminism and *interventismo* in *Interventiste nella Grande Guerra*.

[18] While this wartime phenomenon has been well documented in other countries, with regard to Italy the theme of the blurring of gender lines during the war has only recently emerged, especially through the work of historians Paola Di Cori and Augusta Molinari.

[19] On male hysteria during the Great War in Italy, see Gibelli.

[20] On the gender trouble generated by war, see Curli and Di Cori.

blind by the war, often felt reduced to the level of helpless children.

Although some moderate feminists did emphasize the maternal nature of women's work during the war, arguing that women were naturally suited for organizing charity aid for other women and children, and for caring for the male troops as nurses and loving *madrine di guerra*, the spectrum of female behavior had undeniably expanded, with important consequences also for morality and sexual conduct. Their emergence into the public sphere, and social as well as cultural and political interaction outside the home and the family, led to a loosening of the moral code, while the maternal function was no longer perceived as the only basis for normal female sexuality. Indeed, as early as 1912, during the Libyan campaign that first witnessed the rise of female patriotism in Italy and of nationalist support for war by women, Valentine de Saint-Point's "Manifesto della donna futurista" (1912) and then the "Manifesto futurista della lussuria" (1913) pointed to the power of the female libido as being equal to that of man, and a source of strength rather than shame. Valentine envisioned women as warriors equal to and potentially braver than men.[21] The Futurist indictment of bourgeois morality, and of the subjection and disciplining of women through marriage, along with the traditional roles of spiritual virgin, angel of the hearth, and their polar opposite, the deadly *femme fatale*, was the element that most attracted women to Futurism during the war. As early as 1911, Marinetti's agenda included the legalization of divorce and the abolition of marriage, and was in favor of free love. His political program included female emancipation and suffrage, albeit mostly in the interest of dismantling the existing political order.

Giovanni Amendola and his wife did not exactly have an open marriage, but he had for a time a relationship with the writer and feminist Sibilla Aleramo, while Eva, in 1913 and through 1914, had an intense affair and intellectual exchange with the writer Giovanni Boine, who was seven years younger than she and was a member of the *La Voce* circle and a collaborator of Papini and Amendola in *L'anima* (he died from tuberculosis in 1917). The story of the affair may be gathered from the surviving letters exchanged by the lovers, and the *carteggio* between Boine and Emilio Cecchi. Although not a Futurist, Boine shared the Futurists' (especially Boccioni's) interest in the philosophy of Bergson, and was fascinated by Walt Whitman's poetic vision of cosmic chaos. In fact, Whitman was one of the few "predecessors" acknowledged by Marinetti and the Futurists (Marinetti, *Teoria* 305). With Eva Kühn, and indeed with Giovanni Amendola,

---

[21] The 1912 and 1913 manifestoes by de Saint-Point (the first being an "answer to Marinetti" and a critique of his misogyny) were launched and distributed as flyers simultaneously in Paris and Milan. De Siant-Point, however, who worked for the Red Cross in Paris, became decidedly anti-war by 1916, when she left for Spain along with several artists who refused to serve in the military. On her conflicted vision of warfare, see Re, "Valentine de Saint-Point." English translations by Laura Wittman of the two manifestoes and other texts by Valentine are available in Rainey, Poggi and Wittman, *Futurism*.

Boine had in common an intense concern for the spiritual, and for the exploration of the interconnectedness of spiritual and material things. This spiritual, or rather spiritualist, bent was also prevalent among some of the Futurists, and later in particular among women, for example the Futurists Maria Ginanni, Rosa Rosà and Irma Valeria of the *Italia Futurista* circle, and Benedetta, as well as Balla and Anton Giulio Bragaglia (the photographer, film maker and avant-garde impresario), all of whom developed a strong interest in Theosophy and the occult.[22] While Giovanni Amendola was interested in integrating spirituality with philosophy and Kantian metaphysics, Boine's spirituality was more traditionally religious. The bewildering simultaneity of modern life that excited the Futurists was a source of angst for the young Boine, who increasingly swerved in the direction of an anti-modernist Catholic mysticism, accompanied by an obsession with the notion of sin and by a good deal of misogyny, typical of the *La Voce* circle.

The story of Eva Kühn's adventurous journey by train to meet her lover in Genoa in the summer of 1914, which she later synthetically evoked in her freeword Futurist poem "Velocità," reads like a chapter from Benedetta's later Futurist novel, *Astra e il sottomarino* (1935) and is suffused with the élan of Benedetta's, Boccioni's, Balla's and many other Futurists' paintings of trains rushing through the night, and of the (then still) erotic frisson of crowded train stations, with lovers or loved ones bidding farewell to each other among a mass of anonymous bystanders.[23] During the train journey, Eva had a change of heart, and instead of stopping at the Genoa train station, she went on to Turin, where she met another friend to whom she could confide her agitation and indecision. As Giorgio Amendola comments dryly, "È una storia che indica il clima appassionato nel quale mia madre viveva e che dava allora alla vita della famiglia un tono agitato" (*Scelta* 22). He finally attributes the affair, like his father did, to his mother's mental instability. Yet the surviving correspondence indicates that what worried and upset Kühn was Boine's possessiveness, his intolerable jealousy, and his insistence that Eva must leave her husband and children in order to be his alone forever (Paolino 95-97). This sexual possessiveness was certainly in contrast with the philosophy of Futurism, with which Kühn increasingly sympathized. The correspondence also shows that there had indeed been a growing conflict with her husband, and Eva was in fact thinking of breaking up the marriage, though divorce was impossible in Italy at the time, and women who "abandoned the conjugal roof" were punishable by law, had no right to keep or even see their children, and could even be arrested. Married women had in fact very few rights and were usually their husband's wards, needing the "marital authorization" to undertake any public act. A husband could legally demand separation on grounds of

---

[22] A useful account of the Futurists' interest in the occult may be found in Cigliana.
[23] The train as *locus eroticus* is a motif, albeit a distinctly comic one, also in Marinetti's later *Come si seducono le donne*.

adultery, but he himself could not be challenged unless he flagrantly and publicly maintained a concubine for an extended time. After the affair when Eva's apparent intentions were discovered in the fall of 1914, Eva was committed to a mental institution until she appeared to have regained her sanity and self-control. Giovanni demanded that Boine return the incriminating letters and other compromising documents about the break-up between him and his wife. He eventually had the opportunity to have a man-to-man reconciliation with Boine, whose friend and spiritual kin he was, having been close to him in *La Voce* and *L'anima*'s circles. In commenting on his father's reconciliation with Boine, which was made possible through the mediation of their common friend Emilio Cecchi, Giorgio's tone is one of gratified acknowledgment of men's ability to transcend the messy affairs of the heart and of the body into which women tend to drag them. But beyond this apparently harmless masculine complacency, a more disquieting picture emerges of the cost that women like Eva Kühn had to pay for daring to live like Futurists. The "agitated tone" that Eva gave to the family life and her sexual misconduct were interpreted as symptoms of a mental disorder — hysteria, neurosis, or both. This disciplining and restraining after Eva's "crises" happened repeatedly, but then, Giorgio writes, Eva "tornava e mi sembrava più sana e più bella che mai" (*Scelta* 21).

It was in 1914, shortly before the war, that Eva Kühn had in fact "taken the leap" from what I have called "existential Futurism" to a Futurist aesthetic practice. Presumably both contributed to alienate her from her husband and to make her appear mentally unbalanced. The symbolic gender insubordination implicit in Eva Kühn's adoption of the name of a male Futurist hero, Magamal, which she used to sign her poem "Velocità," is only heightened by the provocative gender ambiguity of the character itself. In the homosocial, and implicitly incestuous and homosexual, transgressive gender economy of *Mafarka* (however deliberately provocative), Magamal is a feminized figure, whose body and gaze take on some of the seductive features of the feline *femme fatale* of the fin-de-siècle.

Era Magamal, il suo fratello adorato, che correva a lui. Era il guerriero adolescente il cui corpo di caucciù balzava impetuoso, vivace e carezzevole a un tempo, nella fiamma volante della polvere sollevata [...]. Egli era quasi nudo, poiché aveva gettata indietro la pelle d'onagro che una cintura di rame stringeva sulla snellezza dei fianchi. Una volontà febbrile faceva vibrare tutte le sue membra sottili che avevano a volta a volta, grazie femminee e sussulti di belva in agguato. "Ebbene, Magamal? [...] Sono tornate le spie? [...] E le hai interrogate?" gli domandò Mafarka abbracciandolo. "Vuoi interrogarle tu stesso?" replicò il giovanetto abbassando lentamente le lunghe ciglia sui suoi grandi occhi di lama, cerchiati d'un'ombra azzurrognola.

(*Mafarka* 31)

The powerful killer gaze under the seductive eyelashes and the eyes encircled by a blue shadow are the somatic marks of the *femme fatale* in fin-de-siècle iconography, an iconography that Marinetti parodically appropriated and turned inside out by attributing the same features to his young hero. In taking on the name of Magamal and becoming a full-fledged Futurist, Eva Kühn symbolically changed gender position and allied herself with the male Futurists. However, it is significant that she should have associated herself with the ambiguous and androgynous Magamal who, although endowed with indomitable will, speed, and agility, also retained a high degree of feminine vulnerability.[24]

According to a letter sent to the Futurist writer Paolo Buzzi, dated Rome, April 29, 1915 (which was eventually published as part of the introductory material to a later edition of his 1915 novel *L'ellissi e la spirale*), in the spring of 1914 while her husband was away, Kühn wrote, over a period of only about forty-eight hours and using a Futurist synthetic style with words-in-freedom, a novel entitled *Eva la futurista*. She sent the manuscript immediately to Marinetti for publication in the journal *Poesia* but, to her great disappointment, Marinetti returned it without any comment. The letter indicates that it was an autobiographical novel based on the motions of her own psyche ("la dinamica della mia psiche"), presumably a kind of stream of consciousness (Buzzi xxi-xxii). In it, and through the enormous concentration and effort involved in composing it, Kühn felt she achieved an "altezza mai raggiunta di virilità." The word "virilità" refers, as is often the case with Futurist writers and artists (be they men or women), not just to masculinity, but to traits that include especially strength, willpower and courage. Although the manuscript is lost (Kühn confesses in her letter that she destroyed it herself in anger and anguish over Marinetti's rejection), the letter is an important document of Kühn's interest not only in Futurist writing, but also in the question of gender. Like other Futurist women, notably Valentine de Saint-Point, Enif Robert and Rosa Rosà, and later men (for example, Fillia), Kühn was interested in the metamorphosis of gender, and especially in the notion of achieving, through an effort of the mind and will, a kind of virile femininity. It is not surprising that in 1914 Marinetti, who at the time was involved with Mina Loy, rejected such a work. After his initial enthusiasm for Valentine de Saint-Point, he was rather taken aback by her attempt to destroy and overcome the difference between male and female. Mina Loy also proved to be insubordinate and unreliable as a fellow Futurist, and although Futurism was a revelation and highly formative for her as a poet, she soon moved away and wrote some hilarious

---

[24] Magamal's vulnerability is associated with a form of female "moodiness" and hysteria in the novel. His brother Mafarka tells him (32): "Oh! lo so, che sei coraggioso! Ma ho in orrore questa tua ridicola sensibilità femminea che ti lancia talvolta in folli esaltazioni e ti schiaccia, poco dopo, sotto debolezze infantili [...] Ascoltami bene! codeste gaiezze subitanee e codeste inesplicabili tristezze, bisogna abolirle, oggi! [...] Ad onta di tutti gli sforzi della tua volontà, il tuo corpo è rimasto tenero e fragile come un corpo succoso di fanciulla. I tuoi occhi, fatti pei baci, non sono, come i miei, spauracchi per gli uccellacci di malaugurio; ma bisogna indurirli, questi occhi, e armarli di artigli come i miei!"

spoofs about the Futurist homo-social sexual politics.[25] Only after women emerged as patriotic Futurists in 1915 and 1916 did Marinetti begin to look more positively on them as worthy interlocutors and even fellow avant-gardists.

Kühn was, however, undeterred by both Marinetti's rejection of her novel and her husband's strong dislike of her Futurist endeavors. In the same confidential letter to Buzzi, Kühn announced that she was preparing several Futurist works, including a synthetic play about Marinetti, a second synthetic play entitled "La donna di tutti e di nessuno" (to present a model for the new Futurist woman), and even an essay on Futurist love. None of these texts planned by Kühn has surfaced, and it is not known at present whether they were lost, destroyed or even ever written. Kühn asked Buzzi to discuss these works only with other fellow Futurists, including Carrà, Boccioni, Pratella and Russolo, but not to mention them to anyone else who might come in contact with her husband: "a nessun altro — non mi dovete tradire — se mio marito lo saprà, mi rinchiuderà" (Buzzi, xxi-xxii). Not only did Kühn have to write in secret for fear of being placed once again in an institution by her husband, but she also felt increasingly imprisoned and embattled, unable to extricate herself from the demands placed on her. In the same letter to Buzzi she wrote: "Non posso avere raffiche di creazione nella prigione in cui mi trovo coi pensieri del ménage, dei bimbi, del guadagno, della società." The use of the word "raffiche" (blasts) reveals how much she saw her Futurist creative acts as bellicose and explosive and in opposition to both her role in the private sphere and her duty as a bread winner in the public sphere, a duty which before the war had been almost exclusively male, at least among the middle classes. Nonetheless, during the war the embattled Eva/Magamal continued to write as a Futurist, if mostly in secret.

Giovanni and Eva, albeit for different reasons, were both interventionists, and took active part in the demonstrations that led to Italy's entrance into the war. Eva supported the war from the Futurist, aestheticizing and quasi-anarchical revolutionary perspective as (in Marinetti's phrase) "the world's only hygiene." In other words, she no longer believed in Tolstoyan pacifism, and embraced instead the notion that war, in spite of its horrifying violence, could bring about authentic change, even an unleashing of liberating madness and chaos, wiping out outmoded systems of thought and reactionary social structures.[26] Kühn also shared with other Futurists, including Marinetti, a boundless love for Italy, a kind of *italianismo* made all the more passionate by the fact that Italy was her adopted country. She, like her fellow Futurists, expected a modern "new" and rejuvenated Italy to be born from the war. For her husband Giovanni, instead, the war was a

---

[25] I discuss the importance of Futurism for Mina Loy even after she was no longer involved directly in the movement in Re, "Mina Loy and the Quest for a Futurist Feminist Woman."
[26] After all, David Burliuk and the Russian Futurists too, in the 1912 manifesto "A Slap in the Face of Public Taste" had urged "throw[ing] Pushkin, Tolstoy, Dostoevsky *et al.* overboard from the ship of modernity" (51).

matter of testing the national unity and the moral fabric of the Italian people. He saw the discipline required by war and fighting as a kind of ascetic practice, a struggle against one's own baser and instinctual nature.

Even as she took part in the irredentist and interventionist demonstrations, Eva grew very concerned about her family in Vilnius, as Lithuania in 1915 was occupied by Germany (Vilnius capitulated to the Germans in September 1915). The Germans exploited the country for the war effort through agricultural requisitions and forced labor. Her parents and most of the family fled to Petrograd (half a million people fled or were evacuated from Lithuania at the time, with great suffering and destruction), returning to Vilnius only after the October Revolution. Eva, like other Futurists, was initially enthusiastic about the Russian Revolution. However, the experiences of Eva's youngest brother, who was drafted in the Soviet army, and the accounts of the subsequent bloodshed when in 1917 the Bolsheviks attacked Lithuania from the East to prevent its independence and spread instead global proletarian revolution, made her and her whole family strongly anti-Soviet.[27] After Soviet occupation in 1920, the city of Vilnius was eventually forcibly annexed by Poland. While he praised the Russian Revolution for overthrowing the Tsarist regime, Marinetti took a decidedly anti-Bolshevik stand, though other Futurists, for example Mario Carli, did not share his views. In 1920, in "Il nostro Bolscevismo," Carli even envisioned a united front of all revolutionary parties and groups. For Marinetti, the leveling ideology of Bolshevism, its internationalist agenda, the notion of a world defined by social classes rather than individual achievement, its — in his view — hypocritical position against the war, and its tendency toward mass social regimentation, were all antithetical to the Futurist passion for patriotic warfare on behalf of the Italian "race," the values of individual genius and achievement (regardless of class), and the anarchic impulse towards absolute freedom, boundless imagination and individual esthetic expression.[28] Eva, who saw Italianness as a spiritual and

---

[27] The new Lithuanian government established itself in Vilnius in 1918, but the Bolsheviks invaded Lithuania and Soviet forces moved into the city in early 1919, followed only a few months later by the Polish forces, which drove the Red Army out but were not welcome by the Lithuanians. In the summer of 1920, the Red Army reoccupied Vilnius. Despite the attempted mediation of the League of Nations, and the convocation of Lithuania's Constituent Assembly in 1920, Vilnius remained a disputed city in the early 1920s and the site of violent and devastating clashes and confrontations. In February 1922, despite vigorous Lithuanian protests, the city and surrounding area were annexed by Poland. During World War Two, Vilnius was once again seized first by Germany and then by the Soviet army, and incorporated into the Soviet Union until 1990, when after the collapse of the USSR it became the capital of the Independent Republic of Lithuania, recognized by the Soviet Union only in 1991, after additional clashes. As Giorgio Amendola discovered when he went to Vilnius in 1971, no trace of the family was left there as all of Eva Kühn's family members were displaced or had emigrated from Vilnius to Canada, Russia, and other parts of the world.
[28] These views are expressed in detail by Marinetti in *Al di là del comunismo* (1920).

cultural rather than biological or racial category, came, however, to share Marinetti's libertarian and anarchic views and his belief in individual excellence and daring, innovative esthetic expression — extended to all aspects of life, including work and even war — as the highest, most sublime achievement of the Italian genius.

5. *Kühn and* L'Italia Futurista: *Cutting Loose*

In the heady days of the interventionist demonstrations in 1914 and 1915, Marinetti appeared more often in the Amendolas' home (Amendola, S*celta* 25). Eva got even closer to the Futurists then, and her friendship (following probably an affair) with Marinetti, [29] was to be one of the most enduring in the history of Futurist male-female relationships. Some of her unpublished, secret Futurist manuscripts from the war years are preserved in the Marinetti papers at the Getty Center.[30] Nevertheless, during the war there seems to have been a reconciliation of sorts between husband and wife. Their third child, Antonio, was apparently conceived when Eva visited Giovanni in Padua, where he was stationed, and was born in 1916.

The year 1916 was also the year in which the new Futurist journal *L'Italia futurista* was first published; the inaugural issue appeared on June 1, with editorials about the war by Emilio Settimelli and Marinetti, artwork by Boccioni and others, free-word visual poems and a prose poem by Maria Ginanni, the first in the group of women who over the next two years would become contributors. Ginanni was also co-editor and on occasion, with all the male Futurists at the front, acted as editor in chief.[31] The first issue also included an excerpt from Bruno Corra's avant-garde and proto-surrealist novel *Sam Dunn è morto*. Kühn, using her Futurist pseudonym Magamal, reviewed the novel in highly positive terms in an article published on September 9, 1917.

With its expressive use of typefaces, white spaces, typographical characters, mathematical signs (+, −, X, =), numbers, telegraphic and syntactically unconnected noun phrases, and verbs in the infinitive, Magamal's poem "Velocità. Parole in libertà" was fairly typical of the Futurist practice of words-in-freedom inaugurated by Marinetti around 1912.[32] Yet "Velocità" is also a fascinating document of Eva Kühn's appropriation from a woman's point of view of the Futurist aesthetic of speed, which Marinetti had turned into a modern

---

[29] Salaris, *Marinetti. Arte e vita futurista* 175-77. Amendola in S*celta* also observes that Marinetti had taken a very central role ("un grande posto") in his mother's life at the time (26).

[30] They include the poem "Il guerriero che torna" (1917) and "Il canto d'amore della donna cosmica" (1918) as well as essays and letters addressed to Marinetti and signed Magamal.

[31] I discuss Ginanni and some of the other women of *L'Italia futurista* in Re, "Maria Ginanni vs. F. T. Marinetti: Women, Speed, and War in Futurist Italy."

[32] The poem is reproduced in the anthology of women Futurists edited by Bello Minciacchi, *Spirale* 158.

"religion" with a manifesto, "La nuova religione della velocità," first published in the inaugural issue of *L'Italia futurista*. Dedicated to Giacomo Balla ("A Giacomo Balla velocissimo") with, as an opening epigraph, two lines taken from a lecture by Boccioni — "Moto esterno . . . /Moto interno . . ." ("External motion . . . /Internal motion . . .) — and a quote from Marinetti incorporated in it — "*Senso del divino*" (parole di F. T. Marinetti) — , Kühn's poem is nevertheless a celebration of the sense of female independence triggered by Futurism.

The poem is divided into two parts. The first is about the typically Futurist theme of moving quickly through space, the exhilaration of speed, and the psychological resonances and mental effects of this experience; the second deals with speed and rapidity as a kind of existential condition, a rhythm of being that involves the ability to radically change and transform oneself. The first part of the poem celebrates the experience of a woman traveling alone by train who seemingly leaves behind the constraints and concerns of her daily life: "Staccarsi, staccarsi — né angoscia, né pensieri." This cutting loose generates a sense of physical excitement expressed in the typically Futurist language of an electrifying, energizing heightening of perception. Although cut loose from any familiar context in the artificial isolation of train travel, the traveler experiences the journey as an intensification of life: "Vita X 100." This intensification in turn takes on autoerotic dimensions. In her ability to be and think by herself, in the "lavorio febbrile" of the mind triggered by the experience of speed, the traveler feels an increasing sensual pleasure ("Voluttà crescente"). The traveler's brain (again in an exquisitely Futurist analogy) is like a telegraph sending messages to itself in a crescendo of desire ("*Desiderio erotico*") and in a final eruption of pleasure: "Fiamme: eruzione del vulcano" (Bello Minciacchi, *Spirale* 158).

The Futurist articulation of sexual with intellectual pleasure takes on a particularly ironic significance in this female-authored poem, given the cultural assumptions in early twentieth-century Italy regarding both women's intellect and women's sexuality. Women were widely assumed in fact to be incapable of reflective thinking, the very activity wittily alluded to in Magamal's image of her brain as a telegraph sending messages to itself. The only intellectual activity women were generally acknowledged to be able to perform was a second-rate elaboration of men's conceptual work. Here, however, Magamal ironizes the very notion of reflective thought, and replaces it with the Futurist concept of "quick thinking," a form of intellectual illumination and intuitive knowledge that resembles the all-too-reviled "female intuition." Both Marinetti and Boccioni valorized quick, instantaneous intuition, a concept that they borrowed in part from Bergson, and, like Bergson himself, attempted to divest it of any feminine connotations,[33] while Magamal mischievously and humorously does the opposite.

---

[33] Le Doeuff points out that Bergson foregrounds intuition when "feminine intuition" is a "full-blown lexical item," as well as a mode of cognition associated with femininity, yet he in no way intends to rehabilitate the intellectual worth of women (16-17).

Even more subversive is Magamal's affirmation of female autoeroticism; not only does she represent herself as intellectually, but also erotically, self-sufficient. Indeed, the erotic charge that leads to her *jouissance* is directly the product of her own intellectual charge. This surprising image not only runs counter to prevalent notions of women being less sexually charged than men, less sensual and less passionate because their bodies are entirely programmed towards reproduction; it also ironically undermines the "official" Futurist sexual ethos (still evident in Marinetti's own 1917 *Come si seducono le donne*), according to which the only female pleasure comes from being possessed and penetrated by man.

The second part of the poem is more analytical and less telegraphic, and it clarifies the existential and psychological value of the Futurist aesthetic of speed for the author:

"Velocità interna: superare crisi dopo crisi velocemente con equilibrio matematico. Trasformare *lava rovente* in *ghiaccio*. Giungere vertice e giù di nuovo precipitarsi nell'abisso — volontariamente e come un fulmine. Ora lampi feroci, ira IRA — ora serenità glaciale. Rinnovarsi in un attimo. Distruggersi. Creare in un batter d'occhio un universo. Ritirarsi dal tumulto della vita in un deserto glaciale e poi in un attimo balzare fuori sulla piazza rumorosa, tuffarsi nel vortice, godere, GODERE. A volontà mutare velocemente il ritmo interno: ora torrente feroce, ora un largo fiume — calmo e maestoso.
Direttissimo sempre pronto per fuggire la stasi, i chiari di luna!
Velocità interna — sei MIA! *sempre. dovunque.*
Sono *Dio!*"

Radically opposed to the image of woman as static, peaceful, home-bound, a-sensual, and tied by the conservative rhythms of human reproduction, Magamal's poem is not only irreverent and iconoclastic in its depiction of female empowerment; it also gathers up the image of a woman with a radical will and power to change. The series of verbs in the infinitive which form the structure of the poem — "staccarsi, spedire, superare, trasformare, rinnovarsi, distruggersi, creare, ritirarsi, tuffarsi, godere, mutare, fuggire" — tells a tale of escape, liberation and metamorphosis. Unlike the patriarchal culture that interpreted her restlessness and desire for change as a form of hysteria and a nervous disorder, Futurism provided a language to articulate and legitimate both. The new female freedom fomented by Futurism accentuated woman's ability to "go out," and to move freely, as well as her freedom to choose to be alone with herself or to plunge into the crowd of the modern city and to take part in the movement of the masses — a freedom celebrated in particular by Rosa Rosà's Futurist-feminist wartime novel, *Una donna con tre anime* (1918).[34] Thus mobilized, woman's desire could

---

[34] The novel was first reprinted in 1919 and more recently in1981 (along with additional texts, including articles Rosà published in *L'Italia futurista*). In English it is available as "Rosa Rosà's *A Woman with Three Souls* in English translation." See also Re, "Rosa Rosà's Futurist Feminist Novel *A Woman with Three Souls*: A Critical Introduction." I

become radicalized in political as well as sexual and existential terms.

In writing her review article on *Sam Dunn è morto*, Magamal used a masculine, rather than feminine first-person pronoun. She was particularly interested in the overcoming of traditional gender difference and the development of a new, post-gender "cosmic" individual — a strong theme in Corra's work, even though its tone is profoundly ironic and irreverent (closer to Palazzeschi's surreal and playful *L'Uomo di fumo* in some ways than to Marinetti). It was in the context of this review article, where she also speaks in highly positive terms of *Mafarka il futurista* (though she is critical of *Zang Tumb Tuum* for its excessive opaqueness) and emphasizes her enthusiasm for the ongoing war, that she took the opportunity to disassociate herself from Theosophy altogether. This position may not have been welcome by some of the journal's editors and contributors (for example the influential Maria Ginanni, as well as Irma Valeria), who were instead deeply into Theosophy, spiritualism and the occult. Kühn wrote about Theosophy that it was "rancida e trapassata." And she added, "la concezione futurista non ha nulla in comune né con la magia né con l'occultismo — odio e disprezzo tutta questa roba — sono cose 'passatiste.'"[35]

In this same article, Kühn refers candidly to her year-long confinement, thirteen years earlier, in a mental institution, and although she does not mention her experience of being locked up again in 1914, she denounces the previous one as "uno sbaglio," an error and an injustice committed against her.

6. *From Mobilization on the Homefront to* Roma futurista *and* arditismo
While Giovanni was at the front, Eva was also deeply involved in assistance to the casualties, including shell-shocked, mutilated and disabled veterans. She worked first with soldiers who had been rendered deaf and mute by shell shock. Instead of keeping the disabled isolated and shut away (shell-shocked soldiers were in fact often subjected to strong and painful electric charges and other forms of aggressive or coercive therapy with which Eva was all too familiar), she was able instead to gain authorization to take them out walking, and even to the theater. She had considerable success. For example, as Giorgio reports, one evening at the Salone Margherita a Sicilian soldier, after seeing on stage an actress who resembled his fiancée, became agitated and loudly called out her name, becoming once again able to speak. While assisting blind veterans, Kühn became so enthused with her mission that she left everything else behind and moved to Frascati's Villa Aldobrandini, where the assistance center was located. She is therefore an example of how the commitment of "the other army" to aid and assistance during the war took women well beyond the traditional maternal role in the household, and helped make their wartime contribution to the fight truly

---

discuss this novel in relation to other Futurist works and gender issues related to war in Re, "Rosa Rosà and the Question of Gender in Wartime Futurism."
[35] This review article has been reprinted in Carpi 189-92.

invaluable.

Kühn was also a faithful wartime correspondent who wrote regularly to her husband at the front,[36] though she also, at the same time, in typical "simultaneous" Futurist fashion, corresponded with Marinetti. The Futurist leader, while he was a soldier, also exchanged letters with several other women, including the Futurists Irma Valeria and Enif Robert. The latter became the author of the wartime novel *Un ventre di donna*, co-signed by Marinetti, whose letters to her are included in the novel, while she was also involved in a relationship with him. As we can gather from Marinetti's wartime *Taccuini*, and as confirmed by historian and biographer Gino Agnese in *Una vita esplosiva*, Marinetti in 1917, when Giovanni Amendola came to visit him in the hospital where he was recovering from a wound, took care swiftly to hide under the mattress a letter signed Magamal (Agnese 186; Marinetti, *Taccuini* 69). While the wartime letters exchanged by soldiers with their *madrine di guerra* were usually chaste, and served the purpose of boosting the soldiers' morale and keep them fighting, letters sometimes also became erotic objects in the highly libidinal atmosphere that paradoxically developed among soldiers, at least occasionally, in opposition and in desperate contrast to the overwhelming spectacle of death and destruction of human flesh and the pervasive sense of precariousness. Marinetti's wartime *Taccuini* are an eloquent testimony in this regard, as is the only partly ironic "seduction manual" that he composed during the war, *Come si seducono le donne*. The book became an instant bestseller among the troops and was reprinted several times, generating a heated debate among men and women on the pages of *L'Italia futurista*, including feminist interventions and critiques by Rosa Rosà and even Enif Robert. In *Come si seducono le donne*, Marinetti wrote among other things, "La guerra creando in tutto e tutti il senso del provvisorio, dell'instabile e del perituro, distrugge nella donna il pudore, la parola data e la invita al pronto rinnovamento del cuore e dei sensi [...]. Ogni combattente deve, per bilanciare il tradimento inevitabile, imbastire almeno sei relazioni epistolari [...]. Una signorina che si rispetta ha almeno tre fidanzati in tempo di guerra" (67-68). He called for an end to emotions and old-fashioned attitudes like jealousy and possessiveness in relationships. At the same time, he urged the mobilization of women on the frontlines and in the trenches: "Sì, un milione di donne almeno in trincea!" (149). Among the women of *L'Italia futurista*, only Enif Robert expressed explicitly the desire to fight at the front, and the regret of not being allowed to do so because she was a woman, though this was not an uncommon sentiment among middle-class and intellectual women. Some, like Elma Vercelloni, even called for mandatory mobilization of women and the establishment of an official female army.[37] In actuality, even if they did not take up arms, thousands of Italian women

---

[36] However, her wartime letters to her husband have apparently not been preserved.
[37] Vercelloni's speech was originally delivered on behalf of the Comitato Armate Femminili at the Teatro Argentina in Rome on March 3, 1918, and then published. Vercelloni, who

"saw action" at the front as nurses, carriers and in other capacities. They risked their lives, were taken prisoners, suffered from violent attacks and displayed bravery comparable to the male fighters.[38] Among the Futurist women on the home front, Maria Ginanni was especially active in composing editorials and commentaries about the war in *L'Italia futurista* that sought to boost morale at the front and women's support of the war.

After the war, Eva Kühn became actively involved with the branch of the upcoming Futurist Party in Rome (the Roman *fascio* was founded in early 1918) and thus witnessed the fusion of Futurism with Arditism,[39] even taking on a new — and, for women, especially unusual — role as public speaker in a political context.[40] She then collaborated with *Roma futurista*, the left-wing, explicitly subversive and anti-bourgeois Futurist journal (1918-1920), financed initially by Marinetti, which was the organ of the Futurist Party, while her husband won the elections and became a member of the anti-socialist and anti-Fascist moderate cabinet led by Nitti.

In its first year of life, *Roma futurista*, edited by Marinetti, Carli and Settimelli, aimed to fuse the political and the aesthetic aspects of the avant-garde and to transform the energy, frustrations and discontent left by the war, especially among the young veteran *arditi*, into a veritable revolution. By this time, Futurism had already gone through the experience of *L'Italia futurista*, where Magamal's poem appeared, had witnessed the affirmation of several Futurist female artists and writers during the war, and had developed a more positive attitude towards women as both creators and political and social subjects. While it privileged the young male *ardito* as the icon of the Futurist revolution, *Roma futurista* at least on paper assigned an equal role to women, supported feminism, and actively sought women's involvement in the movement. As oppressed subjects who would have profited from the overthrow of the pre-war political and cultural status quo, women were considered at the time by Futurism to be potential revolutionaries,

---

sympathized with the Futurist movement, was also the author of a volume of short stories, *Piccola orchestra* (1924), each of which is dedicated to a Futurist artist or writer.
[38] Belzer (103-04) elaborates on this reality, previously unacknowledged or underestimated by historians who adhered to the myth that war was primarily a "male business."
[39] *Arditi* (from the verb *ardire*, to dare) was the name adopted by the Royal Italian Army storm troops during the Great War. Their exploits on the battlefield were exemplary and they gained fame in Italian military history. There was great mutual admiration between Futurists and Arditi, and some Arditi, like Carli and Settimelli, were also Futurists. The *Arditi* were demobilized by 1920 but many kept their weapons and joined forces with the Futurists and the early Fascists. The name *Arditi* was also used in 1919-20 by the Italian occupiers of Fiume. On the Futurist Party and the fusion of Futurism and Arditism, see Berghaus*Futurism* 104-33.
[40] Although we do not know what she spoke about, F. T. Marinetti mentions Eva Kühn Amendola as a speaker at a meeting of the new party then being formed in Rome on December 16, 1918 in his *Taccuini* (397).

and were invited to become militants.[41] The Futurist Party had a decidedly idiosyncratic feminist agenda. Its utopian and populist program not only called for the extension of suffrage to women, but also for divorce and for the abolition of women's legal subjection to men. (Most Italian feminists, on the other hand, as Sibilla Aleramo had pointed out in 1910, were decidedly opposed to divorce.) The Futurist Party went so far as to call for the end of marriage as a legal institution and its gradual replacement by free unions between sexual partners, calling at the same time for the state to replace the senescent patriarchal family in the rearing and education of children (Marinetti, "Manifesto del partito futurista italiano" 1918, 154-55). This program was perhaps too radical even for most Futurist women, and only a few answered the appeal, including Mina Della Pergola, Fanny Dini and Anna Questa Bonfandini, who was in favor of forming a group of female *ardite* to fight for emancipation,[42] and Elda Norchi (Futurluce). Norchi wrote in her eloquent summation of the female experience of war and call for suffrage, composed jointly with Mario Scaparro, entitled "Il voto alle donne": "La guerra è stata la principale forza motrice del progresso femminile. Il sesso debole ha saputo esser forte. E dalle case dove regnavano donne-bambole sono balzate fuori (chiusi i capelli sulla nuca e sostituiti quando occorreva i calzoni alle gonne) le donne-operaie, donne tranviere, donne-carrettiere, donne-spazzine, donne-infermiere, donne-contadine, donne-ferroviere, donne-impiegate."

Yet the atmosphere for women had changed compared to the war years. There was a degree of anxiety and marked resentment among veterans and men in general about "liberated" women who did not return to their pre-war roles in the private sphere. The widespread resurfacing of family imagery in the press expressed a longing, by men in particular to return to the comfort of domestic life, and the embrace of their wives at home.[43] At the same time, there was a campaign to send working women back home in order to allow male veterans to take their place. It was, effectively, a backlash of sorts. Although the Sacchi law of 1919 nominally abolished the "marital authorization," it did not revoke "paternal power," the legal superiority of the man in the family. The notion of a female

---

[41] In an article entitled "Il Futurismo e la donna," published in the front page of *Roma futurista* Sept. 30, 1918, Settimelli once again reiterated that the Futurist "disprezzo" was not against woman, but against the old conception of woman ("contro una concezione della donna e non contro la donna"). He went on, emphasizing how the war had contributed to bring women's value and capacities to the forefront and to everyone's attention: "La guerra ha dato la sensazione delle capacità femminili rispetto alla nazione. E sarà per la guerra che potrà costituirsi in Italia un femminismo vasto e bene organizzato. Noi futuristi, nemici di tutte le prigioni, siamo propugnatori dell'uguaglianza di diritti per gli uomini e le donne."

[42] Questa Bonfandini, "Le donne e il Futurismo." Discussions of the evolution of Futurist women's positions in the postwar period may be found in Salaris, "Le donne futuriste" and Bello Minciacchi, *Scrittrici della prima avanguardia* 140-72.

[43] This phenomenon is discussed by Belzer 160-61.

suffrage was entertained on the basis of women's wartime contributions to the nation, and although the bill initially passed the Chamber of Deputies in September 1919, it was never ratified.[44] According to one of the anti-woman myths that developed and spread even before the war ended, women on the home front had an easy life, and abandoned domesticity only to indulge in wasteful frivolities and luxury, thus threatening to destroy the Italian family.[45] Women thus effectively came under attack, and there was increasingly a tendency to retrench, reverting to older positions and returning to a biologically based view of maternity as woman's only natural and only truly patriotic role. The *Almanacco della donna italiana* from 1920 contributed to spread this view, as did the bestselling *L'anima della donna* by Gina Lombroso (1921).

Eva Kühn, still under the name of Magamal, published an "Appello futurista al popolo d'Italia" in *Roma futurista* in the August 24th 1919 issue, explicitly using the colorful and lyrical language of *arditismo*, and presenting herself as a militant. Yet there is no violence in her appeal, only vehemence, and a highly poetic, heart-felt expression of patriotism, as well as a utopian, idealistic vision of benevolent agricultural colonialism in Africa.[46] The text resonates once again with echoes from Tolstoy's mysticism of the earth, his passion for agricultural labor and peasant work. There is also no specific appeal to all Italian women to become militant suffragists or revolutionaries, nor does Kühn succumb to the new regressive tendency to recast women as merely and mainly mothers. Here instead she naturally envisions women and men together, as full-fledged "Italiani." Kühn asks women, realistically perhaps, and even at this point defensively (considering the cultural and political evolution of postwar Italy, and in light of the ongoing backlash), to welcome back the returning soldiers and, after so much fighting, to enjoy the modest luxury of peace itself, and of being able to love their men, and at the same time, of having the opportunity once again to read, study, write and "sing." Yet she also sees them able to return and finally to enjoy more feminine

---

[44] Schiavon provides an overview of the feminist struggle for suffrage in the immediate postwar period in "The Women's Suffrage Campaign in Italy in 1919," pointing out that "the European-wide postwar gender backlash affected Italian society in the most extreme manner" (51).
[45] For example, in Lo Valvo, *La Guerra e i nuovi destini della donna*, discussed by Belzer, 162-63.
[46] The *appello* reads in part as follows: "Lavoratori e guerrieri della patria — unitevi!/ Parassiti d'Italia, vergognatevi!/ Non è l'ora questa per l'ozio, per gli sfarzi, per lussi sfrenati./ Arditi dello spirito, che arda calma e forte la Fiamma vostra./ Militanti spirituali, all'opera./ L'unico distintivo nostro: lo sguardo sereno il sorriso sulle labra e la mano tesa coll'amore a colui che arde e lavora./ L'unica arma nostra: la fiamma d'amore per il nostro popolo vittorioso ed il nostro verbo lucido: la nostra religione dell'Eroismo quotidiano e della gioia eterna./ L'unica divisa nostra: ardere! lavorare! superare! perché la Patria nostra sia grande e ricca e che dia al mondo la Luce potente. [...] Arditi nelle vostre mani sta la grandezza d'Italia. Tendete lo sguardo e la mano d'aiuto all'Africa che ci chiama [...]. Andate, lavorate la terra sorgente divina di ricchezze senza fondo."

arts such as weaving and the cultivation of exquisite, yet frugal beauty through the applied and decorative arts.[47] These were, in fact, some of the arts in which Futurist women, such as Rosetta Depero, Luce Balla, and Alma Fidora among others, excelled and were allowed to practice in their still largely patriarchal households. Kühn herself had her own original ideas about how to manufacture tactile tables as esthetic objects, based on the principles of Futurist tactilism. Tactilism was an interest that she shared with Benedetta, as well as Marinetti, and that for her was rooted in the experience of working with blind war veterans.[48] Yet Kühn never actually got to enjoy the peace and develop the creativity she envisioned in her 1919 "Appello."

7. From the Futurist-Fascist Campaign to Confinement and Surveillance

Several women, along with Eva Kühn, were involved in the Futurist *Fasci* in Rome; those revolutionary political cells would shortly become associated with Fascism, but were then still a decidedly left-wing movement. In 1919, the Futurist and the Fascist *Fasci* converged and formed an alliance for the upcoming general election. In 1919, in order to be closer to where the action was, Kühn appears to have initiated a move of the family from Rome to a town near Milan, Porto Ceresio (Cerchia 4). Giovanni worked at the time for *Il Corriere della sera*; therefore the move to Milan was fully justified.

As Giorgio Amendola tells us in his memoir, during the Futurist-Fascist electoral campaign in which she took an active role, his mother came into contact with a group of working-class anarchists first in Milan and then in Rome, and struck up an involved and sympathetic conversation with some of them, which evolved into a fertile intellectual exchange and a long-lasting friendship (*Scelta* 43).[49] To Giorgio, anarchism and Fascism appear irreconcilable, and in hindsight he interprets this "strange episode" as evidence of his mother's "mental and political confusion," even though he goes on to admit that the political web which in 1919 connected Futurism to Fascism, socialism, and anarchy, was quite complex and bewildering in and of itself (*Scelta* 43). The clear-cut distinction between a communist left and a Fascist right which emerged from around 1923-

---

[47] "Donne d'Italia! Date vera gioia agli eroi guerrieri che tornano. Siate / grate per la grande vittoria!/ Tessete la tela linda da' colori vivi e belli!/ Ornatevi di perle veneziane: sono più belle dell'oro e dell'argento di / cui ha bisogno la Patria!/ Preparate profumi oleosi squisiti: è ricca di fiori la terra d'Italia!/ Raccogliete aranci, fragole, fiori./ Cantate la gioia eterna, amate e studiate i grandi immortali! Italiani — Eroi — Titani! Lavoratori silenziosi e forti!/ Già spunta l'alba della *Nuova Italia*./ Che dirà al mondo la *Nuova Parola*."

[48] As may be gathered from Magamal, "Polemiche sul tattilismo."

[49] Salaris reports the discovery of a 1919 exchange of letters between Kühn and the anarchist Vincenzo Bianchini, in which, among other things, Kühn described her ideas for a reform of the mental care system and argued the need to eliminate the current system of prison-like asylums for the mentally ill. Bianchini invited her to collaborate in the anarchist journal *L'umanità nuova* (*Marinetti editore* 119)

24 was still quite untenable, to say the least, in the post-World War One period and the early 1920s. For in those years Futurism was at least as close to anarchism as it was to Fascism, and Fascism itself had a strong anarchical component.

After the defeat of the joint Futurist-Fascist list in the November 1919 election, Marinetti was arrested along with Mussolini. Giorgio remembers with shame being taken by his mother to the prison of San Vittore (the same in which he would later be briefly imprisoned as a communist by the Fascists in 1932, during a momentary return to Italy from his exile in France) to visit Marinetti and Mussolini (the latter was released almost immediately, while Marinetti was detained for three weeks), to whom she brought books and food, although her husband Giovanni had been elected to the parliament and had taken his place in Nitti's cabinet. What Giorgio Amendola fails to mention in his memoir, however, is that he was probably allowed by Mussolini to escape to France only through the intervention of Marinetti, who had never forgotten his mother's generosity during his imprisonment. Marinetti, who in 1920 disassociated himself officially from Fascism, chiefly because of Mussolini's refusal to embrace his vehemently anti-clerical program, would never again be actively involved in politics, but in the 1930s he enjoyed Mussolini's guarded respect, and in turn he supported the Duce, although he was leery of many of his policies.

As inauspicious as Eva Kühn's militancy and her initial support for the Futurist-Fascist movement may seem in light of the later history of Fascism and of Fascism's oppressive and discriminatory policies towards women, in 1919 Fascism signified something quite different. It expressed, as we have seen, a yearning on the part of intellectual women such as Eva Kühn for radical cultural, social, and political change. This yearning was deeply frustrated by what was to follow. Giorgio Amendola in his memoir remembers that in 1920-1922, when he was still a teenager, he would go with his mother to the Casa D'Arte Bragaglia in via Condotti (where the Bragaglias had their photography studio) and then Bragaglia's Teatro degli Avignonesi, one of the most lively centers not only for Futurist art, cinema and theater but also for other international avant-garde exhibits and performances, including Dadaist and surrealist works. Yet, in October 1921, Kühn was admitted to a psychiatric clinic near Naples, and then moved to another clinic in Viterbo. In 1922, during a trip home to Vilnius, Kühn was devastated by the stories she was told of the brutality of the Bolsheviks and the Red Army, and the persecutions to which her family was subjected (*Scelta* 56). We are told by her son that, on her return to Italy, where meanwhile the Fascists had seized power and the Amendola family home in Porta Pinciana had become a target for Fascist squads, Kühn, suffering from depression and exhaustion, was again confined to yet another mental clinic, this time in Rome.[50]

---

[50] According to Giorgio (*Scelta* 80), it was the Villa Giuseppina on Via Nomentana. It was a "casa di salute per malattie nervose e della psiche" run by a Catholic congregation of nuns, under the supervision of Prof. Antonio Mendicini.

On his father's instruction, Giorgio went to visit her periodically. Unbeknownst to Eva, Giovanni Amendola was the victim of a retaliatory beating by a Fascist squad in 1923, and again in 1925, which made his poor health deteriorate even more. He eventually fled to France, where he died in April 1926.

Eva emerged from the clinic only in 1934, after more than ten years spent there, having seen her husband one last time in 1925 when, as she recounts, he visited her briefly for Christmas, bringing her roses and sweets. During her internment, the children were cared for and helped by friends of the family, especially Luigi Albertini. Her daughter Ada, who had finished her medical studies and was now officially a physician, finally came to free her "from the hands of the psychiatrists" (Kühn, *Vita* 447). Only then did she learn of her husband's death and was able to read his last letter, written in February, in which, in a brief paragraph addressed to her, he said:

"Aggiungo solo poche parole per mia moglie. Avrei dovuto cominciare da lei: purtroppo le sue condizioni mentali non consentono che questo documento sia consegnato a lei. Chiedo perdono a mia moglie di tutti i miei torti e di tutte le mie mancanze: sono consapevole di non aver reso la sua vita felice, e vorrei poter ricominciare per riparare. A lei perdono ogni amarezza dovuta del resto, non alla natura buona e onesta, ma all'infelice sistema nervoso. Di lei ricordo soltanto il grande amore di cui porto il debito nell'eternità."
(Paolino 102)

Kühn also learned then of her son Giorgio's arrest by the Fascists in 1932, which was followed by his deportation to the island of Ponza, where she was able to visit him in 1935. (Giorgio was freed only in 1937, after which he fled to France, subsequently fighting in the Resistance until the fall of Mussolini). Under Fascist rule, while Marinetti and most of the later Futurists embraced the regime, to which they delegated all political initiatives, Kühn, although granted some occasional and often humiliating work as a translator by the Fascist Ministry of Culture, was not allowed to teach in Italy, though she was able to find a teaching position as a Lecturer in Italian at the University of Vilnius from 1935 until 1937. She was closely watched and placed under surveillance by the Fascist police and by Fascist informers, and followed even during her trips and extended stays in Vilnius. She was portrayed with suspicion and disdain as an immoral woman, perverted and mentally ill, and, at one point in 1937, due to her "foreigness," — in an atmosphere of increasing anti-Semitism — she was even suspected of being secretly Jewish (Paolino 106-07). She was once again committed to a mental institution in 1939 for a few months. Only after the fall of Fascism and the end of World War Two was Eva Kühn Amendola — an exceptional individual but in many ways also a woman who embodied the contradictions and the embattled position of intellectual and avant-garde women in Italy in the early 20th century — finally no longer a woman at war.

University of California, Los Angeles

Works Cited

Adamson, Walter. *Avant-Garde Florence: From Modernism to Fascism*. Cambridge, Mass.: Harvard UP, 1993.
Agnese, Gino. *Marinetti. Una vita esplosiva*. Milano: Camunia Editrice, 1990.
Amendola, Giorgio. *Una scelta di vita*. Milano: Rizzoli, 1976.
Amendola, Giovanni. "Nuovi disordini all'Università di Roma provocati dai futuristi." *Il Corriere della Sera*. December 12, 1914.
Bello Minciacchi, Cecilia. *Scrittrici della prima avanguardia. Concezioni, caratteri e testimonianze del femminile nel Futurismo*. Firenze: Le Lettere, 2012.
———, ed. *Spirale di dolcezza + serpe di fascino. Scrittrici futuriste: antologia*. Napoli: Bibliopolis, 2007.
Belzer, Allison Scardino. *Women and the Great War. Femininity under Fire in Italy*. New York: Palgrave Macmillan, 2010.
Boine, Giovanni. *Carteggio II: Giovanni Boine-Emilio Cecchi (1911-1917)*. Ed. M. Marchione and S. E. Scalia. Roma: Edizioni di Storia e Letteratura, 1983.
Bruno, Giuliana. *Streetwalking on a Ruined Map. Cultural Theory and the City Films of Elvira Notari*. Princeton: Princeton UP, 1993.
Burliuk, David, Alexander Kruchenykh, et al. "A Slap in the Face of Public Taste." *Russian Futurism Through its Manifestoes, 1912-1928*. Ed. Anna Lawton. Trans. Anna Lawton and Herbert Eagle. Ithaca: Cornell UP, 1988. 51-52.
Buzzi, Paolo. *L'ellissi e la spirale: film + parole in libertà*. Ed. Luciano Caruso. Firenze, SPES, 1990.
Carli, Mario. "Il nostro bolscevismo." *La testa di ferro*. February 15, 1920.
Carpi, Giancarlo, ed. *Futuriste. Letteratura. Arte. Vita*. Roma: Castelvecchi, 2009.
Cavaglion, Alberto. *Otto Weininger in Italia*. Roma: Carucci, 1982.
Cerchia, Giovanni. *Giorgio Amendola, un comunista nazionale, dall'infanzia alla guerra partigiana (1907-1945)*. Cosenza: Rubettino editore, 2004.
Cigliana, Simona. *Futurismo esoterico. Contributi per una storia dell'irrazionale tra Otto e Novecento*. Roma: La Fenice Edizioni, 1996.
Curli, Barbara. *Italiane al lavoro 1914-1920*. Venezia: Marsilio, 1998.
De Giorgio, Michela. "Dalla 'donna nuova' alla donna della 'nuova' Italia." *La grande guerra: Esperienza, memoria immagini*. Ed. Diego Leoni and Camillo Zadra. Bologna: Il Mulino, 1986. 307-29.
De Saint-Point, Valentine. "*Manifesto della donna futurista.*" Seguito da "*Manifesto futurista della lussuria,*" "*Il teatro della donna,*" "*Il mio esordio coreografico,*" "*La Metacorìa.*" Ed. Jean-Paul Morel. Genova: Il Melangolo, 2006.
Di Cori, Paola. "Il doppio sguardo. Visibilità dei generi sessuali nella rappresentazione

fotografica (1908-1918)." Leoni and Zadra 765-800.

Di Leo, Donatella. "Eva Amendola Kühn (Magamal: A Futurist of Lithuanian Extraction)." *International Yearbook of Futurism Studies* 5 (2015): 297-326.

Futurluce (Elda Norchi), and Mario Scaparro, "Il voto alle donne." *Roma futurista*, March 30, 1919.

Garretto, Elda, Stegano Garzonio and Bianca Sulpasso. "Eva Amendola Kühn." *Russi in Italia. Dizionario htttp://www.russinitalia.it*

Gibelli, Antonio. "L'esperienza di guerra. Fonti medico-psichiatriche e antropologiche." Leoni and Zadra 49-73.

Guidi, Laura. "Un nazionalismo declinato al femminile, 1914-1918." *Vivere la guerra. Percorsi biografici e ruoli di genere tra Risorgimento e primo conflitto mondiale*. Ed. Laura Guidi. Napoli: Clio Press, 2007. 93-118.

Kühn Amendola, Eva [Magamal]. "Appello futurista al popolo d'Italia." *Roma futurista*, August 24, 1919.

_____. "Henry George e il movimento dei riformatori fondiari." *Nuova antologia di lettere, scienze e arti*, 163 (1913): 275-87.

_____. "Il nuovo metodo intuitivo nell'insegnamento delle lingue moderne." *Italia moderna*. 1907.

_____ "L'ottimismo di Schopenhauer." *Coenobium* 6 (1907): 84-92.

_____ [Magamal]. "Polemiche sul tattilismo," *Cronache di attualità* 5.5 (May 1921): 57.

_____. "La riforma fondiaria di Henry George." *Roma futurista*. August 10, 1919. Rpt. in Filippo Tommaso Marinetti, *Democrazia futurista: dinamismo politico*. Milano: Facchi, 1919. 66-69.

_____ [Magamal]. "*Sam Dunn è morto.*" *L'Italia Futurista* 2:28 (September 9, 2016): 3. Rpt. in Carpi 189-92.

_____ [Magamal]. "Velocità. Parole in libertà" *L'Italia futurista* 1:10 (November 15, 1916): 3.

_____. *Vita con Giovanni Amendola (Epistolario 1903-1926)*. Firenze: Parenti, 1960.

Le Doeuff, Michèle. *The Sex of Knowing*. Trans. Kethryn Hamer and Lorraine Coder. New York: Routledge, 2003.

Leoni, Diego, and Camillo Zadra, eds. *La grande guerra: Esperienza, memoria, immagini*. Bologna: Il Mulino, 1986.

Lo Valvo, Oreste. *La guerra e i nuovi destini della donna*. Palermo: Trimarchi, 1918.

Marinetti, F[ilippo] T[ommaso]. "Al di là del comunismo." (1920). *Teoria e invenzione futurista*. 470-88.

_____. *Come si seducono le donne*. Preface Bruno Corra and Settimelli. (1917). Rocca San Casciano: Stabilimento Tipografico Cappa, 1918.

_____. *Democrazia futurista. Dinamismo politico*. Milano: Facchi, 1919.

_____. *Mafarka il futurista*. Trans. Decio Cinti. Milano: Edizioni Futuriste di Poesia, 1910.

_____."Manifesto del partito futurista italiano." (1918). *Teoria e invenzione futurista* 153-58.

_____. "La nuova religione della velocità. Manifesto futurista," *L'Italia futurista*. June 1, 1916. Rpt. in Marinetti, *Teoria e invenzione futurista* 111-118.

———. *Taccuini 1915-1921*. Ed. Alberto Bertoni. Bologna: Il Mulino, 1987.
———. *Teoria e invenzione futurista*. Ed. Luciano De Maria. Milano: Mondadori, 1968.
Molinari, Augusta. "Autobiografie e vite di donne in manicomio nel primo Nocevento." *Donne e ruoli femminili nell'Italia della Grande Guerra*. Milano: Selene Edizioni, 2008. 111-58.
———. *Una patria per le donne. La mobilitazione femminile nella Grande Guerra*. Bologna: Il Mulino, 2014.
Nozzoli, Anna. "*La Voce* e le donne." *Les Femmes-écrivains en Italie* (1870-1920) *Ordres et Libertés. Chroniques Italiennes* 39-40 (1994): 207-22.
Paolella, Francesco. "'Solo un'immensa fonte di dolore.' Appunti per una ricerca sulle donne in manicomio durante la Grande Guerra." *E-Review Rivista degli Istituti Storici dell'Emilia Romagna in Rete* 2 (2014). http://e-review.it/paolella-solo-un-immensa-fonte-di-dolore
Paolino, Antonietta G. "Eva Kühn Amendola: ovvero l'insostenibile tragicità del vivere." *La famiglia Amendola. Una scelta di vita per l'Italia*. Ed. Giovanni Cerchia. Torino: Cerabone/Fondazione Giorgio Amendola/Associazione Carlo Levi, 2011. 91-116.
Papini, Giovanni. *Autoritratti e ritratti*. Milano: Mondadori, 1962.
Questa Bonfandini, Anna. "Le donne e il Futurismo." *Roma futurista*, February 9, 1919.
Rainey, Lawrence, Christine Poggi, and Laura Wittman, eds. *Futurism: An Anthology*. New Haven: Yale UP, 2009.
Re, Lucia. "Maria Ginanni vs. F. T. Marinetti: Women, Speed, and War in Futurist Italy." *Annali d'Italianistica* 27 (2009). *A Century of Futurism: 1909-2009*: 103-24.
———. "Mina Loy and the Quest for a Futurist Feminist Woman." *Futurist Imperfect. Italian Futurism between Tradition and Modernity*. Special issue of *The European Legacy* 14.7 (December 2009): 799-819.
———. "Passion and Sexual Difference: The Gendering of Writing in 19th-Century Italian Culture." *Making and Remaking Italy: The Cultivation of National Identity Around the Risorgimento*. Ed. Albert Ascoli and Krystina Von Hennenberg. Oxford: Berg, 2001. 155-200.
———. "Rosa Rosà and the Question of Gender in Wartime Futurism." *Italian Futurism, 1909-1944: Reconstructing the Universe*. Ed. Vivien Greene. New York: Guggenheim Museum Publications, 2014. 184-86.
———. "Rosa Rosà's Futurist Feminist Novel *A Woman with Three Souls*: A Critical Introduction." *Italian Futures*. Ed. Albert Ascoli and Randy Starn, *California Italian Studies* 2.1 (2011): http://www.escholarship.org/uc/item/7k625747: 1-14.
———. "Valentine de Saint-Point, Ricciotto Canudo, F. T. Marinetti: Eroticism, Violence and Feminism from Prewar Paris to Colonial Cairo." *Quaderni d'Italianistica* 24.2 (Fall 2003): 37–69.
Re, Lucia with Dominic Siracusa, trans. "Rosa Rosà's *A Woman with Three Souls* in English Translation." Notes by Lucia Re. *Italian Futures*. Ed. Albert Ascoli and Randy Starn. *California Italian Studies* 2.1 (2011): http://www.escholarship.org/uc/item/7k625747: 15-40.
Robert, Enif (Signora Robert), and Marinetti. *Un ventre di donna. Romanzo futurista*.

Milano: Facchi, 1919.
Rosà, Rosa. *Una donna con tre anime. Romanzo futurista.* (1918). Ed. Claudia Salaris. Roma: Edizioni delle donne, 1981.
Salaris, Claudia. *Alla festa della rivoluzione. Artisti e libertari con D'Annunzio a Fiume* Bologna: Il Mulino, 2002.
———. "Le donne futuriste nel periodo tra guerra e dopoguerra." Leoni and Zadra 291-305.
———. "Incontri con le futuriste." *L'arte delle donne nell'Italia del Novecento.* Ed. Laura Iamurri and Sabrina Spinazzè. Roma: Meltemi, 2001. 59-66.
———. *Luciano Folgore e le avanguardie. Con lettere e inediti futuristi.* Scandicci: La Nuova Italia, 1997.
———. *Marinetti. Arte e vita futurista.* Roma: Editori Riuniti, 1997.
———. *Marinetti editore.* Bologna: Il Mulino, 1990.
Schiavon, Emma. *Interventiste nella Grande Guerra. Assistenza, propaganda, lotta per i diritti a Milano e in Italia (1911-1919).* Milano: Mondadori, 2015.
———. "The Women's Suffrage Campaign in Italy in 1919." *Aftermaths of War: Movements and Female Activists, 1918-1923.* Ed. Ingrid Sharp and Matthew Stibbe. Leiden: Brill, 2001. 49-68.
Schopenhauer, Arthur. *Introduzione alla filosofia e scritti vari.* Trans. Eva Kühn Amendola. Introd. and notes Francesco Cafaro. Appendix by Kühn Amendola. "L'ottimismo trascendentale di Arturo Schopenhauer." Torino: Paravia, 1960.
———. *Sul mestiere dello scrittore e sullo stile.* Trans. Eva Kühn Amendola. Ed. Giorgio Colli. Torino: Boringhieri, 1993.
Serri, Mirella. "La futurista. Eva Kühn Amendola." Marta Boneschi, Paola Cioni, Elena Doni, Claudia Galimberti, Lia Levi, Maria Serena Palieri, Cristiana di San Marzano, Francesca Sancin, Mirella Serri, Federica Tagliaventi, Simona Tagliaventi. *Donne nella Grande Guerra.* Introd. Dacia Maraini. Bologna: Il Mulino, 2014. 149-73.
Settimelli, Emilio. "Il Futurismo e la donna." *Roma futurista,* Sept. 30, 1918
Spini, Giorgio. *Italia liberale e protestanti.* Torino: Claudiana, 2002.
Vercelloni, Elma. *Perché la coscrizione femminile deve essere obbligatoria.* Roma: Carlo Colombo, 1918.
———. *Piccola orchestra. Novelle.* Roma, Maglione e Strini, 1924.

Katia Pizzi

From Marinetti's *L'alcòva d'acciaio* to Giani Stuparich's *Ritorneranno*: Gender, Nationalism, Technology and the Italian Great War

Preamble
This article addresses the *Grande Guerra* and modernist imagination in the works of an unlikely couple of authors, veterans and cultural operators: the Triestine novelist Giani Stuparich (1891-1961) and the founder and leader of Futurism Filippo Tommaso Marinetti (1876-1944). In particular, my essay centres on two novels: Marinetti's *L'alcòva d'acciaio*, a triumph of technological masculinity and sexual nationalism, published in 1921, and Stuparich's *Ritorneranno*, a comprehensive and purportedly factual portrait of Triestine society at the time of the conflict, published in 1941. Although their respective approaches to the war are largely out of synch — one is a triumphalist and orgiastic celebration of military effort, the other a sober, realistic and elegiac *tranche de vie* — both novels nonetheless construct and convey significant national imaginings of the First World War. The two novels diverge significantly: while war technology and mechanization take centre stage in Marinetti's war, the maternal nationalism proposed by Stuparich relies on a more conventional set of values closely related to a traditional culture and iconography of ethnic and national identity formation. Whether via machine technology or via a sentimental imaginary of nation building, however, both Marinetti and Stuparich propound a gendered national politics, which ultimately relies on conceptualizations of national and ethnic identity amalgamated with sexual politics and congealing, in particular, around the *topoi* of the feminine and the maternal. Whether in terms of patriarchal sexual penetration (Marinetti) or quasi-sexual mysticism (Stuparich), issues of national identity brought to the fore by the Italian First World War are comparably highlighted here and resolutely associated with lovers, mothers and sisters. An analysis of these two narratives in tandem will shed useful light on the extent to which both writings are underscored by specific politics, helping unpack their gendered nationalism during and after the First World War.

Machines and Warfare
Mechanics, machines and military engineering are historically integrated within conflict and warfare: one of the first mentions of a war implement named *machina* in writing is in Quintus Ennius (second century BC). Both Vitruvius (first century BC) and the anonymous treatise *De rebus bellicis* (fourth century AD) proposed reforms of the art of war predicated upon technical rationalization and

standardized deployment of war machines. However, it was not until the First World War that machines played a large and significant role in conflict, frequently interacting with soldiers on a daily basis. Proponents of war technology in modern Italy, Mario Morasso *in primis*, advocated for and propagated the mystique and the prowess of the industrial war machine, playing a key role in public discourse — see, in particular his treatise *La nuova guerra: armi, combattenti, battaglie* (1914). Even though Marinetti never acknowledged his intellectual debt with Morasso, the latter's discourse around the robotization of future agents within global theatres of mechanized wars, where soldiers are viewed as "nuove milizie meccaniche che si azzufferanno e si lanceranno all'assalto" (159), was influential on Marinetti and other Futurists.

Augusto Platone and other intellectuals of the time became acutely aware of the inevitable mechanization and technologization of conflict.[1] Human slaughter became legitimized through systematic, controlled and professional employment of technology. Time itself became newly homogenized, ticking alongside the atomized, synchronic movement of wristwatches set to the shared, standard time of battle. Soldiers in the battlefields became full-fledged robotic entities, forcibly de-individualised and increasingly fused with the war machinery they operated. The human voice was silenced by the incessant racket of war machinery; the human body itself became a battlefield, the stage of a strife between machines and nature. For Adas, "men are reduced to 'slaves of machines' or 'wheels [or cogs] in the great machinery of war'" (369). Their bodies become machines. In Mumford's words, war itself becomes a "megamachine" where armies are perceived as large mechanisms and humans as cogs of this apparatus. Individuals become reified, pliable to the impelling rhythm of machines like workers on a Taylorist conveyor belt. Anthony Giddens persuasively argued that the systematization of military techniques, especially as concerned the rank and file, was a form of Taylorism *ante litteram*: soldiers were grouped together by technical skills and repeated sequences of regular, single activities, simultaneously responding to preordained command instructions (113-14).

War became an intense and violently dynamic theatre, a deafening and chaotic stage, forcefully spectacular and accessible in the visual and textual flashes and fragments of a reality captured in the fissures of perpetual change and motion. Following Gertrude Stein, Stephen Kern perceives the battlefield as a Cubist painting, as a succession of irregular spaces of equal value (288-301). In fact, the complex body of war itself was a colossal machine propelled forward by the frenzied, compelling rhythm of technology. In short, "World War I was *the* simultaneous drama of the age of simultaneity" (Kern 295; also 288-89). It was the first war of disappearance and consumption, as argues Virilio: "the military livestock quickly jumped on the cattle wagon, but everything was over very fast" (76-77).

---

[1] Platone: "la guerra futura sarà essenzialmente meccanizzata e motorizzata" (12).

Marinetti's Machine of War

At the helm of Futurism, Marinetti treated the war as the ultimate field of agitational and situational politics, a theatre where collective rites of initiation to a mechanical modernity were to be played out. "Marinetti's war is the earthly paradise of the machine" (Wagstaff 156): an intensely idealized and technologized field where the poet's engagement with technologies of destruction is dramatically evident. Indeed, as Lista states, "Marinetti è stato e resta il poeta della guerra, senza rivali in nessuna altra letteratura" (44-45).

War was, for Marinetti, industrial modernity in action. For Marinetti warfare signified the ultimate metamorphosis of human into mechanical, a site where governance of speed translated immediately into military logistics. Borrowing from Lamarck's principles of *philosophie zoologique*, *L'uomo moltiplicato e il Regno della macchina* (1910) posited the mechanical as an agent of multiplication of the human. His manifesto *Guerra sola igiene del mondo* (1915) visualized an environment made of metal inhabited by men whose flesh was made of steel, envisioning a direct correlation between the inevitability of war and metallization of human flesh, with regressive erotic overtones (Marinetti, cit. De Maria xlvi; Schnapp 124-39).

Further, in *Al di là del comunismo* (1920), Marinetti repeats a position originally found in Paul Lafargue, who had argued in favour of machines as a means to free humankind from the oppression of salaried labour (see *The Right to be Lazy* of 1880), a reading later disavowed following Marinetti's alliance with Fascism. Despite his anarchic flare, which earned him the title of "revolutionary intellectual" in 1921 in Gramsci's *Ordine nuovo*, Marinetti makes a clear distinction here between Futurism and Communism, while at the same time flirting all along with Lenin's policies.[2]

In this and further published works, both contemporary and later, an ideal line connects 'mechanical wombs' with 'alcoves of steel' for Marinetti. Technology and national language become integrated particularly in the immediate postwar, much as they did in Germany's Weimar.[3] Marinetti's novel *Gli indomabili* of

---

[2] The article published in *Ordine nuovo* on 5 January 1921 was authored by the revolutionary intellectual Lunacarskij. Gramsci reiterated his esteem in a letter to Leon Trotsky dated 8 September 1922, relaying his satisfaction at the opening of a Futurist exhibition jointly organized by Communists and Futurists in Turin where Marinetti had gone round the rooms in the company of workers. Gramsci, however, became progressively disillusioned with Futurism, as can be gleaned from his *Prison Notebooks*. Claudia Salaris further speculates that Marinetti may have expedited this pamphlet through the press in order to predate D'Annunzio's forthcoming *Carta del carnaro*, a radical script published in 1921 adressing comparable themes; see Salaris, *Alla festa della rivoluzione*, 84.

[3] As Herf observes: "The novelty in the postwar discussions of technology and culture in Germany was that for the first time the non technical intellectuals were trying to integrate technology into nationalist language" (18).

1922 is thrown into relief when aligned with his newspaper clippings, now held at the J. P. Getty Research Institute Library, detailing Marinetti's keen attention for technological advancements in war machinery. Not to speak of a jealously conserved 1935 typescript entitled *Il romanzo della superspecie o la psicosintesi*, a pseudo-scientific rambling by Ruggero Micheloni positing the First World War as springboard of a newly forged cyborg or human-mechanical identity (Marinetti, newspaper clippings) In further pronouncements in the late 1930s, the languages of colonial and erotic possession become conflated into one, as in the case of Marinetti's "L'aerocanzone delle parole nuove," declaimed on Italian radio on 29 July 1939. Here, the engine of the flying machine is feminized, eroticized, objectified and rendered pliant to masculine willpower.[4] As vehicles of erotic possession, Marinetti's trains, planes, tanks and other war machines quickly become subsumed under his aggressively imperialist and masculine identity. In short, Marinetti's First World War is locked in a vision of metallic shine, glamour and virility. He expresses none of the misgivings and disillusion haunting the generation of 1914, which, conversely, will colour Stuparich's memorial, elegiac and low-tech approach to the Great War, as we shall see further down.

In *L'alcòva d'acciaio* (1921) Marinetti's war machine identifies with the "armoured car" or small tank, an extension of human capability and symbol of a desire without limits, a desire shortly to acquire explicitly sexual overtones. The tank had been first introduced on the war scene in 1916, as a means to break the stalemate of immobilized trench warfare. Immediately perceived as a mechanical dinosaur emerging from the primeval mud of the trenches, the tank was hailed at once as a hyper-mechanical weapon, pushing the boundaries of modern technology, as well as a pre-historical monster, reviving ancestral fears and terrors, a testament to evolution running simultaneously backwards and forwards. Though few soldiers actually operated or saw tanks in action, civilians in Britain were familiar with them after being exposed to so-called tank films from 1917 onwards; it is estimated that an audience of 20 millions or so watched tank films. Others would have been exposed to them through cameo appearances in war films, as well as merchandise, such as tank handbags, teapots, moneyboxes and napkins (Tate 72-73). The tank was further anthropomorphized in the British press, becoming a tame but easily disquieting presence, a fantasy able to "produce a fantasmatic, infantile, *and pleasurable* relationship to the war and its objects" (Tate 77). The tank is compact, cocooned and self-contained; its mechanical prowess protected rather than threatened men's vulnerable bodies in battle, making one body with the crew inside. The tank provided the limbs and tentacles of an articulated mechanical creature, (Tate 77-78) affording it pliable and ambiguous erotic symbolism.

---

[4] Marinetti, "L'aerocanzone delle parole nuove," (1). For a debate concerning colonial and anti-technological discourses, see Adas 348-63.

This very ambiguous combination of mechanized humanity, protecting self-sufficiency and erotic pleasure fantasy, sits powerfully at the core of Marinetti's *Alcòva*. Naming and language offer clues to Marinetti's sexual exploitation of this war icon as well. Larger models of early tanks were, in fact, designated as "Mothers" and came in both female and male forms, determined by minor morphological variants. As Tate perceptively observes, "the language of Willie and Mother, male and female, and hermaphrodite, is scattered throughout the early tank writings," and this language is further circumstantial in the British press, war memoirs and literature (78-79). Reassured of his own virility and sexual prowess, man is transfigured and "spiritualized" through his mastery of technology, enacting a fantasy of masculine nationalism and technological domination over nature.

Aggression and sexuality underpin Marinetti's religious patriotism throughout, "a conceit on the analogy of the will dominating reality and being invincible like machines" (Wagstaff 153). The original cover of this novel, censored on publication, featured a small tank bearing an Italian tri-coloured flag penetrating a naked woman, whose breasts were clearly visible, lying in the missionary position (Scudiero). Sex becomes Marinetti's chosen rhetoric of national identity: *L'alcòva d'acciaio* "is all sex: there is not a cloud, not a hill, not a machine that is not described in sexual terms" (Wagstaff 157). For Christine Poggi this stems from Marinetti's fetishistic virility fantasy, "precisely because nature is understood as the locus of the feminine and the maternal, it must be opposed and displaced by both the machine, and its symbolic ally, matter (sheer dynamic physicality)" (24).

The tank offers individual release and disenfranchisement from sexual and cultural inhibitions, the promise of "new kinds of agency — enabling the human body to enter zones which were previously impenetrable". In forward and backward erotic thrusts, the "human subject, like evolution, is imagined as moving simultaneously forwards into the machine age and backwards into the primeval slime — a movement both terrifying and pleasurable" (Tate 83). Providing a fantasy of transcendence and apotheosis for the superman, man is both dead and alive in his metallized shell and armour: now he is truly undead. Indeed, man cannot die as he is already reified. He is therefore truly immortal.

According to Poggi, however, the ultimate, overarching goal of *Alcòva* is patriotic, demanding "a corresponding transformation of the earth itself, from an unmarked, deterritorialized feminine ground, to the delimited and embodied territory of the nation" (31). In highlighting Marinetti's equation of woman with war, Sartini Blum echoes Poggi's views (99). Braun further talks of a "hypermasculine vision of armoured bodies" (11). The mythic penetration of Italy, via its armoured car n. 74, does not merely expose Marinetti's ambiguous eroticization of war technology, but also leads to the articulation of a new and dual, both civilized and barbaric, identity, postulating Marinetti's vision for postwar Futurism in terms of subjection to the authority of the State (Braun 11). As such, Marinetti's *Alcòva d'acciaio* may be sowing the seeds of a "metallization" as understood by J. T. Schnapp; constructing a locus of mechanized, metallic and ultimately chaste mass identity, it is posited as the ideal partner of a fascist revolution and, shortly to come, of fascist demographic campaigns. Not accidentally, the truck deployed in the 1934 travelling mass spectacle *18BL* was significantly called "*Mother* Giberna" (Schnapp 130-31).

Madrepatria
The figure of the mother, particularly the mother of the *caduto* or *milite ignoto*, enjoys unrivalled status in nationalist discourse more widely. As such, it has been studied extensively, together with its implications for memory, commemoration and national identity.[5] In Italy too, the powerful symbolic connection between war, mother and nation is quickly captured and exploited during warfare and in its aftermath. Mother becomes a symbolic blank canvas whose Catholic underpinnings intersect a plethora of diverse discourses and where postwar demographic policies of mourning and commemoration, from national revanchism to *Irredentismo*, are powerfully mobilized and, frequently, even homogenized. Drawing on an undercurrent of national pursuit nurtured within *Irredentismo*, the Italian-Triestine resistance to Austro-Hungarian rule, which led to mystical loyalties as well as enthusiastic enlistment in the Italian rank and file (Pizzi 101-02), Giani Stuparich's novel *Ritorneranno* aims to encapsulate precisely that purportedly feminine cluster of qualities (e.g. emotional nature, cult of the past, custodian of the hearth) perceived as symbolic of nation as well as tradition, order, respectability (Mosse, *Nationalism and Sexuality* 17-18). Historical evidence further testifies that Triestine Italian mothers were overwhelmingly patriotic and it was frequently under their influence that their male offsprings enlisted to fight on the side of Italy. Denied a decisional, proactive role in the public sphere, women seem to have exercised enormous influence indirectly on their children in a pro-Italian, patriotic direction. Phantoms of mothers, wives and sisters crowd *Ritorneranno*, together with much First World War literature of the era from the contended borderlands in the Italian northeast.

For realist novelist Giani Stuparich — war veteran and survivor, haunted throughout by the unbearable guilt of surviving his brother Carlo and his best friend Scipio Slataper, both killed in action — his own mother, Gisella Gentilli, became an epitome of motherhood and most of his fiction is devoted to idealizing her exemplary role. Family-oriented, patriotic, staunchly Italian, Gentilli was a constant source of inspiration for Stuparich who transposed her into endless

---

[5] A large bibliography has amassed around the topic of the mourning, commemoration and nationalism of mothers of dead soldiers in the First World War in the last few decades. To cite only three collective titles, see Evans; Mosse, *Fallen Soldiers*; and Gillis. See also Pizzi, "Maternal Nationalism," in *A City in Search of an Author*, 128-37.

fictional characters, including mother Carolina, the protagonist and *primum mobile* of *Ritorneranno*. Like the Virgin Mary, the mother's face is invariably "santo e lucente," her breath hovers and impregnates the trenches in Stuparich's earlier war diary *Guerra del Quindici* (1931).[6] *Guerra del Quindici* is a fine example of Triestine literature that looks at the Great War as a *summa* of nationalist experience via a maternally inspired *Irredentismo*: "Il cannone romba ora con rabbia soffocata. [...] Fra pelle e carne mi serpeggia un brivido improvviso: 'mamma': pensiero, sentimento indefinibile, come un'essenza che riempie tutto. Mi perdo e mi tremano le gambe" (Stuparich, *Guerra* 8). Defending Trieste and the nation become equated to defending one's own mother. The city itself acquires the status of a "Holy Land", enclosing the mother as if within a sanctuary. Penetrating into Trieste as liberating soldiers is equivalent to penetrating the sancta sanctorum of the city, where mother sits enthroned (Pizzi 130).

Similarly, Stuparich's mother Gisella is the pivot of *Ritorneranno* (1941), set between 1915 and 1918 and the most admittedly autobiographical of all of Stuparich's novels despite its overtly fictional approach. Significantly set during a First World War coloured by Risorgimental values, though written and published in the context of a more heavily politicized Second World War, *Ritorneranno* portrays Trieste in widow's weeds and reinforces maternal nationalism as embodied in the character of Carolina Vidali and, on a minor scale, Carolina's daughter Angela. A comparable, if secondary, character, Angela carries the patriotic flair of Carolina to the streets and piers of Trieste, connecting it powerfully with a broader circle of young Italian women in the Austrian city militantly engaged in pro-Italian activities.

A collectivity of seamstresses, patiently sewing together Italian flags, proselytizing on behalf of the Italian cause, saluting one another in the name of the Italian King, Victor Emmanuel, is juxtaposed to a Slovene nation progressively rising to national consciousness, embodied by the pivotal character Berta, the Slovenian maid in the middle-class Italian household. Berta's experience is also one of being disconnected from her elected motherland, and yet it could not be further removed from that of Carolina and of Berta's contemporary, Angela. Berta's reality is a secretive, hushed one made up of political pamphlets handed out surreptitiously, firmly tied to the Austro-Hungarian motherland so unpopular with her Italian employers. Acquisition of Slovenian national identity (Berta) counterbalances acquired Italian identity (Angela): while the former is descended from Dusan, Berta's nationalist fiancé, the latter follows a strict matrilineal genealogy. As observed by Galofaro (97), an "entanglement" between Italian and Slovenian nationalism is powerfully staged here, via the symmetrical

---

[6] I am drawing extensively from Chapter 3 of my study, *A City in Search of an Author: The Literary Identity of Trieste*

national and identitarian trajectories of Berta, the Slovenian maid of the middle-class Italian establishment — whose national and cultural awakening goes hand in hand with acquisition of literacy and traditional middle class values — and Angela, the educated Italian patriot. Angela, in particular, will take on the focal perspective of a mystical nationalism with sexual overtones.

Could Marinetti's orgiastic copulations with, or through, an armoured car during warfare and Stuparich's patriotic carnival in the context of an impromptu civilian gathering have anything in common? Could "the iron ring of the eternal 'mother image, as Macciocchi has it (69), be at work both in Stuparich and Marinetti? Stuparich's fictional account of the arrival of Italian ships at St. Carlo's pier in Trieste on 3 November 1918, marking the end of the War as well as the onset of Italian rule in Trieste, is related at length in the central pages of *Ritorneranno*. This passage provides compelling evidence of a nationalism so germaine to "female" emotion and emotivity as to translate easily into a state of sexual arousal and orgasmic dispersion. It is worth quoting the passage in question at length:

Un gelo le salì su per le ginocchia, l'affanno del cuore le venne alla gola. Le parve che la superficie del mare s'alzasse, potente, irresistibile. Fu presa da paura: "Non così, non così, è troppo": udì come una lamentevole voce alzarsi dalla propria anima. Poi tante voci le si incrociarono nell'anima: un tumulto. [...] I morti venivano avanti nella luce con le loro ombre, i vivi tendevano le mani ai vivi. La libertà di sentire e di sentirsi irrompeva da ogni parte con una veemenza da togliere il respiro; la gioia era così violenta da far male. Dentro la fiamma del sangue che si ravvivava, tutti i ricordi dei sacrifizi e delle sofferenze, dei sussulti e dei terrori, dei pianti e delle speranze, erano belli, bruciavano chiari come materia secca a un fuoco vigoroso. [...] La visione interiore temprava l'animo a sostenere la realtà. [...] sembrava che il suolo della città si sradicasse per muovere incontro alle navi. Le grida s'erano raccolte in canti, i canti disuguali diventavano un canto solo, le voci una voce sola, un tuono.

(Stuparich, *Ritorneranno* 564-65)

Emotion, affect and a sense of the numinous are powerfully commingled here against the backdrop of national triumph and glory. On the pier, Angela undergoes a veritable mystical experience, where awe for divinity, mystic sexuality and the resonance of voices in the soul, bringing about a dissolution of the threshold between life and death, and a final vision of the purgatorial burning flame. The latter will shortly become an overpowering symbol of nationalism, via D'Annunzio, in Fascism's re-envisioning of ancient Rome. Angela's collapse in the arms of her father Domenico at the end of this emotionally charged scene points to the climax of a sexual-mystical experience, where sexual arousal becomes a conduit for bellicist and national commitment. This emotional charge and dramatic tension are heightened throughout, occasionally degenerating into grotesque bacchanalia. Nonetheless, Trieste emerges as the most patriotic city in Italy, as well as a city crushed down by the weight of its schizophrenic and dishomogenous history: a city of shadow, a city of ghosts.

From Marinetti's *L'alcòva d'acciaio* to Giani Stuparich's *Ritorneranno*

The religious import of nationalism is no novelty. Giuseppe Mazzini, who was crucially if belatedly influential in Trieste via the periodical *La voce*, was no stranger to it. If nation equals representation, a value of symbolic and even existential import, it will be inevitably entangled with the imaginary, including the religious imaginary. The noun itself *Irredentismo* is etymologically rooted in religious experience and discourse and it is safe to assert that in Trieste *Irredentismo* was, in many respects, a secularized form of religion (Hobsbawm and Ranger 303) — a religion so ambitious as to symbolically replace the Catholic Church, traditionally associated in Trieste with the Slav clergy and the Austro-Hungarian Empire. The choice of the Italian nation was comparable to a religious conversion and Trieste carried the enthusiastic response of a novice. The high priestesses of this religion were mothers, sisters and girlfriends, vicarious custodians of patriotic values at home while the soldiers defended them at the front.

Conclusion

Whether through the medium of technology, technologized bodies and war machinery, or via more conventional means drawing on mystical and *Risorgimento* loyalties, women, mothers and female bodies emerge in both Marinetti's and Stuparich's narratives as *foci* of national identity. They are beacons of national values rooted firmly in symbol and culture, even religion, precisely at the challenging First World War moment when the politics of aggressive expansion, land grabbing, and population shifts occur under the name of nation on the international stage. While Stuparich's *Ritorneranno* and Marinetti's *L'alcòva d'acciaio* could be regarded in many respects as polar opposites (stylistically, aesthetically, thematically), they are nonetheless connected by an entanglement of sexual and national politics that informs them both. Written and published after the First World War, contending with radically altered socio-political contexts, both novels nonetheless vividly capture and propound the ambiguous sexual and national politics emerging in the post-war period, where a cyborg-like woman (Haraway) is situated within imageries of war technology or, alternatively, traditional seamstressing, domesticity and low-tech custody of the family hearth. Furthermore, sexuality emerges here as a shared frame of reference within Italian modernity, a *locus* where national and nationalistic discourses are easily accommodated. In their comparable conflation of woman and nation, *L'alcòva d'acciaio* and *Ritorneranno* provide a template for women under Fascism and their ambiguous status, captured between febrile mechanical activism, patriarchal possession, demographic policies and elegiac guardianship of home and nation.

Institute of Modern Languages Research
School of Advanced Study, University of London

Works Cited

Adas, Michael. *Machines as the Measure of Men. Science, Technology and Ideologies of Western Dominance*. Ithaca: Cornell UP, 1989.
Braun, Emily. "Vulgarians at the Gate." *Boccioni's Materia: A Futurist Masterpiece and the Avantgarde in Milan and Paris*. Ed. Laura Mattioli Rossi. New York: Guggenheim, 2004.
De Maria, Luciano. "Introduzione." *Teoria e invenzione futurista* XXVII-C.
Evans, Suzanne. *Mothers of Heroes, Mothers of Martyrs: World War I and the Politics of Grief.* Montreal: McGill-Queen's UP, 2007.
Galofaro, Francesco. "Slavi si nasce o si diventa? La costituzione del Soggetto in 'Ritorneranno' di G. Stuparich." *E/C* 6.11-12 (2012).
Giddens, Anthony. *Violence and the Nation State*. Berkeley: U of California P, 1987.
Gillis, John R., ed. *Commemorations: The Politics of National Identity*. Princeton: Princeton UP, 1994.
Haraway, Donna J. *Simians, Cyborgs and Women: The Reinvention of Nature*. London: Free Association, 1991.
Herf, Jeffrey. *Reactionary Modernism. Technology, Culture, and Politics in Weimar and the Third Reich*. Cambridge: Cambridge UP, 1984.
Hobsbawm, Eric, and Terence Ranger, eds. *The Invention of Tradition*. Cambridge: Cambridge UP, 1983.
Kern, Stephen. *The Culture of Time and Space 1880-1918*. London: Weidenfeld and Nicholson, 1983.
Lista, Giovanni. *Arte e politica. Il futurismo di sinistra in Italia*. Milano: Mudima, 2009.
Macciocchi, Maria Antonietta. "Female Sexuality in Fascist Ideology." *Feminist Review* 1 (1979): 67-82.
Marinetti, Filippo Tommaso. "L'aerocanzone delle parole nuove," 1939, 1-2. Marinetti correspondence and papers. Series I, box 15, n. 2. The J. P. Getty Research Institute Library, Los Angeles.
_____. *L'alcòva d'acciaio: romanzo vissuto*. Milano: Vitagliano, 1921.
_____. Special collections. Series V. Newspaper clippings. The J. P. Getty Research Institute Library, Los Angeles.
_____. *Teoria e invenzione futurista*. Ed. Luciano De Maria. Milan: Mondadori, 1996.
Morasso, Mario. *La nuova guerra: Armi, combattenti, battaglie*. Milano: Treves, 1914.
Mosse, George L. *Fallen Soldiers: Reshaping the Memory of the World Wars*. Oxford, New York, Toronto: Oxford UP, 1990.
_____. *Nationalism and Sexuality: Respectability and Abnormal Sexuality in Modern Europe*. New York: Fertig, 1985.
Pizzi, Katia. *A City in Search of an Author: The Literary Identity of Trieste*. London: Sheffield Academic Press, 2001.
Platone, Augusto. *L'uomo e la macchina*. Roma: Edizioni Futuriste di "Poesia," 1941.
Poggi, Christine. "Dreams of Metallized Flesh: Futurism and the Masculine Body." *Modernism/Modernity* 4.3 (1997).
Salaris, Claudia. *Alla festa della rivoluzione. Artisti e libertari con D'Annunzio a Fiume*. Bologna: Il Mulino, 2002.
Sartini Blum, Cinzia. *The Other Modernism: F. T. Marinetti's Futurist Fiction of Power*. Berkely: U of California P, 1996.
Schnapp, Jeffrey T. *18BL. Mussolini e l'opera d'arte di massa*. Milano: Garzanti, 1996.

From Marinetti's *L'alcòva d'acciaio* to Giani Stuparich's *Ritorneranno* 319

Scudiero, Maurizio. "The Futurist Art Book." Bologna Art Book Fair, 21 Sept. 2007. Public lecture.
Stuparich, Giani. *Guerra del Quindici*. 1931. Torino: Einaudi, 1980.
_____. *Ritorneranno*. Milano: Garzanti, 1944.
Tate, Trudi. "The Culture of the Tank, 1916-1918." *Modernism/Modernity*. 4.1 (1997).
Virilio, Paul. *Speed and Politics. An Essay on Dromology*. Los Angeles: Semiotext(e), 2006.
Wagstaff, Christopher. "Dead Man Erect: F. T.Marinetti, *L'alcòva d'acciaio*." *The First World War in Fiction*. Ed. Holger Klein. London: Macmillan, 1976.

Simona Storchi

Ardengo Soffici's *Rete mediterranea*: The Aesthetics and Politics of Post-war Modernism

The periodical *Rete mediterranea*, entirely written and edited by Ardengo Soffici, was published by Vallecchi on a quarterly basis between March and December 1920. A short-lived project (only four issues were published), it was conceived after the equally short-lived periodical *La Vraie Italie*, which Soffici had co-edited with Giovanni Papini between 1919 and 1920. Although it has received some critical attention, *Rete mediterranea* has not been extensively explored. According to Mario Richter, the magazine was used by Soffici to voice the idea of a national redemption, as he was convinced that the war had shown Italy's maturity and ability to lead other nations (Richter, *Papini e Soffici* 177). Intellectual historian Walter Adamson has noted how *Rete mediterranea* was used to promote Soffici's post-war "retrogardism" and was the result of the artist's increasing detachment from Papini and Prezzolini's views, particularly with regard to Soffici's antisocialism and support for Mussolini and D'Annunzio's occupation of Fiume (*Avant-Garde Florence* 245-47 and "Soffici and the Religion of Art" 60-61; Papini and Soffici 73-80). Simonetta Bartolini too has stressed how Soffici had grown increasingly dissatisfied with Papini's editorial line in *La Vraie Italie*, particularly as it avoided overt politicization. She describes 1919 as Soffici's *annus horribilis*, in that the post-war situation presented itself as very different from what he had envisaged. The treaty of Versailles had resulted in a disappointing outcome for Italy, causing a negative reaction among war veterans, who saw the dissolution of the pre-war world, but could not entertain the prospect of a new one. On a personal level, Soffici found himself at odds with Papini and Prezzolini, just as he no longer had a periodical to use for his cultural and political militancy. At the same time, his artistic development had been interrupted by the war and needed reflection and revision, after four years at the front (Bartolini, *Ardengo Soffici* 353-54). In this context, Bartolini defines *Rete mediterranea* as "la rivista della solitudine, della riflessione, dopo la temperie bellica, del 'richiamo all'ordine'" ("Introduzione" 15). She also stresses the specific post-war dimension of the magazine, by stating,

Rete mediterranea è il naturale sfogo dell'intellettuale maturato nella guerra e tornato a una vita civile carico di un bagaglio umano, spirituale ed esistenziale che non poteva essere deposto in fondo a un armadio con la divisa grigioverde. Al tempo stesso essa diventa il luogo esclusivo [...] nel quale elaborare il lutto provocato dalla scomparsa di alcune illusioni da una parte (la guerra risolutrice, salvifica o, per dirla con il lessico futurista, igienizzante), e di un mondo (quello di prima della guerra, appunto), dall'altra.

(*Ardengo Soffici* 355)

While an atmosphere of *rappel à l'ordre* undoubtedly pervades Soffici's magazine, the inscription of *Rete mediterranea* exclusively within the narrow framework of the post-war return to order seems somewhat reductive, as is the interpretation of the magazine as a personal space created by Soffici to mourn the loss of the pre-war world and its illusions.

This article proposes instead a reading of *Rete mediterranea* which takes into account its strong political component, both in its direct discussion of political matters and in its politicization of the artistic discourse. According to this reading, *Rete mediterranea* cannot be simply considered as "la voce sofficiana in un panorama culturale ormai avviato [...] verso una revisione delle esperienze culturali prebelliche per un recupero della tradizione classica, da leggersi in chiave moderna," as Bartolini puts it ("Introduzione" 15). In particular, the rethinking of the relationship between art and politics makes the magazine an important voice in the post-war artistic and intellectual debates. By focusing on Soffici's position on a number of key themes, both artistic and political — such as the role of the artist-veteran in the creation of post-war national culture, the relationship between classical heritage and modern art, the place of Italy in the European artistic scene, the rise of Socialism and the desire to regenerate both culture and politics after the experience of the war — the article will demonstrate how the Tuscan artist reconfigured the relationship between art and life that had been at the core of the avant-garde experience (Bürger) and reviewed the role of the artist in the post-war context. Finally, the article will shed light on the politicization of Modernism and the forging of ideological links between aesthetics and politics in the crucial transition between the end of the war and the rise of Fascism, which paved the way for the conceptualization of the relationship between culture and politics during the fascist regime.

The Artist-Veteran and the Politics of War Memory
It is significant that *Rete mediterranea* was conceived and published immediately after *La Vraie Italie*. Written in French, the latter had meant to address an international audience and act as an intellectual link between Italy and other countries. As Luca Somigli has noted, the aim of *La Vraie Italie* was to make Italy better known abroad, improve its relations with the other nations that had emerged victorious from the war and foster greater cooperation between the so-called "sister nations," Italy and France, thereby accomplishing both a cultural and a political mission (Somigli 486; see also De Carlis 16 and Adamson, *Avant-Garde Florence* 236). Despite its short life and the disagreements between Papini and Soffici, *La Vraie Italie*, Somigli argues, had been crucial, as it was representative of the crisis of that articulation of the

relationship between art and politics which had marked avant-garde culture and had characterized a number of magazines (such as, for instance, *Lacerba* and *L'Italia futurista*). *La Vraie Italie* was symptomatic of that crisis, for, despite its nationalist programme, it missed, according to Somigli, "the faith in the power of art to renew and transform lived experience by giving shape to modernity and its radical innovations in science, technology and social and economic relations" (489-90).

I would like to argue that at the core of the *Rete mediterranea* project is precisely the attempt to reconfigure the relationship between art and life that had characterized the pre-war avant-garde movements and that seemed to have been lost in the post-war context. In the magazine Soffici reclaimed a political role for art, rethinking the pre-war avant-garde experience and reshaping the artistic and political trajectory of Italian Modernism in the post-war years. After surviving the experience of the trenches, the artist reconfigured his role both as a cultural operator and a veteran, embodying a double function, equally artistic and political. In this context, the experience of the avant-garde was key in the integration of the political agenda into the artistic discourse. As Adamson has observed, the world of 1918 was profoundly different from the one in which the avant-garde had taken shape. The cultural avant-garde had largely collapsed in the war and the sense of political crisis in Italy created the expectation of an impending system change in politics, with Socialism looming larger than in the pre-war years as a result of the Bolshevik revolution ("Soffici and the Religion of Art" 60). After the war, Tuscan avant-gardists, including Soffici, distanced themselves from pre-war modernism not on the question of the latter's project of spiritual renewal, but on their assessment of the aesthetic and political means needed to fulfil it (Adamson, *Embattled Avant-Gardes* 252). Avant-gardism was reconceptualized in terms of a new model, Adamson argues, which entailed a mass movement incorporating the modernist spiritual revolution as the basis for a genuine populist aesthetics politics. These would be nationalist rather than internationalist, reject experimentalism and be based on a communal celebration of heritage and on a restoration of those aesthetic values associated with the great moments of the Italian past ("Soffici and the Religion of Art" 60). What emerges from a close reading of *Rete mediterranea* is, therefore, not so much a retro-gardist "call for order," but a re-elaboration of the avant-garde experience in the post-war context. The aims of *Rete mediterranea* were to reposition the artist after the war, giving him the political legitimacy that derived from having fought in the trenches, to identify the area of intervention for the artist in an aesthetic/political reconfigured field, and to prioritise the creation of a national forum for the discussion of Italian art and politics. Within this framework, the classicism championed by the magazine under the Mediterranean banner proclaimed in the title was not an indicator of a detachment from politics, but of a shift in discourses of engagement and a reformulation of aesthetic politics, in which classical references assumed a political value and in which the artistic discourse was strictly interrelated with the political.

Prior to the publication of *Rete mediterranea*, Soffici had chartered the transformation he had undergone in the trenches in his war writings, *Kobilek* (1918) and *La ritirata del Friuli* (1919), in which the artist had been developing a war narrative marked by a sense of interclass comradeship engendered by the war effort and also some form of communion between the officers and the soldiers. This communion posited unity in a newly found national cohesion, which was equally distinct from the high command of the army and the Italian political leadership (Isnenghi 193-95 and 336). That *Rete mediterranea* is informed by the experience of the war is reinforced by the publication in instalments in the magazine of Soffici's war memoir "Errore di coincidenza." This was the diary of Soffici's hospital stay in the summer of 1917, prior to the events narrated in *Kobilek*, after he had been hit and wounded by shrapnel. "Errore di coincidenza" is a personal recollection of hospital life, which allows Soffici also to reflect on the corporeal dimension of the war, devoting attention to the pain, mutilation, recurrent visions of death and trauma of shell-shock, but also to the human dimension of the war, the soldiers' courage, resilience and good humour, their solidarity and comradeship. The "errore di coincidenza," as Soffici explains, is the chance by which life and death are dispensed by fate and the random events that allow an individual to escape death ("Errore di coincidenza," (a), 243-46).

The focus on hospital life in Soffici's diary moves the attention away from life on the battlefield and in the trenches to concentrate instead on the human repercussions of the war, representing the soldiers in their most vulnerable moment but also showing their courage and resilience. It also focuses on survival, thereby reversing the apocalyptic tendency of war writing (Winter 178-303), and creates a dialectical relationship between life and death, which is reiterated by the memoir's title. The strong sense of camaraderie engendered by the war and the idea of the war as a unifying experience which resulted in a renewed national community, and had featured prominently in previous memoirs, are still present here and they are deployed instrumentally to inscribe the soldiers in a cross-class national narrative engendered by the conflict. The emphasis on the corporeal dimension of the war allows the discourse of the nation to be extended to the bodies of the wounded or the dead soldiers, proposing an almost metonymical association between the soldier's body and the fatherland:

Laggiù è il Carso. [...] Quella soave collina che il sole accarezza amorosamente e tinge dei suoi ultimi raggi, la gioventù d'Italia [...] l'arrossa essa pure e la inzuppa del proprio sangue; in tutto quel riposo c'è anche il riposo di migliaia e migliaia di tombe. Laggiù è la bellezza, ma insieme lo strazio e tutta la passione della Patria.
E allora capisco qual è la forza che m'avvince a quel lembo di terra e di cielo, la cui immagine porterò sempre con me.

("Errore di coincidenza" (b) 352)

The entries of "Errore di coincidenza" create a thread which acts as a narrative counterpoint to the reflections carried out in the other sections of *Rete mediterranea*. The experience of the war underpins Soffici's intellectual, ideological and artistic direction in the post-war years. Nonetheless, as Bartolini rightly points out, the core of *Rete mediterranea* is no longer the narration of the war events but on how they affected Soffici's view of the world (*Ardengo Soffici* 357). The episodes narrated in the memoir reinforce Soffici's position with the consequent legitimation deriving from his first-hand experience of the war. The narrated events and experiences reiterate the significance both of the war as a transformative event and its account as a shaping factor in the narrative of national identity.

The New Nation and the Myth of the Mediterranean
All four issues of *Rete mediterranea* opened with a feature article, which was followed by a section entitled "Ricordi di vita artistica e letteraria," in which Soffici reminisced about his encounters with such artists and intellectuals as Remy de Gourmont, Giovanni Boine, Guillaume Apollinaire and Léon Bloy. A substantial section of the magazine was devoted to a section entitled "Taccuino," a collection of Soffici's personal reflections on literature, art, philosophy and politics, as well as anecdotes of his life. As Soffici's space for unstructured reflection, the "Taccuino" was the most ideologically connoted part of the magazine.

The first issue of *Rete mediterranea* opens with the feature article "Dichiarazione preliminare," a declaration of intents aimed at situating the periodical within the specificity of the post-war context. Soffici's opening statement declares: "Sono uscito dalla guerra un altro uomo; e come tale intendo presentarmi subito ai lettori di questa mia pubblicazione periodica" ("Dichiarazione preliminare" 3). The declaration is followed by a reflection on the circumstances that led to the war, with the expectations that it generated among artists and intellectuals, particularly those, like Soffici, who were committed to the modernization of Italian culture. But what Soffici stresses above all is how the war offered the occasion to rethink the social preconceptions that had characterised the discursive and artistic practices of the avant-garde. The anti-bourgeois rhetoric that had permeated the avant-gardist "revolutionary orgy," as he called it ("Dichiarazione preliminare" 5), was repudiated in the name of a rediscovery of the value of the bourgeoisie. Quoting a passage from *Kobilek*, he declares:

[...] mi rendo conto, dopo un'esperienza di due anni di vita militare, di quanto sia ingiusto e vano il confinarsi, come ho fatto io, in un circolo di gente che fa il nostro proprio mestiere; fra artisti, poeti, filosofi, o sedicenti tali. Questa guerra avrà insegnato a molti di noi, uomini partigiani, membri di *élites* discutibili, quanta umanità, bellezza, spontaneità di vita e di sensi si trovi oltre i nostri confini artificiali, fra i componenti, poco vistosi ma non per questo meno degni, di quella massa, che è poi quasi tutta l'umanità, e che noi

battezziamo in blocco e con disprezzo: borghesia!
("Dichiarazione preliminare" 7; *Kobilek* 27).

As his previous war writings reiterated, Soffici's reappraisal of the bourgeoisie is linked to a critique of the ruling class (Isnenghi 336). Therefore, what Soffici names here as the "bourgeoisie" is to be understood as the petty bourgeoisie, which is incorporated in the more general notion of "la massa" and somehow distanced from the military and political elites. The artist's appreciation of the bourgeoisie is also presented as a polemical rethinking of the avant-garde's anti-bourgeois stance. The war had exposed the illusory character of any form of artistic elitism, repositioning it within the self-excluding attitude which had characterized bohemian artistic circles in capitalist society, and had created the conditions for a reformulation of the relationship between art and society. The special significance of the figure of the artist-veteran allows the artist to rethink his social role; the oppositional attitude and the critique of the social, political and moral values of modernity, that had characterized the position of the artist since the nineteenth century (Wilson 18), are reconsidered in favour of a self-positioning within a new elite, at the same time is artistic and political, who claims to represent the new Italy emerging from the trenches and whose aim is to delegitimize a ruling class whose weakness had been exposed by the war (Isnenghi 336).

Soffici justifies the creation of his new periodical by stressing the notion of *maturità* acquired with the war and by placing a specific emphasis in the role of the conflict in transforming the artistic agenda and the intellectual life of the nation. On a personal level, he explains how the prolonged acquaintance with pain, danger, tragic events, and above all the constant presence of death, have had a sobering effect and instilled a sense of gravity, austerity and purity, resulting in a spiritual catharsis: "In guerra, davanti al rischio imminente e continuo, l'uomo è nudo [...]. In quel terribile agone della morte, tutti appariamo a tutti veri e genuini. E nulla è più grande e bello di questo ritorno umano nella luce all'innocenza prima" ("Dichiarazione preliminare" 14). Such a sense of regeneration brought about by the war led to a rejection of the perceived falseness and vacuity equally affecting contemporary art — particularly in its obsession with "returns"— and politics, on both a national and international level. The artist attributes the rethinking of his attitude to a number of factors resulting from the war, including a renewed appreciation of the formerly vilified bourgeoisie, the consequent repulsion towards an unengaged intellectual class and a revitalised commitment to serve the national cause and promote national heritage, an assertion of the simple values of human solidarity, and a rejection of anything considered "falso and sofisticato". These factors coalesce in a cult of the nation which collapses aesthetics into politics:

Trovo che un culto geloso della nazione nel suo insieme vivo e concreto, storico ed in atto è adesso più che mai una condizione imprescindibile di forza animatrice, del profondo senso dell'individualità, e pertanto di stile originale nel pensiero e nell'espressione lirica. Considero perciò con avversione ogni forma di misconoscenza o tradimento di questa idea luminosa nei secoli, incorruttibile, pregnante e che è la sostanza stessa del nostro essere geniale. Poiché non è possibile ammettere, senza, nello stesso tempo, dar prova d'infantilità, o di ottusità intellettuale, che quello che è la materia stessa della nostra più diretta osservazione, della nostra conoscenza più intima, della nostra creazione come è tutto quello che costituisce la patria — costumi, lingua, luoghi, pensiero e discendenza — possa divenir mai indifferente a chi vive al di sopra degli interessi corporali e transitori.

("Dichiarazione preliminare" 17)

The nation is at the core of Soffici's post-war artistic programme and the self-professed *maturità* is anchored to a strong national agenda. Thus this conviction materializes in a sense of sympathy for, and communion with, what he calls the "anima della stirpe," a cult of the nation and an aversion to any misrecognition of the national idea. Soffici proclaims a belief in an art rooted in historical culture and an admiration for "il semplice, il vero, il reale" ("Dichiarazione preliminare" 18). All this, he claims, must not be interpreted as conservatism or a return to the past, but rather as the sense of personal and collective continuation, in harmony with a self that had been lost amidst the pre-war chaos and that the experience of the war had helped to recover. Simplicity, truthfulness and realism are ambiguously posited both as moral and artistic categories, creating a discourse which conflates the aesthetic and the political. As Emilio Gentile notes, the veterans returning from the war felt that they had a mission to carry out in the name of the nation. Their politics expressed "l'odio verso gli istituti rappresentativi, considerati strumenti di potere nelle mani di pochi politicanti corrotti, e il disprezzo per la politica dei partiti in nome d'una *politica totale*, identificazione di stato e nazione, di produttore e cittadino, di individuo e massa, fusi in una mistica unità di militanti al servizio della collettività rigenerata" (Gentile, *Le origini* 128). The nationalism that had been bound up with Modernism since the end of the nineteenth century, is deployed here to emphasize the equation between national tradition and genuine culture (Adamson, *Embattled Avant-Gardes* 13-14). In this sense, the periodical's title, *Rete mediterranea*, is programmatic. With regard to it, Soffici declares:

Ho scelto il titolo *Rete mediterranea*, per significare la mia intenzione di creare un centro di collegamento fra i punti sensibili della civiltà, appunto, mediterranea, che credo superiore a tutte. Come sono un fervente dell'italianità, così il mio amore e la mia fede si estendono come una rete a tutto quanto di solare è nel pensiero e nell'arte delle nazioni affini, intorno al glorioso bacino, e che all'Italia si riconnette per ascendenza o discendenza. E in quanto al programma, esso può riassumersi in questo. Difesa e illustrazione della stessa cultura mediterranea, con l'affermazione insieme, di un'energia personale nella sua fase di pieno sviluppo.

("Dichiarazione preliminare" 19-20)

By conflating the notion of *mediterraneità*, with all its cultural and political implications, with that of the nation, Soffici proposes an artistic programme in which aesthetics and politics are interwoven in a single discourse. The end of the war and the subsequent return to order proclaimed at an artistic level, far from removing the artist/intellectual from the arena of political commitment, rewrites his role as the creator of an ideology for the new nation emerging from the conflict. The palingenetic stance of the cultural discourse is key to the self-positioning of the intellectual in this new context. The creation of a periodical such as *Rete mediterranea* is evidence of Soffici's self-assigned political mission, reinstated by his criticism of the position taken by such contemporary periodicals as *La ronda*, which deliberately proclaimed an abstention from political matters and the return to formal values (Soffici, "Ritorni"). By distancing himself from *La ronda*'s abstentionist attitude towards politics, Soffici rewrites the agenda for the modernist intellectual in the post-war years, by reworking the legacy of the avant-garde experience and rethinking the relationship between art and politics.

The notion of *mediterraneità*, expressed both by the title and the content of the periodical, alludes to an instrumental use of the myth of the Mediterranean and was employed by Soffici on several levels. First of all it reiterated and highlighted the artistic and cultural link — as well as the political alliance established by the war — that united major centres of artistic excellence in Europe, with particular reference to France and Italy. Therefore, *Rete mediterranea* was positioned, to an extent, as a continuation of the programme carried out by *La Vraie Italie*. However, with respect to the outward-looking position adopted by the latter, rather than focusing on an international audience, *Rete mediterranea* adopted a more inward-looking approach, intent on emphasizing the idea of the primacy of the Italian nation to an internal readership. The amplification of the geographical area, from an exclusive axis established between Italy and France to the wider, albeit undefined, idea of the Mediterranean, served to reposition Italy as the cultural centre of gravity of Southern Europe, thereby claiming the primacy of Italy with respect to France. It also reinforced the opposition between the Northern and Southern European cultures that had dominated the cultural discourse during the war years.[1] The unspecific approach to the notion of the Mediterranean recalled echoes of Greco-Roman classical civilization and reclaimed Italy's central role in the development of Western culture. The Mediterranean was therefore used as a concept that could resonate both at an artistic and at a political level.

Mediterraneanism has a specific place in Western culture and, as Berry Bergdol has argued, one that is characterized by a tendency both towards "radical change" and "atemporal fullness" (xv). The notion is composed of a

---

[1] In this regard, I refer to, for instance, Soffici himself, "Per la Guerra," and his contemporary Papini, "Ciò che dobbiamo alla Francia"; among critics, see Somigli 477; Adamson, *Avant-Garde Florence* 192-95; Gentile, *L'apocalisse* 195-242.

complex articulation of motifs which encompass a celebration of the primacy of Greco-Roman classicism as well as vernacular regionalism and therefore it can incorporate both nationalist and regionalist arguments. For this reason, as Benedetto Gravagnuolo notes, *mediterraneità* is not to be confused with *romanità*. He identifies "many affinities of climate, traditions, topography, and even ethnic traits [...] along the coastlines of countries facing the Mediterranean" (15). The mixing of this plurality of cultures, languages and ethnicities into the notion of *mediterraneità* "can only be re-proposed — or, at least, it has always been reproposed that way — through a mytho-poetic transfiguration and an acknowledged invention"; "The deceit that the Mediterranean myth dispenses", Gravagnuolo continues, "is [...] the transhistorical representation of the past as present. It insinuates the elegant assumption of the *eternal*, [...] the desire for harmony. And it is exactly as *myth*, as a desire for simple and harmonious construction [...] that the concept of *mediterraneità* can and must be evaluated beyond its objective verifiability" (Gravagnuolo 16).

Yet around the 1830s the Mediterranean started being politicized, coming to express "the crucible in which diverse cultural traditions were mixed, synthesized [...], in a process which led to continual transmission, hybridism, and the sponsorship of new inventions" (Bergdoll xvii). Mediterraneanism lends itself therefore both to nationalistic appropriations and transnationalist agendas, relying, as Michelangelo Sabatino has noted, on the many voices and traditions characterising the cultural heritage of the Mediterranean basin (44). Within the specificity of the Italian context, as Claudio Fogu and Lucia Re have argued, Italian culture and the Italians themselves have been invested in a complex process of self-identification with "Mediterranean-ess," which, while marred by intellectual colonization, has nonetheless played a key role in the formation of modern Italian culture, Italian national identity and foreign policy (Fogu and Re 1).

The idea of the Mediterranean had emerged strongly also in the context of pictorial Modernism, Elizabeth Cowling and Jennifer Mundy observe, where it had metamorphosed into the myth of Arcadia, "an earthly paradise protected from the sordid materialism of the modern industrialised world, free from strife and tension, pagan not Christian, innocent not fallen, a place where dreamed-of harmony is still attainable" (Cowling and Mundy 12). They note that at the heart of the Arcadian myth throughout the centuries lurked the potential for profound melancholy, a sense of loss and the knowledge that the ideal can never be attained (12). Such melancholy pervaded the work of Nicolas Poussin and Camille Corot as well as, later, André Derain, Pablo Picasso and Giorgio de Chirico; even when the setting of some of their works was contemporary, there was always an intentional ambiguity, so that the present was seen through the perspective of the past, and thus idealised and made more resonant (12-13).

The association between the myth of the Mediterranean and the idea of *latinità* had also permeated Gabriele D'Annunzio's rhetoric during the pre-war years and was based on the opposition between *latinità* and German "spirit," which placed Italy as the leader of a Latin civilization centred on the Mediterranean. As Filippo Caburlotto notes, the reference to the Mediterranean in this context alludes to a historical, social and cultural heritage from which that leadership had developed. He further argues that these motifs had been appropriated by national irredentism in the post-war years and formed the basis of a nationalism infused with expansionist and colonialist aspirations.

The intersection of such notions and myths centered on Italy's classical heritage and its role in the Mediterranean, therefore, facilitated the politicization of the aesthetic agenda, allowing a simultaneous focus on vernacular nationalism and the transnationalization of the artistic discourse. It could be argued, as Crispin Sartwell does with reference to the classical and the baroque (201), that the Mediterranean provided a "vocabulary" within which artistic and political discourses inscribed themselves, allowing them to conflate.

The choice of *Rete mediterranea* as the title of Soffici's magazine, therefore, was deliberately laden with ideological markers, which underscored the political agenda of the project. The primacy of the Mediterranean was based here on a trans-historical notion which encompassed, yet went beyond, mere political nationalism and placed the aesthetic realm in strict interrelationship with politics. Ultimately, the trans-historical representation of the past as present which was predicated as central to the myth of the Mediterranean would also feed into the historic imaginary that constituted the nexus between aesthetics and politics in Fascism's conception of history.[2]

The Artist as Politician
Soffici devoted a section of the *Taccuino* — entitled "Politica" — entirely to politics, thus exposing his political reflections as a key element of the cultural project elaborated in *Rete mediterranea*. In the opening of the section of the first issue of the magazine, Soffici declares himself not to be political; yet, he continues, in the current moment "i fatti di ordine politico sono spesso così strettamente aderenti, o minacciano di diventarlo, a quelli spirituali ed estetici da dover per forza prenderli in considerazione per metterne in chiaro i rapporti e [...] far del nostro meglio per modificarli a vantaggio, o a minor minaccia, almeno dell'intelligenza e della bellezza" ("Politica" 80). Not only does he, therefore, advocate the artist's direct intervention in political matters, following a practice already tested during the pre-war and war years, but he also establishes a clear interconnection between aesthetics and politics. The legacy of the avant-garde discourse of the reconciliation of art with life praxis, as explained by Bürger in his *Theory of the Avant-Garde*, metamorphoses here conflating the political and aesthetic discourse in such a way as to envisage the

---

[2] On Fascism's historic imaginary, see Fogu, *Historic Imaginary* and *To Make History Present*.

world of politics directly shaped by artistic practice. The "gagliardo disgusto" which Soffici feels for politicians and political matters is overcome in the name of the artist's self-sacrifice "sull'altare dello Spirito e della Patria" ("Politica" 80). The national agenda is therefore at the forefront of Soffici's involvement in politics, assigning to the artist a key role as the gatekeeper of the spiritual life of the nation.

The first declaration of the magazine's section on politics is an exaltation of the war ("Evviva la guerra" is one of the section's subtitles), not only justified as a catalyst for the resurgence of the idea of the nation and of the Italian *stirpe*, but also in its aesthetic connotations: "Viva la guerra d'Italia, nobile e bella fra tutte, con i suoi cinquecentomila morti che sono la nostra più sicura ricchezza" ("Politica" (a) 81). The assertion of the beauty of war is still resonant with the interventionist rhetoric championed by *Lacerba* during the war years; however, the mention of the Italian war dead inscribes the aesthetic component of the war firmly within the sphere of the nation in the post-war context, reclaiming for beauty a political dimension and appropriating an aestheticized post-war memorial discourse. As a veteran, Soffici reclaims the right to justify the war and to rewrite its narrative in regenerative terms, by reconfiguring an aesthetic of the conflict which goes beyond the exaltation of the war machine proposed by Futurism and which encompasses a new relationship between death and beauty. This claim is crystallized in the body of the dead soldier and its symbolic resonance, both as the sacrificial victim from whose blood the nation is reborn and as the life-affirming quality of its beauty (Carden-Coyne 127; Wittman). The palingenetic expectations generated by the war are reiterated and the conflict is glorified as a transformative and spiritual event, which has the ability to cleanse the world and lift man from the sordidness of his appetites: "Essa [the war] suscita nell'individuo d'animo molle e sonnifero le volanti energie, che solo conosce senza di lei il privilegiato che vive la vita del pensiero o del sogno. È una creatrice di valori nuovi, una spargitrice di semi [...]. La guerra è giustizia, nobiltà ed è pietà fratellevole" ("Politica" (a) 81).

Soffici's assessment of the war experience includes a reference to "the people," which reverberates with descriptions of the sort that he had included in his war memoirs. The artist claims to be a friend of the people, of whom he praises "la [...] rude natura, la [...] forza e salute, l'impeto dei [...] grossi canti — e anche la [...] violenza" ("Politica" (a) 82). The hyper-stylized, rather paternalistic, description of the people is coupled with a wish for their material fulfilment and happiness, but also with an appeal to obey their leaders. The mention of the people in Soffici's writings, however, is not only linked to the experience of the war and the subsequently newly found cross-class solidarity, but also to the awareness that, as Roger Griffin puts it, the history of the post-war years would be determined by the masses as a new subject "whose palingenetic reflexes had been awakened by this intensive experience of the end of the world" (162).

Soffici extols the atmosphere of regeneration brought about by current circumstances. The present time is perceived as attractive, full of opportunities and, significantly, "beautiful," where the beauty is generated by the sense of rebirth created by the war:

> Io trovo questo momento incredibilmente bello e attraente. Sento che la storia non ne ha mai avuti de' più sublimi, e che i posteri invidieranno noi che viviamo nel suo corrusco. Pensate! Tutto è in questione: il mondo bolle come una pentola; libertà assoluta di riplasmare noi stessi ed il nostro avvenire. Tutto è da rifare: attrezzi, roba, paesi e filosofie. Si pensa gigantescamente, si può creare con popoli e continenti [...] Vertiginosamente la storia aggiunge forti colori alla sua tela. Ogni momento è pieno di sorprese e possibilità.
>
> ("Politica" (a) 82-83)

Soffici uses *Rete mediterranea* to voice his analysis of Bolshevism, which he reads as a phenomenon of reaction against the bourgeoisie. He is of the view that similar anti-bourgeois reactions are likely to manifest themselves in Western Europe: "[...] la cosiddetta classe borghese è troppo vecchia, corrotta e rammollita per servire da sostegno alle società nuove che si vanno formando. Una forza politica vergine dovrà dunque sopravvenire e questa può essere benissimo quella del bolscevismo" ("Politica" (a) 86). Once again, the object of his attack is not so much the petty bourgeoisie as such, but, as Gentile puts it, "le forme e la mentalità della società borghese" (*Le origini* 163). He expresses little faith in the Italian Socialist leaders and laments, in Italy, the lack of men "di studio, coscienza, fegato" (86) who could lead the anti-bourgeois movement and direct it towards a political programme capable of overcoming chaos and destruction and reassuring the public. Soffici notes with interest the importance attributed to culture by Bolshevism and comments on the particular significance acquired by art at a time of social renewal. Finally, he argues that Russia is an interesting case study in the reconstitution of a national character following the Revolution. He concludes that Italy too might have to undergo a revolution similar to that of Russia to achieve a national renewal (87).

Soffici's analysis of Bolshevism is intertwined in the magazine with his evaluation of the post-war circumstances in Italy. He laments the lack of a political and moral guide, as the Italian political parties are guided by contradiction, ambiguity, confusion, and mendacity. He invokes the creation of a political doctrine which would move away from nationalism, internationalism, democracy, liberalism, socialism and anarchism, and would be the expression of the Italian "race." The cultural reference points for such a doctrine would be Dante, Machiavelli, Mazzini, but also Alfredo ("Politica" (b) 174). Soffici's political analysis stems from his rejection of materialism, which he sees as the cause of the decadence of his age. His critique of Socialism is not so much conducted in terms of its political principles or in relation to its mobilization of the masses — which he considers a sign of strength against "l'abbietto, stomachevole, filisteismo delle nostre classi cosiddette dirigenti" ("Politica" (c) 276) — but it is rather predicated on its neglect of what he calls "le forze spirituali" (276). He argues that the lack of a spiritual dimension makes Socialism unsuitable as a mass ideology and results in a disaffection from the fatherland, which it considers an obsolete concept (277). Soffici's reflections were steeped in the post-war nationalist debates, which promoted the idea of a social revolution which would not relinquish the values of national tradition, seen as the locus of a cross-class identity in which the masses could participate (Gentile, *Le origini* 143). The evocation of a spiritual dimension in the discussion of politics blurs the boundaries between aesthetics and politics. This instance is particularly evident in Soffici's critique of Socialism as lacking an "aesthetic" component, being, as it is, immersed in a vulgar materialism which obliterates the beauty of the nation and its civilization to concentrate on economic preoccupations. He calls for an integration of beauty in history and envisages a political situation which would establish the primacy of beauty:

Ho troppa fede nella fatalità dei grandi destini dei popoli, nella necessità della bellezza nella storia; credo troppo allo Spirito armonioso ed al suo trionfo finale, nella vita nazionale ed internazionale, per non essere sicuro che un giorno qualcuno o qualcosa verrà che, con un soffio violento o un atto fiammeggiante, spazzerà via tutto questo sterco; farà sparire tutte queste vergogne, queste umiliazioni e stupidità; e l'intelligenza, la gentilezza e la bellezza torneranno alla fine a brillar sulla terra.

("Politica" (c) 279)

Soffici identifies in Giovanni Gentile's philosophy the terms for a national spiritual regeneration. Commenting on Gentile's collection of essays entitled *Dopo la vittoria* (1920), he extols the teleological necessity of historical events underscored by Gentile's writings for its spiritual underpinning, according to which any historical event is inevitable and the result of the collective spirit of the nation realizing its destiny. What Soffici admires in particular about Gentile's philosophy is its quasi-religious character. His writings, he argues, "rappresentano [...] il nutrimento più sostanzioso per lo spirito nazionale." "In essi, l'uomo italiano che ha vissuto il fatto sublime della guerra, troverà di tal fatto la ragione profondissima, la giustificazione, non solo, ma l'esaltazione ragionata come di un'epopea della nostra maturità spirituale di nazione risorta" ("Politica" (b) 179). The artist shares with Gentile the sense that the war had been fought for a renewal of the spiritual life of the nation and his belief in a cultural revolution which would revitalize Italy and defeat materialist ideologies (Gentile, *Le origini* 118-20).

The Return to Order and the Politics of Classicism

A reconfiguration of the relationship between Italy's classical heritage and national culture underpins Soffici's articles. He provides an extensive commentary particularly on French art, with the aim of reassessing the French artistic legacy and reinforcing the historical primacy of the Italian tradition and its privileged position as the leader of the artistic renewal in post-war Europe. Within this ideological and aesthetic framework, in an article on Medardo Rosso's drawings, he presents the work of the sculptor as an example of "pretta italianità" — alien to any German or English-inspired mannerism and exoticism — and defines his sculpture as "classical," where the term is used to denote what he considers as "perfetto e definitivo," regardless of the style the artist has chosen to use ("I disegni di Medardo Rosso" 35-41). The definition of classicism employed to describe Rosso's work, intertwined with notions of national character, is opposed to the equally loosely applied notion of "pre-Raphaelitism" (Preraffaellismo), which is used negatively to indicate passive imitation of archaic styles and polemically to describe not only British pre-Raphaelite art, but also such post-impressionists as Gauguin, Van Gogh, Paul Sérusier and Maurice Denis, who, according to Soffici, sought refuge in the past to borrow the artistic rules for the present. Soffici includes Cubism as well as Fauvism, Orphism, Futurism and Dada in this "pre-Raphaelite" tendency and invokes an art that would create a dialogue with pictorial tradition without resorting to the sterile imitation of the past. To pre-Raphaelite mannerism he opposes the art of Cézanne, Renoir and Fattori, who managed to establish a fruitful relationship with tradition, while being modern at the same time ("Preraffaellismo" 71-76). Similarly, in reviewing Carlo Carrà's recently published volume *Pittura metafisica*, he stresses the classicism intrinsic in Carrà's search for the object's essence and permanent quality. He states that

> tutti i veri artisti [...] hanno capito oggi una verità: che, cioè, l'epoca delle ricerche, delle analisi e degli acerbi arbitri deve essere chiusa, e che bisogna arrivare ad una verità sostanziale. E noi italiani non potevamo se non esser destinati a metterci alla testa degli altri in questa indagine per avanzare nella quale abbiamo la guida di tutti i più grandi fra i nostri padri.
>
> ("Pittura metafisica" 78)

Soffici mentions French magazines, such as *L'Occident* and *Nouvelle Revue Française,* as examples of periodicals that had engaged with the need to reconnect modern art with variously defined roots of national culture, as a reaction against the culture of their time. In particular, the idea informing the *Nouvelle Revue Française* was that philosophy, literature and the arts had become self-serving and wrapped up in the individual, forgetting their civic role. Yet, both periodicals were deemed by Soffici to be too "academic" ("Ritorni" 156). Italy too at the beginning of the twentieth century had seen the flourishing of academic magazines such as *Il convito, Hermes, Il rinascimento*, followed by the subversive *Il Leonardo, La voce, Lacerba*, which were in turn followed by intellectual groups promoting a "return" of the values championed by earlier magazines, resulting in sterile and derivative academicism (157-58). While not explicitly mentioned, the reference to *La ronda* is obvious here, particularly in the allusion to the magazine's reverence for Shakespeare and Leopardi, who were heralded in that magazine as literary models.

It was to counter the tendency to academicism prevalent after the post-war return to order that, in the third issue of *Rete mediterranea*, Soffici published his "Apologia del futurismo." In it, he proclaims the death of Futurism ("il futurismo doveva morire; il futurismo è morto". "Apologia del futurismo" 199). Yet Futurism, he argues, managed to renovate the form and content of Italian art and free Italy from its obsession with the emulation of foreign forms of cultural modernity. It regained respect for Italian culture abroad when this was just considered as recycling empty forms inherited from its past glories. Futurism had been, according to Soffici, a triumph of national culture, as it served as an artistic model for other countries: "[...] gli altri hanno dovuto seguirci, imitarci. L'Europa, la *Francia*, hanno preso a modello il futurismo italiano" ("Apologia del futurismo" 205). From an artistic point of view, Futurism managed to renovate the stagnant artistic scene in Italy, catalyse the artistic debate and inject youth and vitality into it, while broadening its intellectual and creative horizons. Futurism — he claims — "accese la passione eroica per la vita e per la bellezza; impostò e risolse con festoso coraggio alcuni problemi che il momento storico artistico imponeva; rinverginì il linguaggio e la tecnica: i modi espressivi delle arti, schiudendo illimitati prospetti alla forza creativa della gioventù italiana" ("Apologia del futurismo" 206). Importantly, Soffici stresses how Futurism had an influence on young soldiers' heroic behaviour in the war: "[...] i futuristi ebbero la loro gloriosa rappresentanza fra i morti, i mutilati e i feriti delle più terribili battaglie. Fra la canea dei suoi rianimati detrattori si notano invece in prima fila gli antichi tedescofili, neutralisti, imboscati e disfattisti" ("Apologia del futurismo" 207). Once again, Soffici coalesces artistic and political discourses. For him, the legacy of Futurism is not only artistic but also, and eminently, political. To return to an order marked by the intellectuals' proclaimed detachment from the political sphere (*La ronda*'s model), he opposes the example of Futurism to reclaim for the artist a political agency intrinsic in the artistic activity. The disenfranchisement from France and the rest of Europe operated by Futurism at an artistic level has a political equivalent in the patriotic heroism engendered by Futurist ideas and ideals. Soffici, therefore, identifies the core legacy of Futurism, beyond its formal implications, in the principle of the indissoluble link between art and life and its transformative potential on a political and social level.

The September issue of *Rete mediterranea* features an article on Guillaume Apollinaire, who had fought in the war and had died as a result of the flu pandemic in 1918, becoming the international emblem of the artist-combatant (Winter 18-22). Apollinaire had been appropriated by Italian artists as a supporter and promoter of the avant-garde but also as a champion of classicism and Latinity (Adamson, *Embattled Avant-Gardes* 110-42). He had become close to Soffici and had followed closely the development of *La voce* and *Lacerba* (to which he had contributed), as his correspondence with Soffici, published in *Rete mediterranea* shows ("36 lettere inedite di G. Apollinaire" (a) and (b). In his article, Soffici highlights the political currency of the French poet's classicism, which he describes as consisting of "assoluti tradizionali, di principi armoniosi e di gerarchie intellettuali [...] ordine e perfezione e limpidità apollinea d'idee e di forme" ("Ricordi di vita artistica e letterararia" 220). He proclaims Apollinaire's classicism as incorporating such characteristics as discipline, a cult of the reason, a sense of measure and balance, both in his artistic and critical activities, interwoven with his *italianità* (Apollinaire was born in Italy). He declares Apollinaire to be "un vero concittadino," as he was impregnated with "lo spirito della nostra razza," whose features were "il senso dell'armonia, dell'ordine, della chiarezza, della grandezza morale e della schiettezza" (222). Even his physical features betrayed his Italian lineage: the "membra proporzionate e aitanti, l'aperta faccia prelatizia, l'occhio nero luminoso e vivo, il capello scuro e la fine bocca" carried a familiarity which was immediately identifiable with the Italian people (222). Apollinaire himself was quoted by Soffici as declaring that Italy was the "mother of civilization." In his memoir, Soffici justifies the combination of Apollinaire's love of traditional order with his notorious interest for the avant-garde by defining him as "sviscerato dalla bellezza antica, fatalmente spinto alla ricerca di una bellezza nuova; per il quale l'idea dell'ordine che gli deriva dalla conoscenza del passato, non è un'idea che viva soltanto di passato ma che vuol concretizzarsi nel presente e per l'avvenire; che perciò l'ordine invoca e persegue nella modernità" (224-25). The figure of Apollinaire is therefore appropriated and used to glorify the artist as a war hero and underscore the interlinking of classicism and modernity.

In the September and December issues of *Rete mediterranea*, Soffici published a two-part review of French art from Édouard Manet to André Derain. While the majority of French artists are criticized for being either mediocre, unoriginal or too preoccupied with technical aspects (these criticisms are directed to Manet and Monet as well as Van Gogh, Gauguin, Seurat, Matisse, Picasso and Derain), only three artists receive praise: Renoir, Cézanne and Degas. Interestingly, both Cézanne and Degas are inscribed in the great Italian tradition. In particular, Cézanne's art is associated with the "tragic and sensual realism" of such artists as Masaccio, Michelangelo, Raffaello, Tiziano, Tintoretto, the Carraccis, and Caravaggio. Regarding Degas, Soffici evokes Michelangelo, Raffaello and Caravaggio — as well as Rembrandt and Courbet — in the description of his style and technique, even intimating the artist's presumed Italian origin. But what associates Degas with the Italian tradition is the "classical" quality of his art, that is, an orderly and harmonious character that makes it timeless ("Bilancio dell'arte francese contemporanea" (a) 261-72 and (b) 364-71).

Soffici's survey of French art conceals, once again, nationalistic concerns. The argument underlying his analysis is that the primacy of contemporary

French art is overstated and that even the most successful French artists are indebted to the Italian tradition. Innovation at all costs is condemned and the reference to the classics is eulogized. The motifs that had underpinned the apology of Futurism are sidelined while some Cubist masters, such as Braque, are deliberately omitted from the review. The predominance of France in the contemporary artistic landscape, with few exceptions, is therefore challenged and the only primacy acknowledged as legitimate is that of the classical tradition defined by the Italian artistic pantheon. Such a critique is aimed at re-stating the primacy of Italian art by reclaiming not only the historical value of the "great tradition," but also its connection to the present and its transformative potential in relation to contemporary art.

Conclusion

While, like many of his contemporaries, Soffici claimed to have been turned by the war into a different man, his cultural project, as it emerges from his post-war writings, was still rooted in the principles that had underpinned much of the Florentine avant-garde project in the pre-war years. These were: a strong nationalist drive, a hostility towards Socialism, the rejection of materialism, and the desire for a cultural, spiritual and moral renewal (Adamson, *Avant-Garde Florence* 264). This rethinking, brought about by the experience of the war, had not resulted in the denial of those principles, but rather in a recalibration process, whereby the nationalist agenda was linked to the quest for the return to artistic tradition invoked across post-war Europe. The politicization of the return to Italy's classical tradition which constituted the basis of Soffici's and many other artists' intellectual projects, combined with the nationalism and palingenetic expectations created by the war, resulted in the belief, as George Mosse put it, that "the spiritual unity of the nation would solve all difficulties." Such spiritual unity was defined as "a resurgence of creativity viewed in aesthetic terms: the dawn of a new world of beauty and of aesthetic form" (Mosse 98; also Storchi and Braun). *Rete mediterranea* constituted an important voice in this debate; it reconfigured the relationship between art and politics, proposing the veteran-artist as the exponent of a new artistic-political elite, capable of capturing the mood of the time and providing spiritual guidance to the new nation emerging from the conflict; it sought to reassess the relationship between the recent artistic tradition in Italy and in France, repositioning Italy as the leading nation in the post-war artistic resurgence and establishing its primacy as the leader of the civilization expressed by the idea of the "Mediterranean"; it proposed itself as a bulwark of anti-socialism, envisaging an impending age of mass politics and invoking a political ideology connoted by powerful leadership, a nationalist outlook, a strong spiritual component and an aesthetic dimension, which would actualize the avant-garde quest to organize "a new life praxis from a basis in art" (Bürger 49). Ultimately, these principles, ideals, and quests culminated in support for the fascist regime, of which Soffici became a staunch advocate. To consolidate his support for Fascism, in 1924 Soffici published an article entitled "Spirito ed estetica del fascismo" (*Lo spettatore italiano*, 1 May 1924), in which he outlined his vision for an aesthetic for the new regime. In it, he proclaimed classicism as the aesthetic formulation of Fascism, where the classical was redefined not in terms of return or reaction, but as an art originating from a deep knowledge of artistic techniques and from the awareness that true art can only be born from an artist's productive engagement with his time. But the classical envisaged by Soffici was also steeped in a moral and political order and principles aimed at reinforcing the national community ("Spirito ed estetica del fascismo"). The return to the classical envisaged in *Rete mediterranea* had found its political counterpart and Soffici, like many modernist artists in Italy, would become an agent of the collusion between aesthetics and politics which defined the fascist regime.

University of Leicester

Works cited

Adamson, Walter L. "Ardengo Soffici and the Religion of Art." *Fascist Visions. Art and Ideology in France and Italy*. Ed. Matthew Affron and Mark Antliff. Princeton: Princeton UP, 1997. 46-72.
_____. *Avant-Garde Florence. From Modernism to Fascism*. Cambridge: Harvard UP, 1993.
_____. *Embattled Avant-Gardes. Modernism's Resistance to Commodity Culture in Europe*. Berkeley: U of California P, 2007.
_____."Modernism and Fascism: The Politics of Culture in Italy, 1903-1922." *American Historical Review* 95 (1990): 359-90.
_____. "Modernism in Florence: The Politics of Avant-Garde Culture in the Early Twentieth Century." *Italian Modernism. Italian Culture between Decadentism and Avant-Garde*. Ed. Luca Somigli and Mario Moroni. Toronto: Toronto UP, 2004. 221-42.
Bartolini, Simonetta. *Ardengo Soffici. Il romanzo di una vita*. Florence: Le Lettere, 2009.
_____. "Introduzione." Ardengo Soffici. *Estetica e politica. Scritti critici 1920-1940*. Ed. Simonetta Bartolini. Chieti: Solfanelli, 1994. 11-60.
Bergdoll, Barry. "Foreword." *Modern Architecture and the Mediterranean*. xv-xix.
Braun, Emily. "L'arte dell'Italia fascista: il totalitarismo fra teoria e pratica." *Modernità totalitaria. Il fascismo italiano*. Ed. Emilio Gentile. Rome: Laterza, 2008. 85-99.
Bürger, Peter. *Theory of the Avant-Garde*. Trans. Michael Shaw. Minneapolis: U of Minnesota P, 1984.
Caburlotto, Filippo. "D'Annunzio, la latinità del Mediterraneo e il mito della riconquista." *California Italian Studies* 1.1 (2010). Web. 28 February 2015.
Carden-Coyne, Ana. *Deconstructing the Body. Classicism, Modernism, and the First World War*. Oxford: Oxford UP, 2009.
Cowling, Elizabeth, and Jennifer Mundy. "Introduction." *On Classic Ground. Picasso, Léger, de Chirico and New Classicism 1910-1930*. London: Tate Gallery, 1990. 11-30.
De Carlis Stefania, ed. *"La Vraie Italie" di G. Papini*. Roma: Bulzoni, 1988.
Fogu, Claudio. *The Historic Imaginary. Politics of History in Fascist Italy*. Toronto: U of Toronto P, 2003.
_____. "To Make History Present". *Donatello among the Blackshirts. History and Modernity in the Visual Culture of Fascist Italy*. Ed. Claudia Lazzaro and Roger Crum. Ithaca: Cornell UP, 2005. 33-49.
Fogu, Claudio, and Lucia Re. "Italy in the Mediterranean Today: A New Critical Topography." *California Italian Studies* 1.1 (2010). Web. 28 February 2015.
Gentile, Emilio. *L'apocalisse della modernità. La grande guerra per l'uomo nuovo*. Milano: Mondadori, 2008.
_____. *Le origini dell'ideologia fascista 1918-1925*. Bologna: Il Mulino, 1996.
Gravagnuolo, Benedetto. "From Schinkel to Le Corbusier. The Myth of the Mediterranean in Modern Architecture." *Modern Architecture and the Mediterranean* 15-39.
Griffin, Roger. *Modernism and Fascism. The Sense of a New Beginning under Mussolini and Hitler*. Basingstoke: Palgrave Macmillan, 2007.
Isnenghi, Mario. *Il mito della Grande Guerra*. Roma: Laterza, 1970.
Modern Architecture and the Mediterranean. Ed. Jean-François Lejeune and Michelangelo Sabatino. London: Routledge, 2010.
Mosse, George L. *The Fascist Revolution*. New York: Fertig, 1999.
Papini, Giovanni. "Ciò che dobbiamo alla Francia." *Lacerba* 2.17 (1914): 249-52.

Papini, Giovanni, and Ardengo Soffici. *Carteggio IV. 1919-1956*. Ed. Mario Richter. Roma: Edizioni di Storia e Letteratura, 2002.

Richter, Mario. "Introduzione." Papini and Soffici. *Carteggio IV. 1919-1956* 5-40.

———. *Papini e Soffici. Mezzo secolo di vita italiana (1903-1956)*. Firenze: Le Lettere, 2005.

Sabatino, Michelangelo. "The Politics of *Mediterraneità* in Italian Modernist Architecture." *Modern Architecture and the Mediterranean*. 41-63.

Sartwell, Crispin. *Political Aesthetics*. Ithaca: Cornell U P, 2010.

Soffici, Ardengo. "36 lettere inedite di G. Apollinaire" (a). *Rete mediterranea* 3 (September 1920): 229-36.

———. "36 lettere inedite di G. Apollinaire" (b). *Rete mediterranea* 4 (December 1920): 309-19.

———. "Apologia del futurismo." *Rete mediterranea* 3 (September 1920): 197-207.

———. "Bilancio dell'arte francese contemporanea" (a). *Rete mediterranea* 3 (September 1920): 261-72.

———. "Bilancio dell'arte francese contemporanea" (b). *Rete mediterranea* 4 (December 1920): 364-71.

———. "Dichiarazione preliminare." *Rete mediterranea* 1 (March 1920): 3-20.

———. "Errore di coincidenza" (a). *Rete mediterranea* 3 (September 1920): 238-51.

———. "Errore di coincidenza" (b). *Rete mediterranea* 4 (December 1920): 320-54.

———. "I disegni di Medardo Rosso." *Rete mediterranea* 1 (March 1920): 35-41.

———. *Kobilek: giornale di battaglia*. Firenze: Vallecchi, 1919.

———. "Per la guerra." *Lacerba*, 2.17 (1914): 253-56.

———. "Pittura metafisica." *Rete mediterranea*, 1 (March 1920): 77-78.

———. "Politica" (a). *Rete mediterranea* 1 (March 1920): 80-88.

———. "Politica" (b). *Rete Meditarranea* 2 (June 1920): 172-80.

———. "Politica" (c). *Rete mediterranea* 3 (September 1920): 275-79.

———. "Preraffaellismo." *Rete mediterranea* 1 (March 1920): 71-76.

———. "Ricordi di vita letteraria ed artistica. Guillaume Apollinaire." *Rete mediterranea* 3 (September 1920): 208-237.

———. "Ritorni." *Rete mediterranea* 2 (June 1920): 153-62.

———. "Spirito ed estetica del fascismo." *Estetica e politica. Scritti critici 1920-1940*. Ed. Simonetta Bartolini. Chieti: Solfanelli, 1994. 156-61.

Somigli, Luca. "Past-loving Florence and the Temptations of Futurism." *The Oxford Critical and Cultural History of Modernist Magazines*. Ed. Peter Brooker, Sascha Bru, Andrew Thacker and Christian Weikop. Oxford: Oxford UP, 2013. Vol. III. 469-90.

Storchi, Simona. "Margherita Sarfatti and *Il popolo d'Italia*. National Classicism Between Tradition and Modernity." *Modern Language Review* 108.4 (2013): 1135-55.

Ungaretti, Giuseppe. *Lettere a Soffici 1917-1930*. Ed. Paola Montefoschi and Leone Piccioni. Firenze: Sansoni, 1981.

Wilson, Elizabeth. *Bohemians. The Glamorous Outcasts*. London: I. B. Tauris, 2003.

Wittman, Laura. *The Tomb of the Unknown Soldier, Modern Mourning and the Reinvention of the Mystical Body*. Toronto: U of Toronto P, 2011.

Jennifer Griffiths

Enrico Toti: A New Man for Italy's Mutilated Victory

> "'Tis the melodious hue of beauty thrown
> Athwart the darkness and the glare of pain,
> Which humanize and harmonize the strain."
> (Percy Bysshe Shelley)

Standards of beauty vary widely across cultures and historic periods as attested to by the fact that the classical statuary of Greece or Rome bears little resemblance to contemporary Playboy or Playgirl centerfolds. If for Kant what constituted human beauty was that perfect exemplum of the human being, the Romantics were clearly drawn to memorialize the beauty of pain, horror and death (Praz). Contemporary artists, activists and researchers in the field of disability studies have recently posed profound challenges to normative standards of bodily beauty. When Marc Quinn's giant version of *Alison Lapper Pregnant* appeared on the fourth plinth of Trafalgar Square in 2005, it sparked some controversy, but Lapper, born with no arms and underdeveloped legs, regarded Quinn's 11-foot-7-inch- Carrara marble sculpture of her naked body to be a powerful assertion that disability "can be as beautiful and valid a form of being as any other" (236). The voices of opposition included those who were concerned that Lapper's image represented an intrusion of the sanctity of Trafalgar Square as a devotional space to the nation and its war dead. David Whiting, grandson of Lord Hugh Dowding, who was killed in the Battle of Britain, felt that "a naked woman should be filling the empty plinth in Trafalgar Square […] ridiculous. Trafalgar Square should be a place where men who have served their country should be honored" (Lyall). Underlying this sentiment is the notion that only a certain kind of disability might be appropriate for display in Trafalgar Square, one that can convey the metaphorical beauty of self-sacrifice via the militarized male body.

Whiting's sentiment points to the enduring nature of a Romantic ideal about beautiful suffering and its application in the construction of a kind of modern masculinity inextricably linked with the rise of nation states. While the Great War is regarded by some as having contributed to a crisis of modern masculinity (Fussell), George Mosse has argued that it "tied nationalism and masculinity together more closely than ever before," adding a new dimension of animal brutality to a concept of modern manliness that was linked to willpower and the idea of "sacrifice for a cause" as "the highest virtue of which masculinity was capable" (*Image of Man* 110-12). Many soldiers imagined war as a test of their manliness and others thought of it as a kind of crucible in which "real" men would be forged. These sentiments carried over into the Second World War as exemplified by Mussolini's assertion in March 1945, "A man who scrupulously avoids war will be anything but a man because only battle completes a man" (qtd. in Koon 22). Despite the rhetoric of modernity that surrounds the technological advances of both world wars, this gender narrative is an old one of the heroic knight on the battlefield whose plate armour, lance and charging steed have been replaced by tank, airplane and/or machine gun.

Yet the remoteness of the modern battlefield and the absence of the dead that had previously helped maintain the conquering hero's masculine mystique were being eroded by the kind of modern technologies that intensified the war experience for non-combatants and civilians. Photography brought home images of the battlefield and its dead, even if imperfect ones, and the discovery of anticoagulants permitted blood transfusions, which increased the survival rates of the wounded, such that large numbers of soldiers returned home with visibly fragmented, mutilated or dismembered bodies. If contemporary prosthetic and surgical technologies have facilitated an impressive re-enabling of disabled veterans returning from Iraq and Afghanistan in our own time, those available to veterans of the early twentieth century, for example tin facial prosthetics (Feo) or uncomfortable artificial limbs (Bourke), were considerably less successful. The war thus forced reformulations of the notion of masculinity as a flawless bodily specimen in response to the numerous visibly fragmented bodies it produced (Bourke; Carden-Coyne; Gagen; Salvante). In this context the image of the disabled male body acquired particular significance becoming emblematic of a kind of moralizing rhetoric of masculine sacrifice, one which served a nationalist purpose.

Italy's "New Man"
"Masculinity," writes George Mosse in his pivotal study of the subject, "was regarded as of one piece from its very beginning: body and soul, outward appearance and inward virtue were supposed to form one harmonious whole, a perfect construct where every part is in its place" (*Image of Man* 5). This notion of masculinity as the total package formed a logical basis for the idea of the body politic that would be put to broad use by nineteenth-century European nationalists. Since the Risorgimento, national welfare has repeatedly and variously been imagined in terms of a metaphor relating the physical and moral health of the human body with that of the nation of Italy itself (Bonetta). Before World War I, authors like Enrico Corradini were still espousing a kind of masculinity that advocated *mens sana in corpore sano* as its key feature (Benadusi 15). Fascism too exalted the cult of youthful physical force, seeing in the perfect male specimen a metaphor for society: "Against the fragmentation and anomie of modern mass society, it placed the harmony, belonging, and identity of the national community" (Koon 3). Although the conjoined image of the Italian nation and the virile male body clearly endured beyond the war, Italy's nearly one million WWI-wounded

presented a serious challenge to totalizing definitions of "real" manhood, a fact that poet and Futurist founder, F. T. Marinetti, seems to have appreciated early on. First published in *L'Italia futurista* in June 1916 and republished in *Come si seducono le donne*, his treatise "Donne, preferite i gloriosi mutilati!" exhorts women to fight alongside men in the trenches in order to be worthy of their love and rhapsodizes about the beauty of truncated limbs: "Donne, fate che ogni italiano dica partendo: Voglio offrirle al mio ritorno una bella ferita degna di lei! [...] Gloria alla pelle umana straziata dalla mitraglia! [...] Questo è il futurismo che glorifica il corpo modificato e abbellito della guerra" (102-03).

Emilio Gentile identifies the First World War as having produced "new ideological syntheses regarding the myth of the nation" that gave rise to the vision of a Greater Italy composed of "New Men," ideals that fueled the cause of what he terms modernist nationalism (*Struggle for Modernity* 5-6). Derived in part from Nietzsche's conception of the Übermensch, he also explains that the picture of Italy's "New Man" as it emerged within the writings of these modernist nationalists was a contradictory one. "The real revolution," wrote Giovanni Papini in 1913, "is in the mind and not at the barricades." Similarly, modernist intellectuals centered around the journal *La voce* envisioned the ideal new Italian as "studious, intellectual, artistic" rather than physically forceful or athletic; yet the Futurists envision the "New Man" as a kind of "new barbarian" or nationalist warrior (*Struggle for Modernity* 35). The existence of such contradictory views regarding the meaning of "new manhood" created spaces for alternative reimaginings of masculine heroism.

The Great War inspired new reflections on a timeless imaginary of masculine heroism in visual culture that has so frequently been populated by triumphant male bodies. The image of the fallen soldier has frequently been mythologized and perpetuated in monuments that draw upon traditional models of ideal youthful Greek masculine beauty and/or Christian symbolism of sacrifice and resurrection (Mosse 70-106). However, after 1916 a new public image of disability arose that insisted on the disabled body as a symbol of the Italian national struggle in World War I (Bracco). One-legged cyclist and would-be soldier Enrico Toti became one of the most powerful and enduring symbols of this phenomenon, emblematic of both Greater Italy and its "New Man" in the wake of their "mutilated victory." War memorials to Enrico Toti help to strengthen the metaphorical link between body and nation still more powerfully by fusing traditional imaginaries of the Greco-Roman athletic masculine ideal and the self-sacrificing saint with those of a fragmented body to create an image of national heroism that resonates with the history of Italian visual culture while re-contextualizing the wounds of the war.

The namesake of numerous streets, piazzas, associations and one submarine, the subject of many rituals, monuments, and one full-length feature film, Enrico Toti and his image have endured well beyond his death. An authority on his life story, Lucio Fabi has observed, "La figura di Toti, per la generazione dei quarantenni e per quelli che hanno qualche anno in più, reassume in maniera singolare uno dei principi stereotipi dell'eroismo bellico, il soldato che suggella con un estremo gesto bellicoso il sacrificio supremo per la Patria" (*Vera storia* 7). Following his death at the sixth battle of Isonzo on August 6, 1916, Toti was resurrected as a mythical figure, the details of whose real life would become more and more obscured as facts were manipulated in favor of fiction by successive governments. The origins of the story that would be widely perpetuated perhaps lie in Achille Beltrame's September-October 1916 cover illustration for *La domenica del corriere* in which Toti is pictured leading a charge against the trenches of the Austrian enemy while brandishing a crutch in his raised right hand and leaning on a rifle with his left. The underlying caption read, "L'eroica fine del mutilato Enrico Toti: ferito per la terza volta, si alza e scaglia la sua gruccia contro il nemico in fuga." Toti's gesture of the raised crutch perhaps came to symbolize Italy's contempt for the "Vittoria mutilata" (Fabi, Vera storia 7); certainly the image of an injured man who, in his final moments, hurls the last element that braces him up against a fall is one of utter defiance in the face of both humiliation and death. However, particularly within the context of the above cultural discourse that fused male body and nation state, it is Toti himself who in some sense comes to represent Italy as an injured body and defiant spirit. In a propaganda leaflet issued in Naples for the VI Prestito Nazionale in 1918, an image of Toti's crutch flying across the trenches is emblazoned with the words, "Che l'Italia non zoppichi piu! Questo volle Toti!" Toti is not pictured, but, at least within the terms of the declaration, Toti and the nation state of Italy are made synonymous and the crutch is used to signify the necessary refinancing of the public coffers.

Those invested in this myth of the nation quickly picked up on Toti's legacy and its relevance in strengthening popular nationalist sentiment. Lieutenant Pietro Bolzon reported that Toti's fame had already been established in the trenches by the time he met him in April 1916. He recorded that Toti "divenne ben presto un simbolo maschio e magnifico di popolo combattente, e i fanti se lo sequestravano gelosamente come pagina vivente del loro oscuro eroismo" (qtd. in Sillani 94). Marshall Gaetano Giardino, said of Toti, "Non è un eroe, ma l'eroe, nell'antico senso Greco [...] che può incarnare visibilmente le virtù latenti di un popolo [...] eletto dal destino" (Fabi, *Vera storia* 11); Gabriele D'Annunzio described him as "il divino dispregiatore dell'austriaco" (Fabi, *Vera storia* 10). The Fascist regime would subsequently adopt and expand on Toti's myth as exemplified by the detailed and emotive elaboration of official accounts of his death twenty years after the fact.[1] Mussolini would identify Toti and another patriot, Francesco

---

[1] Upon receiving the gold medal for military valor the official account of Toti's death read: "Volontario, quantunque privo della gamba sinistra, dopo aver reso importanti servizi nei fatti d'arme dell'aprile a quota 70 (est di Selz), il 6 agosto, nel combattimento che condusse all'occupazione di quota 85 (est di Monfalcone), lanciavasi arditamente sulla trincea nemica, continuando a combattere con ardore, quantunque già due volte ferito. Colpito da

Rismondo, as the very incarnations of the heroism of the Bersaglieri. The Fascist youth, he affirmed, would be trained to idolize Toti as the quintessential emblem of the self-sacrificing citizen: "Tra Misiano che scappa e Toti che butta la gruccia contro il nemico, i fanciulli sceglieranno Toti" (Fabi, *Vera storia* 10-11).

Enrico Toti, Man and Myth
Toti was born in Rome in 1882 and grew up in the area of Porta Maggiore to parents from Cassino (Frosinone). At fourteen years of age he enlisted in the navy and served for eight years; following the death of his brother in 1905, he left the service and eventually found a position with the state railways as a stoker to help support his family. On March 2, 1908, only a year after taking the job, Toti had to have his left leg amputated following an accident in which he was dragged beneath the wheels of a moving locomotive. Although he was left with only a modest state pension, his sister Lina reported that he never lost heart and instead devoted himself to cycling and other interests. After this accident Toti had two traditional alternatives of either relaxing into the life of an invalid or trying to rebuild an image of himself as a whole man via the use of a prosthetic limb. But the optimistic climate of nascent modernism seems to have suggested a third alternative to Toti, who set about raising himself to the status of "personaggio" or public personality (Fabi, *Vera storia* 20). By taking on a number of impressive athletic challenges, including an international swimming competition in the Tevere and a world bicycle tour during which he reportedly traversed 20,000 kilometers across Europe and Africa, he attracted the attention of local and national newspapers. One photograph captures Toti posed on his bicycle departing from the arch of Palazzo delle Esposizioni in Rome in 1911. In May 1915 Toti participated in the city's interventionist demonstrations and, shortly after Italy's entry into the war, set off on his bicycle with a homemade uniform for Trieste and the front lines. His gesture was not unusual in that *La domenica del corriere* reported several similar episodes by women and children in June 1915. Yet, rather than normalizing Toti's gesture, this fact reiterates the reality of Toti's

---

un terzo proiettile, con esaltazione eroica lanciava al nemico la gruccia e spirava baciando il piumetto, con stoicismo degno di quell'anima altamente italiana." Twenty years later this account was expanded to read: "a mezza costa è ferito ad una spalla da un colpo di fucile; cade, si rialza, arranca con la sua stampella; si getta ancora nel combattimento, è ferito al petto una seconda volta, cade una seconda volta [...] pencola ma non cade, s'avventa, balza, sobbalza, incespica, salta, raggiunge i suoi ormai ridotti ad un manipolo [...] quando un terzo colpo lo percuote al petto, non si sgomenta, sta per cadere ma trova ancora la forza di combattere e la stampella, strale incoccato dalla furia suprema di un dio, si leva dal suo pugno di Eroe e sferzando a rovescio la morte s'abbatte sui volti, nelle teste, sulle spalle di nemici trasecolati nella indicibile visione [...] ne afferra la tesa [dell'elmetto], vi avvicina la bocca piena di sangue e alle piume che palpitano all'affannno del suo respiro sempre più stanco dona il suo bacio e la sua agonia" (Fabi, *Vera storia* 13).

marginalized status before the war as a figure whose disability rendered him something other than a full-fledged male citizen, comparable instead to women and children.

Having been turned away on several occasions, Toti eventually received an assignment as a civilian dispatcher at Cervignano. Reputedly he defied orders that prohibited him from any active military involvement to retrieve an Austrian weapon and present it to the commander, who promptly sent him home. In August 1915 Toti is recorded as being back in Rome, where he presented repeated requests to various ministries for permission to return to the front, which was granted in early 1916 thanks to the apparent intervention of Emanuele Filiberto Duca d'Aosta to whom he had written in an undated letter, "Le giuro che ho del fegato e qualunque impresa la più difficile, se mi venisse ordinata, la eseguirei senza indugio," citing his cycling accomplishments as evidence of his physical fitness (Sillani 50). His reassignment as auxiliary volunteer was designed, as before, to keep him out of harm's way, obliging him again to stay well behind the front lines. Apparently Toti was able to obtain a transfer to the Third battalion of Bersaglieri cyclists under major Paride Razzini and appears to have been charged with monitoring lines of communication, retrieving weaponry, and identifying the dead. The details of Toti's final days and eventual death on August 6th are clouded by conflicting accounts. His personal letters home reveal frequent elements of exaggeration and fantasy and it is according to these that he received permission in April to remain in the war zone and display stars like a genuine soldier; however, there is no official record of this claim (Fabi, *Vera storia* 40-44). Likewise, post-facto military accounts that place him at the front of the attack on the morning of August 6th do not match those of contemporary biographers, who report that he suffered terribly from not being allowed to follow the "glorious battalion" (Fabi, *Vera storia* 58). As the only biographer who has attempted to dissect the facts of Toti's life from the possible glorified fictions of his death, Lucio Fabi admits that the task is "un bell'intreccio, per non dir groviglio, tra mito e dissacrazione" (10).

Fabi also identifies three key events in the construction of Toti's myth (*Enrico Toti* 8). First, during a triumphal parade through Trieste, Bologna and Florence, Toti's remains were transported from Monfalcone to be buried at Rome's Cimitero di Verano on May 24, 1922. The service, attended by both family and military, including General Armando Diaz and Marshall Giardino, prompted an episode of public violence that was subsequently attributed to opponents of the war. The second event is identified as the inauguration of a monument designed by Arturo Dazzi and dedicated to Toti in Rome's Villa Borghese on June 4, 1922. The third is marked by Mussolini's pilgrimage to the reputed site of Toti's death, after the inauguration of the Cimitero degli Invitti della Terza Armata del Colle Sant'Elia with King Victor Emanuel III and the Duca d'Aosta on May 24, 1923. The rise of Toti's myth is a clear example of what Gentile has called the *Sacralization of Politics in Fascist Italy*; but while the

Fascist regime nurtured and took full advantage of Toti's transformation from man into national saint, the myth was born in the trenches out of war propaganda's profound need for heroes and in the interest of the royal house, particularly Emanuele Filiberto Duca d'Aosta, commander of the Terza Armata (*Enrico Toti* 8). Furthermore the resonance of Toti's image within the terms of a Christian imaginary ensured that his story would inspire Liberals, Fascists and Christian Democrats alike. Toti's status as a war hero survived the fall of the regime, lasting well into the postwar period, as attested to by David Carbonari's film, *Bella non piangere!* (1955), or the monuments erected at Gorizia in 1958 and at Cassino in 2008. Toti continues to be held up as an example for contemporary Bersaglieri, who greeted Fabi's historic reassessments of 1993 and 2013 with resistance.

Monuments to a National Hero
If, as Elaine Scarry has argued, war "requires both the reciprocal infliction of massive injury and the eventual disowning of the injury so that its attributes can be transferred elsewhere," arguably through acts of omission and redescription, then memorials often serve these sanitizing purposes (64). Toti's case provided a unique opportunity to recast the terms of disability for two reasons: firstly, because Toti lost his leg prior to the war, his injury could be distanced from the mutilating effects of the war on the male population; secondly, his injury could thus be transformed from a sign of weakness into a mark of manliness. Monuments that are dedicated to the memory of Enrico Toti repeatedly evoke Italian visual traditions that synthesize the iconography of the patriotic saint with that of the Greco-Roman mythological hero to legitimize the construction of a paradoxical new model of manhood, which at once glorifies the male body and its ruin.

Each of the three events delineated by Fabi in the construction of Toti's myth reinforced in the public consciousness a sense of Toti as national martyr by activating the traditions and symbolism of Christian history. His remains were retrieved like the relics of the many martyred Christian saints, a shrine was erected, and a pilgrimage made. Beginning with Beltrame's illustration for *La domenica del corriere*, Toti's crutch and, to some extent, his rifle, which in fact he might not have had as a civilian volunteer, became easily identifiable attributes, like those of Saint Paul's sword or Saint Peter's keys, and symbolize his identity as a national martyr. This parallel is perhaps highlighted by the fact that Toti's original tomb at Monfalcone was decorated with a crossed crutch and rifle, translated rather explicitly thereafter on his Roman tombstone into a large palm frond, the element of Christian iconography used to represent the victory of martyrs and the eternal life of the spirit over that of the flesh. Without exception, the war memorials discussed below, those erected in Rome at the Museo dei Bersaglieri and at Villa Borghese, in Gorizia at Piazza Battisti and in Cassino's Piazza Enrico Toti, reiterate Achille Beltrame's initial drawing in their featuring of a crutch in Toti's right hand.

At the Museo dei Bersaglieri in Rome's Porta Pia, the courtyard provides a commemorative space in his honor by way of a monument designed by the sculptor Pietro Piraino (fig. 1). Sitting on a rock base within a circle of rose bushes and against a wall under a dedicatory plaque, his vision of Toti in the trenches on August 6, 1916, recalls Beltrame's early illustration in terms of the presence, rather than positioning, of the crutch. Yet, in Piraino's reimagining, the hero is represented as the fallen soldier, on the ground, with the crutch over his left shoulder, ready to be hurled forward. In this way the sculptor has evoked both the Classical pose of the dying Gaul and the dynamic torso rotation of Gianlorenzo Bernini's Baroque David primed for the toss of the stone in the sling: two of Rome's most iconic artistic treasures. While one evokes a Roman triumph, the other enlists a biblical tale that, more than any other, reminds us of the victory of a diminutive, divinely chosen champion over his gigantic Philistine opponent. This latter artistic quotation suggests a direct comparison between the two heroic figures of David and Toti, and insinuates an ancillary parallel between David and Italy. If the battles at Isonzo were ultimately a futile effort resulting in only a few miles gained at the ultimate cost of a million Italian dead and another million wounded, these battles could ultimately be reimagined via such monuments as a part of a larger war narrative that culminated in the victory of the smaller, younger nation of Italy over the immense Austro-Hungarian Empire. Despite its losses and the terrible defeat at Caporetto, Italy crossed the Isonzo into Austrian territory after an Allied victory in 1918.

By contrast Arturo Dazzi's winning design for Toti's monument on the Pincian Hill (fig. 2) strips the war hero of a uniform, hat or rifle using Toti's naked body itself as a marker of defiance, stoicism and heroism. Recounting the events of the competition and Dazzi's supposedly unanimously chosen models, Guido Guida described the proposed work as one that appropriately captured the spirit of a hero who "moriva con lo sprezzo verso il nemico e la fierezza sul volto per aver guadagnato il suo posto d'onore" (333). With such a statement Guida might equally have been describing Italy's own pride at having won the war and a place at the table with the League of Nations. Toti's symbolic crutch appears once again, this time stretched out behind him at the end of a taut right arm. His stern face and strong jaw point in the opposite direction, looking over his left shoulder and an engaged muscular left arm that props up a frontally positioned, equally muscular torso. With the highly exposed stump of his left leg leaning against a rock formation, Toti's right leg stretches out behind him in an exaggeratedly tense pose, naked heel planted firmly on the ground. In terms of both musculature and posture, the modern hero bears a remarkable resemblance to Antonio Canova's Greek heroes, particularly his *Hercules and Lichas* (1795-1815) or *Theseus Fighting the Centaur* (1804–1819), both of which were executed by the sculptor in Rome and the former of which is in the collection of the Galleria Nazionale di Arte Moderna. These Neoclassical works display the muscular torsos of their respective mythical heroes in frontal view with right limbs extended backwards and electrified with the force of each hero's resolve. While Hercules is about to swing Lichas's frail form over his head to shatter his body against the ground at his feet, Theseus prepares to strike a final deadly blow with the club in his right hand to a centaur that he holds by the throat with his left hand. All three heroes are formally similar, rendered in profile to highlight strong profiles and jaw lines. In so far as Guida argues that Dazzi's work celebrates "un eroe della giovinezza e della vita" with a face expressing "maschia violenza popolana" (331-32), then the artist called upon a familiar visual history of mythological heroism, one which invites comparison with the works of arguably the greatest sculptor of the Napoleonic age. Dazzi's artistic quotations help give Toti new mythical status as an Italian popular hero.

Toti died at the sixth battle of Isonzo and it was during this battle that Italian forces took Gorizia, where a monument designed by sculptor and Bersagliere Mario Montemurro was dedicated to his memory and erected in 1958 (fig. 3). Toti stands at the center of Piazza Cesare Battisti, near the public gardens, on a rocky plinth, wearing the uniform and capercaillie feathered hat of the Bersagliere, with a bicycle resting beside him and a crutch clutched in his right hand. His chest is expanded with what might be a last breath, his arms are slightly elevated by his sides, the fingers of his left hand are partly clenched, and the furrowed brow and open mouth of his face all indicate a body in pain. Toti's furrowed brow and slightly parted lips mirror the facial expression of the famous Laocoon in the Vatican Museums while the position of his upper body recalls Mannerist renderings of Saint Francis receiving the stigmata in paintings by El Greco (1590), Federico Barocci (1594) or Ludovico Cardi Cigoli (1596). All of these images capture Saint Francis's divine rapture or ecstasy with the same slightly opened arms and upward tilt of the chest and chin, a posture that Guido Reni would use again in his painting of *San Filippo Neri in Ecstasy* (1614). The mirroring of these saintly postures suggests that Toti's gunshot wounds somehow correspond to Saint Francis's injuries, both signifying a divine sacrifice and implying a like consecration of the flesh.

Nearly fifty years after the dedication of Toti's statue in Goriza, the municipality of Cassino gathered a committee to erect a monument to Toti in its eponymous piazza in order, according to the city press release, to restore "la giusta dignità ad un personaggio che ha portato alto anche il nome di Cassino nelle pagine di storia" (Comune di Cassino). Egidio Ambrosetti's rendition of the subject was far from unique and it relies closely on the precedents of the monument at Gorizia and Beltrame's early illustration. Toti wears the full regalia of the Bersagliere as at Gorizia, but as in Beltrame's illustration the crutch in Toti's right hand is once again raised over his head as he leans on a rifle in his left. This far more recent memorial demonstrates that the symbolic attributes of Toti's myth have only become more entrenched with the passage of time.

Conclusions

Remarking on "the paradox of the preexistence of an Italian national culture over that of an Italian nation-state," Loredana Polezzi and Charlotte Ross explain that "aestheticized," "regular and regulated," religiously "sublimated" or "youthful, powerful" bodies occupy a preeminent position in Italian "high" art and culture (10). By activating the visual power of Italy's preexisting national culture, Toti's monuments help construct the myth of a national hero in the service of a much broader myth, one that Emilio Gentile has called "the myth of the nation" (*Struggle for Modernity* 2). By infiltrating that canon of regulated and aestheticized bodies, Toti's image as a disabled man is made whole once again by tapping into modernist nationalist fantasies of an Italian "New Man," whose strength of character, dedication to the national cause, and willingness to make the ultimate sacrifice might augur the birth of a "Greater Italy." In attempting to extricate the story of the man from that of his mythic demise, Lucio Fabi reminds us that Toti's motivations for seeking out "la bella morte" were driven by a highly personal desire to be "un soldato e quindi un uomo integro, e non un invalido a cui si fa la carità di un servizio di retrovia" (*Vera storia* 51). Yet, in the service of Italian nationalism, Toti's sentiments were given more universal significance and his myth was manipulated so as to inspire others to make the same ultimate sacrifice.

The visual rhetoric of heroic masculine self-sacrifice is a rhetoric that maintains a powerful hold on the public imagination in the context of contemporary nationalisms and has been re-emboldened by the long series of wars in the Middle East. In Marc Quinn's sculpture, Alison Lapper's disabled naked body resonates with the classical canon of ideal beauty only via the materiality of its white marble, which asks us to look again at the pure nude forms on display. World War I memorials to Toti as a fallen soldier, like the recently mass-produced versions of the Battlefield Cross by artist Richard Rist commemorating the fallen of Iraq and Afghanistan across the United States, are rendered in cast bronze. If white marble reveals the sensuous path of an artist's chisel over the soft stone as s/he considers, traces, and carves the contours of the body, bronze implies a degree of calculated removal from the more sensual or intimate task of sculpting form. It is a hard dark metal that more appropriately obscures formal impurities or imperfections. Alison Lapper's naked form in Trafalgar Square posed a dilemma for some members of the public, perhaps in part because her image demands close formal inspection and reconsideration, challenging the comforting equation that has too often been made between disability and sacrifice, an equation that continues to pervade the imaginary of modernist nationalism and inspire those sacrifices.

The American University of Rome

Works Cited

Belzer, Allison Scardino. *Women and the Great War: Femininity under Fire in Italy*. New York: Palgrave Macmillan, 2010.
Benadusi, Lorenzo. *The Enemy of the New Man: Homosexuality in Fascist Italy*. Madison: U of Wisconsin P, 2012.
Bonetta, Gaetano. *Corpo e nazione: l'educazione, igienica e sessuale nell'Italia liberale*. Milano: Franco Angeli, 1990.
Bourke, Joanna. *Dismembering the Male*. Chicago: U of Chicago P, 1996.
Bracco, Barbara. "Il mutilato di guerra in Italia: polisemie di un luogo crudele." *Memoria e ricerca* 38 (2011): 9-24.
Carden-Coyne, Ana. *Reconstructing the Body: Classicism, Modernism and the First World War*. London: Oxford UP, 2009.
Fabi, Lucio. *Enrico Toti: Una storia fra mito e realtà*. Cremona: Persico, 2013.
_____. *La vera storia di Enrico Toti*. Monfalcone: Edizioni della Laguna, 1993.
Feo, Katherine. "Invisibility: Memory, Masks and Masculinities in the Great War." *Journal of Design History* 20.1 (2014): 17-27.
Fussell, Paul. *The Great War and Modern Memory*. New York: Oxford UP, 1975.
Gagen, Wendy Jane. "Remastering the Body, Renegotiating Gender: Physical Disability and Masculinity suring the First World War." *European Review of History* 14.4 (2007): 525-41.
Gentile, Emilio. *The Sacralization of Politics in Fascist Italy*. Trans. Keith Botsford. Cambridge, MA: Harvard UP, 1996.
_____. *The Struggle for Modernity: Nationalism, Futurism and Fascism*. London: Praeger, 2003.
Guida, Guido. "Il concorso per il monumento a Toti vinto da Arturo Dazzi." *Cronache* 47. 288 (1918): 328-34.
Koon, Tracey H. *Believe, Obey, Fight: Political Socialization of Youth in Fascist Italy*. Chapel Hill: U of North Carolina P, 1985.
Lapper, Alison. *My Life in My Hands*. London: Simon and Schuster, 2005.
Lyall, Sarah. "In Trafalgar Square Much Ado About Statuary." *New York Times*. New York Times, 10 October 2005. Web. 22 September 2014.
Marinetti, F. T. *Come si seducono le donne*. 1918. Firenze: Valecchi, 2003.
Mosse, George. *Fallen Soldier: Reshaping the Memory of World Wars*. London: Oxford UP, 1990.
_____. *The Image of Man: The Creation of Modern Masculinity*. New York: Oxford UP, 1996.
Papini, Giovanni. "La necessità della rivoluzione." *Lacerba* 8 (April 15, 1913).
Polezzi, Loredana, and Charlotte Ross, eds. *In Corpore: Bodies in Post-unification Italy*. Cranbury, NJ: Associated University Presses, 2007.
Praz, Mario. *The Romantic Agony*. 1933. London: Oxford UP, 1970.
"Realizzazione statua di Enrico Toti." *Ufficio Stampa del Comune di Cassino*. Janula, 25 March 2005. Web. 20 September 2014.
Salvante, Martina. "Italian Disabled Veterans between Experience and Representation." *Men After War*. Ed. Steven McVeigh and Nicola Cooper. New York: Routledge, 2013. 111-29.
Scarry, Elaine. *The Body in Pain: The Making and Unmaking of the World*. New York: Oxford UP, 1985.
Sillani, Tommaso, ed. *Lettere di Enrico Toti*. Firenze: Edizioni Bemporad, 1924.

Figure 1. Pietro Piraino, *Enrico Toti*, Museo Storico dei Bersaglieri, Rome. Bronze. Photo Credit: Author.

Figure 2. Arturo Dazzi, *Enrico Toti*, Villa Borghese, Rome, 1919-22. Bronze. Photo in the public domain.

Figure 3. Mario Montemurro, *Enrico Toti*, Piazza Cesare Battisti, Gorizia, 1958. Bronze. Photo Credit: Cristina Beltrami - L'Archivio della scultura.

Silvia Contarini
Pierpaolo Naccarella

La difficile memoria della Grande Guerra nella rivista comunista "Rinascita" (1944-1968)

Introduzione
Dopo avere trascorso quasi vent'anni lontano dall'Italia, il leader comunista Palmiro Togliatti sbarca a Napoli il 27 marzo 1944. Mentre la seconda guerra mondiale continua a infuriare e l'Italia affronta una situazione politico-istituzionale drammatica, Togliatti dedica tempo ed energie alla fondazione di una rivista, "Rinascita", il cui primo numero esce a Salerno nel giugno 1944. Il leader comunista ne sarà il direttore per due decenni, attribuendo con ogni evidenza al periodico un valore strategico: lo scopo sarà di "fornire una guida ideologica" (Anonimo, *Programma* 1) al comunismo italiano e, in particolare, ai quadri del PCI, il Partito comunista italiano (Vittoria, *Togliatti e gli intellettuali* 176).

Una delle principali caratteristiche di "Rinascita" è la grande importanza che in essa hanno le analisi storiche e la commemorazione di avvenimenti storici, come conferma Alatri (*Introduzione* 13), caratteristica che svela sia il "temperamento intellettuale nettamente storicistico" di Togliatti (Alatri, *Introduzione* 14), sia la funzione che il segretario del PCI assegna alla storia per rafforzare il partito e fargli assumere un rilievo nazionale (Vittoria, *Togliatti, la "ricerca oggettiva"* 58).

In questo articolo ci proponiamo di riflettere sulla visione della Grande Guerra — memoria, celebrazione, rivisitazione — proposta nelle pagine di "Rinascita" in un arco temporale di venticinque anni. Perché? La prima guerra mondiale è uno dei massimi avvenimenti storici del ventesimo secolo; essa ha avuto conseguenze rilevanti e durevoli nel campo delle relazioni internazionali come nella vita di ciascuno dei paesi coinvolti e delle popolazioni. "Rinascita" è un periodico di importanza strategica maggiore per il PCI e sarà letto al di là dei quadri di partito, da intellettuali, anche non tesserati; inoltre il PCI aspira a essere partito di massa e di governo, forza politica in grado di trasformare il paese, nei rapporti economici e sociali, come pure sul piano culturale. Come viene rappresentata e analizzata, su "Rinascita", la prima guerra mondiale? Viene dedicato spazio al conflitto? Di che tipo sono gli interventi e chi ne sono gli autori? L'interpretazione resta immutata o evolve nel corso degli anni?

Queste sono alcune delle domande alle quali cercheremo di rispondere, analizzando gli interventi sulla prima guerra mondiale pubblicati nelle seguenti annate: 1944, 1945, 1947, 1948, 1954, 1955, 1957, 1958, 1964, 1965, 1967, 1968. Sono annate in cui si celebra la ricorrenza di date fondamentali della prima guerra mondiale: scoppia nel luglio del 1914; l'Italia vi entra nel maggio 1915; il 1917 è l'anno della disfatta di Caporetto (ottobre-novembre), ma anche quello in cui a Torino si svolgono, ad agosto, moti operai di protesta contro la guerra; le ostilità si concludono nel novembre 1918.[1]

Prima di entrare nel merito, è utile ricordare due avvenimenti legati alla storia di "Rinascita". Il periodico nasce come mensile e mantiene questa periodicità fino alla primavera del 1962, quando diventa un settimanale. Perché questo cambiamento? Togliatti decide di fare della sua rivista uno strumento più agile, "che permettesse una presenza più ramificata e più puntuale" (Vittoria, *Togliatti e gli intellettuali* 173) del PCI nella società italiana, attraversata al tempo da cambiamenti rapidi e profondi. L'altro avvenimento, di poco successivo, è la morte di Togliatti a Yalta il 21 agosto 1964. Dopo la scomparsa del fondatore, il nuovo direttore di "Rinascita" è il dirigente comunista Gian Carlo Pajetta, sostituito nel 1966 dal giornalista e uomo politico Luca Pavolini. Quindi, Togliatti è il direttore di "Rinascita" per tutte le annate della rivista di cui abbiamo fatto lo spoglio, tranne gli ultimi quattro mesi dell'annata 1964 e le annate 1965, 1967 e 1968.

È questo un dato da non sottovalutare, tenuto conto di alcuni elementi della biografia sia di Togliatti sia del suo "maestro", Antonio Gramsci. Nei mesi che precedono la decisione dell'entrata in guerra dell'Italia, Togliatti, iscrittosi al Partito socialista italiano nel 1914, è interventista. Secondo la ricostruzione fatta da alcuni dei suoi principali biografi (Agosti, *Palmiro Togliatti* 12-14; Bocca, *Palmiro Togliatti* 31-39), probabilmente Togliatti condivideva le posizioni di interventismo democratico di Gaetano Salvemini: lo storico e politico pugliese vedeva nel conflitto un'occasione propizia al trionfo del libero scambio in Europa e sosteneva la necessità della partecipazione italiana alla guerra sia in opposizione agli Imperi centrali (l'austro-ungarico e il tedesco) sia per completare l'unità d'Italia (Frangioni, *Salvemini* 53-97).[2]

Nello stesso periodo, un altro giovane intellettuale socialista attivo a Torino, Gramsci, si schiera contro la maggioranza neutralista del PSI (Partito socialista italiano) e adotta le posizioni della mozione presentata da Lenin nel 1915 alla conferenza di Zimmerwald: trasformare la "guerra imperialista" (come tale era percepito dal rivoluzionario russo il primo conflitto mondiale) in guerra civile,

---

[1] La scelta di non procedere allo spoglio esaustivo della rivista, lavoro dal quale sarebbe risultata peraltro una campionatura smisurata ed eccessiva ai fini del presente saggio, è anche frutto di una riflessione sull'importanza cruciale del periodo preso in esame e della funzione celebrativa della rivista, come risulterà chiaro alla lettura del saggio. Sottolineiamo anche che la delimitazione ragionata del corpus, dodici annate su un periodo di venticinque anni, ha prodotto una campionatura sufficientemente vasta (circa 70 interventi) per essere significativa.

[2] Lo slancio interventista di Togliatti è così forte che, dichiarato inabile al servizio militare a causa della sua miopia, nel 1915 si arruola come volontario nella Croce Rossa. Nel 1916 è finalmente dichiarato abile e presta servizio in fanteria e, poi, negli alpini.

cioè in guerra del proletariato contro la borghesia (Vacca, *Gramsci* 348). Vedremo come si posizionerà "Rinascita" rispetto all'interventismo di personalità-culto come Gramsci e Togliatti.

Gli anni quaranta
Procedendo in ordine cronologico con lo spoglio delle annate 1944, 1945, 1947 e 1948, osserviamo che la rivista comunista pubblica una quindicina di interventi nei quali viene citata la prima guerra mondiale, pur non costituendovi l'oggetto principale; nella maggior parte dei casi, anzi, gli interventi le dedicano brevi accenni e la Grande Guerra non è né commemorata né tantomeno celebrata.

Negli anni quaranta, "Rinascita" sembra insomma poco interessata alla prima guerra mondiale; quando affronta l'argomento, il giudizio è intrinsecamente negativo: si è trattato di una guerra imperialistica (Spano, *Appunti sul massimalismo* 270; Alfa, *La rivoluzione sovietica* 289; Astesano, *Come i comunisti lottano* 429-430), nella quale le classi dominanti hanno precipitato i popoli per affermare il loro predominio (Diaz, *Le due libertà* 152). Più precisamente, il conflitto armato, condotto dall'Impero tedesco-prussiano per interessi del tutto estranei a quelli del popolo, aveva visto contrapposti due gruppi di Stati imperialistici, che si erano dati battaglia per realizzare una nuova spartizione del mondo (Anonimo, *La barbarie prussiana* 53 e 55).

Per dimostrare al di là di ogni dubbio che la prima guerra mondiale è stata imperialistica, "Rinascita" ricorre all'indiscutibile autorità politica e intellettuale del padre della rivoluzione d'Ottobre, Lenin. Non soltanto la riflessione che questi svolge sulla Grande Guerra in quanto guerra imperialistica è richiamata da uno dei collaboratori della rivista (La Rocca, *Lenin e la guerra* 134), ma "Rinascita" pubblica nel 1947 un articolo di Lenin risalente al 1923, nel quale il leader bolscevico parla di "prima guerra imperialista mondiale" (Lenin, *L'originalità della Rivoluzione* 280). In altri termini, "Rinascita" sembra fondare la sua visione della prima guerra mondiale sulla riflessione già elaborata da Lenin, anche nell'opuscolo del 1916 intitolato *L'imperialismo fase suprema del capitalismo*, nel quale, riferendosi alla Grande Guerra, Lenin sosteneva che la lotta tra le potenze capitalistiche per la conquista di mercati e territori sarebbe inevitabilmente sfociata in un conflitto armato.[3]

Secondo "Rinascita", la prima guerra mondiale ha avuto conseguenze nefaste sia in Italia, in campo politico ed economico, sia nelle relazioni internazionali. Per

---
[3] Scritto nel 1916 e pubblicato nell'aprile 1917 in russo, col titolo *Imperializm, kak novejsij etap Kapitalizma*, il saggio sarà tradotto in varie lingue, tra cui l'italiano (prima pubblicazione nel 1921). Il testo italiano è oggi disponibile sia in diversi siti (per esempio, nella sezione italiana di Marxist Internet Archive, http://www.marxists.org/italiano/lenin/1916/imperialismo/index.htm) sia grazie a diverse edizioni economiche, a conferma della attualità dell'interesse per le teorie anti-imperialiste di Lenin.

quanto concerne l'Italia, la Grande Guerra, combattuta da masse, in parte politicamente immature, "è stato un fattore importante del successo fascista" (V. C., *Recensione* 159). Inoltre, essa ha prodotto alterazioni negative della "struttura naturale" dell'industria italiana poiché ha danneggiato proprio le industrie che, date le condizioni presenti nella penisola, avrebbero potuto "vivere e prosperare" (Pesenti, *Struttura e avvenire* 235-36). Sul piano internazionale, invece, la prima guerra mondiale ha profondamente mutato gli equilibri, sia rafforzando gli Stati Uniti, dei quali ha stimolato l'attività industriale e lo sviluppo, sia rovinando gli altri paesi capitalistici (Foster, *Esiste una situazione* 13).

In alcune analisi proposte dalla rivista comunista si riconosce nondimeno che la Grande Guerra ha avuto anche conseguenze positive. Il conflitto ha contribuito all'educazione delle masse, preparandole "a realizzare una vera politica marxistica" (Spano, *Appunti sul massimalismo* 270); ha risvegliato i popoli che, nel primo dopoguerra, "ripresero con nuovo e più incalzante vigore le loro rivendicazioni sociali" (Diaz, *Le due libertà* 152); ha fatto cessare il trasformistico compromesso attuato in Italia da Giovanni Giolitti poiché, mostrando a tutti le insufficienze e la debolezza del vecchio Stato liberale, ha permesso al proletariato italiano di porre "la sua candidatura a classe egemonica" (De Rossi, *Dal Partito popolare* 110).

La prima guerra mondiale dunque avrebbe favorito la maturazione politica delle masse, dando loro lo slancio necessario per continuare le lotte con rinnovata foga. Questo "risveglio" suscitato dalla Grande Guerra ha coinvolto non solo le classi popolari e proletarie, ma anche le donne italiane, come sottolinea Rosetta Longo Fazio. Secondo quest'ultima, la prima guerra mondiale è "la grande leva che riesce a muovere le donne [...] a dar loro una maggiore maturità e consapevolezza" e a permettere loro di inserirsi attivamente nella vita politica, economica e sociale dell'Italia (127).[4]

Il principale merito della Grande Guerra che si deduce da alcuni interventi su "Rinascita" sarebbe però un altro. La rivista pubblica uno scritto di Stalin, nel quale il dittatore georgiano, richiamandosi all'autorità di Lenin, cita un passaggio di *L'estremismo, malattia infantile del comunismo*. Secondo Stalin e Lenin, tra le circostanze esterne che hanno favorito il successo della rivoluzione d'Ottobre

---

[4] L'analisi sul ruolo delle donne durante e dopo la guerra e sulla posizione delle femministe e delle militanti socialiste necessiterebbe un'ampia digressione che non trova spazio nel presente saggio. Ci limitiamo a menzionare la condivisibile e autorevole posizione della storica Françoise Thébaud la quale, nel volume da lei curato, dedicato al Novecento, dell'imponente opera *Storia delle donne in Occidente*, dapprincipio ricorda: "L'idea che la Grande Guerra abbia profondamente trasformato il rapporto tra i sessi, ed emancipato le donne in misura molto maggiore dei precedenti anni, o persino secoli, di lotte, è assai diffusa durante e dopo il conflitto. È questo un luogo comune della letteratura e della politica" (25). Per poi concludere: "Preferisco sottolineare, al di là del ruolo essenziale del genere nei sistemi bellici, il carattere profondamente conservatore della guerra in materia di rapporto tra i sessi" (83).

(che, conviene ricordarlo, rappresenta ancora negli anni quaranta il modello e la speranza dei comunisti del mondo intero), c'è stato il fatto che questa è scoppiata durante la prima guerra mondiale. Più precisamente, la Grande Guerra ha contribuito al trionfo della rivoluzione russa per tre ragioni: i grandi gruppi imperialistici, che lottavano tra loro, non potevano curarsi della rivoluzione d'Ottobre; le masse, che desideravano la pace, vedevano la rivoluzione proletaria come via d'uscita dal conflitto armato; infine, la "lunga guerra imperialista", cioè la prima guerra mondiale, avrebbe fatto maturare una crisi rivoluzionaria (Stalin, *Condizioni estere e interne* 311).

Un ultimo elemento positivo legato alla Grande Guerra si evince dalla lettura di "Rinascita": l'esercito italiano ne è uscito "con onore", contrariamente a quanto stava accadendo in quegli anni, affermazione contenuta in un articolo pubblicato nel luglio 1944 quando la seconda guerra mondiale è ancora in corso (Anonimo, *Ufficiali filofascisti* 24).

Presentiamo infine un articolo essenziale, a firma dell'allora vicesegretario del PCI, Luigi Longo, uscito nel numero dell'agosto 1948, dopo l'attentato subito da Togliatti nel luglio dello stesso anno. In questo articolo, chiaro esempio del culto del quale il "Migliore" è oggetto all'interno del PCI, Longo ripercorre le tappe dell'azione politica di Togliatti. Ora, arrivato agli anni della Grande Guerra, così si esprime sull'impegno del capo comunista: "Egli visse, come militante, la tragedia della prima guerra mondiale, la lotta tra sciovinisti, centristi — né aderire né sabotare — e rivoluzionari, dei quali gli operai di Torino presero la testa con le grandi manifestazioni contro la guerra" (Longo, *Il nostro capo* 283). Longo non lascia intendere che Togliatti è stato interventista e ha partecipato al primo conflitto mondiale; il lettore che ignorava la circostanza continuerà a ignorarla.

Gli anni cinquanta
Un decennio dopo, il contesto politico italiano e internazionale è cambiato rispetto all'immediato dopoguerra. Il PCI ha fatto parte del governo italiano fino al maggio 1947, ed è poi diventato la principale forza di opposizione (Colarizi, *Storia dei partiti* 88-117). Il 1947 è un anno decisivo anche nel campo delle relazioni internazionali perché scoppia la guerra fredda, la cui fase più acuta termina nel 1953 con la morte di Stalin, cui faranno seguito la distensione internazionale e l'ampio diffondersi di ideali pacifisti, favoriti anche dal timore permanente di un conflitto nucleare (Colarizi, *Storia dei partiti* 171-81). Nel 1956, a soli tre anni dalla scomparsa di Stalin, il movimento comunista internazionale, di cui il PCI è parte integrante, è scosso sia dalla denuncia dei crimini del dittatore georgiano, fatta in occasione del XX congresso del PCUS, sia dall'intervento dei carri armati sovietici in Ungheria. Il PCI togliattiano sostiene la sanguinosa repressione condotta dall'Armata Rossa, posizione che condurrà numerose personalità della cultura a prendere le distanze dal partito (Colarizi, *Storia dei partiti* 203-10).

Nonostante un contesto così differente, l'immagine della prima guerra mondiale che affiora dalla lettura delle annate 1954, 1955, 1957 e 1958 di "Rinascita" è sostanzialmente immutata. Come nel decennio precedente, negli interventi su "Rinascita" in cui si parla della Grande Guerra — 16 in totale —, essa svolge un ruolo marginale (eccetto in un caso su cui ci soffermeremo). E come negli anni quaranta, viene valutata in modo negativo. Una condanna storica, politica e morale basata sulle seguenti considerazioni:
1) si è trattato di una guerra imperialistica. Questo giudizio è ricorrente (Canzio, *La partecipazione italiana* 171; Amendola, *Il lungo cammino* 627; Fabbrini, *Recensione* 128; Sereni, *Nella vita e nella lotta* 552; Pieck, *Ricordo di Clara Zetkin* 558), e lo si trova soprattutto in un influente testo di Lenin (*1920* 753).
2) Si è trattato anche di una guerra "borghese", che ha rivelato "la stupidità, la bestialità, la viltà, l'immoralità della borghesia, dello Stato borghese, del patriottismo borghese, della 'patria borghese'" (Malaparte, *Autobiografia* 376).
3) La partecipazione dell'Italia al conflitto si è attuata, come afferma autorevolmente Togliatti, "attraverso una brutale violazione della legalità parlamentare, di fronte a un Paese nella sua maggioranza ostile o passivo" (*Attualità del pensiero* 139). Secondo il direttore di "Rinascita", la decisione di fare entrare in guerra l'Italia è stata presa in violazione dello Statuto albertino ed è stata anche politicamente e moralmente illegittima poiché solo una minoranza degli Italiani le era favorevole.

Rispetto agli anni quaranta, tuttavia, la riflessione si concentra particolarmente sulle cause del conflitto. A questo proposito spicca il solo intervento che ha come oggetto principale la Grande Guerra, il cui autore è il padre della rivoluzione d'Ottobre. Si tratta di un rapporto presentato da Lenin nel 1920 in occasione di un congresso dell'Internazionale comunista. Il rivoluzionario bolscevico spiega, con tono appassionato e perentorio, le ragioni per le quali è scoppiata la "guerra imperialistica": è stata la conseguenza inevitabile della "spartizione di tutta la terra" da parte delle potenze coloniali capitalistiche, del "dominio del monopolio capitalistico" e dell'"onnipotenza di un numero infimo di grandissime banche". Secondo Lenin, la guerra è stata fatta "per una nuova spartizione del mondo" e "per decidere quale dei ristrettissimi gruppi dei grandissimi Stati — il gruppo inglese o il gruppo tedesco — avrebbe ottenuto la possibilità e il diritto di saccheggiare, di soffocare, di sfruttare il mondo intiero" (*1920* 752).

L'intervento di Lenin è pubblicato nel 1958 in un voluminoso numero monografico di "Rinascita" intitolato *Crepuscolo del colonialismo*. Nello stesso numero, l'interpretazione leniniana della Grande Guerra è ripresa in altri due articoli: visibilmente, i collaboratori di "Rinascita" si riconoscono nell'interpretazione di Lenin, secondo cui la prima guerra mondiale ha avuto cause essenzialmente economiche in quanto decisa per sapere chi avrebbe conquistato il diritto di utilizzare le risorse e le ricchezze della Terra. Per esempio,

Pacor ritiene che la Grande Guerra sia stata il risultato della crisi di sovrapproduzione di fine ottocento, dell'aumento della concorrenza tra paesi industrializzati e colonialisti e della "lotta più accanita per le materie prime e per i mercati" imposta dai nuovi investimenti resi necessari dallo sviluppo tecnologico (*Ascesa e fine* 696). E Michele Salerno, citando Lenin, precisa che la guerra è stata combattuta dalle potenze imperialistiche per "decidere i destini dei paesi coloniali", cioè "per ridividersi il mondo coloniale" (712 e 714).

Questa lettura economicistica delle cause della guerra era già stata proposta, tre anni prima, dal dirigente comunista Giorgio Amendola, secondo il quale "le forze motrici" del primo conflitto mondiale erano quelle della "grande industria", che "si poneva fini di espansione imperialistica" (*Il lungo cammino* 627).

Inoltre, è inevitabile che una guerra dovuta all'avidità degli Stati coloniali capitalistici abbia avuto conseguenze negative. Lenin, Amendola e Gramsci ne individuano tre: innanzitutto, il conflitto ha precipitato la popolazione dei paesi sconfitti, a cominciare da quella tedesca, "in una situazione di soggezione coloniale, di miseria, di fame, di rovina, di mancanza di diritti" (Lenin, *1920* 753). In secondo luogo, ha favorito l'avvento in Italia del fascismo (Amendola, *Il lungo cammino* 624 e 627). Infine, sempre in Italia, ha danneggiato particolarmente il Mezzogiorno, aggravandone il ritardo rispetto al Nord industriale (Gramsci, *Il Mezzogiorno e la guerra* 151-52).

Quest'ultimo effetto negativo della Grande Guerra è espresso da Gramsci in un articolo apparso per la prima volta nel 1916 nel settimanale "Il grido del popolo", ripubblicato da "Rinascita" nel 1957 in occasione del ventesimo anniversario della morte dell'uomo politico sardo. Ma allo stesso Gramsci e alla sua autorità "Rinascita" si richiama per mostrare che la prima guerra mondiale ha avuto anche conseguenze positive. Quali? Quattro anni di guerra combattuta nelle trincee, si può leggere in un articolo del giornalista e politico comunista Luciano Barca che cita esplicitamente Gramsci, "rompono molte barriere tra operai e contadini, annodano nuovi legami di solidarietà che 'altrimenti solo decine e decine di anni di esperienza storica e di lotte intermittenti avrebbero suscitato'" (747). La prima di queste conseguenze è dunque che la vita di trincea sopportata dai soldati ha favorito l'unità tra le classi sociali più svantaggiate. Su queste ricade un altro effetto positivo del conflitto, ricordato dallo storico Franco Ferri in un denso articolo dedicato alla concezione gramsciana dei consigli di fabbrica e del partito. Secondo Ferri, Gramsci ritiene che la Grande Guerra abbia "messo in movimento masse sterminate di operai e di contadini", nei quali la vita di trincea e i sacrifici hanno "creato la coscienza di nuovi diritti, la spinta a nuove rivendicazioni". Dal conflitto, insomma, esce "un prorompente sviluppo di immense forze sociali nuove e tumultuose" (461).

Le altre due conseguenze positive della prima guerra mondiale, ma relativamente alla Russia, sono enunciate direttamente da Gramsci. Il conflitto ha suscitato in Russia, pur tra miserie e sofferenze inenarrabili, una "volontà collettiva popolare"; esso "ha servito a spoltrire le volontà" che si sono messe rapidamente "all'unisono" (*La rivoluzione contro il "Capitale"* 147), provocando in tal modo un'accelerazione della storia. Sempre secondo Gramsci, "nel sommovimento ideale provocato" dalla prima guerra mondiale, si è rivelata una forza nuova, quella dei "massimalisti russi", cioè dei bolscevichi. Il fatto che il "massimalismo russo" si sia fatto conoscere durante questo conflitto e grazie a esso è, per il politico sardo, un evento di portata storica che gioverà a tutte le nazioni e a tutti i popoli: "[...] al massimalismo russo la storia riserva un posto di primo ordine, superiore a quello dei giacobini francesi" (*Wilson e i massimalisti russi* 148).

Gramsci e i collaboratori di "Rinascita" che lo citano non sono i soli a mettere in evidenza i "meriti" della prima guerra mondiale. Secondo Curzio Malaparte, la disfatta di Caporetto è stata, in realtà, "una 'rivolta' della fanteria, cioè del 'proletariato della guerra'"; per questa ragione, la si può considerare "come l'atto iniziale della rivoluzione comunista italiana" (*Autobiografia* 376). Infine, lo storico Roberto Battaglia si appoggia sull'autorità di Lenin per sottolineare che la prima guerra mondiale ha posto in modo perentorio "le questioni essenziali": o difendere i privilegi e i vantaggi della borghesia oppure abbattere i governi garanti di quei privilegi attraverso l'azione rivoluzionaria svolta dal proletariato internazionalmente solidale (860).

Gli anni sessanta
Negli anni sessanta, "Rinascita" subisce una doppia trasformazione. Da mensile, diventa settimanale, periodicità che consente di seguire più da vicino l'attualità politica italiana e internazionale e, pertanto, di intervenire con maggiore capillarità nel dibattito politico e culturale. L'altra trasformazione è legata al decesso di Togliatti: "Rinascita" perde colui che ne ha elaborato e deciso la linea per oltre due decenni. I suoi primi due successori, Gian Carlo Pajetta e, poi, Luca Pavolini, non hanno certo il prestigio e il potere di Togliatti, che concentrava nella sua persona la carica di direttore di "Rinascita" e di segretario politico del PCI. L'avvicendamento alla direzione del periodico sembra riflettersi sul contenuto degli articoli, che appare, come vedremo, meno costretto all'interno di una rigida griglia politico-ideologica.

Non sono solo la morte di Togliatti e il cambio di leadership a introdurre maggiore libertà interpretativa[5]: il contesto internazionale è mutato. Da un lato, il

---

[5] Le trasformazioni nella leadership del PCI sono notevoli, poiché al carismatico Togliatti succede Luigi Longo, che promuove una gestione collegiale del PCI, considerandosi un semplice "primus inter pares" (Höbel, *Il PCI di Luigi Longo* 57-59). Un altro cambiamento importante in seno al PCI è l'indebolirsi del dogma del "centralismo democratico" con la nascita, dopo la scomparsa di Togliatti, di ben quattro correnti interne (Colarizi, *Storia dei partiti* 342-350).

rapporto con il PCUS, gradualmente si allenta.[6] Dall'altro, l'anno successivo al decesso di Togliatti l'*escalation* della guerra in Vietnam raggiunge l'apice, prima con i bombardamenti massicci sul Nord, poi con la decisione degli Stati Uniti di passare all'intervento diretto, e questo induce i comunisti italiani a accentuare la lettura classista delle relazioni internazionali e, di conseguenza, l'antiamericanismo e il "terzomondismo" (Pons, *L'URSS e il PCI* 30).

Questi cambiamenti si riflettono sul modo in cui "Rinascita" affronta il tema della prima guerra mondiale nelle annate 1964, 1965, 1967 e 1968, nelle quali si trovano ben 37 interventi che parlano del conflitto. Rispetto ai due decenni precedenti, emerge subito la differenza quantitativa (gli articoli sono ben più numerosi), ma la differenza è anche qualitativa: il conflitto è l'oggetto principale di numerosi interventi. Soprattutto, si notano un impegno intellettuale e un livello di approfondimento molto superiori rispetto ai decenni precedenti. A questo non è estraneo il fatto che, nella grande maggioranza dei casi, gli autori degli interventi non sono veri e propri politici, ma storici di primo piano, talora membri del PCI, talora semplici "compagni di strada".

Osserviamo quindi che negli anni sessanta, il giudizio sulla Grande Guerra è ancora più negativo e viene espresso in maniera ancora più netta. Ecco perché: 1) si trattò di una guerra imperialistica (Spriano, *Il "no" alla socialdemocrazia* 5; Lepre, *I partiti socialisti europei* 22; Lepre, *Il revisionismo in Italia* 29; Longo, *Un grave pericolo* 2; Spriano, *Zimmerwald* 19; Secchia, *Il no di Liebknecht* 28); 2) fu una guerra inutile (Longo, *Un grave pericolo* 2; Spriano, *Isonzo 1917* 28); 3) la guerra dissanguò il popolo e rovinò l'Italia (Longo, *Un grave pericolo* 2); 4) l'Italia fu coinvolta attraverso menzogne e pretesti (Longo, *Un grave pericolo* 2); 5) la guerra fu imposta da una minoranza alla maggioranza degli Italiani (De Felice, *Caporetto perché?* 25), come prova "la estrema ristrettezza della base democratica di potere" in Italia alla vigilia della Grande Guerra (Spriano, *L'Italia neutrale* 28).

Questa critica radicale diventa ancora più impietosa quando si tratta di valutare il comportamento e le scelte degli alti ufficiali delle forze armate italiane, a cominciare dai membri dello stato maggiore dell'esercito. I collaboratori di "Rinascita" attaccano duramente gli ufficiali per la loro mancanza di umanità, l'incompetenza e gli errori commessi (Alatri, *Caporetto* 22-23; Lepre, *Recensione* di Emilio Faldella, *La Grande Guerra. Le battaglie dell'Isonzo* 18), nonché per

---

[6] In realtà, per il primo "strappo" ufficiale da Mosca occorrerà aspettare l'agosto 1968, quando il PCI criticherà pubblicamente l'invasione della Cecoslovacchia compiuta dalle truppe del Patto di Varsavia. Tuttavia, già nel memoriale di Yalta (agosto 1964), una sorta di testamento politico, Togliatti teorizza il "policentrismo" nel movimento comunista internazionale. Sarà la nozione chiave per sciogliere il vincolo di ferro con l'URSS, il cui mito si avvia al declino; Togliatti utilizza il concetto di policentrismo per affermare che ogni partito comunista ha il diritto, ma anche il dovere, di elaborare il suo modello rivoluzionario, cioè di trovare la sua via al comunismo (Colarizi, *Storia dei partiti* 250-54).

l'atteggiamento sterilmente e pericolosamente romantico e retorico, che li portava a declamare vanamente "sull'Idea della Vittoria" (Ferrata, *Un anno sull'Altipiano* 23). Non sorprende dunque che le cause della disfatta di Caporetto siano "tutte riconducibili alla condotta della guerra dall'alto, col logorio, la rabbia, la insopportabilità che aveva oramai generato nella truppa" (Spriano, *Isonzo 1917* 29). Detto altrimenti, la lontananza abissale, anzi la vera e propria frattura esistente tra gli alti comandi dell'esercito e i soldati semplici, che erano in gran parte di condizione operaia o contadina, ha generato in questi ultimi un senso di "estraniazione [...] alla guerra dei signori ufficiali", portandoli a tentare di sottrarsi in tutti modi (diserzione, ammutinamento e perfino autolesionismo) a un conflitto al quale si sentivano estranei (Spriano, *I due volti della guerra* 32).

Le cause della prima guerra mondiale restano di tipo fondamentalmente economico: il conflitto è stato provocato dagli "interessi industriali e commerciali" di 'poche cricche'" (Cipriani, *La guerra alla televisione* 19). Esso è stato determinato dalle "forze sociali interessate alla conquista di territori altrui e alla dominazione di altri popoli" (Boffa, *Dal "decreto sulla pace"* 30) e, dunque, in ultima analisi, dal capitalismo, che "porta in sé la guerra, come le nubi l'uragano" (Longo, *Il dilemma della pace* 3). Il peso dell'elemento economico è così forte che, secondo lo storico comunista Paolo Alatri, "sono le contraddizioni degli interessi capitalistici e imperialistici facenti capo alle grandi potenze" che spiegano perché, al termine della prima guerra mondiale, la comunità internazionale deve fronteggiare gli stessi problemi dell'anteguerra (Alatri, *Recensione* di Mario Toscano, *Pagine di storia diplomatica contemporanea* 31). E tuttavia, sulle pagine di "Rinascita", una voce autorevole, quella di un altro storico comunista, Paolo Spriano, si distacca da questa interpretazione in chiave puramente "economicistica" della prima guerra mondiale. Spriano ritiene che sulla decisione della corte e del governo di fare entrare l'Italia nel conflitto abbiano esercitato "scarso peso" le "pressioni guerrafondaie venute da ambienti industriali e finanziari". Esistevano infatti imprenditori che sostenevano la neutralità perché pensavano, grazie a questa, di ottenere commesse dagli Stati in guerra. Inoltre, la capacità degli imprenditori di influenzare direttamente i principali decisori politici era ancora molto limitata. Spriano ritiene che in realtà nell'elaborazione della politica estera italiana siano prevalsi calcoli e paure legati alla politica interna, cioè "al disegno di tenere a freno il socialismo e le spinte eversive con una guerra [...] capace di rinsaldare un equilibrio strettamente conservatore" (*L'Italia neutrale* 28).

Questa lettura delle ragioni dell'intervento italiano nella Grande Guerra è innovativa rispetto alla linea sempre seguita da "Rinascita" che prevale ancora negli anni sessanta. Spriano non vede la prima guerra mondiale come evento imposto dalla brama di ricchezza di capitalisti, banchieri e grandi industriali, come voleva l'interpretazione fondata sugli scritti e i discorsi di Lenin. Ed è questo uno degli esempi più chiari del minore conformismo ideologico e della maggiore diversità di punti di vista che caratterizzano, negli anni sessanta, gli interventi su "Rinascita".

Sulle pagine del settimanale, la prima guerra mondiale è anche oggetto di un'operazione di demistificazione ideologica. "Rinascita" si schiera contro la lettura della Grande Guerra come continuazione del Risorgimento, contro "il mito patriottardo" e il dannunzianesimo proteso "verso il culto dell'eroismo sublime" che hanno aviluppato il conflitto (Argentieri, *Nuovi film di montaggio* 26), contro ogni forma di retorica esaltatrice della guerra (Lepre, *Le lettere di Battisti* 25), "contro l'oleografia ufficiale dei libri di storia patria, contro i canti di vittoria" insegnati nelle aule scolastiche durante il fascismo per celebrare la prima guerra mondiale, contro ogni assurdo nazionalismo (Seroni, *Ritorno sul Carso* 20). La posizione da cui, tra il 1964 e il 1968, numerosi collaboratori di "Rinascita" giudicano questo conflitto è apertamente e nettamente pacifista (Anonimo, *Introduzione* a Jean Jaurès, *Sull'orlo della tragedia* 28; Longo, *Un grave pericolo* 2; Cipriani, *La guerra alla televisione* 19; Spriano, *Zimmerwald* 19; Boffa, *Dal "decreto sulla pace"* 28-30; Ungaretti, *Ritorno sui luoghi* 28; Spriano, *I due volti* 32).

L'orientamento pacifista è confermato dalla decisione di dare in omaggio, a chi si abbonerà alla rivista per l'anno 1968, un libro contenente lettere di due personalità comuniste fortemente ostili alla prima guerra mondiale, Karl Liebknecht e Rosa Luxemburg; un libro che può considerarsi una sorta di manifesto pacifista. Il dirigente comunista Pietro Secchia spiega in questi termini il senso del volume omaggio, del quale la rivista ha pubblicato un estratto già nell'ottobre 1967 (Liebknecht e Luxemburg, *Lettere di Karl Liebknecht e Rosa Luxemburg* 16-17): "La pubblicazione che *Rinascita* offre in omaggio ai suoi lettori nell'anno in cui le forze avanzate e progressive sono impegnate e devono ancor più impegnarsi nella lotta contro la NATO, è quanto mai opportuna". Inutile sottolineare come la posizione sulla Grande Guerra espressa su "Rinascita" tra il 1964 e il 1968 sia influenzata dalle esigenze politiche del momento, ossia dalla necessità di alimentare la campagna svolta dal PCI contro la NATO e contro la guerra del Vietnam.

Non è il solo esempio dell'influenza dell'attualità politica sul modo in cui la Grande Guerra viene rievocata. Gli autori di quattro interventi già citati svolgono un parallelo tra il tempo presente e il periodo della prima guerra mondiale. In particolare, Longo critica gli Stati Uniti perché cercano di coinvolgere l'Italia nella loro politica da "gendarme mondiale", facendole così correre il rischio di restare nuovamente invischiata "in avventure imperialistiche", come già successo all'epoca della Grande Guerra (*Un grave pericolo* 2). Il giornalista comunista Giuseppe Boffa e lo stesso Longo affermano che la politica estera dell'URSS è coerente nei suoi cinquanta anni di storia: dal "Decreto sulla pace" leninista, con il quale nel novembre 1917 si proponeva ai popoli in guerra una pace democratica, cioè senza annessioni né riparazioni, fino alla concezione della "coesistenza pacifica", con la quale negli anni sessanta l'URSS si identifica quasi nella vita internazionale (Boffa, *Dal "decreto sulla pace"* 28-30; Longo, *Il dilemma della pace* 3-4). Spriano, infine, scrive che i contadini e gli operai che si opposero con tutti i mezzi alla partecipazione alla prima guerra mondiale "costituiscono gli incunaboli di quella che nella dimensione della guerra atomica diventerà la ideologia del dissenso" (*I due volti della guerra* 32). Tutti questi autori associano la loro riflessione sulla prima guerra mondiale alla volontà di rendere credibili le posizioni assunte negli anni sessanta dal movimento comunista internazionale.

In ogni caso, su "Rinascita" negli anni sessanta, il conflitto è visto come radicalmente negativo. Se ne indica esplicitamente una conseguenza nefasta, già espressa nei decenni precedenti: la guerra ha rafforzato "indubbiamente le correnti di destra" (Lepre, *Epistolario di Omodeo* 29; Lepre, *Recensione* di Piero Pieri, *L'Italia nella prima guerra mondiale* 33) e, in particolare, il fascismo (Lepre, *Risposta alla lettera di Livia Battisti* 27). All'opposto, le conseguenze positive si riducono a una sola: "[...] è la svolta della grande guerra a porre in luce, in una luce nuova, le forze rivoluzionarie che si agitano nel nostro paese [l'Italia]. E non solo in questo" (Spriano, *Gramsci e Bordiga* 28). Secondo Spriano, la prima guerra mondiale segna un mutamento radicale, che crea un contesto propizio alla valorizzazione delle formazioni politiche rivoluzionarie.

Una memoria evolutiva
Nella riflessione sin qui svolta sul modo in cui "Rinascita" parla della prima guerra mondiale tra il 1964 e il 1968, abbiamo evidenziato alcune differenze rispetto ai decenni precedenti, legate al mutato contesto. Approfondendo l'analisi in questa direzione, si rilevano altri elementi di discontinuità.

In primo luogo, negli anni sessanta, alcuni collaboratori di "Rinascita" ragionano sul ruolo e sull'azione dei Partiti socialisti europei e, specialmente, di quello italiano, alla vigilia e durante la prima guerra mondiale. Nell'ambito di questa riflessione, lo storico comunista Aurelio Lepre critica le forze politiche socialiste affermando che le ambiguità e le incertezze dei partiti membri della Seconda internazionale nel momento della crisi del 1914 sono dovute soprattutto al fatto che, nei vari Stati europei, la solidarietà e la coesione nazionali erano più forti della solidarietà internazionalista tra partiti socialisti (*I partiti socialisti europei* 21-22; *Risposta alla lettera di Renato Risaliti* 31).[7] Tali carenze ed esitazioni non risparmiavano il PSI; col risultato, sempre secondo Lepre, che non solo il PSI non riuscì a sfruttare la guerra per fare la rivoluzione, ma non fu nemmeno capace di saldarsi a quella parte della borghesia italiana che era contraria al conflitto (*24 maggio 1915*).

La posizione di Spriano è diversa, benché come Lepre si mostri critico nei confronti della maggior parte dei Partiti socialisti europei che, non tenendo fede

---

[7] Negli stessi articoli, Lepre mette in luce anche la debolezza ideologica dei dirigenti dei vari PS e la loro integrazione nel sistema.

all'impegno per la pace assunto all'inizio della prima guerra mondiale, passano nel campo del "socialsciovinismo" e appoggiano il conflitto (*Zimmerwald* 19).[8] Più sfumato è invece il giudizio di Spriano sul PSI. Pur apprezzando la "sterzata a sinistra" del PSI nei mesi che precedono lo scoppio della Grande Guerra, sterzata che ne fa "un movimento particolarmente sensibile all'azione di massa, particolarmente intransigente nei suoi connotati di classe", Spriano evidenzia l'"intima antinomia" degli anni di conflitto: il PSI ebbe il merito di "ripudiare ogni collaborazione con la borghesia nella guerra imperialistica", ma le sue componenti riformiste crearono una "situazione di incertezza e di esitazione" (*Il "no" alla socialdemocrazia* 5). Precisa che "la propaganda socialista contro la guerra è stata efficace", senza assumere carattere rivoluzionario, malgrado la maggioranza del PSI avesse una "posizione incerta" e una condotta dai "limiti attendistici" (*Caporetto* 15; *Gramsci e Bordiga* 28).

Un'altra novità, in alcuni articoli pubblicati tra il 1964 e il 1968, è il riferimento esplicito all'anniversario della Grande Guerra (Lepre, *I partiti socialisti europei* 21; Lepre, *24 maggio 1915* 23; Spriano, *Caporetto* 15; De Felice, *Caporetto perché?* 25). Ossia, solo negli anni sessanta la prima guerra mondiale diventa per "Rinascita" degna di commemorazione storica. E, tuttavia, la rivista comunista tiene a sottolineare la differenza tra il modo in cui rievoca la Grande Guerra in occasione di anniversari significativi, come il cinquantesimo dell'entrata in guerra dell'Italia, e le celebrazioni ufficiali, dalle quali essa prende le distanze. I collaboratori di "Rinascita" spiegano che non intendono unirsi al coro delle celebrazioni promosse dal governo perché queste sono vanamente retoriche (Spriano, *Isonzo 1917* 29; Anonimo, *Il 4 novembre di Gramsci* 24; Spriano, *I due volti della guerra* 32) e servono, in realtà, a coprire problemi che sarebbe urgente risolvere (Sema, *Destino di Trieste* 6).

Un'ultima novità risulta dalla lettura delle annate di "Rinascita" comprese tra il 1964 e il 1968. Mentre nei due decenni precedenti ogni forma di interventismo era stata condannata con vigore, ora sulle sue pagine si compie uno sforzo considerevole per comprendere le ragioni della partecipazione alla prima guerra mondiale di due "interventisti democratici", nei confronti dei quali si esprime stima ed empatia. "Rinascita" presenta in termini positivi la figura di Giuseppe Lombardo-Radice, padre di Lucio, dirigente comunista e collaboratore della rivista. Ricorda che Giuseppe Lombardo-Radice era uscito dal Partito socialista nel settembre 1914 perché era convinto che la partecipazione alla guerra contro gli Imperi centrali fosse necessaria per completare il Risorgimento e per fare vincere la democrazia e l'indipendenza dei popoli europei. Aggiunge che

---

[8] La riflessione di Spriano è influenzata da Lenin che, come si ricorda in un altro intervento pubblicato da "Rinascita", polemizzava nel 1917 contro la corrente socialsciovinista dominante "nei partiti socialisti ufficiali di tutto il mondo" (Fabbri, *Il dramma del socialismo europeo* 22).

nell'autunno 1914, lo studioso siciliano era "stimato da tutti [...] per la sua generosità e la sua integrità morale" e fa notare che, coerente come sempre con le sue idee, appena l'Italia entrò in guerra, "si presentò volontario" (Anonimo, *Introduzione* a *Una iniziativa di Gramsci* 32).

L'altro "interventista democratico" di cui su "Rinascita" si parla in termini positivi è lo scrittore Piero Jahier, del quale Manacorda dice che "tese sempre a inserire la prima guerra mondiale 'in un processo di sviluppo della democrazia e della libertà' [...] sia per quanto doveva riguardare i rapporti fra i popoli sia, ancor più, per quanto doveva riguardare i rapporti interni della società italiana" (Manacorda, *Recensione* di Piero Jahier, *1918 L'Astico. 1919 Il Nuovo Contadino* 30). Si ammette dunque che la partecipazione di Jahier come volontario alla Grande Guerra avesse avuto motivazioni nobili, quali la democratizzazione delle relazioni tra gli Stati e tra le diverse classi della società italiana.

Come si è detto, anche Togliatti era stato interventista e aveva sostenuto la partecipazione dell'Italia alla prima guerra mondiale per ragioni simili a quelle di Lombardo-Radice e di Jahier; ma nel 1948, quando Longo — il "numero 2" del PCI — aveva parlato dell'azione politica di Togliatti negli anni del conflitto, una formula era stata pudicamente ellittica: "visse, come militante, la tragedia della prima guerra mondiale" (*Il nostro capo* 283). Il periodico comunista, che in quel periodo condannava ogni forma di interventismo, preferiva non dire che il suo direttore e segretario del PCI aveva sostenuto l'entrata in guerra dell'Italia. Nel 1964, sedici anni dopo la pubblicazione dell'articolo di Longo, il PCI e "Rinascita" sono cambiati. Ne sono una testimonianza visibile i due interventi nei quali si riconoscono e si comprendono (anche se non si condividono) le ragioni dell'"interventismo democratico". Si osservi che quando "Rinascita" pubblica lo scritto su Lombardo-Radice, Togliatti è ancora in vita, mentre è deceduto da oltre un mese quando appare l'intervento su Jahier. Se è plausibile pensare che la morte di Togliatti abbia permesso di affrontare argomenti che, quando il "Migliore" dirigeva la rivista, sarebbero stati difficili da trattare, l'evoluzione della rivista (e del Partito) era comunque in corso.

Conclusioni
Quali conclusioni possiamo trarre dalla lettura di circa settanta articoli, pubblicati su "Rinascita" nelle dodici annate considerate, su un periodo di venticinque anni?

Il primo elemento da sottolineare è che l'interpretazione che la rivista comunista dà della Grande Guerra si sviluppa, almeno negli anni quaranta e cinquanta, all'interno e nei limiti di un'uniformizzante griglia ideologica. La lettura della prima guerra mondiale è monocausale e dunque riduttiva. L'applicazione del dogma del materialismo storico nel campo della riflessione storiografica porta i collaboratori della rivista a ignorare le cause non economiche della Grande Guerra. Nessuna riflessione verte su aspetti socio-culturali: le cause e conseguenze economiche da un lato, le implicazioni ideologiche e politiche dall'altro sono gli unici aspetti che emergono da "Rinascita", un periodico, ricordiamolo, destinato a formare la classe dirigente comunista e gli intellettuali vicini al partito. Questo dogmatismo ha come conseguenza l'impoverimento dell'analisi sulla prima guerra mondiale, della quale "Rinascita" non coglie né la complessità né la portata.

Se non sorprende che una rivista di partito proponga una lettura fortemente ideologica di un avvenimento maggiore, lo studio che abbiamo condotto permette di individuare un'altra caratteristica, più peculiare. Si tratta del rispetto dell'autorità dei "numi tutelari" del comunismo italiano, Lenin e Gramsci, citati dai collaboratori di "Rinascita" come interpreti pressoché infallibili. Un'analisi della prima guerra mondiale fondata su scritti o discorsi di Lenin o Gramsci dà la certezza, a chi si esprime sulle pagine di "Rinascita", di essere nel vero. Il risultato di una tale riflessione condizionata dall'ideologia e rispettosa del principio d'autorità, è stato per due decenni un "giudizio 'canonico'" sulla Grande Guerra, sia di "Rinascita" che del PCI, come osserva acutamente (e polemicamente) la figlia di Cesare Battisti, Livia, in una lettera inviata nel 1967 al direttore della rivista (*Lettera a Rinascita* 27*)*. Sono considerazioni valide fino agli inizi degli anni sessanta quando, grazie alla graduale liberalizzazione che comincia a investire il comunismo italiano, l'interpretazione della prima guerra mondiale evolve.

La seconda conclusione che possiamo trarre è che la memoria del passato e la commemorazione sono condizionate anche dalle esigenze politiche del presente. In altre parole, abbiamo visto che l'interpretazione data dai collaboratori di "Rinascita" alla Grande Guerra risente degli imperativi politici che il PCI ha nel momento in cui essi scrivono (Guiso, *La seconda guerra mondiale* 531-532). Basti ricordare quanto il pacifismo, rivendicato dal PCI negli anni sessanta, condizioni la nuova lettura della Grande Guerra: la condanna è assoluta alla luce dei valori che il PCI intende incarnare e che lo spingono a opporsi con durezza alla politica, vista come bellicistica e aggressivamente imperialistica, degli Stati Uniti in Vietnam e, attraverso la NATO, anche in Europa. Si ricordi anche come, negli anni sessanta, l'influenza della lettura leninista della Grande Guerra si smorzi a mano a mano che il prestigio del Paese-guida si affievoliva; non a caso, diversamente da quanto avveniva nei decenni precedenti, il padre della rivoluzione d'Ottobre viene citato sporadicamente come interprete autorevole del conflitto.

La terza e ultima conclusione è forse quella che più si presta al dibattito e a ulteriori approfondimenti. Si sono notate le difficoltà e gli imbarazzi dei collaboratori di "Rinascita" nell'interpretare, o nel semplice commemorare, uno snodo cruciale della storia e della cultura quale fu la prima guerra mondiale. Alla Grande Guerra, per due decenni, "Rinascita" riserva uno spazio molto limitato. Certo, per il PCI la prima guerra mondiale è un avvenimento negativo, seppure con alcune conseguenze positive, e in quanto tale non è degno di essere celebrato.

Ma se si considera da un lato l'importanza epocale della prima guerra mondiale e dall'altro l'impostazione di "Rinascita", così attenta agli anniversari storici e alla rielaborazione del passato, sarebbe stato legittimo attendersi maggiore attenzione e una seria riflessione su quella che, non a caso, è stata chiamata la Grande Guerra.

Ora, si ha quasi l'impressione che la rivista comunista sfugga a un confronto esplicito e diretto con questo avvenimento. Perché? Le ragioni sono probabilmente legate, almeno fino al 1964, alla leadership del PCI: Togliatti era stato interventista, ma il partito condannava la prima guerra mondiale. Lo stesso Gramsci, che il PCI togliattiano aveva scelto come "padre nobile", si era schierato contro il pacifismo del PSI e per una trasformazione del conflitto in guerra civile tra operai e borghesi. Accanto a queste ragioni politico-biografiche, ce ne sono altre più profonde, attinenti al rapporto tra PCI e nazione, tra PCI e storia nazionale. Pur rivendicando energicamente il suo status di partito nazionale (Gentile, *La Grande Italia* 355-63), il PCI togliattiano apparteneva al sistema comunista internazionale. Esso celebrava i suoi saldi rapporti con la nazione italiana e con la storia patria (Aga-Rossi, *Il PCI tra identità comunista* 300-311), e nel contempo esaltava il ruolo-guida della classe operaia, i legami tra i proletari di tutto il mondo e la solidarietà internazionale tra partiti comunisti. Era difficile in queste condizioni condurre una riflessione organica su un evento come la prima guerra mondiale, presentato da molti interventisti come quarta guerra d'indipendenza, cioè come l'occasione tanto attesa per ultimare il Risorgimento e completare finalmente l'unità politico-territoriale italiana. E altrettanto difficile era criticare un conflitto da cui l'Italia era uscita vincitrice grazie al sacrificio di un milione circa di morti e più ancora di feriti, militari e civili.

Per queste ragioni, particolarmente negli anni quaranta e cinquanta, "Rinascita" tende a eludere un confronto diretto con la memoria della prima guerra mondiale e concede prudentemente uno spazio modesto alla riflessione su di essa. In ultima analisi, il rapporto complesso e problematico con la memoria della Grande Guerra, che il nostro studio rivela, conferma la "doppiezza" del PCI togliattiano, impegnato nel difficile compito di conciliare l'aspirazione a essere un partito nazionale con l'integrazione nel sistema comunista mondiale.

Una interpretazione, quindi, sotto influenza ideologica, allineata alle strategie politiche del momento, limitata dalla prospettiva storicistica ed economicista: la tragedia umana della Grande Guerra e la rottura culturale ad essa conseguente sono ignorate.

Université Paris Ouest Nanterre La Défense
Université Paris Est Créteil Val de Marne

Opere citate

Aga-Rossi Elena, *Il PCI tra identità comunista e interesse nazionale*, in *La nazione in rosso. Socialismo, Comunismo e "Questione nazionale": 1889-1953*, a c. di Marina Cattaruzza, Soveria Mannelli, Rubbettino, 2005, pp. 297-320.

Agosti Aldo, *Palmiro Togliatti*, Torino, UTET, 1996.

Alatri Paolo, *Caporetto: diario inedito*, "Rinascita" 2 (9 gennaio 1965), 22-23.

_____, *Introduzione*, in *Rinascita 1944-1962. Antologia* a cura di Paolo Alatri, 3 voll., Firenze, Luciano Landi, 1966-1967, pp. 9-96.

_____, *L'"era" fascista*, "Rinascita" 29 (17 luglio 1965), 25.

_____ [p.a.], *Recensione* di Mario Toscano, *Pagine di storia diplomatica contemporanea*, Milano, Giuffrè, 1963, "Rinascita" 11 (14 marzo 1964), 31.

Alfa, *La rivoluzione sovietica e la socialdemocrazia*, "Rinascita" 10 (ottobre 1947), 289-92.

Amendola Giorgio, *Il lungo cammino di Gaetano Salvemini*, "Rinascita" 10 (ottobre 1955), 623-28.

Anonimo, *Il 4 novembre di Gramsci*, "Rinascita" 43 (1° novembre 1968), 24.

Anonimo, *Introduzione* a Jean Jaurès, *Sull'orlo della tragedia*, "Rinascita" 31 (1° agosto 1964), 28.

Anonimo, *Introduzione* a *Una iniziativa di Gramsci* [lettera inedita di Antonio Gramsci a Giuseppe Lombardo-Radice, marzo 1918], "Rinascita" 10 (7 marzo 1964), 32.

Anonimo, *La barbarie prussiana nel giudizio di Marx ed Engels*, "Rinascita" 2 (febbraio 1945), 52-55.

Anonimo [Palmiro Togliatti], *Programma*, "Rinascita" 1 (giugno 1944), 1-2.

Anonimo, *Ufficiali filofascisti*, "Rinascita" 2 (luglio 1944), 24.

Argentieri Mino, *Nuovi film di montaggio*, "Rinascita" 25 (20 giugno 1964), 26-27.

Astesano Luigi, *Come i comunisti lottano per la pace*, "Rinascita" 12 (dicembre 1948), 429-32.

Barca Luciano, *La classe operaia nella vita della nazione*, "Rinascita" 11-12 (novembre-dicembre 1954), 746-49.

Battaglia Roberto, *Le tradizioni anticolonialiste della classe operaia italiana*, "Rinascita" 11-12 (novembre-dicembre 1958) [numero monografico intitolato *Crepuscolo del colonialismo*], 852-63.

Battisti Livia, *Lettera a Rinascita*, "Rinascita" 17 (28 aprile 1967), 27.

Bocca Giorgio, *Palmiro Togliatti*, Milano, Arnoldo Mondadori, 1991.

Boffa Giuseppe, *Dal "decreto sulla pace" alla politica di coesistenza*, "Il Contemporaneo" [numero monografico sulla rivoluzione d'Ottobre], supplemento mensile di "Rinascita" 42 (27 ottobre 1967), 28-30.

Canzio Stefano, *La partecipazione italiana alla aggressione antisovietica dal 1918 al 1920*, "Rinascita" 3 (marzo 1955), 171-76.

Cipriani Ivano, *La guerra alla televisione*, "Rinascita" 26 (26 giugno 1965), 19.

Colarizi Simona, *Storia dei partiti nell'Italia repubblicana*, Roma, Laterza, 1996.

De Felice Franco, *Caporetto perché?*, "Rinascita" 50 (22 dicembre 1967), 25.

De Rossi Giulio, *Dal Partito popolare alla Democrazia Cristiana*, "Rinascita" 4 (aprile 1945), 107-12.

Diaz Furio, *Le due libertà*, "Rinascita" 5-6 (maggio-giugno 1945), 151-53.

Fabbri Fabio, *Il dramma del socialismo europeo*, "Rinascita" 33 (23 agosto 1968), 22-23.

Fabbrini Fazio, *Recensione* di Lenin, *La costruzione del socialismo*, Roma, Edizioni Rinascita, 1956, "Rinascita" 3 (marzo 1957), 127-28.

Ferrata Giansiro, *Un anno sull'Altipiano è un libro che non invecchia*, "Rinascita" 3 (16 gennaio 1965), 23-24.

Ferri Franco, *Consigli di fabbrica e partito nel pensiero di Gramsci*, "Rinascita" 9 (settembre 1957), 461-67.

Foster William Z., *Esiste una situazione d'eccezione del capitalismo americano?* "Rinascita" 1 (gennaio 1948), 11-15.

Frangioni Andrea, *Salvemini e la Grande Guerra. Interventismo democratico, wilsonismo, politica delle nazionalità*, Soveria Mannelli, Rubbettino, 2011.

Gentile Emilio, *La Grande Italia. Il mito della nazione nel XX secolo*, Roma, Laterza, 2006.

Gramsci Antonio, *Il Mezzogiorno e la guerra*, "Rinascita" 4 (aprile 1957), 151-52 [articolo pubblicato da Gramsci in "Il grido del popolo", Torino, il 1° aprile 1916].

_____, *La rivoluzione contro il "Capitale"*, "Rinascita" 4 (aprile 1957), 146-47 [articolo pubblicato da Gramsci in "Il grido del popolo", Torino, il 5 gennaio 1918].

_____, *Wilson e i massimalisti russi*, "Rinascita" 4 (aprile 1957), 147-48 [articolo pubblicato da Gramsci in "Il grido del popolo", Torino, il 2 marzo 1918].

Guiso Andrea, *La seconda guerra mondiale nella "memoria storica" del PCF e del PCI (1945-1956)*, in *La seconda guerra mondiale e la sua memoria*, a c. di Piero Craveri e Gaetano Quagliariello, Soveria Mannelli, Rubbettino, 2006, pp. 529-65.

Höbel Alexander, *Il PCI di Luigi Longo (1964-1969)*, Napoli, Edizioni Scientifiche Italiane, 2010.

La Rocca Vincenzo, *Lenin e la guerra di liberazione nazionale*, "Rinascita" 5-6 (maggio-giugno 1945), 132-34.

Lenin, *1920: un miliardo e 250 milioni di oppressi*, "Rinascita" 11-12 (novembre-dicembre 1958) [numero monografico intitolato *Crepuscolo del colonialismo*], 752-53 [dal rapporto tenuto da Lenin al II congresso dell'Internazionale comunista il 19 luglio 1920, pubblicato in Lenin, *L'Internazionale comunista*, Roma, Edizioni Rinascita, 1950, 258-61].

_____, *L'imperialismo fase suprema del capitalismo* [1917], Milano, Lotta comunista, 2002.

_____, *L'originalità della Rivoluzione di Ottobre*, "Rinascita" 10 (ottobre 1947), 280-81 [articolo pubblicato da Lenin nella "Pravda" il 30 maggio 1923].

Lepre Aurelio, *24 maggio 1915: anche l'Italia nella grande strage*, "Rinascita" 21 (22 maggio 1965), 23-24.

_____, *Epistolario di Omodeo*, "Rinascita" 14 (4 aprile 1964), 29.

_____, *Le lettere di Battisti*, "Rinascita" 13 (31 marzo 1967), 25.

_____, *I partiti socialisti europei dinanzi alla guerra del '14*, "Rinascita" 31 (1° agosto 1964), 21-22.

_____ [a.l.], *Recensione* di Emilio Faldella, *La Grande Guerra. Le battaglie dell'Isonzo (1915-1917)*, Milano, Longanesi, 1965, "Rinascita" 38 (25 settembre 1964), 18.

_____ [a.l.], *Recensione* di Piero Pieri, *L'Italia nella prima guerra mondiale (1915-1918)*, Torino, Einaudi, 1965, "Rinascita" 18 (1° maggio 1965), 33.

_____, *Il revisionismo in Italia*, "Rinascita" 1 (2 gennaio 1965), 29.

_____, *Risposta alla lettera di Livia Battisti*, "Rinascita" 17 (28 aprile 1967), 27.

_____, *Risposta alla lettera di Renato Risaliti*, "Rinascita" 35 (5 settembre 1964), 31.

Liebknecht Karl e Luxemburg Rosa, *Lettere di Karl Liebknecht e Rosa Luxemburg*, "Rinascita" 41 (20 ottobre 1967), 16-17.

Longo Luigi, *Il dilemma della pace*, "Rinascita" 47 (1° dicembre 1967), 3-4.

_____, *Il nostro capo*, "Rinascita" 8 (agosto 1948), 281-84.

_____, *Un grave pericolo per l'avvenire dell'Italia*, "Rinascita" 20 (15 maggio 1965), 1-

2.

Longo Fazio Rosetta, *Il movimento femminile democratico in Italia*, "Rinascita" 3 (marzo 1948), 127-30.

Malaparte Curzio, *Autobiografia di Curzio Malaparte*, "Rinascita" 7-8 (luglio-agosto 1957), 373-78.

Manacorda Giuliano [g. m.], Recensione di Piero Jahier, *1918 L'Astico. 1919 Il Nuovo Contadino*, Padova, Il Rinoceronte, 1964, "Rinascita" 40 (10 ottobre 1964), 30.

Nation R. Craig, voce *Imperialism*, in *A Dictionary of 20th-Century Communism*, edited by Silvio Pons and Robert Service, Princeton Princeton University Press, 2010, pp. 408-11.

Pacor Mario, *Ascesa e fine dell'impero inglese*, "Rinascita" 11-12 (novembre-dicembre 1958) [numero monografico intitolato *Crepuscolo del colonialismo*], 694-701.

Pesenti Antonio, *Struttura e avvenire della nostra industria*, "Rinascita" 11 (novembre 1945), 234-37.

Pieck Wilhelm, *Ricordo di Clara Zetkin*, "Rinascita" 10-11 (ottobre-novembre 1957), 557-58.

Pons Silvio, *L'URSS e il PCI nel sistema internazionale della guerra fredda*, in *Il PCI nell'Italia repubblicana (1943-1991)*, a c. di Roberto Gualtieri, Roma, Carocci, 2001, 3-46.

Sema Paolo, *Destino di Trieste*, "Rinascita" 51 (27 dicembre 1968), 6.

Spano Velio, *Appunti sul massimalismo*, "Rinascita" 12 (dicembre 1945), 270-72.

Salerno Michele, *Mito e realtà dell'"anticolonialismo" USA*, "Rinascita" 11-12 (novembre-dicembre 1958) [numero monografico intitolato *Crepuscolo del colonialismo*], 712-15.

Secchia Pietro, *Il no di Liebknecht*, "Rinascita" 50 (22 dicembre 1967), 28.

Sereni Emilio, *Nella vita e nella lotta di Giuseppe Di Vittorio bracciante pugliese, dirigente operaio e capo comunista, si riflettono 50 anni di vita italiana*, "Rinascita" 10-11 (ottobre-novembre 1957), 541-56.

Seroni Adriano, *Ritorno sul Carso*, "Rinascita" 11 (17 marzo 1967), 20-21.

Spriano Paolo, *Caporetto*, "Rinascita" 7 (17 febbraio 1967), 15.

_____, *I due volti della guerra 1915-'18*, "Rinascita" 47 (29 novembre 1968), 32.

_____, *Gramsci e Bordiga nel '17*, "Rinascita" 17 (28 aprile 1967), 28.

_____, *Isonzo 1917: cimitero di noi soldà...*, "Rinascita" 23 (5 giugno 1965), 28-29.

_____, *L'Italia neutrale*, "Rinascita" 35 (8 settembre 1967), 28.

_____, *Il "no" alla socialdemocrazia*, "Rinascita" 4 (25 gennaio 1964), 4-5.

_____, *Zimmerwald*, "Rinascita" 46 (20 novembre 1965), 19.

Stalin, *Condizioni estere e interne della Rivoluzione di Ottobre*, "Rinascita" 10 (ottobre 1947), 310-11 [dalla prefazione scritta nel dicembre 1924 al volume di Lenin *Sulla via d'Ottobre*].

Thébaud Françoise, *La Grande Guerra: età della donna o trionfo della differenza sessuale?*, in *Storia delle donne in Occidente*, a c. di Georges Duby e Michelle Perrot, vol. *Il Novecento* [1992], a c. di Françoise Thébaud, Roma, Laterza, 1996, 25-90.

Togliatti Palmiro, *Attualità del pensiero e dell'azione di Gramsci*, "Rinascita" 4 (aprile 1957), 137-45.

_____, *Introduzione* a Curzio Malaparte, *Autobiografia di Curzio Malaparte*, "Rinascita" 7-8 (luglio-agosto 1957), 373.

Ungaretti Giuseppe, *Ritorno sui luoghi della prima poesia*, "Rinascita" 8 (16 febbraio 1968), 28.

V. C., *Recensione* di Giacomo Perticone, *La politica italiana nell'ultimo trentennio. La crisi della democrazia e la dittatura fascista (1921-1943)*, Roma, Edizioni Leonardo, 1945, "Rinascita" 5-6 (maggio-giugno 1945), 159.

Vacca Giuseppe, voce *Gramsci, Antonio*, in *A Dictionary of 20th-Century Communism*, edited by Silvio Pons and Robert Service, Princeton, Princeton University Press, 2010, 348-352.

Vittoria Albertina, *Storia del PCI: 1921-1991*, Roma, Carocci, 2006.

_____, *Togliatti e gli intellettuali. Storia dell'Istituto Gramsci negli anni Cinquanta e Sessanta*, Roma, Editori Riuniti, 1992.

_____, *Togliatti, la "ricerca oggettiva" e la politica della storia*, in *Togliatti nel suo tempo*, a c. di Roberto Gualtieri, Carlo Spagnolo e Ermanno Taviani, Roma, Carocci, 2007, pp. 58-72.

Consider

ARACNE

FOR YOUR NEXT PUBLICATION.

ARACNE
is an independent publisher founded in Rome, Italy, in 1993. Its mission is to advance research in the sciences, humanities, and arts through publishing works by scientists, scholars, novelists, poets, and journalists as well as through disseminating their works throughout the scientific and academic world and society at large.

ARACNE welcomes proposals of publications, ranging from monographs to miscellaneous volumes, annotated editions, conference proceedings, and didactic materials.

ARACNE's rapidly expanding catalogue already includes more than 2,500 titles, some of which are winners of prestigious awards.

ARACNE has adopted a system of peer reviewing, and its staff collaborates with all contributors in order to publish works of the highest scholarly quality.

ARACNE
allows its authors to maintain copy-wrights of their works. ARACNE avails itself of the most advanced methods of publishing, printing books expeditiously and on demand so that updated editions can be easily made and volumes are never sold out. For further information, catalogue, and series, please visit Aracne's website: http://www. aracneeditrice.it

ADDRESS ALL YOUR INQUERIES TO:

info@aracneeditrice.it

DANTE ALIGHIERI

Le Opere

Volume I

Vita nuova · Rime

A cura di
Donato Pirovano e **Marco Grimaldi**.
Introduzione di
Enrico Malato.

Tomo I

Vita nuova · Le rime della Vita nuova e altre rime del tempo della Vita nuova.

Salerno Editrice
Roma: 2015. Pp. LXXIV + 804.

Premessa di Enrico Malato	XIII
Introduzione di Enrico Malato	XIX
Vita nuova. A cura di Donato Pirovano	
Nota introduttiva	3
Nota al testo	37
Vita nuova	77
Rime. A cura di Marco Grimaldi	
Nota introduttiva	293
Nota ai testi	313
Sezioni I e II. Le rime della Vita nuova e altre rime del tempo della *Vita nuova*	325

STUDI E TESTI

A Collection of Monographs sponsored
by
Annali d'Italianistica, Inc.

ALL VOLUMES ARE AVAILABLE ON PRINT
ALL VOLUMES ARE AVAILABLE ELECTRONICALLY EXCEPT
VOLS. 1, 2, 4

Carmine Di Biase, ed. *"Oh! Mio vecchio William!" Italo Svevo and His Shakespeare.* Studi & Testi 10. Chapel Hill, NC: Annali d'Italianistica, 2015. Pp. X+118.
Editions:
  1. Kindle E-book: Amazon.com
  2. Print edition: Amazon.com
      ISBN-13: 978-0692545522 (Annali d'italianistica, Inc.)
      ISBN-10: 0692545522
  3. PDF E-book: Email annali@unc.edu ($6.99)

***

Email: annali@unc.edu to order the following volumes:
North America: Print copy $35; Print and digital $40; Digital only $ 25
Outside North America: Print copy $50; Print and digital $55; Digital only $25

Rosetta D'Angelo and Barbara Zaczek, editors and translators. *Resisting Bodies: Narratives of Italian Partisan Women.* Studi & Testi 9. Chapel Hill, NC: Annali d'Italianistica, 2008. Pp. 33 + 224. ISBN 0-9657956-8-3.

Thomas C. Stillinger and F. Regina Psaki, eds. *Boccaccio and Feminist Criticism.* Studi & Testi 8. Chapel Hill, NC: Annali d'Italianistica, 2006. Pp. vii + 273. ISBN 0-9657956-7-5

Robert C. Melzi. *The Conquering Monk. The Story of El Mansur, An Eighteenth-Century Italian Cleric who Conquered Chechnya and Daghestan.* With the translation of Boetti's *Relazione* (Turin, Archivio di Stato) and the *Biografia manoscritta* (Turin, Biblioteca Reale). Pp. vii + 95. Library of Congress Control No.: 2004106764. ISBN 0-9657956-6-7

Maria Domitilla Galluzzi. *Vita da lei narrata* (1624). Edition, introduction, and notes by Olimpia Pelosi. Studi & Testi 6. Chapel Hill, NC: Annali d'Italianistica, 2003. Pp. xxxiv + 273. Library of Congress Control No.: 2003114534. ISBN 0-9657956-5-9

Daria Valentini & Paola Carù, eds. *Beyond Artemisia: Female Subjectivity, History, and Culture in Anna Banti.* Studi & Testi 5. Chapel Hill, NC: Annali d'Italianistica, 2003. Pp. vi + 196. Library of Congress Cont. No.: 2003110677. ISBN 0-9657956-4-0

Giuseppe Conte. *Le stagioni / The Seasons.* Studi & Testi 4. Chapel Hill, NC: Annali d'italianistica, 2001. Pp. xvi + 136. Library of Congress Control No.: 2001086991. ISBN 0-9657956-3-2

Massimo Maggiari, ed. *The Waters of Hermes / Le acque di Ermes.* Studi & Testi 3. Chapel Hill, NC: Annali d'italianistica, 2000. Pp. 208. Library of Congress Catalog Card No.: 00-131648. ISBN 0-9657956-2-4

Rosamaria Lavalva. *The Eternal Child: The Poetry and Poetics of Giovanni Pascoli.* Studi & Testi 2. Chapel Hill, NC: Annali d'italianistica, 1999. Pp. 226. Library of Congress Catalog Card No.: 99-072079. ISBN 0-9657956-1-6

Augustus Mastri, ed. *The Flight of Ulysses: Essays in Memory of Emmanuel Hatzantonis.* Studi & Testi 1. Chapel Hill, NC: Annali d'italianistica, 1997. Pp. 360. Library of Congress Catal. Card No.: 97-72098. ISBN 0-9657956-0-8

Annali d'italianistica, Inc., Dey 141, UNC-CH,
Chapel Hill, NC 27599-3170 USA
Fax: (919) 962 5457; Web site: www.ibiblio.unc.edu/annali
Email: annali@unc.edu

Annali d'Italianistica

An Invitation to Subscribe 2016

Volumes 1-21 available online for free consultation:
www.archive.org/details/annaliditalianis212003univ

VOLUMES AVAILABLE:

volume 4 (1986), Autobiography
volume 5 (1987), D'Annunzio
volume 8 (1990), Dante and Modern American Criticism
volume 9 (1991), The Modern and the Postmodern
volume 10 (1992), Images of America & Columbus in Italian Literature
volume 11 (1993), Goldoni 1993
volume 12 (1994), The Italian Epic and Its International Context
volume 13 (1995), Italian Women Mystics
volume 14 (1996), Travel Literature
volume 15 (1997), Anthropology and Italian Literature
volume 17 (1999), New Landscapes in Contemporary Italian Cinema
volume 18 (2000), Beginnings/Endings/Beginnings
volume 19 (2001), Literature, Criticism, and Ethics
volume 20 (2002), Exile Literature
volume 21 (2003), Hodoeporics
volume 22 (2004), Petrarch and the European Lyric Tradition
volume 23 (2005), Literature and Science
volume 24 (2006), Negotiating Italian Identities, Norma Bouchard
volume 25 (2007), Literature, Religion, and the Sacred
volume 26 (2008), Humanism and Post-Humanism
volume 27 (2009), Futurism 1909-2009
volume 28 (2010), Capital City: Rome, 1870-2010
volume 29 (2011), Italian Critical Theory
volume 30 (2012), Cinema italiano contemporaneo
volume 31 (2013), Boccaccio's *Decameron:* Parodying the Christian Middle Ages
volume 32 (2014), From *Otium* and *Occupatio* to Work & Labor in Italian Culture
volume 33 (2015), The Great War and the Modernist Imagination in Italy
Volume 34 (2016), Forthcoming: Speaking Truth to Power from Medieval to Modern Italy
Volume 35 (2017), Forthcoming: Violence Resistance Tolerance Sacrifice

Annali d'italianistica

Subscription Rates
2015-2016

INDIVIDUALS
  North America:
  Subscription for print copy: $30; back issue: $41
  Subscription for digital copy: $25
  Subscription for print copy and digital copy: $35; back issue $41
  Outside North America:
  Subscription for print copy: $45; back issue: $58
  Subscription for print copy & digital copy: $50; back issue: $63
  Subscription for digital copy: $25

INSTITUTIONS
  North America:
    Subscription for print copy: $45; back issue: $51
  Outside North America:
    Subscription for print copy: $60; back issue: $73

AGENCIES
  North America:
    Subscription for print copy: $40; back issue, $46
  Outside North America:
    Subscription for print copy: $55; back issue: $68

Please send your subscription, check or international money order, payable to:

Annali d'italianistica
UNC-CH
Dey Hall 141
Chapel Hill, NC 27599-3170

www.ingramcontent.com/pod-product-compliance
Lightning Source LLC
Chambersburg PA
CBHW071232290426
44108CB00013B/1387